Zodiac Signs

The Ultimate Guide to Aries, Taurus, Gemini, Cancer, Leo, Virgo, Libra, Scorpio, Sagittarius, Capricorn, Aquarius, and Pisces

Contents

Part 1: Aries
The Ultimate Guide to an Amazing Zodiac Sign in Astrology

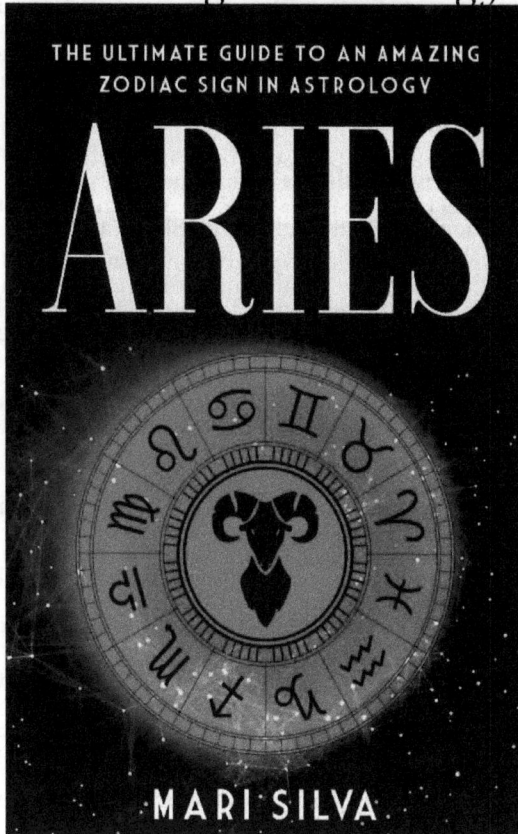

THE ULTIMATE GUIDE TO AN AMAZING
ZODIAC SIGN IN ASTROLOGY

ARIES

MARI SILVA

Introduction

Since time immemorial, humans have been drawn to the sky and the heavens above. As a civilization, we are curious and eager to explore the vast space that surrounds the Earth we live on. The movement of stars and planets is fascinating. In a bid to understand the unknown, our ancestors started mapping the positions and movements of everything in the visible heavens. This fascination has only strengthened with time.

Are you familiar with the phrase, "As above, so below?" It refers to a close connection between the celestial and physical realm and the results of the connection. It suggests the movements of planets and the stars exert an influence on human life and all our affairs.

We live in an extremely busy and complicated world that places great emphasis on scientific truth and discovery. Despite all these advancements, we are still searching for our purpose. When choices constantly surround us, how do we know we are making the right ones? What are we destined for? What is our purpose on this Earth? These are questions we all think about from time to time. If all this sounds familiar, a simple answer is to look up to the stars. This calling to find one's life purpose cannot be fully answered by science. It requires a deeper understanding of the cosmos, and this is where astrology steps into the picture.

If you are fascinated by astrology and wish to learn more about the first zodiac sign – Aries – this is the perfect book for you. Astrology is often referred to as the language of the stars. Rediscovering astrology's ancient wisdom will help you get a better sense of yourself and others in life. Living in an unpredictable world isn't easy. Well, time to rectify this by delving into the fascinating world of stars, planets, and the heavens up above.

This book will teach you everything you need to know about the first sign in the zodiac calendar, Aries, from the basic concepts such as the sign, symbol, elements, and ruling planets to favorable colors and gemstones for Aries. Once you understand the basics, you will learn about personality traits, including Arians' strengths and weaknesses. This is your go-to guide to learn about this wonderful sign. You will discover information that will help you get an in-depth understanding of Aries, such as their compatibility with other signs, tips for a better love life, and how to maintain healthy romantic relationships.

If you have ever wondered about the best career options available for Aries or the ideal work environment, look no further because this book has all the answers. It also includes comprehensive information about the Aries child and all they look for in life. If you or anyone dear to you is an Aries, you made the right choice by choosing this book. Once you have a thorough understanding of this zodiac sign, it becomes easier to understand it and demystify your personality.

So, are you eager to discover more about all this? If yes, let's get started right now! After all, Aries love swift actions and quick results! Channel your inner Arian and learn more about yourself, your potential, and all that life has in store for you.

Chapter 1: An Introduction to Aries

The first astrological symbol in the zodiac is Aries. All those born between March 21ˢᵗ and April 19ᵗʰ belong to this house of the zodiac. It is represented by the horned ram and is governed by the planet Mars. Aries represents new beginnings and fiery energy. If you look up into the night sky, making out the Aries constellation isn't difficult.

Individuals with birthdates close to the intersection of two zodiac signs are known as cusp signs. There are two cusps for every zodiac. For Aries, the cusps are the Aries-Taurus cusp and the Pisces-Aries cusp. The Aries-Taurus cusp falls between the 17ᵗʰ and 23ʳᵈ of April. The Pisces-Aries cusp is between the 17ᵗʰ and 23ʳᵈ of March. Since these individuals "on the cusp" are born close to the two zodiacs' intersection, they often share the traits exhibited by both the signs. For instance, an individual born on April 18ᵗʰ shares the traits of both Aries and Taurus.

Learning about astrology is fun and simple. All it takes is a little time and attention. Before delving into details about the Aries personality and its characteristics, it is important to understand the basic concepts associated with this astrology personality.

Symbols

The ram symbolizes Aries. Since it is the first sign of the zodiac, the positioning is also symbolic. It symbolizes leadership and an intention to pioneer. Positive points associated with Aries include innovation, inspiration, courage, boldness, spontaneity, and initiation. They always like to go first, don't hesitate while taking the initiative, push forward, and keep going even in the face of obstacles.

Did you know the term Aries is derived from the Latin word for ram? It will also bring to mind a battering ram. A battering ram was a tool used in ancient and medieval warfare to break through an opponent's defenses. The astrological equivalent of the spring equinox is when the sun is at 0° relative to Aries. It symbolizes the beginning of the astrological year. The Aries symbol is linked to spring, change, new life, and new beginnings.

The glyph for Aries resembles a single line divided into two. It resembles the horns of a ram, but there are several interpretations as to what the glyph represents. One interpretation suggests the glyph resembles a new shoot that has broken through the earth's surface during early spring. It's a sign of new beginnings and life. The seeds are, in a way, battering their way through Earth's layers to introduce new lives. These tiny and tender shoots are overcoming several obstacles such as dirt, tree roots, and even rocks to push up and out of the earth. This is symbolic of the journey Aries undertake in their lives.

Aries is associated with fire, and so it is presumed to be the early spark of creation through new ideas and concepts. Certain zodiac signs are associated with multiple symbols. For instance, the zodiac sign Scorpio correlates to a spider, scorpion, snake, and even a phoenix, but Aries is associated with only a single sign and symbol. This simplicity, in itself, is symbolic of Aries. Under this simplicity lies raw and direct power that helps with new beginnings.

Another interpretation is that the glyph resembles fallopian tubes. It is not a coincidence nor a far-fetched idea that this symbol is identified with reproduction. Reproduction isn't always about giving birth to a new life; it can be about ideas, too. Aries are extremely creative and have a wonderful imagination. The idea of new life can be in the form of new experiences, travel, creativity, and adventure. So, the association between a symbol of fertility and the Aries glyph is a perfect match.

Now, let's learn about the role of the ram in ancient Egypt and Greece. The ram was associated with power and fertility. It was thought to be a sacred animal in different ancient cultures, especially Greece and Egypt. According to an ancient Greek myth, Poseidon, the god of the sea, took on the form of a ram. It is believed he sired a winged ram with a golden fleece. The goddess Nephele appeared as a winged ram to save her son Phrixus and carry him to safety. To prevent himself from being sacrificed, Phrixus returned the ram to Poseidon. Upon its sacrifice, the ram was immortalized in the heavens as the constellation Aries. There are several versions of this myth, and this is just one version.

Rams were considered sacred and used as temple animals in ancient Egypt. Archaeologists have discovered several pieces of Egyptian art featuring rams. For instance, at the Karnak temple in ancient Thebes (present-day Luxor) there is an entire avenue of lambs that lead to the temple's main entrance. Ancient Egyptian gods such as the sun god, Amon-Ra, were often depicted with the horns or even the head of a ram.

Elements

Do you think about the one thing that sets you apart from everyone else? Or maybe you have wondered about a personality trait that makes you truly unique? Perhaps others appreciate your brilliant creativity. Maybe you are criticized for being aggressive or stubborn. Regardless of all this, the meaning of elements in astrology plays a significant role in your overall personality. The universe is made of energy, and this is constantly flowing between everything present in it. Even science supports this claim and suggests energy can neither be created nor destroyed. Energy can only be transformed from one form to another. We are all part of the same universe, and our electricity is a reflection of the cosmos's energetic makeup.

The four elements in astrology are Fire, Earth, Water, and Air. These elements are present in everything, and they are very much alive, but these elements play a significant role in our lives. The extent to which a specific astrological element influences our life is determined by all the celestial activity which takes place at the exact moment of birth. It is the law of nature for things to be in balance. The concept of yin and yang exists everywhere you look.

Similarly, every element has a corresponding yin and yang. Yin describes feminine energy, while yang represents masculine energy. Striking a balance between the yin and yang is quintessential for one's physical, emotional, and spiritual wellbeing.

There are twelve signs in the zodiac, and each of these elements is accompanied by three signs. Fire and air are believed to be masculine elements, while water and earth are the feminine ones. Feminine energy is more nurturing and sensual, while the masculine side represents communication and action.

Understanding these elements gives a better insight into your personality and general approach toward life. Fire is the element associated with Aries. It is a symbol of creation, passion, and immense energy. When the universe was created, the initial element that was born is believed to have been fire. Fire rules Leo, Sagittarius, and Aries. Over-the-top enthusiasm and passion are representative of this element. It makes you competitive and extremely active.

On the downside, it can also make you quick-tempered and impatient. Tapping into your inner child is possible when you channel this element. Fire is also a source of confidence. As you read more about the zodiac sign Aries, you can see the association between the elements and the overall personality traits they foster. Everything in astrology is intricately connected.

Ruling Planet

The planet that exudes a significant impact on a specific zodiac is known as its ruling planet. This relationship between signs and planets is a central aspect of astrology. Every planet has its own set of unique properties and directly influences the traits and characteristics of all those born under the sign ruled by said planet. If you take a moment, you will realize all the planets are named after Roman gods. These gods' stories will help you understand the significant influence they have on the signs they rule.

The planet Mars rules Aries. Did you know that Mars was the Roman god of war? In ancient Greece, he was known as Ares. Well, now it seems obvious where the planet gets its name. This Roman god has become quite popular today, all thanks to the recent Wonder Woman movie! In the ancient world, Mars was considered one of the four powerful gods. The other three powerful figures in Greek mythology are Minerva, the goddess of wisdom, Venus, the goddess of love, and Discordia, the goddess of chaos.

Mars is the god of war, so this planet is linked to courage, physical activity, and action. It also signifies quick temper, immense physical strength, and courage to stand up for what one believes in. These factors have a significant effect on attraction, romance, and the course of your story. Learning about your ruling planet allows you to harness its power to succeed in life fully. In this section, let's look at Aries's ruling planet.

It might be scary and worrisome to realize your ruling planet is associated with anger and violence. To be fair, who would truly want to be ruled by aggression? Don't worry, because there are several plus points about the god of war. Fighting doesn't always have to be physical. Just because an aggressive planet rules you doesn't mean you will get into physical brawls.

In its true sense, Mars is about fighting for all that you believe in. It is associated with bravery and honor. Remember, the modern idea of war is quite different from the one prevalent in ancient Rome. Ancient Romans believed that war was as much about discipline and strength as destroying and obliterating the other side. The modern connotations of war are negative, but that wasn't always the case.

According to ancient astrological texts, Mars was referred to as the planet of small misfortune. Before you start worrying about this, it's important to understand the context and what it really meant. Don't be under the misconception that Mars will bring discord and unhappiness into your world. Small misfortune doesn't necessarily mean you will be experiencing several misfortunes in your life. Small misfortune can refer to your short temper or a minor argument. Now that you are mindful of what it means, you merely need to be cautious. Controlling your temper is an important life skill, so spend time learning it.

Did anyone ever tell you that you have a quick temper? Perhaps you are called stubborn, argumentative, or extremely opinionated. Are there instances when you experience extreme anger, to the extent that it feels like you are about to burst? Don't think of it as a disadvantage that holds you back. Instead, learn to harness it. Harness the power of anger and direct it toward positive things. Remember, the small misfortune mentioned in the astrological texts will come true only if you allow these feelings to dominate your actions.

This planet is all about leadership. Throughout history, several leaders such as Otto Von Bismarck, Eva Peron, and Al Gore were ruled by Mars. Mars brings with it aggressiveness, fearlessness, and ambition. You need all these things if you want to be a leader. It authorizes you to voice your opinions without backing off. Remember, it was mentioned that war doesn't invariably have to be about violence? Standing up for all that you believe in, despite any contradictory opinions, is a show of strength.

On the downside, your opinions don't always have to be right. Mars isn't known for its recklessness. Even if you believe you are right, chances are throwing yourself into an argument without aforethought is not worth it. Spend time and learn to contain your controversial opinions. Look for diplomatic ways of expression without resorting to aggression.

Mars's energy is traditionally masculine. It is descriptive of one's passion and desire. These two characteristics will trickle into your intimate relationships and love life. From your planet's perspective, anyone ruled by Venus is a perfect match. According to ancient Greek mythology, Mars and Venus were lovers. Venus exudes feminine energy, making it the perfect fit for Mars's masculine one. It doesn't mean Mars is only associated with men. Both men and women have masculine energy in them. After all, masculine and feminine energies are two sides of the same coin. They are nature's yin and yang. Anyone can use their inner masculine strength to voice their opinions and stand by them.

Mars is also associated with physical strength. This is the reason why Aries is physically more energetic than other zodiacs. It doesn't mean everyone born under the sign is destined to be a bodybuilder. It merely means you have greater physical strength and stamina. Harness Mars's energy and transform yourself into your best version.

Colors

Colors play an important role in our overall mood and general attitude toward life. Did you ever notice you opt for bright colors when in a good mood and dull shades when you feel low on energy? We do this subconsciously. According to astrology, certain colors help harness one's energy while others dampen this sparkle. Colors can also give you the extra boost of confidence needed to get through life.

Aries wear their passion on their sleeves. They are confident and sultry. The fiery personality of Aries, ruled by Mars, is closely associated with colors representative of fire. Red might be the initial color that pops up in your head when you think of fire, but several other colors work well for Aries. Blood orange and eggplant offer positive energy that gives them the power required to push through any challenging tasks even when they don't want to. So, the next time you are feeling low on energy or exhausted, try using these colors.

Another color appropriate for an Aries is pink. Pink helps people get along with each other. Since Arians are naturally outgoing and friendly, pink enhances the plus points. The peaceful and helpful energy of pink balances the aggressiveness of an Aries. Now, let's go back to the fire color palette. Orange is presumed to be the harbinger of good luck and is well suited for this sign. Orange prevents you from absorbing any negative energies while harnessing your personal energy and directing you toward good fortune in life. Other fiery colors are yellow and red.

Red is associated with courage, excitement, passion, and success. Success brings about a feeling of happiness and keeps individuals motivated to keep going and do what they are doing. When you are constantly doing things you love or are engaging in tasks you enjoy, you automatically become more passionate and this intensity is harnessed by red. Aries are naturally courageous and brave. Red helps amplify these feelings and channel the energy in the right direction.

All these four traits are quintessential for an Aries if they don't want to feel bogged down. Whether you belong to the Aries zodiac or not, yellow is a color that helps you open up to others. Talking about a complex topic or an issue that is bothering you becomes easier with this emotionally uplifting color. Opening up emotionally is seldom easy. We all need courage and lots of soul-searching to do this. Yellow offers the positive energy required to do this.

Until now, we have only mentioned dark and bright colors. White is also associated with a burning fire. White and cream balance the fiery energy of an Aries. Whenever you feel overwhelmed or overstimulated, including these colors can bring calming energy.

When it comes to colors associated with the zodiac, you don't necessarily have to wear them. They can be a part of any accessory you carry and even included in your surroundings. Depending on your mood and the intensity you wish to channel, choose the different colors discussed in this section. A simple way to include all the colors is by using stones associated with them.

Gemstones

The entire universe is made of energy. Crystals and gemstones are filled with universal energy. Gemstones are not only precious and pretty, but they are powerhouses of unharnessed energy. The unique frequencies emitted by different crystals help support and balance your personal energy fields.

They can be used to leverage the cosmic energy. Depending on the zodiac, different gemstones are suitable for each sign. This section looks at gemstones that can amplify the strengths of Aries and overcome their weaknesses.

Diamond

You might have heard the phrase, "Diamonds are a girl's best friend." Well, it's not just women; diamond is the birthstone of Aries. All diamonds help enhance the properties of Aries, but white diamonds are your powerful allies. They bring with them a feeling of clarity that helps calm the busy mind of an Aries. This clarity lets you see through all the confusion and distractions and find the ability to concentrate on the things that matter. Diamond is not just a gemstone with an Aries, but it also acts as a metaphor. Diamond is the hardest substance known to man, and this is pretty much how Arians appear on the surface. Despite its hard exterior, a diamond shines brilliantly and is beautiful.

Another metaphor that comes to mind about diamonds is "A diamond in the rough." Unpolished diamonds seldom get a second glance. Carbon atoms form diamonds in the Earth's interior due to severe heat and pressure. Similarly, if an Aries is willing to learn from his life experiences, he too will turn into a diamond. With a little polish and chiseling, a raw diamond gets its brilliance. The same analogy applies to all who share this zodiac sign. Skill, patience, and determination are needed to polish an Arian into a remarkable gem. Even if they are rough around the edges, Aries certainly bring with them a unique shine and brilliance to the world.

Aquamarine

Aquamarine is water stone, and it comes in handy to tame the fiery nature of Aries. It brings about a sense of flexibility in an Aries's life. It helps them go with the flow of life's tides.

Amethyst

When Aries set their mind on something, they don't care about anything else until they achieve it. This focus can come at the expense of oneself and others, too. Amethyst introduces a feeling of spiritual likeness to all their endeavors and ventures. It helps establish a better sense of balance in their lives and channel their ambitions healthily.

Carnelian

The fiery energy of the carnelian is a perfect match for the fiery energy present within an Aries. If there were any instances when it felt like you were losing your energy, the carnelian would come in handy. Passion and courage are the two energies that can be harnessed with this stone. If your fiery energy is in overdrive, use caution with this stone. Excess fiery energy can make you self-centered and prevent you from seeing your goals for what they are. The best combination is to use a carnelian with an aquamarine or clear quartz.

Black Onyx

The full-steam-ahead personality of an Aries is further enhanced with black onyx. It helps them see new insights and ensures their actions are originating from a place of personal strength. The energy offered by the stone is balancing and centering, which comes in handy because this personality can get a little overworked and heated. Any fears that might be holding an Aries back can also be overcome with black onyx's healing energy.

Clear Quartz

Clear quartz is a healing crystal. As its name suggests, this stone brings about a grasp of clarity. Passion and ambition are two traits associated with Aries. Clear quartz helps bring a feeling of calmness and clarity so that the Aries moves ahead in the right direction to achieve their goals without forgetting others. The great thing about clear quartz is it can easily be combined with any other crystal. The energy given by all other crystals can be harnessed and amplified by using clear quartz.

Citrine

Since Aries is all about new beginnings, it's important to manifest their energies in the right direction. Citrine helps amplify the Aries's inherent energy of manifestation. Accepting criticism isn't this sign's strong suit. Citrine provides the energy required to accept criticism positively and make the required changes based on the information they receive.

Red Jasper

Aries is not known for thinking before acting. Well, this stone helps them do this. It offers vitality and incredible energy levels that can nourish and support an Aries's energy when depleted.

Garnet

According to the conventional zodiac, garnet is the stone associated with Aries. Its healing properties include success, strength, and courage. Since these are traits associated with an Aries, they are further magnified with the helpful energy of a garnet. It also protects the ever-trusting Aries from those who might deceive them. It's believed to be a vitality stone and offers the energy required to pursue new ideas and bring about new beginnings.

Emerald

New beginnings require a significant amount of hope. Emeralds give this hope. The stone is popularly known as the prosperity stone. The uplifting energy of an emerald is associated with positivity, which is required for the forward-motion thinking of an Aries.

Rose Quartz

Aries are extremely passionate. This stone brings about feelings of unconditional love and selflessness. It helps balance the aggressive nature of an Aries with its subtle and pure energies.

Aries through 12 Houses of The Zodiac

Learning about the various houses in astrology is important. The zodiac is divided into twelve houses, and a different sign rules each. Unlike a regular clock, the zodiac starts from the first house and moves counterclockwise. Every house has certain defining traits that influence your general characteristics.

The Earth rotates, the planets move, and the positions of stars change. At the moment of your birth, different planets were in specific signs and houses. In astrology, each planet's meaning, the house it was in, and the sign it shone on are used to trace one's strengths and possible challenges they will face in a lifetime. When a planet moves into a specific zodiac house, it lights up that specific part of your chart and energizes the given house's different traits. These houses can also predict the unique aspects of your life that will be in focus and the best course of action available. In astrology, the first six houses are known as personal houses and the rest as interpersonal houses. In this chapter, you will learn more about the twelve houses of the zodiac and what they mean for Aries.

1st House

As the name suggests, this is the house that begins the zodiac calendar and includes all the new aspects of your life. First impressions, initiatives, new beginnings, and appearance of oneself are included in this house. The sign positioned at the edge, or cusp, of this house is known as your ascendant or rising sign. Aries rules the First House.

Since Aries starts the calendar and rules the first house, all your personality and qualities are magnified here. It influences how you present yourself to others and your self-perception. In this house, taking any initiative is easy for you, and you are often fearless.

2nd House

Taurus rules the Second House. All the diverse aspects of your life associated with the physical and material environment, including your primary senses, are influenced by this house. The second house governs your self-esteem, income, and finances.

In this house, Aries is rather aggressive when it comes to money management. You are adept at managing any material resources. It also increases your desire and engagement in sensual pleasures.

3rd House

Gemini rules the Third House. All forms of communication, including verbal and non-verbal communication, from how you think to how you talk, are governed by the third house. It is responsible for all the relationships you build with your siblings, peers, classmates, co-workers, and so on in life. It offers deep insight and important information about your immediate network.

Since this house is all about communication, you always have an opinion and defend it vehemently. If left unchecked, the communication can come across as forceful and aggressive. You look for different ways to express and defend your opinions, whether it is in writing or by talking. Aries have plenty to say in this house. Aries is incredibly opinionated here, and their chances of engaging in arguments and quarrels with others also increase. On the plus side, you are also often the first one to make amends.

4th House

Cancer rules the Fourth House. This house represents your home and roots. It forms the foundation for all things, such as your home, privacy, relationship with parents, your children, nurturing abilities, and feelings of security.

This house is all about your home life and family settings. Since the planet Mars rules Aries, aggression can also make its way into the home, but it also brings out your inherent desire to create a perfect place and a safe haven that gives you a break from the tiring realities of life.

5th House

Leo rules the Fifth House. This house is characteristic of romance, tension, creativity, fun, and self-expression. It's reminiscent of the creativity and natural sense of freedom that children have. It essentially allows you to connect with your inner child.

It is all about romance, passion, and charisma, but it also describes your inner grasp of creativity. Engaging in any form of art is a great method of self-expression for Aries in this house.

6th House

Virgo rules the Sixth House. This governs your understanding of service to yourself and society and your overall wellbeing. Anything associated with these things, such as your schedule, fitness, diet, exercise, organization, and routine, is influenced by the sixth house.

In this house, you are a tireless and aggressive fighter. Aries becomes the pack leader in all aspects of life in this house. When Mars rules your work life, you become a go-getter and aren't worried about stepping on other's toes to get what you want. Since it describes your overall health and a sense of service, channeling your inner energy to be of service to others is a great way to allow your Aries energy to flow with no barriers.

7th House

Libra rules the Seventh House. This house is all about the various relationships in life. Whether it is your personal or professional relationships, from marriage to business partnerships, everything is influenced by this house. It gives you a better sense of understanding about yourself and those you associate with. The Seventh House also influences your ability to interact with your loved ones.

Libra describes a relationship with others. From tender loving to the energy required to deal with different aspects of relationships, Aries's life is influenced by the seventh house.

8th House

Scorpio rules the Eighth House. This house influences all things associated with birth, death, sex, and transformation. Magic and mysticism are two significant aspects.

Since Mars rules your life, the passion and intensity you experience are often intensified. This house makes you fearless and releases you to explore the world around you physically, mentally, and psychically without any worries or hesitations.

9th House

Sagittarius rules the Ninth House. All things associated with your personal self, such as inspiration, philosophy, and the extraordinary journeys you go on in life, are influenced by this house. The journey mentioned here is not just representative of little journeys in life, but metaphorical ones, too. It essentially holds the key to the different things that bring inspiration, surprise, and delight to your life.

Your desire is to explore the unknown and learn more, and this house influences desire. It allows you to delve into the deeper aspects of life that others don't concentrate on.

10th House

Capricorn rules the Tenth House. This house essentially influences the different characteristics or traits you want others to notice in you. It is believed to be the mid-heaven and is often used to understand an individual's ideal career path. It governs traditions, honor, public image, achievements, boundaries, authority, discipline, and rules.

In this house, ambition and recognition become extremely important. Whether it is realized in your personal or professional life, you have a willingness to go after the success you desire.

11th House

Aquarius rules the Eleventh House. The eleventh house governs all aspects related to friendship. Whether it is personal friendships or relationships at the workplace, it is influenced greatly by this house.

For the Aries in this house, standing up and fighting for the underdog becomes the norm. Friends become your lifelines. It gives you a lot of energy to participate in activities involving others.

12th House

Pisces rules the Twelfth House. The last sign of the zodiac is about your subconscious mind. It is the center of one's imagination, creativity, and art. In the same way as the first house governs the beginnings, the twelfth house governs the endings.

If Mars is ruling this house, it can become a bit tricky because it can help identify others' aggression even when not visible. All the things in this house are often hidden. With Mars ruling your energy cycle, it helps you become aware of things that are not always what they seem. It gives you a deeper sense of intuition to understand how others behave and to decipher their motives.

Chapter 2: How to Recognize an Aries

We all have a unique identity, and no two individuals can ever be truly alike, but those who share the same sun sign also share certain characteristics and traits. When you know someone's sun sign, you can understand them to a certain extent. On the other hand, if you know the typical sun sign traits, you can guess the person's zodiac sign even if you don't know their birth date. In this section, let's look at similar traits shared by all Aries. Using this information, you can spot other Aries in a crowd.

Aries are extremely outgoing and friendly. Whether it is a kid or the neighborhood grandma, Aries is friendly toward everyone. These individuals cannot tolerate injustice in any form. If you see someone standing up against prejudice and fighting all sorts of wrongs, chances are they are an Aries. They not only stand up for themselves and what they believe in, but they don't mind standing up for the weak too.

To a certain extent, there is a general naiveté associated with Aries. They might seem confident and competent, but they are innocent too. These traits make them fearless on one hand while making them extremely vulnerable on the other. Since they genuinely trust others, their chances of getting hurt are high. Instead of being extra cautious, an Aries believes in learning their lesson, forgiving, and forgetting. This process keeps repeating. If you are naturally trusting of others and are good at forgiving and forgetting, it is because of your sun sign. This is one trait all Aries shares.

One thing an Aries will never run out of is topics for conversation. People of this zodiac sign are adept at talking about anything and everything under the sun. You don't have to think, "What do I talk about?" when conversing with an Aries. Even if you are lost for topics, the Aries will keep the conversation going. This stands true even if an Aries has just met someone for the first time. They love interacting with others and thrive on conversations.

This is the first sign of the Zodiac, and this position brings with it a childlike nature. They are akin to a baby fascinated by his own fingers and toes. This can make them a little self-absorbed but, after all, what else can you expect from a baby? Just like babies, even Aries are focused solely on their needs and requirements.

To a great extent, Aries are guided by actions and behaviors instead of words. They love to talk but expressing emotions doesn't come easy to them. Instead, they are the sort who let their actions speak. On the downside, Aries tend to leave things midway. For instance, they might start out strong and be motivated to complete their tasks. If the task at hand becomes monotonous and routine, they quickly lose interest and want to do something else.

Their childlike nature makes them extremely honest. They don't lie and are brutally frank. With an Aries, you get exactly what you see. There are no pretenses and no façades. Subtlety, modesty, and diplomacy are not their strong suits. They are not afraid to call a spade a spade. In a crowd, if you notice someone who speaks his mind without worrying about what others might think or feel, chances are he is an Aries. They don't beat around the bush and they get to the point quickly.

Confidence, competitiveness, optimism, an open nature, a love of challenges, impulsiveness, a short fuse, and a fear of physical pain are common characteristics of Aries. All those born under this Zodiac also share certain physical similarities. When it comes to facial features, concentrate on the eyes and eyebrow area because it can look like their zodiac symbol. They often have connecting eyebrows and an athletic build. You might or might not see physical similarities in all Aries, but identifying their defining traits is easy.

At work, Aries are the go-getters and fearless leaders. They are the life of parties. At home, they are passionate and make loving partners, spouses, and children. They are always the center of attention and love it. Their fiery energy is hard to ignore, and their passion is unfettered.

Pisces-Aries cusp is a combination of the first and the last zodiac signs. Aries stands for new beginnings while Pisces is about endings. Those born on the cusp of these signs are incredible. They possess the fiery passion of Aries, which is tempered with the calm of the water sign, Pisces. They are instinctive and empathetic while radiating courage and fiery passion. It certainly is a steamy mixture of two important natural elements. Their perspective toward life is more interesting than any other cusp.

To identify a Pisces-Aries cusp, look for an individual gifted at making plans, coming up with solutions, and churning out ideas. They do all this while ensuring they are considerate of others and their needs. Unlike the Aries, who is always in a rush, this cusp sign takes time to come to a conclusion or make plans. They are compassionate and empathetic towards all those they love. Aries are not known to be good listeners, but those on the cusp sign make good listeners because of their Pisces nature.

When the fearless ram is combined with the stubborn bull, the Aries-Taurus cusp is formed. They are fiercely independent, fearless, and headstrong. Since Taurus and Aries are both comfortable in their skin, they can seem extremely self-centered. It is easy to identify those who share a combination of these zodiac signs. These individuals are fun, energetic, courageous, and strong. They are the ones who are not only determined to climb mountains but have the energy to do so in their professional and personal lives. They want to be the best and love to lead their team towards success. They are also strong enough to know they are enough by themselves and don't need anyone else to depend on, but they can come across as stubborn, selfish, pushy, and even controlling. Sharing responsibilities doesn't come easily for this sign. Aries love to assume the role of leader and are good at delegating responsibilities. An Aries-Taurus cusp struggles to do this.

Chapter 3: Famous Aries

In life, some excel while others don't. We are often curious to understand more about the lives of those who succeed. Why does this happen? No, it isn't about luck. The difference between success and failure boils down to certain traits.

Celebrities are well known and are often the center of public attention. Are you interested in learning about popular Arians? It turns out all those who are born under the same sun sign tend to share certain traits. In this section, let's look at famous Aries and their defining traits.

Gloria Steinem

Gloria Steinem was a freelance journalist and one of the most popular feminists of her time. A rather controversial woman, she always stood by her opinions and was incredibly smart and brave. She was a war reporter and later founded her own magazine. She was a strong feminist when society didn't believe in the equality of the sexes. Regardless of whatever happened, she did not give up and stood by her beliefs. All the traits she displayed made her a true Aries.

Lady Gaga

Stefani Joanne Angelina Germanotta, better known as Lady Gaga, is a popular pop icon. She is truly a self-made woman and an Arian woman at that. She wasn't afraid to take on new challenges and went from being a singer-songwriter to a record publisher, a successful businesswoman, a reputable fashion designer, a philanthropist, and even a brilliant actor. Her willingness to take the initiative as well as explore different avenues, and her fearless nature both on and off-stage, are due to Mars' fiery strength that rules Aries. She has no qualms about being herself and is bold and incredibly daring.

Thomas Jefferson

Thomas Jefferson became the President not because of his political ambition, but his incredible leadership. He was a natural-born leader, and his ideas of freedom rang true of his Aries nature. If you ever get a chance, go through his personal history, you will realize he always did what he wanted and knew what he had to achieve. All Arians share these two traits.

Robert Downey, Jr.

Aries are survivors, and they never give up. They can pick themselves up and start all over again regardless of the troubles they face in life. All this is true for Robert Downey Jr, better known as Iron Man. He was nominated for an Academy award in 1992 but ended up in prison in 1996. He truly tested the limits of everything in his life and didn't hesitate. His resilience and fighting spirit can be associated with the fiery planet Mars.

Maya Angelou

Maya Angelou was a world-renowned civil rights activist, poet, and writer. Her famous poem, "Still I Rise," is reminiscent of the Aries spirit to keep fighting despite difficulties and challenges. She was a true warrior and always stood by her beliefs. Her fiery confidence, unshakeable conviction, and fierce fighting spirit coupled with the desire to be of service to others made her a truly exceptional woman. All these traits are typical of the first zodiac sign.

Pope Benedict XVI

Pope Benedict XVI was nominated to lead the Catholic Church in 2005. His natural role as a leader shows his Arian side. Aries are known for their unwavering conviction and beliefs. They do what they want, as long as they believe in it. They are confident and brave enough to stand up for themselves even when others don't. He exhibited the traits of an Aries by resigning from his position as the Bishop of Rome in 2013. He was the first Pope in history who ever renounced their title from the prestigious post.

Leonardo da Vinci

Leonardo da Vinci was a well-known Renaissance artist. Not many people know that he was a musician, inventor, architect, and polymath. He is famous for the Mona Lisa and the Last Supper, but that wasn't all that he did. His curiosity to keep learning and exploring the world around him was true to his Aries nature. Aries are leaders, pioneers, and visionaries. He shared all these traits and channeled his inner fiery passion into becoming a pioneer in different aspects of science and art.

Peyton Manning

The Pro football quarterback Peyton Manning set several records and won five NFL MVP awards and trophies. Aries are incredibly competitive and cannot stand the thought of losing. He displayed this competitive fiery spirit and kept fighting until he attained his goals. In the end, when he retired from the NFL in 2016, he mentioned that he fought a good fight.

Keri Russell, Joan Crawford, Ayesha Curry, Alexander McQueen, Queen Latifah, Bruce Willis, Adam Levine, Gary Oldman, Reese Witherspoon, and Fred Rogers are popular Pisces-Aries cusps. Charlotte Bronte, John Muir, Carmen Electra, Queen Elizabeth II, Kourtney Kardashian, John Cena, Victoria Beckham, Kate Hudson, and Max Weber are popular Aries-Taurus cusps.

The list of famous Aries discussed in the section isn't exhaustive. The list is endless. Why did all these Arians succeed in life? They succeeded because they were true to themselves; they were their own heroes and didn't shy away from challenges and resiliently tackled everything life threw their way. They were committed to themselves and their goals. They were endless, optimistic, and guileless. None of these Arians had success handed to them on a silver platter. Instead, they believed failure was not an option. They considered failure to be a prerequisite for success. If you have any goals in life, go after them. Don't let anyone stop you. Learn to channel your inner fiery energy and passion to get you there.

Chapter 4: Strengths and Weaknesses

All humans have a natural tendency to compare themselves to others. Based on our perception of strengths and weaknesses, these comparisons can make us feel superior or inferior. We are all different and function differently because of our personalities. Instead of comparing yourself to others, it's better to know yourself and your capabilities. We all have certain strengths we can leverage to push ourselves and move ahead in life.

Similarly, we also have certain weaknesses. These weaknesses are not your undoing, but they are simply areas you should improve upon. It doesn't mean you lack something; it merely means there is scope for improvement and learning. In this chapter, you will learn about these differences in Aries.

Strengths of an Aries

The first zodiac sign is Aries, and this positioning comes with certain strengths. Those around them can appreciate all their positive traits. In fact, Aries are blessed with certain qualities that others struggle to develop during their lifetime.

Courageous

Represented by the ram, Aries are extremely courageous. They never shy away from trying new things and take up responsibilities without flinching. They are risk-takers. An Aries always keeps an open mind about discovering and learning something. They love the excitement and don't get overwhelmed, worrying about the possible consequences. Instead, they are brave enough to take the first step when others shy away. The dynamic planet Mars rules this zodiac sign, so Aries are naturally fearless warriors who are ready to face any challenge that life throws their way.

Leadership Mentality

Most humans have a herd mentality, but the ram is a natural-born leader. They like taking control of situations and even helping others attain success. They like uniting others and assume the role of a leader whenever required. Real-life leadership roles are exciting and enticing for an Aries. Whether it's a managerial position or a leadership role, Aries are drawn to it. From team leaders to directors, they automatically step into the shoes of a leader in any situation. Unsurprisingly, most people look to their Aries friends in times of need.

Energetic

Since Aries are the first sign of the zodiac calendar, they are filled with immense energy. They are the people who never get tired or run out of strength if they like what they are doing. Their energy isn't something everyone can keep up with. If you are an Aries, chances are you've been asked, "How do you do this?" or "How do you keep up?" If you like something, there is nothing that can get in your way or derail your energy.

Optimistic Outlook

If you are an Aries or know an Arian, you might know their optimism. Many people are drawn to this personality because of their optimistic vision, regardless of all the challenges that come up in their lives. Instead, they can see their goal and work toward it. They rarely spend their time and energy worrying about all the unstoppable situations or dwell on their past mistakes or losses. They are the ones who are adept at learning lessons that life teaches and quickly moving on.

Generous Nature

Their extremely generous and giving nature makes them kind and understanding. Even if an Aries doesn't earn much, they are generous with their money and give it away without hesitation. They are ready to help others in difficult circumstances, even with their money if necessary.

Passionate

The passion Aries shows is unlike any other. If they like something, the Aries is quickly consumed and driven by it. This passion trickles into all aspects of their lives. Whether this relates to their professional or personal life, they are passionate and rarely give up on things they like.

Creative

If you are ever running low on inspiration or motivation, look to an Aries in your circle. Aries are incredibly creative and can think outside the box. They are innovative, and their imagination knows no bounds. This imagination and creativity become the crux of their problem-solving abilities. Their problem-solving skills, self-confidence, passion, and energy help in their leadership roles. If you are an Aries, you might have realized your loved ones turn to you in times of need. They do this not only because they know you will help them, but they know you *can* help them and come up with solutions to solve their problems.

Ambitious

Aries will take nothing for granted. They are naturally ambitious and set high goals for themselves. They not only push themselves to meet these goals but inspire others, too. They make ideal leaders in society. If you have ever worked with an Aries, you'll understand this. There will be times when working towards a goal becomes difficult, but the Aries will keep you motivated.

Self-Confident

Aries have a natural sense of self-confidence. They believe in their opinions, ideas, and values. Their values guide all their decisions, and they don't hesitate to stand by them. This natural self-confidence is attractive to others. It also gives others the courage to follow them.

Highly Independent

If you are an Aries, you might have been called "adamant" or "opinionated" by others. Well, these things are admired and are welcome in the challenging modern world. It describes your ability to stand by your ideas and opinions because they align with your core values. Instead of listening to others' advice, Aries are eager to experience things for themselves. Their independence comes not only in their vision but their ability to reach those goals.

Trustworthy

Aries are trustworthy and honest. They call it as they see it, but don't do this with any ill intentions. It is in their nature to be honest and open, even if it means expressing their resentment. While talking to an Aries, you can always count on their honest opinion. They are not bothered by others' façades and will be themselves in every situation.

Strengths of an Aries can be summed up as follows:

- Aries are natural-born leaders and risk-takers.
- They are confident and courageous.
- They have immense energy and the passion required to achieve their goals.
- Their passion and creativity allow them to come up with unique approaches to tackle any obstacle or situation in life.
- The inherent sense of optimism of an Aries makes them a positive presence.
- Trustworthy, honest, and generous are adjectives that describe this sign well.
- Their strong sense of independence, coupled with all the traits mentioned earlier, makes them incredibly ambitious.

Pisces-Aries cusps are affectionate, confident, and practical. In comparison, Aries-Taurus cusps are idealistic, bold, and responsible. These cusps showcase the strengths of both the signs they are born under.

Weaknesses of an Aries

It's the rule of nature that there needs to be balance. To every good, there is bad, and to every plus point, there's always a minus. Fortunately, even one's weaknesses can be transformed into strengths. To do this, it is important to become aware of the weaknesses. In the previous section, you were introduced to the strengths of Aries. Now, let's look at a few areas where this sign struggles.

Highly Competitive

No other zodiac sign is as competitive as an Aries. Perhaps it's their first position in the calendar that makes them competitive. Whatever it is, Aries always wants to come first. They cannot stand losing or even the thought of losing. They think of every event in life as a battle. In a battle, there can be only two outcomes: winning or losing. Since Aries don't like losing, the only alternative left for them is to come out victorious. When they don't win, Aries become dejected. From playing games with friends to completing tasks at work, Aries are always competing. An Aries believes life is a competition.

There is nothing wrong with wanting to win, but it is important to choose your battles. Life is not a competition, and you don't always have to win to be happy. Don't associate your happiness with winning because it increases the stress you experience. This competitiveness can also be a sign of an internal insecurity you harbor. Don't compete with others but try to compete with yourself. Try to do your best in everything. Remember, life is seldom black or white. Try to channel your highly competitive nature in a positive way, shifting all your focus on the process and effort instead of the results.

Reckless To A Fault

All Aries have an inherent tendency to try to be the best and the fastest at everything. It often means they make quick and rash decisions. A rash decision is seldom wise. Since they are always in a hurry, they don't have enough time to analyze the risks and consequences of their decisions thoroughly. They love quick results and want to be winners. In their bid to do this, they skip an essential stage in decision making – thinking about results. Aries don't shy away from risks and are always up for a challenge. When it comes to risks, they need to be calculated. A calculated risk can be the difference between winning and losing.

Before you make a decision, take time and think about its consequences. Don't always be in a rush; try to think things through. Your creativity and imagination, coupled with problem-solving skills, give you an edge over others. So, try to make the most of these wonderful traits.

Aggressive Nature

Aries are inherently more aggressive than other signs, and it is often associated with their ruling planet Mars. When these signs struggle to regulate their anger, it results in temper tantrums and outbursts. Since these things are avoidable, learn to regulate your emotions. Anger is a potent yet natural feeling, and unless you control it, it will certainly control your actions, behaviors, and even thinking.

Anger isn't always avoidable, and the simplest way to regulate it is by learning to calm down. Pay attention to your feelings and emotions. Whenever it feels like they are getting the better of you, take a break from your situation. Walk away from the place and put physical distance between yourself and the situation. Take a couple of moments to regroup your thoughts and regulate your breathing. Once you calm down, it becomes easier to review the situation and decide the course of action rationally.

Impatience

Aries always seem to be in a rush. They are incredibly impatient and hate waiting for results. Aries is similar to a super-fast sports car and wishes to live life at a great speed. This is the reason they often make poor decisions. Slowing down or anything monotonous doesn't work for an Aries. This is why they often leave tasks unfinished and switch to other activities if work becomes routine and monotonous. Aries set big goals for themselves and often get to work without evaluating all the possible consequences of their actions.

A simple way for an Aries to tackle their impatience is to become mindful. Don't be in a hurry, because life is not a race. It isn't about hurrying to the finish line; it's about enjoying the journey. Don't get distracted; learn to live in the moment. Stop concentrating only on the results and enjoy the process.

Attention Seekers

Aries not only love attention but thrive in the spotlight. Think of them as actors who need an audience. If they don't get the attention they desire, they can quickly become disappointed and agitated. Aries constantly look for external sources of appreciation and validation. They need listeners and love it when others praise them. Sometimes, they go out of their way to complete certain tasks to make themselves look better than others.

Dear Aries, don't do this. Instead of looking for external validation, concentrate on being the best version for yourself. Once you realize your source of happiness, motivation, and acceptance comes from within, life becomes easier.

Slightly Selfish

As mentioned in the previous chapter, Aries can seem a little selfish, but they are like babies, and it would be unfair to call a baby selfish. Since they are so focused on winning, any behavior that will help them seems okay to an Aries. If they have a goal and wish to complete it, nothing can get in their way. Even if things go wrong, Aries doesn't believe it's a reason to give up. Due to this, Aries's behavior might seem selfish to others, but from an Aries perspective this isn't selfish, and it's only about self-promotion. They concentrate on the results and themselves before everyone and everything else.

The simplest way to get over this seemingly selfish attitude is by tapping into your inner generosity. You don't always have to be in the spotlight or be right. It is okay to accept your mistakes and make things right. It doesn't devalue you. Don't forget about others while concentrating on yourself. Placing yourself first is perfectly acceptable but understand the consequences of your actions, too. Before you do anything, take time and think about your actions and the possible consequences.

Aries-Taurus cusps are easily distracted, often rush into situations, and have a tough time letting things go. In contrast, Pisces-Aries cusps are easily distracted and extremely problematic. These cusps display a combination of weaknesses associated with other zodiac signs (namely Taurus and Pisces) and not just Aries.

Weaknesses of this zodiac sign can be summed up as follows:

- Aries are prone to aggression and are known for their explosive tempers.

- This sign is highly competitive to the extent that they cannot deal with the idea of not winning.

- Aries can come across as selfish and inconsiderate.

- They are also impatient, impulsive, and reckless to a fault.

It is time to tackle your weaknesses and channel them into something positive by concentrating on your strengths. Follow the simple advice given in this section to overcome your weaknesses and to be a better version of yourself.

Chapter 5: The Aries Child

As with adults, even kids have certain defining traits and unique personalities. Most of the qualities we display in adulthood are a magnification of the traits we displayed as kids. It has been repeatedly mentioned that one's zodiac sign influences their personality and characteristics. The same stands true for kids too. In this section, let's look at all the information you want to get a better understanding of Aries kids.

Traits of Aries Children

Aries kids, like the adults, are enthusiastic, innovative, and ready to take on new challenges. They aren't afraid to take risks and don't like to follow others' rules. With their inventive and creative thinking, there is seldom a dull moment. If you don't keep a close eye on them, there may be trouble; these are the kids who don't hesitate to climb the tallest tree in the backyard, leap off the roof, or jump fences. They are impulsive and view life as one big adventure. They cannot sit idle, and keep exploring their surroundings, often to their parent's dismay.

Children born with the sun in Aries often leap before looking or even thinking. These traits follow them into adulthood as well. As toddlers, they rush about, in and out of rooms, often too fast for the parents to realize what they are doing. They often learn from experiences and consequences instead of listening to the advice given by others. Regardless of all the precautions their parents teach them, they prefer to live life on their own terms even from a young age. They love breaking the rules because they are natural-born leaders. They believe in making their own rules. If you have an Aries in your life, you need to be extraordinarily patient with him/her. Teaching them to respect and abide by rules and follow limitations is difficult, but necessary.

These kids are physically active and extremely competitive. The best way to channel their inner competitiveness is by directing them to sports and other physical activities. By adding physical activities to their daily routine, it gives them a sense of structure.

Aries are born leaders. They love the limelight and don't care about what others think. The only thing that matters to them is what they want. Once they set their sights on something, they go after it with everything they have. With a little guidance, you can mold an Aries into an incredible adult. He/she has all the makings of an inventor, a leader, and an entrepreneur. They are brave, fearless, and can rise up to high positions in life. Whether it is class president or the top honcho in a company, Aries will rise to the top.

Aries tend to move quickly, too quickly at times for their own good. Their inability to sit still or think before acting makes them impulsive. Unless you teach them to regulate these impulses, they will get hurt. Quick actions and instant results seem to be the motto for an Aries. This is also a reason why they are easily distracted. An Aries kid might seem motivated and determined whenever he starts something new. Chances are, he gives up before completing the task at hand and moves on to something else. If you don't teach him patience, he will never learn the importance of completion. It takes patience to teach an Aries to be patient.

Do you remember any instances from your childhood when others told you to slow down? Well, did you listen to them? If not, don't expect the Aries kid in your life to listen to your advice either. If you really want them to pay attention to you, start by becoming a good listener. By teaching them patience, you also teach them to think things through before acting.

Moderation isn't a term that exists in an Aries's dictionary. Their strong emotions often guide these kids. Whether it is extreme happiness or rage, all their emotions are amplified. These emotions also make them impulsive. All adults in an Aries kid's life need to be watchful for such behaviors, especially any form of aggression or violence. They are hot-headed and tend to get into fights, squabbles, and arguments.

Aries kids are known to be highly competitive and egocentric. They need constant attention from their caregivers and feel dejected when they don't get it. They also seek recognition for all their achievements and actions. As a caregiver, learn to discourage the little ones' undesirable behaviors from a tender age. Allow them to become assertive without getting angry. Teach them basic humility, because Aries doesn't understand the meaning of this word. Their "Me first" attitude can prevent them from excelling in life.

Arian Babies and Toddlers

Aries kids are not just feisty but are enthusiastic and determined too. They don't shy away from taking risks. This increases the chances of them getting into accidents. In this section, let's look at the defining traits of an Arian baby.

From birth until six months old, these little ones are a bundle of energy and activity. They are unusually friendly and alert. You will mostly see the baby with a big happy smile on his face, but they are exceptionally loud and vocal about their demands. These babies need little sleep and often prefer short naps instead of sleeping through the night.

By the time the baby is 6-18 months old, their overall activity levels increase. They might even start walking and crawling by this time. The Aries's trademark of impatience shows up at this stage. If the baby cannot do what he wants to do or is prevented from doing it, he will get frustrated. When he gets frustrated, prepare yourself for temper tantrums.

Kids are naturally curious, but an Arian kid is more inquisitive than others. As your little one approaches the three-year mark, you can see a visible increase in their curiosity. Be prepared to answer endless questions about everything and anything. "Why?" will become an increasingly common part of your little one's vocabulary. Try to fuel their curiosity and answer the questions as honestly as you can. Remember, they are trying to learn and grow at this stage. They will be incredibly busy and always on the move. It's not just the questions, be prepared for a little rebellious behavior too. Kids, by this age, become argumentative and start questioning authority.

Between 3-5 years, Aries kids start experiencing a variety of powerful emotions. This may be difficult for adults to handle, but it's even more complicated and tricky for the kids. Their overall mood might seem incredibly volatile to you. Your sweet and loving little one can become angry and violent at the drop of a hat. They are sensitive and take everything personally. Aries get frustrated when they cannot perform like they thought they would or if they fail. Their inability to deal with this frustration often presents itself in the form of temper tantrums.

School Age Arian Girls

Confident and unconventional are the two defining characteristics of Arian girls. They have a thirst for adventure that often lands them in unpleasant circumstances. They are fiercely independent. Their inherent adventurous nature makes them fearless and open to taking risks. Don't be surprised if your sweet little girl goes through a wild phase. This is common, and it often mellows down with age. As a parent or a primary caregiver in the Arian's life, be prepared to experience a little difficulty supervising her. Also, prepare yourself to receive an incredibly effective evil eye that communicates her indignation without saying a word. Aries love pushing boundaries and testing others' limits. They don't do this with any malicious intent, but it is their nature.

These girls have immense potential within them. They are full of energy and try to direct their energy toward positive aspects of their life. It's not just their physical energy, but mental energy, too. An Aries girl will often come up with innovative and creative ways of doing regular tasks, which might surprise everyone. At this stage, simply play along and let their creativity thrive and grow. Don't be too restrictive but teach where certain limits are. If you provide her with the right tools and resources, she will become incredibly successful.

Aries love being in control. They love the power rush of being the person in charge. As the Aries girl grows, she will start actively participating in household decisions. In fact, she will expect to be a part of all household decisions. Her pride matters a lot, and it is not a sign of vanity. If you give her the chance to channel her inner energy toward positive activities, she will become successful. She is good at organizing and arranging things. Try to make the most of her creative abilities.

One trait that all Aries share, regardless of gender, is their extroversion. Aries girls thrive in social settings, especially when they are in a controlling position. They might seem a little domineering, but their inherent nature is to take charge. They like leading and tend to reinforce the concept of working together as a team, but there will be moments or circumstances when she doesn't want to be around anyone else. Respect her privacy and give her the time and space she needs for herself. Don't try to push, but do start treating her like an adult. If you treat her like a child, she will rebel. Aries are independent and fiercely protective of this independence.

School Age Arian Boys

There is seldom a dull moment in an Arian's life. This is especially true for school-aged Aries boys. They are always up to something. Their natural desire to take on a leader's role makes them proactive and gives them the courage required to initiate things. If they are initiating something, they are certainly inciting someone else. They have absolutely no regard for structure or rules because they think it curtails their sense of adventure. They are looking for a lot of excitement in life and don't like to be stopped. They want action, and they want it without any break. They are highly active, healthy, and strong. They are highly competitive, so try to guide their energy toward something positive. Get them engaged in sports or anything else that will tire them out physically.

On the downside, these boys might have a tough time completing tasks. They often get tired and bored with projects halfway through and quickly move on to something more interesting. They are constantly seeking excitement and entertainment in life. You might be tempted to get disheartened when your little boy doesn't listen to you anymore. It is his way of asserting his independence. Teach him to be independent without stepping on other kids' toes. Also, teach them the importance of completing tasks. Once he understands the beneficial relationship between the effort that goes in and the results obtained, he will be more motivated.

Aries boys are natural leaders, and they are conquest-driven. They love engaging in battles. It isn't all about physical fights; anything that challenges their intellect or skills is appealing and enticing to an Arian. Be prepared to end up in parental battles. The Arian boy isn't doing this because he is selfish. Instead, he is trying to push your boundaries. Aries are curious and inquisitive. One way they learn in life is by testing the limits to which they can push others. It might seem like his sole purpose is to push your buttons. Resist giving him the satisfaction of the reaction he desires. Instead, channel your energies into teaching him good behavior. Show him better ways to deal with his inherent aggression and angst without locking horns.

Aries boys aren't good followers, and the sooner a parent realizes this, the better it is for the relationship. Instead of engaging in meaningless power struggles, choose your battles wisely. As an Arian grows up, he will undergo a significant motivational change. He will look for ways to channel his inner energies. Inspire and support him during this phase. He is incredibly passionate, and once he learns to harness his energy, he will become unstoppable.

Tips to Deal with Aries Children

Since Aries kids are impulsive, it's important to teach them to rein in their impulses. By helping them develop self-control from a young age, you can ensure that they have better decision-making skills in life. The first step toward tackling this issue is by making them aware of their impulsiveness. Whenever the Aries kid acts impulsively, bring their attention to it, and help them understand why such behavior is problematic in the given instance. For instance, if they constantly interrupt you while talking, tell them it isn't proper behavior. Inform them that you will answer all their questions, but they need to wait. Whenever you modify their impulsive behavior, be certain that you do it calmly. Any negative behavior from your side may harm the Aries's fragile self-esteem.

Slowly teach the child to combat his impulsive behavior. By suggesting alternative behaviors, you are not only encouraging good habits but also discouraging negative ones. Let's go with the examples discussed in the previous section. Whenever the Aries interrupts or disrupts you while talking, suggest he should raise his hand instead. When you teach him this, you are essentially suggesting that he needs to wait for the other person to acknowledge him before he starts talking. If the Aries is rather aggressive and resorts to physical aggression, teach other ways to acknowledge their emotions. Instead of hitting or taking it out on other kids, encourage them to hit the pillow.

It's not just about rectifying improper behavior; it's also important to praise positive behavior. Whenever your child is patient, corrects their own impulsive behaviors, or does anything else you desire, don't forget to praise their efforts. Aries love praise and love to be the center of attention. When your child knows they will be praised, their inherent willingness to listen to your suggestions increases.

Whenever you notice the Aries is acting up, don't punish them. If you do that, it merely creates a negative association with the act they are performing. Also, punishments don't teach good behaviors. Another drawback of punishing a child is it harms the relationship you share. Remember, they are a child, still learning. You are an adult, and you need to take control of the situation. Start by being patient. Take this opportunity to display the behavior you want them to follow. Children learn from others, especially the adults around them, so be mindful of your behaviors around them.

Aries children love to push boundaries. They do this to understand the extent to which they can get away with their acts and behaviors. They are inherently curious, and by pushing boundaries, they learn a lot in life. You should set certain clear and firm boundaries. It's not just about creating these limits but implementing them too. Besides implementing it, make sure that you have set certain consequences if these boundaries are broken. By doing this, you are helping your little one increase their tolerance for frustration. With consequences, the child automatically learns the relationship between an action and its result. If they do well, they will be rewarded. If they do something wrong, consequences will follow.

Children struggle to understand and regulate their emotions. Well, most adults struggle with this, too. To help a child regulate their emotions is important. Aries is a fiery and passionate sign. They can be consumed by their emotions if they are not careful. It's not just anger that is magnified, but happiness as well. Everyone needs to manage their emotions. The simplest way to teach your child about their emotions is by acknowledging them. Even if they are unable to regulate their emotions, acknowledge what they are feeling. After this, teach them to identify those emotions.

For instance, if you realize that your child is looking a little sad or angry, tell them, "I realize that you are a little upset right now." By saying this, you are not only acknowledging their emotions but are also labeling them. Once you label their emotions, encourage them to do the same. Identifying their emotions gives you a better insight into what they might be experiencing and its triggers. Engage in regular conversations about feelings and emotions. Teach them that there is no such thing as a good or bad emotion, but that the only thing that matters is what they do with those emotions.

Now, it is time to teach the difference between feelings and behaviors. For instance, if you notice that your child is angry because they did not get to play with their favorite toy, take them aside and sit with them. Calmly talk to them about it. Tell them that you realize they are upset. After this, calmly state the reason you believe to be the trigger for their anger. By doing this, you are helping them understand what happened. Identifying triggers is an important part of regulating emotions. Never punish your child for their emotions. All you can do is rectify their behaviors.

Arians are incredible at solving problems. They are very creative and can think quickly. Now is the time to use these traits and teach your Arian child how to solve their problems. If you notice that your child is struggling with something, encourage them to solve it independently. Do nothing for them that they can do by themself. It teaches them to be independent and feeds their need for independence. If they get frustrated when they cannot solve the problem, offer assistance.

Encourage them to seek help whenever needed. Since Aries is naturally proud, teaching them to swallow their pride once in a while for the sake of their own wellbeing is important. Many parents make the common mistake of trying to calm their children down as soon as they start acting up. Are you wondering why this is bad? Well, it doesn't teach the child the skills they need to manage emotions. Instead, it merely conveys the message; "Mommy or Daddy will come and fix the problem for you." The child shouldn't become used to such unhealthy attention. Arians love attention, but they also love their independence. From an early age, inspire them to be independent, and they will thrive.

Aries are infamous for being stubborn. This fiery sign is adamant about their wants, needs, and dislikes. They are opinionated to the extent of being exceptionally stubborn. This is not a trait you should encourage; dominating others is not desirable behavior. The simplest way to deal with the stubborn child is by listening to them. Children are smarter than we give them credit for. The next time your child starts acting up, try to listen to what they are truly saying. Most children become defiant when they know they are not heard. If you give them your undivided time and attention, they probably will calm down. Once they're calm, you can talk about desirable behaviors.

Whatever you do, there are two things you should never do. The first one is you should never lose your calm. The second thing you need to keep in mind while dealing with kids is that you shouldn't disrespect them. Arians are sensitive to criticism. This is just an expression of the fiery energy that rules them. If you lose your calm or disrespect them, it will harm the bond you share. Besides this, it can also convey the wrong message that they are not good enough.

One final tip: when dealing with children, make sure there is consistency. If you are inconsistent with the things you say and do, children will get confused. It also teaches them it is okay to break the rules. Instead, all the primary caregivers in the Arian's life need to follow the same home rules. Don't lose your patience while they are learning all this. It will take time and a lot of effort, but your efforts will pay off. Arians are destined for success in life. By arming them with the right tools and skills, you can ensure that they can achieve all their goals!

Chapter 6: Aries in Love

Compatibility with Other Zodiacs

When it comes to your love life, looking at astrological compatibility is a good idea. Astrology helps obtain insight into oneself and the world in general. As mentioned, those born under the same zodiac share several similarities. Certain signs are meant to be together. Think of astrological compatibility as the equivalent of "It was written in the stars." If you believe in destiny or fate, you will understand what this truly means. Zodiac compatibility will help you find a partner who shares similar and complementary traits. This is quintessential for the success of any relationship.

In this section, let's look at the compatibility of Aries with other zodiac signs. Learning about your personality traits and that of other zodiac signs makes it easy to navigate any obstacles the relationship might face.

Aries and Aries

The relationship between two high-strung fire signs is extremely passionate. You both wish to be the alpha in the relationship. It is like playing a game of hot potato, tossing it back and forth. One might submit to another's will or rule but only through gritted teeth. Accepting something without protest doesn't come naturally to this sign, but it helps build the trust the relationship is based on. Aries is a Zodiac paradox. It is the first sign and, therefore, the zodiac's infant. It is also the hero because a warrior planet, Mars, rules it. The paradox is that Aries wishes to save and be saved simultaneously.

There needs to be a regular shift in power from one partner to another in a relationship between two Aries. One cannot always play the knight in shining armor while the other is the damsel in distress. These two roles need to be played by both partners. It is okay to allow your partner to charge in and rescue you occasionally, but there is a fine line that you both need to tread carefully. Letting your guard down and being a little vulnerable is not the same as spiraling into neurotic helplessness. Also, don't get stuck in a state of analysis paralysis where you keep overthinking a specific topic. Remember, no one wants to be saddled with the emotional responsibility of taking care of an overgrown baby. Since Aries are like adult babies, don't forget to keep a check on this side of your personality. Aries are extremely independent and cannot give up on their sense of freedom, even for the sake of a relationship. It is important to maintain separate personal lives while concentrating on creating a life together.

Aries are prone to aggression, and the best way to disperse this angst is through physical exertion. Whether it is going on adventures together or indulging in passionate sex, engaging in physical activity helps remove these feelings. Aries are known for their passion and libido. It might bring the likes of Hugh Heffner to mind, but it also comes with a sense of entitlement. Learn to find mutually agreeable ground and don't get too stuck in your ways. Make your terms flexible here and there; making little compromises and understanding each other's perspectives is important.

Aries and Taurus

When the adamant ram locks horns with the stubborn bull, the relationship will be fierce and fiery. It might seem akin to a Pamplona stampede, but the flames of passion will never die down. Aggression, whether civilized and uncivilized, is a part of human nature. In a relationship between an Aries and a Taurus, it is important to remember you are both extremely aggressive and willful. You are also stubborn and stuck in your ways. Both these signs have a variety of steamrolling tactics to get their way. The first face-off between an Aries and Taurus helps them gauge each other. These signs crave for a partner who will keep them safe and secure. They can do this on their own but look for similar traits in their potential partners. Victoria and David Beckham are the perfect examples of an Aries and Taurus marriage.

Getting together, dressing up, and flaunting your inherent superiority over the rest is something these signs enjoy. It is a sweet deal for both partners. In such a relationship, a Taurus finds an attractive mate they are proud of and a lusty partner to satisfy their libido. On the other hand, Aries has a lifelong partner and provider who supply them with unlimited creativity and lots of playtime, but on the downside, Taurus can become extremely possessive and curtail an Arian's freedom. Since Taurus is naturally indulgent, they need to stay active to keep pace with their energetic Arian partners. The relationship between these two signs is similar to that of two kids at the playground who favor the word "Mine!" Since both these zodiac signs crave attention, it's important for the partners to alternate between the roles of giver and receiver.

Aries and Gemini

According to the Zodiac, Arians and Geminis are best friends. If you are best friends, throwing in added benefits certainly sounds like an excellent idea. It is a great idea, but don't be in a rush. Certain similarities shared by these signs can lead to combustion. They are both reckless, seek instant gratification, and are impetuous. They know what they want and want it immediately. The excitement of playing footsie under the dining table or engaging in an edgy conversation might make them feel like they are soulmates. It's important to be spontaneous in a relationship, but when you combine spontaneity with recklessness, it often leads to poor decisions. If you are not careful, you will probably skydive into City Hall headfirst, believing you are meant to be together, without getting to know each other. You are Aries and Gemini; you both need to slow down.

Since Aries and Geminis make good friends, establishing a healthy and strong relationship is possible. Intellectual chemistry and physical fun are two elements you cannot take away from both the signs. The only thing to remember is to pace yourself. Don't allow boredom to creep in and keep things exciting. To alleviate boredom and understand each other more, engage in activities together. Spend time with mutual friends, learn an activity together, or find a small project to satisfy both your short attention spans. A simple tip: this couple needs to practice turning to each other for advice, especially in moments of vulnerability. Since both these signs are proponents of tough love and impatience, the conversations can quickly become draining. Even a conversation about the vulnerability can quickly escalate into a faultfinding mission. The vulnerable partner might misperceive his partner's advice as a personal attack.

So, learn to be patient and compassionate toward each other. If you can both let your guard down and think things through before acting on impulses, the relationship will be rewarding and wonderful.

Aries and Cancer

Cancer rules the fourth house of the zodiac and is associated with home, family, and motherhood. Aries is the baby of the zodiac calendar. This might bring a rather unsettling notion of an oedipal relationship between these signs. Unless you consciously temper these traits and concentrate on self-development, the relationship will not be healthy. Instead, you will automatically lapse into the roles associated with your signs. Cancer plays the role of a parent while the Aries becomes a child. Aries can come across as a little selfish and self-centered, but it's never with malicious intent. Instead, their crude and clueless style can leave the Cancer partner feeling resentful and dismayed by the Aries's lack of understanding.

The crabs are natural nurturers and givers, but this sign is very vulnerable too. But Aries loves to be coddled and the center of attention. It can trigger Cancer's parental instincts and cause them to indulge the Arians every whim and fancy. In the end, the Aries becomes a demanding and spoiled partner. Even though the crabs have a tougher outer shell, Arians are the real warriors, ruled by the aggressive Mars. Aries love their independence, while Cancer is all about the family. The ram loves and thrives in freedom while the crab can be possessive. There is room for a lot of compromise in the relationship. It can become extremely competitive and increasingly rooted in jealousy. If you both are not careful, it will quickly become depressing. There will be days when both partners are brooding, and their emotions get the better of them. Instead of resorting to the silent treatment, it's better to communicate openly about your needs and desires.

Aries and Leo

Both Aries and Leo are fire signs; they are adventurous, passionate, and love drama. These signs are flashy and outspoken, and each strives to meet their personal agenda. These restless souls need physical and intellectual stimulation. If the conversations become boring or dull, the relationship loses its charm. Since they are fire signs, they are incredibly passionate. This passion also bubbles up to the surface in the form of emotional meltdowns. Neither of them is adept at dealing with their emotional turmoil. It becomes difficult for them to deal with other's emotions as well. These folks thrive on adrenaline, and bring to mind the celebrity couple Jennifer Garner and Ben Affleck. This Aries and Leo duo fell in love while filming the action flick "Daredevil".

Since they are fire signs, both Aries and Leos are independent and love their freedom. They are looking to make their mark on the world and don't like anyone stealing the spotlight. In fact, the relationship hits hurdles when one partner tries to eclipse the other. If one tries to make the other look thoughtless or foolish, it spells doom for the relationship. These two signs mustn't compete with each other. The only person you need to compete with is yourself. The relationship is not a competition, and no one has to be the winner or loser. Learn to be each other's supporters and cheerleaders. Keep the spark alive and don't become complacent. Comfort is not the same as complacency. Once complacency creeps in, partners tend to lose interest in doing their best in the relationship.

Aries and Virgo

Couplings between Aries and Virgo are common. The relationship between these two signs is all about walking the fine line between love and hate. Even though the attraction feels fated and impossible to avoid, it forms a contradictory coupling. Guided by fire, Arians love freedom, and are risk-takers. These people helplessly fall for the parental and prudent Earth signs Virgos are guided by practicality and all sorts of protocols. In a way, Aries is often the flame that touches the gossamer wings of a Virgo. Yet the Virgo willingly flies close to the fire.

These signs come with a natural hero complex which translates into their relationships, too. But the signs are constantly looking for ways to fix each other or expose the other to different ways of life. The first couple of months in a relationship between an Aries and Virgo is exhilarating and thrilling. Aries passion helps awaken Virgo mentally, physically, and even sexually. On the other hand, the cautious Virgo teaches the ram to slow down and look both ways before crossing.

Unearthing new secrets about one's personality is an exciting adventure for both these signs.

The real trouble starts once this hormonal rush goes away. There are certain glaring differences these signs need to negotiate for the relationship to succeed and survive. Even well-intended criticism from Virgo can feel like a direct assault on their character to an Aries. Virgos can feel unappreciated and resentful due to the inherent selfishness associated with Aries. Even after listening to their Arian partner for hours on end, Virgos will not get the credit they are looking for. During the initial stages, this couple tends to spend a lot of time together. Soon, they realize they have spent too much time together and have lost touch with the external world. You must both maintain and retain your sense of individuality in your personal lives, even when together. Virgos need to be careful about their criticism and shouldn't try to change an Aries too much. Similarly, Aries need to stop worrying too much about being in the driver's seat and try to let go of the controls once in a while.

Aries and Libra

Aries and Libra are two opposite signs that get along quite well, but the relationship between these two sides is baffling at times. Aries is all about themself, while Libra is about relationships. Aries is a fighter, and Libra is a lover. These polar extremes come together well because they not only complement each other but each makes up for certain traits the other doesn't possess. Aries is temperamental, rash, and seldom gives others the benefit of the doubt. They don't look before leaping and often think about the consequences after making the rounds. Well, they can learn how to not do all this from their companion, the wise Libra.

But Libra is often extremely accommodating and struggles to say no. It is time for them to learn to stand up for themselves, start saying no, and instead of wondering and overthinking the consequences, start acting. These differences can be a little irritating, but if they harness their positive energy properly, a Libra and an Aries can become a well-rounded couple.

Libras are good listeners and will lend an ear to Aries whenever they want to rant. Arians can also expect sensible feedback and advice from the wise Libras. Aries can help their Libra counterparts fight their fear of conflict and teach them to stand up for themselves. For this relationship to succeed, both need to adjust their internal thermostat. Aries is hotheaded, so they have to learn to regulate their anger. Unnecessary displays of concentrated emotions will quickly imbalance a Libra's internal scales. Compromise is the key to this relationship to work. Libra needs to get away from their lofty ideals and, instead, concentrate on taking the first step. Aries tend to jump headfirst into a relationship, while Libras take all the time they need to decide whether or not it is the right action.

Aries and Scorpio

Mars rules Aries and exerts some control over Scorpios, too. Physical attraction is the first thing that draws these signs together. The sexual attraction is so great that it feels like fireworks are constantly going off when these signs are together. To be fair, neither sign is afraid of a little sexual gunpowder. The high intensity of the watery Scorpio, coupled with Aries firepower, stirs up a charge. However, this match cannot last for long unless the Scorpio has moved into an elevated state. Aries is not a giver, and Scorpio is a withholder. Whenever an Aries reaches out his hand to help Scorpio, their first instinct is to take a step back, which can wound the ram's ego. Aries's energy is extremely consuming and can leave the Scorpio a little scared. These things can become quickly overwhelming for a Scorpio. Therefore, Aries need to temper the raw desire and rein it in.

Aries are independent and outgoing. Therefore, they love spending time with different circles of friends, acquaintances, or even strangers. The Scorpio needs to temper their jealousy and possessiveness. There is no point in trying to control an Aries because no one can truly control them. The problem with this relationship is both the signs are sensitive to the fear of abandonment. To protect themselves, they try to push others away. The self-protection paradox of shutting people off before they leave them will become this couple's downfall.

But Aries believe they are entitled to the best in the world. These signs seem to say, "What's mine is mine and what's yours is mine." When both partners are takers in a relationship, the important question to consider is "Who will be refilling the coffers once they are empty?"

Aries and Sagittarius

These two fire signs are naturally drawn to one another. Chemistry and love don't take long to develop. Each will feel as if they have met the reflection of their soul. These signs are independent, adventurous, favor lust, live life at the moment, and are pumped full of self-confidence which is often mistaken for arrogance. They also share a love for blunt humor, and understand and respect each other's need for independence and space in the relationship. Well, it all seems good, at least initially. Remember, Aries do everything they possibly can when they love someone, but this kind of love doesn't come easily to the ram.

This couple will never run out of topics while conversing. They can talk about everything and anything under the sun, which is one reason they are drawn to each other. When together, even the impossible seems doable, and their natural confidence starts to soar. On the downside, both these signs live in the moment and therefore their perspectives can be slightly myopic. It isn't likely that all their plans will manifest into the results they want. During the times they don't, they both need crash insurance. So, this couple needs to work on looking both ways before crossing. However, they are both prone to bouts of overthinking, which swiftly drain the usual upbeat environment they both love.

Aries's need for attention and affection is higher than a Sagittarian's need for this. It can make the Aries resentful if he feels that he needs to constantly compete with the Sagittarian's busy life and schedule to get what he wants. Aries not only want attention but also think they deserve all this and more. Aries's needy moments can agitate the impatient Sagittarian. When pushed to the limits, the combined fiery anger can quickly burn down a forest. Be mindful of your temper, learn to think before leaping, and be respectful of each other's needs and temperaments.

Aries and Capricorn

Aries is a natural-born leader and always seeks to hold the alpha position in all his relationships. When an Aries and a Capricorn get together, the ram has finally met his match in the goat. The Aries will come to know the goat is a seasoned leader. This relationship is one of the rare instances when the Aries doesn't mind showing some obedience. The natural respect that Capricorn's command comes from the planet that rules them – Saturn. Saturn commands authority, compliance, and respect. If Aries is the firstborn of the zodiac, the goat is the father sign. The difference between these two signs is similar to that of a knight and a king. Both these signs are noble, but one is clearly older and wiser than the other (Capricorn).

Sometimes this can become a deal-breaker for the Aries in the relationship, because Aries value their independence too much, and a Capricorn's natural display of paternalism can become too controlling for the fiery fighter. Even though Aries is prone to throwing tantrums and can behave like a hellish brat, Capricorns are unruffled. In fact, Capricorns can find Aries's tantrums and outbursts amusing. They will give the younger zodiac the space required to act up. Once these two signs understand and accept the cosmic rules, it becomes easier to maintain the relationship. They not only make excellent partners in love but business, too. Aries is the warrior, and Capricorn is the four-star general. Life is viewed as a battlefield, and both these signs try to conquer it with their grit and determination. When put together, there is nothing they cannot achieve when working as a team.

The restless hooves of the fiery ram are tempered with the earthy Capricorn's love for structure and planning. They become daring playmates who continuously excite and amuse one another in and out of the bedroom. Aries are prone to flirting and spending too much time with others. This can make the conventional Capricorn a little jealous. Over time, the goat's fears can be put to rest if the relationship is based on mutual trust and respect. Once these two things are attained, it makes for a supportive and healthy relationship that is sustainable in the long run.

Aries and Aquarius

Aries and Aquarius make a brilliant duo. The romance might not be as exciting as the side-splitting guffaws they come up with. The simple fact that you are both capable of standing your ground, have clever responses, and don't hesitate to deliver hilarious comebacks becomes a turn-on. This casual banter quickly leads to the bedroom, and sex is often playful and experimental. Even if it doesn't lean heavily toward the emotional side, at least not during the initial stages, sex is fun together for these signs. It almost feels as if an Aries has met his twin in an Aquarian and vice versa. If this is left unchecked, you will both soon start feeling more like siblings than partners and lovers in a relationship.

However, Aries aren't known for their attention span and quickly get bored with things. If the relationship becomes too routine, the Aries will quickly lose interest. Aries are known for intense emotional spells and require excessive emotional attention. Aquarius, on the other hand, prefers to keep things light and can seem aloof and distant at times. Therefore, an Aries might feel as if the aloof Aquarian does not meet his emotional needs. Well, all this boils down to communication. An Aries doesn't quit until his problems are solved and will keep looking for ways to solve them. An Aquarian tries to solve their problems with logic or will leave them alone until he can find a solution. An Aries's determination can become too much for the casual and lighthearted Aquarian.

The cool Aquarius and the fiery Aries express their affection differently. The ram's passion and physicality can become a little overwhelming for the Aquarian who isn't always in the mood for constant touching or contact. If you want the relationship between an Aquarius and an Aries to survive, you both need to push yourself into the platonic borders. Engage in activities together, take time to travel, and spend more time talking to each other about emotions. Aquarius needs to realize it is okay to be emotionally vulnerable, and Aries needs to respect the time an Aquarius takes to open up. If these signs develop their independent selves, their reunion will be incredibly exciting.

Aries and Pisces

Pisces is the last sign of the zodiac and Aries the first. They are the quintessential alpha (Aries) and omega (Pisces). They are the dusk and the dawn. One cannot be seen or appreciated without the other. It might look like these signs are extremely different, but opposites attract. Despite all their differences, there is a lot of material to form a relationship. Aries love to be adored and often crave to be the center of attention. The generous nature of Pisces ensures all of the Aries's demands are met. Pisces can do and give anything in the name of love. This kind of love helps the Arian let go of his vulnerabilities and be his true self.

Aries can follow his natural instincts in this relationship while Pisces prepares for celebrations. The only problem with this couple is they both have powerful imaginations and are dreamers. If two dreamers are trying to steer a ship's helm, chances are it will veer off course. Aries is a good leader, but he needs a strong second-in-command. Pisces are often insecure and fall into spells of helplessness, especially under stress. These moody spells can be a little difficult for the Aries to deal with. Pisces are passive-aggressive while Aries are naturally aggressive. By changing your communication styles and understanding how to love each other the way you are, the relationship will thrive and prosper.

Cusp Signs

The Pisces and Aries cusp sign includes individuals who lean toward eccentricity in life. They crave intellectual stimulation more than anything else. Unsurprisingly, they look for partners who offer them this kind of stimulation. Gemini, Libra, and Aquarius are the air signs that can offer the Pisces-Aries cusp the stimulation they crave. The air signs are known for their creativity, spontaneity, understanding of human nature, and the ability to hold their own in a conversation. However, it is always the Earth signs that help balance the energy of this cusp. A person on the Pisces-Aries cusp not only needs a partner who will light up their world but bring about a sense of balance and grounding support.

The Aries-Taurus cusp looks for partners who will help calm their aggressive nature. Their partners need immense patience to deal with the combined leadership and dominance this cusp is prone to. These individuals know no bounds and will love their partners unconditionally. The only caveat is this lover will go away if their partners don't meet their expectations. The best zodiac signs for this cusp include Cancer, Virgo, Libra, Taurus, and Pisces.

They are extremely independent, have wild ways, and require equally strong partners. On the positive side, once the cusp knows they are ready to settle down, they will do anything and everything they can to see their commitment through. All earth signs make for good partners because they will understand your need and desire for success in life. But they will also push themselves to excel. Therefore, you will get all the freedom you need. These signs also look for a partner who will not easily get hurt because of their brash nature. Therefore, air signs also make for ideal companions. Air signs are naturally detached, and it means they will not take your strong opinions personally and will respect your independence. These free-thinking spirits come with their own set of strong opinions, but they understand that no two individuals are alike, and there will be a difference in opinions.

Teen Aries

The teenage years are usually tumultuous. It is slightly more overwhelming for an Arian. Since they are naturally drawn toward exciting things, love looks enticing. However, all the different properties discussed in the previous section about your strengths and weaknesses play a role in your love-life; not just in adulthood, but in your teenage years, too.

Aries are usually self-absorbed and focus too much on all that they want to achieve in life. This can hinder relationships. If all your time, energy, and effort go toward catering to your own needs, you are left with nothing for your partner. Therefore, Aries need to consciously decide to take some time out for their partners.

Aries are self-confident and don't like depending on others. When it comes to love, you need to show your vulnerabilities. It is okay to trust your partner and learn to trust your relationship.

Once the excitement of the relationship fades away, Aries quickly moves on to other things. It is time for a little self-introspection to understand whether the relationship has run its course, or you are simply bored. There are different ways to deal with boredom, not all of which involve ending the relationship.

Learn to manage your expectations in all aspects of life. Aries are often disappointed when things don't turn out the way they pictured. Since Aries are dreamers, they have lofty expectations, not just of themselves but of others, too. This kind of expectation can quickly spell trouble for a relationship.

Aries love to jump headfirst into new ventures in life and their relationships are no different. Try to refrain from doing this. Relationships must never be rushed, and they take considerable time, energy, effort, and patience to cultivate and maintain. Unless you are willing to dedicate these things, the relationship will not last.

Aries First Love

First love is one of the most memorable experiences anyone can have in their life. Embarking on your first relationship is a major life milestone. It doesn't matter whether the relationship lasts or not, you never forget it. When Arians fall in love, they don't hold back. They are direct and forthright toward their lovers. They play no mind games, and there's no manipulation. When an Aries dates someone, the partners know what they are getting into. They get exactly what they see in a relationship.

First love is exciting, and it can be a slightly overwhelming process. Life feels better, and everything looks brighter and beautiful than ever before. All these feelings are magnified for Aries. The passion with which they love is unlike any other. The aggression of the planet Mars directly elevates their passion. Do you remember how you felt when you fell in love for the first time, or your first real relationship?

Aries are dreamers, but they are go-getters, too. Once they set their sights on someone, they go for it with everything they have. Does this sound familiar to you? Well, let's learn more about how Aries deal with their first love and relationship.

Aries is fast-moving and lives in the moment. They seldom pause or second-guess themselves. If an Aries falls in love, it will be swift. There is no other sign that falls in love better than Aries. They are courageous, natural-born leaders and always want to be in the driver's seat. When in love, they will give it their all until they get what they want. Their determination and laser-sharp focus make the pursuit fun and interesting. The excitement of falling in love is intoxicating to them. Well, Aries not only knows this but also appreciates this excitement. It is reminiscent of how a toddler is attracted to a shiny new toy until something better comes along and distracts him. This is how Arians behave in relationships. Falling in love comes easily and naturally to Aries but staying in love is an entirely different ballgame.

Aries rarely get nervous, but in the face of new love or first love, they experience butterflies in the stomach like anyone else. They are not the most expressive of the zodiac signs, and often struggle with subtle conversations. If an Aries likes someone, he will be upfront about it. They are incapable of dealing with overpowering emotions. If it gets to be too much, the emotions will get the better of them. If an Arian falls in love for the first time, he will be honest and direct about it. From grand gestures to simple displays of love and affection, Aries will do it all. It might even feel like their entire world revolves around someone else. Since Aries are often self-absorbed and consumed with themselves, this shift in perception can be difficult. It can bring about a series of conflicting emotions.

If the Aries feels comfortable and happy in the relationship, they will let go of the fear of expressing their vulnerabilities. Aries are courageous and love standing up for themselves. Showing vulnerabilities doesn't come easily or naturally to them. Even if they are passionate, they struggle with being vulnerable.

Aries In A Relationship

Heady romance, passion, love, and unbridled affection are some words that describe an Arian in a relationship. In this section, let's look at how Aries behaves in relationships.

No Holding Back

Aries doesn't know how to hold back, and this is true for their love-lives, too. They are direct, honest, and forthright partners. They will not play any mind games. With an Aries, you get precisely what you see, and there are no façades. Aries can seem a little domineering and aggressive in the relationship, but it never comes from a bad place. All this is done with general enthusiasm and childlike innocence that is difficult to find fault with. Aries bring with them a certain sense of excitement to the relationship, which is intoxicating. This heady mixture of excitement and romance makes it easy to ignore their urge to be in the driver's seat all the time.

As an Aries, you're probably used to always being in control and taking charge. You're the one who always makes the first move and have no qualms about it. With relationships, ensure that you don't come on too strong to your partner. It is okay to take charge but draw a line about respecting the other person's boundaries.

Strong Partners

Aries are extremely strong personalities and look for similar traits in their partners. An Aries cannot deal with a weak partner. It doesn't mean they are looking for individuals who are dominating or manipulative. It merely means they are attracted to individuals who don't hesitate to put in the required effort to make things work. If their partner is clingy, needy, or insecure about the relationship, it probably annoys them. Aries hate pushovers and look for partners who are as feisty and confident as they are.

Heady Romance

Aries love the excitement of falling in love. They enjoy the chase, and it gives them an adrenaline rush they love. Their extroverted nature introduces them to people from all walks of life. This, in turn, introduces them to a variety of potential partners. This, coupled with their contagious enthusiasm, energy, and bold approach to relationships, means Aries usually go through multiple relationships before finding their perfect match. Their confidence, unbridled enthusiasm for life, and healthy libido make them an enticing prospect for potential partners.

Once an Aries is in a relationship, they become protective. Aries are naturally protective of all that's dear to them, and their partners are no exceptions. This kind of attention given by Arians is exciting and endearing. They don't go overboard with their affection but look for a partner who can hold their own. Romance with them is intoxicating. This heady mixture of traits makes them an ideal lover and partner.

Slight Jealousy

As mentioned, Aries can be a little possessive, like a child saying, "It's mine." Once an Aries thinks something is theirs, it is only theirs. This kind of thinking is not a result of any insecurities or malicious thought process. Instead, it is just their childlike nature at play. Aries also love the attention and don't like it if their partner cannot give them the attention they think they deserve. If you have experienced jealousy of this sort, remind yourself to keep it in check. Remember, more for others doesn't mean less for you. Whenever you feel jealous, it is better to talk to your partner about it. A lot of problems in the relationship can be easily solved with open and honest communication.

A Little Impatient

This fiery sign is not scared of taking risks and accepts challenges without a second thought. At times, that leads to poor choices, especially when you don't think situations through. There may have been instances in your life when you thought, "Well, it seemed like a good idea at the time," or "I thought it would turn out better." These thoughts are the result of your impatience. This impatience will follow you into your love-life, too, if you don't pay attention. Aries is not known to be patient or subtle. Therefore, if partners are overly cautious and reserved, it becomes an instant turn-off. Before you come to any conclusions or decide to do anything, it is always better to take a pause and think about what is happening. Not everyone requires quick results the way you do. Learn to be a little patient when it comes to handling aspects of your life.

Commitment

This is a sign that quickly commits to relationships. From an Aries's perspective, flirting and dating are a means to an end. The end they have in mind is commitment. Committing to a relationship is similar to completing the final leg of the race for an Arian. Since they are goal-oriented, committing to the relationship is the final phase of the journey they have set on. They are in it for the long run and will celebrate every win along the way until they achieve their goals.

If an Arian knows his mate is also willing to commit, they are the ones who believe in grand gestures. They will buy flowers and rings and will not wait to make things final. From popping the champagne bottle to celebrating their wins, Aries wants to do it all. It can be a little overwhelming when an Aries does all this. There is one slight problem in how Aries views a commitment. They think of commitment as the final battle they need to win in the war of love to come out as victors. Once they win a war, it doesn't end there. They actively seek other wars to win and another reason to fight. All those in a relationship with an Aries or committing to a relationship with an Aries need to ensure that the battles are reasonable and help each other to find victory. Instead of starting new battles that go against a relationship, you can channel all your energy toward attaining goals on different aspects of your lives together.

A Quick Guide To Dating An Aries

Aries love leadership and are quite assertive. They are organized and choose professions that allow them to express themselves and harness that energy freely. They are passionate, energetic, and love control. If you are dating an Aries or want to date an Aries, here are some tips that will come in handy.

Learn To Be Direct

Aries know what they want and how to get it. If an Aries likes you, you will know. If you caught their attention, expect plenty of eye contact, gestures, and flirty comments. They are honest and don't mince words. Therefore, learn to be direct. Other personality traits of theirs will get in the way, but your best bet is to be upfront about your intentions and motivations. An Aries will appreciate your candor.

Stick To The Truth

Since Aries are honest and cannot lie, they appreciate truth and honesty. They cannot lie to save their own skins and then expect their partners not to do the same. Compared to other signs, Aries can detect lies easily. Stretching the truth might sound like an interesting option to tantalize and engage your potential crush. However, chances are the strategy will quickly backfire. If the Aries detects you are lying, omitting the truth, or are dishonest, things will take a turn for the worse quickly.

Stand Up For Yourself

Aries love to be in control and are known for testing boundaries. They don't do this with any malicious intentions, it's just their childlike nature. The baby of the zodiac calendar often tests boundaries to see the extent to which they can get away with their actions. Therefore, stand your ground and implement your boundaries. It is a sign of self-respect, and an Aries will respect you for it.

Don't give up and stand for all that you believe in, even if the Arian continuously tests your boundaries. Don't try to bargain, and certainly stop over-explaining. Don't backpedal and never leave any room for interpretation in conversations with Arians. When it comes to implementing your boundaries, ensure that you leave a little wiggle room. Your boundaries are a sign of self-respect and acknowledgment of all that is acceptable and unacceptable to you. Remember, you always have the option to leave when things get too much to handle.

Lots Of Socializing

Aries are extroverted and love to socialize. If you are dating an Aries, be prepared to socialize. They mix with different social groups and have a long list of friends and acquaintances. If you are an introvert or lean toward introversion, it can be a little trying for you. However, don't worry too much about it. Aries love spending time with others but love their downtime, too. It means you need to be prepared for endless TV marathons as well as a healthy dose of parties.

Don't Give Up Your Independence

Aries are independent and love their freedom. They look for partners who share similar beliefs. You cannot take away an Aries's need for alone time. In any healthy relationship, the partners need to retain their identity and independence. You both need to have your own lives. Just because you are dating doesn't mean you have to spend every waking second together. In fact, if you become needy or clingy, you will push your Arian partner away. If you are an independent person, dating an Aries is perfect.

Bring Excitement

Remember that Aries are the babies of the zodiac calendar? Well, they are curious and are always exploring things. While dating an Aries, keep things interesting. Everything doesn't have to be a grand gesture, and you don't have to make any radical changes to your personality or life. Instead, try to keep the spark alive. Aries have an incredibly short attention span, and holding their attention will take considerable effort from both of you. They don't like just going with the tide. Instead, they constantly seek excitement in all their endeavors, and their personal lives are no different. Keeping things interesting is important in any healthy relationship. Don't get complacent, and don't let your partner get bored.

Aries are extremely loving. Even if they get a bad rap for being flirty, they are in it for the long run once they love and trust you. The kind of passionate and fierce love an Aries is capable of giving is unlike any other. However, they are a little complicated, too. Open up your heart and allow your intuition to guide the way. Dating an Aries is similar to riding a rollercoaster. There will never be a dull moment, so prepare yourself for the ride of your life.

A Quick Guide for Aries to Navigate Healthy Relationships

Aries make for wonderful and amazing partners full of confidence and filled with an enthusiasm for life. As an Aries, your unbridled enthusiasm, childlike innocence, and zeal for life are reflected in everything you do. You are constantly looking for ways to make life more interesting. Unless life is a big adventure, you don't feel satisfied. When things start to feel routine, you get bored. Therefore, you must constantly look for new places to explore with your partner.

Aries have multiple interests, and that usually means people from all backgrounds may surround them. You have no reservations when it comes to asking others to help you achieve what you want. However, you don't necessarily depend on them to make your dreams come true. Your natural curiosity is important in a relationship because it helps you understand more about your partner.

Arians are focused and determined. They are the go-getters and don't hesitate to take the initiative. This initiative comes in handy in your personal life. You have an immense social circle and the mental and emotional energy required to achieve your goals. You are not afraid to make the first move. This is a helpful skill, especially when it comes to solving any obstacles or hurdles your relationship faces.

Aries like to try new things and are open to change. Your adaptability makes you strong enough to deal with the many ups and downs of the relationship. You are not stuck in your ways and are willing to explore different things until you find something that works for you.

Aries are incredibly kind to others, but they are not the types who will suffer in silence. They are not afraid to call a spade a spade regardless of whether others want to see their perspective. This kind of brutal honesty isn't always welcomed by everyone.

They also tend to act without carefully thinking through the consequences of their actions. It can seem thoughtless to their partners in a romantic relationship. Therefore, spend some time trying to understand what you are doing before you go through with it. Remember, your decisions influence not only the course of your life but the lives of others, too. Don't be thoughtless, try to become considerate toward others.

Don't be scared to let down your guard and be vulnerable. Aries struggle to show their vulnerability. If you cannot do this then developing emotional intimacy becomes difficult in a relationship. Trust your partner and have a little faith in the relationship.

Aries are known to be temperamental and moody. Don't let your mood affect the course of your relationship. You are not the only human being capable of feeling and experiencing different emotions. Others do this too. If you want your partner to be there for you in tough times, learn to be there for them. Try to channel your inner angst towards positive things in life, and relationships become easier.

Chapter 7: Aries at a Party

Humans are social animals, and we live as a part of societies. We cannot live in isolation, and social contact is good for our overall wellbeing. We learn and grow while interacting with others. Our social circle shapes our personal lives and identities. Aries are naturally extroverted and thrive in crowds. For Aries, their social circle matters a lot. In this chapter, you will learn about Aries' friendship compatibility with other zodiacs, tips to form and maintain friendships as an Arian, and tips to cultivate friendship with Aries.

Friendship with Other Zodiacs

Aries

The friendship between two Aries brings together two strong and unyielding individuals. This sign is always open and honest. Therefore, you don't have to worry about any malicious intentions or hypocrisy when friends with another Aries. However, this ego can hamper the bond since these signs are easily offended. They often have a wide circle of friends and acquaintances because they need constant change and stimulation. When you are friends with an Aries, there's plenty of stimulation available, and you don't have to look for it anywhere else.

Taurus

The friendship between an Aries and Taurus is perfect. It brings equilibrium to an Aries's spontaneity and the Taurus's thoughtfulness. The simple fact that they are extremely different from one another merely makes the friendship enticing and charming. It helps create the right balance of masculine and feminine energy. When Aries needs a listener, the Taurus is there for them with a listening ear and good advice.

Gemini

The friendship between these two signs is a beautiful partnership that balances physical energy with intellectual strength. They get along well because the airy strength of a Gemini supports an Aries' fiery spirit. When they work together, they can attain prolific results because of their different personalities and exceptionally good communication skills. It is a complimentary friendship where both benefit from each other.

Cancer

Stability and trust are the primary characteristics of a friendship between Cancer and Aries. As the friendship strengthens, the sense of understanding between the signs also increases. The water and fire elements don't go well together, but they can make an exceptional team with mutual effort and understanding.

Leo

Passion and energy are the defining characteristics of the friendship between Aries and Leo. These two signs are incredibly dynamic, adventurous, and have a healthy competitive spirit. Mutual respect and admiration, coupled with dynamic energy, makes the friendship fruitful to both these signs.

Virgo

The harmony between Aries and Virgo will be long-lasting once they accept each other the way they are. They might be opposing signs, but their differences keep the friendship interesting and exciting. Each sign gets an opportunity to learn more about themselves and discover something new from the other.

Libra

The union of Mars and Venus brings with it a sense of harmony. This makes the friendship between Aries and Libra fulfilling and mutually satisfactory. Libras love collaboration and Aries are incredibly independent. Therefore, there will always be plenty of ground to explore. In this friendship, the signs will never run out of topics to discuss.

Scorpio

Once these signs learn to overcome their naturally dominating personalities, friendship can be fun and exciting. Their shared sense of humor is enthralling, but it can also cause power struggles. If these signs learn to put aside their differences and work together, their combined energy is unmatchable.

Sagittarius

A friendship between Aries and Sagittarius will always be fun and entertaining. Their similar traits and love for excitement make them compatible as friends. However, both these signs are famous for their quick temper. Once they learn to regulate their anger, friendship can be mutually inspiring and beneficial.

Capricorn

Once the Aries and the Capricorn learn to identify and accept their well-defined roles in the friendship, they can work wonders. Since these two signs are naturally competitive, it is important to ensure the competition always stays healthy. Their competitive nature can also create unnecessary trust issues. All this can be easily circumvented through open communication.

Aquarius

The friendship between Aries and Aquarius might be competitive, but it will always be exciting. Both these signs are imaginative and creative. Therefore, they will never run out of activities they can do together. Their shared interests and passions will sustain a friendship, but they are both a little stubborn, and they need to learn about compromising once in a while.

Pisces

The friendship between Aries and Pisces is mutually beneficial. Pisces brings about a sense of stability and balance to an Arian's bossy nature. The first and the last signs of the zodiac make for unlikely friends who will not hesitate to stand by each other's side in times of need.

Whether it is the Aries-Taurus or the Pisces-Aries cusp, these signs love exploring the world around them. Their extroverted nature makes it easy for them to make and maintain friendships.

Recognize an Arian at a Party

Parties are fun and exciting. They help you interact with your loved ones and strangers alike. You get to know many people at parties, and it gives you a chance to unwind. At every party or social event, different types of individuals come together. Some people are superstars, and some are simply overly drunk individuals. Some play a paparazzo role, shot pushers, the babysitter or the parental figure, the beer pong player, the table dancer, self-styled DJ, the freestyle dancer, or the crybaby. Recognizing an Arian is quite simple. Why is it easy? Well, it's because they are usually the center of attention and thrive on all the attention they get.

Aries is like the lightning bolt at a party, one that instantly energizes and electrifies the party's environment. From the moment they arrive until they leave, they demand everyone's attention. The natural urge to seek excitement makes them the life of the party. These individuals are usually the ones who insist that everyone keeps drinking! They are full of energy, and it almost feels as if it's radiating from their bodies. Their naturally competitive nature can also be seen in public or social settings. Whether it is a drinking game or beer pong, Aries will try to win.

If an Aries is hosting a gathering, you will know. Some prefer casual sit-downs, while others love huge gatherings where food, alcohol, and music flow freely. You might not realize it, but the zodiac also plays a role in the kind of parties you host. Since your Sun sign influences your basic personality traits, the type of party you want to host will also differ. Aries not only know how to bring a party to life, but their high energy and positive vibes can instantly uplift the mood. They don't get bothered by the small details and instead concentrate on the environment. They don't need hours to plan a party and host a brilliant one even at a moment's notice. Their natural charisma attracts people to them. Also, if Aries is hosting a party, chances are there will be a variety of individuals. Remember the different types of individuals who were mentioned earlier? You will find them all at an Arian's party.

Aries as a Friend

A typical Aries usually has a lot of friends. They are faithful and loyal to their friends. They are truly dependable. You can always count on your Aries friend to step up for you in times of need. Regardless of the time of the day, if you need them, they will be there for you. If you manage to get past their tough exterior, you will understand how wonderful and vulnerable they are. Aries appreciate friends who can stand up for themselves, are not scared to act, and have a sense of adventure. They demand honesty in all relationships. Even though they are impulsive and short-tempered, their hearts are always in the right place. In an argument or disagreement, be prepared for them to react harshly. The good news is, they are incapable of holding grudges, and the anger passes quickly. All it takes is a smile to make things okay with an Aries. After all, they are the Zodiac's baby.

As an Aries, even though you are a fiercely loyal friend there might have been instances in your life when you have lost a friend or two. It often happens because you have a wide friends circle and don't really realize the value friends add to your life. It can also be because of the self-absorption associated with your sign. Usually, Arians lose friends for personal reasons. For example, if an Aries helps out his friend in times of need, he will expect the favor to be returned. If the other person fails to do this, Aries can be unnecessarily harsh or aggressive because of it. An Aries cannot be friends with anyone who doesn't respect him, or who are not honest. For instance, if an Aries realizes that he's been fooled or taken for granted, there is no going back. It will be the end of the friendship.

How To Be Friends with An Aries

Aries is a fun and optimistic individual. A friendship with them is incredible. They are naturally adventurous, independent, generous, and vibrant. They always take the first step to bring about the change they desire. However, they can also be impatient and moody. If you have an Arian friend or are trying to be companions with an Aries, it is important to consider the personality. In this section, let's look at simple and practical tips for being friends with an Arian.

Understand Them

You cannot be friends with the person if you aren't aware of their traits. This knowledge includes an awareness of their positive and negative traits. Once you get to know this zodiac sign better, it becomes easier to understand why they behave in the way they do. It also gives you an insight into their thinking process. On the positive side, Aries is courageous, generous, innovative, loyal, creative, active, confident, enthusiastic, and fun. They like keeping the overall environment lively and light. They are not the sort to get bogged down by troubles or problems in life. Instead, they look for creative ways to overcome any challenges. On the downside, they are short-tempered, rash, indecisive, aggressive, impatient, and selfish to an extent, not to mention dominating, controlling, and moody.

Attention Matters

Aries love to be the center of attention and will always ensure they get the attention they think they deserve. They love to be in the limelight. So, if you want to be friends with an Arian, give them all your attention. When you are with them, don't concentrate on other things and do let them know you are listening. Arians are also known to have massive egos, and stroking them every once in a while can work miracles for the friendship. However, you don't have to go out of your way to do things for them. Instead, be genuine and offer a few honest compliments.

Their Love for Speed

Aries are not known for their patience. They are swift in both actions and thoughts. A slow-paced life is something an Aries cannot handle at all. This is the reason they constantly keep pursuing different things in life. Unless you can match their speed or pace, you cannot be friends with them. Since they are impatient, they don't like to wait. If you can keep up this pace, you have found a genuine friend for life.

Be Adventurous

There will seldom be a dull moment in a friendship with an Arian. They have exciting ideas and new adventures they want to embark on. Those who are shy or hesitant might need to step out of their comfort zones to accommodate an Aries. It doesn't mean you have to change. It merely means you learn to be more open to life and all the advantages that come your way. If you add some excitement and vibrancy to an Aries's life, the friendship becomes truly rewarding.

Give Them Their Space

Aries love to be around people, but they value their personal space as well. They are fiercely independent individuals who value freedom highly. If an Aries feels that their freedom is curtailed, they will cut all ties and run in the opposite direction. Aries detest individuals who are needy, clingy, and who don't respect their personal space. Since they are moody, they need private moments to regain a sense of balance in their lives. If an Aries says he wants to be alone, give him his space. He will get back to you.

Be A Good Listener

The first zodiac is talkative and often looks for listeners. They are also known for going on rants about different things that bother them. If an Aries is ranting, let them. Don't interrupt, and certainly don't offer any advice immediately. Instead, merely lend a listening ear and let them understand you will be there for them. Despite their brave exterior, Aries are emotionally vulnerable. It takes a lot for an Aries to let their guard down and allow someone else to see their inner selves.

Let Them Control

Aries are natural-born leaders and love to be in control of all situations in life. Whether it is their private or personal life, they always want to be in the driver's seat. Because of their leadership qualities, you can never truly control them. Let them take charge of things once in a while, and learn to take a backseat. When you do this, the friendship will thrive, and you will get to know more about your Arian friend.

Tips for Aries to Form Healthy and Lasting Friendships

Aries love meeting new people and often have a varied circle of friends. In fact, they tend to have friends from all walks of life. Whether it is the neighborhood postman or the kids playing at the park, Aries can pretty much get along with anyone. However, there is a difference between getting along with others and making true friends. In this section, let's look at simple tips you can follow to cultivate and maintain healthy and lasting friendships.

Balancing Act

Aries understand the importance of honesty and sincerity in life. They cannot stand pretense. With an Aries, you pretty much get what you see. They are brutally honest, which isn't always appreciated. Therefore, learn to strike a balance between tact and being real. It is okay to want to be real all the time but learn to gauge your friend's mood before saying anything. A little diplomacy will not hurt anyone and will help strengthen your friendships. For instance, if you notice that your friend's sad face reflects a decision he made, now is not the time to say, "I told you so." Instead, be there for them, and you can offer your insights and advice later.

Learn To Be A Good Listener

Aries expect others to listen to them but are seldom good listeners. Cultivate the patience required to be a good listener. Listening has become a lost art these days, and cultivating this skill will come in handy in all aspects of your life, not just friendships. When you listen to someone, it shows you care and understand. It also shows you respect what the other person is saying. If you realize your friend is talking to you about something, pay attention to what they are saying. Forget about your problems for a minute and listen to them. No friendship can survive if no one takes turns being a great listener. Also, when you inquire about your friend's life and their overall wellbeing, it shows you are interested in all that they have to say.

Make Some Time

You probably have a lot of friends, and there's nothing wrong with this. However, if you want to cultivate and maintain healthy and lasting friendships, you need to make time for your friends. A friendship cannot sustain itself if you cannot offer your time and attention. There might be a hundred things you want to do, but your friends matter, too. Don't forget about giving back to your friendships. Time is one of the greatest gifts you can give anyone.

Don't Try To Be Controlling

As an Arian, it is in your nature to always try to control a situation. However, if you expect others to listen to you all the time or get upset if you don't get your way, it will spoil relationships. Learn to understand that there will be instances when you need to take the back seat. If your friend listened to you previously, now it's time to return the favor and listen to them. It is okay if you're not in charge. Learn to let go of your obsessive need for control and relax instead.

Encourage and Appreciate

Aries love to be encouraged and appreciated for their positive points and all that they do in life. Well, you need to give as much as you get. A relationship cannot survive if there is no reciprocity. Therefore, start showcasing the kind of behavior you enjoy. If your friend is excited about something, share their excitement. Learn to appreciate all that your friends do for you. Don't take the relationship for granted, and certainly do not ignore them.

Dealing With Conflicts

Aries are known to be aggressive and short-tempered. Learn to control and neutralize your aggression without targeting your friends. A difference in opinions is bound to crop up in any relationship. Learning to deal with it positively is important. Just because you have an opinion doesn't mean others are wrong. Understand that there can be multiple opinions, and all of them can be right. One need not be wrong for the other to be right. Remember, not everyone thinks and behaves the way you do. Learn to be considerate of others' feelings and emotions and not just your own. Don't get so caught up in your own life that you don't have time for others. Deal with conflicts positively and rein in your temper.

Chapter 8: Aries at Work

Work is an important part of life. It's not just a means to an end or a form of livelihood, but it is also a part of your life. On average, a usual workday lasts for anywhere between 6-8 hours. It is believed that an average individual spends about 90,000 hours at work. Yes, you read it right, 90,000 hours! That's a considerable portion of your life dedicated to work. Therefore, it is important to ensure you are in the right job and have created the right work environment. Working a job that you don't like will become stressful and frustrating. Similarly, if your profession doesn't play to your strengths, it increases the frustration you feel.

In this section, let's look at how Aries behaves at work, their ideal career options, and tips to increase their work productivity. All the information in this chapter is based on the primary traits showcased by Arians. It will help you make the most of your strengths and overcome any challenges that come your way.

Identify an Aries at Work

Aries are natural-born leaders, and this quality shines brightly in the workplace. They are enthusiastic, driven, and innovative. They are independent and hate routines. It is easy to identify an Aries at work. Did you notice that there is a specific co-worker who always volunteers to do things? Perhaps takes the initiative to organize parties at work or takes the lead in any projects? Chances are, he is an Arian.

Every office has its own water-cooler gossip spot. During breaks, you will certainly find an Arian there – surrounded by a crowd. Since they love attention and interacting with others, gossiping comes naturally to them. However, they will not be spreading malicious lies about others. It is in their nature to be truthful and honest. Playing mind games isn't something an Aries enjoys, and you don't have to worry about vicious rumors being spread by them.

If you ever notice a co-worker who has his headphones on and seems to be lost in his own world, it is likely he's an Arian. Aries are self-absorbed and driven to their causes. It doesn't matter to them whether others understand them or not.

Arians are go-getters, and their fiery passion can be seen in their work. They are competent, versatile, and can adjust to any environment. But they prefer their work environment to be lively and proactive.

Ideal Careers for Aries

Aries is the most competitive zodiac sign. If you have the desire to be the best at everything you do, you are a true Arian. It is no secret that Aries love winning, and there's nothing that can get in their way. Aries love challenges but are impatient. They are extremely courageous, ambitious, and usually take charge of any situation. Perhaps the biggest challenge you will face in all aspects of your life as an Aries is your fiery temper and attitude. Once you rein these things in and replace them with patience, you can make the most of your strengths. In this section, let's look at ideal career choices for Arians.

The modern world we live in is incredibly fast-paced. There is a lot of competition you need to overcome to find the job you desire. Finding the right job helps channel your creativity and gives an outlet for all your creative energy. These factors can help you shine in any area you choose. By analyzing your zodiac sign, you can use astrology to find the ideal career path for you.

Entrepreneur

An entrepreneurial role suits the pioneering ram. They are independent, ambitious, and dedicated. Instead of working under someone else, Arians thrive while working independently. Any entrepreneurial venture, whether it is an online or offline business, is a good fit. Your willingness to take risks and resilience coupled with leadership skills make you a good entrepreneur.

Surgeon

Arians are highly competitive, dedicated, and hard-working individuals. These are three traits that come in handy in the medical field. There are always risks involved when human lives are at stake. Therefore, the challenge is high, and the rewards are incredible. This is something an Arian truly craves. It also puts to good use their analyzing and decision-making skills.

Stockbroker

Aries make good stockbrokers because this profession requires good impulses. Making split-second decisions can make all the difference between profit and a huge loss. Since Aries can think on their feet and adapt to situations easily, you should consider this option. Taking risks requires a certain degree of fearlessness and courage. Dealing in the stock market requires an individual to stay resilient and hold onto a position even in the face of difficulties and obstacles. Well, doesn't it seem like the perfect job for an Arian? Since the risks are so high, the rewards are equally high. All this merely acts as an incentive.

Hotel Manager

Any profession where the Arian interacts with others is a rewarding experience for them. A management position requires good people skills, and Aries certainly possesses that in heaps. They are incredible organizers and can manage things easily. Hotel management jobs are exciting, enjoyable, and thrilling. It also requires the ability to adapt to different situations easily. This, coupled with the fact that the Arian is in a leadership role, makes the job even more fulfilling.

Marketing

Any profession that involves the dynamic and extroverted ram to interact with others is a good idea. Marketing is an obvious choice. It not only stokes the leadership flames in an Aries but provides an outlet for their creative energies. Their ability to stay abreast of changes and their adaptability are two traits that come in handy in a marketing role.

Law Enforcement

An Aries's inherent sense of responsibility and inner courage are what make them ideal for law enforcement. They are not afraid to hold their ground, even in challenging circumstances. Once an Aries believes in something, they don't hesitate to give 100% to see things through. This dedication and their desire to help others make them a perfect fit for law enforcement.

Firefighter

As with law enforcement, any role of public service helps channel an Aries's inner strength, courage, integrity, and willpower. Since fire is the element associated with this sign, they are fearless firefighters.

Military Service

Aries are energetic, and their physical strength is superior to that of other zodiac signs. Once an Aries comes to a decision on something, he will stick to it and stand by his promise. This makes them a great fit for military service. It also gives them a chance to make the most of their inner aggression and channel it constructively.

Professional Athlete

To be a successful athlete, you need a sense of motivation and dedication. Since Aries are driven and willing to take risks, they tend to perform better, even under stressful circumstances. Becoming a professional athlete helps channel their inner strength and puts their immense willpower and perseverance to good use.

Pilot

Aries love doing everything on their own, and this is the reason they are leaders. They can think quickly, adapt to the situation without any difficulty, and are not scared to make decisions even under tough circumstances. These are all the traits a pilot needs while maneuvering an aircraft. Therefore, Aries make good pilots.

Lawyer

Aries are opinionated and don't hesitate to stand up for themselves. If an Aries believes in something, he will stick by it regardless of what others say. This comes in handy in the field of law. Becoming an attorney at law or a criminal defense lawyer will put your effective communication skills to good use. Since Aries are convincing speakers and can impress others easily, this can swing judgments in your favor. That determination, resilience, and confidence make them good lawyers.

Tips to Overcome Challenges at Work

The fearless planet Mars rules Aries, and its element is fire. Therefore, your fiery nature allows you to surpass any obstacles or hurdles that come your way. You are seldom afraid of obstacles or any other hurdles you face in life. Regardless of the field you choose, you will try to be a pioneer in it.

The things worth having in life seldom come easily. There will be obstacles in all aspects of your life. By harnessing your inner fire, you can turn any challenge into a learning opportunity.

Dealing with Impulsive Behavior

Impulsive behavior means rash decisions. Impromptu plans might be exciting to your inner fiery spirit and passion. However, such behavior is seldom desirable at work. Don't allow your impulses to win out, instead learn to regulate them. If you give in to every whim and fancy of yours, you can get nothing done at work. Once you rein in your impulses, it becomes easier to see everything you need to complete. It gives you a better perspective of the challenges and opportunities available.

Don't Be Moody

Don't allow your mood to get the better of you. Remember, you are always in control of your emotions and behaviors. You cannot regulate how others feel or act, but you can regulate your own behaviors. If you allow your moods to dictate your behaviors, you will end up hurting yourself and others in the process. If you get overwhelmed, take a break from whatever you're doing, regain your composure, and then get back to the task at hand.

Regulate your Bossy Nature

Aries are proactive, love taking the initiative, and tackle challenges head-on. These traits make them natural leaders. But remember, you don't always have to be a leader to complete tasks or attain your goals. You can play the role of a team member, too. When at work, you are never alone, and you need to coordinate and communicate with others to get things done. Therefore, Aries need to learn to regulate their bossy nature. Don't try to dominate others. If you believe you have an incredibly good idea, talk to others about it instead of shoving this idea down their throats. Also, just because you have a good idea doesn't mean others are not capable of thinking. Don't believe that you always know best, and learn to become a team player.

Listen to Others

If you want others to listen to you, you need to reciprocate. No one will listen if they know you have no intention of listening to them. Listening doesn't mean just hearing their words. Instead, try to look at things from their perspective. When you consider multiple perspectives, it makes you more objective and improves your decision-making skills. You never know, others might have better ideas than you. Unless you listen, you cannot make the most of the resources at your disposal.

Always Complete Tasks

Aries are easily distracted. If the task gets routine or monotonous, or if something better comes along, Aries get distracted. The babies of the zodiac calendar have the attention span of a child. Learn to concentrate and live in the moment. It doesn't mean you shouldn't concentrate on other things in life. It merely means when you are working on a task, ensure that you see it to its logical conclusion. Unless you complete a task, don't move on to anything else. When you complete tasks and deliver on promises, it makes you trustworthy and reliable.

Tips to Create a Fulfilling Work Life

Planning is Important

Aries are naturally spontaneous and quite impulsive. They do not make detailed plans about what they want to do. Instead, they merely come up with a goal and try to figure things out as they go along. When it comes to work-life, spontaneity does more harm than good. If you have no plans, it becomes difficult to concentrate on the task at hand. Chances are, you end up getting distracted by several other things instead of concentrating on your goals. Once you start planning, you get better at time management. Time management is a crucial skill to establish a work-life balance. Once you figure out how to manage your time better, it gives you an idea of your priorities and the different goals you wish to achieve. It also ensures you have sufficient time left to do the things that you truly enjoy other than working.

Work on Communication

Aries are quite opinionated and make effective speakers. Well, you need to be an effective listener too. You cannot always expect others to listen. Therefore, work on improving your communication skills. Aries are honest, lack tact, and are not subtle; diplomacy doesn't come easily to them. When you combine all these traits, it increases the chances of miscommunication and conflicts at work. For instance, if you believe someone else's idea is not good and say, "That is foolish," or "How did you even come up with such a stupid idea?" this is not helpful. It might honestly be a stupid opinion, but no one likes to be told they are stupid. Learn to manage your opinions and don't come across as a know-it-all. Concentrate not just on your verbal communication but non-verbal communication, too.

Channel Your Creativity

Look for different ways in which you can channel your inner creativity. Your fiery passion allows you to see opportunities where everyone else sees challenges. Trust your gut instinct but listen to your rational brain, too. Don't let go of rationality when it comes to working.

Take Breaks

Aries usually believe they can accomplish anything and everything they put their mind to. This is a helpful and optimistic attitude to have in life. But if you are not careful, you will be overworked. Take on tasks you know you can complete. Push yourself but know your limits. You are not a tireless machine, and all your energy within needs to be replenished. Respect yourself and your boundaries. Take breaks while working, and don't push yourself to the breaking point.

Small Steps

Aries often set lofty goals for themselves. The only problem with such high ideals and goals is it increases the chances of disappointment. Ensure that your goals are small, manageable, attainable, realistic, and time-bound. If you set impossibly big goals, it increases your dissatisfaction and frustration. By managing your expectations, things become easier. Be realistic about all that you can and cannot do.

No Multitasking

Don't try to multitask. When you multitask, it merely increases mental stress and reduces productivity. Your fearlessness, energy, and aggressive nature might make you believe you can tackle everything that comes your way. This is true to a certain extent. Aries are resilient and strong. However, it would be best if you never bit off more than you can chew. If you take on too many things, you will merely burn yourself out, increasing frustration and resentment. Do you remember it was mentioned that planning is important? You can stop multitasking once you start planning.

Chapter 9: What Does the Aries Need?

By now, you will have realized how marvelous Aries are. Whether it is their initiative to be a leader or their loyalty as friends, they are incredible individuals. In this chapter, let's look at simple and actionable tips you can follow to harness your strengths as an Aries and effectively deal with the Aries in your life.

Tips to Harness Your Strengths for Success

• "Fortune favors the bold" is a perfect fit for the fiery Arians. Arians are bold, dynamic, courageous, resilient, and natural leaders.

• The self-confidence emanated by an Aries is unrivaled. They are extremely self-assured, and this trait enables them to charm their way through anything and everything they do in life. Whether it is an interview or a party, they know how to command a room.

• Aries are energetic, active, and goal-oriented. You have what it takes to reach your objectives and never give up. Hold onto your fighting spirit and be resilient.

• The love for adventure is one trait that all the Aries share regardless of their age or gender. Channel your ability to take risks into attaining your goals. With no fear of failure, it becomes easier to put yourself out there. Take risks only when required, and trust your gut.

• Arians are in touch with their impulses and are delightfully spontaneous. If an opportunity presents itself, grab it with both hands before it gets away. Your impulses set you apart from others. Your internal strength and courage are the perfect combination that you can channel toward making the most of any opportunity that comes your way.

• Your self-confidence is a brilliant resource, and you should never let go of it. If you believe in something, stick to it regardless of what others say. Stand up not just for yourself, but also for those who cannot do it for themselves.

• You are resourceful. Use your creativity and innovation to get the desired results in life. You can succeed, provided you put your mind to it. Show initiative and allow your inner leader to shine through.

• Arians have several excellent traits, but they have certain weaknesses, too. The good news is these weaknesses can be easily overcome with a little effort and dedication.

• Aries like to work by themselves because of their entrepreneurial nature. You might have firm beliefs and the ability to defend them. However, it doesn't mean you should ignore others. Learn to become a good listener, and it will help magnify your strengths.

• Be patient in all aspects of your life. When you look for instantaneous results, you often set yourself up for disappointment. Once you master the fine art of patience, success will be closer than it ever was. You have what it takes to succeed but be patient with yourself.

• Don't get so involved in your own world that you forget about everyone else. You are a loyal and loving friend. Learn to reciprocate all that you desire from your friends. When you become self-centered, it causes a lot of friction in your relationships. It also makes you look irresponsible while making others feel as if they have been taken for granted. It is okay to put others first occasionally, and it does not reduce your self-worth.

• Don't be too eager or adamant about always being in charge of situations in life. Learn to let go of this need to be in control, and life becomes joyous. This can be as exciting as being in charge.

• Give others a chance to shine. Learn to celebrate others' victories and spread happiness.

• Rein in your impulses and think before you act. Being impulsive will help you grab onto opportunities. But rushing in isn't always good because the chances of failing are quite high when you dive in headfirst. However, if you think a little before leaping, the results will be worth it.

• Arians are good at adapting to different circumstances in life and are welcoming of change. Hold onto this, and don't become stubborn. If you get too fixated on your ways, you will not get ahead in life. Learn to be flexible without compromising your core values.

• Don't let your ego get in the way of relationships. If you believe in the relationship, never prioritize your ego.

• The ram is ruled by the aggressive planet Mars. It makes you short-tempered and aggressive. Learn to manage your natural aggressiveness. Pick your battles wisely. If you are not mindful, this anger can consume you and remove all traces of happiness from your life.

• You might have a tough time asking others for help, but don't be too proud. Pride is good, but if it prevents you from excelling, let go of it. Even seeking constructive criticism from others will help you see perspectives you may have previously ignored.

• Aries tend to live in the moment to the extent they forget to see the bigger picture. They are also constantly seeking something or the other in life. This can make an Aries seem ungrateful. Practicing gratitude is a great idea.

• It is always our choice as to what we do. Choose to focus your energy on what you have in your life instead of focusing on missing things. Happiness is an elementary concept. It can be as simple as gratitude that you feel. People tend to focus too much of their time and attention on what they don't have. The grass always does seem greener on the other side. If it's not one thing that you want, after achieving it, it will be something else. There is no end to this ever-growing list of wants. Life has become a constant race for having the best of things. How can you ever be happy when all you want from life is more things? Take a moment and appreciate what you have. Only when you can count your blessings will you realize how fortunate you are. Humans in general need to learn to be more grateful. Your happiness depends on your ability to be thankful. Here are a few things that you should do to be more thankful in life.

• Maintain a gratitude journal. Fill this up with moments of sincere gratitude associated with the most commonplace events that take place. It will help to make you more grateful. Think about all the challenges that you have overcome in life. It will help you to become content with what you have in life. You cannot honestly embrace what you have if you don't remember the struggle you had to go through to get it. Here are a few questions you can ask yourself that'll help you with self-introspection. Ask yourself: what you have received from life, what have you given to life, and what troubles have you caused? These questions will help provide some perspective on your life.

• Whether it is school, college, work, or love-life, follow the different tips discussed in this section to see a positive change. You have great potential within, so step up and harness it. While doing this, don't forget to be patient with yourself. Don't get disappointed if you don't see instant results. The results will be worth your while, provided you will make this commitment to yourself.

Advice for Cusps

The Pisces-Aries cusp is a mixture of fearlessness and compassion. They are strong, instinctive, and always have an urge to get going in life. They are also smart, quirky, and fun. However, this sign is quite impatient because of their intuitive knowledge coupled with an impulsive mind.

If you are one of those on this cusp, you don't always think your thoughts through and have a tendency to put them into action before understanding their consequences. A strong sense of empathy and compassion for your loved ones makes you a good listener. You not only listen to them but also offer good advice. However, you do have an entirely different perspective on life. Unless others are willing to share this perspective with you, it can be a little off-putting in social circumstances.

Delving deep into subjects comes naturally to you. All you need is a listener. Your intuition, coupled with an inherent trait of holding onto your beliefs, can make you exceptionally stubborn, especially when someone challenges you. Therefore, learn to let go and enjoy life the way it is.

The same advice also applies to the Aries-Taurus cusp. Your initial reaction in any situation is to try to place yourself in a position of control. This characteristic makes you a good leader, but it can also make your life complicated. To become more likable and improve the quality of relationships in your life, learn to let go. Don't be too harsh on yourself or others. Once you stop being stubborn, you will understand how wonderful it is to care for others and share things with them.

How to Deal with The Aries in Your Life

Learning to deal with the Aries in your life will help cultivate fruitful, healthy, and lasting relationships. To do this, you need to thoroughly understand Aries's nature.

The first sign of the zodiac has an incredibly primal nature. They are the embodiment of ego and free will in its true form. Dealing with the fiery and commanding energy of an Arian isn't always easy. However, any relationship with them is rewarding. If you have an Aries in your life, here are simple tips you can use to enhance the relationship.

• Aries is often compared to children, and rightly so. Children are self-centered, willful, and filled with an optimistic innocence. Those born under the zodiac sign of the ram share these traits.

• Arians are curious, outspoken, loving, and exciting. In a relationship, they look for an individual who helps cool down their fiery nature and balances their energy. However, it is seldom easy to restrict an Arian. An ideal relationship for them is a balance between compassion and independence. They need a partner who appeals to their competitive and inquisitive side and adds a sense of adventure and vitality to the relationship.

• If an Aries likes you, be prepared for a lot of warm hugs and touching. These are the sort who don't waste any time and who do not play mind games. Instead, they accept the challenge, stand their ground, and try to attain what they want. Chances are that the Arian will not be quite happy if he needs to share your attention and affections. The great thing about an Arian in a relationship is their honesty. They make for a loyal, strong, honest, exciting, and fiercely passionate partner in a romantic relationship, provided they are committed to their partner and the relationship.

• Aries always like taking the lead in all aspects of life. They are creative and passionate. All this flows into their romantic lives as well. They are flirtatious, filled with a need for excitement, and radiate immense energy. Once in love, an Arian will truly commit himself to the relationship. Every day with an Aries is filled with surprises, excitement, and a never-ending stream of love and affection.

• The traits, as mentioned earlier, tend to follow them into the bedroom. You never know what will happen next and an Arian enjoys keeping his partners guessing. They are dominant, bold, and competitive. They not only like challenging themselves in bed but also aim to please their partners.

• Aries might seem tough, strong, and brusque on the outside. Once you get through these layers, you will realize how vulnerable they are. An Aries often struggles with an underlying fear that they are unworthy of love. They also have abandonment issues and tend to get hurt easily.

• Having an Aries as a friend is one of the most fulfilling friendships you can ever make. They are the embodiment of everything that's adventurous, playful, and happy. Nothing will be average or normal with an Arian. They are honest, loyal, witty, and one of the more supportive of the zodiac signs.

• All the traits an Aries exhibits are what he looks for in his relationships in life. Aries respect individuals who are honest, have integrity, and don't mind standing up for themselves.

• Aries are the true babies of the zodiac calendar. They seldom think about how their words or actions can influence those around them. They know nothing about diplomacy and cannot sugarcoat their feelings. They usually hurt others, trying to protect their pride. If an Aries is upset with you, the best you can do is keep calm. Don't give in to the natural urge to react, and allow them to cool down. Once they are calm, you can talk to them about it. Aries might be the first person who gets angry, but he is also the first to cool down.

- It is quite easy to know when an Aries is upset. Aries is bound to experience extreme mood swings and give in to their emotions. When an Arian is sad, they are not angry, but they allow impulsivity to get in the way. Even their overall energy levels seem visibly toned down.

- It does not take much to make an Arian happy. They love it when they are the center of attention. They appreciate it when others take notice of them. Something as simple as spending time with a good friend or engaging in physical activity can fulfill their needs.

- At their best, these signs are natural leaders. They are always seeking to learn and grow in life. They play multiple roles in every relationship in their life. They are happy and hold onto their sense of optimism, even when the going gets tough.

- At their worst, Aries is rude, selfish, and often plays the devil's advocate. All their strengths become their weaknesses when they're at their worst.

- Aries are often conflicted. They seek adventure, but they also desire to be of service. They cannot get on with a boring and mundane life. However, they also want to ensure the relationships in their life are not fleeting. They have several insecurities that others might not see. They live with the constant fear of being abandoned by their loved ones.

- Do not try to set any limits on the freedom expressed by the Aries in your life. Instead, give him all the time and space he needs for himself. Once he feels comfortable with you, your life is about to get interesting.

Conclusion

We are all curious to learn more about ourselves and the world in general. One way to satiate this curiosity and get a stronger sense of yourself is by turning to astrology. Astrology is a wonderful subject and is incredibly fascinating. After going through the information in this book, you probably have a better understanding of yourself. It might feel like all the pieces are finally falling in place. We cannot discount the influence of planetary movements and stars.

From ancient times, humans have always looked to the skies for answers. Sailors use the positioning of stars to chart waters. Similarly, learning about astrology helps chart a course for your destiny. All you need is a willingness to learn and an open mind toward astrology.

In this book, you were given all the information you need to understand the Aries zodiac sign. Whether you are an Aries or have an Aries in your life, this information will come in handy. It not only gave you a better understanding of yourself but your life in general. This book will act as your guide while you learn about Aries. From the basic characteristics of this zodiac sign to their strengths and weaknesses, ruling planets, houses, elements, and colors, there is plenty you will have discovered within these pages. You will also have learned about how to deal with and raise an Aries child, as well as read some tips to help them unlock their true potential and help you understand them better.

Besides this, you were given information about creating and maintaining healthy relationships, tips for a good love life, a compatibility chart of Aries with other zodiacs, and everything associated with relationships for Aries. It also included information about Aries and their social life, friendships, and how they function in the world. Other helpful information in this book included the ideal career choices for an Aries, how they can function effectively and optimally at work, and the ideal workplace and home environments. By using all this information, it becomes easier to navigate life as an Aries.

So, what are you waiting for? There's no time like the present to leverage this information and harness your power as an Aries. Start using the different tips given in this section to live a happy and prosperous life. The practical suggestions in this book will help improve your relationship with other Aries you encounter in life.

Part 2: Taurus
The Ultimate Guide to an Amazing Zodiac Sign in Astrology

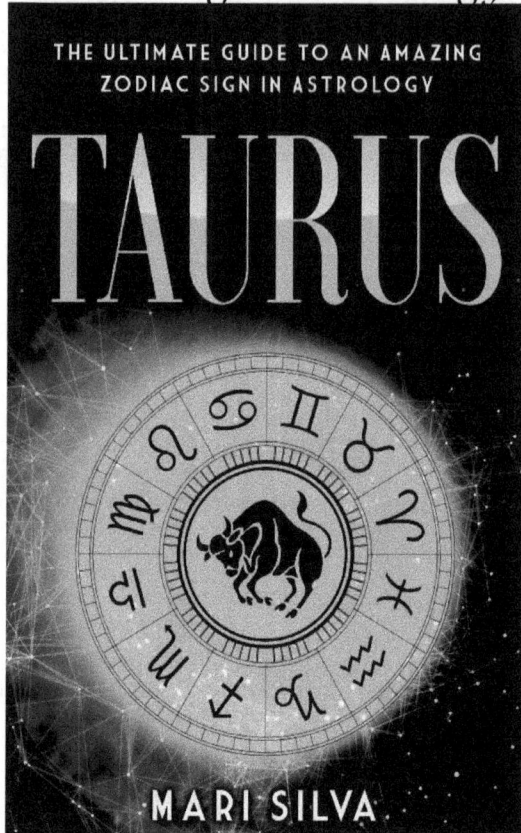

Introduction

The Taurus is one of the earliest zodiac signs, and it's believed to have originated from actual bull worshipping in ancient Mesopotamians, often called "The Great Bull of Heaven." If you aren't familiar with astrology, you will want to read the first chapter of this book carefully, to get a thorough understanding of the parameters that govern the world of zodiac signs. From symbols to planets, the world of zodiac signs is much bigger than you may think.

Taurus people are known for their ability to put up a fight if push comes to shove. Taurus' stubborn nature makes for a very stubborn worker who will always get the job done. Giving up is a fate they seriously despise. The confidence a Taurus has is based in reality, and it's deeply grounded in their belief in themselves. The aura of stability surrounding Taurus people is a great asset in climbing up the corporate ladder and acing the interview.

You will be hard-pressed to find an elegant party that is not hosted by a Taurus. While some signs may find them a bit too formal when it comes to planning parties, a Taurus host knows what they are doing down to the most minute details for hosting events. It's hard to shake off the perfectionism and organization traits of a Taurus regarding any project they do. You will even find them hanging out by the DJ, trying to help with the music choice.

Zodiac signs are often contrasted together by the comparison of weaknesses and strength; not everyone enjoys the same cup of tea. You can always know a Taurus by observing their thought process. It's no wonder why everyone seeks the advice of a Taurus because of how logical and sound it is, built upon facts and realistic perspectives. The more serious the situation is, the more valuable you will find the advice of a Taurus. A Taurus knows how to inject a dose of common sense at the right time, helping others become more grounded in reality and centered. This book will detail the traits that make Taurus a logical thinker and a problem solver.

The generosity of a Taurus is always apparent to both strangers and loved ones. A Taurus has no problems giving themselves to those who they love, preferring to put others before themselves any given day. They hardly play any games and always go for a direct and straightforward approach to gain the trust of the surrounding people. Organization, kindness, understanding, and patience are all popular points of strength that a Taurus has.

A strong zodiac sign comes with its own vulnerabilities. There is no such thing as a perfect sign without any weakness, especially when you consider that the signs complement each other. Taurus people are on the jealous side because of how much work they put into relationships. They may not be the most active people when they don't have serious work to do, preferring to relax instead of doing a fun activity. Some may say a Taurus can easily become possessive with people and objects when things get out of hand.

If you are the lucky parent of a Taurus child, you might be in for quite the ride. Many people are under the wrong impression that Taureans are unstable and angry, but you will be surprised to learn how fun and sensitive they are. Understanding your child's ticks and how they develop a strong personality as a Taurus is important. A Taurus child will happily learn, but their stubbornness may give you a hard time in certain situations. Raising a Taurus child will be referred to later in this book, as you become more familiar with the zodiac sign's personality traits and specifics.

If you are a Taurus, you probably remember how you stuck to your favorite toys and games once you found something you like. You may even remember getting a lot of scolding from your parents because of some ill-tempered destructive sessions. Knowing a young Taurus can help you raise a child and get in touch with your inner child to solve complicated problems deep-rooted in the past.

If you are a Taurus looking for love or receiving love from a Taurus, you may find the compatibility chart in the later chapters useful. Knowing which zodiac signs sync well with a Taurus can help save you a lot of trouble at the beginning and even help solve problems later. As you follow a Taurus teen's love life, you can understand what they find attractive. From the first relationships to the longest ones, a Taurus's traits are dominant and consistent, which should help to know if you are in a relationship with one.

As you continue reading this book, you will learn how to navigate the ups and downs of life with a Taurus. If you happen to be a member of this mighty zodiac sign, you will learn how you can sustain a healthy relationship or repair a damaged one. Tips and hacks related to a Taurus will be presented in a manner that allows you to take quick action and reflect freely on the points you need to highlight.

As you reach the later chapters in this book, you will have acquired some serious insight into how the Taurus mind works. Research is important, but you will want to make sure that you turn knowledge into action. The later chapters focus on helping the Taurus or their friends better understand such a complex zodiac sign. This will also greatly reflect on the career paths that a Taurus should excel and other paths that may not interest them in the long run. The more you learn about the Taurus, the more interested you will be in its infinite potential. You can always read the chapters independently if you'd like to focus on a certain key aspect related to this zodiac sign.

Chapter 1: Introduction to Taurus

As it falls in the middle of spring, Taurus embraces all those born between April 21 and May 21. It comes second in the 12 Zodiac signs, right after Aries, and the Bull symbol represents it. Out of the four Zodiac elements, the Taurus shares the Earth element with the Virgos and Capricorns. These Earth elements are known for their practicality, stoicism, determination, ambitiousness, and love of worldly pleasures.

It's no wonder that Taureans love worldly pleasures in whatever form they take; after all, the planet Venus rules them. It's only fair that they take after her beauty, hedonism, artistry, and passion for pursuing luxury and comfort. If you're curious about how this divine ruler has shaped the Taurus sign, you're in for a treat. Let's get started!

The Traits of a Taurus

If you're a Taurean, then you've probably realized that you can sometimes be a little too stubborn. But if you have a Taurean in your circle of friends or family, then you know that you can't go wrong with keeping a Taurean around. Taureans are loyal and honest to a fault - and that's how you know they will always have your back. They're also intelligent, dedicated, and hardworking. They're generally gentle, but they'll be fierce if they must be - they just really hate being pushed around. If you're wondering where a Taurean is, you should probably visit their home. There are few things they love more than the comfort of their own homes.

With such an intriguing collection of traits, let's get an overview of everything that makes a Taurean who they are.

Taurus Strengths

It's quite common for Taureans to be described using the following words:

- Rational
- Grounded
- Perseverant
- Aesthetic
- Patient
- Sensuous
- Chilled
- Responsible
- Reliable
- Stoic
- Practical
- Devoted
- Honest

Owing to their well-grounded, practical, and realistic nature, they're able to rationalize every situation and keep their emotions in check. This rational mindset makes them able to push through their way in life, achieving whatever they've set their minds to. Besides their unparalleled love for luxury and pleasure, they are usually determined to pull ahead of everyone else to enjoy life as it's supposed to be lived: a lifestyle for the rich and fancy. If one motto described their lifestyle, then it would undoubtedly be "Work Hard, Play Harder."

If there's one thing they value, it's honesty above all else - so expect a severe reaction if you try to pull a fast one on a Taurus. Not only will they be one step ahead of you, but they'll also call you out on your dishonesty and lose trust in you.

Taurus Challenges

There's always a challenging trait that comes with their strengths. After all, strengths and challenges are two sides of the same coin. Here's what the other side of a Taurean's coin would say:

- Obsessive
- Fussy
- Stubborn
- Greedy
- Uncompromising
- Possessive

Too much determination can turn into an obsession, which is popular with Taureans. This obsession can go either way: a work perfectionist or a pleasure-seeking procrastinator. It's usually a combination of both, which is quite a paradox.

It's only natural for Taureans to be stubborn. After all, they make sure to rationalize everything and think ten steps ahead of everyone else before taking any action. This level-headedness and foresight often lead them to trust in their opinion and judgment above others, making others think of them as stubborn. Despite their foresight, sometimes they can fail to see the bigger picture due to this stubbornness, making trial and error the only way to change their perspectives.

With their lifestyle, Taureans are not very fond of change. They will have absolutely no problem following the same routine for years without feeling there's anything wrong with it. But they will find facing sudden changes wrong, and they will fuss over everything and how things should be the way they expected it to be. Did we mention they hate surprises? Because they do. They aren't afraid of voicing their opinions either, even if it's in straight-on challenging authorities.

Taurus Likes

Following the footsteps of their divine ruler, Venus, Taureans love pleasure. They're sensuous, tactile, and like comfort. This makes the list of their likes and interests include the following and more:

- Luxury
- Comfort
- Music
- Romance
- Cooking
- Gardening
- Working with Hands

- Fancy Lifestyle

Taurus Dislikes

But you can expect a Taurean to steer away from any situations resulting in:

- Unexpected Changes
- Drama and Complications
- Insecurity
- Synthetic Material

The Fixed Quality

With Zodiac signs, many factors affect their traits. The sign's element plays a significant role, and we'll know how Earth affects the Taurus. Besides the element, each sign also has its own modality.

Technically, the modality is like the operating mode of the sign. It's how the sign expresses itself and sets itself apart from other fellow signs. There are three modalities: cardinal, fixed, or mutable. A cardinal quality marks the start of the season, and its signs are often described as leaders, traditional, rational, aggressive, and overly cautious. A fixed quality falls in the middle of the season, and fixed signs are considered stable, persistent, reliable, stubborn, and resistant to change. A mutable quality falls at the end of the season or in-between seasonal changes. Mutable signs are flexible, adaptable, versatile, restless, and unpredictable.

Out of these modalities, the Taurus shares the fixed quality with Aquarius, Leo, and Scorpio. Falling in the middle of the season, the Taurus represents stability and consistency. They'll fight anything that poses any danger, no matter how remotely, to their sense of stability and security. Their sense of security is built on the comfort of the known and familiar. When you think about it, these Taurean traits are what you need the most after facing a big bang (read cardinal signs) and before looking for a new adventure (read mutable signs), and that's what makes Taureans the anchor of Zodiac signs.

The Earth Element

Not only is Taurus a fixed sign, but it also belongs to the Earth element. That makes it the most static of all the 12 Zodiac signs with a resistance to change. While some might describe this as stubbornness, Taurus remains constant in all of its glory for a valid reason.

Taurus falls in the middle of spring, right where life invites you to enjoy its harvest and luxury. It represents life's pleasures and comfort, the physical body, and the food we eat. It doesn't change because that's what we need at this time of the year; it's there to influence all the other signs to be inspired by life and what it offers and make use of each moment. After all, the Earth element is the essence and core of all the other elements and their most solid foundation. It's there to help them achieve all materialistic goals, purposes, and desires.

When looking at Virgo, Capricorn, and Taurus, one can easily see how they excel at work and simultaneously make the most out of life's pleasures. They teach us how to manage our finances and reach ultimate heights - not only are they're hardworking and persevering, but they also follow a practical lifestyle that steers away from drama and unnecessary emotional complications.

It's clear that these traits help anyone associated with the Earth element reach greater heights, but the path they take may be too boring for the other elements. Earth signs can follow the same routine for years, having found their sense of peace in the familiar. They often dread any changes that will throw their lives right out of proportion and turn it upside down. They will prefer to settle for a life where they don't feel happy or appreciated enough, emotionally, intellectually, or financially, just to maintain the sense of security they've created for themselves.

Since one of the biggest challenges for any Earth sign, especially the Taurus, is dealing with sudden change, it creates a lack of compatibility with the Air element. Signs associated with the Air element are the fastest and most unpredictable, but that's also why Taurus needs the Air elements to grow and prosper. The best way to balance the Earth element, especially when they're stiff in their ways, is to adopt the Air's mindset.

To find balance, an Earthling would have to integrate new activities into their routine. They'll need to build a habit of seeking new coffee shops, going for a morning walk, socializing in new networks, and dynamic exercises that get their bodies moving. Dance lessons, stretching classes, and modern music are usually good places for a Taurus to start.

While a Taurean is conditioned to questioning everything, they do and second-guessing every new activity they pick up, they can ease their overthinking by creating a more meaningful sense of purpose for all the changes they adopt. By connecting this purpose and getting in touch with their emotions and rational mindset, they'll be able to stop regretting these actions.

The Taurus Constellation

The Taurus constellation has been discovered from 5000 to 1700 BC - before we were even alerted to the Aries' sign. It's been linked to cave paintings dating around 1500 BC. Still, there wasn't a definitive sign describing the Taurus until Babylonian astronomy came around and dedicated the Bull symbol. It's also been known as the Bull of Heaven or The Bull in Front.

The constellation hosts two open clusters: the Pleiades and Hyades, which extend through the Taurus constellation until the beginning of Gemini. The Taurus zodiac signs aligned to the Taurus constellation right until Equinox's precession, which changes its positioning. As of now, Taurus holds the place of the second 30 degrees of the Zodiac circle, right after Aries. While Aries represents the beginning of life and spring, Taurus sustains what Aries has started and holds life in all of its full bloom.

The Taurus History

Being one of the oldest constellations to have been discovered, not surprisingly, to find many myths and history linked to Taurus. The Bull symbol had been adopted in various mythologies due to its essential role in the agricultural calendar. You'll find myths and tales about the Taurus Bull in ancient Babylon, Egypt, Sumer, Assyria, Akkad, Rome, and Greek.

You may be familiar with the Taurus in the Epic of Gilgamesh, where the Goddess Ishtar sent Taurus to assassinate Gilgamesh as a punishment for his advances on her. You might have also heard about the Sumerian Goddess of sexual pleasure, fertility, and warfare, Innana, where she had been closely associated with Taurus, but if we went into the most infamous myths surrounding the Taurus, we won't have to go any further than ancient Greek mythology.

There are primarily two significant stories about Taurus in ancient Greek mythology, both of which are associated with Zeus, the king of all gods. The first myth was a story of false facades, where Zeus disguised himself as a white bull to seduce the legendary Phoenician princess, Europa. It wasn't long until Europa noticed Zeus, disguised as a bull kneeling in front of her, and fell in love with his charm and meekness. That's when she decided to hitch a ride on his back, where he traveled with her across the water to Crete, where she gave birth to three of his children. The story didn't end with a happily ever after - at least, the happily ever after wasn't with Zeus. Europa then escaped and married Asterion, the king of Crete, and her sons inherited the throne after him.

The second myth sheds light on the infidelity of Zeus to his wife Hera, where he had an affair with Io, her priestess. Hera was soon to discover the affair, and that's when she executed her revenge. She cursed Io into a cow that would forever be stung by a gadfly, forcing her to live a life void of settling and comfort. Eventually, Io sought refuge in Egypt, where Zeus restored her original form. Later, she gave birth to his son, who ruled over Egypt after Zeus and a daughter.

These myths build a close correlation with the Taurean man's personality. They tell the story of a powerful and unparalleled man, taking us into the details of his journey as he pursues love, passion, sexual endeavors, and earthly pleasures. They show how even the most influential man will put on a false facade to seduce his love interest and then abduct them on a journey across the world.

They also show how the worse traits can get the better of a Taurean when the planets in this sign are being challenged regarding their dignity and principles. When that happens, the worse side of the traits can take over, giving way to adultery and infidelity, where a married man can have an affair even with his wife's sisters and closest friends.

In short, the myths about Taurus paint a vivid picture of a wandering bull faced to deal with the consequences of his actions. They're someone who had betrayed the closest of friends and the most sacred of relationships, after which they've lost it all. They're forced to wander the Earth's distance looking for what they once had and ruined, trying to find something similar in the process. Little do they know that the only way they can get this love back is by making structural changes in their perceptions and beliefs - which is the most challenging task a Taurean can ever be asked to do.

The Bull Symbol

Taurus is represented by the Bull symbol, specifically, the face and horns of a bull. The origin of the image is assumed to have started with ancient paintings in a cave dating to 1500 BC, but the more definitive theory links the bull to the shape of the Taurus constellation. Regardless of the origin, the Taurus Bull is strongly linked to fertility, growth, and peace, correlating with the beginning of spring and the blooming of life. It's during this season that nature bestows upon us the most benefits and plentiful harvests.

Looking at the Bull in its daily life, it becomes clear how accurate its representation of Taureans is. You'll always find the bull relaxing in nature, surrounded by peace, quiet, relaxing aromas, and lush flavors. If that's not the best description of a Taurus in their natural habitat, we don't know what is.

Ruling Planet: Venus

The Divine Venus rules Taurus. She's represented by a symbol of a circle, indicating the divine spirit above a cross, referring to practicality and physical matter. The symbol speaks volumes to the necessity of bringing the divine to earth; to integrate art and beauty to the materialistic and worldly desires.

Venus is the planet of pleasure, love, sex, fertility, prosperity, desire, beauty, artistry, creativity, satisfaction, and gratitude when it comes to traits. She's not dissimilar to Aphrodite, the Greek Goddess. This combination of tender traits makes a Taurean excel at whatever they do, never forgetting to leave his or her artistic and creative touch in his or her masterpieces. That's why they make great cooks, lovers, artists, and gardeners.

These traits also make them the most loyal and supportive of friends. They appreciate honesty above all else, but they have little tolerance for conflicts, criticism, and emotional blackmail. This combination of traits makes them careful to let people into their lives. Although, when they do, they expect loved ones and rely on them, on an emotional level. Some people might even describe them as needy, obsessive, and possessive. Despite that, they still have the rational side that allows them to see reason and have sound opinions in conflicts and chaotic encounters.

The Second House of Possessions

According to the Twelve-Letter Alphabet of modern astrology, there are twelve houses in the birth chart. Each Zodiac sign rules over its corresponding house, which makes Taurus the ruler of the second house. If the second house is known at all, it's known for its possessions, personal wealth, and security. The house aligns perfectly with the Taureans' love for earthly pursuits and worldly pleasures.

If we go back in time and explore classical astrology, we'd find that Venus had a high affinity to the fifth house. In Venus' words, she found joy in exploring the creativity, sexuality, and pleasure that came in the birth chart of the fifth house. The fifth house was also known for another trait and is popularly described as the house of good fortune. That explains why Venus is often related to good luck, prosperity, fertility, and sexual desires.

Taurus Gemstone and Color

Not surprisingly, the gemstone or birthstone of Taurus is Emerald. The green of the birthstone is the best representation of a Taurean's nature, the prosperity, and the blooming of fields. It's also the color of wealth, something we've learned that Taureans are especially fond of. Taurus also responds to Rose, Quartz, Sapphire, Amber, Aventurine, and Garnet. These birthstones enhance their emotional, physical, and mental health. Naturally, the lucky color of a Taurus is green, owing to its Emerald birthstone. It also responds well to light pink and white.

Mantra and Purpose

Looking at a Taurean's nature, they get their sense of security from their possessions. They're conservative, preservative, and stable thanks to the mantra playing in their head with the words "I Have." Repeating it gives them a sense of purpose in their endeavors and encourages them to build structure, reliability, and stability in their lives, relationships, and goals.

The Taurus Man

With the Taurean man, finding another sign of similar strengths will be hard. You'd be hard-pressed to find someone who is as strong, loyal, trustworthy, honest, tender, patient, and generous as a Taurean man. He'd be willing to go out and beyond to make their partner feel loved and appreciated. Often, he will never pay attention to other flirtations and subtle hints - if not for anything other than he didn't even notice these advances.

He's willing to go all-in into the relationship, which makes him take his time doing so. He'd never rush into the physical aspect of the relationship without making sure he connects on an intellectual level with his partner, and that always takes a lot of time until he feels secure enough to trust their partner. He puts honest communication and transparency above all during this process, as he hates all forms of artificiality.

In return for going all in, he expects the same from their partner. As loving and tender as he can be, he'll be quick to be immovably unforgiving if his partner had betrayed him. But he can get too comfortable in his stoicism after settling in with a partner, owing to his calm and consistent nature. To get a sense of dynamicity in his life and how he can avoid boredom, it will be worthwhile if he takes up sports or outdoor exercises to be more grounded and get ready for action.

The Taurus Woman

Nothing charms a Taurean woman like appealing to her romantic side. You'll need to take your time doing so since she expects you to keep courting her slowly and consistently, even after starting a relationship with her. Just like the Taurean man, she knows that the mental and intellectual connection comes before the sexual bond, so she'll rarely jump into a physical relationship without thinking about the rest of the aspects.

One of the most important things for her is feeling loved and secure, requiring transparent honesty and open communication. False facades and games don't impress her, and she'll be quick to call you out on it. But she appreciates both simple and grand gestures of romance; after all, she takes after her goddess Venus. Once she feels secure enough, she'd give her soul, body, and mind to her partner without a second thought - if he remains faithful to her.

The romantic and tender side of a Taurean woman doesn't make her weak. On the contrary, she remains one of the most practical, reliable, and robust signs of all the zodiacs. She'll be ready to commit to a lifetime with the right partner and plan for a life with children and other blessings, but it takes a lot of patience and effort to unlock all her outstanding traits. She can be distant, preserved, closed, and set in her ways. If she lives with a feeling of guilt, it can eat up her inside and prevent her from ever feeling satisfied.

The Taurus at Work

Taureans love money. They love all forms of luxury, and they know that it doesn't come without working hard and making enough cash to sustain their luxurious lifestyle - so they go all in. You'll find that Taureans are among the most dedicated, capable, creative, practical, and hardworking people in whatever field they work in. Whether they're employees or managers, it won't make a difference because they'll do the job perfectly. They'll quickly establish a routine and focus on the task at hand, regardless of what's happening around them. Perhaps the only downside to their strong work ethics is that there's a fine line between dedication and obsession - something that Taureans often cross readily without noticing. Their obsession with work can turn them into perfectionists who expect everyone to go the extra mile, just like they do. They reward themselves for their hard work by playing and enjoying the luxuries of life even harder.

The Taurus with Money

As someone ruled by the second house of wealth, you'd expect a Taurean to be good with finances - and they won't disappoint. They're able to make do with both small and large salaries, planning their lifestyle according to their financial state. They'll never forget to leave some savings for a rainy day, and they'll consider their responsibilities, retirement saving, and both short and long-term goals.

The Taurus with Friends

Taureans thrive on the sense of stability they make sure they build for themselves. It's common to find a Taurean depending on this sense of peace with their circle of friends either, possibly even managing to maintain all their childhood friendships strong and precious. Once they let you in their life, they'll be some of the most loyal and supportive friends you have. They'll make it a point to keep nurturing your relationship and maintaining a healthy, honest, and pure bond that can last a lifetime. They're the Hufflepuffs of the zodiac signs.

The Taurus at Home

The ultimate form of stability for a Taurean is building a home with their family and living happily ever after. They're people who value family above all else, so you can expect them to show their love, support, and reliability to their parents and siblings from as early on as they can talk and move. As they grow up and take their paths in life, they'll settle with their loved partner and plan for ways to fill their home with laughter and happiness. They'll fill the house with kids and appreciate every second of the day, and they'll never say no to host a gathering of family and friends.

Chapter 2: Taurus Strengths

Having a Taurus in your life can be a blessing in disguise. They are sophisticated characters with more traits than meets the eye. You will need to get to know them to understand what is going on in their minds and how they think. Those born under this zodiac sign are interesting characters with numerous capabilities and strengths. Exploring those strengths can be quite a journey itself. If you were born under this sign with the sun, feel proud and unique, as you will come to learn how worldly your character can be. Here is everything you need to know about Taurus's strengths and how you can identify them in yourself if you're a Taurus or in someone you know.

Key Strengths and the Science Behind Them

Determining a zodiac sign's strengths in astrology is not something that some people just guess or make it up. A whole science behind it makes it easy to spot these positive traits and work on nourishing them if they are not too noticeable. This science is represented through three modalities, and they are basically the way each zodiac sign expresses itself. The modality types are fixed, mutable, and cardinal. With the case of a Taurus, they follow the fixed modality. To understand how Taureans express themselves, it is essential to understand the different modalities and how they work. Each modality has a mix of signs that make up for all the elements, which are Fire, Air, Water, and Earth.

Cardinal

This modality is the oldest one in all the groupings. Its signs are Aries (Fire), Libra (Air), Cancer (Water), and Capricorn (Earth). These characters are adventurous and outgoing. They express themselves loudly and say whatever they think, which is a positive or negative trait depending on the context and the situation. The Cardinal signs like to assert their dominance and leadership wherever they may be.

Fixed

With the fixed modality qualities, the Taurus can be seen shining along with other signs like Leo, Scorpio, and Aquarius. The Fixed signs are steady in their elements, making their strengths visible and noticeable as you get to know them. Their steadiness can often make them seem stubborn, but they are believers and stand for their beliefs no matter what the obstacles are. Taurus is an Earth sign, which makes Taureans even more determined and stable, but do not take no for an answer, and they get what they want in any way possible. They are not exactly revolutionaries or big fans of change, but they do like things happening their way. You will often see Taureans leading steady, fixed lives like their modality, where there is little room for surprises.

Mutable

Looking at the Mutable signs in comparison with other modalities, they are all about the change. Mutable signs are Sagittarius, Pisces, Gemini, and Virgo. Those born under these signs and have the mutable qualities are ever so restless. They always like to be active and, on the move, and they appreciate the change to a great extent. Settling for anything is not their strongest suit, and they can sometimes be a little chaotic. They are great communicators, making it easy for them to form friendships with those with other modality qualities like the Taureans.

Work Capabilities

The Taurus personality is very hardworking and determined. You can see them shine when they are at work or taking on a certain project in their careers. You can easily spot a Taurean in your workplace, as they will show great ambition and tenacity regularly. They can be a little competitive, but that is a good thing, as they will keep everyone around them on their toes and up for the competition. They are likely to become team leaders quickly and early in their careers. Those born under this zodiac sign are like seeds waiting to grow with the right nutrition, especially for succeeding in their fields and careers.

When you think of a Taurus's work capabilities, always think about discipline and punctuality. In specific fields like agriculture or admin management, those born under this sign will be excellent for the job. It is rare to see Taureans not being punctual or missing any details because they were too laid back or unfocused. But they are responsible and precise in their every move.

They can also be some of the most creative artists you have ever come across. Those with a Taurus personality are abstract in their way of thinking. This allows them to create exciting pieces of art and express their thoughts in a unique way you will not see with anyone else born under a different star sign. They are disciplined even in their art, which helps them notice beauty in everything to portray it in their artwork. Their artistic and musical taste is as classy as it comes. Even if they don't practice art themselves, they can still appreciate it when they see it. If you have a Taurus in your inner circle, it will be relatively easy to see how much they are interested and entertained by different artwork.

Since art is not just painting or listening to music, Taureans can excel in other creative fields like construction. This field needs hardworking, pragmatic, and artistic individuals, and it is super easy to find all these traits in a Taurus individual. They will add their sophisticated personal touch likely to change the way any construction work they get their hands on for the better.

Positive Social Aspects

Taureans are not necessarily perceived to be very sociable, but that doesn't mean it's a bad thing. Them being loners at times is a great strength. They are adaptable, and they can do things on their own with no help from anyone. They are human, though, and they still need some form of social interaction. When you get close to a Taurus and become their friend, they will be loyal to you for as long as you show them respect and appreciation. Do not mistake their loyalty for weakness. They will stand by you no matter what you get yourself into, but if you ever take that support for granted, they will not look back to the friendship they had with you twice.

One of the great things about Taureans is that they are also very consistent. They do not like change; you can go for months or even years without speaking to them and come back to find them the same. They are not easily influenced by others or by the world around them. That is why it is almost impossible to find a Taurean who has changed over time or become a different person than what you used to know.

Another great quality that is rare to find in any other sign but easy to spot with any Taurus in your circle is reliability. Whether the Taurean in your life is your friend, partner, or even mentor, you can always count on them to get things done and have your back whenever you need them. You won't have to ask them for anything twice as they will have it in the back of their minds until they can get you what you need or have asked of them. Responsibility is their middle name, and you can always count on them to seize the day.

Taurus with Family

Every family has a rock, someone they can rely on and go to when things go south. If you look closely at all the members of your own family, you will come to notice that the rock of the family is often a Taurus. Family is always the main priority for a Taurus. They do not take household matters lightly and can be protective of their loved ones. They might struggle to show their love for those they care about, but deep down, they would do anything for them, and that makes them powerful characters. They will often show their love to those in their home subtly by preparing special meals or spoiling them with lavish gifts.

Being good with kids is also one of the main qualities of this star sign, as they are funny and understanding. Taureans are perfect fun aunt or uncle material. They will spoil all related kids and shower them with love and attention. If they have children, they are likely to be mini versions of themselves. Whatever they ask for, they will probably get in the end. The main things any kid needs growing up are supportive parents, and a bull character is precisely that. They are overprotective with their children, but they would do anything for them.

Similarities with Other Signs

The qualities and traits of a Taurus are unique but are not that rare. You can easily spot certain positive characteristics like those of other zodiac signs. This can sometimes make it challenging for people to know on the first encounter whether the person in front of them is a Taurus, but by understanding the similarities and slight differences these characters have, you can tell them apart.

Taurus is an Earthly sign, which means the similarities it has with other earthly signs are numerous. Capricorn and Virgo are very grounded signs that share the stability trait with Taurus. They are all big fans of security and balance and might not always like surprises. Not that they won't know what to do if they experience shock or an emergency. Taureans share that trait with Capricorns and Virgos, where they will take charge if any emergency occurs or surprise event and deal with it responsibly and effectively.

In terms of similarities with other signs following other elements like water, air, and fire, Taureans share particular social traits with Sagittarius and Scorpio. With Sagittarius, both zodiac signs love their families more than anything and will do anything for them. They can be great parents and will always prioritize their loved ones over anything else. Scorpios share positive social traits with Taureans, where they are also reliable people who show support to those they care about and are reliable when times get tough.

Taureans share an essential trait with fellow earthly Virgos. They are both sensual signs with a unique, artistic sense that allows them to think creatively and logically. Every step they take is calculated, but they are practical and can adapt to any situation they are put in to be comfortable yet productive. You will not need to take care of these two Earthly signs as they can take good care of themselves and others. Taureans, Virgos, and Capricorns are all committed beings who can get things done with or without anybody's help and will show unmatchable results full of creative thinking and innovation.

Compatibility with Other Signs

Every zodiac sign has its match; it is the people they feel most comfortable around and understood by. With Taurus, they are compatible with fellow earthly signs and other star signs. When it comes to overall compatibility, they can easily get along with Capricorns. They also follow the same modality traits and will find comfort in one another. It is easy for a Taurus to open up when they are around someone they feel comfortable with, and that is something Capricorns can offer them. This trusting relationship helps a Taurus feel more confident in sharing personal experiences and can easily exercise self-expression.

Because Taureans love stability so much and can easily thrive in an environment where they have plenty of experience and people they trust, they might not always get along with signs like Gemini or Aries. These signs are all about change and adventurous surprises, which Taureans might not like much. Yes, they can adapt if they face such a surprise, but they would not appreciate it.

Two Taureans can get along well and understand each other's needs and wants as they have similar experiences in life. Their powerful traits will thrive together in such a relationship, whether it is a romantic or strictly platonic one. Even if the other Taurus in your life is a family member, you will quickly come to notice that being around them is comfortable and reassuring as their way of thinking is the same as yours.

Just because Earth rule Taureans, it does not mean they cannot get along well and share similar traits with other signs and elements. In fact, signs that follow the water element are often a perfect match in a work environment and a home environment. Earth and Water go hand in hand in nature, and that is a similar case to other zodiac signs.

Spotting the Strengths in Others

If you have a Taurus in your life you know and love, then it'll be easy to spot their most formidable characteristics and capabilities. But if you do not know the person that well, then spotting these strengths might be a challenge. but you can find these strengths the more you spend time with them and get to know their back-story. The life experiences a Taurus shares with you can quickly make you realize just how resilient they are and what they can do. Not all Taureans share the same strong and positive traits, and it's rare to find them all in just one person. People are different; you are likely to find a bulk of traits in one person and another set of strengths in another.

You can learn more about a Taurean's positive traits by seeing how they spend their time. If they are into artistic activities, you will understand that their sense of creativity is higher than anything else. If they like spending their time working or laboring, you can find that they thrive on earnest hard work when they are on their own, and they are committed to whatever task they have at hand with nobody else's help. They can have all the strong traits of a bull or just a few. It is up to the surrounding people to discover what they excel at.

Being a Taurus's friend will help you get a better insight as to what their personality is like. They will be a good friend, for sure, but whether their loyalty is their best feature or their reliability, which is what will differ from one Taurus to the other. You can simply ask them what their strongest skills and characteristics are, but it is always more exciting to discover these traits for yourself as you get to know a Taurean.

Spotting Your Traits

If you are a Taurus yourself, learning about your strengths might be a little more challenging than what you would expect. Not everyone knows what he or she is good at and where he or she excels in life. You can have all the right traits and qualities within you and still not know they are there; you might not even know how to utilize them, but it need not be that way forever. Digging deep within yourself and your emotions will help you figure out where you can shine as a Taurus and what fields will be a perfect match for your capabilities.

Start by looking at your hobbies and interests. If there is something that you particularly love doing, even if it is nothing too major, then that might be your strongest suit, and you need to nourish it. For example, if you like doing any form of art in your spare time, then that can be your real calling, and focus on making a career out of it or occupying yourself with your artistic side more often.

Taureans often prefer working alone and having an independent life. That can be an asset within you never knew about. Leading an independent life can help people discover more about themselves and see the full extent of their capabilities. It will help show how responsible a Taurus can be and how well they can take care of themselves on their own.

Strength Myths

People often think that the myths about any zodiac sign are just about their weaknesses or what they cannot do or even who are they are or are not compatible with. But there are a few common myths about a Taurean's strength that can be misleading for those with a Taurus within their network or who were born under the Zodiac sign themselves.

Among the most common myths about Taureans is that they are easygoing and mellow. That is not any far from the truth. They are adaptable beings that make the best of a situation they might find themselves in, whether it was good or bad, but they are not easygoing as that trait is overpowered by them being determined and wanting things to go a certain way, one that gives them comfort and stability.

Another trait that Taureans are often mistaken for is being overly confident. They are confident in themselves and their abilities, but they are not so confident that it makes them irritate to others. You won't have to worry about a Taurus stealing the show or taking all the attention. They like getting things done in peace – drawing no attention to themselves. Of course, they will appreciate it when their efforts are recognized, but they won't go around trying to show them off.

When Does a Taurus Really Shine?

Having character strength is not something that comes and goes, but is something that a person develops and grows over time. There are certain seasons and times when your zodiac sign will shine and come to light. The Taurus season is when a bull's positive traits come out to show obviously. That is from the duration of April 20 to May 20 every year. They will be the most like themselves and can reveal a lot of liveliness and success during that period.

You can also see a Taurus in their element when doing something they love and are passionate about regardless of the season. It could be working in the field of their dreams or spending their time with loyal friends or family members they love and appreciate, which is when all their positive and robust qualities become obvious and come to life.

What a Taurus Needs to Excel

Anyone needs to be placed in the right environment for their most vital abilities to shine. With Taureans, they need to be surrounded by a reliable support system just like themselves to excel in whatever place they are in. These characters like stability and having constants they can go back to whenever they need to. When they find themselves in a comfortable environment and surrounded by a loving network of individuals they are compatible with, you will see them becoming the best version of themselves. Taureans need honest people around them who will tell them all they need to know straightforwardly, sugarcoating no facts. They are pragmatic people who respond well to logic and can handle anything they encounter when they have all the facts.

Taureans are not complicated beings. They are very straightforward thinkers who go through life with a lot of determination and ambition. It is almost impossible to shake a Taurean's faith in anything they believe in. If you treat them right, they can be your best friend and most loyal confidant. Whether you are a Taurus yourself or have a Taurus in your life, you must learn about what makes those born under this sign special and unique. They are loving and kind, and anyone would be lucky to have them in their life.

Chapter 3: Taurus Weaknesses

Like all signs in the zodiac, Taureans have their fair share of shortcomings that need to be addressed. Building on the Taurean's practicality and positive traits we discussed in the earlier chapter, understanding one's 'weaknesses' is an essential tool in understanding how to deal with a Taurus. If you have a Taurean in your life or are one, you know how this can help reach the stability this sign incessantly seeks and thrives for. Unlike other books on the market, you won't just find an explicit list of a Taurus' weaknesses; instead, you will come to understand the why behind every trait.

In this chapter, you will also learn how each weakness can be made them work for you or your Taurean friend or acquaintance instead of against them. This is a book you will want to pull out every time you are ready to go deeper and gain a more profound sense of self. Otherwise, if you are not a Taurean yourself, you will still need this book to know how to best interact with every new Taurus you come across in life. One thing you need to remember, as an avid astrology fan, is that we can't just pool all Taureans together, which is why you will find a separate section dedicated to the weaknesses of Taurean born on the cusp towards the end of this chapter. But for now, let's focus on the Taurus natives:

Stubbornness

There is a good explanation as to why a double-horned bull is the symbol of the Taurus sign. Taureans are stubborn – so incredibly stubborn that it takes a lot to make them even budge to change their minds about something or someone. If you have a Taurean in your inner circle, you know how hard it can be to convince your Taurean friend to see your viewpoint or even meet you in the middle. Taureans don't do "middles," which can make it very challenging for other people to always accept this single-minded approach. Fellow fixed sign peeps like Leos, Scorpios, and Aquarians may find cultivating a harmonious relationship with Taureans challenging, but to Taureans, it's not about being stubborn because they wholeheartedly believe that their way is the right way.

And most of the time, their stubbornness results from their strong aversion to change, as we mentioned earlier in this book. Unless you have an eloquent and well-thought argument, you'll never convince your Taurean husband to invest in a new dryer instead of fixing the one you have for the third time! While it might sound like you're never going to win with the Taureans in your life, there are tricks that you can use to work around this challenging trait.

Do Not Corner Taureans

Like all people, when put in an uncomfortable situation, Taureans will be triggered to activate defense mechanism. To have a smooth relationship with your Taurean spouse or friend, don't take communication in the direction of your word versus theirs; instead, listen to what they have to say first and then add on to their ideas. You may win them over by making them feel that you are on the same side rather than using unnecessary labels like "your idea" vs "my idea."

Maintain Honest and Open Communication

To more easy-going signs, dealing with a bull-headed Taurean can be depleting and consuming. but this shouldn't be an excuse to avoid engaging with your Taurus friends altogether. On the contrary, aim to have an honest and ongoing conversation to gain their trust and encourage them to become more lenient in your relationship.

Give Them Time

For example, rushing your Taurean son to get into the school night routine after having been on long summer vacation will backfire. It will do you both good if you accept that he will need more time before he can get into the new routine. Though, not only should you accept it, you need to show him you understand and that it's ok, and that you are here to support him if/when he needs your help.

These simple changes in perspective can be all that you need to cultivate a more constructive relationship with the Taureans in your life. But what if you are a Taurean yourself? How can you overcome your stubbornness and not let it get in the way? Here are techniques that you should try:

Pause and Think Before You Act

Often, even if you can't openly admit it, like most Taureans, you have this belief you can do things better than others. You also think that whatever others are suggesting, your ideas are probably superior. But this mentality can push your loved ones away because they feel like you don't need nor value their inputs.

An excellent way to work around it is to pause and take a deep breath before you judge someone's idea as good or bad. Teach yourself to listen more and that not everything that happens in front of you needs a reaction. Over time, you will become more accepting and can easily allow others to have their way occasionally. Still, this will need some time before getting used to, but if the intention to change is there, you will eventually see results.

Get to Know People Around You on a Deeper Level

This technique alone can help you immensely with your stubbornness. When you become intentional about getting to know people around you better, you will learn to trust them more and become more willing to embrace their thoughts instead of insisting on yours. Especially if you are still young or starting a new job or moved to a new country, the only way you can become successful in such scenarios is to show your interest and respect towards other people. Don't give your new coworkers a reason to avoid working with you because you are too fixated on having your way all the time. Express interest and curiosity in others and see how this will improve your relationships and make them mutually rewarding.

Get Out of Your Comfort Zone More Often

True, you are a Taurean that hates change, but you're also persistent by nature. If you set your mind to becoming less stubborn, you will do whatever it takes to make it happen. One of the great ways to do so is to put yourself in situations you would typically try to avoid at all costs. If you aren't big on social gatherings, try to go out more and hang out with people from all walks of life. This way, you will become exposed to various mindsets and backgrounds, which will compel you to become more tolerant. With time, you won't need to enforce your viewpoint over everyone else's.

What's interesting is that your friends and family are likely to start giving you compliments and patting you on the back for becoming more flexible, even if you don't see it yourself yet. But when you give yourself some time and space to experience each of the above, you will feel more comfortable in your relationships and become more accepting of new situations.

Possessiveness

Taureans are possessive creatures, whether it's about people or worldly possessions; they like to claim ownership of what's theirs. With relationships, this trait can be suffocating to their partners. A Taurean's possessive nature is a byproduct of their insecurity and inability to celebrate other people's successes. It either makes them feel less than or insufficient as humans, so they overemphasize ownership. If you are in a relationship with a Taurean, don't take it as a sign of lack of trust; otherwise, you won't be able to continue together. Possessive Taureans can only thrive in relationships where their partners can accept belonging to them and become an extension of themselves.

Besides being possessive with people, Taureans are also possessive with their possessions and they rarely accept having others share their belongings, or their wealth. Being skillful with money, possessive Taureans usually come across as greedy and ungenerous. Even though that's not wrong, that's not usually their intention. If you are having a hard time teaching your daughter born under Taurus about the importance of sharing, or you're dating a Taurean and have trouble enjoying a peaceful relationship, there is a way out. Here are some tips that might help:

Show Compassion

Dismissing possessiveness as an unaccepted trait won't get you far with Taureans, but it will make it even harder for them to trust you, and they may shut you out altogether. A better approach is to show compassion and acknowledge their feelings. For example, you can discuss the recent blowout you had with your jealous boyfriend in a more understanding and loving way. Start by expressing your appreciation for his love and then ask what would make him feel more comfortable moving forward. That you took this tone instead of blaming and pointing fingers will encourage him to relax and show more faith in you.

Involve Your Taurean Friends

Rather than ignoring your Taurean friend, involve them more in your plans. Give them your time and attention so they can feel safe and loosen up a little. When you're going out with other friends, ask them to come along, this way, they'll be sure that you aren't trying to replace them.

Be Possessive

If you can't fight them, join them! That's not to suggest you base your relationship on mutual smothering attention. Instead, you can try to reciprocate your Taurean partner's possessive feelings in a more loving and caring way since it's how they express their love.

As a Taurean, even if you aren't ready to own up to this personality trait, pay attention to the tips below so you can apply them once you are ready:

Self-Analyze

Not to be confused with self-criticize. Self-analyzing is more about getting to know you better and analyzing your underlying insecurities and inhibitions. Pay close attention to what situations trigger your jealousy or possessiveness. Ask yourself the hard questions and dig deep to find the answers. You can also work with a therapist if you believe that your actions are wreaking havoc on your closest relationships. It won't be an easy journey, but it'll be eye opening and eventually comforting.

Always Give Others the Benefit of the Doubt

To you more than others, this is essential to cultivate healthy relationships. Before you jump to conclusions because your boyfriend was late in calling you back, run the million possible scenarios in your head first, then wait for him to call. Not only will this help you calm your mind, but it'll also give your partner the chance to relax and live more authentically without constantly worrying about your possessive behavior.

This trip applies not only to romantic relationships. If you are having a hard time at work delegating to your team members some of your responsibilities, you can follow the same approach. Make yourself believe that your employees want what's best for your company because it reflects on their livelihood. Also remind yourself that doing this job means they already have the needed skills and experience. The more you talk yourself into seeing the good in those around you, the more you'll be able to keep your controlling tendencies in check.

Keep Yourself Busy

As an excelling hard-working Taurus, this shouldn't be a problem for you. Focusing on other things than those that trigger your possessive nature is an easy way to weaken the effects they have on you. Try a new sport or hobby that can keep your mind occupied instead of running wildly when free. It's doubtful that you will turn into a mild-tempered individual who doesn't respond in provocative situations, but you will become more mindful of your actions, and you'll find that you'll do a better job of not hurting the ones you love.

How to Overcome the Fear of Change

Whether it's in their personal or professional lives, Taureans not only despise change, but they also fear it. To Taureans, change is not an idea they can easily entertain, even if their lives depended on it. If you're a Taurean yourself, you know that even the thought of change can be enough to cause you anxiety. This sign likes stability and prefers to live a predictable life where everything goes as planned and expected. To other more flexible signs like Geminis or Leos, Taurus' aversion to change is a huge turnoff, but other insecure signs like the super-sensitive Cancer rely on the 'stable' Taurus to take the lead and keep things steady.

Taurus' fear of change is influenced by their strong belief in structure and always wanting to be in a setup where they can expect what's coming next. This might explain why changing their mind doesn't come easy either, as they don't know how to deal with an unfamiliar outcome. Yet, this quality is usually more sabotaging to Taureans themselves than to those around them. For example, a Taurean in a failing relationship will usually take longer than others before pulling the plug once and for all. Even with their career, although most Taureans are career-driven and successful, it usually takes them a long time to admit that their job isn't a good fit and that they need to find a new one. To learn how you can best deal with the routine enslaved Taureans in your life, you can try these tips.

Taureans Hate Change

You might be coming from a good place wanting to help your Taurean friends open up to life after a bad break up but pushing her into it might do more harm than good. It's better if you can offer her the support and company that she needs until she chooses to move forward herself. You can take her out and go on fun trips together, but you shouldn't be doing more. When under pressure, Taureans can become aggressive, pushing away their loved ones because they don't know how else to react.

Nurture and Encouragement

Raising a change fearing Taurean child can be daunting to any parent. You'll always be worried about them because you know how changing schools or a new teacher can be too much for them to handle, but the best thing you can do is to be there for them. Show them you believe in them and will always have their backs. Besides mouthing the words, let your actions speak for you. Cheer them on from the first row when they play their first soccer match at their new school. With time, you will see that your child will become more willing to cope with change instead of complaining about it like they usually would.

Fear of Change

People born under the Taurus sign are usually realistic, but their fear of change can prevent them from standing back up after falling. Your job as a friend is to help them find the silver lining. Talk to them about the lessons they should learn from a bad experience and then give them the space to make the needed changes to move past it.

A deeper understanding of the reasons behind your fear of change can be just what you need to overcome it. Here are tips that you can try for a little push to make the necessary changes,

1. Grow Your Faith

Most of the time, change is brought upon you when you're least expecting it. The only way you can break free from your fear of change is to have more faith. Trust that everything happens for a reason and that no matter how things go, it'll ultimately be for the greater good. When you train your mind to believe that the universe is working for you and not against you, you will find it easier to accept the idea of change.

2. Commit to Change

While this might sound counter-intuitive, it's an amazing way for a stubborn and persevering Taurean to tip the scales in your favor. They say that the best defense is a good offense in football, and that's exactly what you should do with change. Instead of always being on the receiving end, being someone who doesn't like surprises, take the initiative, and start the change yourself. Try something different every day. These can be as simple as changing your coffee order or taking a new route to your office. These small and simple actions will train your subconscious to accept change as a part of life when done consistently. You will no longer see it as something that you need to avoid wholeheartedly.

3. Tap into Your Practical Nature

Among the 12-star signs of the zodiac, you are by far one of the most practical ones. Tap into your practicality to conquer your irrational fear of change. Starting a new job? Focus on the higher salary and all the status that comes with the new title. Being wealth-driven and someone who appreciates the finer things in life can be enough to make you forget about your fears.

4. Avoiding Change

Yes, you read that, right! Whenever you can, and if it won't set you back in life, you can always choose to avoid change. You shouldn't feel shamed into welcoming change with open hands just so other people don't think of you as another stubborn Taurus. If a particular way of life is working for you and you aren't hurting yourself or anyone else, then decline that overseas job offer and stay put.

5. Laziness

This varies from one person to another, but in general, Taureans are relatively lazier than others. Again, this comes from their need for stability and lack of enthusiasm for experiencing anything new. Laziness is obvious in Taurean children. If you have a Taurean child in the family, you can clearly see they are not the outdoorsy sporty type; they prefer to hang out in peace indoors. But don't despair because there are things that you can do to make them more active.

6. Don't Over Spoil Them

Over-spoiling lazy Taurean kids is a recipe for disaster. With their lazy demeanor, having all their wishes granted will only make them grow into entitled unappreciative adults. Teach your Taurean kid about the importance of working for what they want. For example, if your Taurean daughter has been asking for a new pair of sneakers, give her chores to finish and pay her the money to buy them herself. This way, you will be encouraging her to do something purposeful instead of idly lying around.

7. Be a Good Example

Steady Taureans appreciate consistency. You can't expect them to follow your advice if your actions contradict your talk. The best way to inspire your Taurean friend to get moving is by showing them the active life you lead. Making them understand that it's the right way to live if they want to live a long healthy life will probably urge them to do the same.

If you are a lazy Taurean yourself, you can:

8. Start Small

Doing simple, consistent changes is the only way you can reverse your laziness curse. Instead of deciding on a whim to work out every day, aim for 2-3 days/week, and then add, more as you go.

9. Take Frequent Breaks

Because motivation doesn't come easy to you, schedule infrequent breaks where you can recharge and clear your mind before you get back and finish the tasks at hand.

Cusp Taurus

As promised at the beginning of this chapter, if you are born on the cusp of Taurus, you will find something for you here. Besides the native Taurus qualities, being on the cusp means that either Aries or Gemini influences you, which are the signs adjacent to Taurus.

Aries-Taurus Cusp

Being born on the Aries-Taurus cusp means you were born on the cusp of Power. You are resilient and authoritative, but having this fiery personality often puts you into a lot of trouble because you can't just stop and think. Even though you don't intend to, you tend to offend those around you with your careless ways. This can drive away even your closest friends and family. Though, if you want to make sure you use your powers to your benefit, don't overlook kindness. More than others, your words can use a little-sugar coating to balance out your bluntness. Throw in a smile, and you will be able to avoid alienating the ones that you love without losing yourself in the process.

Taurus-Gemini Cusp

As an individual born on the cusp, you are full of energy and zeal, but you tend to overindulge and rarely know when to stop. Whether it's partying or eating, there's no stopping you. This behavior can take a toll on you mentally and physically and leave you feeling drained. The best way to overcome the imminent burnout is to practice self-control consciously. Have an ongoing conversation with your mind to stop you from devouring the entire bag of chips in one go. Over time, you will be able to keep this destructive behavior in check.

Taureans are highly influential and one of the strongest signs. As you have read in this chapter, their weaknesses mainly emanate from their rigidness and inflexibility. In the following chapters, you will get to see how the above weaknesses influence how Taureans act in other aspects of life, including love, work, and family.

What to Avoid as a Taurus

Naturally, there are some negative traits that a Taurus may have, and they can make life much more difficult if left unchecked. It's easy to become a bit self-absorbed due to the highly focused dynamic that a Taurus maintains. It's crucial to identify behavioral tendencies that are not healthy for you and know how to maneuver yourself into safety.

Self-Indulgence

Getting carried away is one of the bad traits of Taurus people. This can mean that they may over-indulge themselves to guarantee that the fun never stops, which develops a habit of procrastination. Being perfectionists, they can still maintain a great professional path, but they can easily stray away if their ambition is drowned in self-indulgence and hedonism.

Laziness

Even though Taureans are greatly ambitious, they aren't the most active sign. It's always harder for people who value perfectionism to start something due to the fear that it won't turn out as planned. A Taurus should always keep their priorities straight and focus on starting the task quickly instead of being shackled by hesitance. Keeping a distinct line between work and leisure time is very important if you want to maintain a healthy schedule.

Materialism

A sign that is governed by Venus is bound to have a knack for shiny and expensive things. It's common for Taureans to think that life is all about financial success. While financial freedom is great, it's not the only thing in life worth working for. Being flexible and appreciating the little things in life can help Taurus overcome a lot of difficult challenges.

If you are a friend of a Taurus, you will learn a lot of information that can help you with developing better communication with them, in addition to helping them out in a pinch. Not knowing the best traits you have and what you need to develop your character further can be such a huge waste in the case of a Taurus. As mentioned in this book, a Taurus possesses an abundance of outstanding characteristics.

Chapter 4: The Taurus Child

If you are lucky enough to be the parent of a Taurus, then you should count your blessings. Taurean children are among the easiest to bring up and can grow to be unique human beings. By knowing everything there is to know about this sign from an early age, parents will be able to nurture all the right skills their child possesses and help them develop their strengths effectively. Your child's characters will start appearing from early on, even as a baby. Babies born between April 19 and May 20 are like no other newborn. Here is everything you need to know about them as a parent or someone who is expecting a baby Taurus in the family.

Characteristics

Baby Taureans begin their life and approach every action they take differently. They are not like every other kid you will meet. They can be very calm and even shy at times. Parenting Taureans is all about taking into consideration their emotional attributes as well as logical attributes. They won't always express how they feel in words. It can rather be seen in their actions and how they interact with their parents, other family members, or even different people in their social network as kids. Sometimes, you might need to give them their space for them to feel comfortable and be able to find comfort with themselves.

If one of the parents is a Taurus themselves, they might understand their child's needs even more than themselves. Remembering what it was like to be an earthly born kid and how it can sometimes feel like nobody in the world fully understands the way you think or feel can be quite helpful for a parent when it comes to raising their Taurean child. It'll help them relate to personal experiences from the past and understand how their child might think and why they can sometimes behave the way they do.

A Taurus child has a wide range of bold characteristics. They are stubborn, emotional, loving, and warm. They are pretty much born to grow into their roles as family-oriented people. They can have a deep connection to their mothers, but they love everyone in their family just because of the blood ties they share. They are also relatively calm, so they won't be as irritating as some kids might be and are not likely to give you a hard time even if they are upset over anything. Teaching them a lesson won't be difficult since they like to listen and follow the rules. Overall, they are obedient kids who are likely to grow to become successful adults with great potential.

Taurus Children at Home

All children are most comfortable when they are at home, as it is where they have maximum personal space while still being surrounded by loved ones. It is a perfect balance for a Taurus child, and it's the ideal environment to shine. It might not always be comfortable at home with a Taurus kid as they can sometimes become too stubborn, and their parents may lose their patience. When they are set in their ways, the parents need to understand that negotiating logically is the key to resolving arguments in such cases. Of course, with a child, mature logic might not be the way to go. Nonetheless, if you explain all the facts to them and let them in on how you're thinking as a parent, they might just get along with you and become less stubborn.

Parenting is all about learning your child's traits and seeing how you can help them develop their strengths and manage their negative traits into positive ones. If a parent is rational enough at home with their kid, they will become determined individuals rather than stubborn ones. They will also end up being responsible adults who have a lot of respect and appreciation for their parents as Taureans already have strong ties with their families from the second they are born. Children born under this star sign are affectionate and cuddly even as babies, so all it takes for them to grow up and become considerably achieving adults is to be loved and respected in their own homes.

Taurus Children at School

When it comes to education, Taurus children respond particularly well to sensory learning. They are children with really heightened sensory skills and can learn a lot by using every single one of their five senses. Kids belonging to this zodiac sign are both logical and methodical learners. It can drive their parents and teachers crazy at times when they do not respond well to homework or practical work assigned to them. Yet, adults can easily notice how they still achieve great results with tests, for example. That is because these children take in the information, fully understand it, and analyze it in their tiny little brains, then move on with their lives. They might not all be geniuses or book worms - maybe some are - but they follow a systematic approach in learning that works slowly and steadily until they eventually win the race.

Subjects like math and physics can be where these Taureans shine the greatest. Alternatively, they can do great in sports and art classes and have a great musical ear. They might not be as great when it comes to theoretical subjects and things like learning languages or history and such. Because they are logical and like to count their every move, they work much better with the sciences and can achieve excellent results in such subjects.

Taurus Boy Traits

A male Taurus is an individual with a mind of his own. As children, Taurus boys won't be pushed around under any circumstances. They will do things in their own way and on their own time, or the parents must suffer through hell on earth. Parents can overcome this issue with their boys by showing them a lot of love and affection. Over time, their attitude will improve, and they will learn to compromise for the sake of their loved ones, but only their loved ones. Taurus boys will never be bullied or stand for the bullying of anyone else either. They are the ultimate definition of an alpha male. Leave them in a room with other kids their age, and they will dominate in a matter of minutes.

Generally, boys love their mothers more than anyone else in the whole world. This bond can be even stronger with a Taurus boy than any other kid born under a different star sign. This results from Taureans wanting a lot of love and compassion because it brings them a lot of joy and satisfaction. They are confident in themselves, and that confidence begins with the love that a mother shows them during their early years. A dad's attention is essential too, but motherly love is what can make a difference in a Taurus boy's upbringing.

With their social circle, whether at school or with their friends or relatives anywhere, Taureans are not one who will stand shy in a corner waiting for someone to include them. They know how to make their way into a group and even lead the room on certain occasions. Attention is not exactly what they seek, though they like to be respected and acknowledged in everything they do.

Taurus Girl Traits

A Taurus girl is born to rule from day one. She is not one to be told what to do. People work on her schedule, not the other way around. Organization is her middle name, even as a child. It is also essential to realize from early on that if a baby Taurus female does not like something, no amount of persistence by the parents will ever change her mind. This can apply to food, toys, and even specific places. She will be very vocal about her feelings and won't shy away from an argument.

The Taurus girls are great listeners. They like being told stories, especially when it was from or about their parents when they were younger. They can also be close to their grandparents. If a Taurus girl is the parent's firstborn, the grandparents will probably spoil her rotten with lots of cuddles and love that a Taurus girl will adore.

These young women can be cute, yet so mature for their age. You cannot deceive them because they will bust you almost instantaneously with their sharp mind. They are tenacious and determined, so no matter what creative skills and tricks the parents come up with to get them to do something different, their attempts are likely to fail. The Taurus girl often finds it somewhat amusing to witness their parents' failed attempts to drive them off their course and simply give up in the end to the girl's wishes, but they are not wild children. They are predictable and enjoy stability and discipline in all arrays of life as they grow up.

Hobbies and Interests

One of the many great things about Taurus children is that they are committed to whatever they put their minds to. As soon as they develop an interest in something or have a specific hobby, they are not likely to back out as other children might. Sometimes, this can make them seem a little obsessive which might not always go well with the parents, but it is essential to realize this trait is healthy. It helps them commit to more necessary things in life as they grow old and never back away from anything they've started.

Taurus children are often interested in activities and hobbies that involve set rules and disciplines to them. Chaotic games and messy activities are not something they'll ever enjoy. They enjoy mind games and puzzles that fire up their logical thinking skills, where they can analyze everything and conduct smart tactics. Board games and card games might also seem exciting for them though it might differ from one child to another.

Among the hobbies they might take on and show a keen interest in from early on are artistic hobbies. They might enjoy painting or playing music. That is something that the parents will need to notice and nourish from the early stages in their little kid's life. If these skills and hobbies are well nourished by parents, the kids can grow up to be brilliant and creative people who produce unmatchable artwork.

Stability and Routine

Change is not something that any Taurean appreciates. As soon as they can express themselves a little, even as toddlers, they will show signs of liking stability and routine rather than surprises and sudden changes. Familiarity is everything for these kids, whether it is with people, places, or even food. Taking them to new places to meet new people can be quite a challenge. Though, this might get easier as they grow a little older and go to daycare or school. As soon as Taureans find themselves comfortable with those around them and develop a sense of familiarity, they become the friendliest kids in the world and can talk and laugh and simply be themselves. Otherwise, they won't be comfortable in any new environment, and it will quickly show in their attitude.

Developing a routine with a Taurus kid is one of the easiest things a parent can do. It is recommended so that both the child and the parent can live in harmony together. This routine should be applied to everything from setting a tight sleeping schedule to planning meals every day and making sure the day goes according to a set plan with almost no room for surprises. This routine can make a parent's life so easy, especially with Taurus toddlers since it will allow them to plan their days according to their babies. They'll also be able to find some time for themselves occasionally in the middle of the busy schedules.

Exploring the Senses

Taurus kids experience everything in life through their senses. They will smell, taste, hear, see, and feel every little thing and every detail around them. As soon as they are born, they will start grabbing things and putting everything they see in their mouths after analyzing it with their eyes and noses. As they become toddlers and manage to support their body weight to crawl, anything within eye level from them will probably go into their mouths.

With taste, these kids love to eat. So, parents are not likely to face any issues with them in that regard, but they might find themselves in love with a small selection of food items and not want to try anything else for a while. Parents need to keep on offering their kids healthy alternatives occasionally, without forcing them, and they will eventually come to try them on their own.

These children might also cling to certain toys or cuddly bears as they explore their senses and look for extra affection. Parents should not deprive their kids of that and instead try to encourage them to develop their senses healthily. They can do this by offering them educational toys that can allow them to utilize all their senses effectively.

Emotional Stability

Taurus children have very grounded personalities. They like things done a certain way and only like a selection of items, so if they are offered alternatives or surprised by sudden changes in plans, they can throw manic tantrums. Taurus kids usually are very calm and emotionally stable just if everything is being done their way, and they are getting enough love and affection. The minute there is a change in their routine, they can quickly turn destructive and aggressive until parents cave and give them what they want.

It is the responsibility of the parents to avoid encouraging this behavior. They can do so by having rational discussions with their kids. It's crucial to explain everything logically and lay down all the facts and consequences. Appropriately punishing the children when they become aggressive might also be necessary. This needs to be done to manage these episodes of anger and teach Taurus children rational self-expression.

Staying Active Outdoors

Among the things that Taureans, as kids, excel at is being active outdoors. They are not lazy children who sit at home all day doing nothing or merely playing video games. These kids are explorers who like to feed their natural curiosity by going outside and learning about the world. They may not turn out to be athletes, but they can still do well at certain sports. Simply going outside and soaking in the sunlight can be everything they need to thrive.

Taureans are earthly beings that enjoy everything this planet offers. Exploring the great outdoors by using all their senses is something that will allow them to develop their positive traits and learn more about the world. These children particularly love being outdoors with their parents as they can form a bond with their family and earth as their primary element. Consider taking your children to the backyard or to the park where they can see you in natural surroundings and maybe even hear some fun music in the background while they play and stay active. This can be great for a developing Taurus child.

Physical Traits

Young Taureans are charmers. They have attractive features and almost always take the family's best genes. Since they love being active and engaging with the world outdoors, they are usually fit and maintain a healthy figure growing up. Even with food, although they can be picky eaters, they typically prefer healthy meal options. Their faces are super friendly and cute, making them easily approachable by other youngsters their age at school or any playground.

Artistic Skills

Creativity and innovation are second to any Taurus. That is why they can become great artists or make a successful career for themselves in that sector. It all starts when they are young, even as early as when they are toddlers. They will be way too interested in music and dancing. They can also be keen on drawing and creating their own little masterpieces. Some might even show an interest in cooking by helping their parents in the kitchen then attempting to prepare their meals. Their parents should encourage all these artistic skills so they can develop into successful artists.

Taurus children are born natural artists and just need the right guidance to flourish. They might not necessarily grow up to be painters or dancers, or even singers. They may find their calling in the creative sector in general. If their skills are nurtured and supported as kids, they will grow to become innovative adults. All it takes is some parental support and guidance in the right direction when they notice they have a keen artistic sense in one form of art or another.

Best Toys for Taurus Children

All children love toys; there is no exception to that fact. The only thing that differs from one child to another is the type of toys they enjoy playing with. With young Taureans, they enjoy toys that tickle their five senses and artistic skills. Little musical instruments might be the best toys for babies and toddlers. They will have so much fun grabbing the musical kit and playing songs all day long. Coloring books and drawing sketches might not be toys, but they are something that an older Taurus child would enjoy.

The Taurus kids might also enjoy toys they can use outdoors to get active. Getting them a bike is a great step for the parents since they'll have a fun time playing outside and staying fit. Parents might also consider letting their little Taurus children play in the garden or the dirt. Get them digging toys and a kid-friendly gardening kit.

The Best Books for Taurus Children

Little Taurus children often surprise their parents with how much they love to read. Even those who are too young to read books themselves enjoy having some quality time with their favorite adults who read bedtime stories for them. Books about exploring nature and fictional characters in the wild can be quite intriguing for Taurus kids, and it will help them with their vocabulary and understand the world around them. These children also love gardening considering their element is Earth. Books about gardening and trees will be perfect to teach them a thing or two about nature. This is bound to keep them keen and eager to take on tasks like gardening and caring for plants on their own.

Best Activities for Taurus Children

Parents often want their kids to commit to any beneficial activity when they are young to develop their skills early on and nourish them as they mature. Some parents take their kids to different educational classes, like learning new languages or new skills. Others enroll their children into sports teams to see if they have a knack for sports and maybe a future of being an athlete. Children born under this earthly star sign are big fans of artistic and outdoor activities. So, when parents are choosing a suitable activity for their Taurus boys or girls, they should remember that.

Creative classes, whether it is drawing, singing, dancing, or music, are an excellent option for these kids. These courses won't require them to be too active, yet they will get enough activity to thrive as they grow up. It is a way for them to unleash their inner artists and begin a successful creative journey in that sector.

Another activity that works perfectly for these kids is any outdoor activity that takes them into the wilderness. Things like hiking, camping, fishing, and gardening can be of real interest to the Taurus children from a very young age and can help shape them as they grow up.

Parenting Tips

Raising a child is no easy task. It is full of emotional and physical challenges for both parents, and it is something anyone expecting a child should remember before their babies are even born. For raising a child born under the Taurus zodiac sign, particular challenges might be more manageable than others. As your child grows older, your parenting skills need to change and develop to keep up with their needs. Every minute your little Taurus child grows up, you will need to treat them differently according to his or her developing maturity.

Early Years

Baby Taureans need a lot of love and affection. As they grow older over the years, they will need that outpouring of love and affection, but as infants, they need it a lot more than any other time in their lives. If parents cuddle their newborns and shower them with love and kisses, they are likely to stay calm and even smile and laugh for them all the time. As soon as your babies become toddlers, encourage them to develop their hobbies and interests, and get them to stay active as much as possible. This will allow them to use all their senses and grow up to become more creative and aware.

Teenage Years

Being a teenager is hard on both parents and kids, and that is always the case. When you have a Taurus child verging on their teenage years, they are likely to show a different side of their personality as they try to learn more about themselves. It is a period where they want to be loved and supported by their parents and try to seek some independence from them to do things their way. Stubbornness might be the highlight of this period with Taurus teenagers, and it is the parents' job to manage this behavior with them by having logical discussions and laying down all the facts.

Youth Years

As your child gets to the end of their teenage years and becomes an adult or a young adult, they will leave from under your wing slowly, which is not something that many parents find easy to accept. But parents must realize that their children will always love them and appreciate them even if they are not living under the same roof and following the same rules. The quicker they accept that the better parents they can be for them in their journey of growing older and experiencing the world as tenacious bulls.

Being blessed with a Taurus child is an exciting and adventurous experience. If you have been a Taurus baby yourself, you can realize how the journey of growing up can be a rollercoaster of emotions and challenges. Taureans are easy to raise if they are well understood and supported by their parents. They are just like any other kid needing lots of love and affection to thrive in the world and become successful adults with stability in their lives.

Chapter 5: Taurus in Love

Relationships are what make life a wonderful journey. Finding someone you love that loves you back can be one of the best things about embarking on a new relationship. If you fall for a Taurus, then you should count yourself lucky. These celestial bulls are all about good taste, so that a Taurus is falling for you too says a lot. Those born under this earthy zodiac sign can be great partners. They are loving, loyal, and kind to their loved ones. It is doubtful for a Taurus to be described as a heartbreaker. Whether you are a Taurus yourself or think you are falling for one, here is everything you should know about Taureans in love.

What they Look for in a Relationship

Taureans love being in love. Affection means a lot to them, and they will do anything to get it and shower their lover with it. When Taureans dive into a relationship, they are in it for the long run. Flings and one-night stands do not interest these celestial characters as they are all about stability and commitment. They will not pressure their partner into committing too quickly or suffocate them with how much they want a long-term relationship. Although, they will clarify it from the first minute of that relationship they are after a stable commitment built to last.

While you are together, a Taurus won't ever stop fighting for you. It is a known fact that Taureans are stubborn, but if you are dating one, think of that stubbornness as passion. They will do anything for their loved ones and continuously work on improving their relationship with their partner. It is fair to say they come first in the zodiac calendar competition of the best lovers.

Why they are Great Lovers

The perfect lover criteria often differ from one person to another. But some fundamentals make a great partner – which everyone can attest to. These fundamentals are what make the relationship so strong and stable for those looking for long-term commitments. Being romantically involved with a Taurus should make you expect certain things you would not usually get with anyone born under a different star sign. Here are characteristics you should expect:

Loyalty

Trust is the basis of any healthy relationship. Those who want stability and peace of mind in their lives always seek loyal and committed partners they can count on and trust with their hearts. That is something that can be easily found in a Taurus. They are intensely loyal and devoted to the person they are with, against all odds. They do not need a "for better or worse" vow considering that is just how they operate anyway. As soon as they find someone who makes them happy, they are theirs for the long haul and will notice no one else under any circumstance.

Romantic

First impressions of a Taurus may not always reveal just how sensitive and romantic they are but being in a relationship with one is often like living in a fairytale. Taurus individuals are all about affection and showering their partners with love, and they are never afraid to show it at every chance they get. They are touchy-feely and love to cuddle with their other halves to express how much they care about them. They also appreciate the nice things in life. So, expect a Taurus to spend a lot of money on their partners, showering them with fancy gifts and trips every now and then just to spoil them and treat them right. The only thing a Taurus expects in return is mutual love and respect and showing appreciation for all their efforts.

Depth of Emotion

Talking about emotions and being vulnerable around others is not something that many people can do. For dating someone, they must show you this side of them and be open with you so you can get to know them fully. Taureans have no problem opening up to their loved ones and having deep conversations about their emotions or becoming vulnerable around them. They won't expose their feelings that deeply unless it is with someone they fully trust and love. So once a Taurus opens up to you, know just how special you are to them. These conversations are what can make a relationship with a Taurus stronger, and you'll both be ready to face everything that life throws in your way.

Ambitious

Being in a long-term relationship with someone means having to think about the future at one point or another. It is not just what the future has in store for the relationship itself, but what it will be like for the individuals in this partnership in terms of their careers and personal lives. Planning is something of second nature to a Taurus. They are extremely ambitious and always look forward to becoming better and more successful at anything they set their minds to, whether it's a career or a personal endeavor. Surprises are not something they like, so they will have a set plan for everything they would like to achieve and accomplish in their life. If they have someone they care about, they will include them in that plan for sure.

Passionate

Taureans are stubborn; that is an undeniable fact. Still, if you are in a relationship with one, this stubbornness is more likely to turn into a passion. Those born under this zodiac sign fight for everything they believe in at all costs. So, if they believe you are the one for them, they will fight for you tooth and nail, remaining dedicated to you against all odds. It will not matter what the world thinks about your relationship or what anyone ever says to bring him or her down. Once they have their heart and mind set on someone they believe is partner material, they will show their passion for them and do anything it takes to keep them around.

Dedicated

A Taurus is known to be a hard worker, but hard work does not just stop at the office or at them being a little workaholic. They carry that trait in everything aspect of their lives. Dedication to their loved ones comes naturally to a Taurus, so their partners should never have to worry about them not putting enough effort into the relationship or giving it their all. These Taurus individuals do not go through anything unless they are not willing to put their hearts and souls into it and tirelessly give it everything they have. That includes their romantic relationships where they'll be obsessed with their other half, in a healthy manner, and will likely do anything for them.

Mysterious

The initial period in any relationship is always full of mystery and electricity. The couple wants to learn all about each other and impress each other with their character and personality. Taureans can be a little mysterious at first and not show all their cards at once. They will still try to impress whoever they have their eyes on, but they will not open up too soon. Once they do confide in their partner and share things about their past and what they are like, one can quickly see they have a lot more than what meets the eye. It is one of Taureans' most attractive things since they only allow certain people to knock down their walls and get a glimpse into their souls.

Turn-Ons and Turn-Offs

Loving a Taurus is not a complicated task. They are simple beings that only need some love and appreciation to thrive in any relationship. The biggest turn on for a Taurus is the ability to understand them so well and being sensual around them. Planning simple dates not too extravagant or too cheap can be the best thing a partner does for their Taurus lover. Taureans are very conscious about their finances, so they do not need someone to spend crazy amounts of money on them to make them happy. Instead, they would rather spend long hours with their lovers talking about important things and spending quality time together in the mornings and evenings.

When it comes to a Taurean's turn-offs, they are not ones who appreciate feeling like they are "plan B." They do not expect their lovers to prioritize them a hundred percent of the time either, but it is always nicer when they are right up there on their second half's priority list. Nothing can get on a Taurean's nerves more than canceling plans at the last minute. These earthy characters are all about planning and hate surprises to their very core. So, if they plan and trust they are doing something with their partners and they cancel it suddenly, it can start massive arguments. Similarly, Taureans love it when their lovers put effort into the relationship. So, if at any point they get the feeling that their partner is not putting in any thought as to how they woo their second half and instead settle for just anything, a Taurus will close off from the relationship and lose interest quickly.

Best Matches

Finding your perfect match can be challenging. Everyone wants to be loved and understood so they can thrive in a healthy relationship. That is why people often go on tons of dates before they can finally say they have found "the one." But analyzing your star sign compared to other star signs can be just the thing you need to find your other half. Every star sign has some compatibility with other star signs; it is just about finding that perfect celestial match made in heaven. Since a Taurus's main element is Earth, they get along well with fellow earthy signs. Here are some of the best matches for a Taurus and how their relationship will be like.

Virgo

Virgos and Taureans can be the most peaceful couple you ever get to meet. They both hate drama and are all about being straightforward with one another. This pair of earthy beings are as sophisticated as they come. They are logical thinkers who weigh all the facts and have rational discussions concerning their relationship. People will often describe this couple as a lovely duo. They like minding their own business but are super friendly to others, and it shows in the way they treat everyone around them. They are extremely traditional, and if they live together, their spirits will reflect in their home through a display of creativity and warmth. Occasionally, the couple can be a little judgmental, but it won't be too aggressive or offensive to anyone. Taurus and Virgo are open-minded and intellectual people, which is likely because Venus rules them both.

Pisces

These two-star signs are a sensual match ruled by the planets, Venus and Neptune. Taureans and Pisces getting together can only mean one thing, and that is living a luxurious and comfy life. This couple fancies gourmet meals and has a knack for expensive wines and sophisticated events. Taureans do not always flaunt their love for lavishness, but with a little encouragement from their Pisces partners, they can go all out. Those born under the Pisces star sign are imaginative and in touch with their emotions. This makes them perfect for Taureans who love talking about in-depth topics and delving into their emotions with their trusted partner. This couple is amazingly dynamic and in control of their relationship in a way that does not allow emotional build-up to ever hinder their love.

Capricorn

Taureans are known for being stubborn occasionally. Capricorns are perfect for them in that regard as they can easily match their persistence and reach a compromising balance with them every time. This duo goes well together, especially with their love and passion for work. They can both be workaholics, but their ambition and determination to succeed in their relative careers is what might bring them together in the first place. Financial stability is the number one priority for this duo, so you are not likely to find them arguing over money as they are both quite sensible with their expenditure. Although both star signs love organization and plan for every little detail, Capricorns can have a bit more discipline than Taureans. It would not cause arguments, but Capricorns tend to push their fellow Taurus partner to do more and stay motivated than they would outside the relationship.

Taurus

Occasionally, the stars will align for a bull and bull match to happen, the perfect definition of a power couple. This pair is all about being slow and steady. They are in the relationship for the long run and are committed to one another. They are a power couple due to their love for love. They appreciate the beauty of one another and can be affectionate behind closed doors. Ruled by Venus, they usually live in a house more of an art gallery than a home. As Taureans have high artistic senses and appreciate the beauty in everything, they like displaying their creativity if they live under the same roof. The home of a Taurus couple is usually the heart of family gatherings. This pair loves their blood ties and looks forward to bringing everyone together on all occasions. They can host lavish parties and reunions always warm and inclusive. The power pair are also likely to be great parents, as they can set an example in love and discipline that any kid would be lucky to have.

Worst Matches

Just as there are star signs that are always compatible together, there are ones that just don't. Some of these matches might be nice and dreamy initially but can become a failed relationship too soon. There are some exceptions to these rules, usually if one person, usually not a Taurus, will compromise to make the relationship work. Yet, these exceptions are so rare, and when found, the relationship might not be as happy or healthy as one would want. If you ever find yourself involved with someone from an opposite star sign, you will need to give yourself some time to think about what you might be getting yourself into and whether or not this relationship is doomed from the start.

Gemini

Stability is everything for someone born under the Taurus zodiac sign. They are very traditional beings that are very grounded and love having everything done so it fits with their chill lifestyle. Geminis are the opposite of that; they are outgoing individuals who are hot and cold and all about new adventures. Pairing those two together can be a disaster in the making. At first, they may think that they are balancing each other out, but eventually, clashes are bound to happen, and it can break the relationship completely. Free-spirited Geminis and traditional Taureans are rare to have many things in common, if anything at all, and that is not a good foundation to start a healthy relationship with.

Leo

The chemistry between those two celestial star signs can be great, but that chemistry can lead to a nuclear explosion in the end. Stubbornness is something they share, and compromise is not something that any of them is ever willing to do. Lions love being in charge but so do bulls. When placed together in one pair, it can end in one of two ways, either a complete disaster where arguing is the only thing these two ever do or taking over the world together as one fierce, dynamic duo. The success of a lion and a bull in a romantic relationship is a rare event, but it is possible. But usually these two signs do not see eye to eye as they are always in a power play that rarely ends well.

Libra

Taureans and Libras are both ruled by the planet Venus, which is famously known for its great passion and sensuality. However, with these two signs, the cardinal elements are just not suitable for each other, with one being Earth and the other being air. This makes a relationship between those two an uncomfortable and often an unsuccessful one. Earthly signs always look for stability and traditions, whereas those following the cardinal element of air are always buzzing for change and adventure. It can be frustrating when these two come together as they want to feel loved and share their love of nature, but it often comes across in the wrong way, leading to their inevitable separation.

Scorpio

A Scorpio and a Taurus's traits can be seen as opposites; these two just won't get along on much of anything. It is not only in romantic relationships, it's even in social relationships, that they go neck to neck. The two-star signs often have a love-hate relationship because of their differences, but that is often a deal-breaker for them for getting romantic. Each is always trying to mark their territory and prove that they are in control, which never works in a healthy coupling.

Loving a Taurus Woman

Falling for a Taurus woman can be the best feeling in the world. These women are affectionate and caring and will shower their partner with unconditional love. It is not the suffocating love that people often escape from, but it's the kind that humans need to feel special and wanted. If you are lucky enough to love a Taurus woman, then you should always make her feel like the queen she is. Never try to change her or tell her she is not enough; she does not like feeling she must compete for your love. Also, public displays of affection will not always feel right for her. Though, remember that compliments are always nice to hear anywhere, especially if her loved one praises her in front of her close family and friends, whom she holds dearly in her heart.

Loving a Taurus Man

The way to a Taurus man's heart is through emotional support and appreciation. These men can seem a little standoffish when you first meet them, but when they fall for you, all their walls will be broken down. They expect their partners to take them and make them feel understood and loved through all odds. Small gestures will go a long way in your relationship with a Taurus guy. Things like asking about their day or giving them little compliments every now and then can make all the difference in the world. These men thrive on routine and stability, so surprising them is not a good idea. Instead, try to plan things together and see what they love to do on their time off so you can work on your relationship more often and bond in a healthy manner.

Attracting a Taurus

Taureans are all about long-term commitment. If you are looking to settle down and maybe even get married at some point, then he or she can be your perfect match. Attracting them can be done by showing them you are looking for the same things they are. Being a grounded person on good terms with their family and likes expressing their feelings to others appropriately and healthily can get you on top of a Taurean's list. They are suckers for family-oriented individuals passionate about the important things in life. These celestial beings also love being involved with someone who cares about their career and has a lot of ambition that allows them to succeed in life.

Signs a Taurus is Interested

A Taurus is not too obvious for showing how they feel. They take their time and try to be subtle at first just to see how the other person responds. Taureans like giving subtle hints to test the waters, and once they feel like the person on the other end are interested too, they will go all in. Some signs they will give are things like checking up on the person they are interested in more often. They'll send texts and messages and show a lot of interest in their lives and how their days are going so they can let the person know they care about them.

A Taurus often shows they are into someone by asking him or her for advice occasionally. Taureans are very stubborn and mostly do whatever they want and like to do. So, if they genuinely ask for advice from someone they are interested in, it is a clear sign they are falling hopelessly in love.

Perfect Date Ideas

Dating a Taurus can be a magical time. They are all about showing love and affection to their other half, and for planning a date, they expect a whole lot of romance to be involved. They are also active people who like going out in nature and spending some quality time with their partners. That is why planning a date with your Taurus lover is simple if you know them. Here are some date ideas guaranteed to tickle a Taurean's fancy.

Hiking

Going out in the secluded nature trails with their favorite person can be the perfect date for a Taurus. It can be packed with delicious snacks and some candles or roses to make it even more romantic. Essentially, this kind of date just ticks all the boxes. It gets the Taurus to go out and get active and use all their senses and allows them to feel free while being showered with love from their partner.

Movie Night

Romance is a Taurus's middle name. They are also big fans of traditions and love being at home where they can be themselves. Bringing all those elements together in a magical movie night with a nice dinner can be the best thing you do for your favorite Taurus. It is romantic and cozy and is all about showering each other with love and attention away from the rest of the world.

Couples Massage

There is nothing more relaxing and enjoyable than getting your sore muscles massaged at a spa, especially with your loved one. This date idea allows a Taurus and their partner to get in touch with all their senses and relax together in a calm setup that fits their relationship's theme. It is the perfect getaway to let loose together and come out feeling refreshed and more connected to your partner.

Falling for a Taurus can be an exciting experience. It is also likely to last for a long time, a lifetime if the stars are aligned for you. When dating a Taurus, it is vital that you let them be themselves without judging or asking them to change. They will do anything for their loved ones, but not if they feel insecure. Remember always to express your love for your Taurus partner through compliments and showing care for them through all the odds because that will give them all the reassurance they need that they are loved and wanted.

Chapter 6: Taurus at Work

After covering Taurus's personal life in the previous chapters, let's peek into the professional side of this zodiac sign. In this chapter, we will discuss a Taurean's career and workplace characteristics.

In general, a Taurus is a hard-working, reliable, and determined employee or boss in the work field. However, certain weaknesses could massively ruin their chances of gaining success. Let's take a detailed look at how the Taurus is like in the work field and what can stop them from achieving success.

Best Career Choices for the Taurus

A Taurus is ambitious, dependable, and hard-working, which makes them great workers and leaders on the professional front. Based on their traits, a Taurus should focus on these career paths.

1. Chef or Restaurant Manager

Taureans love and appreciate food. They like to try new recipes and are often curious about different cuisines. Among other zodiac signs, Taurus individuals are the emerging food aficionados. And so, they can make great chefs, as they love to cook and feed others. Besides preparing delectable dishes, they will also ensure that the presentation of each dish is optimized. If they don't want to cook but still manage projects around food (due to their knowledge and liking for food), they can also make talented restaurant managers. Taureans have impeccable organization and planning skills. They can easily manage and instruct restaurant workers, waiters, cleaners, and other staff.

Candace Nelson and Brad Leone are two famous Taurus chefs.

2. Interior Designer

Since Taurus holds an apprehension for art and culture, they make amazing designers. Interior design is an excellent choice for this zodiac sign due to their impressive organizational skills and ability to transform a space. They also have a knack for talking to homeowners and convincing them to follow a particular home transformation plan. While individuals with Cancer and Libra as zodiac signs are also equally talented at this job, the Taurus can pave their path in this discipline due to their desire for perfection. Besides interior designers, Taureans can also work as fashion and graphic designers. Since they are keen on knowing and learning about aesthetics, this career option is an excellent fit for a Taurus.

Donatella Versace and Tan France are two famous Taurus fashion designers who are well known for their knowledge of aesthetic and styling skills.

3. Banker or Financial Advisor

Also known as a manager of money, a person with this zodiac sign can look into money handling and organization as a plausible career option. Due to their meticulous and pragmatic attitude, Taureans can also become competent bankers or financial advisors. Since they are wise and resilient, they have been deemed an asset within this discipline. Besides bankers and financial advisors, they can also look into financial administration and accountancy as a career option in this field. Another reason this option is great for the Taurus is that they are skilled in the calculation and tremendously reliable for accuracy.

4. Botanist or Agriculturist

This sign loves nature and wants to be around flora and fauna. If you are a Taurus and are partial to spending most of your time outdoors and around nature, this career option is the most suitable. Besides their passion for nature, their meticulous skills and knack for details will make them talented botanists and researchers in this field. This discipline requires a person to follow a pattern and take a methodical approach, which is a perfect career option for a Taurus. Other suitable sub-disciplines include farming, landscaping, and gardening.

5. Politician or Leader

Taureans are known to be stubborn and do not budge until they convince the other person. At times, this can lead to arguments. But if a Taurus uses this trait for their benefit, they can become a successful politician. Also, their organization and attention to detail will help them make better decision-makers. They are independent, determined, and quick on their feet. As a Taurus, if you pursue a goal, you will go to any extent to achieve it. This is a much-needed trait in most politicians. If becoming a politician is not their cup of tea, they also make competent leaders, such as the CEO of a company or an entrepreneur.

Some famous Taurus politicians include Pope John Paul II and Queen Elizabeth II.

6. Singer, Composer, or Musician

Taureans are artistic and have a great sense of style, music, food, and other cultural interests. Even though they are pragmatic by nature, their artistic sense is exemplary, which is also surprising. With music, they are extremely gifted. If you need new song suggestions, you can always turn to a Taurus. This quality can also be turned into a successful career as a musician or singer. And they can work for endless hours with the same scrutiny and attention to detail, which is required in a music career. You will find them working until they have achieved perfection.

James Brown, Billy Joel, and Sam Smith are some famous Taurus musicians and singers.

7. Manager or Executive

As mentioned, Taureans are blessed with management skills and can be extremely resourceful. This makes roles like management and executive direction fit for this zodiac sign. Also, since they are not shy, they like to take the plunge and lead others within this discipline. A manager or an executive must stay on top of their game and lead their team, which is another reason it makes a perfect job description. Also, since these two positions offer a higher chance of getting a bonus or a promotion, the Taurus usually prefers it.

8. Makeup Artist or Beauty Blogger

A Taurus has an impeccable aesthetic taste and a knack for beauty. They focus not only on their looks, but they also have a distinct perception of beauty around them. When paired with their eye for detail, they can make talented makeup artists or beauty bloggers. This zodiac sign's ruling planet is Venus, which explains their tenacity of becoming a beauty blogger. Anything related to beauty is a great career choice for a Taurus, but know that succeeding in this discipline will take some time. Even though it will be difficult initially, you will enjoy every bit of this journey, which will make it easier for you to succeed. This is also partly due to your tenacious nature.

9. Vet or Pet Sitter

Your love for animals can be converted into a career option. Two such options include being a veterinarian or a pet sitter. While the former requires you to have enough patience to study and graduate, the latter does not require formal education. Both these options let you be near pets most of the time, which is something a Taurus will love. Also, a Taurus is reliable, which makes them great pet sitters. As an individual with this zodiac sign, you can also consider other similar jobs, like pet grooming, dog boarding, or pet taxi. Since you are also blessed with management and organizational skills, you can make relevant appointments and start your own pet company. Consider other options like dog training classes and grooming equipment stores as well.

Worst Career Choices for the Taurus

1. Doctor, Nurse, or Medical Practitioner

Any sub-category within the medical discipline requires time and patience and is not a strong suit for Taurus. Individuals with this zodiac sign work hard to achieve their goals; however, they are not well known for practicing patience. First, it takes years to graduate as a doctor or medical practitioner, which is difficult for this zodiac sign. Second, they want to achieve their goals within a lesser time, which may lead to rushing mistakes. Any kind of error is unavoidable in the medical field.

2. Human Resources

A job role as an HR sounds boring and mundane, which a Taurus will hate. Since people with this zodiac sign usually look forward to new and challenging tasks, this job may be too modest for them. An HR's responsibility is to narrow down the gap between the company and employees, which needs time and patience. While the Taurus can easily manage the organizational skills and even excel at it, they might just not have the patience to deal with employees' complaints. Let's not forget about a Taurus' stubbornness that could potentially get in the way of their job role and cause trouble in the company.

3. Teacher or Professor

Again, this role is difficult for the Taurus to portray, as it needs them to be more tolerant and accepting of others. Since kids don't easily listen to elders, it can be difficult for them to manage such scenarios. Also, if a kid and a Taurus come face to face, their stubborn natures can cause a never-ending debate. No one is ready to yield, which can cause trouble for the Taurus as a teacher.

These best and worst career options for this zodiac sign should be considered when picking a field. Consider your skills and strengths at a personal level and make a wise choice.

Where Does the Taurus Fit in an Office Setting?

Various scenarios in an office setting involve employees being near the water cooler and gossiping about other employees, planning social events, and managing informal gathering, or putting on headphones and are engrossed in their work. Where do you find a Taurus in such workplace scenarios?

The Taurus loves their share of gossip and will want to discuss it with their close friends. If one of their coworkers is also their best friend, you are likely to see them in the office cafeteria or near the water cooler, where they occasionally meet to pass along fresh news. Also, since they are social, they always look forward to parties and informal gatherings. If you need a party planner in an office setting, hire a Taurus. Their impeccable organizational and management skills make them competent event planners. It is difficult to find a Taurus engrossed in only work.

Since they can be lazy, dependent, and often too distracted, they are less likely to be seated at their desks, completing their work. They either hover around the workplace, looking for others to finish the task or are distracted by their phone or other unimportant matters.

A Taurus boss is rarely seen in the office, which gives other Taurus employees the freedom to roam around and complete tasks at his or her own pace. Also, since the boss is usually unaware of the day-to-day tasks and accomplishments, it is easier for a Taurus to take credit.

Obstacles at Work

A Taurus at the office or a work setting can be surprising. While they have many strengths, their weaknesses can often overpower their personality. This affects not only their work and productivity but also their mental health. To resolve these weaknesses, first learn how to detect them.

If you are a Taurus or are working around one, you may notice one or more of these obstacles or weaknesses in their work and performance.

Taurus as a Coworker or Employee

1. They May be "Bonus Oriented"

Due to their materialistic nature and need to live a luxurious life, most individuals with this zodiac sign constantly seek a bonus or a promotion. For this, they often overwork and try to achieve their goals quickly. While it is beneficial for the company, it might affect the quality of work. If they fail to achieve their bonus, they might get extraordinarily disappointed or disheartened, dampening their productivity and will to work.

2. They Can be Too Lazy

A Taurean's lazy nature can pose a threat in their path towards success. Although most Taurus employees are ambitious, they often get lazy during group projects or when it is a collective responsibility. They may rely on their coworkers to get the job done, which can delay the deadline. Even if they agree to contribute, their lazy nature can disturb their working pattern, which will cause unsatisfactory results. If a Taurus puts 100% effort into his or her work (which many achieve), he or she will probably be the best employee in a workplace setting. However, their laziness often keeps them from being one.

3. They Can Easily Get into Fights

Due to their stubborn nature, a Taurus can easily pick up a fight with their coworker. Debates and arguments are frequent with a Taurus as a teammate. They not only argue with their coworker but can also get in occasional tiffs with their boss. It is difficult to win an argument with a Taurus, even if you are right. While it hardly matters in an informal setting, this attitude can majorly affect a company's performance and goals.

4. They Can be Too Social

While it doesn't harm their personal life, a social employee might be seen chatting and making plans during office hours. They are often distracted during work due to their need to be social. If one of their coworkers is also one of their closest friends, they are often seen socializing, which can affect their quality of work.

5. They are Dependent and Take Undeserving Credit

A Taurus has the potential to develop innovative ideas; however, they are occasionally not bothered to do it and let their coworkers take charge. Besides, if their coworkers complete the project on time and accomplish the goal, the Taurus employee takes the credit.

Taurus as a Boss or Group Leader

1. They May Want to Achieve Too Many Things at Once

As a Taurus boss, your main goal will often involve completing a project or wrapping up a deal as quickly as possible. Taureans are very ambitious go-getters and will fight their way to achieve success. While this is beneficial for the company, it may affect your employees' mental health. Not everyone can work as quickly as a Taurus, and they should understand that your employees have their own pace and can get only a certain number of things done within a designated period. If you're a Taurus boss, try to take things slowly and take one step at a time. Follow a plan to get closer to your goal. Even if it takes time, you are bound to succeed.

2. They Can be Bossy and Insensitive

If your Taurus boss doesn't get what he wants, he may become too bossy and even lose their temper occasionally. When it comes to working, they disregard their employees' and co-founder's feelings and won't think twice before uttering harsh words. While it is casual for them, certain words and remarks could hurt their employee's sentiments, which might even affect their performance. In extreme cases, a Taurus boss can even make personal remarks, which is unacceptable. Employees under all circumstances should abide by their rules and regulations, which are written in stone. Failure to do so could trigger the Taurus boss, resulting in a hard time for the employees. Even if a Taurus rarely gets angry, their casual attitude towards treating other people, especially when the latter are wrong, can come across as mean and rude.

3. They Refrain from Accepting Their Mistakes

Even if they are unclear about their expectations, they are not ready to accept their mistakes initially. The need for the right takes a toll on their employees. A Taurus boss usually briefs their employees in a way they deem "perfect" and "detailed." While it is typically the case, they can sometimes be too vague due to impatience. In this case, the results are unsatisfactory and not up to their expectations. Conversely, a Taurus boss can sometimes blame their employees instead of accepting their mistake.

4. They are Unable to Take Risks

While this can lead to favorable outcomes sometimes, a leader should possess the courage to take risks to lead their company to success. The Taurus boss prefers to play it safe, resulting in losing potentially successful leads and deals. Individuals with this zodiac sign cannot face the fear of uncertainty. Taking risks is all about being aware and affecting, which is not a strong suit for Taurus. While being a risk-taker is rare, a leader or a boss should possess this skill to achieve success.

Once you determine the traits of a Taurus in a work setting, you can then help them resolve these issues so they can lead a successful work life.

Tips for a Fulfilling Work Life

Since a Taurus can be too lazy and stubborn they are likely to face failure in aspects of their career if they don't turn things around. As a Taurus, work on your weaknesses and polish your strengths for personal development and get closer to your goals. Since you already know your weaknesses, it is time to navigate them to gain a fruitful professional life.

Here are some work tips for individuals with this zodiac sign:

1. Take Charge of a Project

While a Taurus can be too lazy to contribute to a project as a coworker, they are the complete opposite as a team leader, as mentioned in the previous chapters. If you want to improve your lazy nature and contribute more to the workforce, take charge of a project. Be a leader and put your organizational skills to proper use. A Taurus team leader is an excellent addition to the company and will become reliable and push their fellow teammates to do their best. This way, a Taurus will learn to pull their weight and drive the company towards success. At the same time, they should initiate new ideas and projects with a detailed plan likely to gain approval.

Taureans make promising leaders, which is why you should work as one. If your boss doesn't recognize your talent and is skeptical about appointing you as the leader, you must prove yourself first. Throw your lazy veil away and work to prove yourself. Come up with innovative ideas and a detailed plan to increase your chances of being appointed as the group leader.

2. Take More Risks

While it is easier said than done, taking risks is imperative in a workplace setting, especially if you are the company's boss or CEO. Since the Taurus lacks the courage to take risks, it is difficult for them to take the leap. To let go of this fear and build courage, try to acknowledge your fear. Being vulnerable and knowing of this feeling can help you build the courage to take risks. If you know the dangers and fear involved in a particular risk, you become more prepared to overcome them. What is the worst that can happen? What could go wrong? To what extent will it harm the company or employees? Questions such as these will also help you overcome the fear of taking risks.

Taking risks will help your company and make you more confident and resilient as a person. It is necessary to develop your personality too. You'd be surprised to know your potential. Last, build more skills and develop your skills to gain the confidence to overcome risky situations. You must be patient, as being a risk-taker is not easy.

3. Learn to Compromise

There is a fine line between being levelheaded and being stubborn. While the former usually relates to being wise and making the right decisions, the latter often leads to a downfall as it relates to the need for being right (even if the person is wrong). As you already know, the Taurus is probably the most stubborn of all zodiac signs. A Taurus should learn to compromise and let things go. Failing to do so can affect their personal and professional life. They may even lose touch with valuable acquaintances and job prospects. If you cannot put your foot down, it is necessary to turn this situation around.

To do this, learn to listen to others. Do not speak or interrupt others before they have finished. Even if you disagree with someone, let him or her speak before you put your viewpoint across. Before you assert domination and mark all prospects as "no", take a minute to evaluate the situation and talk only when you fully agree. At times, spontaneous reactions and quick decisions can lead to misunderstandings and even arguments. So, listen carefully before you speak. Also, know that you are not always right. Remember this when talking to someone. More important, remember that not everyone has to agree with your opinion. Let go of this expectation and learn to compromise.

4. Improve Your Communication Skills

While the Taurus doesn't face an issue to communicate with others, their stubborn nature can cause a rude and mean tone, even if they don't mean it. Improving your communication skills will help you in the professional field to impress your boss. It is a necessity for most zodiac signs.

Besides speaking, effective communication skills also involve proper listening. Let the person finish their lines and focus on the critical parts. Try to maintain eye contact. This shows you are listening to the other person and are acknowledging their opinion. It will also help you focus on the crucial parts of a conversation, which will ultimately help you make acceptable comments. When your time to respond, be humble, and help others realize that you have been listening to the entire time. Whether it's an employee you are talking to or conversing with a delegate on an important business lunch, focus on the way you speak and listen to achieve the best outcome.

5. Overcome Procrastination by Minimizing Distractions

Due to their laziness and need to procrastinate, a Taurus may witness delayed success. Even though they can achieve success through their talent and organizational skills, their laziness can be a significant obstacle. To overcome this, minimize distractions and incorporate anti-procrastination strategies. Since procrastination is deeply ingrained in one's behavioral pattern, it's challenging to turn it around in less time. However, one must try to succeed and achieve their goals.

The first step towards overcoming procrastination is to realize your problem. Once you do, stop beating yourself up and promise yourself to turn the situation around. Second, minimize distractions such as mobile phones, electronics, and food. Since you are lazy to work, you often find distractions that fuel your boredom. To avoid this, keep your cell phone and electronics locked in a drawer and keep food away. Besides this, try other anti-procrastination strategies such as making a to-do list, rewarding yourself for accomplishing specific tasks, or asking someone to keep track of your progress.

These tips will help a Taurus excel at work and push them to achieve their goals. Implementing these tips will also help you to work on your personality and make a positive change in your personal life.

As you learned, the Taurus at work can either make or break the entity they are working for. While they possess numerous strengths, their weaknesses could lead to a major downfall in their performance and productivity. The best way to combat this situation is to recognize these flaws and improve them. If a Taurus does it, they are bound to succeed.

Chapter 7: The Social Taurus

Most Taureans possess unparalleled social skills and a need to make friends. In this chapter, we will look at how a typical Taurus behaves in a party or an informal setting.

Taurus Friendships

In this section, we will talk about how Taurus makes friends and functions in general. When it comes to making friends and sustaining long-term friendships, a Taurus gives 100%. They hardly make friends, but once they do, they are in it for a long haul. Even though they consider "friends forever" to be a cliché, they abide by it. It is challenging to attract a Taurus and be their friend, but the bond is fruitful once you do it. The Bull is not only loyal but also possesses a great sense of humor.

If you are in pain or feeling down, call a Taurean friend to get a dose of laughter because they are witty and know how to make people laugh. Also, they remember important dates, events, birthdays, and anniversaries of people close to them. With a Taurus as your best friend, you can expect a grand celebration on your birthday. They will never let you modestly celebrate any important dates. Even if you don't like it, you must put up with their grandeur and celebrate your day as they prefer. This shows they take friendships seriously and want their friends to stay happy and content.

It is difficult to be friends with a Taurus as they are too picky with people they allow in their inner circle. And so, you must work at winning their heart and gaining their trust. Still, you will always have to put up with their stubbornness, which is difficult. Also, since a Taurus is often suspicious of others and their intentions, being close or best friends with them is a major challenge. For them, outsiders always seem to have an agenda that can affect their personal and professional lives. You can't blame a Taurus for thinking this way, as they often encounter people who take advantage of their loyalty. This weakens their trust in people, which also explains their pickiness. And they are honest and expect honesty from their friends too.

Taurus Friendship Grid with the Other 11 Zodiacs

In this section, we will examine the friendship compatibility of Taurus with other zodiac signs.

Taurus and Aries

Aries is governed by the symbol of Ram, which makes them impulsive and always seeking adventure. While a Taurus prefers to take things slow and experience one step at a time, an Aries usually takes the leap, which often causes an imbalance between them. Though, since Aries is direct and straightforward, you prefer to hang out with them. They directly tell you what's on their mind, which feeds your impatient soul. There is usually no beef between you two. Also, you don't mind exploring new arenas and going on occasional adventures with your Aries' friend. But Aries prefers to hang out with a Taurus due to the latter's carefree and sensible attitude.

Taurus and Taurus

Surprisingly, a friendship between these two similar signs turns out to be relatively stable. You can rely on each other and always count on your Taurean friend when you are sick or in trouble. As a Taurus, if you are looking for practical assistance and advice, you can always turn to another Taurean. They are always aware and quick on their feet to give you the best practical advice possible. Whether job assistance or a suggestion for a good doctor, they always have an answer. Due to their relaxed nature and earthy humor, they enjoy each other's company and look forward to spending time together. Even if you don't like adventures, you won't mind enduring new experiences such as wine tasting, a visit to the amusement park, or a spa retreat with them. One major downside to this friendship is that both friends can get into an unending argument. Due to their stubbornness, none will back off easily.

Taurus and Gemini

A Gemini is known to be whimsical, which is quite the opposite of a Taurus' apparent traits. They are not as practical as you and may make you question their actions. While they are constantly seeking adventure, a Taurus prefers to follow a routine, which is quite the contrary. A Gemini friend prefers to spend money on the best experiences, whereas a Taurus friend prefers to save every penny earned. As you can see, it can be difficult for these signs to become friends. Even with, a Gemini's sense of humor and a Taurus' practical and methodical approach always balance the two, which sustains the friendship. For the friendship to last long, a Taurus must put up with a Gemini's unwillingness and steady movements, whereas a Gemini has to be patient.

Taurus and Cancer

This pairing is one of the few friendship bonds that can last for years, which is rare with this zodiac sign. Cancer always vents or puts their thoughts and aspirations in front of their Taurus friend. The Taurus doesn't mind listening to their Cancer friend even if they call at midnight. Both signs are there for each other through thick and thin. Their friendship is loyal and everlasting. While a Cancer admires your perception towards life, a Taurus friend appreciates the other's executive abilities, which brings a perfect balance to the friendship. If a Taurus manages to put up with a Cancer's moodiness and a Cancer rarely minds a Taurus' stubbornness, the friendship is bound to last long.

Taurus and Leo

Despite being different personalities, certain commonalities between a Leo and a Taurus bring these signs together. Their appreciation for luxury, materials, and the finer things in life is unparalleled, which often brings them together. Also, both signs are highly creative, which brings up interesting topics of discussion, most of which are related to art, museums, photography, and other cultural implications. Both signs also match in terms of impeccable organizational and management skills, which they find attractive about each other. For the friendship to last long, a Taurus must put up with Leo's ego, and a Leo must ignore a Taurus' calculated steps.

Taurus and Virgo

Both signs love nature and being outdoors, which brings them closer. Friends of this zodiac sign are often seen on an adventure, a picnic, or random evening walks. As a Taurus, if you are looking for practical assistance and problem-solving skills, you can always turn to a Virgo. But if a Virgo needs financial advice and management, they can ask their Taurus friend for help. A Taurus may find a Virgo friend annoying because they act as neat freaks. But they tend to ignore these tidbits because a Virgo friend also ignores a Taurus' stubbornness.

Taurus and Libra

Since both signs share the ruling planet Venus, they hold an inordinate desire for beauty and art. Within this discipline, your tastes may marginally vary. For instance, a Libra may prefer exquisite or contemporary artists, whereas a Taurus will stick to antique or classical art and expression forms. While a Libra is more social and is often seen in a bigger group of friends, you prefer to stick to one or two of your closest pals. Even though a Taurus possesses the ability to be social, they prefer to stick to their closest friends. One significant difference between these two signs is that a Taurus is organized, whereas a Libra is all over the place, often without an organized plan. Also, a Libra friend has the tendency to change their mind quickly, which leaves the Taurus friend confused. Since a Taurus prefers to follow a plan, they may find this trait to be annoying. For the friendship to last long, a Taurus must put up with a Libra's spontaneity, and a Libra must let go of a Taurus' attention to detail.

Taurus and Scorpio

Even though a Taurus and a Scorpio are completely different, their friendship is often long-lasting. While they share some similar interests in dance, art, wine, and culture, a Taurus despises a Scorpio's evasions. Yet, this friendship is based on mutual respect and admiration for the opposite astrological sign, which is why it survives for a longer period. They continuously learn from each other. For instance, a Taurus appreciates a Scorpio's viewpoint and passion towards life, whereas a Scorpio wants to learn money management from a Taurus. For the friendship to last long, a Taurus must put up with a Scorpio's manipulation, and a Scorpio must ignore a Taurus' stubbornness.

Taurus and Sagittarius

While a Taurus is calculative and calm most of the time, a Sagittarius is extremely enthusiastic, which contradicts their natures. A Taurus monotony and ability to repeat things, outfits, and activities are puzzling to a Sagittarius. What's more, puzzling is their new and enthusiastic response to the same old activities. Even if you eat the same lunch every day, your excited reaction is mystifying to your Sagittarius friend. As a Taurus, if you need to incorporate some change in your life, you can always turn to a Sagittarius. But if a Sagittarius is looking for a light-hearted conversation or needs some cheering, they can ask their Taurus friend for help.

Taurus and Capricorn

These two are Earth signs, so they share similar traits, personalities, and aspirations. Even though you both are too picky, you bond quickly. This is because you understand the other's mindset and help them reach their goals. While a Capricorn yearns respect and stature, a Taurus adores and yearns beauty. Both need a comfortable and steady life. A Bull can help the Goat find a job, one they deserve, and put them in the spotlight. A major difference between these two signs is their working style and pattern. While a Capricorn works hard with no rest, a Taurus' laziness may be off-putting for them. Other than this, there is no serious reason for the friendship to weaken at any point.

Taurus and Aquarius

This friendship will be challenging for both signs. However, they know how to navigate their way through difficulties. Their interest and need for material possessions can often be a major difference between these signs, sometimes even a threat. While an Aquarius is least bothered about accumulating materials, a Taurus finds pleasure in it. Also, a Taurus prefers to be near his friends, whereas an Aquarius likes to be alone most of the time. However, since both signs appreciate each other for their strengths, this friendship can be enduring.

Taurus and Pisces

A friendship between these two signs is probably one of the easiest and light-hearted bonds among other pairings. Pisces possess a great sense of humor and creative skills, which a Taurus adores. But a Pisces admires a Taurus' practical approach and common sense. They both have something to offer in their friendship. For instance, a Pisces learns finance management and organizational skills from a Taurus, and a Taurus friend picks up creative skills from a Pisces. For the friendship to last long, a Taurus must put up with a Pisces' unpunctuality, and a Pisces must ignore a Taurus' inflexibility and stubbornness. To overcome these minor annoyances, find a hobby that you'd enjoy together.

Signs that Don't Get Along with Taurus

The complex interrelationships between the signs matter more than many people think. While it shouldn't be a deal-breaker, it should help you understand more why some of your relationships with friends or family are the way they are.

Taurus and Aries

Aries is one of the most active and competitive signs, making them often clash with Taurus. The definition of fun for both signs is different, which is why they usually have drastically contrasting interests. If they can cooperate to a greater extent, they can push each other to accomplish great goals. A Taurus can help Aries go through something that they rarely have the discipline to go through, while the Aries can open diverse paths that the Taurus was too conservative to approach.

Taurus and Gemini

Gemini doesn't have a long attention span, which usually results in them finding themselves in a million different things. This overwhelming divergence can cause them to stretch themselves too thin, which is the opposite of what a Taurus would do. Taurus appreciates familiarity and comfort zones, allowing them to focus on a single task or activity until they perfect it. They can both help each other out as one provides the other with different and useful perspectives.

Taurus and Sagittarius

The clash between Taurus and Sagittarius is basically about the unknown. Sagittarius thrives for tackling the unknown and unfamiliar territories. Taurus avoids the unknown and prefers to be surrounded with as much security as possible. This problem can become apparent in romantic relationships as their interests can create a big gap. Depending on the understanding of both parties, it is possible to find satisfying compromises.

Signs that Get Along with Taurus

Knowing which signs to look for can help you skip a lot of hassle. There is nothing wrong with looking for compatible signs that can make your life easier. Finding complementary signs can push you forward in your professional and social life.

Virgo and Taurus

Both Virgo and Taurus are earth signs, which means they have a high probability of enjoying each other's company. Both signs are known for their reliability and practicality, making them a great duo. A Taurus can provide enough stability to a Virgo to create a foundation that frequently allows the Virgo to push forward and reach its target. Having a Virgo as a friend or a partner is always a good idea as they are focused and provide matching energy.

Libra and Taurus

Earth and air-based signs are not usually the most compatible, but this rule may not directly apply to a duo composed of Libra and Taurus. It's believed that the Venus connection between the two signs makes them relatively stable. The emotional and subjective perspective of Taurus finds its polar opposite in the objective view of the Libra. They can match each other's tones and create a bridge that allows them to focus on what's important. These two signs are an excellent match for romantic and platonic relationships.

Pisces and Taurus

Earth and water are a great combination with the zodiac signs. The relationship between Pisces and Taurus is a dynamically synchronous one. Pisces complements the relationship with their devotion and idealism, while Taurus makes sure that they don't go off the grid with their realism. This can make a Pisces and Taurus duo quite powerful as they both can reduce the other's weaknesses. A loving relationship between the two can last for life, navigating problems as they go with great determination.

Taurus at a Party: Social Life

In this section, we will describe a party scene and see how the Taurus fits in.

If you are at a Taurus' birthday party or informal gathering, you are bound to have a blast. Since the Taurus has an eye for details, they are likely to throw a grand party to impress their guests. Also, since they're also major foodies and know their way in the kitchen, be ready to try delicious dishes at their party.

At someone else's party, a Taurus can be found meeting and talking to new people. They seem comfortable and are often seen with a drink (mostly a classy liquor type) in their hand. Even if they are in a corner, they seem to grab everyone's attention. They keep an eye on their close friends and make sure that they are fine. More important, they look out for their friends and make sure that they are not making a fool of themselves.

Why Does a Taurus Make a Great Friend?

Although a Taurus has many weaknesses, they are often minute and can be overlooked. Their strengths overpower their weaknesses, which makes them a loyal and reliable friend.

Here are five reasons friendship with a Taurus is valuable:

1. They Will Always Stay by Your Side

Even if you committed grave mistakes in your relationship, a Taurus believes in giving second chances. They will even help you correct your errors and get back on your feet. They are reliable and will always stay by your side. Also, if you desperately want to share a secret but not spread it further, you can rely on a Taurus, as they are secret bearers. They are loyal and will not spread gossip.

2. They Have a Solution to All Your Problems

Even if you mess up, your Taurus friend will have some solution to help you solve your issue. If you find yourself amid a crisis, call your Taurus friend up and let them help you. Even if you don't ask for help, they will do anything to make sure that your life is sorted. Whether it's an emotional family crisis or an intense project deadline, you can count on a Taurus to get you out of trouble. With a Taurus as a friend, your fridge is always loaded with beer, and your Netflix is paid every month.

3. They Oversee All Events

Whether it's your birthday or a school event, a Taurus will put their organizational skills into action and throw the best event one can imagine. Their impeccable management sense and attention to detail make them a valuable friend who can organize any event with little help. No wonder they make great managers. Even if it's your dog's birthday, they will always turn up with a doggie treat and candle.

4. They Will Show You the Better Side of Life

Due to their appreciation for food, art, culture, and luxury, they will guide you to life's finer things occasionally. With a Taurus friend, you can explore new restaurants and cuisines, take museum tours, or go wine tasting. This zodiac sign loves to eat and possesses a knack for cooking. With a Taurus as a friend, you will try new food and learn about the culinary world. Even if you can't afford to go out to a restaurant, a Taurus will whip up something delicious in their kitchen.

5. They Will Give You Expensive Presents

While this shouldn't be the sole reason to befriend a Taurus, it's an added benefit that not everyone is blessed with. A Taurus has expensive taste and prefers to use grand and luxurious material goods. Their clothes, shoes, bags, and gadgets are often high-end, and name brand. They not only want expensive things for themselves but also want their friends to experience luxury. Whether it's your birthday, graduation, or any other important event, your Taurus friend will always shower you with expensive gifts.

How to Foster a Taurus Friendship

As you can see, friendship with a Taurus is super valuable. However, their weaknesses can often get in the way and spoil your bond. To overcome this, go through these tips that will help you foster a Taurus friendship and sustain it for a long time.

How to Foster a Friendship Between a Taurus and Taurus

Even though both Taureans live through and understand their nature, certain aspects can clash and threaten their friendship. If you are a Taurus and want to sustain your friendship with a fellow Taurus, consider these tips:

1. Try to be More Understanding

The biggest problem that two Taureans can face in a friendship is a never-ending debate due to their stubbornness and argumentative nature. The only way to resolve this is to be more understanding. One or both Taurean friends must practice understanding, or it can cause a dent in their friendship. The first step is to listen. Instead of arguing and filling your head with a big "No" as they speak, listen to their viewpoint, and put yourself in their shoes. At times, they may have a point. The key is patience and an open mind.

2. Give Them Enough Time and Space When They are Angry

As Taureans friends, both of you may get easily angry and triggered due to your short tempers. If both of you get in a heated argument, give each other time instead of bombarding them with more viewpoints. Since a Taurus' temper dies down quickly, it is easier to resolve the issue when you give them enough time and space to think and contemplate the situation. Also, this zodiac sign despises drama in their life, which is why they resort to comfort and happiness after some time.

3. Make More Indoor Plans

If a Taurus earns money, they will likely spend it on a cozy home and luxurious material possessions. As a fellow Taurus, you too would prefer to stay indoors in your elegant home. To make plans with your Taurus friend, consider cooking together, watching a movie at home, ordering food, or getting a takeaway. Plans like these are more precious for two Taureans than to explore the outdoors. It will also give you enough time to learn about the other's whereabouts.

How to Foster a Friendship Between a Taurus and Other Zodiac Signs

As you learned through the friendship compatibility chart of a Taurus with other zodiac signs, a Taurus is a loyal and reliable friend. Though, certain negative aspects portrayed by other zodiac signs could affect their friendship with a Taurus. Here are three ways to maintain and foster a friendship with a Taurus:

1. It's All About Persistence

Since a Taurus is stubborn and wants things to go their way, the only solution to overcome similar situations is persistence. It is difficult to deviate from their plan and timetable. If you want a Taurus to follow your way without offending them, be persistent and polite simultaneously. Mention your desire occasionally. Even though they are stubborn, they will listen to you because this zodiac sign values friendship. At one point, they will realize the importance of putting their foot down and following their friend's wishes. Even if they say no to the first offer, keep insisting. They will eventually let their guard down and let you have your way.

2. Pay Attention to Important Dates

Taurus values important events and dates in their life. If you forget their birthday, graduation, anniversary, or other significant events, it may be difficult for them to forgive you. Every detail in a Taurus' life is important to them. So, as their friend, it should be important to you. To remember important dates, mark them on the calendar or set phone reminders. Celebrate with them instead of just congratulating or greeting them for the occasion. This is enough to make them happy and retain their loyalty.

3. Be Honest

A Taurus is an honest friend and expects you to be sincere. If they catch you lying or cheating, they will never forgive you. They may even break their friendship. Losing a Taurus in your life means losing an honest, loyal, and reliable friend, which is a rare kind. Even if the truth sounds bitter, never lie to a Taurus as they can easily decipher the difference. Due to their suspicious nature, they may cross-question your intentions too. They also hate it when someone gives a fake compliment. Dishonest flattery is off the charts. Be honest, even if it may offend them because it is better than lying and losing them forever.

A Taurus is a loyal and reliable friend who will show you the brighter side of life. Once you learn to put up with their stubbornness and laziness, they have a lot to offer. Their resilience and management skills are a lesson to be learned.

Appreciating Yourself as a Taurus

It's common for Taurus people to sell themselves short. This is to be expected from a sign that always shoots for the best and never retaliates until it gets what it wants. A Taurus needs to look at how far they've come and appreciated the progress that they've put. They are quite envied thanks to the effort and dedication they put into their lives. The discipline and responsibility needed to move on in life properly is something that Taurus has an abundance of. You can't expect people to respect your achievements if you don't respect them yourself.

It's time to look at success as a curve that's composed of a series of learning steps that you are gradually climbing. Don't expect that you must invent everything from scratch to be successful. You've already accomplished a lot, and it's never a good idea to think of the hard lessons you've endured as something to be swept away in disregard.

One problem that Taurus people struggle against is their attachment to the material world. A lot of the world's wealthiest people are Taurus signs. When you're dealing with low self-esteem problems, stop for a second and look at what you own, whether it's a Mercedes or a great career. Enjoying the luxuries you've collected over a long time is bound to make you understand that you're doing more than okay.

Just like any sign, Taurus has its merits and flaws. But a relationship with a Taurus will always be a great one.

A zodiac sign that aligns with Venus, the goddess of love, is going to be a strong advocate for big romantic gestures. The Taurus's love for ensuring that everything is planned and perfect makes them take quite a long time to get into a romantic relationship. They aren't just looking for any relationship, but the one. You'll always find their partners amazing because they are only attracted to the best. If you're in the early stages of dating a Taurus, you may find it difficult to catch their full and undivided attention, but once they choose you back, they will show a great level of genuine loyalty for a long time. If you happen to be the Taurus, you might want to take it easy when it comes to looking for perfection and try to enjoy people as they come with their good and bad.

Being a friend of a Taurus comes with its benefits, such as being trustworthy and loyal, but it's also important to know how to handle a Taurus's constant search for perfection. They may find it hard sometimes to match their standards, especially with sure signs like Aries, who can get very competitive. Fortunately, Taurus prefers to always go with the truth, so you don't have to keep an eye out for malicious lies or backstabbing.

Conclusion

As you finally start to understand your needs, complementary signs, and many other things about your sign, it becomes time to put it into action. You'll want to review your points of strength and weakness as a Taurus and see how you can improve them.

If you have a Taurus friend, count yourself lucky. There are a lot of great benefits you can enjoy due to the Taurus's nature and little quirks. While many people may be under the wrong impression with their temper, there are many things they might not know.

If you are a Taurus, expect most of your friends to come running to you for advice, whether it's about something romantic or a career decision. If there is one sign that's almost officially licensed to advise others, it will probably be Taurus. Common sense is their strongest ally, so is their ability to interpret situations on the move and multitasking. Separating emotions from individual situations allows them to see the problem from a vantage point. This gives them a more conclusive perspective. Making use of pros and cons lists is an excellent way for a Taurus to analyze almost any situation systematically. If emotions are running high, and the situation is getting out of hand, a Taurus can keep you grounded in common sense and logical thinking.

The Taurus is known to be one immovable rock when it comes to their preferences in friends and lovers. Many signs may switch partners or friends fast, but the Taurus sticks to their choices once they fixate their eyes on someone. They are looking for a way to enjoy the most out of what life offers, and that is done by keeping a balanced routine that builds their relationships upon love and trust. They are great friends you want to have your back in good and bad times.

A Taurus is actively interested in keeping their loved ones protected at all costs. They enjoy it rather than thinking of it as a chore like many other signs. A Taurus knows how to avoid making someone uncomfortable or uneasy, whether it's by giving him or her space or providing him or her with what they need. They have no problems taking on others' burdens, even if it means they must carry it all alone.

If you have a Taurus friend, you can expect to witness the finest things in life in multiple areas. Whether it's great music or obscure restaurants no one has heard of, they will travel to the ends of the earth to find something truly fitting to their taste. They also can appreciate almost everything and give it its fair share of thinking, which is one merit of being logical thinkers.

The perfectionism that a Taurus has whenever they are trying to improve themselves, or their work is simply inspiring. Having a Taurus friend can influence you to reach beyond what's at your fingertips. They are quite popular for their sense of self-control and ability to curb their appetite for activities that may stall their professional or artistic life. They simply find it uncomfortable to not be the best at what they do.

Creativity, love, stability, and aptitude are all great qualities of those born under the Taurus sign. Taurus' are a great gift to the universe, and we are blessed to have them in them in our lives.

Part 3: Gemini
The Ultimate Guide to an Amazing Zodiac Sign in Astrology

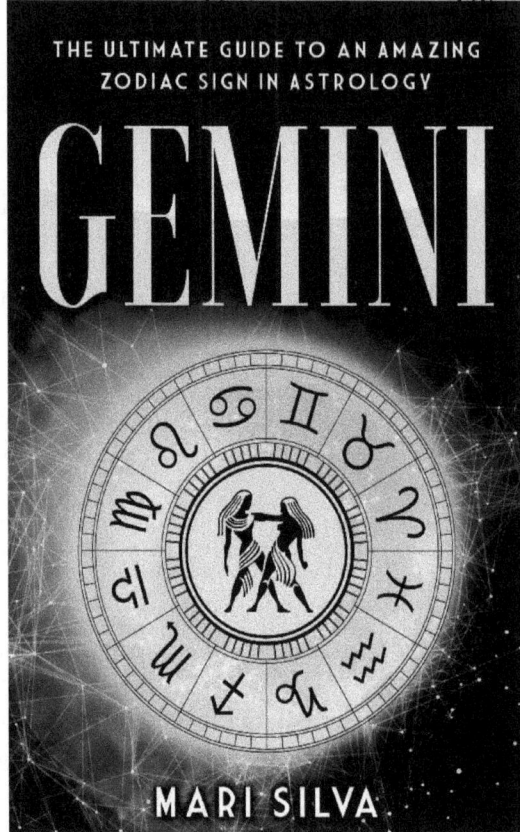

THE ULTIMATE GUIDE TO AN AMAZING
ZODIAC SIGN IN ASTROLOGY

GEMINI

MARI SILVA

Introduction

Magazines, newspapers, and other glossy commercial items have ruined the fascinating allure of astrology. Many individuals acknowledge this as an amazing phenomenon that has also been recognized as a formal field of study. If you are one of those individuals, then you have come to the right place. This expert guide has been created so that interested readers (like yourself) can find out more about people, stars, charts, and the planets that govern us.

The most interesting aspect of astrology revolves around the prediction of one's personality via charts and signs, but we must tell you that it is not quite as simple as that. This field has been recognized as one of formal study because of the very logical nature of the predictions it makes rather than the mockery presented by various forms of media. There is a science behind it that starts from the birth/natal charts. Through the birth charts, people can pinpoint the location of the Sun, the moon, and other varied planets/stars to predict what sort of personality they will have. Birth charts were very expensive to make; as technology evolved, it became a pretty straightforward and easy task to perform. Now, you can get them from various sites online by just inputting your birth time. It is worth mentioning that this process is free!

These outlines can then help determine what traits a person is likely to inherit. These predictions are not always black and white. This is why it is so annoying to experts in the field when they see how horoscopes are presented in magazines. There is a range of signs given off of the birth chart that is employed to forecast different aspects of a person's personality. The sun signs are the twelve symbols that are most commonly depicted in western astrology. Many people already know these through their birth date, but moon signs are also utilized to predict personality, behavior, and emotion rather than basic attributes and talents related to an individual.

The focus of this book will be on a more specific topic rather than tackling the entire spectrum of this enormous field known as "astrology". The focus will be on one of the sun signs called "Gemini".

This introductory chapter will examine the significant features of this sign and why this study is fascinating. It will also discuss how to use this resource effectively by explaining the value of each of the different chapters to the subject matter.

The Gemini

May 21 to June 20 is the period that encompasses people born with the Gemini star sign. Gemini, the name itself, is not English, but Latin. The Latin translation of this word means "twins." There is a lot of truth to this translation because one of the most common personality traits that Geminis are branded with is their duality. This means that Geminis are more suggestive than other signs out there, and that what they express can be completely opposite of their mood a couple of minutes earlier. This does not mean they have difficulty deciding on what to do or have "bipolar" tendencies! It just means that their personalities are unique, as they will be more expressive of this dual nature. If you are a Gemini, then you can attest to this trait!

This section delves into common aspects related to this sign (like the duality aspect); more detailed explanations can be found in the chapters below. We will also discuss key information that all Geminis should recognize about their star sign. Without discussing such material, this guide would be incomplete.

The very first thing that Geminis should know is the symbol and the glyph commonly used to represent the star sign. There are differences between the two terms (symbol and glyph) that are explained in this session. A zodiac sign's symbol is a more graphical representation of the sign and is often represented by Greek mythology characters. In our case, the "Dioscuri" twins are often the representing symbol of the Gemini star sign. Castor and Pollux were sons of Leda but had different fathers, even though they were twins! This may sound weird and fantastical, but they prove to be a very accurate symbol since they represent two contrasting personalities. This symbol emphasizes the dual nature of this star sign.

A glyph is an elemental symbol used in many aspects of typography. People often agree upon a glyph to represent a set of symbols or characters in a complex chart or in other functions. So, zodiac charts also have their own set of glyphs, where each one represents a star sign. Many zodiac magazines and articles available in the world use the terms "symbol" and "glyph" interchangeably. We have clarified this to make it easier for the reader to understand the jargon that revolves around star signs. The glyph for the Gemini star sign is the Roman numeral two. It also characterizes this sign's dual aspect but is much easier to write/make than the symbol for this star sign. Other glyphs in the zodiac charts also hold significant meaning and can be easily decoded if pondered. For example, the Sagittarius symbol revolves around a "centaur" (also a mythical creature from Greek mythology) that is known for being an archer. Its glyph is a simple bow and arrow drawing. Now that you know about this important difference, it is time to learn more about Geminis.

Each sign is assigned a "ruling planet" through which their personality's main pattern can be derived. Ruling planets prove that zodiac signs have a major link to astrology, and learning about this connection will clear up all of your misconceptions.

Planets are the major deciding factors of everything that is expressed through the zodiac signs. This first appeared to happen when early astrologers observed the planets and their energies and drew parallels to zodiac signs and their qualities. Since Neptune, Uranus, and Pluto were not identified at that time, they were not appointed any signs. Modern astrologers have associated these newly-discovered planets with signs as this sector of science continues to grow and make new discoveries. These got matched up with the zodiac signs after the 18th century, while other older pairings have been left unchanged. These associations may keep changing as further explorations are made in this field, but an important question arises: how are planets used for interpreting zodiac signs?

To answer that question, we must examine the details that astrologers provide when looking at charts. First of all, each sign has a ruler planet (or two) whose energies and qualities are a primary influence over dimensions of someone's personality. If your sun sign is in Gemini, then your ruling planet is Mercury. Greeks first matched up planets to seasons and not to these signs. Over time, astrologers developed complex techniques that led to more specific forecasts (rather than season-long predictions). The planets are like an archive or a data set used by astrologers every time they want to interpret a natal chart. They look at constellations of planets according to their position within the sign to predict major personality traits. The ruling planet and the sign are both focal points for the astrologer when looking at house cusps in a chart. This leads us to another key element used in zodiac interpretation: "houses."

The main translation of zodiac charts depends upon "houses" that the astrologer chooses beforehand. Houses form a chart, and their positions are based on location and time rather than on a date. For example, in a birth chart, if an astrologer knows the exact time of birth, then he/she will derive a very accurate interpretation. Often, the exact time might not be known, which restricts the astrologers to using the sunrise as an instrument in house calculation. This may not yield correct results for the astrologer.

As seen in the example above, the estimation of houses in a chart depends on Earth's movement along its axis and the Sun's orbit. But the difference of opinions (mathematical differences) amongst astrologers has created numerous ways of calculating houses and thereby produced a range of different "house systems." Different traditions (cultures) had their own ways of doing things, and so had different house systems as well. For example, in the Hindu tradition, houses were known as "Bhavas." But one of the most common systems known to the western hemisphere is called the "Placidus" system.

Generally, the houses are a division of the "ecliptic" plane. This plane contains the orbit of the Sun as viewed from the Earth; many house systems also regard the movement of other stars and planets in our galaxy. The Placidus system divides the planetary and star movement above and below the horizon. This division takes place in equal-sized parts, and the number of houses is twelve. The first six houses usually denominate spaces below the horizon, and the other six are associated with being above.

Houses depend on the exact time, and so this is a time-oriented system (Astro Dentist, 2020). Giovanni Magini developed this process around the 16th century, but mathematician Placidus Titis refined it; thus, the process is named after him. The system cannot be used for regions beyond the polar circles because of mathematical complications at the time of its development.

There are many other house systems like the Koch system, Capmanus, and Regiomontanus system, but the explanation of each can take up this entire guide, taking the spotlight away from our topic. This limited explanation of houses was deemed necessary to include since it gives a historical and scientific background as to how horoscopes work.

Another insight into the history of the development of this field is reflected in an image of a traditional zodiac sign and house dial. It shows an old dial that was constructed to represent divisions according to houses depending on the time of day. The idea behind it seems to be that of a sundial. The shadow that the Sun makes seems to predict the position of time in the "plane" being used, but its correct way of functioning does not matter to us since the focus is its historical significance. It shows how far astrology has come from physical dials that needed experts to predict the positioning of planets at the time of birth to having websites that do that for you. This explanation should give the readers an immense understanding of how everything is working in the background when someone is having their horoscope predicted. So, astrologers effectively fuse the house system (relating to the Earth's axis) along with the zodiac wheel (related to the Sun's movement) to read charts and make predictions or horoscopes.

Coming back to the main topic, a connection can be made between the houses and how they relate to the signs. Each house is viewed as an area/part of life and is ruled/associated with a Sun sign (like Gemini). Many astrologers understand houses as being ruled by a sign, just like how the signs have a ruling planet. This understanding has been derived from the fact that each excels at that particular part of life (the part of life that is represented by the house).

The third house is usually considered to be ruled by the Sun sign Gemini. It has a modern title as well as a traditional Latin name. The modern title is "the House of Sharing." From the title, you may have guessed that it is related to communication. It has been rightly linked with Gemini since it has already been established that Geminis do not fear being overly expressive. The third house is associated with all forms of information, starting with basic talking/thinking and covering all forms of electronic transmission.

An interesting fact about the third house is that it covers relations with the community, neighbors, and siblings. This means that a sign located within this house in the natal charts will have decent relations throughout their lives. Handling such relationships is a pretty hefty task that comes naturally to Geminis, which also proves that they have been rightly placed in this house.

Another key thing to note about houses is that astrologers draw various conclusions when different planets transit through each house. So, if a planet transits through the third house, the signs associated with them receive integral information about their community/network. Usually, Geminis are born in such months that the alignment of the planets allows them to share the ruling traits of these two aspects — the houses and the planets/stars.

The next thing that anyone should know about zodiac signs is their association with the four basic elements. Throughout its development, scholars have associated zodiac signs with fire, water, air, and earth. Interpreters can yield better predictions since the relationships with these elements can have parallels to the exchanges between the signs associated with them. For example, the earth needs water to thrive (nourishment for growth), and water naturally exists on the earth, so water and earth signs can typically be good soulmates. Aries, Leo, and Sagittarius are considered fire signs, while Taurus, Virgo, and Capricorn are earth signs. Similarly, Gemini, Libra, and Aquarius are air signs, and Cancer, Scorpio, and Pisces are water signs. There are a lot of complicated interpretations of these elemental categories (triplicities) that take into account planets and the different signs but explaining that can be very cumbersome and is better left to an astrologer. What we need to concern ourselves is with the implications of Gemini being an "air" sign.

These four components are very relevant to this study as their combinations effectively create the world around us. So, it is up to us to recognize the type of energy that each of these elements demonstrates to better understand the output of their combinations. Each element comes together to shape a sign and its natural traits, enabling the sign bearer to be who he/she is. This elemental interpretation adds another layer of complexity to our topic, and piece-by-piece, we will eventually unravel the entire onion! The intricacy that is added allows astrologers to conceive a more complex and accurate chart, which leads to realistic predictions.

Air is usually deemed to be the element of intellectual people, as they seem to thrive on mental connections. All air signs are good at communicating, and they also deal reasonably well with others' arguments. The outlook on everything is changed when viewed through an air-sign bearer's eyes since their analysis is usually unique, and their thought process is also very special. The particular quality of an air-sign bearer is their ability to be empathetic. They can understand another person's pain and hardship if they focus on a case for long, and they might do just that since they are also highly curious individuals.

In general, the air means the surrounding space, and it is very important for human survival. Just like that, wisdom is vital for the spirit to thrive, and air bearers are known to be knowledge bearers. This is a vital trait for air signs due to the analytical nature of their thinking. It does not mean that they are smarter than everybody else around them, but they are more well-rounded than others because of their mental ability to process everything around them at a much faster rate. Their capacity to listen and reason plays a huge part in being well-rounded, allowing them to become a good communicator as well (PeacefulMind.com, n.d.).

The negative aspect of this sign is the self-evaluation that accompanies the mentally- inclined nature of these individuals. They tend to evaluate themselves more harshly than they do the world. This is probably a positive thing in many cases, but in others can be demoralizing... but the slumps in life are commonly followed by good times, and this self-evaluation is bound to bring better results sooner rather than later for air signs. Air signs also have a specific standard for themselves that they will go above and beyond to meet every time. This is usually associated with staying clean, maintaining their hygiene, and meeting a certain job performance model, among other things. This egoistic nature makes them excel in particular parts of their lives, but it can be tiresome in other parts.

Air signs are usually empathetic, as discussed, but are known to hold a grudge if angered to a certain extent. They are also prone to physical violence at times since their anger is not forgotten, unlike the fire sign's rage, but one thing to note here is that it is very hard to tick them off, and so if you did anger them, then you are probably wrong! The grudge may disappear almost immediately if you try to work things out with them because of their empathetic nature and their ability to listen to others. The air signs have been associated with blue, white, and yellow colors and have a liking for specific stones. Gemstones are the next important talking point about Geminis.

Gemstones are a very integral part of zodiac theory since they help in unlocking certain "powers". They are like birthstones but have been branded by astrology as being associated with the Sun signs. Each sign has one or two gemstones that can help in certain aspects of their lives. Gems are known to have protective and healing powers that compel a lot of people to keep them in their houses or with them at all times. A few also believe them to be lucky for them and can be very superstitious about their gemstones!

For the Gemini sign, the agate and the pearl are two very common stones. They represent the colors that the air signs have been associated with and are a reflection of their persona. The mentally active Gemini can benefit from the grounding essence of their stones. They can be reminded of being calm and can get through very tough situations if they use this stone as an ornament that they keep close to themselves at all times. This is also known to be a spiritual protector and can help from energy drains and eliminate stress. It has a divine aura that can aid in mental stimulation as well as decision-making. Many Geminis are very particular about their agate and pearl ornaments and carry them everywhere to support themselves with tough decisions (Melorra, 2020).

Now that all of all the zodiac interpretations key elements are covered, you will have a sense of where these predictions come from. This is key to understanding yourself and the sign that you are associated with in a more profound manner. These interpretations can be used to comprehend all the other chapters that follow, since they will focus on Gemini's personality traits and relationships. These explanations are also very useful for figuring out other signs like the Aquarius sign, since both of these signs lie in the air region. This guide's method of explanation is from "bottom to top" rather than being a top-down description. This means that the concepts are explained first, and then the big picture is drawn in the end. We find this way to be much more intriguing since all the views explained in this introduction are key to the explanations in the following chapters.

Different Gemini Profiles

It would be useless to just tell you about the zodiac signs' basic traits without a proper explanation since that information can be found anywhere on the Internet. This guide divides a person's life into many aspects/periods so that it is easier to explain the traits of this Sun sign. Another advantage of this unique style is that it allows greater readability and navigation through the guide. This means that you, as a reader, can go to any chapter and look for the relevant information in a tireless manner. It also makes it much more relatable and interactive. This session gives a brief introduction to each of the different profiles that the following chapters explain so that you know which one you can categorize yourself into.

The basic Gemini temperament is always active in all life stages, whether you know about it or not. This is something that more people need awareness about, and so is presented as the first chapter of this guide. It explains the basic and most evident "strengths and weaknesses" of the Gemini personality trait. It can be associated with all ages and every Gemini in any stage of his/her life.

Children are different from adults since they have virtually no responsibilities and a unique outlook on life. Many of the key traits that Geminis show in their early life result from their inquisitiveness. This might be the first sign that the child is following a set Gemini path, which leads to an overall balanced identity in the future. Adults should let them harness this personality, as they will grow into their mentally curious and analytical selves in a few years.

Geminis at work operate differently, so this is also a profile to analyze. This can be true for everyone since we all behave differently in different social surroundings. They have a unique skill set that is essential to excelling at many jobs, and so Geminis can be observed engaging in analytical debates and problem-solving their way through tough social situations as well as carrying out the job itself. They can form strictly professional relationships and enjoy their work at the same time. They work with excellent conviction, and their analytical skills help maintain their interest in their tasks. This is a very interesting profile that is associated with many working Geminis and can be accessed in the fifth chapter of this guide.

Geminis at other social gatherings behave in a very different way than when they are at work. This profile is perhaps the most talked-about profile by many astrologers when predicting their horoscope. At events and parties, they are always engaged in fun, humorous, and engaging debates since they are the Masters of Communication. Their spirit thrives on this activity and is constantly forcing the Gemini bearers to earn new people's trust. This allows them to make friends more easily than the other signs. This interesting analysis is discussed in more detail under the heading of the fourth chapter.

When in love they also present a compelling case. Their dual nature can be observed frequently in relationships, and can be the cause of their undoing. At the same time, it can also prove to be the main factor in keeping the relationship working. They are unique people, and so their love life is as complicated as it is unique.

Within the safe spaces of their homes, Geminis are also pretty different from any of the other profiles we discussed. Since they have higher mental prowess than other people, they can get bored quickly. So, while at home, they are always looking for something to occupy their time. They can also lose interest in their tasks because of the very dominant duality trait.

A few of the most popular Gemini celebrities are Sir Ian McKellen (most famous for playing Gandalf), Octavia Spencer, Amy Schumer, Tom Holland, Heidi Klum, Angelina Jolie, and Michael Cera. People who follow them can recognize key Gemini traits in their behavior after going through this guide!

Chapter 1: A Quick Primer – Suns, Moons, and Houses

Astrology is one of the world's oldest languages, using zodiac signs, planets, and houses to create your birth chart. This chart maps where the stars, sun, moon, and planets were at the time and place you were born. If you ever wondered why the full moon had a strange effect on you, this is why.

There are three primary points in your birth chart, mapping your personality - the sun, the moon, and rising. We all know our sun sign, but few of us are aware of our moon and rising signs. Understanding what all this means can influence everything you do in life.

All three - the sun, the moon, and the rising sign - are all in one particular zodiac sign on your chart. Each zodiac sign is in an elemental group - water, earth, air, or fire - and has a quality associated with it - cardinal, mutable, or fixed. Each also has one planetary ruler.

The Sun Sign

The sun provides your identity, what you shine out to everyone. It is the force that drives you on to be the best you can be. It represents your life experiences and your individuality, the energy type needed to help revitalize you, and how you recharge your batteries.

If your sun sign is one of the air signs - Libra, Gemini, or Aquarius - you express yourself intellectually and use social settings to recharge and revitalize yourself.

If your sun sign is one of the fire signs - Aires, Sagittarius, or Leo - aspiration and inspiration motivate you, and you use physical activity to revitalize yourself, along with pursuing specific life goals.

If your sun sign is one of the earth signs - Virgo, Taurus, or Capricorn - practicality and materialism motivate you. You revitalize yourself through productivity, heightening your senses, and working in the physical, not spiritual, world.

If your sun sign is one of the water signs - Pisces, Scorpio, or Cancer - emotional desire motivates you, and emotional experience and intimacy with people revitalize you.

The Moon Sign

Your moon sign represents your identity's soul, the subconscious part that nobody sees. This is the part of you that drives your emotions and helps you feel pain, pleasure, sorrow, and joy. It helps you understand how and why you react the way you do in emotional situations.

If your moon sign is one of the air signs - Libra, Gemini, or Aquarius - it represents how you react to change and evaluate it objectively. Social interaction helps you align with your inner self, as it does when you express ideas.

If your moon sign is one of the fire signs - Aires, Sagittarius, or Leo - you use direct action to react to change. When you express confidence, turn your back on negative self-talking, and show your strength, you align perfectly with your inner self.

If your moon sign is one of the earth signs - Virgo, Taurus, or Capricorn - you face change with stability and steadiness. Working towards your personal goals and being productive helps you to align with your inner self.

If your moon sign is one of the water signs – Pisces, Scorpio, or Cancer – you use emotion and sensitivity to face change. When you feel something deeply, you align with your inner self, but you must never forget to put self-love ahead of anything else.

The Rising Sign

Your rising sign is also called your Ascendant sign, and it represents your personality socially. It relates to whatever zodiac or sun sign was rising over the Eastern horizon at the time of your birth. It represents your physical body, the style you present to the world. It is a combination, a manifestation if you like, of your outer and inner world, helping you understand your approach to life and the type of energy your physical body needs.

If your rising sign is one of the air signs – Libra, Gemini, or Aquarius – you are friendly, curious, mentally quick off the mark, and you like to talk. Your approach to life is often in line with wanting to understand everything and everyone you meet.

If your rising sign is one of the fire signs – Aires, Sagittarius, or Leo – you are an active person, blunt, confident and to the point. You have a lot of physical energy and use it to your advantage to make your mark.

If your rising sign is one of the earth signs – Virgo, Taurus, or Capricorn – your focus is mainly on the physical world, and you are matter-of-fact. Your approach to life is steadfast, and that helps ground other people, especially when life is stressful.

If your rising sign is one of the water signs – Pisces, Scorpio, or Cancer – you are empathetic and sensitive; your environment has a direct influence on you. Your approach to life is an emotional and deep one.

The Twelve Houses

When planets visit any of the houses, that part of your chart will light up, adding energy to the specific House's traits. Astrologers use these houses to predict the areas in your life that will come into focus, allowing you to determine the best course of action at that time.

Houses 1-to-6 are the personal houses, while the last six are the interpersonal houses.

• 1st House – The start of the zodiac, the very first of everything, including self, impressions and appearance, fresh starts, leadership initiative, and new beginnings. Ruled by Aries, the sign on the 1st House cusp is your ascendent or rising sign.

• 2nd House – Relates to your physical and material environment, including your senses – touch, taste, smell, sound, and sight. It is ruled by Taurus and is responsible for self-esteem, money, and income.

• 3rd House – Rules communication, including gadgets, talking, devices like cell phones, and thinking. Ruled by Gemini, it covers community affairs, travel, schools, communication, libraries, your neighborhood, and siblings.

• 4th House – Ruled by Cancer, this House lies at the bottom of the wheel and is responsible for foundations, including your privacy, home, parents (especially your mother), security, children, TLC, and nurturing.

• 5th House – Ruled by Leo, this House is responsible for self-expression, color, drama, fun, romance, attention, and play.

- 6th House – Responsible for health and service, including organization, schedules, fitness, nutrition, exercise, healthy living, and routines. Ruled by Virgo, it also covers your helpfulness and what you do for others.

- 7th House – This House is responsible for people and relationships. Ruled by Libra, it covers professional and personal relationships, matters associated with those relationships, marriage, contracts, and business dealings.

- 8th House – One of the more mysterious houses, this one rules sex, birth, death, mysteries, transformation, the merging of energies, and deep bonding. Ruled by Scorpio, it rules property, money, inheritance, real estate, and investments.

- 9th House – This House rules long-distance and international travel, the higher mind, inspiration, foreign languages, optimism, expansion, broadcasting, publishing, and higher education. Ruled by Sagittarius, it also covers religion, gambling, risk-taking, luck, adventure, ethics, and morals.

- 10th House – The topmost House on the wheel and the most public, this House rules incorporation, public image, structures, tradition, honors, fame, awards and achievements, rules, authority, discipline, and fatherhood. Ruled by Capricorn, the cusp is also known as the Midheaven, giving astrologers an idea about your career path in life.

- 11th House – This House is responsible for groups, friendship, teams, technology, society, electronic media, social justice, networking, rebellion, and humanitarian causes. Ruled by Aquarius, it also governs eccentricity, originality, surprises, sudden events, astronomy, invention, and science fiction.

- 12th House – The final House governs endings, like the last stages of any project, loose ends, the afterlife, completions, surrender, and old age. Ruled by Pisces, it also governs separation, hospitals, institutions, hidden agendas, jails, secret enemies, the subconscious mind, creativity, film, arts, journals, and poetry.

Chapter 2: Gemini Strengths and Weaknesses

Like any other human, Geminis excel in several aspects of life while struggling in others. Significant research and studies have highlighted certain personality traits attributed to Geminis. The best part is that Geminis can now know and understand them using this guide.

Strengths

Geminis are often gregarious and sociable human beings. They are enthusiastic about social gatherings and excited to meet and talk to new people, but this does not mean that they are annoyingly chatty. If you have a friend who is a Gemini, notice what piques their interest. They are likely keen on deep things in life or any specialized discipline, and that is what they love discussing with their peers.

But this does not imply that Geminis cannot talk about anything else. They thrive in conversations and love giving their two cents' worth on everything. This quality gives them an edge in small yet crucial everyday discussions. For example, Geminis find it relatively easy when journeying through high school and college. Making friends or interacting with the institution's hierarchy comes easily to young Geminis.

If you are a Gemini, you probably love parties and parades. If you ever host a party, make sure to have Geminis on your guest list – they will make the best out of anything. Their excellent conversational skills allow them to hold a crowd and make every person in the room feel welcome. With exceptional interpersonal skills come brilliant flirting skills as well. Geminis flourish on dates. If you go on a date with a Gemini, you will notice how hard they try to make you feel comfortable. They make sure you have fun-filled experiences while simultaneously enjoying themselves. A date with a Gemini is bound to be a heartwarming day, but more on that later.

Along with being a brilliant conversationalist, a Gemini uses their outgoing nature to be friendly with others. Rather than being cocky when conversing, Geminis are gracious and kind with whomever they interact with. No matter how enthusiastic they may be, they care about the perspectives of those on the other side of the table. They can have themselves heard along with hearing out others. This trait makes Geminis perfect pacifiers or moderators.

They like to mediate conversations and try their best to accommodate each and every person sitting with them. Need someone to break the ice between you and your crush? Ask your Gemini friend to be your wingman. Are you too shy to strike up a conversation with a group across the court? Ask your Gemini friend to join you for the day. Want to clarify a misunderstanding between yourself and a loved one? A Gemini should be able to patch up the two of you. With a Gemini, you are highly unlikely to feel left out in a conversation.

Besides being loquacious, Geminis are more than often exceptionally energetic and zestful people to have around. They not only know to talk with enthusiasm, but they also physically express their excitement about things they deeply care about. Their body language gives them away and describes the notions they have in mind. This makes Geminis very jovial people to be around. They may perform impersonations of someone or tell a story by acting a few parts of it to make it look hilarious. No one makes more of the day than a Gemini does. They detest boredom and tend to keep themselves actively busy, either by doing productive work or killing time with close friends. Their huge tank of energy helps them to be active and social. They take a long time to tire themselves out and retire to their beds. Look around in your social circle and see which people are the liveliest of them all. See how many Geminis you find.

Another positive trait Geminis possess is the ability to stay optimistic. Geminis tend to find happiness in the smallest of events that take place during the day. They hope for the best and do not waste time worrying about what fate holds for them. Geminis always live in the moment. They are likely to be happy all the time unless something serious comes up. They do their best to keep themselves, and everyone around them, full of joy and optimism all the time.

If you have a Gemini friend, you may have noticed that they are very cheerful and oddly optimistic about things in life. They do not give in to petty unfortunate events, like a lousy exam or a small car crash, and let it ruin their day. Geminis live their lives to the fullest. They wake up every day as an adventurer and go to sleep hoping to enjoy the next day as well. Their optimistic attitude also makes them excellent sympathizers. A Gemini can uplift those who feel low and help them regain their confidence; they always inspire other people to be happy and positive. If you have been facing a lot of stress lately, ask your Gemini friend for help. They will graciously help if they can.

One of the better strengths a Gemini can benefit from is adjusting and adapting to situations quickly. Gemini is always craving new ventures. They are comfortable taking on new things every other minute. They are capable of shifting their attitude and adjusting it to the situation at hand. If you are a Gemini, ask your loved ones to rate your improvisational skills. There is a good chance of you scoring a solid nine out of ten. Notice how your Gemini friends respond to sudden changes in activities around them. It is like having a supercomputer's speed in reacting to scenarios, and this is not an overstatement. Even in life-changing yet gradual transitions, they quickly process it in their head and adjust to the flow. Recently shifted to a new house or city with a Gemini sibling or parent? Notice how they adapt to their new home within a week. If your Gemini son or daughter just joined college, you need not worry. As long as you keep in touch, they will thrive there.

The same applies to spontaneous plans and gatherings. Most Geminis are explorers and want to try everything at least once. The word "no" just does not seem to be in their dictionary. They like planning spontaneous adventures and trips and will tag along on short notice. They make time for joyful occasions, and that is what makes them such good friends, colleagues, and team members. Working late at night on a deadline at the office with a Gemini? Ask them to join you on a drive around the block. Chances are they might respond with a better crazy idea for spending the next few minutes. Reminisce on any sudden plans you were a part of. Was it a Gemini friend who came up with the idea in the first place?

The fact that Gemini is able to contribute to any discussion indicates their intelligence. Any person who can talk with you for hours on a diverse set of topics and be kind and considerate while doing so is bound to possess a remarkable intellect. Usually, these people are Gemini. Besides being companionable, they are known and observed to have an inquisitive mind. They like learning more about almost everything.

As mentioned earlier, Geminis despise getting bored. This is the reason why they welcome new ideas and intriguing knowledge with both arms. It is easy to find Gemini engrossed in books or seated in seminars that others generally avoid. Did you just read a new book and have no one to talk about it? Mention it to a Gemini, and they will get back to you with their critical insights. Gemini students tend to ask fascinating questions. That is the reason teachers and professors are likely to develop a liking for Gemini students. On the downside, they might be judged as know-it-alls to their peers, but it might be the same with academic exams.

A Gemini prefers intellectual understanding over ideals. If you are a Gemini, you may find it hard to accept something until you have seen the proof. You tend to not care about noisy news on the television. Instead, you seek credible sources for your research and try to understand each aspect before accepting it. Even once you do learn something new, you crave updates and further insights on the matter. This intuition fortifies you against rumors and fake claims. The beauty of being a Gemini that it is highly unlikely for you to be wrong, or at least ill-informed.

Being clever with a lovely sense of humor is another one of the many perks of being a Gemini. When with friends, they like partaking in banter a lot. Belonging to an "air" sign, they are generally empathetic people with a long fuse. Instead of being sensitive about it, a Gemini may reply with a snarky comment. No matter how hard you hit them, they avoid being triggered and outraged right away. They do keep a count of what is happening, but not in the form of a grudge.

While history shows us many great Gemini thinkers, like Blaise Pascal, intelligence does not necessarily refer to great thinkers. Gemini is quick in finding solutions to everyday problems. They do stunningly in situations that require immediate answers. They do not need to know the laws of matter and motion to escape hectic traffic. Similarly, they know how to react to urgent moments in sports like football, squash, badminton, etc. Notice how good your Gemini friends are at riddles. Being Gemini allows you to breeze through daily challenges that other people might surrender to.

Intelligence combined with proficient speaking skills and an improvisational attitude makes for a lethal asset for Geminis. They can think quickly on their feet and react well to situations. You may call them "quick thinkers" as they are able to make informed, rational choices in a short period. If you are a Gemini, you will be sought after the most when building a team, as you have the social and intellectual skills to be a crucial team member. The team is most likely to revolve around a Gemini as well.

Weaknesses

While Geminis flourish in several aspects of life, they do have a few shortcomings. As you may notice, most of these flaws are just the flip side of the benefits that being a Gemini brings. Not all Geminis must have each one of these defects. It depends on how they live their lives and tackle these weaknesses. This book will also highlight a few tips other Gemini use to overcome these mere limitations. They might or might not work for you.

While Geminis may appear to converse with a group of people benevolently, their habit of accommodating everyone might make them look two-faced. At one point, they might favor any issue, while at another point they might completely disagree with the same proposition. By embracing a set different of opinions, Geminis might end up being dishonest to themselves. They tend to mix up their own beliefs while conceding other people's thoughts. This process confuses many fellow Geminis and throws them into a spiral of self-doubts. So, one weakness a Gemini may struggle to deal with is bewilderment regarding themselves. Look around at your Gemini peers. Have you noticed them having multiple opinions or contradicting insights on any topic?

The next two problems we will be discussing stem from the weakness mentioned above. While Geminis might have a hard time figuring out what they really stand for, they also deal with nervousness when making crucial life-changing decisions. With doubt in one's own beliefs comes doubt in one's actions. If you are a Gemini, you may notice that you are indecisive at times. For instance, we discussed that most Geminis easily adjust to a new home, but the process of selecting the house is not a Gemini's cup of tea. They tend to be critical about the smallest details, so much so that they build hundreds and thousands of choices in their heads. Selecting or choosing is the worst situation for a Gemini.

Ever been to a shopping mall with a Gemini? Just give them a set of clothes to choose from and see how long they take to pick their favorite. In their head, they might be thinking of many things; the latest trend, a magazine or actor they saw, a friend's suggestion, the price, the number of times they might wear that clothing or only what they already have in their wardrobe. While it may make sense to make informed and calculated discussions, scrutinizing every single thing tires them out. It is better if you do not ask a Gemini for a choice of movies on movie night. They might fuss over it unnecessarily, ultimately watching whatever the majority decides. This is the reason they love going with the flow and tagging along in events.

Another negative trait attributed to Geminis is their fondness for materialistic gain. Gemini people are usually shortsighted when it comes to identifying the inner beauty of someone. They are dazzled by the fineness and grandeur of the world. They want the same class and beauty that impresses them for themselves as well. While it is common for anyone to be attracted to charm and intelligence, Gemini tends to overlook the hidden yet meaningful aspects of things, people, and places. Understandably, they may try to associate themselves with rich and attractive people and end up getting disappointed.

While most Gemini makes very good friends, a Gemini might ditch their close friends for someone with a lot of charm and beauty. This can be detrimental to not only the maturity of Geminis but also their social life. They are likely to lose friendships like this and may end up having fewer shoulders to cry on. The worst part about this is that Gemini is likely to repeat this mistake and spiral down into the dark abyss. Just as they find happiness in little things in life, Gemini should also embrace people for who they are rather than what they outwardly look like – a lesson most Geminis learn the hard way. Did you recently go through a broken friendship? Was it a Gemini? If so, what do you think were the reasons?

Belonging to the element of Air, Geminis usually fail to connect their thoughts with reality. Geminis happen to be people who believe more in theories rather than actual practice. They may appear to be idealists who believe anything is possible. They are mostly driven by sheer will. While the raw will is good for people lacking motivation like Geminis, it blinds them from the practicality of their thoughts and opinions. This may also be seen when Gemini requires something they do not need. They seem to face a "disconnection between introspection and actuality" when making decisions (preparingforpeace.org, 2020). This can easily be noticed when Gemini is confronted with blame for something they did not do. Even though parts of them may be puzzled regarding what wrong they may have done, they are likely to apologize since it is the nobler thing to do. You can do a short experiment on your Gemini friend to see this. Try blaming your Gemini friend for losing something you gave him/her. How do they react? This trait can play heavily in circumstances with higher stakes. To fix this, we recommend Gemini friends develop assertiveness and awareness of their immediate surroundings.

Since Geminis are usually hungry for knowledge, they are prone to impulsive thinking. For instance, a Gemini hears a different opinion or theory about something; they are likely to change their own perceptions due to that influence. We do not mean to imply that Geminis do not think for themselves. Instead, they get, once again, easily puzzled when shown a set of opinions or thoughts. If they do not discover the truth through their research, they fall prey to bewilderment. In the worst-case scenario, this could lead to reckless decision-making after wholeheartedly believing and changing their thoughts on a topic. This impulsive reactionary behavior may also stand in the way of their accomplishing long-term goals. They may feel motivated for a certain task one day but might leave it hanging the next. For this very reason, Gemini struggles to deal with casual, gossipy rumors. It may not be right to ask the person themselves, and any other source they may listen to will only add to the list of stories they heard. While Gemini is stunning in conversations head-on, they hate these sorts of "Chinese whispers." Notice this amongst your Gemini peers. How indecisive do you think are they?

The same impulsive attitude may apply to emotional behavior. While Gemini may have a high temperament, they are likely to burst out in front of anyone once they reach their limit. They remember what was said and meant, pile it up in memory, and execute a reactionary response once overload reaches its limit. Gemini may greet you with a bright smile like an angel or yell at you with a horrifying expression like a devil. This may lead to many Geminis to go through breakups or broken friendships. They may end up being aggressive to a colleague and ruin their relationship with them forever. Any Gemini should work on their emotions if they tend to do this a lot. Since they are likely to react quickly, it is also likely that a Gemini might say something wrong or hurtful. To regulate this behavior can be extremely stressful for Geminis, especially if they do this more regularly. While Geminis should try to control their impulsiveness, other peers belonging to other signs should learn to cut them a bit of slack wherever possible. Are you a Gemini going through similar circumstances? Try explaining it to your loved ones and ask them for help.

If you are a Gemini, you may find it challenging to sustain your motivation when working on a month-long project. This may because you experience a change in priorities or may simply get bored. If your school hours consist of long raw lectures with barely any extra-curricular activities, you may not enjoy school as a Gemini. Geminis do not thrive in routines, especially when the activities are restricted, boring, and repetitive. They barely have any fixed routine and tend to go along with whatever life throws at them. This makes Geminis blind to the big picture in life, relationships, friendships, and careers. The requirement to always keep themselves entertained and engaged is a Gemini's biggest weakness. Since they like delving into multiple topics of their interest, they may pile a lot of stuff on their shoulders, more than they can carry. If you are a Gemini, you might want to keep track of all the commitments you make and when delivery is expected. Losing track of time is easy for anyone, especially a Gemini. They may sacrifice hours to procrastination, only to fulfill their hunger for amusement. Being a good friend, you should try to keep tabs on your Gemini friends and help them see the big picture.

Gemini is curious and craves knowledge about everything they can think of. While being a seeker of knowledge may be a charming quality to possess, many Geminis take it a step too far by getting deeply interested in other people's lives. They might want to be continuously updated about events and changes in everyone's lives. This behavior can rightly annoy anyone they converse with. They may worsen a person's mental health if they ask a bad question and unknowingly attack their insecurities.

Have a small scar on your cheek? A Gemini will be sure to ask you about it and the story behind it. Just came home from the dentist? Your Gemini sibling will want to know all that happened. Went on a date recently? Your Gemini neighbor will ask you every single detail. If you have a Gemini friend, notice how much they may encourage you to share your secrets. Even though this may help them build friendships, most people may find Geminis nosy due to this trait. Geminis, being the conversationalists they are, might appear to be intruding when interacting with new people. Not everyone they meet will want to answer questions like where they live, how many boyfriends they have had, or how their childhood was. If you are a Gemini, start observing caution when asking questions and talking. What is your question about? Think of any way your question may hurt the person.

While Gemini may be kind and empathetic, they are usually undependable. Their indecisiveness takes a toll on them, and they tend to become irresponsible with the task at hand. This is why Gemini is less sought after when seeking advice. No matter how religiously they may have committed initially, many Geminis fail to get the job done. They pile up too much work, not knowing when to stop. Ultimately, they leave most of it incomplete and miss their deadlines. Normally, a person will rely on someone who is specialized in the field, committed to the work, confident, and self-aware. The fact that many Gemini find trouble while evaluating themselves make it difficult to rely on them. A Gemini may get bored when preparing a tedious long Excel sheet. The next thing you know, they spent the rest of the day on Netflix or shopping. If you send an invitation to a Gemini of an event way before the day, they will probably cancel it as the day closes in. It is not like Geminis are rude or arrogant. It is sheer irresponsibility that stems from their inherited characteristics and leads them astray. If you are a Gemini going through the same situation, we recommend making to-do lists and limiting the tasks you commit to. While Gemini might have a hard time helping others with work, they will not let anyone down for a fun night out.

As we discussed earlier, Geminis are judged as having many personalities. People may judge them as two-faced or people-pleasers. Even in astrology, Gemini represents "duality". It is not really a Gemini's fault here. They may only be trying to accommodate and be friendly to people. The problem lies in when they overdo it and accidentally make others uncomfortable. Judging by how indecisive Gemini people can be, they might be visualized as people with unstable personalities.

We discussed how Geminis struggle to find what they actually stand for. They may fret in their head over contradictory opinions, unfair reactions, or differences in treatment for different people. For instance, a Gemini may profusely criticize their local government for mismanagement but when talking with someone in favor of the government, they might discuss other reasons for the incident and justify the government's efforts as sufficient. This two-faced behavior further adds to the unreliability of Geminis. Gemini can suffer excruciatingly from this flaw, as they are likely to lose friends, acquaintances, and clients.

Generally, Geminis are amazing and charming personalities. Their strengths enable them to get along with people quickly. But they tend to struggle in their social lives when they overdo their loquaciousness and unintentionally make others uncomfortable. Other negative traits are only the flip side of their strengths. Gemini should work hard to strike a balance between the two without giving up the type of person they essentially are.

Chapter 3: The Gemini Child

Children are the joy of people's lives; they remind them of how simple life was once, but kids are commonly misunderstood, which enables the adults around them to make uneducated decisions about their growth and needs. If you have Gemini children and want to understand a few of their actions, then you have come to the right place! This chapter will cover all the common traits and characteristics of Gemini children that adults can consider peculiar. The last section of this chapter aims to focus on the differences between young Gemini girls and boys. This is an important section as there are a few critical differences that not a lot of people are aware of. It can help you in understanding the young Gemini boy or girl in your life!

This chapter can also be an interesting read for young adult and adult Geminis that seek to reminisce about their childhood, since it will bring back all those memories that you thought you had forgotten! All the explanations below arise from the universal components of zodiac astrology that were discussed in the introduction of this guide (common elements were ruling planets, houses, natal charts, gemstones, and much more).

Common Traits of Gemini Children

The very first significant action in a child's life is talking. Mercury rules Geminis, so essentially, they become efficient communicators later on in life, but this ability to articulate begins early. Gemini children start talking (or mumbling words/gibberish) slightly earlier than other toddlers. Do not be afraid of this early action since Gemini children have this "expressive nature" discussed at the start of this guide. If you are a Gemini, then you should probably ask your parents about the time you first started talking. You'll probably hear that it was earlier than your siblings. Parents are recommended to encourage this behavior by performing activities (or using different forms of media, such as music) that are designed to bring out this expressive nature. If nurtured correctly, the children can then go on to inherit their ability of articulation!

This does not mean that if your child resides on the quieter side of the talking spectrum, there must be something wrong with him/her. A surprising amount of Gemini kids are on the quieter side, but they are quick-witted and charming when they need to be. This quick-wittedness also means that they have the ability to articulate efficiently since they are constantly in a dialogue with themselves. Even if they are not talkative all the same, you still have to stick with the same routine that was explained in the earlier paragraph. As parents, you have to surround your Gemini child with books, music, puzzles, and other such media that will allow them to keep on having their inner dialogue.

In both the cases explained above, the Gemini child is always expressing his curiosity in different forms. This means that along with being charming and quick-witted, the Gemini child is also very curious. This characteristic will evolve with time and will play a major role in the traits explained in the adult life profiles in the chapters that follow. Remember this when reading those chapters.

Another common trait that Gemini children have is their ever-changing interests in things. The duality concept that is clear in many Geminis in the world takes its roots from this stage in their lives. At this early stage, Geminis are very interested in examining, performing, and conducting new activities/things. It is often observed that they also shift from one activity to the next very quickly too. This means that Gemini children are often interested in a combination of different experiences rather than focusing on extracting maximum utility from just one experience. This also results in the kids getting bored much more quickly than other kids, since they want new activities so often.

Gemini parents have their work cut out for them since they always have to find new things for their kids to do. As a Gemini, you can understand this since you also probably did the same thing as a child. This results in adult Geminis also getting bored easily. With a lot of free time, Geminis will be always on the lookout for random chores and interesting projects to invest their time in. This trait also emerges from the curiosity characteristic discussed earlier.

These will be the first few signs of the dual-nature personality that your Gemini child will soon inherit, but one positive can be drawn out from this trait! Geminis that change their minds often are also known to be adaptable and great problem solvers since they are used to facing different situations.

There is also a negative from this dual-nature ability. Gemini children are so focused on diversifying their experience that it is hard to make them focus on one particular activity. This may hinder their ability to focus, and in turn, affect their abilities. We recommend parents allow them to experiment with different experiences, and as they get older, their minds will develop naturally. This natural development will allow them to live a satisfactory life since they will not be pressured to learn one craft; rather, they will have a combination of different experiences to boost their capabilities.

Gemini kids also start to crawl at a very early age because of their curious nature. To feed their curiosity and expressive nature, they often go into places that other babies will not go. Any Gemini parent should baby-proof their entire house, as once their child becomes an explorer, they will leave no space untouched. Parents are also advised to keep a close eye on their Gemini children for their safety. They need to be extra careful with a Gemini child since their curious nature can get them into dangerous spots around the house. This trait grants the baby more freedom to move around, but it also means that the baby will sometimes not like to be confined in small spaces. The Gemini child will find this restricting experience an obstacle to fulfilling their "mental" hunger. So, in many ways, parents of Gemini children should be relieved that they need not put a lot of effort into parenting since allowing the Gemini child to develop naturally is the best way forward!

All the traits above can be observed frequently in the home, but they can be translated into different traits when the Gemini child is at school. The school is one of the first places outside of the home that a child gets to experience, so it is fairly obvious that he/she will exhibit different traits there. The next few traits are often observed amongst Gemini children when they are at school.

The first common trait is the unpredictable nature of Gemini kids. Due to the dual and unpredictable nature of the children, they may do something that means trouble for them or someone else in the school, but it can also mean that many positive things are also possible because of this unpredictable nature. Due to this curious and unpredictable nature, it is difficult for a Gemini child to follow a strict schedule. This means the child might exhibit many negative behavioral traits. Since going to school is an activity that follows a strict schedule, the child may throw tantrums in classes or during other activities if they lose their interest and follow their free souls. Following a strict sleep routine is also important for going to school. Unfortunately, that too is tough to ask from a Gemini child because of this trait. All of these combined can create an uninterested individual that may be rebellious when they move into their teenage years.

All of this should not worry a parent because of the following traits that are quite positive for a school-going Gemini child. A Gemini Child is a very good socializer since they have an infectious and endless energy that can attract all sorts of people. They can thrive in social situations and activities in the school. This allows the children to be well-liked by their peers as well as the school staff. They are sure to reap the benefits of building a strong relationship with the community. This stems from Gemini's ruling house that is deeply associated with positive relationships with the community and Gemini's siblings. If these relationships last for a long time, they can positively or negatively impact the Gemini's life during their adult years.

The dual nature of the Gemini can make it difficult for children to choose. This can become an obstacle in situations like a verbal class activity or deciding their lunch in the cafeteria, but this can easily be navigated through with a little guidance. The Gemini child is very responsive, so adults will know immediately about their wants and needs. They can then use this information to offer them guidance.

These traits summarize the life that your Gemini child will follow inside your house as well as in their school. It is useful to know about these traits because the next part of this section will explain how you can use this information. The following paragraphs of this section will cover the basic needs of a Gemini child. As parents, you can offer an environment that encourages their growth by fulfilling their needs according to their zodiac sign. Gemini teens and adults can also read the next few paragraphs to learn a few tricks about how to navigate through their negative traits.

The most important thing that can be derived from all the above traits is that the Gemini child reacts positively to joyful interaction and mental stimulation. They always need to talk to someone or to be occupied in something that challenges their mental capabilities. If parents continuously talk to and make sounds at their children (positive interaction), the child will respond in positive sounds and broken words. As parents, you need to invest in good literature and fun activities (like puzzles and board games). Hopefully, these games will keep your child interested in them for a while before you need to think of something new and fun. This cycle of investment and interest should continue until the child automatically finds something that grabs their attention for longer than just a few weeks/days.

Parents also need to take care of their children in the sense that they always need to keep an eye on their curious movements as they may run into something dangerous. It is good to baby-proof the house because Gemini babies need this protection more than other types.

Most of all, a Gemini child needs a patient parent who can guide them through their toughest choices. Making choices can be a recurring challenge in their life, and if they have a stable influence to guide them through it, then they may grow up to be very well-rounded people that boast an array of experiences to boost their capabilities.

Differences Between Young Gemini Boys and Girls

There are a few personality differences that are dependent on the gender of the child. Astrologers claim that parents, as well as Geminis, need to understand such differences to better navigate through their lives. This section will give a short overview of those differences so that you can make well-informed decisions in the future.

The main difference between these two genders is their forms of communication. Now, this information might not be applicable to all the Geminis of the world but since it is frequently reported, it may be helpful. The male child has a different way of communicating than the girl, even though both of them are pretty expressive. The female child may address her curiosity by asking a lot of questions. When we say a lot, it might be an understatement. These questions will range from simple ones to very complex ones, which will require you to research them online, but the male child is always looking to put his quick wits to good use and is always up for a practical joke or two.

Both of them still retain their basic traits discussed earlier in the chapter but how they use them is a bit different. Another trait that is utilized differently is the duality aspect. Girls tend to shift their interests a lot more than boys. They may appear interested in something on one day while doing the opposite thing on the other. Boys are unpredictable, but they tend to stick to their interests more often than girls.

Another rare trait that is sometimes not found in Gemini girls is the ability to multitask efficiently. Gemini boys tend to multitask frequently in their teens and build up the ability so that they can access it in their adult life. Women have a natural tendency to multitask, but it is less frequently reported in Gemini girls than Gemini boys.

There are more differences but those can arise on a more individual basis rather than a collective basis. Thus, they were not included in this section. The differences that were selected are a common representation of a Gemini boy and a Gemini girl. Parents can use this information and link it with their children's needs to make better decisions about their wellbeing.

Chapter 4: The Gemini in Love

To trust a person and to offer your entire self to them can be a daunting task. So, falling in love with someone can prove to be difficult for certain people, as they struggle to open up. It is even more challenging for people to find themselves a perfect partner to marry. Finding someone who is perfectly compatible with your personality and will perfectly complement you is very difficult. Rarely do people find the right person that will not leave their side until the end of time.

Every person's personality traits are unique, and to find this person – someone with complementing characteristics – can be a hard task. Even if one finds the perfect person, they might struggle with various obstacles in the relationship. Be it a girlfriend and boyfriend or a husband and wife, everyone faces challenges in their relationships. Many manage to surpass these challenges, while other relationships are shattered due to the pressure of these obstacles. The key to the success behind a long-lasting marriage and a happy couple is the expectation of these hurdles. If people expect these challenges, they will be better prepared and have the ideal mindset to survive the issues and save their relationship. You might think that finding love and dodging these challenges might be a matter of luck. You are wrong. What if I tell you, finding love and holding on to it for a long time can become easy with the understanding of your horoscope and your birth chart? No, I am not kidding. Your star sign describes what kind of personality you have inherited, and if one is aware of these traits, they can find their perfect partner with comparable ease.

So, if you have a crush on a Gemini in your neighborhood, college, or workplace and want to discover the right way to pursue it, then you have found the right book. Similarly, if you are in a happy relationship with a Gemini and want to know any obstacles that you need to be cautious about, this book is perfect for you too. In this chapter, we will explore the compatibility of a Gem with other star signs. We will learn about how the personalities can clash or contrast and how they can start their exploratory journey of finding their first love. We will focus mainly on Gemini's attributes and tips that will help you date a Gemini. It will also cater to a Gemini by looking at various topics from their perspective. It will serve as a place for a Gemini to understand their habitual reactions to love and provide a guide for them to navigate a healthy relationship.

When you are a teenager, you have a lot of emotions and have inherited expectations from the people around you. When it comes to love, a teenager finds it difficult to navigate this relationship and find the starting point to go about it. Expectations, fears, or excitement often blur their thoughts. As explained before, Geminis have dual personalities, and searching for love can be difficult for a teen Gemini. They can be confused by the dual personalities that might guide them in opposite directions. This section will help a Gemini, especially a teen, understand love and be aware of the expectations to carry.

First, let's emphasize Gemini's dual personality trait and how it impacts their love life. Imagine being on a night out, dancing carelessly, and having the best time of your life. You have your friends around, and you are the most comfortable that you can get. A stranger comes up to you, and you both start talking. As a Gemini, you like conversations and are very easy to talk to. When you get back home, you think of going out on a date with this person. A Gemini can feel they are too young for it, or even if they go out on a date, they might not pursue it further. The thought of love can frighten a few young Geminis, as they think it will shackle their freedom, but a Gemini needs to realize their dual personality and that a decade down the lane, they might feel that they are too old for love. Anyway, a Gemini will never think that it is the correct time to explore their love options. They will either be too young, too old, too busy, or too free to get involved in a relationship. A Gemini, especially a teen, needs to realize that there is no time for love - it is timeless.

There is not an age bracket for finding true love. Fearing that love will restrict their freedom is not the right thought process for a Gemini. Despite being great lovers, Gems distance themselves from commitment even if it's what they desire. They love adventures and exploring different interests. There is no organization in their life as they strive for spontaneous thrills. So, it is important that Geminis keep this in mind because the fear of losing time and freedom can cause them to miss out on the right person. Just make the leap when you find someone you love unconditionally and who respects your interests and personality. The kind of people who will gel well with you and be compatible with your complex personality is explored in the next section.

Second, as we briefly talked about before, most people are buried in expectations when it comes to the topic of love. Having expectations is human nature and something that everyone does, but the Geminis are some, if not the only, people who doubt the expectations they have. Being so energetic and social, they think it is difficult to find someone who can mirror their zeal for adventure and travel. They also doubt that anyone can match their intellectual capacity, their desire for funny, entertaining conversations and intellectual, witty conversations other times.

Young Geminis need to be assured that there is someone who can and will match their love for adventures and fulfill the needs of their dual personalities, but expectations can limit your experience; in this case, never settle for less. Gems need to be constantly in search of the right person and persevere until it happens. Note that this does not mean that you look for someone who is perfect or a perfect clone of the perfect person that you have imagined. Instead, look out for those who just fulfill your emotional, spiritual, intellectual, and physical needs. Keeping this in mind will allow you to make the right decisions that you do not regret in the future.

Now that we have highlighted the two most significant things that can often spoil the experience of finding love for a Gemini. Let's approach this topic from the perspective of an outsider trying to impress a Gemini.

First, try to talk about something they might not know. Geminis are very inquisitive people and crave learning. Talking about your dreams, hobbies, and passions, especially something that they do not know about, will excite them and make them more interested in you. Your uniqueness will attract the Gemini's attention and will cause them to come back for more, as there is a possibility that there is more that they can learn from you. Also, it is essential that you are original. Do not repeat yourself or copy the same old trick. Geminis tend to get bored easily, so treat every chance that you have as your last chance.

Second, Geminis like to struggle. Try to act disinterested in the Gemini, and they will work to earn your attention. This might annoy them initially, but it can allow you to strengthen your bond in the long run. It will also make them appreciate you in the relationship more. Play this move cleverly because overdoing it can cause them to repel from you.

Last, try to make a Gemini feel comfortable in his or her own skin. Geminis are mutable, which means that they can change with time or change with the flow of the situation. This was touched upon before and is also evident through their symbols, which means "twins". Rather than restricting them from exhibiting their various personalities, allow them to remold themselves at their own convenience. This will make them feel comfortable with you, as they can put their true self at the show. Moreover, if you can be spontaneous with plans and trips, it will make Geminis happy and can leave a good impression on them.

These are a few of the significant things that Geminis need to consider when exploring love and non-Geminis when trying to pursue one.

Now that we have touched upon these things that will make your journey of finding love a little smoother let's talk about things from the other perspective. We will cover how to react from the perspective of someone who is in a relationship with a Gemini. The next section will equip them with ideas about how to respond in the relationship. In the next section, we will discover a Gemini's compatibility with the rest of the zodiac signs. We will explore the relationship in a manner that can cater to both Gemini and other zodiac signs. Be mindful that these are the traits that only their sun suggests, but a conscientious effort from both parties can alter any differences.

A Quick Guide to Dating a Gemini

The previous part of this chapter has explored different techniques when trying to engage in a relationship with a Gemini, but things take a different turn when you find yourself in one. You might encounter situations that you have not been in before and might find yourself exposed to aspects of your partner's personality that you have never seen before. In these scenarios, one needs to know how to react and tend to their partner's needs. To make a relationship last, it is vital that you understand your partner and act appropriately towards their needs.

This section will list a few pointers that can come in handy for someone in a relationship with a Gemini.

Listen to Your Partner

Geminis love to talk endlessly. It is a significant part of their personality, and they are curious to know more about things. Do not burden yourself with thinking of a topic for discussion; instead, let the Gemini take the lead, because they will have various topics in mind to chat about. Just be careful not to interrupt the Gemini during this conversation because they might think that you are not interested.

Be Patient with Your Partner

When going into a relationship with a Gemini, you should expect that their moods and behavior might change regularly. They can be fun and happy one moment and can get angry and grumpy the next. In these situations, you should not allow their behavior to get to you. Refrain from taking it personally and try talking to them, inquiring about what is bothering them.

Do Not Force Gemini's to Make a Decision

Duality nature once again presents itself here. Due to this personality trait, a Gemini might be stuck in confusion over two available choices. One part might want the first choice, while the other part of their personality might be inclined to pursue the second option. Confusion between having Indian or Thai food on a date night can be one of these situations. If you find yourself in a similar situation, then do not force your choice on them. Gemini hates it. Instead, you can approach such problems by making a suggestion. Note that even if you frame your preference so that it comes across as a preference rather than a decision, it will allow you to dodge any arguments. So, instead of forcing them to have Indian, you can rephrase it and say, "We had Thai last night, and I heard there is a new Indian restaurant that has opened down the street. Should we try something new today?"

Never Break the Trust of a Gemini

Geminis are very loving and enjoy the company of humans. So, it makes a lot of sense that they invest a lot of their trust in their friends and partners. After you have broken their trust, Geminis might forgive you and accept you back into their life, but you will never be able to regain their trust. This is because Geminis are intellectual people and choose to think beyond their emotions. This characteristic allows them to forgive quickly.

Additionally, do not expect to go behind a Gemini's back and think that they will never find out about it. Geminis are very inquisitive characters. If they sense any secret, they will try to find it out. This is why you should always be honest and upfront with a Gemini. They will prefer honesty instead of a lie any day of the week. No matter how harsh the reality is, they will appreciate it.

Do Not Try to Control a Gemini

Geminis are free souls who are always in search of their big new adventure. Geminis do not like anyone navigating their life for them. They prefer exploring and finding their path in life. If you try to set restrictions on your partner or control them in any manner, then you might find your Gemini partner to be very unhappy. Allow them the freedom to explore the world on their own and be respectful of this decision of theirs but if you find Geminis lost and in trouble, then reach out to them and offer them your support. Geminis might like independence, but they also like companionship.

Do Not Take What a Gemini Says as Binding

You might notice that Geminis often act contradictorily. This is because their personalities are multi-dimensional, which often confuses them at times. So, if a Gemini tells you that they want to go on a walk tomorrow, then do not take it as a definite truth. They might wake up tomorrow morning and feel like going to the gym rather than on a walk. So, be aware of such possible scenarios occurring in your relationship. In these situations, rather than forcing their former decision on them, you should encourage them to pursue their new desires. If this situation extends to them canceling plans, then do not be upset. If it bothers you, then talk to them about how their behavior affects you. Accusing them of being unavailable and flaky will not be the right approach to this situation.

These were a few tips to keep in mind if you are in a relationship with a Gemini, but in the next chapter, we will discover a Gemini's compatibility with the rest of the zodiac signs. We will explore the relationship in a way that encompasses both the Gemini and the other zodiac signs. Be mindful that these are the traits that the sun suggests, but a conscientious effort from both parties can change the outcomes.

Love and Other Zodiac Signs: Compatibility, Obstacles, and Navigating Love

In astrology, predicting compatibility based on behavior which itself is assumed from the interaction of suns, moons, and planets, is quite big. People in huge numbers look at their horoscope and consider their compatibility with other zodiac signs when looking for a serious relationship but there is not any evidence to support the claims made in these charts.

They predict compatibility based on zodiac signs that emerged in the Western culture in the 1970s and are referred to as synastry. In this approach, the astrologer actively makes birth charts for each person through various methods. They then compare these birth charts to predict how well both the involved personalities will align.

The compatibility charts adopt a very popular approach when making predictions. They take into consideration the rising sign of each person. The rising sign refers to the zodiac sign that emerges from the eastern horizon at the time of a person's birth. Many also take into consideration the position of moons and planets, but to produce accurate predictions based on those positions, you have to know the exact time of birth, as the positions change with time. In this chapter, we look at compatibility based on the sun signs since looking at other factors will only complicate our understanding. We will look at what obstacles can arise in a relationship, how well two zodiac signs match in terms of love, and we will also look at how compatible they are in bed.

Every zodiac sign is unique and is defined by its traits. As discussed before, these traits play an important role in every person's love life as their ruling planet administers them. In this section, we will match Gemini with other zodiac signs and figure out how well their compatibility rates and find any obstacles that might arise. There are twelve zodiac signs in total, and we will explore all, one after another. This might get long, so let us hurry up!

An Aries and a Gemini together is an interesting match. While Aries is an enthusiastic group of people, Gemini is psychologically gifted. A Gem will try to mimic the energy level and the passion of Aries, even though they might not feel that way intrinsically. While mimicking your behavior to fit in, they will ignore all the things you are condemned for (like being too angry) and focus on the good side of your personality (like your empathy). The Aries will dominate such relationships, but Gems will have no problem steering the wheel and will not hesitate to throw in their ideas and advice about what to do next. One best part about this relationship is that Gemini will not get offended easily. It is hard to offend them, and even when you do, they get over it quite easily. In modern relationships, most of the problems arise from one person disrespecting and offending the other. This will not be the case here (at least not for a Gem) as they are very thick-skinned and not a fan of holding grudges. Neither of these people are jealous, clingy, or emotionally over-demanding. An Aries will ignore the Gemini's sides that other people might usually point out and criticize them for, but the most significant challenge for these couples come from the lack of excitement to finish a venture. These people love starting a new project or a task in their life and lose the excitement midway. The allure of a new idea distracts them as they lose sight of what they have already started.

Taurus and Gemini might be a terrible match because it can end in an agonizing skirmish of demeanors in the relationship. A Taurus is usually tricky, but their stubbornness is accentuated when in a Gemini relationship; as discussed before, Gems are highly expressive and exceptionally lucid. This relationship might feel like a ball (Gemini) ricocheting off the wall (Taurus). Not only this, but Taurus does not reciprocate Geminis love of chaos. Gems loathe routine and are impatient people, while Taurus prefers a sense of organization. This might result in many arguments, but Gemini, being masters of negotiations and articulation, will have an edge in these too. This will further frustrate a Taurus who will lose an argument despite knowing that they were right. Moreover, it might be difficult for a Taurus to keep up with a Gem because they are active and social.

Although everyone appreciates hard work and dedication, no one likes chaos and rampant disregard for efficiency. This might also stretch to the bedroom where both of their sleep schedules might not match. Gemini's social personality might also not sit well with Taurus since they might not be as eager as a Gem on a night out. This might raise questions over commitment for Taurus, as on a night out alone, a

Gem will not hesitate to talk to strangers at the bar or dance with someone on the dance floor. Taurus might fear that such actions might lead to something that can harm the relationship. If you want this relationship to work out, you need to be ready to make sacrifices and adjust. Compromise is important in this relationship, or you might find it too demanding and exhausting.

A Gemini and Gemini pairing is only suitable as long as it is limited to a friendship or casual flirting. The energetic personality and the chaos-loving character can often clash and accelerate the relationship to destruction. Being very active and hardworking, this couple might find themselves too busy to share alone time. Often romantic times might not be planned but rather occur naturally. Since both of these people will be disorganized and will be lacking passion, they might find themselves lost in the relationship. Figuring out where they stand in the relationship might be difficult, and both will be scared to commit to one another. It is possible that both of them might play mind games with one another and purposely and falsely lead each other on.

There has to be a person who can think emotionally and one that can be intellectual in a relationship. There is also a requirement for someone to entertain, so no one loses interest. When two of the same zodiac signs are brought together, their strengths and weaknesses are magnified, and this can influence the nature of the relationship. Since Geminis are social creatures, together they can be amazing friends, but the lack of passion and emotion usually means they may not make a great romantic partner.

Cancer and Gemini relationships can either be excellent or end badly. Gems are entertaining human beings who are always searching for a little fun. On the other hand, Cancers are intuitive individuals and very empathetic. Cancers are usually reserved and try to keep their social circles small. Gems are social creatures, and this is why both their personality traits are clashing. On a date night, Cancers might prefer eating-in, while Gems might like to eat-out. Cancer can offer a sense of security to the partner and comfort them and give them the attention they need, while the Gem can be the source of adventure in the relationship, keeping it young and interesting. These different traits can provide a balance in that relationship that can, in actuality, work well, but this balance will not come naturally; rather, the couple will have to work on it. Similarly, clashes can arise because Gems prefer to be a free soul, while Cancers like their home and family. This means that a Gem might not be ready for commitment when Cancers are seeking it.

Fights might arise because Cancers can perceive Gems as emotionless, lacking empathy, and stubborn. At the same time, Gems can view Cancers as over-emotional and too needy. These differences will only resolve if both the people realize that each of them is different, and rather than getting angry, they try to learn from their differences. Acceptance will make the relationship last a lifetime.

Leos and Geminis are similar in many ways and also different in various fashions. Like Geminis, Leo is also very social and enjoys going out. They both want to be the topic of discussion and want the entire room to notice. This couple can have a nice time competing for the spotlight, but it can also lead to struggles as they both compete for the same thing. Being sociable, both of them are always looking for ways to entertain each other. They can have a good laugh in this relationship and feed off each other's positive vibe, but beware, because Leos can be dramatic and a little extravagant. Gems might not appreciate this behavior, as they value analytical behavior more than impulsive, let alone extravagant. Although Geminis might enjoy this trait eventually when traveling to new places with their Leo and benefiting from this trait's entertainment perspective. And most Leos take casual flirting quite well, but a few may not correctly interpret the intentions. So, Leos might be quicker in expecting commitment than Gemini. If this is to happen, it is better than you clear your intentions about flirting at the start of the relationship.

Another clear difference between both these zodiac signs is that Leos prefer organization and work hard to prevent chaos. The Gemini, as stated before, is disorganized and enjoys the thrill of a chaotic environment. Overall, this relationship is very compatible, both emotionally and physically.

Gemini and Virgo are both good communicators and can effectively convey their feelings and frame their arguments. They have very sharp minds and often think from the head, and do not allow their judgment to be clouded by emotions. Virgos are not clingy and are not excessively demanding in a relationship, but they might misinterpret a Gem's casual flirting with other humans. In such times they can become far more possessive than any other human being. The advantage of firmly framing your arguments and thinking rationally will allow you to resolve many conflicts in the relationship.

Virgos are very dedicated to their work and can stress about the deadlines and their duties. Arguments might occur because Gemini, being disorganized, might not take their concerns seriously. Moreover, Virgos might also come across as problematic, as they have the tendencies to critique and pick on minor details. Virgos are also big on smart spending. They like to make efficient use of their money and make their purchase decisions after quite a bit of thought. On the other hand, Gems are spontaneous and can make big purchases for the sake of the thrill. So, money can also contribute to conflicts in the relationship. Overall, they both make a great match since Virgos are down to earth and can tend to a Gemini's needs.

A Libra-Gemini relationship is a perfect relationship per the books. They both are very compatible with each other, and there are no downsides to pursuing this relationship. You need to be cautious about exhausting the spark in the relationship by over-using it. Geminis are flirty humans, but they might find "the one" in Libras. Both of these zodiac signs are intellectuals, and debates in this relationship will be interesting. Arguments might erupt through these debates, but people in this relationship will easily forgive each other. The love for travel and adventure is also common among both of these zodiac signs. Unless there is a storm outside, neither prefer to stay indoors. They like social gatherings and will eagerly join each other to go to events. Libra's enthusiasm and positivity will stand out to a Gemini, and these attributes will bring out the better in a Gem. When this relationship gets serious, Geminis should beware because Libras will be the first to think seriously of marriage. Gems are adventurous, but this time they will cave in. Being indecisive, marriage might take a long time arriving, but they both will come to this chapter sooner or later.

A Scorpio is often considered a dark personality, especially when its traits are looked at in isolation. So, this Scorpio-Gemini relationship might be a struggling battle since Gemini's are full of heart. As far as bedroom antics go, Scorpio makes a wonderful and fulfilling partner but there will be an evident emotional battle in the conflict. Scorpio signs are mysterious characters, and this will attract a Gemini to them, but this mysterious character also demands privacy. So, Gemini will have to respect their privacy; if not, then the Scorpio will erupt.

Scorpios are highly instinctive humans and also secretive, but they are good at understanding people and their intentions. Gemini might often find them talking to their partners in this relationship about their own troubles in order to seek Scorpio's advice since they are good with people and have an excellent understanding of their nature. Because of this intense trait of Scorpio, a Gem might find them too possessive. Similarly, Geminis might be perceived as immature because of their playful nature that is often on exhibition during the worst possible time. Also, Gems might not be bothered by how they are perceived, but Scorpios will be. Scorpio will also want to dominate the relationship and be in control. If there are not significant compromises made, this relationship will not last long, even considering it is a very unlikely match. Compromise and respecting each other is the only way to make it happen.

Geminis are naturally attracted to Sagittarius because of their personality, which happens to be quite fun. They are very inquisitive humans and prefer being in a social environment where their sharp intellect can be displayed. Both the people in this relationship like steering conversation toward enthralling topics, and communication between both the people will be great.

Geminis have a wide array of hobbies and interests, while Sagittarius likes to concentrate their interests and be very passionate about them. Each partner will likely introduce the other to newer interests and activities during this relationship but Sagittarius' personality trait of being open and blunt might be found annoying by many Gems. Sagittarius is very self-opinionated, while Gems try not to judge people and situations and be analytical rather than emotional. So, Sagittarius being bluntly honest might not be appreciated by many Gems and may cause conflicts in the relationship. Sagittarius prefers a civilized debate instead of the casual exchange of ideas. They might hold a Gemini responsible and at fault for not choosing a side and passionately defending an idea. This might cause a Gem to think of their partner as shallow, while Sagittarius might think of a Gem as irresponsible. Still, neither accusation is true about each other's personality traits. Whether these things annoy the people in this couple will unfold later in the relationship, but the couple will have a lot of fun. Both the zodiac signs are funny and outgoing. They love adventures and are always looking for something to do. They also have a similar sense of humor and can track sarcasm well. This is why the Gemini-Sagittarius relationship will always be energetic and have the spark despite the differences. According to the zodiac, both these people will be complete opposites of each other. This relationship will go well or will be a disaster. It will depend on how early they get bored with each other.

Capricorns are a very complicated personality. They are a combination of passion, hard work, humility, and determination. The Capricorn's sexy and entertaining side is reserved for their friends and loved ones, and they do not leave it on exhibition for anyone else. A Gemini might be only exposed to a serious personality, making them feel like a parent rather than a lover. Capricorn's ability to be focused on their goals and be very organized clashes with Gems' spontaneous and chaotic personality. Although a Capricorn can be sexy and romantic, they might express this emotion through a series of practical actions rather than plain cheesy and hopeless romantic behavior. This might cause a Gem to perceive a Capricorn as dull. This perception might also come to a Gem's mind because Capricorn handles money and lives their life with considerable care. Capricorns like to be careful with money and save for an unfortunate situation when it can help them. A Gem likes to spend it as it comes.

Additionally, Capricorns like a sense of predictability in their life and to know what is in store. They like to like to organize their every step and practice what they want to say in a conversation beforehand. So, they do not like spontaneous plans and socializing. Geminis, on the other hand, love going out and can go on a new adventure every day. Initially, Capricorns can expect to enjoy the light-hearted and entertaining personality of Gems. Still, it will soon fade out if none of the involved parties are ready to compromise or understand the other's personality. Sex will also be fun and cheery in the beginning, but that too will become too predictable and, thus, boring – especially for the Gemini.

Aquarius is a very confident and exciting bunch of people. They like to have deep conversations but also have a fun and entertaining side to them. They can be perceived as cold, but they are very intellectual and unpredictable in an entertaining fashion. This is the reason why an Aquarius-Gemini relationship will be perfect and should be pursued without any hesitation. Even if the relationship does not work out too well, the people will find lifelong friends in each other.

Geminis and Aquarius do not form opinions about another person because they do not care how people perceive them, and as a result, they do not judge people. The Aquarius and Gemini duo makes a great match because of this. Moreover, Aquarius finds the indecisive and chaos-loving nature of Geminis attractive rather than dull, unlike most of the other star signs. However, Aquarius can be a little reserved when expressing their commitments and romantic feelings to their partner. This trait might have been a threat to the relationship with a Scorpio, as they need continuous attention and validation from their partner. In the case of a Gemini-Aquarius relationship, this trait is harmless as both are not clingy and possessive. None of the people in this relationship will be emotional, and both like to have witty and intellectual debates.

Aquarius strives to be unique, and this trait will provide a thrill to the relationship since both like an adventure. This adventure will extend to the bedrooms too, where the Aquarius will be able to keep the Gemini on their toes romantically. This relationship will survive hardships and struggles as long as the personal boundaries of each person are respected. The only downside to this couple is that they both hate doing chores, but who cares when you are busy having adventures and making memories.

Pisces are very emotional and loving humans who think intuitively. A Gemini-Pisces relationship might not work out because of clashing personality traits. The very emotional character of Pisces is not compatible with the intellectual personality of Gemini. Gemini prefers to live their lives to their fullest by being adventurous and benefiting from the thrill that any situation can provide. They might find Pisces holding them back due to their demanding personality. In the relationship, Pisces will look for validation, and they will be needy for attention and love. Pisces can be passionate lovers and can be very unconditional, but Gems do not connect to deep and emotional love. Their idea of love is rooted in the emotional connection and the resulting friendship and joy. Because of this emotional love, Gemini will be repelled and back off from this relationship. This action will cause Pisces to feel insecure in the relationship and make them even needier for reciprocation and validation.

Gemini takes nothing seriously, while an Aquarius can have firm beliefs and can be too vulnerable and emotional about certain things and issues. This problem also extends to humor. Gemini's sense of humor can be possibly offensive for Pisces, as it can unintentionally hurt their sentiments. Geminis will, therefore, have to be very cautious around their partner. They might also find themselves turning around the mood of Pisces, who can be pessimistic and sad at times. Last, like Scorpio, Pisces, too, need their space to recharge for the day but unlike Scorpios, they do not do well in social settings, and a Gemini-Pisces couple might find themselves arguing about going out or not.

The above evaluations are made after considering the interaction between the sun signs. If you read the compatibility breakdown above and found that you are not best suited with someone you like, then do not be desperate. There are various other planets and astrological connections that can impact a relationship and can influence the compatibility between two zodiac signs. To better understand your compatibility, you can get an official astrological reading from an astrologist. If the answer is still the same as you find in this book, you can work on the differences mentioned and embrace them. Any relationship can be saved by respect and compromise.

A major part of a relationship is the intimate moments that you share together. When people search for a partner, they look for someone who can fulfill their emotional as well as physical needs. It can be challenging to keep a relationship afloat if one person values sex more in the relationship than the other person. Considering every partner's needs and catering to their needs is the crux of the relationship but in terms of sex, this can get difficult if one person in the relationship does not want to have sex while the other one does.

Many people often define a healthy relationship as the quality of sex that people are having in a relationship. Sex can be a deal maker or a deal-breaker for Gems when pursuing a relationship. Below, we will explore how the match of different zodiac signs fare in terms of compatibility when it comes to sex.

The sexual chemistry with a Gemini is not the best that Aries has experienced with their prior partners. Aries are people who need a certain sense of conflict to enhance their sexual urges. Aries-Gemini sexual chemistry will be intense, and the passion and creativity of the Aries will be welcomed and appreciated in the bedroom by a Gemini. Aries are also likely to dominate in the bedroom, and a Gemini will appreciate this dynamic. Gemini is excited by verbal lovers and will like it when Aries talk to them about their plans. Last, Gemini will also be more adaptive in the bedroom and become more daring to match an Aries' drive.

Gemini people are experts with their narratives in the bedroom, but this is not a Taurus' forte. Taurus is great at the physical act in bed but not at conversations, which Geminis like. Being adventurous, Geminis are also very experimental in the bedroom and will try everything at least once. They might prefer a quickie once in a while, and might try to break away from the routine to keep things interesting. This is something that a Taurus will be less likely to lean towards.

Being fun personalities, a Gemini-Gemini couple prefers light casual sex to something with a lot of emotions. They like stimulating their sexual desires through phone calls, texting, and acting. They might be perceived as superficial by other zodiac signs since they are repelled by emotional sex, but they will fully satisfy each other and will never get too clingy, allowing the other person to have their personal space.

Cancers like to have sex that has meaning, and which is deep and emotional. This clashes with the personality of a Gemini who prefers fun to emotions. Gemini's sexual desires might not be fully satisfied by Cancer because they might feel that their styles do not match. Similarly, Cancers might also feel dissatisfied. This dissatisfaction can be eliminated if they both appreciate each other better. Communicating with a Gemini when they need a cuddle can help Cancers. Similarly, if something is lacking for a Gemini, they can communicate it to their Cancer partner.

Leos and Geminis also have great chemistry in the bedroom. The sexual chemistry is great between them, as Leo loves when Gemini vividly pronounces their plans about what they wish to do in the bedroom. They both appreciate the light, sexual fun in the bedroom, which, as we have seen, is not reciprocated by many other zodiac signs. They both like being adventurous in the relationship and might experiment outdoors and indoors. This relation is a great start for a Gemini/Leo to overcome any manner of embarrassment or shame they face with their sex life.

For Virgos and Geminis, emotions in the bedroom do not matter, but this can be a problem as the sex might lack any form of intimacy in a Virgo-Gemini relationship, but this couple might also like this relationship because it is not needy and respects their personal space. Virgos can be a little too predictable for Gemini in terms of sex, and they might soon get bored with it. This couple also appreciates good phone sex or role-play. Geminis might take the dominator's role in the relationship while Virgo will be the submissive one.

The imaginative sense and the physical capabilities of a Libra and Gemini are so brilliant that they will certainly have a great time in the bedroom. Both of these people bring different dynamics to the bedroom. Libra brings romance into the relationship, while Gemini brings the aspect of adventure. This relationship will be characterized by fun role-playing before sex and various seductive games that will be the source of energy.

Although the emotions and passion of the Scorpio during sex complement the fun-loving approach towards sex by the Gemini, it will not last in the long run. Eventually, a Gemini might find this relationship to be too demanding, and the emotional aspect might be a massive turnoff for them. Scorpio and Gemini have opposing needs in bed, which might make sex unsatisfying for both parties after a time but understanding the needs of each other can deter you from experiencing such problems. It is not so bad to adjust, and it is not as self-sacrificing as it sounds. And Scorpios are very amenable to experimenting in bed, and their sense of spontaneity and unpredictability can keep things interesting.

Between a Gemini and Sagittarius, sex will be light and fun, and the couple will be very spontaneous and adventurous in their sexual encounter. They both equally enjoy experimentation in the bedroom and will try new things. This couple might take things out of the bedroom and involve themselves in risqué things. Both of these people are intellectuals and chatting will be part of the date, but sex will entail more than conversations in this relationship. Geminis love the sex drive of a Sagittarius, while the verbal aspect that Geminis bring to bed excites Sagittarius. This relationship can be molded into a long-term commitment if both the people make adjustments and think level-headedly. If things go smoothly, this couple also has chances of ending up married.

Capricorns and Gemini both love light-hearted sex, and this aspect will be appreciated in the relationship because there will be no restriction or expectations to behave. There will be extreme passion in the relationship, and Capricorns can teach a Gemini more about physical performance and push it to be more than just talk. Further, Capricorns have great stamina in the bedroom and can be very passionate when matched by the experimental nature of a Gemini, but there are chances that this passion will soon be overshadowed in the long term when feelings of dissatisfaction settle in.

Aquarius and Gemini will be a great match in bed since both of them are not very needy and clingy. They will take things at a fast pace and taking their clothes off will not take much time. They will start having sex very early on in the relationship. Additionally, these zodiac signs do not necessarily have to be in a relationship to have sex. They can be friends and occasionally also have sex without blurring the lines of friendship. They can also concoct very erotic tales for their bedroom due to their imaginative and creative traits. This means that both people can always maintain the excitement in the relationship. In short, they both are very compatible, both in and out of the bedroom.

Pisces like to have a deeper meaning and emotional bond when they are having sex, whereas a Gemini does not like when emotion is tied to sex. Rather, they like it fun and exploratory with no connection, but a lot of experimentation. This difference in what they consider as good sex often allows the passion to fade out soon. After a short term of having sexual intercourse, things start to get dissatisfying in the bedroom. When Gemini tries to be independent, it increases the insecurity experienced by a Pisces. This causes a Pisces to be needier, and a Gemini might not provide them the validation that they might be longing for. If the people involved in this relationship can think level-headedly and compromise to conform to the other's needs, this relationship can withstand many obstacles.

This will help you explore your love options if you think that sex makes up a considerable amount of your life and it's of significance to you. But like the previous section, this section is also based on the sun and does not take into account the birth time-specific aspects –planets and moon positions.

Chapter 5: The Social Gemini

Geminis have a unique persona that can lead them to have prosperous social lives. The following chapter discusses the entire social profile of Geminis. This entails a detailed analysis of different social situations and the Gemini relationship with other zodiac signs. Reading the following content can help Geminis navigate through tough social situations. This chapter is also essential if you have a Gemini companion in your life and you want to better understand them. You can pick up useful pointers that will eventually help you to grow your rapport with your Gemini friend.

The Social Map of a Gemini

By now, most of Geminis' common traits have been discussed, but this section will cover those traits relevant to social situations like parties. Social situations like the workplace will not be covered in this chapter as those are considered separate profiles discussed in future chapters.

Gemini has been described as the most social zodiac sign on the zodiac wheel due to its communication and curiosity traits. These traits lead them to build a sound relationship with the people around them. Interaction with their community is also part of their ruling house trait, so they do not have to look far for satisfying connections. These connections mentally stimulate our Gemini subjects, so we have to look at something similar when we are looking at social situations, such as a party.

Depending on their birth charts, people inherit different traits from their signs/ruling planets. Most Geminis have this burning curiosity to know more about life. Keeping this in mind, it is safe to assume that Geminis are among the most extroverted people at a party. Geminis are often interested in the audience/participants at an event or party rather than the party itself. Their innate ability to communicate effortlessly is a gift that is used very wisely in such situations. Their ability to articulate well is one of their strongest suits and can get them through the worst misunderstandings in life.

Geminis also have the ability to adapt to different situations. They can rewire their brain more quickly than a few of the other signs if faced with a situation they were not prepared for, since they have basically faced their dual nature during their whole lives. Both of these abilities help in approaching random strangers and connecting with them at a human level. These traits make random interactions easy and natural for the Geminis.

An ideal night out for a Gemini involves bar hopping with a couple of their closest friends. They will always be open to thoughtful conversation at the bars in exchange for a few drinks. Engaging in conversation will satisfy their mind while the activity around them will make them feel as if they are in their most natural element. Whether a Gemini is single or not, they will always have a fun night out if it involved bar hopping activities.

Geminis have a couple of other traits as well that can help them navigate through a party. Geminis are independent souls; thus, they do not fear doing things on their own. This means that they want to do more than just dancing or drinking at a party. So, partying with them will contribute to a fuller experience rather than it just being a wasteful night that ends up giving you a hangover. Depending on their individuality and their house positioning (cusp positioning), Geminis may range from seeking a very wild party experience to a fuller experience, but one thing is for sure: no party is a dull party with a Gemini.

An ideal party for a Gemini will start off normally, like any other party but it is only a matter of time before the Gemini gets bored and leaves or does something to make it more interesting. A lot of interesting strangers should be part of the party so that the Gemini can exercise their traits and have thoughtful exchanges all night long. Another feature of an ideal party for the Gemini includes a lot of wild party games. "Wild," in this case means absolutely entertaining and fun, and in many cases, it can get immensely personal as well. The Gemini teens and adults like such games that bring out the personal details of a person's life since they are always looking for something interesting to chat about.

Another trait of social Gemini is to get involved in the gossip that goes around. Geminis will never admit this, but they love to gossip since that too is a part of communication, and it brings out many interesting details (from people's lives) to satisfy their mental cravings. As a Gemini, you can relate to this last detail wholeheartedly since we know you will not admit it to anyone else in reality.

A few Geminis (who have unique birth chart positioning) may not follow most of the traits explained above for a social setting. It depends on the cusps and houses that the astrologer draws out, but different activities can bring out the best of them at a party. Many can be carefree while others can decide to engage in activities only. It really depends on the individual's personality, but the basic traits of the Gemini may still be observed often.

Another factor decides how Geminis interact and behave with different people in a party (or a social setting). The zodiac sign of the person that you are interacting with also matters. Compatibility is a metric that astrologers often use to decide whether two signs will be compatible with different activities/stages in life, such as love, marriage, friendship, sex, and other similar things. We can examine the Gemini's relationship with each of their zodiac compatriots to see who will bring the best out of them. Our results will also show us why Geminis might react negatively to a person at a bar or at a party.

Gemini is very compatible with Aquarius as both have pretty similar traits and are looking for things that the other is willing to offer. They will never run out of topics to talk about and do share a few of the split personality traits, meaning they can shift from activity to activity throughout the party extracting the most fun from each one. Aquarius and Gemini make a good match in many aspects of life, and this social aspect can also yield a wholesome friendship between the two. They can link up pretty quickly but both of them rarely have similar feelings towards something.

Libra and Gemini both represent social people, so they will always have playful chemistry between them. They may even become best friends, but it may be a clash of two alphas at a party. Joining forces might make a lot of people jealous, and they may get looks from other people throughout the party. Libras may find this as validation, but Geminis have fairly different emotions, and so their emotions do not coincide.

Gemini and Aries are described to be more of a hot and cold match. During a party, the opposite aspects of their personalities can attract each other while other aspects may become a turnoff. This situation is when an air sign meets a fire sign, and it can get pretty adventurous and passionate really quickly.

Leo and Gemini are a few of the more egoistic signs, and their conversation can make both of them appreciate each other. Their differences are what attract each other, and so this too is a fire and air match.

Sagittarius and Gemini can have an instant connection based on how similar they are. They can be amazed at how similar they are once they talk at a party, but being too similar may not allow both of them to take this friendship further.

Gemini likes attention, and Taurus is one sign that is willing to give it. Interaction between them at a party is sure to bring out a fruitful relationship, but how long it will last can be questioned; however, it would be fulfilling for the moment.

Gemini and Pisces can form a unique connection that focuses on their creativity. At a party, they can go on and on about their creative sides. Both have different emotions and may not get each other in the long term.

Scorpios have an intense personality and are a straight challenge to Gemini's personality. Geminis can be intrigued or repelled by it but if they have an initial conversation that goes well during a party, then they have probably found someone who can keep them in check.

Cancer and Gemini have fairly positive compatibility because Geminis want to feel appreciated and want attention, and the Cancers can give it to them, but the Gemini's tendency to become uninterested fairly quickly might not allow this relationship to foster.

Capricorn and Gemini may not be the perfect partners in a relationship, but their connection can be pretty fun at a party. The Capricorn's posing will put off the Gemini, but their curiosity can carry them through an entire conversation. It might not be fun, but it will still be interesting.

The Gemini and Virgo combination is not the best connection that a Gemini can have at a party. Virgos have too many walls, and at first, the connection might be interesting, but the Gemini will eventually feel uninterested and run away from it.

Many of the best connections that a Gemini can have are with other fellow Geminis! This combination will be fun for the Geminis as well as everyone else at the party or at any other social situation. This is mainly due to how similar both of those people will be and how they will instantly make all of their life decisions. They will also relate to each other's lives, which might be the start of a budding friendship.

Gemini Friendships

Ever wondered why you cannot seem to start up a conversation with your Gemini classmate? There are a couple of straightforward ways for people to befriend Geminis, and this section will talk about a few of those ways. This section is also important for Geminis if they want to learn about how to make friends while navigating through their zodiac traits.

Geminis are not afraid to express their opinion, and so you are better off just initiating the conversation and let them take the driver's seat. Geminis are pretty confident, so complimenting them may work at first but building their self-esteem regularly will get you nowhere in the relationship. Try to contribute to the conversation by mentally stimulating them. You can do that by bringing in new debates and controversial opinions to prove them wrong. Geminis think that they are pretty smart (which may be wrong), and so debating with them is pretty fun. You can build nice chemistry by doing this, and eventually, Geminis are going to consider you as a fun indulgence. Doing so allows things to stay interesting, which will be an attractive proposition for the Geminis. Geminis will go wherever their curious mind takes them, so it'd be hard for them not to indulge in a fun and thought-provoking conversation where they are allowed to have the center stage.

Eventually, you can also help Geminis decide between two strong choices/opinions since they may find it really difficult to decide on their own. This will also add another layer to the dynamic of your relationship. You can give your own opinion about the two and then your final verdict for what they should choose. Such small things can also turn into a thought-provoking conversation that can keep the Gemini interested. Always remember to talk about different things as talking about the same thing is eventually going to bore them.

A common issue that people come across when trying to befriend a Gemini is their lack of interest in them, but Geminis might be preoccupied with other tasks as they are also described as a social butterfly. They do not just have a couple of close friends, but a lot of them, so you have to wait your turn and be patient with them. Once the thought of you pops in their mind, they are sure to respond positively. This is a common trait of the Gemini that people need to compromise on, as this is how they are hard-wired. You cannot change it; you can just be patient with it and reap this newly formed relationship's fruits.

Another pointer about befriending a Gemini is that if you want to spend time with them, you have to be ready for many movement activities. Geminis do not like to stay in one place for a very long time and so need a change of scenery every few hours. This is the effect of their trait of getting bored easily. Make sure to suggest any good places that you have in mind when they ask to move away from where you initially are. This way, you can control the situation, which might otherwise lead to someplace you do not find amusing. In this paragraph, the emphasis is on "suggest" as Geminis do not like being told what to do. Make it sound like it is a mutual idea, and hopefully, they will follow suit.

Geminis are pretty intelligent and easy to talk to, but if you are a Gemini, then you can relate to the next few tips that take you through the critical parts of maintaining your friendships. Geminis have a lot going on because of all the traits discussed in the guide, so it is difficult to focus on one relationship at a time. Their innate nature suggests having the excitement of knowing everything and talking to everyone. Knowing everything has its downfalls as you may cause relationships to fall apart by spilling secrets. As Geminis, this is something that is very hard to resist as they have a lot on their mind, and it is wired to communicate and articulate efficiently.

It is hard to keep your free-spirited nature in check, but if you focus on knowing less "secrets," then it will be easier for you to keep relationships. It is difficult to move a relationship forward without knowing intimate secrets about the other person, but it is possible. Many people do so and have been doing so for a while now. It is all about finding the right crowd who recognize your traits and then choose to tell you stuff even after knowing about them.

Another thing about you as a Gemini is that you always think about loving yourself first and may forget about your friends at times. This is because of two reasons. The first is that this is the innate nature of Geminis; they regard themselves as smarter individuals who deserve attention. This makes people feel like Geminis are narcissists, but that can be far from the truth. Perception is key, and in this case, it matters how you come across to others. The other reason why this is true is that you have so many friends that you may often neglect a few at times.

A straightforward tip for this case is to minimize your friend circle, but we all know that will not work for a Gemini. You should start to focus more on other people, especially your friends. This way, even when you are alone, you will be thinking about the small details they told you a few days ago. This way, you can always buildup relationships that you are focusing on rather than letting the good ones fly by. Many will think that they are being ghosted or ignored, and so they'll eventually stop making that effort of becoming your friend. Focusing on the smaller details and reciprocating them will show that you care about them and are making an effort to let them know that you love them.

More about all of these tips are covered in greater detail in the last chapter of this guide. The last chapter focuses on a Gemini's needs from the perspectives of a Gemini and an outsider so that better and prosperous relationships can be created.

Chapter 6: Gemini at Work

Professional career choices are a significant part of any person's life. Deciding what you intend to do for the rest of your life can be alarmingly difficult for anyone. In this book, we will be exploring the possible careers Gemini may adopt. We will be referring back to the strengths and weaknesses discussed earlier to understand the reasons behind a specific career discussed.

The ideal way towards sustenance and survival is to play your strengths. As discussed earlier, Geminis are natural conversationalists and highly adaptive, but they despise boredom and prefer exciting and challenging tasks to monotonous routine work. If you are a Gemini, you will do poorly at a job that you force yourself into. Geminis do what they genuinely want to do. They are known for doing their job with passion and dedication, but only if they enjoy doing it. At the same time, they struggle to make crucial decisions due to their indecisiveness and might be reckless at times. Before we dive deeper into careers suitable for Gemini, think about the possible careers that Geminis thrive at. Also, think of which jobs they might hate. What jobs do the Geminis you know of do? Are your Gemini friends playing to their strengths?

Best Career Options for Gemini

Following their creative and outspoken personality traits, Geminis will make excellent journalists. Excellent speaking skills will help them interact with many people they may come across in their professional work. Interviewing people of influence is likely to come easy to Geminis. Using their fascinating creativity, Geminis can come up with intriguing questions and perspectives. Any journalist is obligated to know the news inside and out. This is where Geminis can use their inquisitive nature and comprehensive researching skills. They can patiently observe a situation from all sorts of point-of-views and build questions and ideas as a product of their research.

Furthermore, journalism is not a boring or stagnant field. In our modern world, there is always something important happening in every country on the globe. So, Gemini journalists are rarely found bored with their work. They embrace the new daily occurrences gladly and work on them religiously. Being articulate with the pen as well as with the tongue is another strength Geminis can benefit from in this line of work. By gathering an expansive range of knowledge, Gemini journalists are more likely to get recognition and accreditation. Since they intuitively hate bias, they are also deemed credible. Anderson Cooper and Ian Fleming are two of the most famous Gemini journalists we know of. If you are a Gemini, it is recommended you try interviewing and researching for a time. Not only might you enjoy it, but you might also be good at it.

A profession similar to that of a journalist is a presenter. Television show hosts, news reporters, and live presenters are all jobs that Gemini are meant to thrive at. These occupations demand interpersonal skills and confidence, and Gemini seems to have those in abundance. Due to their proficient way of communication, many Gemini may even make better presenters than journalists.

Having a sweet spot for conversations, Geminis might end up learning multiple languages if they move to a foreign land. This potentially can make Geminis excellent translators. The ability to research extensively on a language may be tedious for the rest of us, while a Gemini may devotedly learn a new language. Multilingual people often make good ambassadors as well.

Another suitable profession for Geminis is a tour guide or travel vlogger. Gems love traveling around the world, from city to city. They love the freedom of expression as well as the freedom of mobility, and this job just might fulfill that. Being a good tour guide or travel-blogger requires resourcefulness, communication skills, and adaptability. Not surprisingly, Geminis check all those boxes. Being a tour guide is about being clear and kind with your tourists, something Geminis seem to be comfortable with. How can one forget the creativity of a Gemini when it comes to having fun? They will never leave their tourists bored and can be a treat to be with on an adventure. Moreover, Geminis tend to be comfortable in front of the camera and fully express themselves. Their love for exploring can take them to the farthest point from wherever they may stand.

Art is a field that will fully utilize the creativity of a Gemini. In our modern world, art can take various forms, including poetry, writing, videography, painting, and so on, but the commonality between all these is creativity, adaptability, and variety. Geminis tend to excel in these aspects and hence, usually do way better than other people as artists. Geminis with eloquent and melodic voices should lean towards becoming singers. Those who are praised for their witty humor should try their luck as comedians. Those who are quieter than their fellow Geminis should try drawing or painting to show their unfulfilled creativity. Acting is notably common amongst Geminis as it not only gives them a platform to showcase their communication skills but it adds excitement, challenges, and fame to a Geminis life. Did your high school recently host a theatrical play? See how many of those actors were Gemini. If we look at the Hollywood industry, a few of the most reputed names born as Gemini are Morgan Freeman, Kanye West, Paul McCartney, Prince, and Michael Moore.

Geminis also make amazing salespeople. They use their kind, energetic, and sociable personalities to convince potential customers. They see each person as a target and selling the products as their challenge. Being good social learners, they know when to step back and be respectful at the same time. Marketing also requires hectic surveys and research, something Gemini are reasonably good at. Be it getting their voice heard or getting their products sold, Geminis are gifted in both.

Another profession that Gemini can take up is that of a lawyer. A proficient and qualified lawyer can think differently, outside the box. The profession requires a substantial amount of research, learning, and exploring. Many lawyers continue to study even after cementing their industry position, as there is always something new to learn. Looking at this profession on the field, lawyers get bombarded with all kinds of different cases. A more empathetic Gemini lawyer can take on pro bono cases and help those in need. How can we forget the amount of public speaking skills a lawyer requires? A Gemini is sure to have the right attitude to become a lawyer.

The last career option we have for our fellow Gemini is the profession of a teacher. If you look closely, this profession seems to be perfect for a Gemini. Teaching requires the power of persuasive speech. Teachers should be able to communicate difficult topics to their students in the simplest form possible. Alongside that, they are obligated to get each student involved in the class discussion in one way or another.

As discussed earlier, Geminis are naturally outspoken, energetic personalities. They are capable of engaging the masses of students with the least compromise possible. Their active presence enables them to do anything to get the message across. They tend to develop enjoyable ideas and activities to enhance learning and convert a boring and dry class into an interesting one. Like university lectures or seminars and other higher levels, Gemini lecturers will relate to the young adults sitting in front of them. They are more likely to build healthy student-teacher relationships in a small amount of time with their students. The even better drive this profession may give to Geminis is the opportunity to interact with many young minds inside the classroom. Throughout their lives, Geminis hope to continue learning new things. This mindset is necessary for thriving as a teacher, which further strengthens Geminis as one of the best candidates for becoming teachers.

These were the professions that not only put fellow Geminis at an advantage but may also be fulfilling for them as human beings. It is perfectly fine if a Gemini opts for a career not discussed earlier. In the end, the case of choosing careers becomes subjective and depends on what a person truly feels and wants but there are a few professions that are not likely to be compatible with Gemini.

We know that Geminis are interested in an adventurous life. Gemini heavily dislikes any profession that ends up being monotonous in practice. Profitable and professional careers like accountants, bankers, clerks, factory workers, etc. tend to involve complex yet similar procedures every day. Professions that do not include a lot of communication or discussion are more than likely to put a Gemini to sleep instead of extracting rapid productivity from them. They always crave spice in their lives and run away from everyday office jobs. Ask around your Gemini friends who may be an accountant or a banker. Are they wholly content with what they do for a living? Chances are they might hesitantly say "no".

But it does not mean that Gemini will never make good bankers or office clerks. Being a Gemini provides you the ability to adapt quickly. If you are Gemini working at an office and seek excitement every day only to get disappointed, we recommend you be your workplace's life. Greet everyone with that bright smile of yours every day you walk in. Maybe treat your closest colleagues on a Saturday night after getting a proposal accepted. Leave a thank you note for everyone, from your boss to your janitor, to make his or her place as wholesome as you may like. You have the power and energy to uplift a crowd of people. Another tip is to make the best buddies at your workplace. This will, for sure, get you out of bed just to see their sparkling faces. Try decorating your workstation a bit with stickers and post-its if you are allowed.

Apart from the aforementioned career options, it is equally possible that another profession may intrigue you. Being loquacious beings, Gemini should find any career that lets them harness their raw interests. Look for careers that keep you entertained. Geminis adore a profession that allows them to teach and learn simultaneously. Had bad grades in academia? Do not worry. See if becoming a gym instructor or beauty trainer piques your interest. Geminis want a career that is both fun and productive at the same time. So, start by listing what is that you enjoy doing the most. When making career choices, ask yourself a few questions. Will I be consistently challenged while doing this? How will I be able to learn anything new through this job? Generally, try your best to get comfortable with your profession as quickly as you can. Only then can you truly excel in your career.

Compatibility with Your Colleagues

There is no denying that individual motivation, dedication, skill, and persistent hard work lie at the core of a professional's success. But to be able to contribute to a firm, society, organization, or even a small project, excellent teamwork and intelligent leadership are what really define the end product and its success. In this section, we will look at Gemini as potential leaders or bosses, as well as see how compatible they can be with their peers in the workplace.

By now, we know that Geminis are excellent with people. They tend to catch up with what their colleague's mood is, their likes, and dislikes. Their proficient interpersonal skill help keep their team gelled together for the entirety of the project but their weaknesses, like indecisiveness and inconsistency, may limit their progress in the long run. Keeping Gemini's characteristic traits in mind, let us discuss what a Gemini boss would be like.

A typical Gemini boss is likely to be an intelligent, innovative, yet impulsive workplace member. They arrive at work full of energy and tend to charm their workers with the sheer energy they bring. A Gemini will give his heart for the sake of their profession. Their passion for their work mainly fueled the effort and hard work they put in to reach that position in an organization. If a Gemini makes it to the top as a boss, no one doubts his or her commitment to their work line. So, their co-workers find them incredibly charming and inspiring. Looking at a Gemini boss and their loyalty should be enough to motivate the workers and employees around them.

When it comes to actual practical work, Gemini bosses prefer verbal collaborations and constant feedback. They are likely to have early morning meetings and multiple discussions throughout the day. Every worker and employee will have a say in a meeting led by Gemini bosses. During these meetings, it may seem like everyone is the boss because of the amount of attention the Gemini boss gives them. Are you working under a Gemini boss? You are likely to get tired of the number of meetings they may call everyone in for, but these collaborations and conferences keep a Gemini going at work. The exchange of ideas, discussion, critique, and diverse set of insights fill their tank of information, which they need to make decisions. The more information a Gemini boss has, the better chances are of their decisions of being effective and efficient. Apart from sharing and learning insights, Gemini bosses regularly celebrate small successes to keep everyone motivated. The discussions may even conveniently shift from productive work-related meetings to chatty personal conversations. This probably stems from the eternal hate that Geminis have for monotonous working environments.

Geminis believe in teamwork more than individual brilliance but that does not mean that they restrict their workers to the ideas of the masses. Geminis hate being micro-managers and dictating to their employees. They despise the conventional dogmatic style of management at work. Under a Gemini boss, workers tend to have full control over how to go about their tasks, as long as they deliver effectively and in a timely fashion. If anyone wants creative freedom at work, they will thrive working under a Gemini boss. This may be because Geminis themselves crave creative freedom at work. They do not like being strictly instructed on doing their job and continue reflecting the same when they become bosses. Many Gemini bosses may even have a special group of people to deal with less important responsibilities. They may be delegated full or majority of the control over many tasks while retaining their say in final decisions.

One of the biggest strengths of being a Gemini boss is being able to carry the team together for the project's length. Gemini bosses thrive in communication and are also open to ideas and proposals. They want to be continuously updated on any news that may have taken place. Most Gemini bosses have an open-door policy. Just came up with an idea you think will benefit the project? Walk straight into your Gemini boss's office. He will be ready and open to hearing your propositions.

Geminis are able to keep their workers motivated easily. They tend to appreciate small things like regularity and a sense of initiative a worker may show. They celebrate their personal joys to develop their sense of belonging at work. They also encourage their workers to interact with each other as much as they can. They might assign a task to two separate departments to increase productivity and let their workers get to know each other. This is beneficial for a project, especially one that consists of a lot of collaborative tasks. Thanks to the Gemini boss, the overall chemistry between the workers improves, and the project flourishes.

A Gemini boss is very comfortable when it comes to solving the company's urgent problems and overcoming unforeseen hurdles. They can improvise and adjust when it comes to sudden changes in situations. With their diverse knowledge and experience, they are able to figure out a way through excruciating circumstances. A Gemini boss champions anyone when it comes to reacting to emergencies. They are quick to give valuable suggestions and keenly analyze what others have to say. This makes Gemini bosses excellent managers during a crisis. They do not panic under pressure and keep themselves composed while working.

While Gemini bosses may not be strict managers, they are amazing observers. Being committed to their job, they are peerless when it comes to analyzing and keeping track of the activities of those working under them. They are quick to point out and discuss the mistake made by their team workers and calmly communicate and rectify it with the one at fault. While it may be a little embarrassing to be observed and critiqued at work, employees working under Gemini bosses progress and improve comfortably than the rest. If they start looking up to the Gemini boss as a mentor, they will notice significant growth in their professionalism and productivity at work. In short, those working under a Gemini boss are on a shortcut to self-improvement.

One of the best things about the Gemini bosses is that they create a gratifying workplace experience. Geminis themselves prefer fun in parts of their lives, which is reflected when they become bosses. A Gemini boss thrives in work that he enjoys and believes the same to be true for his or her workers. They may occasionally have games night or contests with rewards for the winner. Apart from motivating every member under them, they will individually socialize with them for hours. Furthermore, most Gemini bosses themselves lead very social and extroverted lives. They tend to have a lot of fun, so anyone will want to work for them because it is enjoyable.

But just like any human being, Gemini bosses are likely to struggle in certain ways. They have a few weaknesses that they need to work on to get the best out of themselves and their profession.

Gemini bosses tend to change directions and shift priorities throughout the process. They are flexible in managing these changes. They tend to react quickly to changes, and that may lead to a variety of different decisions in a short time. They may appear to be undisciplined and inconsistent with their workers. While this practice may have the benefit of keeping the workers on their toes, it tends to be annoying and exhausting. Hence, working under a Gemini is often difficult. The workers may not know what to expect every week. If you are someone who prefers the conventional dogmatic methods of working, you are likely to struggle to sync with your Gemini boss. Do you or know someone who works under a Gemini? Notice how frenzied the routine working under them can be. This inconsistency is what may make a Gemini boss less effective as a leader. No matter how much they try to keep everyone on the same page, they might leave people behind in the hustle and bustle. If you are a Gemini boss, you should be extra careful not to overload work on those under you. Try to work on your consistency if you find it hampering the productivity of your workers.

Gemini bosses are always prone to be distracted. They do well at work only when they are devoted and concerned about it. If they fail to keep themselves motivated in a project, they will probably seek that thrill elsewhere. This may lead to sloppy and miscalculated decisions, which can prove to be painful to the workers and the project itself. Procrastination, random trips, and delays in meetings are likely to get a Gemini boss fired by those higher in the hierarchy. To deal with this shortcoming, Gemini bosses should have a personal assistant or an employee whose job is to keep them on track and get rid of any distractions. A good friendship with an equally motivated individual from the workplace can also prevent a Gemini from falling astray. Other than this, Geminis themselves should continue with their jolly ways at work to keep themselves interested and devoted.

We know that Gemini bosses are not the perfect leaders. So, they need an exceptional team and the right environment to lead a project. If you work at an office or firm under a Gemini boss, you can always be sure to have an exciting and thrilling day, but it can also get difficult to deal with them at times. In those situations, the best choice is to go and calmly talk with your Gemini boss. They are good listeners and empathetic people and will tend to any concerns you may have. If we have learned one thing, it is that Gemini bosses and their workers all should be equally driven to work to be compatible with one another.

It is more than likely that Geminis may not end up becoming the boss of any team in their professional careers. In those cases, they may end up and employees and collaborators on a project. To know your compatibility with everyone may be exhausting and almost impossible but we have made it easier for you, as in this section, we look at how compatible Geminis are with other astrological signs at the workplace.

The first compatibility we will check is between Gemini and Aries. Aries are people born between March 20th and April 19th. Usually, Gemini and Aries get along very well. Both tend to have extremely energetic and adventurous personalities. If motivated by the same cause, they are most likely to have common ground and work together but there may be instances where Gemini and Aries might find problems working together in a partnership. When working with an Aries colleague, Gemini should be careful of maintaining their space at professional work. Since both have curious personalities, they are likely to bump into each other's work when working on the same project. When sharing your ideas with an Aries, a Gemini should be careful of presenting only an excerpt of concepts. Having long discussions on a variety of ideas can lead to a lot of wasted time, as Aries might not take things seriously.

Geminis have creative and inquisitive minds, which can help them to come up with brilliant ideas. On the other hand, Aries are energetic people who might do an excellent job in carrying out the plans a Gemini envisions. By complementing each other and rectifying each other's mistakes, Aries and Gemini can form a healthy professional partnership. If you are a Gemini with an exciting business idea, it is in your best interest to partner up with an Aries to get the job done. Profession-wise, Aries and Gemini will work together very well as marketers or salespersons.

People born between April 19th and May 29th belong to the astrological sign called Taurus. When it comes to working with a Taurus, Gemini might feel like dropping out of the partnership instantly. Taurus people are usually industrious, cautious, and pragmatic. They are dogmatic about the way of doing things. On the other hand, Geminis are adventurous and creative people who seek excitement at work. Both seem to have opposite personalities. While a Gemini will prefer multitasking, a Taurus will strictly adhere to their rules of performing one task at a time. Similarly, a Taurus might not welcome the open-mindedness a Gemini may offer. In practicality, it may be very difficult to build and fuel a healthy partnership between Gemini and Taurus at work but by bringing opposing ideas to the table, they can benefit from one another. For example, a Gemini might work on new creative ideas for marketing their product, while a Taurus will manage the hectic day-to-day activities like accounts, orders, finances, etc.

As we discussed earlier, Gemini is a sign of duality. So, having two Geminis on board is equal to having four people on your team. A partnership between two Geminis might lead to a lot of confusion and arguments. Both the Geminis will function as an idea creation machine. You can never run out of ideas with two Geminis in your office, but it is equally likely that both may debate on which, out of the many ideas they come up with, will be the perfect one. To a third person, two Geminis working together might look like two little siblings fighting over the last piece of cake, but these fellow Geminis will thrive under these fanatical conditions. To be able to collaborate effectively, a team of two Geminis will need a supervisor. Loss of excitement at work will mean a fall in the productivity of both the Geminis. If you are a Gemini at a workplace with another Gemini, you can always switch duties rather than starving from boredom.

People born between June 21st and July 22nd are born under the astrological sign of Cancer. If you thought Taurus was the opposite of Gemini, you were slightly off the mark. Cancers are people who prefer security and insurance instead of anything else. They tend to be conservative and introverted in nature when meeting new people. Meeting a Gemini can be an overwhelming experience for a Cancer, especially if the Gemini straight away handles the long-term goals while Cancer focuses on the ideas and other day-to-day activities by themselves. One shortcoming of this partnership will be that both are prone to overlooking small mistakes that can compromise the project's success.

Capricorns are people born between December 21st and January 21st. Capricorns are consistent, regular, sincere, and professional people, especially in their line of work. They are very strict about deadlines and try their best to deliver on time. Furthermore, Capricorns demand respect from their peers. They are quick to react to insults and jokes about them. At the same time, they know how to appreciate others when they see sincere dedication and productivity.

A partnership between a Gemini and Capricorn is unlikely to work out due to the difference in personalities. Being respectful is necessary to work with a Capricorn. Since Gemini tend to be talkative, they are most likely to annoy a Capricorn. A casual joke by Gemini can hamper the partnership but if both the Gemini and the Capricorn understand each other and be considerate, they can pull off tremendous accomplishments together.

People born between January 21st and February 20th fall under the astrological sign of Aquarius. Aquarius is known for its visionaries and thinkers. They believe that sheer will is the most fundamental driving force behind any accomplishment. They are sincerely dedicated to their vision and do not compromise on any obstacle that may interfere. These qualities make the partnership between a Gemini and an Aquarius unstoppable. Both Gemini and Aquarius aspire to achieve a range of things in their lives. While Gemini may lack the motivation to work, Aquarians are the perfect people to refill their tank. This partnership can bring forward a lot of influential ideas. If both Gemini and Aquarius are on the same page, they can achieve incredible success. One shortcoming of this partnership is the lack of practicality and an excess of idealism. Both Aquarius and Gemini tend to float around in a pool of incredible thoughts, but they lack when it comes to meticulous planning and implementation. This may lead to a waste of a lot of hard work. Nevertheless, both Gemini and Aquarius are likely to get along well and accomplish success with mutual optimism. The best collaboration between the two will have the Aquarius sort the long-term projects, while the Gemini deals with the day-to-day activities.

Pisces are people born between February 20th and March 20th. Similar to a Taurus, Pisces are introverted people who like to work silently on creative projects. While Gemini may announce their lives to them, Pisces will still stay reserved and mysterious to their colleagues. This may not be good for the partnership with a Gemini, who will then get bored and demotivated to work with their colleague. Pisces also demand freedom while working. This will not be good news for their Gemini partner because they will be left without someone to discuss or plan with. Overall, the two signs are not compatible to work together at a workplace but both Gemini and Pisces are known to be creative people. If somehow their ideas and imaginations coincide, a partnership between them can work out. With compromise and mutual understanding, they both can be teamed up to carry out a task.

While astrological signs may or may not be compatible together at times, one can always work out a relationship with the other through mutual compromise and understanding. If you are a Gemini, try reaching out to your fellow Taurus and Capricorn colleagues. Sit and talk with them. No relationship is impossible.

In this chapter, we extensively discussed possible careers perfect for fellow Geminis. We also saw how compatible they might be with peers at their workplace, with regard to the astrological sign to which they may belong. This chapter's purpose was to inform you more about yourself and others as members of the workplace. We highly recommend our readers to use the teachings to understand one another and figure out ways to work together.

Chapter 7: What Does the Gemini Need?

Being such a complicated personality, where they often have more than two personas, Geminis can often confuse themselves. As mentioned in the earlier chapters, these obstacles can hinder their experiences as children, at work, and as lovers. Although all the personality traits, be it a Gemini or any other zodiac sign, should be taken as a strength and celebrated, they can often make things difficult when not suppressed or altered according to their situation. For example, if someone is in a long-term relationship, they cannot shy away from commitment because there has to come a time when their relationship's fate will rely on their attitudes towards commitment. Sometimes, people do not realize the impact their characteristics can have on a person or a situation.

This book has covered the attitudes and actions of a Gemini in a workplace, at a social gathering, as a child, and as a lover. We have also discussed the compatibility of the Gemini with other zodiac signs, allowing them to smoothly manage their love life and choose their partners after educating themselves about what they will offer and how they will impact them, but we have yet to discuss how a Gemini can work around their personality's difficult parts. This chapter is designed to do so. Here we will explore various tips that can allow a Gemini to be a better human being by emphasizing traits that can give rise to problems or tension. We will also be looking at this aspect from the perspective of a friend or a loved one. We will explore how they can help a Gemini get around those personality traits and fashion a better situation. This will also inform them of any expectations they should keep in mind during an interaction with a Gemini.

For a Gemini

- Use Your Intelligence

Geminis are very gifted individuals with great intellect. They are equipped to think better than most people and have a higher IQ than most of the people. Being an air sign, they are very quick at thinking and are great learners, but they have no sense of organization despite this gift. Their smart and charming personality can allow them to achieve huge success in their future life, but this is compromised when they procrastinate and do not commit to the long-term. This is where they need to use their intelligence and make their decision strategically. Planning and structuring their future can safeguard them from the unexpected turns and bumps that life has to offer. Their spontaneity and adventurous nature are a defining trait of their personality, but they should only be explored in situations where they do not face a significant trade-off. Securing a well-paying job can offer them opportunities to explore more countries and experience more things. They need to clearly draw a line where this adventurous behavior is acceptable and does not compromise the quality and opportunities of their life.

- Don't Fear Emotions

Geminis have a dual faceted personality, which can make them contradict themselves. They also have an outgoing personality, which allows them to meet people and experience things that someone of another zodiac sign might miss out on. Their easy-going personality will enable them to be a good co-worker and an approachable person, but Gemini does not like emotional connections. This trait might sometimes be appreciated, but it can also make them lose out on friendships and relationships that need a certain sense of emotional reciprocation. Although valuing intellect over emotions is great for arguments, a small ounce of emotions needs to be introduced in relationships and friendship. They need to be emotionally present to appease other people and make them feel like they care. This will allow them to hold on to ties for a long time.

- Don't Be Indecisive

Being a mutable sign, Gemini often questions a decision. One personality suggests that they should do it, while their other personality pushes them away from the decision. This indecisiveness is also birthed from the fear of the repercussions that they might face if they make the wrong choice. Geminis need to let go of this fear and allow their adventurous trait to overtake their fear of eradicating indecisiveness. If a Gemini has a strong instinct favoring one decision over another, they should go for it.

- Keep Your Moodiness in Check

Moody behavior is also a product of the twin personality trait of a Gemini. They might find themselves switching from one decision to another and changing their emotions regularly but do not confuse this with them having any "bi-polar" tendencies; it's just that they can quickly change how they think. This behavior can extend to changing a date plan with a girlfriend at the very last moment, but this behavior is not just limited to changing plans. A Gemini needs to keep other people's emotions in mind when making sudden changes and when experiencing mood swings.

- Keep Your Sarcasm to a Minimum

Geminis are quick and witty individuals with a great sense of humor. This is the reason why they get along with so many people and can be the center of attention wherever they go. Their humor also employs a lot of sarcasm that might be misinterpreted by many people. A Gemini should stay considerate in order not to offend anyone. They can play down their sarcasm in a setting where they realize their sarcasm might not be fully understood. Instead, they can keep the conversation fun and cheery and allow their humor to be comparatively gentle.

- Don't Keep Secrets

Every person has secrets that they are trying hard to hide from people. These things are something that people are not proud of but the decision to tell these secrets or keep them solely relies on the individual. But one has to realize that by letting go of secrets, they are in a way freeing themselves of the fear, restriction, or anxiety that it might be causing. Geminis being very happy and disconnected from emotions, tend to have a lot of secrets. Keeping these secrets can be very emotionally taxing and might consume a lot of their energy. Geminis might be missing out on fully living their lives solely because they are too scared to let go of these secrets. Emotionally opening up to people and sharing your personal secrets with them will allow a Gemini to live life more adventurously and freely than they now are.

- Prepare Before a Meeting

Geminis need an intellectually stimulating conversation to vibe with. So, prepare a witty or funny dialogue that you can start to allow a Gemini to take an interest in you. This will also make you be on the same wavelength as a Gemini. If you do not have anything prepared, do not worry. Just ask the Gemini questions from the conversation they are having. Questions appeal to the curiosity of a Gemini, and they will make you part of their conversation. You can use this tip to get to know a Gemini better and become friends with them.

- Be Acceptable

Gemini is a mutable sign; their double personalities can often make them appear to be inconsistent human beings. As stated before, they can have mood swings and suddenly change plans. Their tendency to say one thing and act on another might frustrate many people, especially those close to them but friends have to accept a Gemini for who they are and look at the positive traits. This dual personality trait also means that Geminis are very adaptable human beings who reform their attitudes to fit in with different people. For example, in a posh setting, they might carefully present themselves while being very cheery and loud in a group of friends.

- Ignore Immature Behavior

Geminis love to be the center of attention and relish making people laugh. Although they are very intellectual people, they can be silly and loud in a social setting, like at parties. Many people might perceive their entertaining gestures as superficial and overly flirtatious. They will actively try to impress people and get a laugh out of them, but those who do not share the same humor might be bothered by it. If a Gemini is failing to suppress their sarcastic humor in such a setting, people who do not like such behavior should try to ignore it. If their actions bother you, then divert your attention to somewhere or something else. Gemini does not intentionally mean to bother or offend people, so try to understand them and not hold this against them.

- They Have Other Friends

Geminis are naturally very extroverted people, and this has been proven and verified through evidence and research. They love making conversations and interacting with humans. They are always on the lookout for change and can get bored easily with relationships and people. This is why you should keep a considerable number of friends and acquaintances and not heavily rely on a Gemini company. You should not feel offended if a Gemini is not answering your calls or replying to your texts because they might be occupied with another adventure. They will come back around when they feel like it is the right time for them.

- Don't Tell Them Your Secrets

Sharing a secret with a Gemini is one of the bad decisions that you might make. Thinking that a Gemini will hold on to your secret until the end of time is a wrong perception that you have. Being very social and interacting with many people, the secret might intentionally or unintentionally slip out of a Gemini. If it is intentional, then it will not have slipped out of malice, but rather as gossip that is too interesting not to hold a conversation about.

These were a few of the things that a friend with a Gemini should be mindful of. The purpose of these tips is to smooth the relationship that you have with a Gemini so that any arguments or misunderstandings can be identified and deterred easily. These tips will allow you to strengthen the bond and understand a Gemini at a much deeper level than anyone else.

Conclusion

We started with the horoscope phenomena and ended on a positive note about how relationships could prosper if people focused on their zodiac signs. As you can now confirm, there is a lot more to the zodiac than people initially suppose. All the inner workings have been communicated in the introduction. Readers must familiarize themselves with the introduction as it can be extrapolated to all zodiac signs on the zodiac wheel. The best chunk of information has been summarized to only the important details in the introduction so as not to compromise readability. Information about ruling planets, houses, cusps, natal charts, and gemstones has all been covered to show the astrologers' inner workings. An immense amount of mathematic application is required on the part of astrologers to make just one prediction. After reading this guide, Geminis can confirm that there is a bit of truth to all of those predictions.

The focus of this guide was on the different profiles that have been discussed in the book. From a human's birth to living out their entire life, all the profiles have been discussed in great detail. An entire chapter has been dedicated to each profile just so all the different perspectives about that profile can be cleared up.

This guide has tried to cover both perspectives that exist around this sign. The first one is about the Geminis themselves, while the second one is about the perspectives of the other signs. This allows the guide to be more complete than any other resource available on a similar topic. This is the ultimate guide to the zodiac sign known as Gemini!

Part 4: Cancer
The Ultimate Guide to an Amazing Zodiac Sign in Astrology

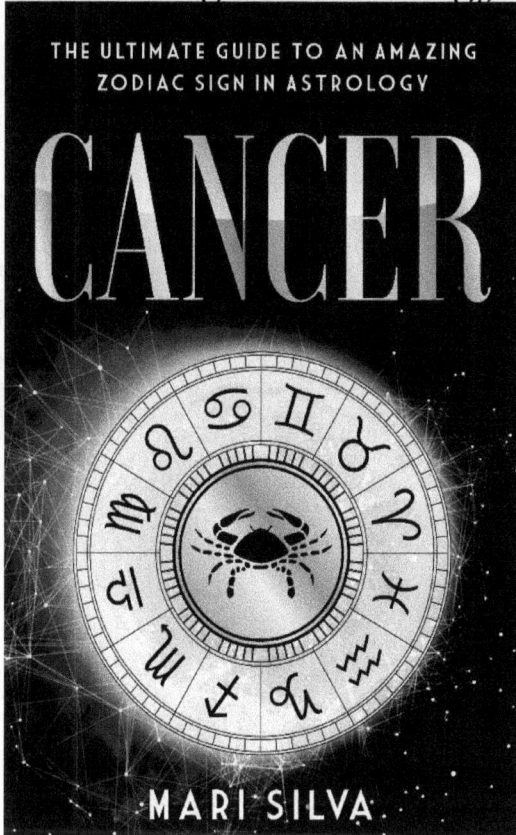

THE ULTIMATE GUIDE TO AN AMAZING
ZODIAC SIGN IN ASTROLOGY

CANCER

MARI SILVA

Introduction

Perhaps you've had an interest in astrology for years, or maybe even decades, but you've never stretched past the generic information in newspapers and online. This ultimate guide walks you through every season and major element in a Cancerian life. Prepare to learn about your sign or the sign of someone you know and understand what it truly means to be a Cancer. You're not just born between June 21st and July 22nd; you're more than a crab that might be a bit sensitive. So many elements play into astrology, and the daily horoscope readings are just the cherry on top of a massive sundae.

The universe is in constant motion, and the ebb and flow of daily life feel a bit of that movement. When looking at astrology, there is a blend of science, belief, and phenomenon that has sparked rampant intrigue across the globe for centuries. Astrology is recovering quite a bit of its former craze, and people are beginning to question or wonder about the extent of the science behind something that seems fun and light-hearted. Astrology can tell you about your personality, emotional process, and even how you might interact with other people. This book is a great way to get an in-depth look into each element of being a Cancer or having a Cancer in your life. Use it as a chance to explore yourself, understand different facets of your personality, play to strengths, and overcome natural weaknesses. Cancers are truly unique people who can face adversity, give sincere sympathy, and call up a strength within themselves that they may not have known to be there at all. Read on to find out more about the Cancer sign.

Chapter 1: A History of the Zodiac and Cancer, the Great Crab

We've lost endless volumes of knowledge through the ages, but one element of daily life that is making a resurgence is the Zodiac. Understanding the heavens, celestial bodies' movements, and the universe's impact on our lives each day is grabbing quite a bit of attention again. The Zodiac goes by many names. It is also known as the western Zodiac, as there is an Eastern Zodiac or the Chinese Zodiac. The twelve signs that make up the western Zodiac, also called houses, referring to both the sun and moon signs. These name fluctuations are relatively common knowledge, but they're the best place to start.

Throughout this text, you'll have the opportunity to learn about the fourth sign, Cancer. We'll refer to the western Zodiac as "the Zodiac" to keep things simple as we dive into the complex nuances of what it means to rule under the moon, how the term "cardinal" affects you or your loved ones, and what is so unique about this water sign.

To get started let's ease into the process by looking at the science and history behind the Zodiac. Astrology is still a science. It looks at the movements of celestial bodies, but it delves into the realm of theoretical and analyzes the impact on human affairs and the natural world. Fortunately, most of the research done on this was started thousands of years ago by a few of the best astrologers and astronomers from our world's ancient civilizations.

How the Zodiac Came to Be

At the beginning of the first millennium, Babylonian astronomers divided the heavens into the ecliptic Zodiacal signs. That sounds complex, but essentially, somewhere between 1,000 and 500 B.C., these astronomers began watching these twelve signs move across the sky in different positions through the seasons. After noticing their patterns, it was made into the Zodiac wheel well-known among people who follow astrology. This gave birth to astrology, but many of the stories and beliefs associated with these signs, and the constellations that are the Zodiac houses, stretch long before Babylon into Grecian and Egyptian studies and fables.

The earliest indicator of using the planets and stars to understand our world arose from those first Babylonian studies. In Ancient Babylon, the astronomers, who at the time were also in charge of astrology, would track the motions of Venus to identify planetary omens of bad times or good fortune to come. But we also know that the Egyptians employed planetary tracking, labeled constellations, and used planetary movements to make agricultural decisions. Babylon receives much of the claim to fame as Egyptians did not extensively document their tracking processes or respond to the movements. The major shift within the western Zodiac that delivered the system that we know and understand today took place in 330 B.C. when Alexander the Great conquered Egypt; Egyptian and Greek astronomers and people could then work together and exchange information they independently found about mathematics and logic. Together, they established strict rules such as the thirty-degree segmentation of the houses. They're also responsible for giving purpose to the Zodiac's circular structure which the Babylonians constructed. Eventually, they aligned their positions in the sky to the seasons and correlated the movements to other stars and planetary changes. At this point, ancient astronomers laid out the foundation of what we know of astrology's scientific and mathematical elements. Many significant developments have come, but the old traditions accumulated over thousands of years remain in place.

It's well worth noting that the Egyptian, Greek, and Babylonian cultures aren't solely responsible for the Zodiac. Hebrew practice, specifically the Hebrew Bible, aligns with many astrology points and is primarily the reason for a few of the most well-known characteristics of people born under specific Zodiac signs. Unlike the other cultures, the Zodiac's Hebrew elements looked explicitly at the quarter-landing signs or signs that directly affected the seasons changing, rather than looking at all twelve signs equally. The Hebrew contribution to the Zodiac mostly revolves around Leo, Taurus, Aquarius, and Scorpio. But just because these teachings don't have a hyper-focus on Cancer doesn't mean that their research, studies, stories, and culture don't impact the sign. Thomas Mann authored a novel called "Joseph and his Brothers" which looked at Israel's twelve tribes, assigning each to a specific characteristic associated with a singular Zodiac sign. The creatures representing Leo, Taurus, Aquarius, and Scorpio all appear as the quarter signs in the Book of Ezekiel. It acknowledges that these are the signs that align with the lunar year of the Zodiac. A bit later in this chapter, we'll evaluate these, and you'll see much more of this throughout the book as well.

As the Zodiac developed and appeared in more cultures worldwide, people began associating personality traits and characteristics with different Zodiac signs. This stretches as far back as Egyptian and Grecian times when they represented celestial figures that came with stories, fables, and even godly worship. The signs emblems, symbols, and roots that we know today came as a result of all of this rich history melding together over the years. One major moment that brought these observations and thousands of years of study together occurred in the 15th and 16th centuries. During the 15th century, astronomers began working with *volvelle*, or movable devices, to work out the sun and moon's positioning with respect to the Zodiac. During the 16th century, those mechanisms were used to give more foundation to each of the signs, and then 16th-century artists began cultivating pictorial representations with this new information.

Sun Signs and Moon Signs

As a quick overview, there are twelve Zodiac signs, also called Sun Signs. Because we know more about the sun's changing situation with the constellations and celestial bodies, Sun Signs are favored, but there are also the moon and rising signs.

The twelve signs of the western Zodiac include Aries, Taurus, Gemini, Cancer, Leo, Virgo, Libra, Scorpio, Sagittarius, Capricorn, Aquarius, and Pisces. Each name of the Zodiac ties to a direct constellation that matches up with the dates of when the sun is in that house. They gained popularity as a result of the astronomer Ptolemy, who tracked the movements of the constellations in conjunction with the sun's position, one of the reasons we refer to them as sun signs.

Cancers are born between June 21st and July 22nd when the sun is in the house of Cancer the Crab. This book is going to dive into exactly how Cancers work and how the world around them might impact them on different levels. Each person presents a unique representation of their sun sign. Still, they're also affected by their moon sign, Rising Sun Sign, and other astrological elements that go beyond the basics of their sun sign. As you read through this, we hope that you can gain a complete understanding of how changes in astrology and the founding principles impact your life or that of a Cancer that you know.

Moon signs are a bit different from sun signs, and they're far more difficult to calculate. With a sun sign, you simply have to know your birthdate, and then you know your Zodiac sign. But the moon signs change constantly; you must know your birth date and the hour of your birth. Sometimes even the difference of a single minute can change your moon sign. Your moon sign depends on calculating your full birth date and the place and time to calculate the moon's position at the moment of your birth. Many quick and easy online calculators do the complex work for you as long as you have the basic information.

So, what do moon signs do? A sun sign is taken as an indicator of personality, and essentially your charge or frequency within the universe. A moon sign plays less into your personality and more into your emotions and management of those emotions. Cancers are notoriously private, but also sensitive. That sensitivity can make them especially in-tune with their moon sign. For a quick example, and we'll have many of these throughout the book, someone born on June 30th of 1995 at nine in the evening in Los Angeles would have the moon sign of Leo. They would have all the personality traits of a Cancer but would process their emotions in a much more "Leo" way and may be more likely to step outside of their shell from time to time. With a Cancer-Leo combination, this person might feel less self-critical or may not care as much about what others think when compared to a Cancer-Cancer combination. But the traits of a moon sign differ slightly from the characteristics of the mirrored sun sign. Those with the moon sign of Cancer would be high attuned to other's emotions and would likely be highly sympathetic, a real-life empath.

The last of the Zodiac signs that deserves a fair amount of attention is the rising sign. This is a form of your sun sign correlating to your outward style or what you project to the world around you. If your sun sign is the energy or vibration that you have in connection with the universe, then the rising sun sign is the vibration or frequency you emit specifically when you're around others.

Calculating a rising sign also requires knowing your place and time of birth. The example we used above of the person born on June 30th would result in a Capricorn ascending sign. That means that Capricorn's sign was rising to the suns position at the time of this person's birth. Again, the rising sign depicts the more social version of their personality. In the example, the person might have a greater sense of outward accountability and responsibility. A person with a Cancer ascending sign might be shy or wary of new people and might seek outright isolation. Cancer-rising people are often inherent introverts or extremely low within the extraversion scale.

How Can Learning About A Sun Sign Impact You?

When science seems so certain, but the authority figures behind it seem unreliable, many people turn back to the tried-and-true astrology approach. A National Science Foundation poll from 2014 indicated that more than half of Millennials believe astrology to be a science.

The foundations of mathematics and logic which drive astrology play a bigger role than other less scientifically-founded astrology elements. But even though less scientific elements of astrology can offer a lot of insight into a person's personality, communication preferences, and daily approaches to life, it's a mixture of fun and science. Take a look at how celestial movements may have affected your birth, childhood, love life, career path, and many other life elements.

Having a spouse, friend, child, sibling, or even co-worker born under the Cancer sign can be quite a mystery. This is, without a doubt, one of the most intriguing signs in the Zodiac, and it offers an allure that draws people into the unknown. People born under the Cancer sign can be strong but sensitive and possessed of all other oxymoronic combinations. If you know someone was born under the Cancer sign, then you've seen these opposing personality traits work together seamlessly to deliver an action-oriented, empathetic, and productive person.

When looking at the history of Cancer and the constellation representing that house, it's clear that there are many strong elements, underlying weaknesses, and essentially human traits. The constellation Cancer, which is Latin for "crab", lies in the northern sky. It is nestled between Leo and Gemini, has a 20° north declination, and has many star clusters but most notably the Beehive. The constellation story goes back to Greek mythology and is occasionally represented by a crawfish or a lobster. The story goes that this is the crab that pinched Heracles while he was fighting the Hydra.

After pinching Heracles, the crab was crushed. Hera, the goddess of women, marriage, and family, was an enemy of Heracles and rewarded the crab for its valiant efforts by placing the crab in the heavens.

For many people, the Zodiac is a bit of fun, but knowing your sign's roots, position, element, and other minute details can help you understand parts of your personality. Knowing in-depth information about Zodiac signs can help one be very insightful into the lives of people born under each sign. The Zodiac history, the heavens' movements, and the stories tied into the constellations are woven throughout the Zodiac and feature heavily in our lives. Is it any wonder that a sign celebrated by Hera represents a mothering nature? Throughout this book, you'll get an in-depth look at the different seasons that a Cancer will go through in life and how you, or your friend, can make the most of their natural strengths. Along with understanding and building upon those natural Cancer strengths, they can learn how to work around the possible downsides as well.

Being a Cancer, or knowing and loving one, is an extraordinary thing. Here you'll learn what Cancers are like on their own, a seldom-approached element of their life. You'll also have the opportunity to learn more about Cancers as children, the careers they thrive in, and how they are affected by the ever-changing presence of the heavens and the surrounding energy.

Chapter 2: Cancer Basics

Everything you need to know about the basics of Cancer in astrology is in this chapter. While much of this information is common knowledge, you'll have the opportunity to assess the information associated with these basic elements that are often glossed over online or even in most horoscope books. What does it mean to be a water sign? You might know you're a cardinal sign, but what is that, and how does it impact your life?

These are the questions we hope to discuss as we review the fundamentals of the Cancer sign within astrology and begin our deep dive into Cancerian lifestyles.

The Fundamentals of Cancer Life

Cancer is the sign of the great Crab, it's the fourth in the Zodiac Circle and is for those exclusively born between June 21st and July 22nd.

An overview of all Cancer fundamentals:

- Born between June 21st and July 22nd
- Ruled by the Moon
- Water element
- Cardinal
- Represents the Chest or Torso

Of course, many other fundamentals come with being a Cancer. It's likely that as Cancer, you have various positive traits associated with the sign, such as a great sense of loyalty, powerful intuition, and empathetic nature. You may also experience the natural drawbacks such as moodiness, pessimism, and being rather suspicious of those around you.

Cancer life always comes back to these core elements. The positive traits, weaknesses, and relationships all root in Cancer's element, ruling planet, quality, and even power colors or crystals.

What a Cardinal Position Means

Even those who follow their horoscope or the Zodiac often neglect their sign's position or quality element. Cancers are in a cardinal position or offer a cardinal quality, which is important not only to the sign's history but also to the two core elements of most Cancerian personalities.

Common personality elements of cardinal signs include:

- Ability to overcome challenges with ease
- Affinity and acumen at the hands-on approach
- Perceived as natural leaders

Within the Zodiac, there are four cardinal signs: Aries, Cancer, Libra, and Capricorn. These are identified as cardinal signs because they are reactive or important, because they mark the turning point of a season. The word itself, cardinal, stems from the Latin word for important, and these signs occur at key times that would have been highly important to ancient civilizations. Although we don't put much thought into changing seasons now, the beginning of the summer solstice stood as a pivotal moment in the year for almost every ancient civilization that contributed to astrology.

The summer solstice takes place on June 20th, with the house Cancer taking it over the following day. On ancient Greek calendars, it was evident that the summer solstice and entering the house of Cancer were important to the culture. The summer solstice began a one-month countdown to the Olympic Games, brought forth the Festival of Cronus, and during this time of change and celebration, the Greek social structure was completely ignored. Everyone from royalty to slaves participated in the celebrations openly. Pagan traditions for the summer solstice were midsummer, and even Native American tribes had solstice celebrations and traditions.

Being a cardinal sign and understanding the many celebrations that occurred at this time of year is important because it explains a lot of the Cancer personality. Cancerians are known to have a wishy-washy nature; they often change their minds, and their emotions tend to ebb and flow with greater variety than non-cardinal signs. Cancers may be wary of change when it's put into motion by others, but when they're in charge, the change is impactful, even though possibly temporary.

Within the four cardinal signs, there is further division. Cancer is seen as the emotional well or the heart of the cardinal signs. Cancer is already emotion-driven as a water sign, and as a cardinal water sign, Cancerians push the limits for feelings and communication.

The Cancer Element – Water

Having twelve houses, each of the astrological signs is attached to an element. Cancer, the crab sign, is attached to the water element. Typically, water signs are emotionally sensitive and generally self-protective, which ties into their sensitive nature. They must be certain of their emotional grounding and make decisions that don't make much sense to others because Cancerians are looking at every possible angle before deciding what to do.

Key traits of water signs:

- Extremely observant
- Intense emotional connection
- Often lost in thought (Cancers tend to get lost in the past)
- Crave inclusion
- Mysterious
- Creative and innovative thinkers

Often, water signs are led toward the arts and useful hobbies that can help others. But why water? Cancer, represented by the Crab, seems quite at home in the water. The earth is habitable because of water, and we engage with water every day through humidity, snow, steam, vapor, and of course, water in its liquid state.

Water signs can lack direction, feel listless, and be lost in decision making. Cancer's cardinal position makes it prime for water-signs advantages while mitigating many of the downsides. Other water signs like Scorpio may tend to lack direction, but Cancers' cardinal position pushes them with considerable momentum. Cancers may change and are indecisive at times, but there is no hesitation in decision-making and no sensation of listlessness when they choose to do something.

Water signs are also known for being in tune with their emotions. Again, their experiences with emotions depend on their position within the Zodiac. As a water element with a cardinal position, Cancers are subject to a lot of emotional change and receptiveness. To offer a comparison to another astrological sign, Pisces is also a water sign, but they're in the mutable. When it comes to the combination of water and the mutable position, Pisces tend to be emotionally static and, rather than receptive, assistive. So Pisces would, at a point, stop listening and rush off to do what they think is best, where Cancers tend to listen to the troubles and offer little advice but rather let the person in need take the lead.

Ruling Planet

Sure, the moon might not necessarily be a planet, but it is vital to the Cancer sign and has a pivotal contribution to astrology. Within astrology, the moon is recognized as the fastest moving element in the universe in terms of relative motion. As a fast-moving planet, the moon is known for its tendency toward change, and it greatly affects each person's unique star chart. Moon astrology is a vital element of overall astrology, and as we mentioned in chapter one, the moon isn't just a planet recognized in astrology. It also comes with an assigned moon sign.

The moon represents all things that we would find within ourselves, such as preferences, dislikes, fears, emotion, and the soul itself. As a sign ruled under the moon, Cancers are known for their peace-loving nature and their ability to understand emotion within themselves and within others.

If you're feeling disappointed with the moon as the ruling planet, we're going to dive directly into the high level of importance that the moon plays within astrology. First, the moon begins its starting point in Cancer, it starts in the fourth house, and it ends in Scorpio. That means that Cancer is the first moon sign, and Scorpio is the last. Second, the moon itself is more likely to experience interactions with asteroids or meteors, given that it lacks an atmosphere. This means that it is far apart from any other celestial entity, with its only close relation being the Sun.

Finally, the Sun and the Moon have more relationships in astrology than most people would imagine. We mentioned that there are Sun Signs and moon signs. We also mentioned that both the Sun and the moon lack an atmosphere; that differentiates them from any other celestial entity. Our final point in the moon's importance as a ruling planet and specifically as Cancer's ruling planet is that the Sun and the moon are not competitors.

The moon is an aide or an assistant to the Sun. Across the endless civilizations, there is a clear divide between light and dark. But it is the moon that brings light into the darkness of night. Many fables and beloved stories recognize that the moon and the Sun are closely tied because the moon itself reflects the light of the Sun and provides that light to disrupt darkness.

With the moon as Cancer's ruling planet, Cancerians are in a uniquely powerful position to disrupt darkness, forge new light, and provide swift change for inner elements of ourselves.

Various Houses

Cancer is within the House of Moods, the fourth house of the Zodiac, and the ruling planet being the moon further enhances that presence of emotions. That is further enhanced by their water element, which ties directly to feeling, and even further by their quality as a cardinal position tying them to change.

Not all signs have this grand buildup of a singular characteristic or core element for their personality. It's pretty rare, which makes Cancerians truly unique. They are within the House of Moods and Emotions, but their planet represents emotional awareness. Their position indicates times of change, and their element is that tied to emotional connection.

Cancers have another affinity, that for the house, family, and home. Cancers will often feel a deep attachment to home or a deep need to create a home of their own. They often surround themselves with the people that they hold dear, whether that's blood relation or otherwise, and create a home environment wherever they land.

Power Colors

Tying back to the moon itself, Cancer's power colors are silver, cream, gray, and white. Not only should you feel a surge of energy and positivity when wearing or donning these colors, but others around you should feel it, too.

Understand the meanings of these colors to get more aligned with your Cancer power colors. Silver largely represents grace and sophistication, while cream or beige represents calm and serenity. These two colors can do well in your living space, as well as your closet.

Cancer Personality Traits

With the Cancer sign, it is easy to see how each sign's element leads into the other. There is a strong overarching sense of emotion, change management, and introspective attention. Being a Cancer ruled under the moon as a cardinal quality and home to the fourth house produce many Cancer personality traits that clearly make sense.

Cancers are often emotional, which is no surprise. But a few of the most famous Cancerians have shown off their emotions in drastically different ways. Elon Musk is a Cancer. Although he works in the Sciences rather than the Arts, it's evident from his passionate speaking and presence that he's largely ruled by emotion. Few can forget the emotional impact evident on Elon Musk's face when his rocket was a success.

The 14th Dalai Lama and Nelson Mandela are both notable Cancerians showing the true depth and complexity of this sign's personality traits. Kind heartedness, love for others, and an emotional connection to others in the world are present in these two outstanding figures.

When exploring the importance of the ruling planet for Cancer being the moon, it was emphasized that the moon's rule is to shed light in the darkness. One of the most astounding traits in the Zodiac falls to Cancer, and it's their innate ability to spark happiness in others even when they themselves are not feeling great. There's a long list of Cancerian actors and entertainers who made careers out of this personality trait. Most notably perhaps is Robin Williams. Would anyone else have made such emotionally charged movies such as "Patch Adams", "What Dreams May Come", "Aladdin", "Jack", or the many others to which he lent his talents?

Other entertainers and comedians that have used their ability to bring happiness and dive deep into their emotions include Patrick Stewart, Dan Aykroyd, John Goodman, Kristen Bell, Nicole Kidman, and Meryl Streep.

Cancerians are often shy and typically need a lot of time alone. Still, they are pulled into the spotlight because of their tendency to be natural leaders and their inclination toward kindness and positivity. Combining these personality traits can turn people into natural leadership roles such as running a household, running a company, or helping people in their life without any official leadership title.

There is a special mention for those born within three days of June 21st or July 22nd, otherwise known as the cusp. While you are still a Cancer and everything you've read here still applies to you, it may be slightly muddled or altered depending on the cusp sign. Typically, those of the Gemini-Cancer cusp have an enhanced version of most of the Cancer personality traits and respond with greater enthusiasm to the Cancer sign's foundational elements. They are often more loyal and more likely to ebb and flow between moderate or extreme emotions. It's almost as if the spring to summer transition heightens the change and celebrational elements of the Cancer sign.

The Cancer-Leo cusp, which spans from July 19th to July 25th, is a different story. While these Cancerians are usually empathetic and in tune with themselves, they're offset by the purest fire sign. When the highly emotional Cancer and the ego-driven Leo meet, you get someone who's confident and empathetic but possibly to the point of being overzealous or even manipulative. Those born on the Cancer-Leo cusp might be more inclined to take active leadership positions, drive change, and insert themselves into causes they care about that require an assertive hand. It's a stark difference from the calm, kind, and sensitive Gemini-Cancer cusp.

It's the culmination of the very foundation of the Cancer sign which resulted in many Cancerian strengths. The personality traits listed here are not outright strengths, but they can lend themselves towards being a positive force or a negative element in a Cancer's life.

Chapter 3: Cancer Strengths

Motivated by deep emotional connection, recharging through intimate time spent alone, and developing family relationships within their inner circle are just a few ways of seeing Cancer people from an outward perspective. But much like a crab, all the good stuff is under the shell, and that outer appearance doesn't prepare anyone for what lies beneath. Cancers are well-known for their strengths and appreciated as many of the most compassionate and strong characters among the Zodiac. These individuals are often sought and kept as lifelong friends because of this combination of strengths.

If you were born under the fourth house, then these strengths may seem like natural parts of your personality. They may not even seem like strengths to you, as many of Cancerians' strengths also lend themselves to weaknesses. Almost all of these strengths are a double-edged sword, but that makes it even easier for a Cancer who understands themselves to play up their strengths often and in doing so lower, if not eliminate, many of the weaknesses they face as parts of their personality.

If you know a Cancer, then these strengths won't surprise you, and it's likely that you've experienced the benefits of many of these strengths frequently. Friends, spouses, and family members of Cancer people often love having them around because of the strengths they bring into everyday situations. Those who know Cancerians should be careful not to take advantage of these personality traits or extort them explicitly for their own benefit. Typically, Cancers aren't aware of their many abilities and what they bring to the table because they're so often concerned with the other people around them. When a Cancer person recognizes that they're only kept around for specific elements of their personality, they tend to recede and feel used. They don't stick around long when it seems like they aren't truly loved, but only appreciated for one part of themselves. Cancers want pure, unconditional love, not to be kept around for someone else's benefit. You'll see through their many strengths that Cancerians can benefit from their own strengths as much as anyone else can, and that they can set healthy boundaries to make sure they're not taken advantage of and that their interactions are mutually enjoyed.

Compassionate and Empathetic

Those born under the Cancer sign are among the most compassionate and empathetic people you'll ever meet. But compassion and empathy are two different strengths that Cancers have. They're combined here because of their similarities and their roots in emotions and feelings.

Compassion, or being compassionate, has a core in suffering and pity. The word "compassion" has a Latin root of *pati*, and that root word means "to suffer". Giving someone compassion means connecting with them in their suffering and relating to their pain. That relation and connection are like lending that person a bit of strength. Essentially, Cancers have the innate ability to say, "You're going through something rough, and I'm here for you. I understand you and know that you're so strong for getting through this." That is compassion. Cancers know that the other person doesn't always need them to jump into action, sometimes they just need to hear a sympathetic acknowledgment of what the sufferer is facing.

Female cancers are more likely to have higher levels of compassion. Male cancers do have compassion, but they may have higher expectations of the other person involved. Male and female Cancers have different nurturing ways, and often, female Cancers offer more sensitivity, whereas male Cancers offer a bit of a push in the right direction. Having compassion, showing condolence, and offering pity all come down to the heart and head sensitivity that Cancers experience as water signs. When it comes to the elements that make up the strength for a Cancerian, it's obvious that this is their most prominent strength no matter their gender, and it can even break down the barriers that cusp babies might feel. Those on the Gemini cusp might have more of this trait than those on the Leo cusp. Gemini, as an air sign, has a lot more in common with this water sign, whereas Leos, as a fire sign, often contradict the very strength that Cancers possess.

Empathy is a different matter; a strength for others, but often a drawback for an untrained Cancerian. Empathy is a skill that Cancers need to learn, even though it's a natural part of their personality. Cancers are natural empaths, but they don't naturally align with this skill from birth; it is something that they have to dedicate time toward developing.

The definition of empathy is the action of understanding and being aware of the feelings of others. This definition expands to include experiences, thoughts, feelings, and emotions of others, either past or present. When discussing empathy as an ability, we're talking about the inherent ability to take understanding those emotions, feelings, and thoughts to a deeper level. Empaths don't just understand; they experience the feelings, emotions, and thoughts as if they were happening to them directly. They feel it as raw and as openly as if they experienced the event or feeling first-hand. As children, these kids have huge feelings that any other sign as a parent may see as overwhelming or outright unmanageable. But Cancerians need to develop this skill as though it were a school subject, psychic ability, or athletic skill. They must engage in empathy practice and be receptive to their abilities as they develop and adapt. When properly prepared, a Cancer could be the go-to counselor in the family, workplace, or among friends. They are often the ones to solve problems and work through people-problems in small groups. Cancerians are aces at cognitive empathy, making them excellent with people even when they're introverted.

Because of these two abilities, Cancer should never lack genuine friends and should always understand complex or advanced emotions far beyond their years. They understand the effect on those who experienced an event first-hand but always offer the compassion to exercise their understanding in accepting the person's experience as unique to them.

These two abilities go back to two distinct elements in this Zodiac sign. First is the connection to the moon and the moon's representation of the soul, emotions, and all things "under the surface". Second is their root in the ocean, where emotions run deep and the desire to connect with others goes even deeper. Even those on the cusps will have powerful elements from these strengths in their daily lives, and these two strengths lend themselves toward a third: listening. These two elements come together to create excellent listeners. On a good day, the sympathetic and emphatic Cancerian can bolster others' confidence and strength, as well as their own. On a bad day, they can use these strengths to manipulate a situation in their favor or, inversely, become overrun with emotion and seclude themselves. But even when alone, or even when using their abilities for their own ends, it's not the worst results of these two strengths. Cancers aren't prone to manipulation and often use it as a last resort when they feel extremely vulnerable, so even at the end of a bad day, this is still a strength for the Cancer.

Ability to Find Happiness

Where many signs see happiness or despair, light or dark, the crab likes to scuttle sideways and walk the fine line between the two. Their ability to approach situations in unexpected and indirect ways often allows them to find happiness where it seems that there's nothing to be found but dissatisfaction.

When J. K. Rowling wrote the famous line, "Happiness can be found even in the darkest of places, if only one remembers to turn on the light," she may as well have been talking about Cancers specifically, and you'd better hope that you have a Cancer around in dark times. Without a doubt, they'll be the ones to find the light switch, strike the match, or pull back the veil to let the light in on the world.

That doesn't mean that Cancer's aren't plagued by bouts of darkness occasionally, but usually, they're at their most despondent when this happens. It's not common for Cancers to go through bouts of deep depression or experience chronic depression, but lower levels of discontentedness are likely seasonal. It isn't any shock when you learn that a Cancer experience Seasonal Anxiety Disorder or simple rounds of the Winter Blues.

Cancers are naturals when it comes to bringing happiness and contentment to the forefront. Suppose you notice that a particular Cancer, perhaps yourself, leans toward a pessimistic disposition. In that case, this could largely be attributed to your moon sign, as you may have congestion in managing your heightened sensitivity to emotions. That congestion or pessimism could be an effect of the self-preservative nature of Cancers. Cancers are more highly attuned to their moon sign than any other astrological sign, and their heart and head sensitivity to emotions often mean that their moon sign can dampen this strength if they don't know how to manage it properly. Understand a bit more about your moon sign and know that each astrological sign's moon-sign effects are different from the sun sign effects. For example, those born under the Cancer moon sign are less likely to accept change and are often deeply rooted in familiarity and security. They may be less likely to see the good in various opportunities or less inclined to look for a solution when they would rather sulk. This is quite different from the Cancer's sun sign inclining them to find light in the darkness. Explore your moon sign more to understand how you can use this strength to the best of your abilities.

This strength ties back to the cardinal element of the sun sign for Cancer. As a cardinal sign, they're leading the changes in life, knowing that there's always something positive or beneficial on the other side of that change. They tend to live in the realm of perceived abundance and often are happy with circumstances and material possessions far below their means.

A special note for Cancer-Leo cusps: this may be a struggle. Balancing the regal and somewhat materialistic Leo tendencies with this Cancer happiness should be easy, but you might occasionally feel torn.

Concerned About Fairness

Cancers are advocates for justice in the way that they see as most fair. They're often the ones to foster a compromise agreement between two or more people that are struggling to agree or work together. This strength comes from the house and element. Not only are Cancers attuned to the mysteries of the ocean, but also its naturally stable ecosystem. There are undercurrents, currents, and natural changes, and Cancerians feel all of that. In their mind, things should work a certain way, within reason. They're looking at compromise and what it would take to create win-win scenarios with little effort. But when it's evident that one person is outright unruly or unfair, then they step in with their claws.

Very Loyal

Their loyalty level is definitely a strength, but it does lead to the negative side-effect of leaving them averse to seeing unsavory elements of their friends or family. Their loyalty is above par, and they substantiate it with honesty, good listening, and genuine concern. These are the people who prove their loyalty by listening and working with their friend, colleague, partner, or family member toward accepting or correcting any situation. To get their loyalty to such a high level, Cancerians often develop solid friendships very early in life and then cultivate new relationships with an air of caution because they know what they may have to put into a relationship.

This strength makes them exceptional friends and employees. They are great when they have a particular person to direct this loyalty towards, which often leads Cancerians into long-term relationships. Even though Cancers enjoy time alone, they often feel at their best when they're in a stable relationship, and they're usually the ones who bring that stability. A person in a relationship with a Cancer needn't have any trust issues, but they might struggle to keep the Cancer happy and match this level of loyalty. Cancers don't expect much more than standard loyalty; they don't expect people to match their loyalty level, although it often brings out the best in other signs as people feel the need to reciprocate what they've received from a Cancer. Cancer's loyalty isn't just a strength for others to benefit from; it often means that they have the best connection with their friends, spouse, and close family members. They can trust the people in their lives without a doubt because of this loyalty, and that loyalty brings out the best qualities in others.

When it comes to lost trust Cancers have different ways of responding to loyalty changes. For example, if faced with a cheating spouse, a woman Cancer might place loyalty over self-preservation. This is part of their personality, they love this person, and they're loyal because of that love so voiding that loyalty wouldn't just be a loss of that person in their life but the love they experience as well. It may be self-protective to stay and reap what they can from the relationship until the trust is so diminished that the loyalty has no foundation and crumbles.

A male Cancer, or a Leo-Cancer cusp (man or woman), would likely end the relationship immediately because their loyalty is more malleable than that of a female Cancerian. Even Gemini-Cancer cusp people may turn away from a relationship if they feel their loyalty was exploited or unappreciated.

Overall, a Cancer's loyalty is a strength because of what it brings into the Cancer's life, not because of what they give to others. They cultivate better friendships and can count on people more reliably than other signs because of their innate loyalty which tends to bring out the best in those around them.

Imaginative

Cancers see unexpected ways of approaching life, whether it's something fun and explorative or something technical. Cancers are many of your top problem-solvers for people issues, and they have a great capacity for creative imagination as well. This can seem like a Cancer is shutting down, because they're usually secluded or enjoying alone- time when they're utilizing their creative side. Cancers don't always want alone time to get away from people, although it might seem that way; they really just want the chance to explore and imagine without distraction.

Cancer men do best when they're left to their own devices and can think about everyday things like driving or shopping. They'll often come up with off-the-wall ideas, although they may not always follow up on them. Cancerian women usually need alone time or dedicated time to imagine and explore creative pursuits. They don't want someone intruding on their thoughts, and they don't want distractions pulling them away from their interests. Cancer-Leo cusps may be more prone to exploring their imaginative gifts in both communication and creative fields with other people around them. They may take on group projects or lead innovative ideas from start to finish.

Cancers typically prefer to work with little supervision and virtually no restrictions, as they don't want anyone putting a damper on their ability to work creatively and spend time imagining. This Cancerian strength lends itself to others in many ways. They often tend to attract others who are creative as well and foster deeply loyal connections with them. Cancerians may also use this strength to build up people going through a rough patch or find creative solutions to people's problems. Overall, these strengths make them one of the most precious signs within the Zodiac, as nearly all of these strengths benefit others as well as themselves. Cancerians aren't prone to an excessive ego, making them extremely selfless and caring. Their deep connection to the moon and the ocean, balanced with the cardinal-sign ability to adapt to change, means that they're constantly thinking about what they can do for those around them in a way that also allows them to protect themselves. It's astounding how one sign can bring so much happiness and clarity to the world.

Chapter 4: Cancer Weaknesses

Let's talk about weaknesses because we all have them, even the Leo's, who tend to believe they're the baddest lions in the universe. Those who are Cancer-Leo cusps may be all too familiar with this over-confident mindset, and the fact that they may even openly believe that they're outright unstoppable, invincible, or completely without fault. Everyone has faults, even Cancer-Leos, and of all the possible faults, Cancerians really have it pretty easy.

Across the board, their weaknesses are similar, except for Cancer-Leo cusps, who feel a few of these faults a little harder than the other Cancers. Often these weaknesses appear in flares or as spurts and then subside quickly. The drawback is that it seems Cancerians are prone to extreme mood swings and that they're inconsistent. That's true sometimes, but Cancers just can't help it. They feel big feelings, and when the mood strikes, they can be needy, too connected to the past, or prone to passive-aggressive outbursts. These usually surprise everyone else around them because, on a typical day, Cancers are kind, understanding, generous, loyal, and enjoy their alone time. So when they suddenly turn on a friend or become angry that they don't receive enough attention, it's quite a shock. These weaknesses can all be overcome, and it's reasonable to expect Cancers to learn how to live with them in a way that helps them build their strengths at the same time.

Unexpected Neediness

Typically, Cancers are the ones who offer emotional support for everyone around them and then retreat into their alone time for a good recharge. But occasionally, they don't retreat, and instead, want all the attention from those they love most. This unexpected change often puts people on edge because they're not sure how to handle a needy Cancer who typically needs space but now they want attention. This is very confusing for everyone else, and when a Cancer is having a bad day, that confusion, as far as they are concerned, is not *their* problem.

Cancers put up a stoic front and act like they're perfectly fine on their own and aren't reliant on anyone. But once you get close to a Cancer, you'll see the softness beneath their shell; it's clear that Cancers are high-maintenance. They're the kid that's too cool for school but really just needs a good hug and someone to show them that they don't need to present such a hard face. This weakness often comes from being overloaded or putting too much of themselves into others. Their natural inclination towards sympathy, empathy, and the need to make sure things are fair can leave them too drained to recharge on their own. They want someone to swoop in and offer comfort. Unfortunately, when they're in these moods, they're also a real Negative Nancy, which generally drives people away and worsens this mood.

So what can people, and specifically Cancers, do to handle this?

How to Overcome Neediness

Cancers can learn to manage their neediness independently, but perhaps the best approach is to have a regular regimen to offset this weakness and drive it into the dark. The way to handle this weakness is by scheduling and planning various things that will deter neediness by ensuring that the Cancer gets the attention they need from others and that they allow themselves to have alone-time.

Try the following to deter this weakness and make sure you don't unexpectedly get too needy or turn into a Negative Nancy:

- Have a weekly appointment, event, or phone call with people who can provide you with undivided attention.

- Dance and get moving to boost those feel-good hormones.

- Meditate to have time alone dedicated to processing the overwhelming feelings that you might have bottled up throughout the day.

- Watch or listen to comedy often; everyone needs to lighten up a little, and for Cancers, this should be a prescribed practice.

- Find a fun way to spend one-on-one time with another person.

Let's look at two Cancerians to see how they manage these. One male Cancer listens to a comedy talk radio while driving to and from work, or in the morning on his days off. It keeps his mood up, but also gives him something to discuss with a close friend who loves talk radio. He also has a scheduled time that he meets with his brother and a shared friend. They sit together every Friday night, sometimes at a brewery or sometimes just over pizza at one of their houses, talking and sharing until the early morning hours. It's all the attention he needs and gets him through the rest of the week as a low-maintenance Cancer.

The other Cancer is a Cancer-Leo cusp female. She's exceptionally needy, and she knows it, but it's not something she's proud of, so she puts up a front and spends a lot of time alone until finally, she snaps. Usually, she snaps once every month, or every other month if she's really doing well. But she's found that meditation can help deter the solar flares of neediness, and what helps even more is dancing. Doing it around other people helps her get attention while bonding through movement. She attends a Zumba class or does a few dance videos with a friend at home to spend time around others in a positive way. But sometimes she just needs to tell a close friend that she wants a little more one-on-one time.

Ruminating on the Past

Cancers will sit and hold on to the past. Because of their sensitivity, they'll forgive, or they say they do, but they never forget. A scar from the past is always an open wound unless they invest in recovering and re-stabilizing that relationship. This particular weakness is a sneaky one because Cancers can often benefit from spending time evaluating the past. Cancerians are highly capable of looking at what happened in the past and the changes that are happening in the present and using that information to produce a more favorable result in whatever they're doing. This goes wrong when they get into a negative spiral, which Cancers are prone to do.

Cancers can usually shed light and happiness onto situations that seem dark or foreboding to others. They're not so good at doing that for themselves. When a Cancer gets into a negative thought cycle, they can spend a lot of time looking at what they've done wrong and what situations have affected their life negatively. It's really up to them to turn this around and to pull themselves out of this negativity, but that is hard for them to do.

But why does this happen? Often ruminating on the past is a result of their ruling planet, the symbol, and their mode. The keyword that embodies a Cancer is "feeling" and that is because their ruling planet, the Moon, is responsible for emotional awareness and attunement with the soul.

Additionally, the Cancer symbol – a crab – is important because crabs molt, and in doing so they retreat into comfort often found in the past. They will also spend a lot of time holding onto key elements from the past that won't be present when developing or finding a new shell.

Finally, being a cardinal sign means that Cancers are exceptionally prone to change, and with every change comes an evaluation of past events. It is absolutely necessary for a Cancer to evaluate the past and use it to guide them into the future. Unfortunately, there is always the hazard of finding negativity in the past, and that can dramatically influence a Cancer's current mood and outlook. It is a significant weakness, but a necessary one.

How to Overcome Ruminating

One of the key factors that contribute to this weakness or bringing this weakness out is planetary movement. Typically, Cancers have a lot of control over how they deal with the past, and their openness to change allows them to move easily into the future. But certain planetary movements such as Mercury or Venus in retrograde can bring greater attention to past events that have negatively affected Cancer.

One way to work around this is to be aware of planetary movements and prepare yourself for how they will probably affect you. For example, when Venus moves into the house of Cancer, there's likely going to be an emphasis on your past romantic relationships. You might find that when Venus is in the house of Cancer, you tend to sit and think about where past loves to have gone wrong. But if you know that this is going to happen, you can embrace it and frame this in a way that's going to produce a positive result. Instead of thinking about what has gone wrong, Venus entering Cancer is the opportunity to evaluate what you took from those relationships. Even when Cancer has had an extremely negative relationship in the past, they can evaluate how they came out of that relationship as a stronger person. You can do this with each house and develop a better understanding of how a certain planet in the house of Cancer, a planet in retrograde, or part of an eclipse can impact your awareness and feelings about the past.

So, the first advice is to be aware of your birth chart and how different houses and planets impact your view of the past. The second piece of advice in handling this weakness is to document and give validity to those feelings. As a Cancer, you should already know that emotions and feelings are as real as the person who's experiencing them. Validating those feelings or acknowledging them as real gives them substantiation and allows the Cancer feeling them to move forward.

You can document and give validity to your feelings about the past by journaling, perhaps using a Voice Journal. Not everyone is comfortable putting their thoughts to paper or putting their memories down in a catalog format. Cancers can simply grab their phone or computer, open voice memos, and then speak openly. It's important to note that this is a type of emotional dumping ground. There shouldn't be any filtering or evaluation in this first part. After all the feelings are out, Cancer can then evaluate the relief of that process how they felt when they were able to get out those emotions and speak them into the universe.

Moodiness and Passive-Aggressive Nature

As a direct result of hiding their feelings, Cancers are prone to letting their feelings pile up, and then they get moody. Unfortunately, they often lash out at the people they love most, even for small problems. They can be great for months, but then they hit a point where a sink full of dishes or a minor frustration such as traffic can set them off.

Moodiness and passive aggression are possibly the biggest weakness for Cancers because this is an almost daily issue, and it largely impacts those that they're closest to. It's likely that their spouse and family members are going to be receiving the brunt of sudden mood changes and passive aggression. Don't be surprised, if you're close to a Cancer, to find snarky post-it notes or receive underhanded text messages. This can come about because of household chores, broken promises, or even things that were said months ago.

The moodiness that Cancers experience is often a result of the surrounding people. This is a downside of being an empath, someone so open to the surrounding emotions. Their passive-aggressiveness is often the Cancers trying to self-protect by not putting their emotions on their sleeve, but still addressing the underlying element of their dissatisfaction.

How to Overcome Passive Aggressive Tendencies

You shouldn't expect Cancers to make much progress in handling their moodiness or refraining from occasionally lashing out through a passive-aggressive attack. This is just a version of the-scorpion-and-the-frog syndrome; it's simply in Cancer's nature to be receptive to emotions, and that naturally produces moodiness. In a turbulent time of their life, particularly during their teenage years, there may be no hope for escaping this moodiness. Cancers need to understand how to accept and process emotions and not be overwhelmed by others. As they learn to do this, they will need time to self-reflect.

There is an opportunity for those who are close to Cancers to help. They might help by reducing how much personal expectation they put on their Cancer friend or family member. If you are a friend or spouse or family member of a Cancer, then be sure to begin your conversations with a clear outline of your expectations.

Another way that people can help Cancers avoid passive-aggressive outbursts is to acknowledge any issue on the table. Asking a Cancer what's wrong will not get you anywhere. They will probably say "nothing" and then storm off; but sitting down with them and letting them know that this is coming from a place of genuine concern can result in the conversation going much differently. Suppose you comment to a Cancer that they haven't been themselves lately, and you'd like to know why; you can start easing into the issues at hand. Make sure that you keep the conversation focused on feelings because that's where Cancers work best. Put the discussion in their hands and let them lead the way. Try asking how they've been feeling lately, or why it is that they've been acting so differently.

If you're a Cancer and would like to take a serious role in reeling in your passive-aggressive tendencies, then consider having at least one consistent creative outlet for your frustrations. Many people report a lot of success with journaling, but some people have trouble remembering to do this daily. They find themselves only journaling during either exceptionally positive or exceptionally negative moods. The idea of reeling in your moodiness means that you need to evaluate your emotional state consistently and how it may be affecting others. So if you can't journal consistently, then consider an alternative.

A few do sketching for a set amount of time each day or take a photo every day. Even just going for a five-or-ten-minute walk once a day can be your creative outlet. Think about it this way; if you take the opportunity to explore your emotions while taking time to yourself, then you won't take your frustrations out on those closest to you.

There are a thousand-and-one ways to accomplish this, and you can certainly find something that you enjoy doing every day that could give you more control over your emotions.

Ultimately, each one of these Cancerian weaknesses contributes to the whole of a Cancer's personality. Those Cancer-born are going to be far more in tune with their emotions, and have a greater understanding of other's feelings, too. You can see how these are all a natural result of the Cancerians' openness to everyone else's emotions while having to process their own. If anything, Cancers are often overwhelmed, although they keep that information to themselves. If you are a Cancer, then know you need to take time to process everything you've experienced during the day, including other people's emotions. Unless you take time for yourself to recharge, these weaknesses can easily rule over your life. Whereas taking a few steps to take care of yourself, you'll find that you're using your strengths more often than these weaknesses. If you know a Cancerian or are close to a Cancer, then be sure that you communicate clearly and don't just expect them to listen. Initiate conversations that allow Cancer to explain their feelings and what they are going through, too. Keep in mind that Cancers tend to worry, and they may spend more time worrying over falling to these weaknesses than perhaps they should.

Chapter 5: Cancer and Planetary Movements

Planetary movements affect everyone, but they impact each sign differently. Understanding planetary movements and the objects within the universe is leaning more about science and astrology. This was the foundation of astrology, and it still largely affects how we interact with the world around us and how we feel within ourselves.

All planetary movements are taken from the earth's perspective, i.e., how they interact with the Earth's position in the universe. Each planet symbolizes different life elements or inner personality traits, but outside of the primary planets there are also special points and asteroids, often called luminaries. All of these can impact our lives directly or impact the people around us and indirectly affect our day-to-day happenings. Here are a few of the ways that planetary and luminary movements directly impact Cancerians and how to understand and accommodate the effects of these changes.

Planets and Their Relation to Cancer

Each planet represents different aspects of life, and they impact signs differently as well. There are two factors in the resulting effect; the first is that the planet enters a specific house. The second is that the person may have different experiences with that planet being in that house, as a result of their sun sign. Let's look at the relationships between your sun sign and the planetary movements in the heavens.

Mercury

Mercury in mythology is the messenger of the Gods, and so, Mercury is the planet of communication. Mercury represents not only communication but also language, intelligence, mind, and the ability to reason. Mercury takes three to four weeks to transition between signs, and retrogrades for about three weeks three or four times per year; there are a few unfortunate signs that feel the full effects of a Mercury retrograde more than the others.

Cancers often have problems with Mercury because Mercury is an unemotional planet. That lack of emotion goes directly against the core of a Cancerian personality.

For those born with Mercury in their star chart, they'll likely come across as more emotional or sensitive than they are. Mercury, however, increases the external awareness of the internal workings of a Cancer-born person.

When Mercury enters the fourth house, the house of Cancer, things get a little dicey. When Mercury is in your house, it can seem like you're overwhelmed with ideas about the past, politics, psychology, and creative pursuits. While Mercury is in your house, your emotional dissonance will often mean that you don't have the energy or clarity of thought to take action on any of these ideas.

Venus

Venus, goddess of love, ruler of Libra and Taurus, represents both love and money. People often oversimplify Venus's impact. Venus takes between four and five weeks to transition between signs. The planet goes into retrograde once every eighteen months, and it does so for about forty days, which means that it's likely to impact two signs rather than one.

This planet symbolizes the ideas of beauty, social interaction, and pleasure. For Cancers, their attachment to art, social interactions, and emotion make Venus an important planet. Venus in Cancer often provides a high level of security in relationships. Cancer's born with Venus in a prominent point in their birth chart may have underdeveloped egos, be exceptionally picky or moody in finding love, and become cold or detached as a method of self-protection. Venus entering the fourth house often means that Cancers are at the top of their game in creative endeavors and seek out social events during this time.

Mars

Representing the ancient god of war, Mars rules over Aries and transitions between signs every six or seven weeks. Mars often stirs sexual desires, competitive natures, passion, and aggression. People often say if you're going to do something big, then wait until Mars is in place. Essentially, Mars stirs our animalistic natures, which can go extremely well or absolutely terribly.

Those with Mars in Cancer on their natal chart are defensive in almost every aspect of their life and can become extremely manipulative with other's emotions. They spend extraordinary amounts of time worrying and dwelling in the past.

When Mars enters Cancer, Cancerians become extremely protective of those around them. They fear the animalistic sides that come out in people, and when it involves the house or family, they worry that people will ruin relationships or family connections. This time is when Cancers are most prone to leadership and a bit of bossiness.

Jupiter

Ruler of gods, do we need to say more? Why is Jupiter pushed to the side so often? Well, perhaps because Jupiter spends about twelve months, sometimes thirteen, in each house; it isn't often that you're directly affected, although you're always indirectly affected. In 2020, Jupiter will begin to move into Aquarius, so there are a few more years before Jupiter enters Cancer.

Jupiter represents growth, optimism, the lifestyle of abundance, and luck. Sagittarians enjoy that luck of Jupiter on a daily basis.

When Jupiter is present in the ascending position on a Cancerian's natal chart, it can help that person better manage their money and have good fortune. When it's descending in their chart, it can push them to actualize goals more often and strive for security, which may or may not come easily.

When Jupiter enters the fourth house, it places a high volume of rewards in family matters and personal happiness. People are easier to appease at home, there are fewer arguments, and people easily make warm connections.

Saturn

Ruler over Capricorn and symbolized by the Greek titan Cronus, the Father of Zeus, Saturn represents limitations and restriction. Saturn takes two or three years to transition between signs. Generally speaking, Saturn represents law, discipline, responsibility, and obligation, which all tie back to restrictions and limitations.

Saturn in the fourth house often makes everyday fun feel like a chore and chores feel like torture. Cancerians are emotion-driven, and they enjoy the freedom given by their cardinal mode and water element. Saturn takes a long time to transition houses; this doesn't happen often, but it'll last for a while when it does.

Uranus

Uranus takes seven years to transition and represents unpredictable change, eccentric appeal, rebellion, and revolution. Uranus is the god of the sky and rules over Aquarius. This house celebrates originality and scoffs at tradition. Uranus hasn't been in Cancer since 1956, but eventually it will come around again. When that happens, expect big changes in how we all understand our emotions and connect with those we love.

Now, Uranus is probably in one of your houses on your natal chart, and what you can expect is to have quite a bit of instability in that house. For example, if Uranus was in the tenth house, which traditionally rules over career, you might find that you jump from job to job, have no distinct career ambitions, and may purposefully dive into careers that seem outside of your personality.

Neptune

Ruler over Pisces and symbolizing intuition, imagination, delusions, and dreams, Neptune takes between ten and twelve years to move between signs. It's also the planet of mercy and compassion. But those with a strong Neptune presence in their star chart may also be prone to addiction, deceit, and trickery.

Pluto

Pluto takes at least twelve years to move between signs and sometimes up to fifteen years. It represents rebirth, transformation, power, and death. This planet rules over Scorpio and corresponds to Hades, the ruler of the underworld.

Pluto left Cancer most recently in 1939 and won't re-enter it any time soon. Cancers might evaluate their natal chart to identify where Pluto might affect them, and they should expect to experience fears, impulses, and big changes in that house over the course of their life.

Sun

The sun is the representation of personality, understanding of self, and ego, and is the giver of life. It influences all signs within the Zodiac in terms of people understanding themselves and connecting with their choices. It's the foundation of the sun signs and rules over Leo, who are not likely to let others forget that they're the center of the universe. It takes one month to transition between signs.

To say that the sun is in a house means that there's a special focus on that force within people's personalities. Cancerians will probably feel the strongest effects when the sun is in Cancer, and they'll tend to focus more on family and happiness.

One element that the sun provides in astrology is the idea of learning within one's self. Your sun sign is your astrological attunement; we look to the sun for answers, and those born in any given sun sign will often seek out answers to issues relating to their sun sign. Cancers will find themselves constantly learning about emotions and feelings. Cancerians have a natural drive toward curiosity about inner feelings and the emotions which drive themselves and those around them.

Mercury in Retrograde

Mercury in retrograde is one of the biggest events that happen on a regular basis when it comes to planetary movement. Mercury will go into retrograde three or four times per year and directly impact communication, which spells trouble for many people. Retrograde is when a planet is moving away from Earth, as happens when the planet laps the Earth as they are orbiting the Sun. Because Mercury completes its orbit in eighty-eight days, it is in retrograde (relative to Earth) three or four times throughout the year, and each retrograde lasts for about three weeks.

Communication

When Cancerians experience Mercury in retrograde, they really tune in to their emotions, because they are under the sign that is affected most by that particular retrograde. Mercury is not defined as masculine or feminine, but instead shape-shifts and morphs to adopt the house's characteristics. When Mercury retrograded within Cancer in 2020, it was an emotionally turbulent time for most people, but exceptionally for Cancerians, who found that they had trouble communicating with those they loved most. It affected communication and family.

But if Mercury were to retrograde in Venus, the communication troubles might only impact relationships or, specifically, new relationships. When Mercury retrogrades and impacts a house or a sign that is largely associated with tradition and stability, there's the opportunity for a positive impact. Whereas when Mercury retrogrades in an unstable or flighty sign, there are greater chances of bad news. For example, if Mercury were to retrograde in Uranus, which is largely known for unpredictable change, then you might expect every possible thing in your day-to-day life to go wrong.

No matter where Mercury is when it enters its retrograde, Cancerians should always expect an emotional overload. This overload occurs because of how many people around them feel the retrograde impact while they're also handling this struggle.

Mercury is in retrograde; a Cancer will openly be more emotional, more sensitive, and likely to lash out at those around them. They will have an uncharacteristically short temper and not have patience when it comes to communicating clearly.

Solar Eclipses

Solar eclipses are a huge deal for everyone in the Zodiac, and it doesn't matter which house the eclipse happens in, nor do the Sun and Moon signs present during the eclipse. Solar eclipses are so significant because of their rarity, and they will always affect Cancer- born people because of the presence of the moon during the eclipse.

Solar eclipses happen at the same degree within the same house every nineteen years. Because a solar eclipse took place in 2020 in Cancer, there won't be another Cancerian solar eclipse for 19 years. But every solar eclipse that takes place between now and then will still impact Cancers because, without the moon, there is no such thing as a solar eclipse.

In a nutshell, a solar eclipse is a "moon sandwich." The Moon takes a special place between the Earth and the Sun, and when it comes to astrology, that's exactly what's happening. The moon and everything it represents is eclipsing the Sun and everything it represents. Emotions and feelings take precedence over ego and self during these times.

The Moon's Phases for Cancer

Cancerians have a special issue to manage when it comes to planetary movement. They must consider that the Moon moves through the houses and that the fourth house, their house, is receptive to the effects of different planets. But they must also consider the phases of the Moon.

In astrology, the moon represents the unconscious mind, and Cancers are inherently more intuitive and connected to other people. The moon has two particular phases that directly impact Cancerians that don't impact other signs.

The moon cannot retrograde, but it can become full or new. A new moon and a full moon are excellent times for Cancers to balance home and work. It allows them to sustain a higher security and stability level than what is normally available during a waxing or waning moon.

Key points in the year involve the new moon occurring in Cancer, which happens from the end of June to the beginning of July. Then there are times when the full moon is in Cancer, which only happens from the end of December to the beginning of January. But throughout the year, as the moon waxes and wanes, it impacts Cancerians regularly.

Ongoing Planetary Tracking

Throughout this chapter, we repeatedly mentioned how planets move, and we've also mentioned a star chart or a natal chart. There are many systems online which generate a complete natal chart based on your birth information and birth location. Although you can always meet with a professional astrologist to have a complete star chart constructed for you personally, these are fairly accurate.

The star chart is your starting point and can provide a lot of insight into your personality, which goes beyond your sun and moon signs. Each planet has its own sign. Depending upon which house they were in during your birth, they will have great or little effect on you. For example, you may have been born in Cancer, you might have even been born with a Cancer moon sign as well, but if you were born with Mars in Virgo, then you may be more practical and logical than other Cancers. You might find that you naturally create systems, especially for managing the home and managing your career. That doesn't mean that you are less Cancerian, it is just another facet of your personality. It doesn't disconnect you from the water element or your emotional connection to those around you.

Now, as the planets and luminaries move throughout the heavens, those will also impact you to a certain degree. Unless you want to work closely with a professional astrologist, it's best to check planetary movement regularly through an online astrological map. These maps typically update daily and show you which house the Moon is in, which house your moon sign is in, and other planetary movement elements that might impact you, such as Mercury in retrograde. Because Cancerians are so in tune with the world around them and others' emotions, they can often benefit more than others when it comes to ongoing planetary tracking. Cancer-born people are extremely receptive to those around them, so a nearby Aquarius or Taurus having something impactful in their star chart could affect the Cancers in their life. Be aware of and receptive to planetary tracking.

Chapter 6: The Cancerian Child

Eventually, everyone spends time thinking about or reflecting on their childhood. They might do this well into adulthood or even start the evaluation process as a teen. Cancers often experience their best qualities in their most heightened state as children. Cancerian children can be a pleasure to raise, but they can be extremely emotional and flip from one emotion to another in a matter of seconds. It's not simply because they're an emotion-driven sign.

These mood fluctuations happen because Cancer children are very receptive to the changes in planetary positions and changes within the universe. When a planet goes into retrograde or into a new house, Cancerian children will often feel the response to that before any other sign, at any other age.

As a quick overview, a Cancer baby or child is sympathetic and intuitive, but they require a lot of extra attention. Cancer children are often very demanding until they hit an age where they begin to explore their creative and imaginative side. As Cancer children begin to understand and grab hold of their imagination, they become very independent.

Understanding Yourself as a Child

What were you like as a child? Well, if you were born under the Cancer sign, then you were probably prone to be a bit stubborn, throw the occasional tantrum, and as an older child leading into your preteen years, probably spent quite a bit of time entertaining yourself. Of course, things like the first order, the signs of your parents, and your siblings' signs can all play a role in how Cancer children grow and develop.

What Cancer children can repeatedly deliver into any family unit is a spark of light. It goes right back to the moon being the only entity in the universe that can reflect the light of the sun. Cancer children may experience slumps or feel like they're in a rut, but they are often very concerned about keeping others happy. You may have sacrificed quite a bit as a child for the benefit of others, even for keeping adults in your life happy. This is often particularly true of firstborns in the family or children that have a large age gap over their younger siblings. Firstborn Cancers, both male and female, are often prone to developing their leadership skills earlier in life and will probably seek out leadership roles in their adult career.

Cancers that are middle children are more likely to be a bit sulky. Whereas middle children are often known for their outbursts, Cancers are more withdrawn and shyer. It's likely that they'll actively seek out love rather than attention, and as children, they'll quickly cultivate a tight-knit friend group that they'll keep for a long stretch of time.

I can see when Cancers are the baby of the family. They are that free kindred spirit. They might seem reserved, but they're certainly not as shy as other Cancer children. These children will often develop deep and intimate relationships with your family members, and they're definitely the type of children to see their older siblings as heroes.

It's likely that regardless of your birth order, you had very nurturing qualities as a child. This is seen in Cancers that have had a very hard childhood as well as Cancers that have had a really easy childhood.

They generally enjoy time alone but really want to spread that love and affection to the people around them. Sometimes Cancer children do this to their own detriment, where they may be giving more love than they're receiving, or they may find themselves constantly craving the attention of the person in the family who shows the least interest in them. Cancer children can have trouble building self-confidence and trying new things. It can initially seem like a setback, but many Cancerians blossom during the later teenage years.

What Cancer Children Need

So, what do Cancer children really need to thrive? Regardless of the parent's sign, there are a few things that parents of Cancer children should do to address the Cancerian needs specifically. First, they need to make sure that they're giving enough attention to this child. Even if you received a ton of attention as a child, you might have had that constant want for more. Children that are born to the fourth house are often under this insatiable appetite for attention and praise.

It can get to the point where Cancer children just want to sit next to somebody or watch TV together. They don't necessarily need a lot of one-on-one, hands-on time but they need a lot of quiet time together.

As Cancerian children develop, they need a bit of space. Their privacy becomes very important to them, especially between the ages of five to nine. As Cancers go through childhood, they go through more of an emotional journey than other children. While they certainly need mental and physical nourishment as well as family time, there are emotions that they are just going to have to learn how to process on their own. For many children, this emotional journey as a Cancer can seem really taxing. You might notice that they often nap or turn to sedentary hobbies such as watching TV rather than sports.

If you're a Cancer, you might remember being told constantly that you needed to go outside, that you needed to be spending more time with friends, or that you need to play with siblings. Although it's frustrating hearing these things as a child, that is exactly what I call childhood. A parent is going to help pull them out of their shell so they can become comfortable in trying new things on their own. It can also help Cancer children develop social skills early in childhood where they might otherwise stagnate. Catholic children are well known for their ability to make it in life, and when they make a friend, it's often lifelong. But they get into a pattern of, once they make one or two good friends, not socializing outside of that immediate circle.

In short, Cancer children need nourishment and encouragement. Parents of Cancer children should focus on helping them develop skills that can offset certain Cancer weaknesses such as moodiness and the inclination to be alone. They should also put direct effort into providing the attention needed to nurture a Cancer and the space they need to digest the day or particularly troublesome events. As a result of Cancer's empathetic abilities and emotional receptiveness, it's possible that even a family disagreement could result in the Cancer child needing time alone after a bit of cuddling or special attention.

Parenting a Cancerian

So many people wonder how exactly they can parent a Cancerian child when they're so emotional and needy. They're emotional and intense, and often parents feel lost or as though they can't get anything right.

As infants, you might feel completely drained because they constantly need to have a good cuddle. These children may be impossible to put down. After you get through that first hard year of infancy, you can see the Cancer child flourish, and parents of a Cancer will need to pivot. Parents of Cancers need to be authoritative from a distance. Their child needs a physical connection with their parents, but they may demand too much or use their needs to evade discipline.

Here's an example of a typical Cancer child interaction:

The child picks up an item they shouldn't have.

Mom: Put that down right now.

The child puts the item down.

Mom: Thank you.

The child picks up the item again.

Mom: Put that down.

Child: But mom...

Mom: Put it down, or timeout.

Child: Mom, please.

Mom takes away the item.

The child doesn't cry but instead hugs the parent. It's a form of manipulation that children use unintentionally. But this is a prevalent technique used by Cancer children. When other children would get mad, Cancer children become apologetic or even act as though they're experiencing shame for not complying or not appeasing the authority figure. That is why parents need to be authoritative from a distance. Clearly, parents need to set boundaries and take actions for safety, such as taking away potentially harmful items or having rules in place like not walking in the street. But how do you enforce these when your child only wants more attention and love after being scolded? Parents for Cancers have to be strong and lead communication. When you're calm, and the child has had an opportunity to process the interaction without getting immediate "forgiveness," then you can both talk. Because Cancers are so empathetic and receptive, Cancer children can often have deeper discussions than most children. When parenting a Cancer, don't shy away from emotionally intense discussions or explaining your feelings; it can help the child overcome stubbornness and understand their sympathetic nature.

A word of caution, Cancer children are more likely to fit into assigned labels. If you tell a Cancer child that they're "bad," they'll feel that way. If you tell them that they're a "bully" or "stubborn," they will be toward that behavior even though it hurts.

Cancer Teens

Teenagers come with emotional turbulence, but a Cancer teen is an outright conundrum that absolutely baffles parents. Sometimes they'll want to spend more time with their family than anyone would ever imagine from a teenager. The next day they're picking fights with everyone. No one is safe from this hormonal, emotional, irrational, loving, and kindhearted person.

Cancer teens demand privacy, and when a parent or sibling violates privacy boundaries or quiet time, they feel outright betrayed. Don't search a Cancer teen's room or get into their items without an invitation. It's probable that you won't find much, anyway. Typically, Cancer children will keep their friends right into their teenage years. Their friends may fall into bad habits or shady situations, but if not, great; you can pretty much count on a Cancer teen sticking around with people they know.

When it comes to simple check-ins, a "How was your day?" question can set red flags off in a Cancer teen's head. If you're prying too much, they'll just become more secretive and retreat from the parent.

What you can expect from a Cancer teen is a high level of motivation. It may not necessarily be for school, but they'll find a passion, and it'll likely follow them all through life; and, it's probably for one of the arts. Cancer teens are often leaders among their peers if they're passionate about local news or activism.

How can you help a Cancer teen develop? Here are some ways to help them grow and flourish:

- *Allow them personal responsibility.* Ask them to cook one night a week or take on a task to make their own.

- *Acknowledge how they help the family.* Cancers can have all different types of love languages, and as a teen, it can be hard to pin down that teen's preferred language. Maybe fit a few different approaches for appreciation into your day. Say "thank you", offer an incentive or reward for their efforts, pick up one of their chores, or do something special for them once in a while.

- *Drop unnecessary rules.* Cancer teens tend to rebel against nonsense or anything that they don't feel is important. Don't set an arbitrary bedtime for no particular reason, and make curfews dependent on the situation. For example, instead of saying "Remember that your curfew is 11:00 p.m.", you can say, "Oh, it's prom night, you'll probably be out late. Let's make it before 1:00 this time." Or, for example, "If you can't get home from John's house before 10:00, ask if you can stay the night." That way, they don't have the sword of Damocles hanging over their head at every turn.

- *Indulge their self-expression.* As with any teen, they're figuring out their personal preferences, what they like and dislike. Because Cancers are so emotional, this is a little more important here than with other teenagers. Avoid comments that put down their personal preferences without any good reason. For example, "You call that music?", or "I can't stand that, turn it down." In both instances, you can ask for the volume to go down without asserting that you don't like what they like. Cancer teens still crave that connection to their family, and they want to have a connection with you; they don't want to hear that you hate something they love.

Cancerians as Parents

We couldn't leave a chapter about Cancerian children without some discussion of Cancers as parents. Cancerian parents are widely celebrated as the best nurturers in the Zodiac. They're not just great parents because they're intuitive and empathetic; it's because they remember exactly what it was like to grow up as a sensitive and emotional child. Cancers have the innate ability to hold on to the past, and they don't forget the hurts or the joys of childhood.

This particular element is one of the few places where male and female Cancers really differ. Cancerian fathers are the fun parents, the ones who let the kids stay up late and eat junk food, the ones who can connect with them on an emotional level. They protect their children and can be fierce if they're threatened. But, as much as they're a papa bear or daddy crab, they also want to be their children's friend and to shower them with affection.

Female Cancers make prize mothers. They're the loving authority that nurtures and/or disciplines as the situation demands. They're overprotective, and on occasion can be a bit overbearing. Often, they love the labor of mothering, and they're the type to have a fully loaded schedule with shuttling kids to all sorts of activities. They tend to remember from childhood how their parents did or did not encourage creative exploration and self-explanation.

If you grew up as a Cancer child, take pride in knowing that you can give your children that dream childhood of affection, connection, and provoking constant growth. You might have had a hard run through the teenage years, but they prepared you for everything that you would face through adult years. The emotional ebb and flow often subsides in the later teens and allows Cancers to take all their lessons learned through childhood to become the best parents.

Chapter 7: Cancer in Love

Cancers are often applauded as the best lovers in the Zodiac. They are sensual, emotional, and passionate, which seems like a recipe for success in any romantic relationship. Unfortunately, they also tend to be a bit needy, but that is something that any sign in the Zodiac can adjust to in consideration of what they're getting from the Cancer person.

Cancers surprisingly have quite a bit of trouble when it comes to love, and there's a clear reason for it. Let's address this challenge in romance before we dive into what a Cancer is like when they find their mate.

While Cancers are certainly the best lovers in the Zodiac, they often can't find another sign that can reciprocate that level of love, compassion, and emotional connection. It might seem like the solution is that Cancers need to find other Cancers, but typically Cancers aren't compatible because of how needy they can be and how much they crave alone time. With Cancer-Cancer relationships, it's common that they struggle to be on the same wavelength because they're both exceptionally receptive, but also demanding. Later on, we'll discuss Cancer's compatibility with each sign, but know that typically, the Cancer-Cancer connection isn't the simple solution for Cancers receiving the love they need. Another avenue that Cancer's often find themselves on is to connect with a fire sign, which we'll evaluate individually as well, as these relationships are either made for the stars or absolute disaster.

Ultimately, Cancers have epic romances, and they're deserving of only the best. When they share too much of themselves, they are at risk of being overrun. Their natural inclination toward leadership makes them likely to dominate a relationship, but they're looking for someone to guide the way toward happiness in a partner. Relationships for Cancers are usually wonderful or tumultuous.

"Catching Feelings" is Fairly Literal for Cancers

The slang term "catching feelings" almost exactly describes how Cancers fall in love. They start talking to someone, and then suddenly, they don't just have a crush, they're head over heels. It's a vortex for Cancers, they love *love*. They love other people and experiencing the emotions of a new romance. Their sensuality and understanding of emotions make them fall hard and easily.

Cancers are exceptionally attuned when it comes to love and their physical sensations. When it comes to sex, Cancers want to have nearly an act of worship, and they start thinking about it early on. Most Cancers don't pounce on the idea of moving too quickly on the physical side. But when it comes to emotions, they are often found *running* into relationships, or at least fantasizing about it. The joke about imagining a wedding after that first message is particularly true for Cancers. They're dreamers with lots of love to give, and they hope to receive a lot of love in return.

When it comes to dating, Cancers can be a bit cagey. They like getting to know people, and sometimes the relationship can stagnate and result in great friendships but no relationship. Cancers may also enjoy the dating process and continue that element of the pursuit deep into their relationship, making for a truly fruitful relationship. They love discovering, but Cancers ultimately want to find long-term, slow-burning love in comfortable, low-stress settings.

Intimacy and Physical Love

When in bed, Cancers make long and passionate love. They aren't the ones to bring in toys, shower sex, or props. They want an act of passion approaching worship. Cancers want eye contact, cuddling, and lazy days spent in bed. A lot of these tendencies play into the Cancerian water element. There's a ton of intimacy, but it's reserved for a few in most cases. Cancers aren't usually promiscuous, although they love getting to know people and might occasionally dip into isolated bouts of promiscuity.

Cancer Women and Cancer Men in Relationships

"Mars... Venus", and all the other business, but the undeniable fact is that men and women are different. It's hard to argue that they're overly different, emotionally and psychologically, but Cancer men and women have separate ways of expressing their needs when it comes to love and romance.

Cancer men tend to be soft, loving, and occasionally nurturing, but you have to put in a lot of hard work to get through that shell. They protect themselves at all costs, which means that a partner might get used to a low-maintenance, highly independent partner only to hit the level of trust necessary for the Cancer man to unleash his softer side. Cancer men often believe in chivalry but may be apt to hide this as they know that their partner might crave higher independence levels or even put off by traditional romance or courting.

It's important to address the fact that Cancer men are easily hurt, and if they're hurt once, they're not apt to forget it. One misstep could mean the end of the relationship, or it taking weeks or even months to rebuild lost trust.

Cancer women in love are the true moon maidens. They want to be wooed and romanced... but, Cancer women take a bit of time to warm up. They are generally stand-offish and suspicious of potential partners. They don't want to get hurt, but they also don't want to waste their time. Unfortunately, for all their suspicion and guardedness, many will find themselves giving much more in a relationship than they'll get out of it.

Because Cancer women, like Cancer men, are self-protective but also ruled by feelings, they do a good job of hiding emotions that they think aren't welcome in the relationship. The Cancer woman specifically may keep a lot of her emotions to herself until she reaches a breaking point and then unleashes a hurricane of emotion. They aren't the crazy girlfriend; if the partner makes it past that initial hurricane, they should have smooth waters ahead (unless they don't learn their lesson, in which case the relationship may be doomed or at least off to a rocky start).

Cancer Compatibility

Overall, Cancers have a high compatibility rate. Here's the overview for each sign's compatibility with Cancer and the specifics about what to expect in these different relationships.

Cancer and these signs have the highest level of compatibility:

Taurus

The Taurus is a steadfast and passionate lover, which can work out quite well. As a fixed sign, they can help ground a Cancer man or woman, and they're likely to catalyze intense physical chemistry.

Pisces

Cancer and Pisces will have an intense ride, but it can be magic if they meet each other at the right point in life. A mentally mature Cancer and a mentally mature Pisces can make lifelong mates that have a nearly unmatched emotional connection. They dream together, plan together, and share that bond for years.

Scorpio

Two water signs that are meant for each other, there's a magnetism that draws these two together. Even when epic fights happen, it certainly doesn't mean the end of the relationship is near. The emotional eruptions are just part of these two signs being together. Fighting could be an outlet that allows them to appreciate each other more once their emotions stabilize.

Aries

Expect well-matched intimacy but little else. This fire sign is the "dry" fire sign and the least compatible with any water signs, but especially with Cancer. The communication in these relationships takes a lot of effort. Is it impossible? No, but it takes work from both sides.

Gemini

Cancers and Geminis get along quite well, and if you're looking for a love that has a foundation of friendship, this could be it. Don't expect as much passion in the bedroom but enjoy the open communication.

Cancer

This could be the best or worst relationship you might have as a Cancer. It's possible that you find someone you click with and that you're emotionally aligned to, or it could turn out that one of you is always on opposite ends of the emotional spectrum.

Leo

As the pure fire sign, Leos offer Cancers a chance at a passionate and steamy romance. Leo's are egotistical and can have trouble communicating, but they can shower love the same way that Cancers do in a relationship. It's important that the Leo and the Cancer work out who is the leader in the relationship.

Virgo

Virgos are highly compatible, but they can be combative with Cancers when it comes to emotional demands. Virgos are generally very private people, and that works out well when Cancers want their space. But then there are those other times.

Libra

There are few signs that don't fit well with Libras, and there are few signs that don't play well with Cancers. These two seem like they'd be perfect as they're both kind-hearted and concerned with fairness, but they don't mix well. Cancers are too good at sniffing out fakeness, and Libras aren't happy to handle an emotional rollercoaster.

Sagittarius

These two will have tons of fun together, but probably not result in a long-lasting relationship unless the lighthearted Sagittarius can accommodate Cancer's ever-changing mood. And of course, unless the Cancer can keep up with the wild Sagittarius ambitions.

Capricorn

There's high compatibility here and a moderate level of communication. You shouldn't have any problems easing into a steady relationship with a Capricorn so long as you both remember that you're prone to quiet bouts.

Aquarius

Expect almost no communication here. While Cancers are great listeners and Aquarians are great talkers, these two just don't align when it comes to delivery. Of course, there is an opportunity to overcome communication hurdles, but generally, the air and water combination is a little lackluster for the emotional Cancer.

Water and Earth

Water and earth mixtures are more like the edge of the beach than the mud that people imagine. These signs include Taurus, Capricorn, and Virgo. Cancer has the ability to soften a few of these signs, which are typically very reserved and private. But in doing that they may open a box of emotions they weren't prepared to handle.

There should be a balance between earth signs offering practical help and encouragement, with the Cancer leading communication efforts.

Water and Fire

Water and fire signs are passion bottled up until the top blasts off. It's a steamy combination that can be all right or all wrong. There are particular issues with the fire signs as they're a bit different from the other elements. Fire signs include Aries, the hot moving toward dry, Leo the pure fire sign, and Sagittarius the hot moving toward wet.

Typically, a Cancer doesn't have much to gain besides intimacy or friendship from an Aries or Sagittarius. There's either a lot of passion or a lot of fun. With Leo, there's the opportunity for a relationship, but it could be disastrous.

There's also the risk that a fire sign could make the water sign feel dried up, that they may not receive the nourishment they need. At the same time, fire signs may feel that the water signs douse their burning inspiration.

All the same, Cancers frequently jump into relationships with fire signs because the feelings and emotions at the start of the relationship are too intense to turn down.

Water and Air

When it comes to water and air, you almost couldn't ask for a deeper connection until we get to water and water combinations. Air signs create a strong foundation for water to communicate their feelings and dream lofty dreams. These signs often feed off of each other very well and encourage each other to move forward. The downside is that these are often friendships, and sometimes cultivating the communication with Cancer opens up emotions, and air signs aren't always stable when it comes to long-term commitment.

Water and Water

Now, water and water are a match made in heaven. After all, we're looking to cultivate an ocean, not be a lonesome pond. But there's a bit of challenge because sometimes these couples see too much of themselves in their partner. They'll need to understand when their partner wants alone time, and when they can merge together and spark their emotional bond.

How to Catch a Cancer's Eye

It sounds like such a cliché, but you really just need to be yourself. Cancers are too empathetic and perceptive to be fooled by manipulation. If someone is doing anything but being authentic, even if they're just trying to play it cool, a Cancerian can tell. So, don't ever try to manipulate or fool a Cancer; they can always tell.

Then, make time for them. If you manage to land a date, know that you might have to do a fair amount of the talking. But filling the air with conversation doesn't mean that you're running the show. Make time for them and direct the conversion in a way that invites them to do more than just listen; offer engagement. Additionally, it's best to ensure that this one-on-one time is distraction-free. Grab a meal and talk. But leave your phone and other devices off or on silent. Cancers hate to break the mood when they're in the getting-to-know-each-other phase.

Finally, have real conversations. Don't talk about surface topics like the weather, traffic, or the latest shows. Cancers are excellent conversationalists, but they don't often employ that skill because they're such great listeners. Finding someone who draws out this element in their personality is something really exciting, and Cancers love to explore people and even themselves. Give them a chance.

So, how should you approach Cancer? Start direct. They don't like muddled communication. If you like them, say so, and then give them a bit of space but don't fully disconnect. Chat through the day or a few times a week, making sure that you don't come on too strong or abandon them completely.

How to Communicate with Your Partner if You're a Cancer

If you're a Cancer, you might have noticed through this chapter that any time there were genuine troubles, it was due to communication. Communication plays a vital role in every relationship, romantic or otherwise, but when dealing with a partner, it's vital that you keep those lines of communication open. Cancers do have a tendency to shut down unintentionally, and often their partners can perceive that as getting the silent treatment.

Look for everyday ways to communicate, and when you can't find the words, send images, gifs, or even memes. Embrace text messaging, and send video messages; that way, you don't have to video chat, but instead, you can send a personal message without worrying about having a full conversation.

You might also consider being blunter than what seems normal or polite. Cancers like to ease into discussing their feelings because they're so wrapped up in everyone else's. If you're feeling mad, flustered, or needing attention, then be blunt about it rather than trying to keep that emotion buried. Only when Cancerians don't address their needs, especially emotional needs, do they have these blow-up fights with their partners or mates. It's likely that any problem in a relationship involving a Cancer and anyone else has its root in unaddressed emotions. Address the emotions you're experiencing directly, rather than trying to address the other person's needs first.

Finally, give some consideration to their sign. The compatibility outline above is a general guide, but if you're both aware of your strengths and weaknesses, you can have a successful relationship with signs that may initially seem incompatible. Romantic relationships rely on personalities coming together and two people being interdependent, which is possible in a variety of combinations. But if you're with someone who is refusing to work through difficult communication or understanding emotional needs, then it's not likely you'll see any substantial change in the relationship itself. Seeking out strong relationships is something that Cancers are very good at. They're often very content being independent until they find someone with whom they can be themselves and enjoy the time.

Chapter 8: Cancers at a Party

From the outside, Cancerians are walking conundrums. Many other signs see them as simply impossible to understand, and one of the reasons for this is their varying degrees of social interactions. Again, from the outside Cancers seem like introverts, but on the inside Cancerians know that they not only love a good party, they love hosting one. Cancer-born people often feel drained when they're around extreme emotions, but they usually enjoy the happy vibes at a party.

Cancerians also enjoy a bit of pampering and attention from time to time. Cancers tend to spend more time at a party with a small group of people, and when they're hosting, they make sure they're not spreading themselves too thin. Overall, it's surprising, but Cancers love to party, and they love social interaction when they can control part of the environment. Here are a few of the deeper insights into how Cancerians enjoy time around others and what they can do to make the most of that time.

Cancers Party to Unwind

Cancers have two ways of unwinding. The first is the more notable, and the more gossiped about, need for seclusion. Cancerians do like to hide away from the world; it's very crab-esque of them. But they are just as likely to host a small get-together and use that as an opportunity to recharge. In fact, this is one of the best ways for Cancer-born people to learn to overcome their most prominent weaknesses.

Because Cancers are so easily affected by others' emotions, they have trouble separating the good from the bad in many situations.

Think about it for a minute... when you go to work, you probably get a mix of good and bad emotions. You might have a coworker who's excited for a big trip with their family and another coworker who feels like he's stuck in a dead-end job and hates his life. Cancers pick up on both of these. But a party with people you know and love is a different experience.

Throwing a party with your closest loved ones has a high probability of turning out a good time and everyone being happy. That's why Cancers love a good get-together, but they're not one for raging parties.

If you're trying to imagine a Cancer having a great time at a party and being able to unwind, then think of more of a kicked-back affair as opposed to a frat party. We're talking about a bit of barbecue, maybe casual drinking, and really good conversation. When Cancers party, they don't have music that drowns out conversation, or the focus itself is on the music and the conversation is about what's playing. They do best when they're offering home-cooked meals to their friends and spending time around people they know they'll enjoy.

Now, a Cancer-Leo cusp might find more enjoyment in the big party scene. They might plan out these experiences well ahead of time to ensure that they can emotionally prepare but being extremely social is one of those characteristics that come out in the Cancer-Leo cusp. These people might find greater joy in planning to attend a big event such as a well-established rave, concert, or seasonal event. Even those people who fall on the Gemini-Cancer cusp will probably enjoy partying for the sake of fun more than pure Cancers. But both Gemini-Cancer and Cancer-Leo cusps should expect the same recharge effective when attending small gatherings.

Prefer Consistency Over Novelty

Male Cancers are prone to enjoying parties more than female Cancers are. They're traditionalists, and they understand that socializing is part of regular life. They want to plan their social encounters, and in doing so it may seem like they're setting up a very old-school-style affair. It's likely them, a few male friends, moderate drinking, background music, and reserved for Friday or Saturday night. Their innately loyal nature and dependability often mean that these consistent and traditional get-togethers happen regularly. The friends of this Cancer likely know to show up every Saturday night whether they receive an invitation or not. In fact, a Cancer might occasionally take the liberty of not sending invites to see who shows up anyway.

Even female Cancers prefer to party with a bit of consistency over novelty. These are not the type of people who want to go with other people's spur-of-the-moment ideas, but female Cancers are known for occasional spontaneous streaks. They are typically less traditional than male Cancers and tend to use their imaginative or creative side more often when seeking fun. These moments of spontaneity aren't the crazy "let's go jump off the bridge" situations; they're usually just last-minute plans. It's likely that a female Cancer will realize she has an empty weekend and invite over a few close friends.

It's likely that female Cancers also have standing plans with the most important people in their life. For many, that is something to the extent of a Sunday dinner, Friday date night, or after-work drinks with coworkers. It's this degree of consistency that allows the Cancer to unwind and relax with people that she enjoys being around frequently. There's often too much uncertainty for either a male or female Cancer to enjoy themselves when it comes to novelty. You can expect that Cancerians aren't really big on theme parks or summer festivals unless they can plan out all the details and/or create a consistent schedule. For example, a Cancerian might not want a one-time trip to Disneyland. But, if they live in Southern California or Florida, they might get a season pass so they can go as often as they like and do things at their own pace. They would not use these outings as a party and would likely shut down the idea of using highly eventful or hyped-up locations for parties such as family get-togethers or class reunions.

Cancers When Party Planning and Hosting

Although Cancers seem shy, there's a lot that they manage when it comes to socializing. Part of that comes from a need to control new interactions, but they are good at slowly growing their circle of friends and often mix friend groups when others would keep them separate. Because of this, they seem like that one person that knows everyone, and everyone knows them.

But planning and hosting are exceptionally demanding, and it's one of those triggers that can set off moodiness, frustration, and a full Cancer shut down. Cancers work best as mediators and orchestrators. They are the ones who make the right decision when it comes down to a few choices, but when they have to go out and find all the options, research them, and make the decision, things go wrong. Decision paralysis or decision fatigue is common among party-planning Cancers.

On the fun side, we can say that Cancers should grab a glass of Pinot Grigio and enjoy a weekend at the winery rather than a Friday night at the bar. We can also say that Cancers are rather sensuous, and they want a head-to-toe pampering experience. A good salt scrub and a hot shower followed by a full body massage would do just the trick for Cancer-born individuals.

These are the fun things that you find in magazines about how to find the best spa package or the best cocktail to make your weekend stand out. The truth is that Cancers don't need all of this. They aren't the ones looking for things that are just right; if anything, they're looking for elements of the parties that are just right for everyone else. They're the ones who are likely to make a menu and/or a drink menu and contrive the entertainment based on what they think everyone else would enjoy. Never forget that Cancer-born are the mothering archetype of the Zodiac, and they don't just want to nurture; they want to deliver a happy experience.

If you're a Cancer who wants to entertain more often or enjoys entertaining, then take the leap and get help. Ask a friend and use those Cancer charms to get the help that people want to give. You listen, and you know what people want and how they are best capable when it comes to helping. Say to your friend, "You always have the best games at the kids' parties, could you help with this party?" Or "Hey, what do you think would be great for our Saturday bar-b-cue? You know good food!"

Again, Cancers want to use a party's opportunity to draw out those good emotional vibes and enjoy everyone around them being in a good mood. They don't want the planning process or the party itself to feel like a chore, and to avoid that, they'll often ask for help to put together a party or to ensure that things go as planned. It's one of the few times that Cancerians ask for help, and they certainly deserve it!

Who is the Cancer at a Party?

If you were to try to ascertain each person of the Zodiac Trope at a hypothetical party, then the Cancer would be the one sitting outside by the fire pit. You'll likely find them with a couple of close friends, but they're not going to be the ones circulating and talking with people that they don't know or aren't comfortable around. Additionally, Cancers are likely the ones who are going to call it an early night (unless they're hosting the party). When Cancers are hosting the party, they don't mind it going well into the early morning hours. But when a Cancer knows that they have the opportunity to go home and genuinely unwind, they'll take it.

All too often, other signs feel like Cancers aren't happy at parties. They don't understand that even if a Cancer is just sitting outside quietly with one or two friends and food, they're having a good time. Cancers are not the ones who are going to have a good time getting up on the bar and dancing. They're also not the ones who are going to have a lot of fun from typical party games.

It's also likely that Cancers are quick to put down ideas for parties that seem more like a novelty. Things like gender reveal, baby showers, wedding rehearsal parties, and anything else that seems superfluous won't be at the top of a Cancer's priority list. The one exception to this is if the Cancer is planning or hosting the party for someone they love. That mothering and caring instinct will drive them to throw parties that they believe the person who is the focus of the festivity will enjoy. Even if they're not keen on the idea of the party, they'll usually go along with it to make another person happy.

Chapter 9: Cancers at Work and Career Paths

Cancers are especially industrious people. As a water sign, they're able to employ their mystery, creativity, and kind-heartedness in their work. Their sensitivity and high level of intuition can lead to trouble in finding the right career path and following through.

The characteristics of a Cancer make them a hard-working, loyal, and exceptionally diligent employee. These people will pay attention to very specific rules and have that keen eye for detail that many employers love. When they take on a professional role, it's a commitment. Cancerians are not the type to move from job to job frequently. It's likely that even when they feel ready to move on, they'll stay for an additional year or two, feeling that they owe their employer something.

How do Cancerians Act with Their Coworkers?

As coworkers, Cancers tend to lean one of two ways. They're either the energetic and positive force on the team that encourages others to reach new success levels or the opposite. It's important not to forget how moody Cancer can be at times. Suppose they feel jaded or underappreciated in the workplace. In that case, it's often that they're the ones on the team pointing out the negative aspects of the work environment with little insight into how to solve these problems. Cancers work best with a bit of autonomy, but they don't enjoy working alone. They need to work with a team of people they believe are competent, but who contribute differently. It's not enough to have a team of nice people. Cancers want to work on a team of forward-thinking people who contribute new ideas, even if they don't particularly agree with them. Cancers want everyone to explore their creativity, and they do tend to bring this out in other people. But, if you're a Cancer yourself, you might know all too well that this is only the outside perspective. To your coworkers, you're possibly an outstanding team member who is supportive and helps the team grow. But that may come with a deep internal struggle to be heard and to communicate what you have to contribute to the team. There are often two ways of looking at things, from the inside and the outside. For Cancers in the workplace, every day has this divide. Cancerians must find a career path or at least an employer that they truly enjoy. As an emotionally-driven Cancer, taking a job that makes you unhappy is not a long-term option.

In what type of jobs might Cancers perform best and find personal satisfaction? As natural caregivers and counselors, Cancers thrive in roles that allow them to help other people. That doesn't always mean that they're going to be a nurse or professional caregiver, although those are both excellent careers for Cancerians. It might be in a role that helps people help themselves, such as teaching or working in management. Additionally, many Cancers find satisfaction in providing help in everyday ways by working as a mechanic or an electrician. The overwhelming suggestion that you'll find for a Cancer career path is that they should lean towards the arts. Unfortunately, although creative, many Cancers struggle in artistic careers because they're not achieving satisfaction through other elements of their personality. If you have an artistic inclination or want to pursue a career in an artistic field, then make sure that you surround yourself with ways of expressing your kind-heartedness, generosity, and desire to do good for other people.

Realtor

It's a bit of a shock to recommend a Cancer work as a realtor, but there are a great many ways that Cancers thrive in real estate. First and foremost, they're helping people find a home, and that's not something that many people can say they've accomplished. Secondly, real estate is more of an art than a science. You have to know what your client wants and what they expect even when they can't describe it themselves.

A new couple may say that they want a simple starter home within their budget and mentioned that they're planning on growing their family quickly. When handling this, a Cancer may recognize that yes, they do want a starter home. But they also want a house with enough bedrooms for multiple children and probably an extra bathroom.

Furthermore, working as a real estate agent provides the perfect level of teamwork and autonomous work. Real estate agents are almost always independent contractors, but they work with a real estate broker's office and use collective resources. It's likely that as a realtor, you'll participate in weekly team meetings and be called upon for expertise if one of your teammates is having trouble with a sale or with paperwork.

Overall, working as a real estate agent allows Cancers the opportunity to develop themselves, work with others, genuinely help their clients, and guide people through a process that they may only go through once or twice in their life. Working as a real estate agent allows Cancers the opportunity to develop themselves, work with others, genuinely help their clients, and guide people through a process that they may only go through once or twice in their life.

Chef

Working as a chef is the first artistic career path mentioned on this list. Earlier it was mentioned that working as an artist, musician, comedian, or writer might not exactly fit Cancers. Simply producing creative work isn't enough for Cancers. Instead, they should find a profession that allows their Cancer traits to thrive while they also explore their creative inclinations. Chefs do exactly do that. Often, Cancers can get substantial personal satisfaction from crafting delicious meals for people.

We're not talking about your run-of-the-mill cook. If you're looking to be a chef, it's best to get formal education or training but with a celebrated chef if at all possible. We're talking about working your way into restaurants that people go to feel good, rather than blasting through a drive-through for something to ease a bit of hunger.

We're not talking about your run-of-the-mill cooks. If you're looking to be a chef, it's best to get formal education or training under a celebrated chef, if it all possible. We're talking about working your way into restaurants that people go to for a fine dining experience, rather than blasting through a drive-through for something to ease a bit of hunger. Explore your artistic abilities while delivering outstanding performance in this sometimes thankless profession.

Interior Design or Design Professional

An interior-design professional helps people take an average house and make it a lovely home. Cancers love helping, they love crafting, and they usually enjoy creating beautiful things. There's a strong sense of reward when they're able to finish a job.

Unlike the realtor profession, most interior designers don't work in an office with other people who work independently as well. Instead, interior designers are usually independent contractors entirely on their own, or underlings to another designer's operation. Keep in mind that

Cancers are natural leaders, and in creative pursuits probably won't do well just taking directions from another person (unless they're new to the field and deliberately engaged in learning). Cancers are often passionate about learning, so taking the lead from a respected person in the field isn't a problem in that situation. But taking the lead from another person when the Cancer simply wants to exercise their passion, creativity, and desire to explore, doesn't suit them well.

You might have the option to open your own design firm or work freelance, finding clients on your own. In many cases, you might find a work partner, who should be a good friend that can work with your clients while you design away.

Social Worker

It's no surprise that Cancers should be in the recommended service field when it comes to social work. Social workers have the ability to deliver actual help to families and children, rather than just mandate reports to alert the proper offices of their suspicions.

Social work also explores another area unique to Cancers. They're often attracted to mystery because they're a water sign and the ocean contains its own air of mystery, and as a social worker, there's quite a bit of opportunity to investigate and research.

Nurse or Caregiver

Nursing and caregiving is hard work, there's no doubt about it, but Cancers never shy away from hard work. Imagine long hours of helping people, jumping into emergency situations and high-stress environments with a calm cool because you're the one that's there to help.

Cancers that are high-energy might enjoy nursing more than caregiving. They may have more reliable schedules that offer a bit more flexibility with three days off, even though it means working twelve-hour shifts or being on-call through the rest of the week. Longer stretches of time off also allow Cancerians the opportunity to recharge fully, where other jobs might not offer that same benefit.

As a caregiver, Cancers can get too receptive to their patients' emotional despondence and that of the family members that do or don't appear. Cancers are almost always natural empaths, and it can be hard to find so much sadness or grief right in the workplace. But for many Cancerians, this is a welcome opportunity to help the person and the family through this rough process. Many Cancers can take it. They're well-grounded and less susceptible to the effects of feeling the negative emotions but still apt to understand them and help others navigate the choppy waters that come at the end of life. It's likely that the Cancerians who are up to this task have an earth-element moon sign, such as Virgo, Taurus, or Capricorn. Occasionally those with a fire moon-sign might also be able to rise to the occasion.

Essential Services - Electrician, Mechanic, etc.

Essential services have always been around, and only those who do the work understand the reward of a job well done. Carpenters, electricians, plumbers, and mechanics are the ones who truly understand the personal rewards of a career path where you can get your hands dirty and feel dog-tired at the end of the day.

Cancers' unexpected payoff in this type of field isn't that they can run through their energy or work mostly alone with their thoughts; it's that these services help people in ways that no one imagines until they need that support. What would happen if your refrigerator went out today? What about an air conditioner breaking down in the middle of a summer heatwave? Who do you call when your power goes out, or your car won't start? Cancers love feeling needed and helpful, and these professions tick both of those boxes.

Mechanics and electricians have the opportunity to tell people that their problem is gone, or that they can fix it. Unfortunately, they do also have to sometimes deliver the bad news that the problem requires replacement rather than repair.

What Makes Cancers Happy at Work?

Most of the time, Cancers have that strong drive toward commitment, so they want a career, not a job. Of course, the trick to finding a long-term career is to find a position or industry where you can thrive and experience happiness or contentment. Look at which Cancer characteristics are most present in your personality and use them to help you think out different career options.

These traits and the list provided here are only a starting point. Look at the career options that interest you and identify whether your personality is suited for a long-term career in that field. There are often countless ways that you can use your key characteristics, and it's evident from the high volume of Cancerian entertainers that being an extrovert or outgoing person isn't a requirement to fit into careers that initially seem out of the realm of a Cancer.

Chapter 10: Cancers On Their Own

Cancers not only love their time alone; they thrive in it. If you're a Cancer feeling overwhelmed, lost, listless, or just a little down, then take a day to yourself. Cancers don't need another person to be happy, and they are perfectly capable of making their own fun. Although they're emotional and have a deep connection to their family, they'd rather be alone if they don't have a partner. If they don't have a great family situation, they'll make their own, and it might take time, but usually, Cancers don't mind.

Not all Cancerians are introverts, and there are a few differences that come with cusp-born Cancers and between genders. There's an overarching element of comfort in solitude, though. Nearly all Cancers will need time to themselves to process their emotions, recharge, and prepare to face the next hurdle in front of them.

Cancers Need Alone Time - Even the Extroverts

To understand the relationship that Cancers have with their inner selves and why they do so well alone, we need to briefly address the subject of extroverts and introverts. Of the Big Five personality traits, extroversion is the one that receives the most attention. Technically, there isn't any such thing as an "introvert"; those described as such are just very low on the extroversion scale, and the lower on the scale, the more energy they lose around other people. Parties, social situations, and even just going to work if you work around many people can be extremely draining if you're low on the extroversion scale.

Adopting the term "introvert" to describe anyone low on the extraversion scale, we can assume that anyone drained by gatherings is an introvert. But it doesn't quite work out that way. Cancers aren't just drained because they're around people; it's because they're feeling and sensing all of those people's emotions. Cancers don't have to be introverted to enjoy time alone; even the most outgoing of Cancers will need time to recharge.

It's easiest to see this with Cancer entertainers. Unlike Leo, Sagittarius, or even fellow water-sign Scorpio celebrities, Cancers are overly protective of their alone time and their family's privacy.

To take a quick look at how extroverted or introverted-but-charismatic Cancers stack up to other signs, here's a list of a few celebrities by sign:

- Kylie Jenner – Leo (Rather open, with private life)
- David Dobrik – Leo (Rather open, with private life)
- Chrissy Teigen – Sagittarius
- Brad Pitt – Sagittarius
- Ariana Grande – Cancer (Fairly private)
- Robin Williams – Cancer (Private)
- Tom Hanks – Cancer (Private)
- Michael Jackson – Cancer (Private)

You might notice that there's a pretty evident pattern here. Cancers are more private, or to themselves, even though they can get in front of immense crowds and spend most of their time entertaining. How introverted and extroverted you are can depend on your sign, but Cancers again have a unique twist on this subject. Cancers both love people and become overwhelmed by others' emotions. It is a combination of them being a water sign, ruled under the moon, and their house representing the family. They are apt at communication and they easily dial into others' emotions, but all of this is overwhelming for them. Cancers that are low in extroversion could be more susceptible to being overwhelmed by the external emotional input and need more time alone. But how do Cancers spend their alone-time?

Crafting and Exploring

Cancers don't waste the time they spend alone the way that many other signs would. They use that time to be industrious, while also bolstering the explorative elements of their personality. They're prone to picking up new hobbies, crafting, or creating in any way possible. You'll likely find a Cancer unexpectedly picking up various hobbies and dropping them just as quickly.

Many Cancers will even use their downtime to connect with people in different ways, such as through large interactive online games or online communities.

But why all the crafting and exploring? This boils down to a mystery of Cancerians, and exactly why these signs can't keep their hands still is not exactly clear. We know that they're extremely industrious people, which is often attributed to the Moon's speed as it rushes around the earth. Cancers don't sit still, although they enjoy the occasional lazy morning before jumping into action for the rest of the day.

If you are a Cancer and looking for a way to get the most out of your downtime so you can recharge without lazing around all day, consider testing out a few different hobbies. You don't have to commit to one hobby, and you don't have to give weeks or months of your time to one pursuit.

Try these to boost your creativity and exploration during your alone-time:

- Pick up a few art supplies from a local shop
- Follow a YouTube video for painting, knitting, crochet, woodworking, or similar.
- Write a short story or record one on your voice memos.
- Put together a jigsaw puzzle, diorama, or scale model from a box (no stress in picking the "right" items)
- Try a new safe-but-thrilling adventure such as a flight simulator or diving into a story-led game (Role-Playing Game, or RPG).
- Read up or watch YouTube videos on a skill you want to improve or wished you had.

Now, if you are the friend, spouse, or close relation of a Cancer, you want to make sure you don't impede on this alone time. Cancers are not necessarily people that need to be told that they've done a good job. But when they explore crafting or have fun doing something new, they're trying to do this outside of the eye of judgment. They're doing it for themselves, but they can't just turn off their sensitive nature. Cancer men are less likely to be sensitive to judgment, but even they may feel a deep sting of their work receiving negative feedback.

So, if you walk into the room and say, "Wow, that's a really great miniature," their general feeling will be that they produced something, and now judgment or criticism has tainted it.

Cancers are often overly emotional, and when they're coming out of their alone-time, that part of their personality may be exacerbated. When Cancers seek alone-time, it's because they need to recharge, and if you invade that with your opinions and judgments, they don't have the opportunity to recharge, and they are pushed back into alone-time for even longer. They may appear to be using this time to put their feelings out there into the universe, but it's still a private affair.

One of the primary issues that Cancers struggle with, and everyone around them silently criticizes, is that they usually don't stick with more than one or two creative pursuits. They may have one or two hobbies that they go to for comfort. One male Cancer explains that he enjoys music, and because of that passion, he plays multiple instruments; he would even like to learn more, but he usually returns to the bass as his comfort zone and when he's performing with others. His secondary hobby is a well-known MMORPG (massive multiplayer online role-playing game) where he can explore even more crafting while following different storylines and engaging with others on the game's terms.

One female Cancer reports that she spends her alone-time writing screenplays; often these go unsubmitted, but she enjoys her time writing and will continue this hobby. As a secondary hobby, she enjoys crocheting, and often uses this hobby to make unique and handmade gifts for family members because she's confident in the quality of her work and her abilities.

Both the male and female Cancer mentioned here often stretch themselves beyond these hobbies. They've both tried painting, foil art, charcoal sketching, and many other things besides. The male Cancer tinkers with various electrical projects using spare or old parts to make new-ish items such as Frankenstein alarm clocks, motion detectors, and radios. The female Cancer often tries solo pursuits that take her outdoors, such as hiking, geocaching, and photography.

Why do Cancers do this? There are a few reasons behind their love of crafting and exploration and their ability to recharge when alone while also being rather busy.

1. The moon moves quickly through space, and as such, Cancers are happiest when they are in motion as well.

2. Born to the fourth house, Cancers are often looking for ways to cultivate elements of themselves that their family can enjoy too. This is where we see the rise of hobbies that offer entertainment, such as musical performance, photography, and producing crafted goods.

3. The moon, representing the soul and all things that rest beneath the surface, has Cancers constantly trying to understand themselves better. They want to know what it takes to make them content, happy, and rested.

Thinking Through the Past: The Good and The Bad

Cancers are extremely sentimental people, and they tend to revel in the past. They can spend hours going through family memories and attempting to preserve those memories through representations such as photo albums, slideshows, and journal entries. We wouldn't be surprised seeing a Cancer find an extremely creative way to preserve their memories and those personal moments that are extremely important to them.

But as sentimental people, Cancers can fall into a vortex of negative thinking on their own. They can spiral from one memory to another and then to another with very little effort. Cancerians, especially Cancer females and those on the Gemini-Cancer cusp, may have to work extra hard to move past this negative vortex. They should have a list of things or activities they can do for comfort and recharging to help pull them out of negative thinking.

For example, a Cancer woman or a Gemini-Cancer cusp person may have conditional statements to help them enjoy the past rather than get stuck in it:

• If I am feeling down and cannot get out of it, I will try a new independent hobby

• If I am stuck in the past and it's making me feel bad, I'll write (or voice memo) about the experiences and what I learned from them or how they made me stronger.

• If the first two steps don't work, I will call a supportive and positive friend to come by and spend time with me.

Although Cancers do need quite a bit of alone time, it's usually best to spend time with people they know are a positive force when they get stuck in this negative thinking pattern. Because of their heightened emotional sensitivity and their empathic abilities, being around someone who emits positive energy naturally can help lift up a Cancer. Cancers are recipients of outer energy, so their negative energy isn't going to affect those around them; instead, the nearby positive energy will affect the Cancer.

Male Cancers and those on the Cancer-Leo cusp need to take a different approach. It's often that this segment of Cancerians will need to embrace that time alone and really recede into themselves for self-reflection and to analyze or pick apart those negative memories.

Male Cancers are sensitive, but they work harder to keep their feelings and emotions to themselves. They wouldn't venture out into the world, try something new, or spend time with another person when they're feeling extremely vulnerable. For male Cancers, this is an easy equivalent of molting. When crabs molt, they will create or dig a cave and hide away; others will engage in ingenious scams that make them appear dead and unsavory to predators. This is exactly what a male Cancer is doing when they are facing internal turmoil. They hide away, protect themselves and their feelings, and eventually emerge with a new shell.

The Cancer-Leo cusps need uninterrupted alone-time for a different reason. Let's look again at the creatures which embody the Zodiac signs. We already discussed the crab's molting habits, but now there's the presence of the lion. Female lions sleep between fifteen and eighteen hours per day, while male lions sleep about twenty hours per day. This is a good indicator of the basis for an often-overlooked Leo element. Cancer-Leo cusps often require even more time to recharge. Leo's may not have the extremely sensitive disposition that Cancers do, but they wear out eventually, and when they do, they shouldn't be disturbed. Don't poke a sleeping lion, and don't mess with a molting crab. That's the combination you have when a Cancer-Leo cusp gets into a negative cycle of thinking or gets stuck on past events. They just need to accept what's happening, rest, recharge, and emerge when they are ready to face the future again.

Cancers Need Time By Themselves

Don't doubt the ability of a Cancer to thrive independently and build new experiences all by themselves. Cancers are the family house, and they do crave deep emotional connections to the few people they allow into their inner circle. They create families of their own, whether that's blood relations, friend circles, or even workplace families. They're often the nurturer and a subtle leader for any group, which can make it seem as though they constantly need people around to feed off that element of their personality.

That is the outward perspective, and Cancerians know that perspective is only one side of the coin. On the other side, you have their well-developed imagination and creative personality, which isn't usually the focus of a group setting. One of the reasons why Cancers love diverting into alone-time is that they have the opportunity to explore these elements of their personalities that they may keep secret from those around them. Anything that may appear as vulnerability is often reserved for alone-time, and that's one of the ways that they create these new experiences independently.

With the preference and ability to create something independently and then allow others to experience it later through social media, the internet, or even just sharing it with close friends, Cancers really excel at this approach. They're able to explore new hobbies and creative pursuits without limitations and then, when they are confident of their abilities, they can present what they've created to those they love and trust.

Cancerians do tend to hold on to the past, and if they weren't a cardinal sign, that might be of some concern. Under the cardinal mode, and as a water element, Cancers are prone to change. We even see this in their symbol, the crab. Crabs molt often, don't have one single home throughout their lives, and live in an ever-changing environment. Many Cancers particularly struggle with this tug-of-war between holding onto the past and moving into the future. A Cancer can learn how to balance between using the past, understanding themselves, and then creating new experiences to strengthen themselves. Then they can really thrive in almost any environment. It's the idea of using the past to create sustainable change into the future that they struggle with throughout their first few seasons in life.

During childhood and their teenage years, this particular issue will arise often, but as they get deeper into adulthood, they're able to grab hold of the new experiences they crave and use the past to direct their future. The key to achieving all of this is to develop that balance through alone-time, and the Cancer allowing themselves to spend time within their shell in order to understand themselves better.

Chapter 11: Cancers in Friendships

One of the best astrological blessings anyone could ask for is having a Cancer close to them in life. Very few signs don't mix well with Cancers (the most notable being Libras). But even Libras can often benefit from the overwhelming warmth, kindness, and generosity that comes with having a Cancer in your life. If you are a Cancer, then you should be proud of how you lift others up and bring out the best in the people around you.

It often seems like Cancers make a lifestyle out of taking care of the surrounding people. They're usually the best listeners in the group, are quick to jump in when someone needs help, and are extremely generous on a daily basis. But this often makes Cancerians constantly moody because of how much they give to the surrounding people. If you're born into the house of Cancer, then you should have higher expectations of the people around you. The one exception to this is the people born within the Leo-Cancer cusp range in which the Leo tendency to have high expectations may have nullified this issue.

If you know a Cancer and have a parent or a romantic relationship, then you should take extra care to consider their feelings and energy level. Be observant, and this chapter should have a heavy impact on you with lots of advice on what you can do to be more considerate of the Cancer in your life. As a Cancer, you should use this chapter to help you understand what to expect from others in your life.

Cancers as Friends

It's no surprise that Cancers are outstanding, once-in-a-lifetime type friends. They're family people, but to them, the family goes beyond blood. They're also extremely protective, which often means that they jump in to defend their friend when a disagreement breaks out.

If you're a friend of a Cancer, then you already know that they're always there for you and they always have your back. But you might also know that you're generally the one who also feels the pain when they're having a hard day.

Cancers love spending time with their friends in their domain, though don't be surprised if you're often the one inviting people over rather than going to a friend's house. They're also the ones to host a party, which is fairly surprising when you consider how often Cancers are more inclined toward introversion. Cancerians thrive around people that are in high spirits and, at the same time, love having a few close friends together. You can also count on Cancers to either make tasty food or arrange for the best in town.

Cancers are the "helper" friend. They listen, and their creativity from their connection to the moon and ocean makes them excellent problem solvers. Cancers generally love helping their friends smooth over any issues in their life, but they can go for long stretches of time pulled into themselves for self-reflection or to recharge.

There is a stark difference between male and female Cancers when it comes to friendships. How they make them, how many they have, and how they interact don't starkly contrast, but they go about the friendship process in different ways. Take Carrie Bradshaw of Sex in the City, a Cancer if there ever was one. She's passionate, creative, and deeply in touch with her emotions. She has three good friendships, and everyone else is really a passerby. But these friendships mean the world to her. When she's fought with friends, it has often led to many other areas of her life falling apart, which is exactly what happens in a female Cancer situation. Her friends are also predictable.

It's not just that they fit standard female HBO series tropes, but that they make sense for Carrie; she's attracted to people who communicate in mildly different ways, share similar interests, applaud her work, and have different personalities.

Male Cancers use a different approach. They're extremely self-protective, and it's usually hard to find a fictional male Cancer character because they're so hard to understand, especially in their approach to friendships. A few of the most prominent and accurately depicted male Cancerians include Walter White, Deadpool, Ron Swanson, and Peter Parker/Spiderman. What do these guys have in common? They don't really have friends. None of them. Why? Well, some of them don't have friends because they've undergone extremely traumatic events in their life and have lost loved ones, which make them afraid to make themselves vulnerable again. But Spiderman and Deadpool aside, the other two just aren't very friendly. On the surface, Ron Swanson is about as welcoming as a cactus, and Walter White wasn't much better, maybe as inviting as a shaved cactus.

But both of these characters played out a key trait among Cancers. They protected their family and the few friends they'd collected with everything they had. Walter had a few exceptions, but even in a few disputable key points, he felt as though he was doing the "right" thing for his loved one. Ron Swanson surprised viewers again and again with thoughtful but small actions of friendship, all the while putting up his strong front. This is exactly what you should expect on the surface level from a Cancer guy friend. But what about the deeper level? That's family. You can't just be a male Cancer's friend; you end up being part of the family for as long as you're willing to stick around.

Let Them Have Their Space – Physically and Mentally

Want to know how to irritate a Cancer into a week of the silent treatment? Ask, "What are you thinking about?" once too often. Depending on your Cancer friend, once more might be once too often.

How do you know when they just want alone time, and when they're more quiet than usual because something is bothering them? Anyone can answer this question correctly with one big shrug. The truth is that you'll only know based on your experience in that relationship. Cancers have an ebb and flow when it comes to their emotions, much like the tides being set in motion by the moon.

Cancers dedicate as much time and energy as possible to listening and helping others. So, when they want alone-time, they're really not asking for that much. They simply want to be left alone for a few hours, or a day, or two. But for anyone who's not a Cancer, this can be complicated to navigate. When Cancers are upset, they become quiet and often withdraw or become passive-aggressive. When Cancers need time to process the day, they withdraw and become extremely quiet. They may not want to talk about what's on their mind. In fact, the Cancer in your life probably just wants to be left alone in a room undisturbed.

It's very likely that the Cancer you know has a pet project or a variety of hobbies they want to explore and spend time working on, but they don't want other people involved. So what can you do? The best advice is to give them their space. If this person suddenly becomes quiet, don't take it as a personal offense. Don't take it as if they're giving you the silent treatment, and don't feel like you should jump up and do something. Often the best solution with Cancers is to let them take the lead. This is not like dealing with a fire sign that will blow up in a catastrophic outlash if they feel like they're not in control; Cancers are water signs, and they're usually not so over-the-top. When a Cancer wants peace, give it to them and know that they'll come around either completely fine or have a bone to pick in a calm, premeditated manner.

For Cancers, understanding your feelings and having a productive conversation after you've had a chance to think about the situation is key to keeping your beloved relationships. Many times, a Cancer is quiet, and they're not mad; they're just overwhelmed and need time to rest. This most often happens when Mercury is in retrograde or when Mercury enters Cancer. The ties between emotion and communication are always worn thin, but when they react in a way that aggravated the bond, it often means that the Cancer will shut down temporarily. That shut down is like performing maintenance or processing time. They need to recharge, and many Cancers innately know that if they try to communicate during these times that it could spell disaster.

A Cancer Will Always Communicate Their Emotions - Learn to Listen

We've spent many chapters looking at the various ways that Cancers present themselves and how they interact with people. It's easy to say that they put on a strong face, that hard outer shell, but that they're really a big softy on the inside. But that's the surface view of it. Cancers are in tune with everyone else's emotions, and they often suffer because others who aren't Cancers just can't understand them. But with practice, maybe years of practice, it is possible to understand how a Cancer communicates their emotions.

One of the most common myths or inconsistencies within modern astrological reporting is how Cancers wear their hearts on their sleeves. This couldn't be further from the truth. If you're an earth or fire sign who just isn't so receptive to Cancerian energy, or even an air sign, you might be too easily distracted to pick up on these tiny glitches in their behavior.

Let's look at one Scorpio and Cancer couple who've gone to professional counseling for their marriage. Now, the Cancer female will often put up the front that everything is fine. But it isn't fine, and the more communicative Scorpio knows that, and constantly asks the Cancer what is wrong and what he can do. That's not effective, clearly, but he doesn't understand whether she just wants alone-time, or if she's overwhelmed, or if something else is wrong.

Over many years, with the help of marriage counseling, the Scorpio has come to learn that when his wife is knitting, there's no reason to bother her. But, when she's doing domestic tasks that she often hates, such as dishes or ironing, that's the time to worry. He's also learned that when she spends time with friends, it's not because she wants distance; it's because she needs a different kind of attention, and he's put his Scorpio jealousy to the side. He takes these little cues so that he can understand what's going on in her mind. He has stopped pestering her about what she's thinking about and why she gets quiet from time to time.

Cancers are always communicating their needs and desires; it's on the other person in their life to pick up on that. This seems extremely unfair, and in many relationships or friendships, it is. Cancers that are having a tough time, or are outright depressed, can be extremely manipulative with other people's feelings. Be extremely careful in certain times of planetary movement concerning the planet Venus, as it can lead to romantic troubles, and when Venus is in Cancer, or the Moon is in Taurus, there can be great times or absolutely dire times. These changes can rock Cancers dramatically and cause unpredictable extremes. If you have a Cancer in your life, just be careful to understand their tiny hints that they're putting out into the world, hoping that someone picks upon them.

If you're the friend, spouse, parent, or child of a Cancer, there's a bit of relief ahead. The good news is that once you discover these little quirks and determine how to navigate them, you can make tremendous leaps in your relationship, whether it's romantic or otherwise.

Cancer Friendship Compatibility

Just like romantic relationships, friendships come with varying degrees of compatibility issues. The best friendship combination is a Cancer and Cancer friendship; these two truly get each other, but sometimes they can be a little too similar and get on each other's nerves, especially when they're both being moody. The next best option is for female Cancer and male Pisces, and the bond can become so deep that it almost feels psychic. The two can have deep conversations but really aren't meant for a romantic relationship. Pisces can inherently understand and respect Cancer's need for alone time. But, when it comes to male Cancers, they typically tend to prefer time around earth and fire signs. Male Cancers may find the best of friends in a Taurus, or even an Aries. For male Cancers, it's the differences that make the friendship; they want someone who is almost the opposite of what they are, to expand their world.

• Aries – Generally, for males a great friend; for women or Cancer-Leo cusps, too much to handle.

• Taurus – Great friends all around

• Gemini – Gemini-Cancer cusps know this is a friendship made in heaven, but other Cancers could take it or leave it.

• Leo – Cancer-Leo cusps know to stay away from their own kind, but pure Caners know that a Lion can bring in a ton of fun and get them out of a negative funk.

• Virgo – A grounding friend that will appreciate a Cancer the way they deserve.

• Libra – Too similar to make great friends, but good for the occasional brunch date or concert outing.

• Scorpio – Hot stuff here; a Cancer and Scorpio can make best friends for life!

• Sagittarius – This earth sign is a little too crazy and a little too self-interested to give a Cancer proper attention when they need it. Not a friendship meant to last.

• Capricorn – Great friends here, and they are often outstanding at helping each other get through hard times.

• Aquarius – Possibly the worst friend combination for a Cancer; unless you share many interests with an Aquarius, you're likely to fight constantly.

• Pisces – A friendship for the ages, although you can both bring out an unexpected competitive edge in each other. Watch out for mothering tendencies!

There are many elements that go into making a friendship compatible, and the most important one is the ability to communicate effectively. Special notes here on Aquarius and Sagittarius; these are not the best options for Cancers because of communication difficulties. An Aquarius is apt to under-communicate, and they care much more about logic and reason than feelings and fairness. Meanwhile, the Sagittarius is likely to over-communicate and overwhelm the Cancer with trivial day-to-day problems and powerful emotional frequencies.

What Cancers Wish Others Knew About Being Their Friend

In the chapter on childhood, we mentioned that Cancerians make fast friends when they're young, and then as they're older, they begin to put up a bit of a wall. So, adult Cancers will frequently turn down invitations; sometimes it's because they're genuinely busy, sometimes they're not up to the task of being around so many people, and sometimes they just don't want to do it. They may also have regular plans or routines that they refuse to break for any reason. Here are a few of the top things that Cancerians wish other people knew about being their friend.

- When a Cancer doesn't accept an invitation, don't stop inviting them.

- Go with the spontaneous ideas; they're guaranteed fun.

- Don't ask Cancers to do boring things that don't allow for conversation, such as watching a movie.

- Expect a balance of leisure and activity, although it's completely unpredictable.

Overall, Cancers are excellent friends, but they can seem like a lot of work. They're worth all of it, as they are the best listeners, among the most loyal, and without a doubt, fun.

Chapter 12: What Does a Cancer Need to Thrive?

Cancers are not as simple as they seem, but there are a few tried-and-true ways to help a Cancer thrive. There's so much available in the way of personal development that it might seem daunting even to approach the subject, much less to consider taking action. Wouldn't it be easier just to let things be? Not really. To thrive, you need to manage your weaknesses, play to your strengths, and satisfy various elements of your personality.

Cancerians might have troubles confronting their past, or for that matter, confronting much of anything or anyone at all. They might so often support others so much that they miss out. There are many times that people born under the Cancer sign give too much of themselves to others. To thrive, they need to implement a few ways to handle their day-to-day life. With routinely expanding their horizons, it's possible for Cancers to thrive in almost every situation, even when they're sensitive or feeling a bit more emotional than usual.

Work Hard, Play Hard, Rest Often

The Moon is constantly working to reflect light and brighten the night, and Cancerians often find themselves doing the same. They strive to bring light into everyone else's life, and to ensure that they're managing their needs as well as the needs of others, and take advantage of the opportunity to rest, they have to plan accordingly.

Cancer-born people play hard. Of course, that may not mean that they're out bungee jumping, going to raves, or thrill-seeking. To them, creating and exploring their natural curiosity is play. They can spend hours exploring a new hobby that they may drop the next day. Cancers tend to pick up and drop hobbies very quickly, although they likely keep one or two hobbies throughout their life. These people won't need constant reminders to practice musical instruments, put in time at the easel, or go out and snap photographs regularly. The hobbies that Cancerians pick up and keep throughout life are likely part of their regular schedule. One example of a male Cancer hobbyist photographer is proof of how far a Cancer person will go to dedicate time to play. This particular male Cancer does photography on the side, and, at pretty low rates, he offers wedding photography, pregnancy photography, and family photos. He has every weekend booked out for months, which means that he doesn't spend those weekends enjoying time with friends or relaxing at home alone. This is his version of play, and it brings him great joy. Most Cancerians have something to this effect going on in their life.

Another example is a Cancer-Leo cusp who enjoys music. This person uses a different approach to listening and engaging with music; instead of just letting the radio play, she's very intentional with her musical habits. She listens through albums from start to finish and avoids things like iTunes and Spotify. Her curious nature, which comes from Cancer, has paired with the more traditional elements that spawn from the fixed sign Leo. She listens to about two-and-a-half hours of music each day, and all of it is done with purpose.

Now, it's easy to see how Cancerians play hard, and they enjoy it. But they also work hard, and they tend not to enjoy that so much. Those born under the Cancer sign are more likely to seek out a career that actually resonates with them. It might tie into one of their many hobbies or fit directly into their high receptivity to other people's emotions. Many within the Cancer sign serve other people in one way or another through careers such as nursing, teaching, homemaking, and service industries. Even when Cancers have this outstanding degree of reward coming to them on a daily basis, they often overwork themselves. They're the ones who feel absolutely drained by the time they finally get a day off.

That degree of feeling drained brings us to the next element of Cancer in life: resting often. Not all Cancerians are introverts. But you'll often see that if there is an extroverted Cancer, they're likely in the cusp of either Gemini or Leo. Male Cancerians are more likely to be hard introverts, while female Cancerians tend to open up their friend circle a little more than the males do.

All the same, every Cancer needs time away from others, to rest and recharge so that they have complete control over the scope of emotions in their environment. They must schedule and plan out having this alone-time because they get extremely moody and passive-aggressive without it. It's not unusual for a Cancer, if they go a little too long without getting this opportunity to recharge, to lash out against those that are closest to them. If you're a Cancer, you should plan the times you're going to have to yourself. You might do this when you know that others are going to be out of the house, or specifically wake up early or stay up late to have this time alone. If you know a Cancer in your life, then make sure that you're giving them a certain degree of courtesy when they start to become reclusive.

Move Sideways Through Life

When asked how you met your Cancer friend, or when asking a Cancer how they met any of their friends, you're in for an interesting story. The famous sideways scuttle of the crab is present in everyday Cancer interactions. They rarely enter someone's life in a straightforward method; instead, they scuttle into place.

One great example is of one of the male Cancers we've cited throughout this book. He met his romantic partner through his brother, who was dating a woman who was friends with the person who would become his wife. This is the type of Sideways Shuffle that Cancerians have in their relationships, romantic or otherwise. One of the other male Cancers used as an example in many of these chapters met his best friend through a mutual acquaintance that neither he nor his best friend actually likes spending time around. When they would show up to this person's gatherings out of courtesy, they found they enjoyed spending time together, and the friendship blossomed from there.

Beyond relationships, Cancers may experience this same sideways walk when it comes to their career. Those born under the Cancer sign will probably move into a career path that suits them well based on their personality elements and sheer convenience. They may have helped an elderly family member through later years in their life and realize that that caretaking came quite naturally to them. So it's no surprise when they got a job offer as a professional caretaker for another elderly patient and find themselves more or less entrenched in that field.

The sideways walk is a fun way for Cancerians to look at life, and they often use it to analyze their major milestones retrospectively. When they look back on how they met their best friend or significant other, found their dream job, and similar life moments, they can smile knowing that they didn't take a direct path at any of those turns.

Plan and Then Make a Plan B

One struggle that most Cancer-born deal with regularly is planning and organization. There's a lot of discussion from chapter one to this point about the Cardinal mode along with the presence of the water element and the Moon being the ruling planet, all resulting in constant and frequent change for Cancer-born. That means almost any plan a Cancerian makes is doomed before it even has the opportunity to go into motion.

Cancers should make a plan. In fact, the moon itself represents reaping the benefits of work already done; the moon reflects light already created by the Sun. The downside in the human realm is that you can't reap the benefits of work already done if you don't put in the work, to begin with. To accommodate this, Cancerians should make a plan, but they should also have a Plan B.

As with dominoes, one fall tends to lead to another, and Cancers will find that that is often the case with planning. When a Cancer-born person makes a plan, and subsequently a back-up plan, it's important that they don't focus too much on that original plan not working. If anything, they should learn to expect that their plans will not go exactly as intended, but that they'll reap an abundant and pleasant outcome in the end, anyway. Cancer should plan for their own peace of mind, and to understand what they should expect in the upcoming days or weeks. They should not fall apart into an emotional mess the moment that their plan doesn't work.

Record Your Memories and Give Them Rest

Because the Moon is so closely tied to the idea of an inner self, and the crab has that distinctive outer shell and soft interior, Cancers tend to lose themselves in thought, and particularly to thoughts of the past. Many Cancers have absolutely astounding memories, but they may put themselves into a negative spiral by reveling in memories that they can't change, and that are hurtful to revisit.

Without a doubt, there are always benefits to be found when reviewing old memories and retrospectively analyzing how you've moved through life (especially when you're prone to moving sideways and using unexpected methods). Cancers should take careful action to record their memories accurately. Many suggest journaling, but a lot of people, even Cancers, have trouble remembering to journal regularly.

We suggest using journaling, voice memo recording, or even a creative outlet such as photography, painting, or entertaining to help keep an accurate record of your memories. After you document your memories in one form or another, allow them to rest. Those born to the Cancer sun sign are exceptionally in touch with emotions, but they have trouble reflecting on their own emotions and assessing the energy that they're bringing to the environment because they're so receptive to everyone else's. When they give their memories a rest, they allow the surrounding environment to be peaceful.

Learn to Thrive Where You Are

Many Cancers report that they need seclusion and isolation and that their moodiness is something that others just have to accept sometimes. With careful planning, a solid routine, and a deep understanding of their strengths and weaknesses as a Cancer, the Cancer can fit right into almost any situation. They do well in social situations because they're often so well-liked and easy to get along with. They do well on their own because they're creative and don't need another person to entertain themselves or feel content.

The combination of being a water sign, being the Cardinal mode, under the Moon as the ruling planet, and represented by the great crab has led to a very strong personality type for Cancers. This comes with so many benefits it's almost impossible to understand them individually because they work together as a whole. This combination is truly unique, and few other signs have such a consistent presence between their element, mode, ruling planet, and symbol. They are the purest of the water signs, open to change, and ruled under the planet that symbolizes inner self, change, and emotion. Without a doubt, a Cancer is very understanding, compassionate, and caring. It is up to them to understand exactly how they can use their strengths in their everyday lives and how they can overcome a few of their weaknesses. Through the aspects of life discussed in this book, particularly those in the chapters on strengths and weaknesses, a Cancerian, even one exceptionally moody, overwhelmed, and a bit crabby, can learn to thrive.

Conclusion

Now that you are well armed with some in-depth knowledge of Cancerians, we hope you can apply this information to your daily life. Sometimes we forget to look back on the past stories that had some dramatic impact upon our world. The story of the crab who took on Heracles is a symbol today for what people can truly do, and Cancer's spot in the heavens shows that in strength and understanding, there is just reward. Cancerians often find themselves sympathetic and moved by other people's actions. But other key Cancer traits, such as an inquisitive nature or a protective tendency, may shine within your particular personality.

Use the information here to guide you through daily actions and decisions. A Cancerian is often a key decision-maker, even if they don't know it. One of their absolute strengths is a mirrored weakness: they aren't fully aware of their impact on those around them. We hope that you can assess your strengths, navigate through your weaknesses, and look to the future with hope and confidence.

Be sure to continue to track the planets and stars, and survey how those changes in the universe impact your life. Building awareness and continuing the use of astrology is often as rewarding as it is fun.

Part 5: Leo

The Ultimate Guide to an Amazing Zodiac Sign in Astrology

THE ULTIMATE GUIDE TO AN AMAZING
ZODIAC SIGN IN ASTROLOGY

LEO

MARI SILVA

Introduction

Do you prefer being the center of attention or the queen bee in your group? Do you always feel on top of the world when someone gives you even the tiniest compliment? Do you care deeply about your family and friends? If you answered yes to these questions, you are probably a Leo! Go ahead and ask someone around you who has these traits; it is highly likely that they are a Leo, too.

Leos are born between July 23 to August 22 and are represented by a Lion as their sign. As a Leo, you might have heard people calling you warm, generous, and even vain at times. Leos are of an interesting zodiac sign, one that allows a perfect balance in their traits. While they are bright, chirpy, funny, and talented, they can also be stubborn and downright rude at times. Apart from this, Leos have many more layers to them. If you are a Leo or are concerned about one, you've come to the right place, because this book is all about the Leo and what makes them tick.

In this book, you will get a deeper understanding of the sign, which includes Leo's strengths, weaknesses, career paths, love and relationships, tendencies, and social behavior. The book will also give sound advice which will be useful in various settings such as parties, the office, or at home.

Whether you are a Leo or desire to know one, this book has got you covered. It explains everything about Leos - from birth to old age, rising signs, moons, suns, followed by explanations backing their tendencies, characteristics, and compatibilities.

This book provides you with the basic information needed, and then digs deeper, teaching you the lesser-known parts of this zodiac sign. It explores not only the traits and compatibilities of a Leo, but also the reasons behind them. In other words, it bridges the gap between a total 'newbie' book and an overly long dissertation and can be used by more experienced astrology buffs to brush up on the particulars of any given aspect of Leos.

Read on to learn more about this sign.

Chapter 1: An Introduction to Leo

Leos are born between July 22 and August 23 and are popularly known as the "Queens and Kings of the Zodiac." They are well known for their leadership qualities, creativity, confidence, and socializing skills. On the other hand, Leos are disposed to offensive degrees of arrogance due to their narcissistic and egotistical nature.

Before we delve into this sign's deeper aspects, it is necessary to understand the basic traits, characteristics, and information of this zodiac sign to strengthen the foundation of your knowledge.

Leos are mainly known for their fragile nature in terms of wanting and seeking attention. When they get the attention that they think they deserve, they seem to be the happiest creatures alive. It is difficult to decipher a Leo at first sight, or in one meeting. If you really want to know them, you must spend more time with them.

As a Leo, you are the star in your group and are always at the top of your game. Your caring and protective nature, especially toward your family, is praiseworthy and attractive. Your aura is bright, and you lighten up any room as soon as you enter, but you are always defamed for your arrogance, stubbornness, and constant need for attention and validation. As a Leo, you need your fair share of attention and always want to be in the spotlight.

Let's look at the elements, symbols, ruling planets, houses, colors, lucky numbers, gemstones, and most common traits of all zodiac signs to make a fair comparison with Leos.

Aries (March 21 to April 20)

Symbol: The Ram

Element: Fire

House: House of Self, which represents resourcefulness, beginnings, initiatives, and physical appearance.

Gemstone: Coral

Colors: Red

Lucky numbers: 1 and 9

Ruling planet: Mars

Most common traits: The most prominent trait of Aries is their competitive spirit and the need to achieve goals. Other than that, Aries are:

- Extremely creative and are blessed with an incredible imagination power
- A positive influence on others around them
- Full of enthusiasm and drive
- In need of constant attention and praise
- A bit self-centered and do not let people come too close

Taurus (April 21 to May 20)

Symbol: The Bull

Element: Earth

House: House of Value, which represents materialism, money, possessions, self-worth, cultivation, and substance.

Gemstone: Diamond

Colors: Pink, blue, and green

Lucky numbers: 2, 4, 6, 11, 20, 29, 37, 47, and 56

Ruling planet: Venus

Most common traits: The most prominent trait of Taurus is its ambitious nature. Other than that, the individuals bearing this sign:

- Possess a strong sense of intuition
- Are extremely dependable
- Always look for intimate and serious relationships
- Are extremely stubborn
- Have strong moral values

Gemini (May 21 to June 20)

Symbol: The Twins

Element: Air

House: House of Sharing, which represents generosity, distribution, achievements, siblings, communication, and development.

Gemstone: Emerald

Colors: Yellow and green

Lucky numbers: 3, 8, 12, and 23

Ruling planet: Mercury

Most common traits: The individuals bearing this sign are extremely social and possess a talent for making new friends easily. Other than that, they:

- Are super smart and energetic
- Have a bubbly nature and a positive aura
- Are funny and strategic
- Are known to be two-faced
- Have a need to over-analyze their environment

Cancer (June 21 to July 22)

Symbol: The Crab

Element: Water

House: House of Home and Family, which represents heritage, ancestry, roots, bond, comfort, neighborhood, security, and tidiness.

Gemstone: Pearl

Colors: White, orange, and silver

Lucky numbers: 2, 7, 11, 16, 20, and 25

Ruling planet: Moon

Most common traits: Individuals with this zodiac sign are extremely empathetic and are able to establish deep connections with others. Along with this, they:

- Are known to be the caregiver
- Possess a loving nature
- Are partly governed by their emotions
- Can be a bit difficult to deal with in intense situations

· Can be a bit crabby due to recurring mood swings

Leo (July 23 to August 22)

Symbol: The Lion

Element: Fire

House: House of Pleasure, which represents entertainment, risk, enjoyment, romance, self-expression, and creativity.

Gemstone: Ruby

Colors: Orange, red, white, and gold

Lucky numbers: 1, 4, 6, 10, 13, 19, and 22

Ruling planet: The ruling planet of Leos is the Sun. Just like the Sun is the center of the solar system, Leos prefer to be the center of everyone's attention. Other planets revolve around the sun, which makes this for the same metaphor from another perspective.

Most common traits: Even though we will discuss Leo traits in depth later in the book, let's take a brief look right now at Leos' prominent traits:

> · Leos want to be in the spotlight all the time. They want constant attention and validation from the people around them.

> · They are warm, bright, and giving. Leos are known for their generosity and are often appreciated for their giving nature.

> · They have expensive tastes. Leos can be materialistic and often indulge in expensive and luxurious objects, even if they cannot afford them.

> · Leos are stubborn. They do not listen to most people and often resort to their own rules and decisions. Even if the other person is right, Leos will try their best to prove them wrong and win the argument anyhow.

> · Leos are frontrunners. They have impeccable leadership skills and are ready to lead a team. Their personality and wise decision-making skills are appreciated by others, which makes it easier for people to follow their advice.

> · They are brave and protective of their family and friends.

> · Leos are passionate and romantic. When you are in love with a Leo, expect passion and heat in your relationship. Leos will expect the same in return. If they don't get it, be ready to console and comfort a snubbed Leo.

Virgo (August 23 to September 22)

Symbol: The Virgin

Element: Earth

House: House of Health, which represents strength, employment, vitality, healthcare, and skills.

Gemstone: Emerald

Colors: Brown, beige, yellow, orange, green, and navy

Lucky numbers: 5, 14, 23, 32, 41, and 50

Ruling planet: Mercury

Most common traits: Virgos need to help people around them, which makes them extremely dependable. They are:

- Super practical and hardworking
- Usually trying their best to keep people around them happy
- Resourceful and intelligent
- Believed to be obsessive perfectionists
- Despised for their criticizing nature

Libra (September 23 to October 22)

Symbol: The Scales

Element: Air

House: House of Balance, which represents marriage, partnership, business agreements, contracts, and equilibrium.

Gemstone: Diamond

Colors: Pastels, especially blue and green

Lucky numbers: 6,15, 24, 33, 42, 51, and 60

Ruling planet: Venus

Most common traits: This sign is extremely social and can make friends easily. Other than that, the individuals of this zodiac sign are:

- Full of wit, morals, and manners
- Extremely charming
- People pleasers
- Known to be great problem solvers
- Codependent

Scorpio (October 23 to November 22)

Symbol: The Scorpion

Element: Water

House: House of Transformation, which represents rejuvenation, birth and death cycles, resources, finances, karma, and self-transformation.

Gemstone: Coral

Colors: Dark red, scarlet, and rust

Lucky numbers: 9, 18, 27, 36, 45, 54, 63, 72, 81, and 90

Ruling planet: Mars

Most common traits: Scorpios are known for their ambitious nature and super-serious attitude towards work and their career. They are:

- Serious about relationships and can dive in too deep
- Extremely trustworthy
- Super-curious and in love with mysteries
- Controlling and hard to figure out
- Often suspicious about everything, which makes them paranoid

Sagittarius (November 23 to December 21)

Symbol: The Archer

Element: Fire

House: House of Philosophy, which represents culture, expansion, law, ethics, travel, and foreign affairs.

Gemstone: Yellow Sapphire

Colors: Purple, red, pink, and violet

Lucky numbers: 1, 4, 8, 10, 13, 17, 19, 22, and 26

Ruling planet: Jupiter

Most common traits: People bearing this sign are probably the most curious of all. They possess a thirst for knowledge and information. Other than that, they:

- Are hardworking
- Are always exploring new pursuits
- Possess incredible storytelling skills
- Are believed to be know-it-alls
- Often talk over others

Capricorn (December 22 to January 19)

Symbol: The Goat

Element: Earth

House: House of Enterprise, which represents career, society, government, motivation, authority, and advantage.

Gemstone: Blue Sapphire

Colors: Dark brown and black

Lucky numbers: 1, 4, 8, 10, 13, 17, 19, and 22

Ruling planet: Saturn

Most common traits: Capricorns are ambitious and put their career over anything else. Other than that, they:

- Bear a drive and unending passion for their work and achieving milestones
- Are known to take initiatives
- Form excellent leaders
- Have a slight need to control everything
- Do not believe in "me" time and work hard endlessly, which explains their stone-cold demeanor toward others

Aquarius (January 20 to February 19)

Symbol: The Water Bearer

Element: Air

House: House of Blessings, which represents effort, friends, groups, communities, belongings, volunteering, associations, love, and wealth.

Gemstone: Blue Sapphire

Colors: Turquoise, blue, green, and gray

Lucky numbers: 4, 8, 13, 17, 22, and 26

Ruling planet: Saturn

Most common traits: This sign loves their share of independence and wants freedom in every aspect of their life. Other than that, they:

- Have a unique personality that helps them stand apart from the crowd
- Are always looking for ways to change the world
- Are creative thinkers

· Often have controversial opinions in debates and conversations

· Feel the need to push their "unique" perspective in any matter

Pisces (February 20 to March 20)

Symbol: The Fishes

Element: Water

House: House of Sacrifice, which represents retreating, seclusion, refuge, intuition, luck, healing, peacefulness, and completion.

Gemstone: Yellow Sapphire

Colors: Sea green, violet, purple, and lilac

Lucky numbers: 3, 7, 12, 16, 21, 25, and 30

Ruling planet: Jupiter

Most common traits: Probably the kindest individuals of all signs, Pisceans are dreamy and passionate. Along with this, they:

· Are able to establish deeper connections with people

· Are extremely creative and positive

· Come up with new and imaginative ideas

· Are often lost in daydreams and are absent-minded

· Can get easily overwhelmed

Famous Leos

In this section, we will learn about a few famous Leos and their defining or most prominent Leo traits.

1. Barack Obama

This personality ranks number one on the list. An ideal leader, motivational speaker, and a compassionate human being, Barack Obama is probably the most significant Leo in the world's history. Born on August 4, 1961, Barack Obama is popularly known as a former U.S. President. Naturally, due to his leadership qualities, Obama tends to steal the spotlight in any setting. His speeches can be moving, bold, and clever. He is intelligent and possesses the ability to make a crowd follow him. Along with this, he is curious, possesses great communication skills, and can motivate a huge crowd merely by his presence.

Defining Leo Trait: He is a born leader. His charm is addictive, and people respect his opinion as a leader. We all know about the changes he made in the United States during his presidency and leadership.

2. Arnold Schwarzenegger

Schwarzenegger is another popular personality in the world of acting and fitness. He was born on July 30th, 1947 and has motivated many young adults to partake in their fitness journey and achieve their goals in this direction. Arnold is known to be kind, generous, and warm, which comes from the Sun sign of Leos. As witnessed in the past, Arnold is not able to take criticism easily and hates being ignored. He is a creative being and wants to show it to the world. His world revolves around drama, luxury, movies, and theatre, which is a prominent Leo trait in him. If you give him love, he will return an equal or greater amount of love to you. He often likes to be the center of attention.

Defining Leo Trait: He feels frustrated and discouraged when he cannot prove his worth. He will work hard to make a point and stand true to his word.

3. Bill Clinton

Another U.S. president with a strong and significant presence in world history, Bill Clinton is a Leo with strong traits of this sign. Born on August 19th, 1946, Clinton is another Leo that has proven his leadership skills as a Leo. While he did prove his leadership qualities in the professional and political world, his personal life was also dictated by his prominent Leo traits. He was known to be a womanizer with irresistible charm, if not looks. Women were smitten by his charisma and personality. His spouse was ready to let pass many of the negative traits that most Leos possess, which explains the strong bond between them. Lastly, when Clinton was in power, he had a motivational aura around him. The knack for drama in most Leos explains the controversy that surrounded the president.

Defining Leo Trait: As a Leo, Bill Clinton has proven his leadership qualities along with being a charismatic person and a strong personality, right from his younger days.

4. Napoleon

Born on August 15th, 1769, Napoleon Bonaparte was well known in the world for his military skills and for seizing the French emperor's title. As a Leo, he wanted his fair share of the spotlight. Even though this phenomenon was not literally named in the olden days, Napoleon always managed to be in the center and commanded others with authority. He was a brave fighter and leader in the military.

Defining Leo Trait: His bravery, the need to be the ruler, and leadership skills are apparent Leo traits.

5. J. K. Rowling

Famously known for her *Harry Potter* books and movie series, this author was born on July 31st, 1965. Her strong and charismatic personality captures the room as soon as she enters. She is also believed to be warm, kind-hearted, and generous, which are the Sun sign's indicators. Her generous trait is proven by the fact that she donated a major amount of her earnings to charity, which led to the removal of her name from the list of billionaires in Forbes. But she has recently been in the news for her new book and infamous "trans" comments, which explains Leos's penchant for controversial or dramatic gimmicks.

Defining Leo Trait: Her most prominent Leo trait is creativity. Her flair for writing and imagination skills are powerful, which aligns with some Leos. Also, her generosity is another powerful Leo trait.

6. Madonna

Born on August 16th, 1958, Madonna has been a popular figure since her youth. She is known for her confidence, singing talent, and exotic beauty. Madonna has always loved to be the center of attention and continues enjoying her fame and limelight. Her Leo traits are so centered that she can be deemed the epitome of the zodiac sign. Also, she can work on multiple projects at a time, which is a lesser-known Leo trait. She has been the center of many controversies and has somehow always managed to be in the spotlight.

Defining Leo Trait: Her charm, personality, and talent are some of the most apparent and positive Leo traits. The need to be the center of attention is her major Leo trait.

"Placing" a Leo

Even though Leo behaves the same in most settings, you can still notice subtle differences in their behavior due to a change of surroundings.

Leo at Home

While a Leo at work or in any other public setting is at the top of their game, they want to be in their own cocoon at the end of the day to release stress and take some "me" time. A Leo at home is more relaxed as they take time in their space to unwind and contemplate. In fact, when work and socializing become too extreme for Leos, they will often disappear and stay at home for a couple of days until they have their energy back. They want time off from the chaos of the world. Home is where they take time to recharge and return stronger, but even at home, Leos can be found exploring new options and skills. Give them just a day to relax, and they will be doing something new.

Leo at Work

At work, Leos take charge of a project or any other follow-ups where leadership qualities are mandatory. They are driven, motivated, and put in a 100-percent effort to achieve their goals, but they make sure that they are validated for it. If any of your colleagues are a Leo, you will find them near the boss most of the time. They will also try to make their work more noticeable. They want their boss to praise and appreciate them. If they don't receive positive feedback, Leos will sulk and even throw tantrums. If you are a Leo, you might notice yourself throwing a fit whenever you receive constructive criticism in an office setting.

Leo at a Party

Leos at a party are the show stealers. Their irresistible charm and extroverted nature attract people to them. If you are a Leo and are alone at a party, you will immediately find company and make yourself comfortable. Leos have no problem or awkwardness when they meet new people. They are spontaneous and masters at building new relationships in a jiffy. At a party, you will find a Leo either dressed too extravagantly or at the center of the stage; Leos love attention and will often engage in such meager attempts to garner attention.

Leo Cusps

Individuals born on the edge of two zodiac signs belong to a "cusp". These individuals have a combination of traits relevant to both signs. At the same time, you can also expect these traits to clash, which results in the unique personalities of those on cusps.

There are two cusps for every zodiac sign. In the case of Leos, they form cusps with Cancer, which precedes the Leo sign, and Virgo, which follows the house of Leo. Within these cusps, you can expect individuals who are entirely different from each other because of the Sun's dominance. An individual belonging to each cusp will possess qualities depending on the Sun's direction and powerful stance.

Cancer-Leo Cusp (July 19ᵗʰ to July 25ᵗʰ)

If the sun falls toward the Cancer sign, the individual will be too expressive, social, and a complete extrovert. Basically, the individuals born on this cusp are introverts who are on their way to becoming extroverts. They are also blessed with creative skills and generous nature. Sharing and receiving gifts will be routine for these individuals. But if the Sun is on Leo's side, the individual feels vulnerable from the inside and possesses a lot of insecurities; it is very easy to hurt such individuals. People in this cusp can be at the top of their game one day and feeling sad and depressed the next. The sudden change in their mood results from the trait combination of both signs.

They behave like children and are stubborn. Even if they are hurt and feel insecure inside, they will not show it. Instead, they will mask it with a playful spirit. People born on this cusp are creative, courageous, loving, generous, and often self-absorbed, but they seem to be emotionally blocked at times.

Leo-Virgo Cusp (August 19ᵗʰ to August 25ᵗʰ)

If the sun takes Leo's side within this cusp, the individual will turn out to be a perfectionist. They will have an air of creative freedom and the need to express themselves. But if the Sun takes the Virgo's side, the individual is more expressive. A combination of these traits will form a person who is a perfectionist with a creative and playful flair.

People belonging to this cusp are always excited about beginning a new journey, especially if it is going back to school to begin a new term after a long summer break. An interesting aspect of this cusp is that people from both signs possess different egos. Virgos serve others while Leos expect others to serve them, which brings an interesting imbalance to this cusp. They will readily serve you, but with a flair of pride, almost with a portrayal of obligation. While they still behave like divas (which is a prominent trait in Leos), they will also arrange and fulfill their tasks on time, as most Virgos do. While this cusp is still a perfect choice for an actor or a celebrity in the entertainment industry, the Virgo side of this cusp is more apt to be a director.

Some Fun Facts about Leos

While learning their basic traits, elements, and other foundational information is necessary, you should also know a few fun facts about this sign.

· Leos love drama. They can be seen in or anywhere near a dramatic situation. Truth be told, Leos in high school would form a Drama Kids Club as their clique. Also, due to their fondness for drama, their ideal location would be Hollywood, California.

· Leos are believed to be addicted to shopping. Even if they are, or are about to be, broke, they will find a way to shop and acquire the things they like. Leos are known to be stubborn, so they will get what they want at any cost. Since shopping is an addiction, their desires often revolve around new clothes, shoes, and other luxury items.

· Leos will prefer a spiced pumpkin latte in Starbucks.

· An exotic phrase that suits Leos would be *la douleur exquise*, a French phrase that translates to "the pain of unrequited love," which describes their need and passion in relationships and love life.

· If they were to choose or assign a Harry Potter house in the zodiac, all Leos would most likely fit in Gryffindor.

· Given their need to be a star and in the spotlight, they would prefer a clothing item that is sparkly or anything that grabs attention. The glamor and pizzazz that comes from clothing items often enthrall them.

If you are a Leo, most of these fun facts will be relatable. As an exercise, think about other fun facts that relate to other categories with your traits. Consider categories like music, movies, books, seasons, food items, etc., and note them down.

Chapter 2: Strengths and Weaknesses of a Leo

After acquiring some basic information on the traits and other aspects of the sign, we will hop on to this sign's strengths and weaknesses.

Strengths or Positive Traits of Leos

Among the several positive traits of Leos, these stand out the most:

1. They are Warm, Bright, and Bring Love to People in Their Lives

Leos love and are loved by the people in their lives. They possess a bright and warm personality, often a sign of their ruling planet, the Sun. They love their family and friends unconditionally and bring peace and happiness to their lives. They are highly dependable, which attracts people. To top that, Leos are kind, compassionate, and polite, which makes them seem brighter.

A Leo will make sure that their family and friends are comfortable. Their hospitable nature is always welcoming. Whenever Leos meet someone, they immediately make them feel at home. But do not take advantage of their kindness, as they will easily pounce and take revenge without remorse.

2. They are Charismatic

Wherever they go, Leos take the lead stance and seem like the most important person in the room. Their personality, presence, and character collectively make Leos charismatic. Due to this charm, Leos can attract whoever they want, eventually making them stay for a prolonged period. A person's charm is often dictated by their positive traits, which explains Leos's charismatic personality. They are loyal, brave, good looking, and confident enough to personify charisma.

Along with this, they are also blessed with a great sense of humor. Their wit and jokes help them get where they want to go or fulfill tasks with ease. The charismatic personality of Leos is so magnetic that it is often compared to a moth attracted to a flame. Leos attract people and keep them entertained. Besides this, Leos possess power and are driven by ambition, which adds to their charm and powerful personality.

3. They are Social and Can Easily Build Relationships with People They Have Just Met

Leos have no trouble approaching strangers at parties or opening a conversation with people they have just met. Whether it's chit-chat with the staff at the convenience store or meeting a professional in a formal setting, Leos have it easy. They'll say "yes" when you propose to go out and don't have that "I just want to stay home" attitude that other signs have by default. You can call them extroverts who make others feel comfortable. They are highly likely to interact with people they find interesting or who share similar traits.

If you are Leo, you have nothing to worry about in a social gathering with strangers. You will easily befriend others and make yourself comfortable in any setting. If you are not a Leo, you will likely be approached by one. Leos just love to be around people. They cannot be alone and always look for opportunities to go out and socialize. Their extroverted nature triggers them to throw parties, social events, or small informal gatherings like weekend dinners to meet people.

4. They are Born Leaders

If you need anyone to lead a group project in your school or office or make important decisions as the leader of any pack, you can always turn to a Leo. They are reliable and take charge of any situation. They are quick on their feet and can decide easily, helping you navigate urgent situations that require spontaneity. Decision-making ability is needed in most leaders and is thoroughly fulfilled by Leos. As a Leo, your aura is regal, and you instantly inspire people to follow you. Even though you like being the center of attention, you work hard to earn it; it is not merely handed out to you, which is another reason why you want to take charge and lead the group. Leos also have an intuition that pleases the crowd which is why they are often in command and motivate their followers.

Consider the trait of being social in most Leos. They not only want to throw parties and meet people, but they also want to be in charge of the celebrations. Leos like being the host and leader in any event. They love to take charge of any formal or informal situation. Whether it's a political agenda, a national leader, a CEO of a company, or a host of a party, you can always rely on Leos to take the lead and make informed decisions. They never quit and work hard to accomplish their goals.

5. Leos are Highly Protective of Their Loved Ones

Leos guard their family, friends, and other precious relationships as much as they can. Their brave nature helps them tackle any obstacles and make sure that their loved ones are safe and at peace. They will go to any length to keep their relationships intact. They value their friends and family too much and will fight until their last breath to protect them and their relationship. If there is even a slight chance of the relationship being in trouble, they will try their best to fix it. Leos are extremely passionate. They give and want passionate love, to a point where it can get intoxicating.

Leos are known for their bravery and confidence, which enhances their protective trait. Since the Fire symbol guards Leos, they are passionate and put in all their energy to protect what they love. Leos' bravery trait is related to their protective nature and the willingness to perform risky activities. Leos are not easily intimidated by fearful circumstances and will take risks. Leos rarely say no and are most excited about activities that most people refuse to undertake. From going on dangerous hikes to investing money in a business, Leos do not fear risks. They are extremely adventurous.

6. Leos Forgive Easily and are Honest

No matter how much or how deeply they are hurt, Leos forgive easily and will give another chance to the people who have wronged them. Be it breakups, marriage, friendships, or casual relationships, they want to keep the people in their life, but for them to forgive others, they want an apology, and a sincere one. They don't hold grudges, which keeps them cheerful and happy most of the time. This positive trait of Leos lets them keep precious relationships intact.

Leos are probably one of the most honest signs in the zodiac. They stick to their word and pay all debts. When it comes to keeping promises, you can always rely on this sign. They are honorable and do what they say, but if they feel like they can't do it, they will say so to keep you from building false expectations; this saves both parties time and helps them move on. Their honesty is another reason they form good leaders and can lead a team to success.

7. Leos are Creative and Entertaining

They possess creativity and the perception to see things differently, which keeps their creative juices flowing. They are often seen trying out new hobbies and activities. If you have a Leo in your inner circle, you may notice that they are always up to something. Their passion for adventure and exploration is never-ending; it makes them joyous company with whom you like to spend time.

Equally, Leos have a great sense of humor that keeps the people around them entertained. Leos are not only entertaining but can also stay entertained themselves. Their constant need to do something and try new activities keeps them busy and enhances their skill set.

Weaknesses or Challenging Traits of Leos

Having gone through their strengths, let's now discuss weaknesses and challenging traits of Leos that could cause trouble in their lives.

1. Leos are Impulsive

At times, Leo can be quite impulsive. While taking immediate action without thinking twice is useful in some circumstances, it can also lead to a lot of problems. Let's take an example given earlier – investing in a business. It is a huge risk that needs concrete assumptions and demands calculated steps. You cannot simply jump to a decision. Even though Leos make informed decisions, this trait's spontaneity can also result in a major downfall due to unforeseen circumstances.

But when an opportunity comes knocking on their door, they will usually think twice before making a decision, which saves them from trouble. Their impulsive nature only kicks in when they get an idea and want to implement it. They just cannot wait to see an idea of their own taking shape, which results in impulsive decisions. When they are handed something they think twice, but they are quick to take the risk when they come up with their own plan.

2. They Can be a Bit Controlling

This weakness of Leos can lead to a failed relationship. Sadly enough, Leos do this unknowingly. Until they realize their controlling behavior, it is often too late. When this trait overshadows others, they could end up losing their partners. Many people break up with their Leo partners, ending relationships that lasted more than a decade.

For Leos, it is important to realize the nature of their controlling behavior and work at it. Failing to do so can result in incompatible relationships which eventually result in breakups or divorces. Their controlling behavior is also a reason for their stubborn nature because they feel they are right all the time; they believe it gives them the authority to control their partners and family. If this trait is strong in any Leo, they might repel people or even lose them forever.

3. Leos are Often Stubborn and Defensive

They are not ready to listen to others. When they desire something, they will go to great lengths to achieve it. It is helpful in occasional situations, such as achieving your career goals or working hard to buy a luxury car, but in situations where Leos should step back and listen to others, such as a topic of discussion in a social gathering, they often agree to disagree. Often, this stubborn attitude comes across as arrogance, unbeknownst to the Leo.

Also, when they are not allowed to have certain things, they don't listen and try hard to get them anyway, by any means. For example, a diabetic Leo will find a way to eat that chocolate bar that they craved. When someone says that they are not allowed to do something or that they are wrong, they will fight back to prove otherwise. Their defensive nature can be problematic. This nature of arguing and defending until they turn blue in the face is not appreciated by other signs, which is one of the few reasons for being repelled by a Leo. It doesn't matter whether they are right or wrong; if Leos think that they are right, they will do anything to prove their point.

4. Leos are a Bit Egoistical

Leos are probably the most egotistical among the zodiac signs, which can often be problematic. For the Leo, their large egos can be a major problem. They cannot handle criticism well and are easily offended. Even when they face constructive criticism, they can take it too seriously.

Their egos also pave the path to their selfishness. Leos feel that they deserve everything and more. They often put their needs in front of others, which makes them appear selfish and even greedy. Even though they realize this act is selfish, they hardly care and are unwilling to compromise. Due to their intelligence, they always feel they are above everyone else, which also explains their need to be in the spotlight. The hard part is, they manage to gain it somehow. The sense of entitlement is combined with their ability to take advantage of all opportunities thrown at them, feeding their ego even more. Their egos also make them believe that the world revolves around them.

5. They Cannot Deal with Their Insecurities

Leos are well aware of their insecurities and can be easily and deeply saddened when someone targets their insecurity, becoming even more insecure. In other words, their egos can be deemed their biggest insecurity. Since Leos have this urge to be perfect in the way they look, perform tasks, and every other aspect of their lives, any grievances against or pointing out of their insecurities can be too hard for them to handle. If it continues for a long period, they might even break. In a way, targeting their insecurity means pointing out their imperfections, which could also steal their spotlight. No Leo likes or wants that.

They want to be respected and praised all the time. If not, it could take a major toll on their self-esteem. Even if you don't mean it, they will take things personally and keep thinking about it time and again.

6. They Need Constant Validation

Leos need attention and constant validation. They make a show of not caring about others' opinions, but deep down, they need attention and love. A prolonged absence of validation can make them childish until they get enough attention. They feel the need for approval from others, even from people they have just met. When they work hard for something and do not get the praise they deserve, Leos can become too angry and even desperate to get their work noticed. Their usual thoughts are, "I deserve to be praised for something I achieved in less time than others," or "Why hasn't anyone noticed my hard work yet?"

This trait of seeking attention can drive them to show off and boast about their achievements, which is an attempt to come across as acceptable. They try hard to show what they are and want others to perceive them in this way, but their pride will never let them admit that they need constant validation; this trait is toxic and needs to be worked on for them to come across as humble and grounded. It is not easy, but with practice, it will come to them.

7. They are Unable to Bear Losses

Leos can be deemed hopeless romantics. They do need attention, but they are ready to give equal attention. But a minor inconvenience, insult, or loss in relationships can leave a deep scar in their hearts. In cases such as breakups and divorces, they not only get hurt but are also not able to bear the loss. In intense situations, this could lead to a major downfall and chaos in a Leo's life.

8. They Can be Too Materialistic

Leos are attracted to expensive objects and indulge in luxury. They tend to over-shop, and it is difficult for them to stop. If they like something, they will try their best to own it, no matter how expensive it is. To some degree, they will also judge people who are unable to afford or give them expensive objects.

How to Navigate Leo Weaknesses

If you are a Leo, possessing the weaknesses mentioned above is natural. Knowing about them is half the battle won, but you should also focus on navigating these to improve your life.

1. Set Long-Term Goals

Leos are impulsive and will take risks to see their idea to take shape in reality, but at times, this spontaneity can lead to failure. To combat this situation, a Leo should set some long-term goals. These might help a Leo to make more focused decisions and fulfill their goals with ease. Even though this approach takes time, it is a sure-shot way to achieve success.

So, how can a Leo set long-term goals? The first step is to define them. Ask yourself relevant questions like, "What do you truly desire?" or "Where can you see yourself in the next five years?" These questions will help you narrow down realistic milestones. Make sure that they are relevant, realistic, and achievable. If your goals are not achievable, there is no pointing in writing them down. To make them more plausible, cut them down into smaller goals or steps that will eventually lead you to the bigger picture. So, design your goals accordingly. Last, do not give up. If your ultimate goal is to buy your dream house, work hard toward it, and make it happen. Your smaller goals will be to save money and conduct research for the best properties in your locality. As a Leo, you will naturally have the drive to work hard and fulfill your goals.

2. Focus on Your Actions Instead

When a Leo finds themselves in a dramatic setting (which is quite often), they will likely reply with a snazzy comment or even swear at the other person. This tendency should be controlled and avoided. If you truly want to answer them in an impactful way, show them with your actions. If your boss bashes you for not reaching the goal sooner, work harder to achieve more than anyone in your office in the next quarter instead of answering back defensively. Ease up on the drama and divert your attention toward achieving your goals instead of adding to the drama. As they say, "Focus your attention on turning lemons into lemonade instead of throwing them at others."

If your impulsive nature wants you to reply with harsh words, count to three before you say something. Even though it sounds clichéd, it does work. It will save you from saying something that you'd later regret. Try the "Big Gulp" action, where you signal yourself and make yourself more attentive. Also, take it one step at a time. Do not burn yourself out to achieve far-reached goals. Take it slowly and keep going at a steady pace. Consistency and patience are key to fulfilling your goals.

3. Try to Put Others' Needs Before Your Own

As a Leo, your selfishness might seem more apparent at times because you have obviously put your needs ahead of others.' It makes you come across as selfish, needy, and greedy. Individuals who know about this negative trait of Leos often try to take advantage of this, especially in a work setting, so it is necessary for you to navigate this negative trait and focus on others. Even though it is fair to consider your needs too, focusing too much on yourself will make you selfish and put you in a negative light. To navigate selfishness and put the needs of others before you, you must first acknowledge this behavior. It is believed that the more selfish people are, the less they realize the decree of their selfishness. So, reflect on your behavior and ask whether you are selfish or not.

Next, reflect on and realize what others are going through. For instance, if a grocery store clerk is rude to you, it could just mean that they are upset or having a bad day. At times, it is not what it looks like on the surface. Try to assume the best of the other person. Instead of thinking, "It's me against the world," change your mindset to "We should conquer our goals together." If your needs are still important, take what you really want and cannot do without. While you are doing that, make sure that you are not causing an inconvenience to others.

4. Prevent Arrogance

Leos are known to be arrogant and often look down on others. Even though they don't mean it, their regal aura and pompousness make them look arrogant. Sadly, Leos don't realize their pompousness and arrogance as they believe it to be self-confidence, which is perceived otherwise by most signs. This arrogance can even affect a Leo's personal relationships and career. Before it's too late, every Leo should learn to control this behavior.

The first step to combat arrogance is self-realization. Once you realize that you are arrogant, not self-confident, it will be an eye-opener. Increase self-awareness and try to perceive your behavior through others' perspectives. For this self-realization to occur, look for signs in your behavior. A cocky attitude, constant interruption, playing the blame game, and giving unnecessary or unsolicited advice are all signs of arrogance. Treating everyone around you as a competitor or the constant use of condescending words or phrases add to the arrogance factor.

Once you achieve this realization, you have won half the battle. Next, try to be compassionate to others and yourself. Don't take yourself too seriously and try to laugh at yourself. It shows humility and modesty. Treat yourself and others with kindness. Accept mistakes and try to learn from them. Don't try too hard to hide them. Lastly, enjoy your own company and do something that makes you happy and calm. Even though it will take time, consistent practice will help you combat arrogance. Since this is one of Leos's biggest weaknesses, overcoming or learning to navigate it will help you clear the blockage you previously had to succeed in life.

5. Stop Yourself from Buying Items That You Don't Need

Most Leos feel the urge to indulge in luxury and buy expensive objects, even if they cannot afford them. Since they want to be appreciated for their expensive taste, they will buy an item, even if it means emptying their savings. One simple way to prevent this is to put a stop to shopping urges. To do this, you must first acknowledge the fact that your attachment to materials is toxic and irrelevant. Attaching yourself to materials sets up a self-perpetuating cycle in life. The more you buy, the more you will want. It is why many people are resorting to the concept of minimalism, which implies that you must live as simply and minimally as possible, with only the objects that you need and not everything that you think you want. This practice has proven to bring inner peace and joy to people who have followed it for many years.

To control your urge, the first step is to put your needs in front of your wants. Before you decide to buy something impulsively, ask yourself whether you truly need it or not. If it's just a want and not a need, hold off on the purchase. Think about where you can put the same money for better use. Invest it somewhere or add it to your savings. Another way to stop impulse buying is to avoid going to the mall or shopping area entirely. Once you are near such an area, you will automatically be compelled to buy. So, to avoid impulsive buying, avoid going to the mall in the first place. If your friends ask you to hang out at the mall, avoid it at all costs. Yes, it will be difficult for you to resist, but you must learn the value of putting your needs in front of your wants.

Another trick is to freeze your credit card. If you don't have a credit card, never consider getting one. Cancel your credit card or freeze it until you learn to control impulsive buying.

While Leos are blessed with more positive traits, their small weaknesses can be navigated easily to bring their best personality forward. Even though they are stubborn, they are often regarded as the most generous, warm, and intelligent individuals in a room. Once they manage to navigate their weaknesses, they can easily achieve their goals and succeed in life.

Chapter 3: The Leo Child

In this chapter, we will talk about Leo children and the traits they express. You will also learn how Leos interact with other kids and what they can do to improve their relationship with other children.

Leo as a Child

Leo kids are usually generous and warm. They are full of energy and radiate positive vibes. They are often enthusiastic about their life experiences and endure every moment with happiness. Even though they look confident and tough from the outside, it is highly likely that they are vulnerable or even scared on the inside. They possess a touch of vanity, which hasn't developed fully. They look confident, but if you mess with them, it could hurt them deeply. In extreme cases, it could even destroy their self-esteem.

If you are a parent to a Leo kid, you may have to reflect on your tone when disciplining your child. Harsh or mean words can lower a Leo kid's confidence. It is then difficult for Leo kids to get back on track. So, maintain composure and train or discipline your kid in the right manner. Every Leo kid is on a constant hunt for approval and appreciation. Whether it's their parents, teachers, friends, or even guests at home, Leo kids will try their best to glean a word or two of praise. They are not shy and will enthusiastically perform a nursery rhyme or dance to hear a few claps from guests.

From a young age, Leo kids will look in the mirror, dress up, and try to gain everyone's attention around them. When they receive enough praise and appreciation, they will work harder to gain more attention; this is why they usually turn out to be successful, even if there is an ulterior motive attached. The confidence and skill set from a young age is another reason Leos have excellent leadership skills. Since the Lion represents Leos, they are blessed with natural leadership skills.

Leos are so talented and skilled that they might attract opportunities from a very young age. They are skilled enough to be actors in plays or even TV commercials. If they get selected to the football team, it's no surprise either. Leo kids will never shy away from the prospects of becoming popular and will make the most of all opportunities. Even if they don't do well initially, they will develop their skill set on the way and will ultimately excel.

Besides this, Leo kids are known for their honesty and loyalty. They will never lie, even if they will end up in trouble. As a parent of a Leo kid, you should reward them for their honesty; it will inspire them to be honest in the future. Leo kids are also known for their firm morals. Rewarding Leo kids for their honesty and morals are more important than praising them for their sense of style and looks. Otherwise, they will grow up paying more attention to the way they look instead of the way they behave.

Leo kids will make you laugh. Since all Leos have an ingrained sense of humor, they are likely to crack you up. They are likely to be the leader of their group. Since they are bossy, they might be arrogant with other kids. Teach your child the importance of giving a chance to others. Make sure that they learn to give up arrogance. One way to handle this situation is to enroll them in scouting camps. These camps teach kids to be leaders, be humble, and to put their best skills to use to progress in life. Given Leos's talent and creative skills, scouting camps are the best way to mold their personality and character from a young age.

Leo Kids at Home

Leos at home are the same - chirpy and enthusiastic. You will always find them exploring or investigating new areas of their house. They will either show their creative flair by coloring on the walls or stay busy spreading their Lego set all across the floor. Basically, you will find a Leo kid up to something unusual.

They are the naughtiest but also the funniest among their siblings. Even if their parents don't admit it, Leo kids are their most favorite. If they are learning to ride a bike, they will keep trying until they learn perfectly. Failure is not an option for them; they will fail multiple times but still get up and keep at it until they achieve their goal. For Leo kids, quitting is better than accepting defeat, which changes somewhat when they mature. To build their confidence, help them accept defeat; teach them the importance of making mistakes, and learning from them. Teach them not to give up but also not to put too much emphasis on winning. Even if you don't teach them the definition of winning, this sign is already born with it.

Leos at home are often seen busy in various activities, most of which are set up by their parents to teach them new skills. As a parent of a Leo child, find their creative outlet, and set time aside for them to practice at home, usually after school. It can be painting, origami, cooking, or even board games that develop their memory. Building these skills at a young age is necessary, and since Leos are already blessed with creativity, intelligence, and curiosity, it is easier for you to convince them to follow their creative outlet.

Leo kids might also force their parents to get a pet. They love animals and are natural caregivers. Since Leos are full of passion and have a lot of love to offer, you can expect this trait to be a part of their natural personality. Another reason Leo kids like pets is that they are always ready for snuggles. When Leos don't get attention for long, they can always resort to their pet, who is ready to shower their owners with immense love.

Leo Kids at School

Leo kids at school will often hover around their teachers to hear words of appreciation for their finished homework or a drawing they made in art class. If they don't get the attention, they will make a fuss about it and even throw tantrums to gain their teacher's attention. They excel at studies and are often top of the class. Whether it's an art class, drama club, or the sports team, Leo kids are often seen excelling at everything they participate in. They also inspire their friends and classmates to perform well. If a class has two Leo kids, they are most likely to compete. It begins with healthy competition initially but might soon turn into fights or even hatred. Since Leos want all the attention to themselves, they will hate sharing it with the other Leos in their class.

Leo kids are often the star of their young friend group. They lead the pack during classwork or when they decide to play a prank. They are influential and trigger their friends to take part in any activity. It is also because of their bossy attitude. Other kids follow the Leo kid and often want to be like them. If a friend in the group has misbehaved or played a prank on someone, the kids' parents will question the Leo kid first, who is most likely the group leader.

On the playground, you will see them running around energetically and playing cheerfully. They have an impressive physical strength, one that outruns the others. You'll often spot a Leo kid on a monkey bar or climbing up on other installations without fear. Their daring and fearless attitude inspires them to explore new areas and objects, even if it's playtime. Keep an eye on them as they could end up in dangerous situations easily.

Leo as a Parent

Leos make great parents and are often known to be generous, warm, kind, and wise. Like themselves, they want their children to enjoy every moment and make the most out of the opportunities thrown at them. Since Leos are extremely confident, they want their kids to portray their best self, too. They will make sure that their kids are the best dressed in the room and will not mind if their children show off a little. Leos will give enough playtime to their kids and let them have plenty of fun. They are not as restrictive as other parents of different signs and understand the need to have enough freedom. Since Leos are never used to being enclosed or on a shelf, they understand the importance of liberty and give their kids enough.

In exchange, the children of Leo parents usually turn out to be open-minded, creative, and confident. They might catch traits of vanity from their Leo parent, but it is often harmless. Leo parents push their kids to do their best and provide them with all resources they need. They are keen on developing their kids' artistic and performance skills and support their creativity.

There are some downsides, though. Leo parents are so focused on their kids that they often ignore their social life, which is very unhealthy for a Leo. At the same time, their kids can get too demanding due to being pampered. If you are a Leo parent and are facing such an issue, you can schedule playdates for your kids. It will give you time to socialize with your friends and build your kid's social and communication skills. Or you can appoint a babysitter.

After all, you are a Leo; you have the need to rule and be in control of your life. Even before you had your kid, you retained your interests and adjusted them to your busy schedule. By taking time off, you can also pay more attention to your kid, which will not seem like a duty after that. It's a great practice for you and your child's development. You will notice the difference in the long run. Even if you are not a parent, keep these points in mind for when you become one. Your child will thank you.

Leo Kids with Leo Parents

While you already learned about Leos as kids and as parents separately, you might be curious to learn about Leo parents with Leo kids. This pairing is extremely interesting as both individuals need their own version of the spotlight. Both of you possess warm personalities with a bright and radiant aura. You enjoy each other's company and always try to learn a new skill together. As a Leo parent, you are mature enough to give up your share of the spotlight to make sure that your kid gets enough attention. You are attached to and in awe of your kid. Their skills, confidence, and generosity are something that you appreciate every day. Make sure that you praise your kid every day and guide them to become a better person.

Even though you both display tough demeanors, you are soft and vulnerable on the inside. Your Leo kids are even more easily hurt than you are. Try to protect your kids by showering praise and affection. It will help them forget about the incident and motivate them to focus on the positive side of life. Make sure that affection and praises are real, as Leo kids will have a sharp sense of detecting fakeness. Your affection and attention are needed to make your kid stronger.

When two Leos meet, differences are bound to arise. Once you and your Leo kid get into a fight, it is very difficult to arrive at a verdict. Neither of you will back off easily, which is the stubbornness trait of Leos. While you want the best for your kid, they will not appreciate your refusal to indulge them. In moments like these, it is your spouse who settles the quest, as neither of you will accept defeat. It is also likely that one of you will hurt the other's feelings. Even though you hate it, you don't like losing, especially when you are trying to fight for your kid's betterment.

What a Leo Kid Needs to Thrive and Feel Comfortable

As you learned, certain weaknesses in Leo kids need to be navigated for them to develop a positive personality and character. At the same time, certain positive traits should also be used in the right way to mold the skills of a Leo child. As a parent of a Leo, it is your job to do that from the onset.

Here are a few ways to do that:

1. Find a Way to Dispel Their Energy

Since Leo kids are extremely energetic, their parents should find ways to channel all that exhilarating energy in the right direction. For instance, enrolling them in a swimming class, gymnastics studio, or a football coaching club are some smart choices to put their energy to the best use. It will not only help them develop athletic skills but also enhance their socializing skills. If they are consistent and perform well, they can also take it up as a serious career choice, but before you enroll your Leo child in any class ask them their preference, as they would follow their passion more enthusiastically. It might turn out that they don't even like sports or such related agendas.

2. Be Patient with Your Leo Kid

Since Leo kids are stubborn, they must be handled with patience. Whether it's refusing to wear a certain outfit or being adamant about not finishing the vegetables on their plate, your Leo kid can be too stubborn and refuse to listen to you. It is difficult for a parent to get their way with a Leo kid, as they don't listen and only do what they want to. Due to their short temperament, they are also bound to throw tantrums when you don't listen to them. Even though this stubbornness trait can help them deal with bullies in school, it has a higher chance of affecting them negatively. Dealing with their stubbornness with patience is key to handling and diminishing it. Pair it with a little exasperation to handle it better.

As a parent of a Leo child, it is necessary for you to stay calm and be patient during intense situations. For example, if your kid is being stubborn about completing their homework, be patient, and think about dealing with this situation calmly instead of scolding them. To combat this situation, you can say, "Look at your friend, he is getting such good grades. Bet he does his homework every day. No wonder he is always top of the class." Since Leos want to be at the top, they will be driven to take the top spot for themselves. You will notice your Leo kid instantly turning to their homework.

3. Teach Them Moral Values

Sudden outbursts and throwing tantrums in public places are a common scene for most Leo kids. At some point, it becomes so normal that most parents get used to it, but it could affect their personality and personal life when they grow up. The best way to control this situation is to teach your Leo kid the importance of values and moral behavior. The importance of being gentle, calm, and composed should be repeated for your kids to grasp the entire concept. At the same time, you must behave similarly. Since kids copy their elders, it is highly likely that your child will copy you, too. If you are calm and can handle the situation calmly, your kid will reflect the same behavior as well. Lastly, pat their backs to calm them down. When throwing tantrums, your little monsters are full of rage and annoyance. Stroke their hair or pat their backs to make them calmer and soothe their anger.

They will also feel disappointed upon being rejected. They tend to think that they have to be perfect to be loved and respected. Teach your Leo kid that it is okay to be comfortable in your skin and achieving perfection is impossible. If they are not taught at an early age, they often burn themselves out to achieve all goals, even if it means sacrificing food, sleep, and inner peace. Most importantly, teach them these moral values in private, especially if they have made a mistake. If you point out their mistake in public and try to correct it in front of others, they will feel hurt, and it might even pierce their pride. If you hurt a Leo's pride, you are automatically added to their bad books.

4. Play Calming Music

Calming music offers therapeutic benefits to all living beings. Its soothing effect is equivalent to meditation, which relieves stress and improves concentration. It is a useful way to make your Leo kid calm down and maintain their composure. Kids' brains start developing at a tender age and playing calming music stimulates your kid's brain and enhances its functionality. Studies have proven the positive effect of calming music on brain development. Since Leos possess a liking for music and dance, playing music will keep them active, improve concentration, and enhance their skills. Not only calming music, but you can also play the music that your kid prefers. Whether it's a meditation tune, a pop song, or a lullaby, any tune will help in developing a Leo kid's brain. Since Leos are creative and have a fondness for music, dance, drama, and any other cultural mediums, they might even take it up as a career.

5. Set a Routine for Them

Make a bedtime routine a thing. Give your Leo child tasks to do before they go to sleep; this, of course, involves brushing their teeth and changing into nightclothes, but can also include other household chores such as taking the dishes to the kitchen or straightening their room. Make sure that the tasks you give them are not silly, and that they feel them to be important – after all, your Leo child feels like a king and needs to feel important and worthy of the tasks. The routine helps them unwind their energetic attitude and makes them more grounded. They also learn some organizational skills, along with the importance of being organized. And they learn the value of helping others and working as a team.

Your child is most likely to respond to this exercise and help you because Leo kids are generous, understanding, and full of energy. Also, by giving them bedtime chores, they feel needed. Slip in other silly tasks within the list of chores, too, such as picking up their clothes off the floor and putting their socks in the washing machine. If these tasks are on the list, they will do them relentlessly. To make it more effective, ask your kid to cross off a task once it is done. It will give them a feeling of accomplishment, which is what most Leos live for.

6. Make Sure That They are Brought Up in a Loving and Positive Environment

Leo kids need positive reinforcement and praise to stay happy and motivated. While you shouldn't spoil them with unnecessary praises, it is important to keep them on their feet – this is true with kids of any sign. Since their brains, character, and personality develop at a tender age, they should always be surrounded by positivity and love. If so, you will find your Leo kid responding more positively. They will always carry a bright aura, a smile on their face, and infectious energy that motivates other kids, too.

If the Leo child is a girl, you might find her to be too clingy. This behavior is often a result of fear to show emotional commitment, which often comes in the absence of healthy relationships. Once she gets even a bit of affection and love, she tries to cling to it and doesn't let go easily. To correct this, make your household a loving environment. Show her that affection and love are normal and that she'll always be loved. At the same time, teach her the sense of loving others and giving it back.

As you learned, Leo kids are supremely talented, curious, generous, and warm beings. As a typical trait of a Leo, they need their spotlight at school, at home, and on the playground. They will try their best to garner attention and affection from their parents, teachers, friends, and guests. If molded in the right way, their personality oozes charm as they grow up, but they can be too stubborn and do not yield easily. Also, they are fierce and loyal. If you break a Leo kid's trust by lying, they will turn a cold shoulder toward you, even if you are a parent. Even though they will forgive you easily and give you a second chance, they will hardly forget it and may bring it up the next time you repeat the mistake. Lastly, Leo kids are extremely confident, which will help them achieve their goals with no hassle. Pair that up with their creative skills, and you will have a leader in front of you.

Chapter 4: Leo in Love

We have now arrived at one of the most awaited parts of this book, which covers relationships and Leos in love.

Leos are passionate and fiery when it comes to love. Yes, we are talking about a mad, passionate, and intoxicating love that we often see in movies and read in books. They are not only excellent lovers in life but are also sensual in bed, but if left alone, Leos are brave enough to walk alone without any hesitation. They either love hard, or they don't – there's no in-between. If they love passionately, they expect the same in return. If you have a Leo for a partner, they will go to any lengths to prove their love and keep you safe. They expect the same in return, however; one wrong move and they are easily turned off. So, make sure that you are honest and able to reciprocate a Leo's love.

Compatibility with Other Signs

In this section, we will draw out a compatibility chart for the other zodiac signs and determine the most compatible sign for Leos.

Leo and Libra: While Leos are known for their competitive spirit, they would rather share the spirit with Libras instead of competing with them, and both traits will enjoy their spotlights. Not being competitive about it with Libras helps Leos attract them as potential long-term partners. If they enjoy being in each other's company and let their partner enjoy their part of success and spotlight, and even encourage them and participate in the celebration, all will be well.

Leo and Scorpio: Leos get more spotlight compared to Scorpios, which is not really an issue for the latter. In fact, they participate in the celebration and appreciate Leos for their achievements, but Scorpios do want their share of power, especially in a relationship with a Leo. If they don't get it, they could end up in a huge fight that could even destroy the relationship. Since Scorpios are known to choose and fight their battles wisely, there is a balance between these signs until one gets too hungry for power.

Leo and Sagittarius: Probably one of the most compatible pairings of signs, Leos and Sagittarius form a great couple and live their lives peacefully. There is hardly any drama in their daily lives. They create and achieve goals together. They enjoy each other's company so much that they divert their attention to accomplishing tasks that will help them reach their goal sooner. They talk less and do more. Along with this, they always have busy schedules and are rarely found at home because of their seriousness toward their career and goals, in which both signs support each other at every step. The fun-loving and adventurous nature of Leos is often well complemented by a Sagittarius.

Leo and Capricorn: These two signs are less likely to be attracted to each other, but when they are, they form a strong couple that is concerned about their reputation. This couple will work hard to establish their reputation and make sure that others see them as they want them to. While the need to be respected is stronger in Leos, Capricorns have a strong work ethic and are goal-oriented, which makes them shine in their professional peers' eyes. If they set their minds to it, this couple can win the world and achieve all their goals.

Leo and Aquarius: Aquarians and Leos have a higher chance of being sexually attracted to each other; this attraction often leads them to indulge in a non-vanilla relationship that is often casual. It is hard for these two signs to get involved in a serious relationship because they hardly have anything in common, but if they set their minds to it and work harder to make it happen, they can emerge as a strong couple. If you are a Leo and want to get into a serious long-term relationship with an Aquarius, you should make every effort to know the person inside and out. Since you do not have many similarities, knowing your partner will help you sustain the relationship.

Leo and Pisces: When compared to Leos, Pisceans are needy and want more attention, especially in relationships. Their need to be loved, nurtured, and understood falls on their partner. If a Leo does not fulfill the need, the relationship could end sooner. Also, Leos are stronger and more confident compared to Pisceans. The latter can easily crumble under serious circumstances and lack confidence; this is when Leos bring the balance with their high confidence and strength. If a Leo truly loves their Piscean partner, they will go to any lengths to protect their partner and nurture the relationship. In fact, in a Piscean and Leo relationship, the entire responsibility of handling and stabilizing the bond falls on the Leo. Also, the mutual understanding between both signs keeps the boat sailing, but if a Leo feels tired of being too strong over a prolonged period, the relationship could break.

Leo and Aries: Another great compatibility bond, Leo and Aries are known to be good friends and partners. Both these signs love spending time with the other. Even if they do nothing together, they feel comfortable in each other's presence. One peculiar trait that this couple possesses is that they have zealous and jealousy-inducing social tendencies. Deep down, they don't want their friend or partner to spend time with others and have the tendency to get jealous easily, but with understanding and trust, they can easily get over the jealousy factor.

Leo and Taurus: Since Leos possess the need for attention, a Taurus can get easily agitated. They don't appreciate the need to always getting validated, which triggers a Taurus; this could make them jealous and cause bigger problems in their relationship. A Taurus barely knows that they deserve to relax and take time off their busy schedules, whereas a Leo will always feel like being on edge.

Leo and Gemini: While none of these signs excel at "adulting", they can stay busy having fun all the time, which will alleviate the stress of responsibility. They know that they are in charge of their lives, bills, and survival, but they may fail to face this reality and cover this denial phase by playing together too much. They enjoy each other's company and rarely need a third person to have fun. They make each other laugh and only take responsibility when something falls out of order.

Leo and Cancer: Like a Taurus, a Cancer does not enjoy Leo's attention-seeking trait. They feel that their need for attention and validation is insincere, shallow, and inauthentic. While they do not want the spotlight on themselves, they also do not appreciate Leos always wanting to be in the spotlight, but once a Cancer gets to know a Leo, they can tolerate or let go of this need and flow with it easily. While they do not appreciate it, it doesn't have to bother them either. Since both these signs are massively different from each other, they hold the potential to complement and support each other.

Leo and Virgo: The relationship between both these signs is more mature compared to other pairings. They are open and ready to accept each other's strengths and weaknesses, resulting in an extremely mature and happy relationship. These signs are quite compatible and help each other at every step of the relationship. A Virgo doesn't mind a Leo taking the spotlight, which is appreciated by the Leo. This pairing proves that real balance can exist in relationships.

Leo and Leo: A Leo dating a Leo can be volatile at times as both need to be in the spotlight. Unless the partners are mature or are ready to let go of this weakness, the relationship can be too toxic; this is particularly witnessed in Leos who are in the same profession as their partner. A Leo couple who are both doctors or architects can often end up in a never-ending argument due to their need to be the star and their stubborn attitude. Leos who want to be in a serious and long-lasting relationship must find a balance and make it work somehow. It can only be achieved if one or both partners agree to take a step back when things are heated. But since Leos feel the need to be validated, they often give compliments and pay full attention to each other.

The teen Leo's first-time relationships, or acting on an attraction, can be interesting. Teenagers are often quite immature and don't know what to say or how to behave in certain circumstances, and this can be a major backlash for Leo teens exploring their first relationships. Leos need attention and want to be validated. It is a trait that is heightened in their teenage years when they are transitioning into adults. Their call for attention will be extremely loud in this phase, which could make things worse, but since they are attracting people their age, this can go both ways.

In an entirely opposite scenario, teenagers or other Zodiac signs might ignore Leo teens' attention-seeking trait. They may not understand the constant need for attention. Most teenagers of all signs will show similar behavior, which will make first relationships either too easy or too hard.

Most teen Leos are charming, good looking, have a great sense of style, and attract others to them. If you are a Leo and like someone, ascertain whether they have a problem with your garnering attention or not. If you belong to another zodiac sign and are attracted to a teen Leo, you will find them in big groups and difficult to approach.

So, what approach should teen Leos take to explore their first relationship? The wisest advice is to take your time. You must work on your pride (which comes from the Lion) as it could throw you off balance and make you rigid. Your teenage years are where your character and personality grow rapidly, so you must take enough time to build yourself before you find love. Since teen relationships for Leos might fail due to a lack of understanding, immaturity, and the inability to find a balance between both partners, it is wiser to wait for a few years.

First Relationships and Falling in Love

While falling in love and maintaining a relationship is easy for Leos, it can be very difficult for them to find an ideal partner. Even though the Lions are ready to go all-in, it takes time for them to find a partner who aligns with their needs. Even if they find someone, being in a long-term relationship is harder, the reasons for which will be explained in the next section.

Leos are open to dating and will take every shot at it. They are open-minded and do not hurry to judge a person without interacting with them properly. They savor every phase of dating – from feeling the butterflies to taking it to bed, and don't mind doing it all over again. For them, even dating is like an adventure; the more you explore, the better you know.

They do build a set of expectations before going on dates. They want their dates to behave and turn out in a particular way. If not, it can be disappointing for Leos, and they might take some time before going on the next date. It is highly likely to happen, because it is difficult for Leos to find an ideal partner. Only the lucky few rarely struggle in the dating world. At the same time, they do not mind going back to past relationships and giving them another chance. As Leos are extremely forgiving, they expect a person to change and behave up to their expectations. If this happens, they also occasionally find true love with exes or past dates.

In the bedroom, Leos get steamy and wild. They are passionate lovers, even on their first date. Due to their adventurous nature, they might also suggest videotaping their experience, if the partner is comfortable with it; this also explains their fondness for dirty talk. If you want excitement in your first relationship or date, you can always count on a Leo. If you are Leo, you must find someone who is ready to jump on the crazy bandwagon with you. When it comes to sexual encounters, the partners of Leos are lucky as Leos don't tire of pleasuring their partners, but they expect the same in return. So, if you are up for it, you will have a long ride in the bedroom.

Leo in Marriage or Long-Term Relationships

In this section, you will learn about the obstacles that may occur in a Leo relationship and how their traits (which were briefly explained earlier) influence the relationship.

· You might not like your Leo partner garnering attention. If you are someone who likes attention too, the relationship could turn into a competition, which is unhealthy. On the other hand, if you don't like attention but don't like others seeking it, it could also cause trouble in a long-term relationship with a Leo.

· They will act childishly if you don't give them enough time. It could be difficult to keep your Leo partner satisfied when you are under a lot of stress.

· Their fiery temperament can be quite a handful at times. If you disagree with anything they say, their temper can be explosive, which can lead you into an endless pit of arguments. They will go to any length to prove their point and win the debate (even if they are wrong), which can be extremely frustrating.

· If you cannot afford expensive things and gifts, your Leo partner might lose respect for you. While this is not always the case, and they give enough time for development, constant failure can be too off-putting for them, which could end a long-term relationship.

A Quick Guide to Dating a Leo

If You are a Leo

Two Leos as a couple can either be very strong or quite disastrous. Since they both equally need attention and do not appreciate anyone else being in the spotlight, the other person might become insecure. But Leos know and understand the feeling of being in the spotlight which gives them some leeway around each other, but this comes only with balance. If the partner is not mature enough or lacks understanding, it could lead to a breakup. So, before you date a Leo, talk to them about this. If they are not really into horoscopes, they will initially not believe in this foresight and immediately jump into a serious relationship. You are then responsible for carrying it off smoothly.

If You are Another Zodiac Sign

Depending on your zodiac sign, you will either love or despise your partner, in which case you will break up with them soon. While Leos are cheerful, hard-working, and passionate, their constant need for attention will either be off-putting for you or will hardly matter to you. If you are a Sagittarius, you have a high compatibility chance with Leos as you are least bothered about fame and wanting attention. On your first date, you will notice your Leo date flirting with the bartender or server. It is unintentional and far from being intended to make you jealous. They are just trying to squeeze in their occasional need for attention. You and your date know that you are the one going home with them. Also, it is highly likely that your date will dress well. They will appreciate it if you do, too, but make sure to draw the line early, as overshadowing them can steal their spotlight, which they will hate.

Attracting and Dating a Leo Man

Leo men prefer to feel like a king and want to be treated as one, especially by their partners. To seduce a Leo man, divert all your attention to treating him like a king and make him feel important. Just like Leo women, Leo men are also attracted to drama, so make sure that you add enough drama elements in your narration and overall experience with him. If you really want him to like you, give him respect and compliment him every once in a while.

He likes to hear compliments about his looks, so slip in tiny compliments like, "I like how your lips crinkle when you smile," or "Your big eyes are distracting." Do not make the compliments too obvious. Keep it low key; Leo men appreciate that and might even shake to a tiny dance in their heads. Also, make sure that the compliments are genuine. You do not want to come across as fake; Leos are smart, and they will instantly peg your fake compliments. Don't merely say it for his sake; mean it. The best part is you won't have to dig deep for compliments. Leo men are gentle, compassionate, and kind, which are easily complemented traits.

If you give him this treatment and attention, a Leo man is bound to reciprocate similarly and shower you with equal love and care. Once you attract a Leo man, be ready to be showered with gifts and passionate love. If you truly love him, you must show patience and prove your worth to him. Leo men need the assurance that their partners are strong and capable of handling tough situations in relationships. If you succeed, a Leo man will love you endlessly and passionately. If you really like a Leo man, be prepared to face some struggles, as Leo men are constantly on the hunt which means you might face serious competition from other women.

Keep trying and seducing him the way he likes, and if you succeed, you will be rewarded for it with gifts, luxury, and royal treatment. At the same time, be happy always and do not complain. Leo men adore cheerful women who can match their energy. Show him that you have a knack for adventure and are ready to explore new places with him. Leo men will love that and be attracted to you instantly, but when the time comes, prepare yourself to endure the adventure. Simply saying and not doing it can be a major turn off for Leo men, which could also mean that you were lying just to impress him.

Lastly, Leo men want their partners to be conscientious of how they feel. If he loves someone deeply, he will not show it easily, but he is 100-percent devoted to this relationship and always considers himself as the hero in the relationship. He gives you assurance and keeps you grounded. He proves the phrase "everything will be alright," to be accurate and reliable.

Attracting and Dating a Leo Woman

Just like Leo men, Leo women, too, need constant attention, praise, and compliments. All women like compliments, but Leo women are particularly keen to hear comments on their looks and personality. But understanding Leo women can be too complex. There is a major mix of positive and negative traits, so much so that finding a middle ground is too difficult. While some men with other signs can easily put up with Leo women, others prefer to stay away, especially if they hate someone who constantly seeks attention. If you are among the latter, you might want to rethink your decision to date a Leo woman.

Also, while dating a Leo woman, you must shower her with gifts, luxury, and this goes without saying – lots and lots of attention. Basically, a Leo woman should be the center of your world. Unless you are madly in love with her, this is next to impossible. If you are ready, make a note of all her rules and follow them religiously. Failing to do so can trigger her easily, and she will leave without giving you a fair warning, but since Leos forgive easily, she might take you back after a sincere apology. Just make sure that this doesn't happen in the first place because Leo women are hurt easily, and it is very difficult for them to get over losses.

Jealousy is a prominent trait in Leo women. Once she senses another woman in your life or close to you (even if it is platonic), she will leave you without giving you a chance to explain. Be careful and clear about your relationships with other women. As you know, Leos are controlling, which is very evident in Leo women. They will not listen to their partners and will try to control them. If you date a Leo woman, she will most probably decide what you can wear, eat, and do. She'll rarely let you have your own way. She will dominate you, but you will create a liking for it and let her control you because you know that she wants the best for you.

To attract a Leo woman, you must make her feel that she is one of a kind. She enjoys luxury, so an expensive gift once in a while will make her happy. Along with expensive gifts, this sign also appreciates worthy deeds. Choose an expensive and chic restaurant for your first date, because for Leo women, first impressions matter. If you are rich, you have a better chance of being accepted as a partner; this is due to their liking luxury and expensive materials. If you have nothing to offer except pure feelings, you might not stand a chance.

She is passionate in bed but does not appreciate games and experiments. The more love and passion you show her, the more a Leo woman will reciprocate equally or with even more love in return. She will be instantly attracted to you if you prove your worth and come across as a strong and independent individual but show her that she can depend on you. Treat her like a queen, care for her, and love her passionately.

A Quick Guide on How to Navigate a Healthy Relationship

Some Useful Tips for the First Date

If applied on your first date, these tips are bound to impress your Leo date and take it one step ahead. Even though some of these tips were briefly covered in the earlier sections, this short guide will sum up and offer extra ways to impress your date effectively.

· Let them choose the location. If you are planning to go on a date with a Leo man or a Leo woman, let them choose the location for the first date. They will likely choose something extraordinary, bizarre, or out of place because of their knack for adventure. They also want you to explore new places with them, so go along with it. After all, going to a place they prefer is better than choosing a place they might not like, which is a risky move when trying to make a first impression.

· If they give you the choice of selecting a location, they will appreciate a place known for its peculiar setting, expensive food, or class. It can be an expensive restaurant or even a musical play, since Leos love drama. Take them to a fine diner or dainty restaurant after the musical or theatre play. Give their curious souls variety and choices to devour. By doing this, you are allowing their creative inner child to come out, and this effort of yours will stay imprinted on their mind for a long time. If you really want to impress them, seek something adventurous and completely off the wall like a river-rafting experience or a hot-air balloon ride. Since they are into exploration, they will love the idea.

· Go for the finer things. Leos like everything luxurious, classy, and expensive. If you are at a restaurant, order the finest wine and try something new to eat. They prefer an expensive taste and like those who show and possess a liking for the finer things. If you are meeting a Leo woman for a date, buy her exotic and beautiful flowers that match her classy taste.

· Reach for the check or, at least, convince them to split it (if they reach first). Even though Leos will take charge and insist on paying the bill, they will appreciate it when you make an effort.

· If you are in a club, they might ask you to dance with them; remember their need to be in the spotlight, and don't say no. They like energetic people and want you to join them. Even if you hate dancing, make an effort. It doesn't matter if you suck at it; it's the effort that counts.

· Compliment them in a conversation. As mentioned earlier, do not forget to give compliments. It will put you in their good books instantly, and they will develop a liking for you. If you show interest, they will also show an interest. Get a bit touchy, but not in a creepy way. Leos are seasonal flirts and don't mind occasional sensual touches. When you first meet them, give them a huge hug instead of a handshake. Touch their hand when you feel excited or while giving a compliment; this mainly works when you are on a date with a Leo man. With a woman, it could come across as creepy and uncomfortable, so act accordingly.

· Give them a lot of attention, especially if you are meeting them with other friends. If a Leo gets lost in a crowd and does not get attention, they might feel snubbed. When they try to steal the spotlight, give them attention, and make them feel important among other people. A Leo man or woman will remember that for a long time and appreciate your concern.

How to Navigate and Sustain a Long-Term Relationship

Even though attracting and dating a Leo man is difficult in the beginning, it can be extremely rewarding in the long run. Your Leo man does need attention and assurance initially, but once he gets it, he will protect you until his last breath. So, dedicate yourself 100 percent to this relationship.

Here are some effective ways to navigate and sustain a long-term Leo relationship:

· Give equal love and passion. Leos are warm and compassionate. When they give love, they want to receive an equal amount or more back. So, to sustain your relationship, love each other passionately.

· Leos are extremely loyal. Needless to say, cheating can ruin any relationship, but with Leos, it will leave a deep scar for a prolonged period. They will break up with you and feel deeply hurt and bruised as their loyalty was never reciprocated. So, stay loyal, which is key to every relationship.

· Go above and beyond with flattery. If your Leo husband looks dapper in the new suit, tell him that. If your Leo wife is rocking the new heels, tell her that you cannot wait to be beside her in bed. Build a foundation of flattery, and you will have a long-term relationship; more importantly, a passionate and happy relationship.

· Amp up the drama. If you find an opportunity to show or let your Leo partner experience any sort of drama, do it. Since Leos love tiny doses of drama now and then, this will keep them exhilarated and excited.

· Do not hold them back. Leos are born leaders and have a strong desire for authority. If they want to build a new business, let them; if they want to lead a group project in their company, encourage and support them. Holding them back will stifle them, which is the last thing they want.

· You might have to lower your guard and listen to them. Leos are controlling, stubborn, and don't listen to others. Unless you think that they are absolutely wrong, you must listen to what they say. Failing to do so could result in fights, which could also mean the end of the relationship. If certain fights seem to get out of hand, give them time to reflect on their thoughts, and cool down.

· Don't let past mistakes or encounters ruin your present. Leo men despise it when you bring up the past and throw it in their face. Being the practical beings they are, they would rather divert their attention to the present and solve it. While it is hard to get an apology from Leos, they will sincerely apologize when they realize their mistake, so keep away from fishing for apologies. Let them realize it on their own and act accordingly. At the same time, they also do not entertain any kind of passive-aggressive behavior. Consider it a complete no-no as it could ruin your relationship completely.

Leos in love are either too rewarding or completely disastrous. If you really like a Leo and want to reap the benefits out of your relationship, you will have to put in some effort and have a lot of patience in the beginning. If you manage to navigate your relationship in the said manner, you will emerge a strong couple.

Chapter 5: Leo at a Party and with Friends

Even though we already discussed the brief traits of a Leo at a party, we shall take a look at it in detail. In this chapter, we'll discuss Leos's ability to befriend others, Leos in a typical party scene, their behavior and interactive ability, and follow up with a look at the mechanics of fostering a Leo friendship.

The sign of Lion indicates the pride of Leos, which is also shown in their friendship. Compared to other signs, Leos take utter pride in their friendships and their ability to make new friends. They will go out of their way to prove their friendship and assert a positive disposition in this area. However, they might not like friends who take the spotlight and attract attention more than they do, so they carefully measure their stance and decide to move ahead accordingly. Someone who looks, dresses, or performs better than them can be a serious threat, and Leos would rather keep them away than fear the absence of attention.

Despite this feeling, if a Leo really likes a person and wants them to stay for a prolonged period, they will support them and try to get over the feeling of not being validated enough.

Leo Friendship Grid with the Other 11 Zodiacs

The friendship of Leos with other zodiac signs is quite interesting, especially with a few of them. Even though Leos are sociable and make friends easily, you can witness a peculiar platonic relationship with each sign.

Leo and Libra: The friendship radar of these two signs is strong. It is more about admiration. Both signs like and admire each other's qualities and are inspired by their respective positive traits. For instance, a Leo will always go to their Libra friend for book, music, and movie recommendations, given their impeccable taste in art. Their subtle charm and grace are captivating. Instead of being paranoid, Leos also admire Libras and prefer to learn a thing or two from them. On the other hand, Libras love the way Leos live. The glamor and pizzazz surrounding Leos is something that most Libras would also like to experience. Both signs are charming, but Libras are more subtle and do not shout it out loud.

Leos, on the other hand, don't hold back. They snap at waiters or growl at bartenders if they don't get the service they expect. Being the master of etiquette they are, a Libra friend might feel shy or even embarrassed in these situations. They cannot be as bold as Leos and would prefer to diffuse the situation in a calmer tone. Leos are annoyed by the indecisiveness of Libras. When they are on a shopping spree or in a restaurant, a Libra might take a lot of time to decide the clothes to buy or the food to eat, which is quite annoying for the impatient Leo. Their impulsive nature cannot wait and compels them to buy both. These two signs must let go of these minor differences to celebrate a beautiful friendship bond.

Leo and Scorpio: Both signs are passionate, which could result in an intense friendship. For Scorpios, the most attractive trait about Leos is their warmth and affectionate nature because Scorpios face frequent dark impulses which can be eliminated, or at least, avoided in the presence of bright Leos. Their vibrant nature cuts off all negativity, and

Scorpios prefer to experience that once in a while. The friendship between these signs has numerous confusing moments. It is difficult for Scorpios to decipher their need for the spotlight, while on the other hand, Leos are always confused about the privacy factor of Scorpios.

Once both signs get into a fight or even a minor debate, both will fight until the other party agrees, which is nearly impossible in a friendship between a Leo and a Scorpio. As a Leo, you will fight until the other accepts defeat, which is also the case with your Scorpio friend. To avoid the chance of this ruining your friendship, the safest bet is to avoid getting into a fight in the first place. Surprisingly, this trait of Leos is what draws them to each other. Scorpios give Leos a heated and stimulating conversation, something they could even learn from. Even though both parties will hopefully agree to disagree, there is always some valuable take-away from these encounters.

Leo and Sagittarius: These two signs get along well, especially compared to other pairings. In fact, this pairing is probably the most popular and compatible. The sign of Sagittarius, which is the Archer, is extremely compatible with the Lion, the sign of Leos. They are represented by fire, which means that they are equally passionate and share a liking for adventure and exploration. Even though a Sagittarius prefers being alone, a Leo's social skills will drag them along in a crowd, which introduces a perfect balance. A Sagittarius will not mind being dragged. When these two signs plan to go on an adventure, it is usually one of their best times spent together. While any time spent together is valuable for these two signs, adventurous experiences always excel. It is also because both signs healthily challenge each other and bring out their daring sides. In other words, they bring out their best courageous selves and inspire each other to achieve their goals. When a Sagittarius and Leo become friends, nothing can stop them from achieving the things they want.

At the same time, they mold themselves to present their most acceptable selves in front of the world. They try to be what others want them to be, mainly to garner attention. However, when they are with each other, they can easily let the guard down and show their true selves. They bond not only over adventures and exciting trips but also over a warm cup of tea. They enjoy each other's presence and can stay for hours in comfortable silence.

Leo and Capricorn: As a Leo, even though you are the life of the party in most settings, others still admire the presence and authority of Capricorns in the same room. Instead of being intimidated by their presence, you also admire their personality. Capricorns want things their way and will make them happen at any cost. So, if you are the master of snapping at someone for attention, consider Capricorns to be above you. Due to this, there might be tiny tiffs in a friendship between a Leo and a Capricorn. If given charge, Capricorns could even beat your leadership skills.

However, to sustain a friendship between these two signs, it is wise to find a real balance and join hands to win together. For instance, the Leo can take center stage, and the Capricorn can back them up by being the backstage authority, which is more crucial in any event. Give them the backstage or behind the scenes, and they will happily hand the center stage to you. This pairing is one of the strongest. Tiny annoyances from both ends include a Capricorn's pessimism and negative outlook toward life and a Leo's ego and impatience. However, these are malleable, avoidable, and should not affect the friendship too badly.

Leo and Aquarius: For Leos, Aquarius is probably one of the most diametrically opposing or contradictory signs of all. However, since opposites attract, this forms an interesting friendship pair. A Leo's need for constant validation and affection differs from that of an Aquarius, who hardly cares about anyone's opinions and doesn't feel the need to be validated. While Leos are more warm, extroverted, and lively, Aquarians are more reserved and prefer to be on their own. Similarly, while Leos think with their heart and let their emotions get the best of them, Aquarians are more practical and think logically.

If there are so many differences between both signs, what makes the friendship so interesting? One reason is loyalty. As you already know, Leos are loyal and are known to be one of the most trustworthy signs. It is an attractive trait that draws others and keeps them in their lives. Just like Leos, Aquarians are also known for their loyalty, which brings both signs closer. Once you, a Leo, are friends with an Aquarius, you will never ditch each other for impromptu dates or other reasons. Also, Aquarians will never talk behind your back or share your secrets with others, which makes them a trustworthy friend. Instead of facing minor annoyances, you might face certain confusing situations. For instance, your Aquarian friend might always talk in abstractions or try to have nuanced conversations with you, which can be confusing. But your conversations might mainly include fashion, drama, or grooming products, subjects which are not their cup of tea.

Leo and Pisces: Pisces are usually shy, which makes you want to protect them. As a Leo, your protective trait is brought out, and it brightly shines when you are around a Piscean. Pisceans have fragile egos. To help combat this, Leos often give occasional compliments to Pisceans to lift their spirits. Sometimes, Leos also give them expensive and thoughtful presents. Due to these gestures, a Piscean friend values friendship with Leos and is intrigued enough to keep the bond for a long time.

At the same time, Pisceans return the gestures by having an open mind and always lending their ears to Leos. Pisceans tolerate the nagging of Leos and actively listen to them. They offer sympathy and even comfort them if need be. Pisces don't like to be tied down and are free-spirited; since Leos can be possessive of their objects and even relationships, it might seem imposing on Pisceans. They want to explore their options and meet new people, which Leos don't like or appreciate. At times, a Pisces friend drives Leos crazy because of their absent-minded nature. Since Leos prefer a little perfection, certain absent-minded habits such as wearing mismatched shoes or socks and forgetting their wallet at home can be annoying. But, again, it is something that can be ignored and overcome easily.

Leo and Aries: These two are represented by the Fire sign, which represents their warm and affectionate nature. These two signs are gentle with each other. Like Leos, Aries are passionate and enthusiastic about most things in life. Due to this, both signs are always up for an adventure, which can strengthen the foundation of their friendship. When both signs are together, everything is more upbeat and elevated. For instance, when a Leo shares a normal joke with an Aries, it is ten times funnier to them. Similarly, any mediocre dish will taste better if it is made by one of the two.

There are a few negative repercussions in this friendship, too. While Aries dislikes Leo's aversion to calculated decisions (Leos are usually spontaneous and impulsive but will be too timid to make a decision that is not theirs to begin with), Leo despises their brutal honesty. Also, gaining attention and being in power could create some issues. Leos like to be in the center, and Aries want their share of power. However, both these signs usually come to an agreement as they like each other's company and don't want to ruin it. They would rather have fun together than ruin it due to such petty differences.

Leo and Taurus: These two signs are extremely different – the way they think, dress, eat, and perceive life. However, Leo and Taurus do share some similarities. For instance, both signs love luxury. They are fond of everything expensive. Another similarity is loyalty. Both signs are extremely loyal and will hardly ever cheat on their partners, friends, or any circumstance in life. Thirdly, both signs need a lot of attention. The Taurus follows the Bull sign, which means that they could equally be stubborn. If they want to eat something that the Leos don't like, they'd still prefer it anyway. Also, since both signs need attention, they could compete for it time and again, but in a healthy way. It is extremely difficult for both signs to yield, which could grow grudges.

However, this is not the case with close friends. If a Taurus and Leo decide to be close friends, they would hardly worry about the other grabbing the spotlight. Both will be given equal and fair chances to hold their center without feeling snubbed. The secret is to look beyond each other's weaknesses and celebrate their strengths. As a Leo, if you are able to do it, you will have a strong Taurus friendship that has the potential of lasting a lifetime. Also, you can learn a thing or two from each other. For example, a Taurus can learn some fashion tips from a Leo, whereas a Leo can learn money-saving tips from the Taurus.

Leo and Gemini: Gemini are bubbly, high-spirited, and have an air of lightness around them. Despite their age, they seem eternally youthful. Most Leos possess a serious demeanor, which can be treated with the playful aura of a Gemini. In fact, Leos want to bring their inner child out but are unable to do it. A friendship with a Gemini can bring that out and fuel a Leo's childish spirit. With a Gemini, a Leo feels radiant and happy and forgets their worries and stresses for a brief period. Every moment with a Gemini is fun and filled with joy.

With a Gemini, you can get into food fights or play a prank in public places, but the Gemini will handle the situation or clean up the mess. Leos are too high-maintenance to clean up any mess, which is a minor annoyance for Geminis. However, since they enjoy their time together, a Gemini doesn't really mind. On the other hand, Leos appreciate and also despise their Gemini friend's urgent need to clean things up and make everything perfect. Also, Geminis are unable to focus on a particular aspect for a long period, which annoys most Leos. These tiny annoying details are not really a big issue and can be easily avoided, which both signs successfully do, and it results in a precious friendship between both these signs.

Leo and Cancer: Most Cancers are moody, which could pose a threat between both signs. Cancer usually broods or is in a bad mood over minor inconveniences, which really annoys a Leo because Leos are warm, bright, and chirpy most of the time. At the same time, it is difficult for a Cancer to comprehend the sunny mood of their Leo friend. However, they do try to learn and adapt. Even if they cannot do that, they mostly let it go. Cancers are loyal and protective, which is also true with Leos. These similarities attract both the signs to each other.

A Cancer friend is extremely caring and wants the best for their friends. As a Leo, you can expect your Cancer friend is cooking up and putting your favorite dishes on the table when you visit their house. They make sure that their friends are comfortable. Also, a Cancer friend will always compliment a Leo, which is another reason Leos prefer to stay with Cancers. It doesn't stop there; as a Leo, you give equal love and care. Like other pairings, you will have your minor annoyances and tiffs, but both signs understand that friendship is more important.

Leo and Leo: Friendship between two Leos is imperative in terms of disclosing their full potential, talent, and beauty. As a Leo, a fellow Leo will understand and truly comprehend your personality without you even trying to explain it. You, too, will appreciate and be impressed by the bundle of talent that your Leo friend possesses. Both of you will be able to fully understand each other and satisfy the needs of a Leo in friendship. You will be drawn to each other in the first meeting and might develop a strong rapport within the next few. Once you befriend a Leo, be ready for inside jokes, frequent hugs, and occasional compliments. In a way, it will be like looking in a mirror and trying to understand your alter ego.

However, there might be some downsides to this friendship pairing. Your strong egos and constant need to be in the spotlight will affect your friendship. As you know, Leos hate sharing attention, which can affect your developing friendship. You will feel that your problems are bigger than your Leo friend's; your friend might feel insecure about the attention you are fetching. If you want to develop a friendship that will last long, this selfishness and the need to be at the center must be avoided or eliminated. If you are capable of doing this, your friendship and bond will be rock solid and indestructible.

Leo and Virgo: Virgos are known to be fastidious, which can be a bit annoying for other signs. However, Leos love this particular Virgo trait and even want to learn a thing or two about it. After all, this Virgo friend of yours will make sure that you are dressed nicely with a perfect hairdo. Basically, a Virgo will never let a Leo be embarrassed due to bad dress sense (which is highly unlikely anyway), bad hair, or even with food stuck in their teeth. Since Leos are all about showbiz and looking good, they will love having a Virgo friend around. Above all, Virgos don't need the spotlight and don't mind Leos having it all, which forms a perfect balance.

Since Leos always return favors and give equal importance to others, they will never fail to complement their Virgo friends. They appreciate the intelligence and practicality of Virgos, which boosts their fragile egos and makes them look on the brighter side of life.

Even though it sounds perfect, there are some downsides to this friendship. Virgos are all about etiquette; they despise seeing Leos throwing a fit now and then. On the other hand, the neuroses of Virgos are enough to drive a Leo crazy. Again, just like other friendship pairings, try to let go of these tiny grievances as it could cost you a beautiful friendship.

How do Leos Behave at a Party or a Social Gathering?

Leos love parties and informal social gatherings. They not only get a chance to glam up but also garner a lot of attention. Such events are a great opportunity for Leos to make friends and meet new people, some of which can be useful contacts for the future. Parties are a place where Leos can unleash their true wild side and be crazy. They love to sing, dance, and enjoy every moment. Whether it's a round of "Never Have I Ever" or mere board games, Leos are up for everything as long as it is fun.

Leos are well known for their ability to make friends and increase their circle. With friendship, their motto is "the more friends you have, the easier life is." Out of the contacts they build, they slowly choose people who could have the potential of turning into close and life-long friends. At times, they don't even have to choose; if it is meant to be, Leos will automatically grow fond of them and suggest ideas to spend time together.

Whenever Leos enter a social gathering, they imagine a red carpet being rolled out for them. They dress to impress, which automatically puts them in the spotlight. As soon as a Leo steps into a room, they are bound to turn a few heads. Not only because of the way they dress, but also due to their personality.

When Leos meet new people, they instantly connect with them, mainly because of their heightened confidence. Not everyone has the confidence to approach others and start a conversation out of the blue. They take command, not only the conversation but of the room, and rule until it's time to leave. Also, they usually will leave early, especially if they are not getting enough attention; if, on the other hand, they are, they might even stretch an all-nighter. Since they are easily bored and distracted, they might nudge their partners to indicate the "it's time to leave" signal. You will rarely find Leos in quiet night outs where there are merely a few people unless the night out includes only their best friends.

They also have a tendency to flirt with waiters and bartenders to get free drinks and complimentary desserts. If you are short on money and still want an extra glass of beer, you can rely on your Leo friend. They will use their charm to get what they want. Even if not for free stuff, Leos flirt to gain attention. It gives them occasional spasms of joy and is enough to make their night legendary.

According to the personality traits of Leos, they are best suited to a pool party. It's a perfect chill-out event for Leos where they can meet and socialize with a bunch of friends at the same time. Since this sign is always up for something extraordinary and outdoorsy, a pool party is the perfect setting for a warm summer afternoon. If you are a Leo, chances are you will invite even your frenemy to show your hospitality and skills as a host. In other words, you'd want to show off and make them jealous. Even though it sounds petty, Leos don't mind doing it repeatedly.

If Leos throw an indoor birthday party or host a dinner, they expect their guests to dress nice, but not nicer than them. Close friends and guests of host Leos know this and ensure that they are appropriately dressed for such events. Unless you are decked to the nines, you will fail to impress your Leo host. This sign tries to create events from the smallest moments in their life. Whether it's a housewarming, welcome party, or a farewell, they will ensure that there's a party or an event just around the corner. If that's the case, they will divert their attention and stay excited until the time arrives. They will already know what they are wearing and make sure that everything is arranged perfectly. After all, a Leo is known to be an amazing host, and so, everything has to fall in place.

How Leos Make Friends and How to Foster a Leo Friendship

As mentioned earlier, Leos possess the natural ability to make friends easily and socialize with no trouble. They have a lot of contacts and friends, and their network is huge. Their social skills are commendable. They can easily converse with a stranger, reply to texts, slide in DMs on Instagram, and make plans instantly. One moment they are talking to a person in the department store, and the next moment they are invited to Leo's happy hour. Leos just need to "click" with others, after which they are your friend or at least a contact on your phone.

While Leos do give 100% to maintain their friendship and keep their friends happy, they expect the same in return. Their chirpy and bright aura attract people, but it is difficult for others to maintain a long friendship with Leos. Only those who can tolerate stubbornness and don't care about the spotlight can be good friends with Leos. In other words, friendships with a Leo is not easy.

Due to this, they will have fewer friends, and this contradicts the fact that they can make friends easily and often have a large group completely. Here, we are talking about real friends, with whom Leos prefer to share their feelings, and the ones whom they consider family. These friends that stay will last long, probably for the rest of their lives. They stay because they are able to tell a Leo their best and worst. They made an attempt to know the Leo at a deeper level, which unraveled their true personality. Not everyone is able to do that with a Leo. If the Leo is not close to you, they will rarely share their feelings. If they do, feel honored. As a friend of a Leo, it is your duty to praise them and make them feel wanted constantly. If you give enough love and attention to your Leo friend, expect the same in return. Once Leos realize that their friendship will last long and cement this belief, they will make sure that their friends are happy and comfortable. Exchanging expensive gifts is usually an unspoken tradition, given the expensive tastes of Leos.

Another reason Leos are unable to keep and maintain all friendships for long is that they are difficult to pin down. They have planned all their time, and their social schedule is always tight. Even if someone wants to strengthen their friendship bond with Leos, they cannot find time for individual meetups. Your best shot would be to attract their attention in a social gathering or when you are in a group. If the first few attempts succeed, you have a better chance of entering the Leo's private group of friends. Having a Leo for a friend is valuable as they are not only the life of the party but will also go to any length to foster their friendship with their besties.

The Value of a Leo Friend

To befriend a Leo, you must show them your bold side. Leos love those who live fearlessly and out loud. Leos are brave and appreciate others who possess the same quality. Leos feel instantly attached to those who share the same traits and thoughts.

When a Leo approaches you to talk, they will make you feel comfortable. They are the major carriers of any conversation. To keep their attention and take the friendship to the next level, listen carefully. Even though they will not talk about anything personal or share their deepest secrets with you, they probably will spill some beans or even gossip about the happenings around them. They do love their dose of drama. Even if you don't like gossiping but want to be friends with a Leo, nod along and try to be an active part of the conversation.

It is also highly likely that a Leo will talk about some new place they want to check out or slide in a statement or two about their latest expensive purchase. If you want to be in Leos's good books, compliment them often; it is the cheat code to building a friendship or relationship bond with Leos. Give them compliments and make sure they get their dose of attention frequently. If you are easily annoyed by this habit, you must reconsider your desire to build a friendship with Leos as it is their natural trait.

Here are three reasons a Leo friendship is valuable:

1. A Forever Bond

If you manage to get close to a Leo and know all their life secrets, you have locked them in for life. Leos are master connectors. It is difficult for other signs to befriend them; however, once they share their inner secrets and feel close to you, this friendship is bound to last for the rest of their lives. In fact, Leos become a part of your family and treat you like one of their own.

2. They are Generous

If your best friend is a Leo, expect expensive presents on your doorstep occasionally. Leos are generous, giving, and kind. They always have a plan to surprise you with presents and plans out of the blue. It is always rewarding to be with a Leo. Not just with gifts; Leos are generous with other aspects of friendship too. If you face any trouble in life, Leos will try their best to help you overcome difficult situations. Whether it's financial, emotional, physical, or any other issue, Leos will ensure that you get out of it and help you as much as they can.

3. Life with Leo Friends is Exciting

Leo friends are always up to something. They have a plan devised for the next gathering or "hang-out". You will always find yourself in a new restaurant, exploring new places, or going on an outdoor adventure. They cannot stay in one place and will drag you along. If you are an introvert who likes staying indoors, being with a Leo will change your social life completely. You will meet new people often and find yourself in crowded parties or clubs. The strange part is, you will enjoy it and ask for more. Also, since Leos are the life of the party, you will also be perceived as an A-lister and conceded commensurate importance.

How to Sustain a Leo Friendship

Here are some ways to sustain a Leo friendship and maintain it for the long-term.

· If you are a Leo and want to befriend a Leo, you both must arrive at a mutual understanding to let them share the spotlight with you. As you know, Leo friendships can be difficult due to the fact that they despise sharing the limelight.

· Go on adventures. A nice way to hang out with your Leo friend and strengthen your friendship bond is to invite them on adventures. Forest hikes, amusement parks, wine tasting tours, etc., are some great ways to lure a Leo into spending time with you and explore new places at the same time.

· Let them take control. Leos love to be the boss, host, and leader of any formal and informal event. If you are okay with the choices and decisions of your Leo friend, let them plan the schedule while you just enjoy the ride. Being the perfectionists they are, you will never have a dull moment, so enjoy every bit of it. Even if you want to be in charge, Leos will somehow fight for their stance and never allow you to take control. To avoid such fights and keep the friendship flowing for long, simply give up and let them have their way.

· Never lie to them. Leos are honest, loyal, and true to their word. They will never lie to you and will expect the same in return. Failing to do so will make them paranoid about your friendship, and they will never trust you again. If there is something that you are afraid to tell your Leo friend, you may resort to lying. However, if your Leo friend finds out, it will cost you your precious friendship. It's safer to be honest. Leos are known to be forgiving and are ready to give second chances. Also, they will appreciate your honesty.

· Compliment them often. While they may not get enough compliments and attention from strangers (which they will hate), it is your duty to make your Leo friend feel wanted. By compliments, we are not talking about giving fake compliments that might make them overconfident and vain; give real compliments that will lift their spirits.

To sum up, a Leo friend is generous, giving, caring, warm, and the perfect host. They might demand their need for the spotlight and validation, but other than that, a Leo friend is extremely valuable. They will return equal affection and make you feel valued. Whenever you are in need of a friend, a Leo will stand close by you and try their best to pull you out of trouble. Along with this, they will be honest and loyal until their last breath.

Chapter 6: Leo at Work: Career Paths for Leos

This chapter talks about Leos' career paths and how they behave in a work setting.

Great Careers for the Leo

This is an interesting topic of discussion. As you know by now, Leos possess a range of distinct personality traits, which can make it difficult to place them in a particular spot. It also gives them a chance to consider different career paths tailored to their traits. Let's check out a few of these career options and why Leos should consider them.

1. Broadcasting

Since Leos are lively and confident, being a broadcaster is an excellent choice. This career option lets them take the spotlight and allows them to be heard. TV and radio broadcasting are two niches within this discipline. Depending on your preference, you can choose either of these. Leos enjoy talking and are blessed with excellent communication skills, which makes this option a great fit as a career. Whether it's TV or radio broadcasting, a Leo will own the spot and add more pizzazz to turn the broadcast into a success.

As a Leo, if you have parts of Sagittarius or Gemini in your horoscopes, you should definitely keep this career option on your list. A PR executive is another great career option for Leos. Rumor control, sending and maintaining press releases, and navigating crucial information are important tasks of a PR executive. If you are a shy Leo who likes their occasional share of attention, this role is apt for you. It not only lets you maintain a private life but also gives you a dose of public attention every once in a while. Other career options in this line are life coach, on-air host, and nutritionist.

2. Designer

Leos can be great designers due to their passion and creative skills. The best choice for a designing career can be graphic or fashion. It is an excellent career choice for Leos, especially if they have parts of Aquarius or Virgo in their horoscopes. They are good at creativity, but they are also known for putting themselves out in the market. While other signs do creative work and wait for others to notice them, Leos try to display their work and make it noticeable. Since the design discipline is highly competitive, Leos will try hard to navigate their way and be noticed.

You already know about Leo's love for clothing, fashion, and glamor, which is well-served in the fashion industry. They know how to dress well and try to dress others in the same way. Even the fashion industry is highly competitive, but Leos know how to make the most of all opportunities. They will find a unique way to display their work, market themselves, and excel in any discipline. They are not afraid of competition and will face it like a true Lion. The confidence of Leos will help them tremendously in any design discipline.

To get into graphic or fashion designing, you first need to build your creative skills. Try to strengthen your observational skills and perceive objects differently. If you are into fashion, research and find your niche. Take relevant courses or build your own design portfolio after some practice. Apply to design agencies or work as a freelancer. The discipline of design doesn't need a degree, so if you are thinking of changing your career, it is never too late.

Coco Chanel, Yves Saint Laurent, and Michael Kors are some famous Leo fashion designers.

3. Actor

As you know, Leos love their share of drama. They prefer to be in and around anything dramatic and possess a flair for theatre. They love watching movies and theatre plays, which are also great ideas for first dates with Leos. Acting is a great career choice for this sign as it offers glamor, pizzazz, attention, and drama, all in one place. Also, the red carpet and spotlight are perfect for Leos. You will notice a ton of actors and actresses with this sign. If you possess a talent for singing or dancing, you can also become a musician, which gives an equal amount of center stage.

Other sub-niches within this discipline include theatre artists, theatrical agents, and stage directors. Even if they cannot act, they get to be a part of the acting profession, which is enough to garner the required attention. Also, Leos get to show their management and organizational skills with this job position. In this job, they interact with famous actors, casting agents, and other significant figures of the movie industry. Any other profession related to this career option, such as art direction, museum director, lighting design, and costume design is suitable for Leos. Sandra Bullock, Daniel Radcliffe, Jennifer Lopez, and Lisa Kudrow are a few famous Leo actors and actresses.

A modeling career is also an appropriate choice for Leos. They get to be in the spotlight (quite literally) all the time, and they garner the attention of all the people in the room. Besides this, they get to be a part of the glam world. Walking for designers and wearing exquisite outfits and makeup is the dream of most Leos. If they excel in what they do, Leos can easily make it to the top.

Those Leos who cannot make it to the top due to high competition can also pave their path by being social media influencers and endorsing products of big brands. As a social media influencer, you can get a lot of followers and be showered with validation, which is heaven for most Leos. Besides that, Leos are also known to be great marketers due to their ability to convince people; this helps them sell the products they endorse. The best part is, you get to keep products you endorse from various categories – makeup, cosmetics, electronics, clothes, etc.

4. Standup Comedian

Yes, Leos can be comedians too. Their youthful, playful, and charismatic nature is addictive. Also, Leos are naturally funny. They can crack a joke or two out of the blue. Leos are great entertainers, and, using their bubbly and confident nature, Leos can make great standup comedians. They also get their share of spotlight and attention, which, as you know, Leos love. As a Leo, if you have parts of Sagittarius or Gemini in your horoscope, you should definitely keep this career option on your list. This career will not only give you fame but is also extremely rewarding. Also, if you are very good at what you do, other opportunities will come knocking in no time.

Some famous Leo standup comedians are James Corden, Teddy Ray, Victor Pope Jr., and Drew Lynch.

How to become a standup comedian: The best way to start is through social media. Social media platforms like YouTube, Instagram, and Facebook have billions of users collectively, which is a wide audience to entertain. These platforms allow you to share clips of your standup comedy. Before you begin recording and sharing your clips, write funny narrative scripts that usually revolve around one or two topics. Practice a lot and hold a dummy performance session in front of your friends and family. Take honest feedback and implement the changes; then record and share on social media. Slowly, once you gain popularity, you can get help from agencies that hold shows by selling tickets.

5. Advertising and Marketing

Their extroverted, creative, and sociable skills make Leos great marketers and advertisers. They can convince people to buy products and can be great at sales. Their chirpy and bright aura will make people believe that they are investing in something worthwhile. You, as a marketer, will, of course, work behind the scenes. However, your creative skills need a push to convince potential buyers to take some form of action. Leos can channel their creativity through persuasion, which is what makes a good marketer great. Leos have the creative ability to create exceptional marketing strategies that work most of the time.

As mentioned earlier, Leos can also specialize in other sub-niches within this discipline, such as social media marketing, salesperson, and product development. Since Leos are open to exploration and want to experience change, they make excellent salespersons. Also, they fit well in any role; whether it's in retail, as a product line manager, or on the business management team, Leos will make sure that they get their share of commission and tips. Their skills benefit any brand and help them increase sales.

6. Orator, Motivational Speaker, or Spokesperson

While this isn't a conventional career choice for all, motivational speaking can be a great choice for Leos. They possess a leadership skill that inspires them to speak in public. When they speak, they portray a sense of authority. Leos are fiery and full of passion, which gives them the fire and motivation that reflects within their speeches. They inspire others to achieve their goals. Even if the speech is a bit weak, Leo's aura and passion will uplift the listener and motivate them to achieve their goals. If you want someone to take charge of a platform and direct others toward success, Leos are your go-to.

This career position is suitable for Leos as motivational speakers, spokespersons, salespersons, publishers, and commodity traders. As a spokesperson, you can either represent your company during interviews or during meetings with venture capitalists. Leos can sell a product or service with ease. They convince people with their charm and sincerity, which also makes them a great fit as marketers and advertisers (more about this in the next section).

7. Makeup Artist or Hair Stylist

The beauty industry is also a great career option for Leos as they love glamor and always try to look their best. Their approach to beauty and glamor is quite serious. They want to look good themselves and want others around them to look their best. They love makeup and exquisite hairstyles. Due to these traits, they can become successful makeup artists and hairstylists. Since Leos have an exquisite taste for distinct hairstyles, they have this natural ability to conceive and cultivate a suitable look for others (whether it's a hairdo or styling their outfits).

Even though Leos are usually indecisive about their own hair, you can count on them to style *your* hair. At the same time, Leos will keep their clients entertained, which will inspire them to return. Other sub-niches and professions within this discipline, also suitable for Leos, are beauty editor, spa owner, and shoot stylist.

8. CEO or Director

As you know, leadership skills are thoroughly ingrained in most Leos; this is why the position of Chief Executive Officer is ideal for Leos. They can motivate and lead a group of employees in any company. This zodiac sign, which the Lion represents, possesses all the qualities required to be a boss. If you are a Leo, you are likely to be chosen for this role. However, make sure that you are ready for it and work hard to make it happen. Being promoted to the position of CEO is not easy. It takes years of hard work, patience, and effort to reach the top. However, since Leos already have the drive and creativity, they merely need to put in the effort and be patient. Also, know that this job is difficult, so be prepared to face unrequited stress.

The same applies to the role of Director. Next, in line with the CEO, the role of a Director is also to lead their group of employees and handle important decisions within the company. As Directors, Leos will extract specific work from their employees and make sure that they are on top of their game. They will get their way by any means and move forward toward just one goal, which is the company's betterment. Also, ordering and bossing around is something that most Directors do, which, as you guessed, is favored by most Leos.

9. Architect or Landscape Designer

Leos are filled with creativity and imagination skills. At the same time, their communication skills are impressive. Collectively, these traits will make them talented architects who can visualize, and design spaces tailored to any client's needs. Architecture also partly involves problem-solving, which Leos are good at. Creating spaces and plans for buildings is something that Leos would love to do, not only to satisfy their creativity but also to impress others. Since architecture is the most visible form of art (imagine drawings being converted into tall buildings that actually exist), they get a solid chance to gain some serious validation. Whether it's an educational facility, a residential building, or a corporate skyscraper, Leos can design it all.

Besides architecture, a similar field is landscape designing. If the Leo has parts of Virgo, Cancer, or Taurus in their horoscopes, this field is the ideal choice for them. Leos appreciate earth and nature, and this discipline lets them explore and experiment with nature. Since Leos are all about attention, it might also show in their work. Their designs for clients are highly likely to garner attention. For instance, their architecture and landscape design might be the loudest, most exquisite, or attention-grabbing on any street. It is less likely to blend within the context unless that is specifically suggested by the client.

10. Lawyer or Judge

Leos are stubborn and will stretch their arguments to prove their point until the other person agrees or gives up. This trait might be well-suited for career positions like a lawyer or a prosecutor. Moreover, Leos respect law and order, a trait rarely found in other signs. Even if they are a beginner in this career, they will climb to the top by showing their talent and using their charm. Their admiration and importance for order and organization are noteworthy, which is also another reason why Leos make successful lawyers and prosecutors. They take pride in fighting for justice and bringing peace to society. It is also a great boost for their egos, which is why they enjoy this career path.

You can also put it this way: a career path that serves law, order, and justice day in and day out might fuel most Leos' narcissistic nature. However, this is not true in all cases. It depends on the opportunity, position, and luck of a Leo. Also, since some Leos do not prefer to argue or are more reserved, this career path can be a bit questionable. However, it has mostly proven to be fit for Leos, so you can consider it if you are a Leo. Their way with words, ability to seduce, and convincing power will make Leos renowned lawyers known to win most cases. Even if the judge is strict, Leo lawyers will twist words and feed their own perceived thoughts to win the case.

11. Writer

Leos also make amazing writers as they love to tell their story and always have a narrative at hand. Their creative skills also enhance their writing style. As writers, Leos need to follow a set of guidelines while having the freedom of creativity, which is a perfect balance for all Leos. As a Leo, if writing fascinates you, try to delve deeper and start your research. Pick a niche – fiction, non-fiction, fantasy, horror; it doesn't matter as long as you are thoroughly invested in it. Try to make the most out of your creative skills and research. As a writer, you will also get a chance to show and sell your work, which will give all Leos the validation they need.

On the other hand, you should also take a look at certain career paths that are not fit for all Leos and should be avoided often as not.

Here are a few of them –

1. Secretary

Leos want to be the boss, and they are worthy too. As you now know, Leos possess excellent leadership skills. They don't like being told what to do. Leos can become great CEOs and bosses, leading the company toward great success through their calculated and wise decisions. Also, people listen to them and not the other way round. They want to apply their mind, which is not quite possible with a secretary's job. They always want to express themselves and despise those who instruct them. With a secretary position, they would feel enclosed and robbed. The feeling of achieving great goals and accomplishing formidable tasks is absent in this position, which is why Leos should probably not consider this position.

2. Retail Worker or Waiter

Even though we mentioned that Leos could work in retail, do not consider this option unless you have no other job positions available. Whether it's retail or waiting on a table, you would absolutely hate the idea of serving others. At times, customers will be rude to you, which is the last thing Leos desires. Their short temperament will make it more difficult for Leos to control the situation, and they will most probably snap back. In retail, most customers want to save money, even if it means letting go of the latest fashion trends. As a Leo, you cannot understand this mindset and hate serving such customers. Leos, who are usually well dressed, will automatically repel frugal people who save money during shopping. While it is not entirely wrong, Leos will never welcome or accept this attitude. If they find a customer who spends as little money as possible, they will stop trying to please them and refrain from giving the best customer support. Assisting is one thing they hate, and they would rather be the one spending money.

As a waiter or waitress, taking orders from customers is also a big no-no for them, especially from the ones with an air of authority around them and that treat others with a lack of respect. Leos would rather be the customer and order their food than be the ones taking orders and serving grumpy customers. If a customer is rude, Leos are most likely to reply with a rude tone, which could cost them their job.

3. Hotel Housekeeper

Again, this position demands Leos be in a lower position with a boss always above them. Being the frontrunners they are, Leos would hate it when the hotel manager comes to check on them every once in a while. Also, if you forget to lock a room or misplace a key, you might get a good bashing. While they already want to be in the top position, this extra bashing and criticizing will make them hate their job even more. Leos can't take criticism well; they are easily offended and refuse to correct their mistakes immediately. If you are in need of some urgent cash, you can take it up as a temporary position, but think twice before you decide to take it up as a permanent job.

Basically, any job that requires Leos to work under someone should be reconsidered by this sign. Unless it is temporary or holds the potential for promotion, rethink your decision before moving ahead.

Where Does the Leo Fit in an Office or Workplace Setting?

Leos love drama, so it's likely to find a Leo near the water cooler or any other popular gossip spot. They judge easily and hate anyone who doesn't think as they do. As you know, it is hard to fight a Leo, and once you do, you might end up in their bad books forever (unless you are their best friend). They will pounce easily and hold their guard. If you are a Leo and have another Leo in the same company, chances are you will become friends and gossip about other employees. However, you will always be in a constant battle for stealing the spotlight.

Some Leos are reserved, which makes up for a very tiny percentage of this zodiac sign. If your workplace has a reserved Leo, they will quietly sit at their desk, minding their business and completing their tasks. However, they will still fish for compliments and want their due credit. Also, it will be difficult for them to handle criticism.

How do Leos Excel at Work?

Even if Leos are hungry for attention and validation, having a Leo on your team is worthwhile. Their strong sense of responsibility, work ethics, and intelligent minds make a solid employee who will reach and fulfill all project goals. A boss usually counts on a Leo to give them ideas regarding their next project, design strategies, and to help other employees move forward. It is highly likely that a Leo will be chosen to lead the next project. Any office team looking for an employee to be the lead speaker in any presentation or conference will always turn to a Leo.

Also, they know their way around fulfilling tasks. Leos are most likely to fulfill a task by finding a smarter route instead of working harder. They will either trick their subordinates into completing a task or find a simpler solution by racking their brains. And being the group leader, they will put the best minds on the project to increase the success rates.

All in all, creativity, a strong sense of responsibility, work ethics, and smart working techniques make a Leo a valuable employee. However, beware of their presence around you as they could easily steal your spot and are more likely to get the promotion. Even if you show a better performance, they will charm and influence your boss, which will automatically make them a better choice. Lastly, Leos are extremely loyal, which means that you can trust them with their decisions, and they will never cheat.

If all goes well, your company will be blessed with a deserving Leo as your boss, who is courageous, intelligent, and responsible.

These reasons also explain why Leos make great businessmen. They portray an authoritative tone, which most entrepreneurs should possess. They demand what they want and are not afraid to speak up. If they see anything wrong happening in the company, they will immediately redirect their stance and make sure that all employees are at the top of their game. Their ambitious drive is infectious, and they display a massive amount of strength and stamina to fulfill their goals. If you have a Leo for your boss, they will accurately gauge your worth. While they need attention, they will reciprocate a similar amount of appreciation and attention to their employees who perform well under their leadership.

Also, since Leos are open to risks, they are most likely to open a business and succeed rather than work as an employee and take instructions from someone else.

Obstacles a Leo Might Experience at Work

Now that you know the career paths that you can tap into, let's take a look at the negative traits of a Leo at work and how those could affect their work and productivity.

1. They are Impulsive, Which Can Lead to Bad Decisions

Most Leos are impulsive, which can lead to some repercussions, especially of the emotional sort. Even though Leos are quick with decision making, an impulsive nature can drive them to take ill-advised actions.

2. They Might Feel Snubbed at Times

A Leo likes and wants their share of validation when they fulfill a project. If the boss doesn't appreciate their work, they might feel low or even angry. They want their share of credit and others to appreciate their valuable presence in a team, especially if they have helped to sign a lucrative deal. Whether it's a big project they handled or maintaining a small winning streak in the workplace, they will want appreciation for all instances. If it's an important overseas project, be ready to praise your Leo subordinate as they will need the extra credit during such significant instances. While Leo bosses do praise their employees for their efforts, extremely self-centered Leo bosses will take all the credit. Even though it is less likely, you can expect this to happen.

3. Leos Can Suffer from Occasional Spells of Laziness

This is mainly due to getting bored and distracted. While Leos do have a strong sense of responsibility, they are often distracted, and this results in laziness and procrastination, which is unacceptable in a work setting. Whenever they feel lazy, they find a way to get things done with less effort or give it to their team members. Surprisingly, even when they are lazy, they get things done on time.

4. The Workplace Can be a Bit Melodramatic

You already know how Leos love drama. They are dramatic in their personal life and tend to show it when they are a bit overworked or don't get their share of attention. They are either too snubbed or will create havoc in the workplace. With Leos around, you will occasionally face tense situations due to some aspect of their nature.

Tips for the Leo to Achieve a Fulfilling Work-Life

Learning and being aware of your negative traits is half the battle won. To win it all, you must work on your weaknesses and navigate them to achieve success in your work life.

1. Set a Routine

Even though Leos have a strong sense of responsibility, they can, at times, be too lazy and distracted due to their impulsive nature. If you are a Leo, you will find yourself daydreaming about the next big purchase on your work desk, which will ruin your daily goal plan. To save yourself from being distracted, you must set a routine. Plan your day by making a list of your tasks; this will not only help you stay on track, but you will also fulfill your tasks sooner.

2. Work on Your Communication Skills and Techniques

If your ultimate goal is to be the CEO of your company, you must work on your communication skills. While smooth-talking is a part of a Leo's charm, being a boss might require a more authoritative yet calmer tone, one that your employees will listen to and follow. Practice your communication skills by engaging with other people, listening to others, taking time to respond, and simplifying the message. It is also necessary to make eye contact and work on your body language while communicating with others, especially if the other person is a significant figure within your discipline.

Also, Leos can be a bit arrogant, which is quite apparent in their tone. Even if they don't mean to offend someone, their tone can give them away. This is why Leos should work on their communication skills; it will help them climb the corporate ladder rapidly and help Leos control their egos.

3. Prepare or Discover Your Creative Outlet

Your creative outlet is telling yourself that you need some "me" time. When you are always busy and unable to take time out for yourself, you become exhausted and delay your goals. Everyone needs a break. Finding your creative outlet will keep you enthusiastic in all areas of your life and help you combat distractions and procrastination. Whether it's a karaoke night or a DIY project, your creative outlet will help you develop new skills while you enjoy your break time. Finding and pursuing your creative outlet is necessary to keep your mental health in check and give you your well-deserved break.

If something is not letting you sleep at night, it could be your creative outlet. Pay close attention and acknowledge the idea. Is there a thought nagging you all the time and depriving you of sleep? Does your house need re-modeling? Are you stuck with a business idea? What is it? Reflect on your thoughts and work toward them. Another way to find your creative outlet is to find a creative studio in your locality. It can be an art studio, a music arena, or a book reading club. Dig deeper and find a space that calls out to you.

4. Find Your Inspiration

This is related to what you learned above. Your inspiration will help you maintain the drive and keep you motivated. Do you want to start a new business? Have you always dreamed of authoring a book? Are you looking forward to changing your career? Take the step and stay inspired. Even though Leos are motivated and motivate others, they might feel stuck at some point, which is when finding one's inspiration helps. Even if you don't have a recurring thought or a plan, try new things and find a new passion. Join an acting class, take up baking, open your candle business; take the leap, and do what makes you happy. Leos are bright and creative individuals and finding their inspiration and passion will always keep them on their feet.

To sum up, Leos at work are usually reliable and commit their mind and soul to achieve their goals. At times, they can be distracted by laziness, and their impulsive nature can get in their way. Once Leos apply the tricks mentioned above, they will climb the corporate ladder quickly and fight their way to taking over leadership. They make excellent bosses and CEOs, and they have a knack for conducting smooth business. Give the required attention and credit to Leos in the workplace, or you will have an easier time calming them down.

Chapter 7: What does the Leo Need?

In this chapter, we will discuss some effective ways for the Leo to maximize and make the most of their traits and to navigate the tougher parts of their sign. Even though we discussed the important traits, strengths, weaknesses, and how to navigate them, let's discuss some quick tips to summarize these methods and help the Leo take better control of their lives. These tips are simple to apply in the Leos' everyday life and create the highest impact.

As You Learned, a Leo Would Need the Following

Attention and Spotlight: As you clearly know by now, a Leo wants their share of attention and spotlight. They cannot bear it when someone else takes the center stage.

Respect: The attention they get should be genuine. They can easily spot fake gestures and will automatically push away from them. With a Leo, give respect to earn respect.

Passionate Love: Leos are extremely passionate and want equal love in return. Whether it's a romantic relationship or a one-time sexual encounter, they will please their partners with a burning passion.

True Friendship: Leos make friends easily but take some time before they get close to someone. They expect loyalty, trust, constant support, and respect in a friendship, which makes for true friendship.

Luxury: Leos want everything luxurious and expensive. They give expensive gifts and want the same in return. Give some cash to a Leo, and you will find it being wasted on an unnecessary luxurious item.

These are the basic necessities that a Leo wants in all areas of their life.

Quick Tips for Leos

1. Polish your Personality or Image

While you are already working on building your personality every day and trying to be the best version of you, Leos should focus on creating their identity and discovering a unique trait. It will help you polish your image and help you to stand apart from the crowd. Since you like attention, this quick tip will help you regain the center stage. Make sure that you are building an image that reflects self-promotion. For instance, if you are building a new business or designing a new logo for your brand, this unique aspect of your personality should reflect in other aspects of your life, too. It will further polish your image and help your brand stand apart.

Whether it's your email address, brand logo, or business card, the things you use and design should reflect you. Add the colors you like and the ones that represent your aura. Even though it is a long shot, this tip will help you get more recognition in the professional world and push your business toward success. Your face represents your brand and vice versa. So, it is necessary to make a good impression, part of which comes to you naturally as a Leo.

2. Eat More Sun-Ripened Foods

The food you eat directly affects your physical and mental health. Leos are advised to consume sun-ripened foods, and local organic is best. Since the Sun sign governs Leos, sun-ripened foods will keep you close to nature and make you more radiant. Sun-ripened food is also known to make a Leo feel good, healthier, and more energetic. These foods include sun-dried tomatoes, grapes, apricots, chilies, hot peppers, and dates.

Sun-dried harvest is usually free of chemicals, harmful pesticides, and is extremely healthy. Sun-drying fruits and veggies increases the shelf life and helps to keep health benefits intact; the best part about sun-dried food is that it retains all nutrients and can be used for a prolonged period. Have a few sundried foods daily to improve health and look more radiant. Even though eating sun-dried food should be a priority, try not to miss out on the occasional indulgences to retain your sanity, too. Have that slice of cake or a piece of chocolate that you have been craving.

3. Smile and Laugh More Often

Naturally, smiling and laughing more often will make you look more radiant, brighter, and attract people to you. People are attracted to those who have a positive aura, which is often seen in people who are always happy. Even though Leos seem bright and radiant, smiling and laughing more often will boost your immune system and enhance your heart health. You worry less, which reduces stress and improves mental health. Also, the more you smile and laugh, the better people you will be attracting to you. It will help you develop better connections in your personal life and attract opportunities in the professional world.

Try to take time out and meet your close friends often. Plan outings or invite them to play board games. Try more activities that make you happy. Watch comedy shows or stand-up acts. Along with that, play with your kids or your younger cousins to unleash your inner child. Lastly, attend fun outdoor events such as concerts, amusement park trips, or even a day at the beach to feel happy and obtain inner peace.

4. Take Care of Your Physical and Mental Health

While this applies to all signs, Leos must particularly focus on their physical and mental health as this sign is usually proactive and expends its energy aimlessly. Eat right, exercise at least thirty minutes every day, and drink a lot of water. Pay attention to your diet and try to add as many nutrients as possible; this will improve your physical health and stamina, and help you lose or maintain weight. Besides this, you should also practice mental health improvement exercises such as meditation and yoga. Improve your sleep pattern and get seven-to-eight hours of sleep every night.

Besides your mental and physical health, you must also focus on your spiritual and emotional health. Take care of your heart and give it the proper time to heal and develop, especially if there has been a traumatic situation. It will also help Leo men express their feelings, as they are the ones who hold back. Have a heart-to-heart conversation with your loved ones, practice chakra yoga to open your body's chakras, and practice self-healing. Focus on exercises that open your heart chakra.

5. Add More Warm Colors to Your Color Palette

The Sun sign that rules Leos make the individuals of this zodiac sign seem warm and bright. The bright colors of the sun should also be adopted by all Leos and added to their color palette. Hues like red, orange, and yellow should be a regular part of your color palette. The things you wear, use, and eat should include these colors in some form. These bright colors will enhance your personality and make you more attractive. Your liveliness and playful spirit need just a touch of these colors on and around you.

If you still prefer to stick to darker shades, add some bright accessories, such as a belt or a hat with a yellow or orange touch. These colors also reflect the fire element and the burning passion within most Leos. Do not be shy about wearing a warm-colored outfit with a dash of bold red lipstick. As a Leo, you are likely to carry this look with confidence and make a bold statement. Apart from outfits and accessories, add warm shades in accents of the things around you, such as your rug, sofa, curtains, towels, etc.

Quick Tips for the Friends of Leos

1. Let Them Have the Center Stage

Even though we mentioned this tip earlier, emphasizing it is crucial. Since Leos live for attention, they will despise being friends with someone who will take the spotlight. If you value your Leo friend, let them have their share of attention and enjoy their moment. Whether it's a karaoke night or a birthday party, let them be in the spotlight. Even if you don't prefer to share the spotlight, try to be cooperative and support your Leo friend's wants. If you want to go an extra length, encourage and hype your friend by telling one of their funniest stories to the crowd or complimenting them in front of everyone.

These sly techniques are a way to win your Leo friend's heart and stay close friends in the long run. Since Leos like to be validated, they will automatically feel more valuable and closer to you; this is particularly helpful for those Leos who are shy and more reserved. They want to be validated but are unable to garner attention. As their friend, take the initiative and help them experience the attention they often crave. Basically, let them shine.

2. Never Try to Take Advantage of their Situation

As you know, Leos are extremely loyal and trustworthy, and they expect the same in return. Their generous and loyal trait can make them seem unreasonably kind, which some people mistake for being naïve. If you claim to be their best or close friend, you will never take advantage of their generosity and kindness. Once Leos figure out your true intentions are not in their best interests, they will lose respect and the trust invested in you. While it is easier for them to forgive you, it will be difficult for them to forget. Do not exploit their liberality, knowingly or unknowingly.

Do not try to reap the benefits of their cooperative attitude. It will take them no time to reciprocate harshly. You will notice them unleashing their wrath and bringing their inner Lion out. Do not trigger Leos by breaking their trust in any way. Try your best not to make them angry.

3. Be Good Listeners

When Leos are hurt or are in pain, their hearts are heavy, and they want someone to listen to them. As a friend of a Leo, they might turn to you at times. Let them vent and feel lighter. Do not listen to give advice; only listen to what they say, which makes you a good listener. Even though it might seem a bit unpleasant or repetitive, sit through it because that is what best friends do. If they can trust you listening to them during unpleasant situations, they will try to maintain the friendship and be drawn to you with the passing of time.

When they vent, Leos generally let out all their anger and frustration, which is enough to make them smile. After calming down, they develop an ability to think rationally. Don't interrupt them when they are venting. Let them blurt it all out and express their deepest regrets in front of you. To calm them down, try to comfort them by being empathetic.

For instance, if your Leo friend says, "I was trying to call you for two hours as I wanted someone to talk to me and you were unavailable," you should reply, "I understand that you needed me during those intense hours, and I should have been there for you. I can understand that it must be frustrating."

Apart from these tips, you should shower your Leo friend with presents, compliments, and flatter them as much as you can. Try to be sincere about your feelings as Leos can easily spot it if you are fake.

Conclusion

To sum up, let's describe the personality traits of Leos in three words – vivacious, passionate, and theatrical. A Leo is like a lion in the savannah - the powerful king. Leos are powerful lions in the concrete jungle who try to pave their own paths and emerge victoriously. They know how to take the spotlight, are always curious, extremely creative, and born leaders.

Leos at home, work, and social gatherings are almost the same – they are curious about everything and always ready to try new skills. And their supreme talent and leadership skills are impeccable and a hit with others.

If you are a Leo, try to align your weaknesses and strengths in the right direction to achieve your goals and create the best version of yourself. Work on your stubbornness and vanity. At the same time, take proper advantage of your strengths.

If you are a friend, parent, or partner of a Leo, you must pay a lot of attention to them and handle intense situations with ease. Show them affection and let them have their center stage in public settings. If you are trying to impress, seduce, or date a Leo, dress nicely, give expensive presents, and compliment them often. Make them feel wanted and important.

As a Leo, this information will not only give you better control over your life and relevant dimensions of it, but you will also be able to change your life significantly. If applied correctly, this book's advice will help you excel at work, with your relationships, and at social events, which will ultimately build your confidence and help you succeed in life.

It is now time to put this information, tips, and advice into action and win the world. Good luck!

Part 6: Virgo

The Ultimate Guide to an Amazing Zodiac Sign in Astrology

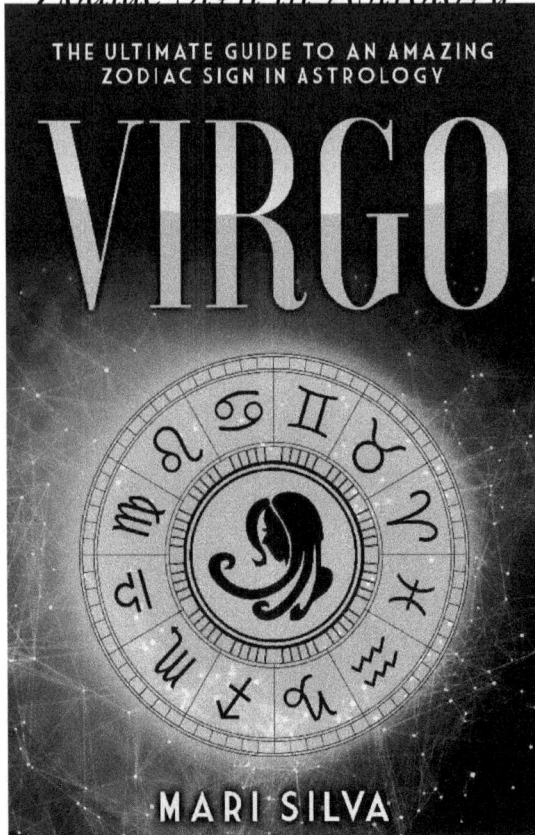

Introduction

An understanding of astrology can alter your life. It has done so for many other people across the planet; me included. Astrology brings the hidden corners of your entire being to light. It is a way to expand your awareness of yourself and others. Your compassion for yourself and your environment depends on it. Your past grows much clearer, and you get a glimpse of your possible future.

Astrology can alter your perception. Once you understand your place in the stars, it becomes impossible to perceive the world like you used to. This field is filled with terms just as poetic as they are objective, fueling your curiosity, and stimulating your intellect. As you probe deeper into the mystical ways of astrology, every human is transformed into a mystery waiting to be understood.

The crown of it all is that astrology presents an unmatched way of discovering yourself not just as a member of a zodiac sign, but as a personalized assortment of abilities and qualities. You are someone whose personal essence reflects the cosmos. Many individuals believe that astrology merely categorizes people into twelve places, but they couldn't be more wrong! Astrology teaches that every one of us is liable to be subjected to universal desires and needs, and that we are all completely and exquisitely unique.

Astrology is as old as time itself and is a constantly evolving system that possesses a variety of dimensions and can be perceived in several forms, from Chinese astrology to Vedic astrology or Western astrology. This book is centered on the Virgo zodiac sign of Western astrology, but it also has many sublevels, branching off into other zodiac signs when the need arises.

Astrology is an unbiased tool used to understand others and yourself. It is used to embrace opportunities, confront adversity, analyze relationships, and make simple choices. For centuries, man has been very fascinated with the stars and the way they affect us all. It's only natural for you to be intrigued by astrology; to wonder about all the many ways these heavenly bodies might affect your day-to-day life.

If you're reading this book, then it means you're particularly captivated by the Virgo — if you aren't one yourself. Whether you're a Virgo, or you're simply seeking to understand the Virgo in your life, you are in luck! This book contains all you need to know about the zodiac's Virgo sign.

Finally, astrology has nothing to do with predestination or fate. It leans more toward propensity and possibility. It is more about maximizing your strong points and acknowledging your weak ones. With astrology, you can finally understand people and align yourself with the universe. Like Sir Francis Bacon once said, "The stars do not compel, they impel." No truer words have been said.!

Chapter One: An Introduction to the Virgo

When you say to people, "I'm a Virgo," you're usually talking about your Sun sign. What's a Sun sign, you ask? When the Sun goes around the Earth year after year, it passes through the zodiac's twelve signs, taking a month in each one.

As for astrology, the Sun is a planet. You could call it the most powerful planet, and you'd be right. In terms of horoscopes, the Sun has the most influence in how others perceive you, how you express yourself, and the motivations and reasons you have for wanting to achieve the goals you've set for yourself.

Your Sun sign offers a big-picture depiction of your personality. Think of it as the outline of a drawing before it's filled in with more details. To have a general idea of yourself as a Virgo, or of your Virgo friend or family member, then the Sun sign will give you what you need to know.

If you've ever read up on Virgo astrology and felt, "Well, that doesn't seem particularly accurate," it's because your Sun sign only gives you the foundation of your personality. Other than the Sun, there's the Moon to consider. A study of your birth chart would likely show that the Moon is in a much different zodiac sign altogether than the Sun.

All planets within your birth chart can be of a different sign, and this makes you a complex, unique individual. Imagine if all Virgos were the same! That would make for a not so fun world — not that Virgos aren't fun. They're amazing - once they let you in.

The only path to know who you are is to look closely at the whole birth chart rather than just focus on your Sun sign. Even when you have all the information you need, understand that you're human. This means you're a dynamic being.

The signs may show you the type of person you are, but in the end, you get to say what you are and what you become. However, knowing the attributes of a Virgo will go far in helping you have better relationships with them. If you're a Virgo yourself, it will help you understand yourself and how you can connect with the world around you in a mutually beneficial way.

Sun Signs and Their Divisions

Before we dive into the Virgo fully, I must help you understand the zodiac signs' various groupings and divisions. We begin with dualities.

Dualities

All twelve zodiacs belong to either the masculine or the feminine, with six falling under each category. We know this grouping as duality. While there are certain preconceptions about what it means to be masculine or feminine, this doesn't imply that one is better than the other. Think of them as neutral qualities, and little more.

The feminine is magnetic and receptive and has nothing to do with being weak, passive, or negative. On the other hand, the masculine is energetic and direct. This doesn't mean that it's better than the feminine; it's just what it is.

A better alternative to describe the feminine trait is to say that all feminine signs demonstrate a quiet strength in being self-contained and possessing inner resolve, while the masculine signs display their powers through outwardly directed action.

The masculine types are Aquarius, Libra, Aries, Leo, Gemini, and Sagittarius, while the feminine types are the Taurus, Pisces, Cancer, Capricorn, Scorpio, and last but not least, Virgo.

Triplicities

We can also split the twelve zodiac signs into groups of four, with three signs to each group. These groups are called triplicities, and they each represent one of the four components: Earth, Air, Water, and Fire. These elements make up the basic characteristics of the twelve types.

Earth signs — Virgo, Capricorn, and Taurus — are stable and practical thinkers. Air signs — Libra, Gemini, and Aquarius — are communicative and intellectual. Water signs — Cancer, Pisces, and Scorpio — are in touch with their intuition and emotions. Finally, the Fire signs — Leo, Aries, and Sagittarius — are enthusiastic and often active.

Quadruplicities

We also split all zodiac signs into three groups of four, known as quadruplicities, all of which signify particular traits. There are three qualities in particular:

- Cardinal
- Fixed
- Mutable

The cardinal signs are regularly the most outgoing and enterprising of the lot. They're the ones who start things. If you want someone who is an innate initiator, you can turn to the Capricorn, Cancer, Libra, and Aries signs.

The fixed signs are Scorpio, Leo, Aquarius, and Taurus. They're not open to change, which can be good since they finish and perfect what they start, rather than initiate things.

Mutable signs are Virgo, Gemini, Pisces, and Sagittarius. They're versatile, quick to adapt, and flexible. They're open and able to adjust depending on the circumstances they're facing.

The thought to remember that there's no zodiac sign with the exact combination of elements, dualities, and qualities. Thanks to the unique combos, all signs naturally express themselves differently from one another.

Polarities

This is the final grouping of zodiac signs, where two signs are assigned to a group. We call each grouping a polarity, meaning to comprise opposing signs with conflicting natures. Let's quickly look at the polarities:

- Where Sagittarius is all about philosophy and higher mental activities, Gemini is all about self-expression.
- Aquarius is all about large-scale ideals and hopes, while Leo is about creativity and personal pleasure.
- Libra is focused on partnership, while Aries is about individuality.
- Capricorn is a sign that's about public life, while Cancer is about life at home.

• Scorpio is about shared possessions and building legacies, while Taurus is about their personal possessions.

• Pisces are all self-delusion and dreams, while Virgo is about self-advancement and function.

Each sign of the zodiac has its lucky days and numbers, special colors and plants, jewels, metals, places, and so on. They too, have their positive attributes and their challenges. I'm not suggesting you live your life by this. As a Virgo, you're more than welcome to wear other colors besides Virgo colors, and to try playing the lottery on any day of the week besides your lucky one; it wouldn't mean the end of the world. However, you might find it fascinating to try experimenting with what you're about to learn. Since this book is all about the Virgo, we shall now turn our attention to just this amazing sign.

The Virgo (August 22 — September 22)

Here's a quick guide on all you need to know about being a Virgo.

• Your duality is feminine.

• Your triplicity or element is Earth.

• Your quality or quadruplicity is mutable. You are discriminating, practical, modest, and reserved. You're an industrious person with a piercing analytical mind, willing to painstakingly seek knowledge and understanding in all you do.

• Your ruling planet is Mercury. This is the ancient god of commerce and communication. This planet oversees reason and intelligence and predisposes you to be a bit high strung or "mercurial."

• Your symbol is The Virgin. The Virgin represents pure motives, industriousness, modesty, and service. You use your talents to help other people. The typical depiction of the Virgin has her holding a sheaf of wheat. This sheaf represents you using your skills, knowledge, and ideas to the benefit (or nourishment) of everyone in the world.

• Your glyph (a written symbol) represents the Virgin because it is the pictorial representation of the human sexual organs, untouched and without blemish. Your glyph has two curved lines (one crossed) and a straight line. This signifies the way you interweave emotions and feelings with wisdom and practicality.

• Your dominant key phrase is *I Analyze.*

• Your polarity is the Pisces. Where the Pisces is about self-deception and buying into illusions, the Virgo is about responsibility and personal-improvement. Where the Piscean revels in imagination, dreaminess, self-delusion, escapism, and vagueness, the Virgo is quite practical and grounded.

• The body parts ruled by the Virgo include the intestines and the nervous system. As a Virgo, you're quite susceptible to illnesses caused by nervous tension and stress. Ulcers are a common concern with you.

• Your lucky day is Wednesday.

• Your lucky numbers are 3 and 5.

• Your magical birthstone is Sapphire, which gives you peace and tranquility of mind, and keeps you safe against injury and illness as you travel.

• Your special colors are Gray and Navy Blue, which both signify a refined taste.

- Your cities include Paris, Heidelberg, Boston, and Strasbourg.

- Your countries are Greece, Turkey, West Indies, and Crete.

- Your flowers are the pansy and morning glory.

- Your trees are nut-bearing trees.

- Your metal is Mercury.

- Your animals are small, domesticated pets.

- Your challenge: As a Virgo, you can't help but interfere, offer criticism, and appear unemotional. These features can make others get angry and violent, so you want to be aware of that.

A-List of Famous Virgos

1. Beyoncé
2. Zendaya
3. Idris Elba
4. Taraji P. Henson
5. Salma Hayek
6. Keanu Reeves
7. Lili Reinhart
8. Keke Palmer

The Virgo at Work

You'd be hard-pressed to find any better boss or employee than a Virgo. You work really hard, and you're intelligent, an undeniable asset. When people need to get jobs done, you're the best woman or man for the job.

One of your strongest traits is your attention to details — even the incredibly small stuff that most individuals won't notice. You're not the kind to be sloppy. You'll be damned before you pass off something that's even remotely incomplete as finished.

You're careful about the decisions you make, and you have a precise process for getting things done. Sometimes your particular work process and awareness to detail make it hard for the others you work with, since most of them would rather move things along as fast as they can. But you are not willing to sacrifice quality for speed, and so you're comfortable getting everyone to take a moment and go through the project at hand with a magnifying glass so you can work all the kinks out. As a result, perfection is something you tend to achieve.

At the office, you're analytical, practical, hardworking, loyal, and gentle. These are your strengths. Alternatively, you are critical of yourself, wondering if you delivered your best and if you shouldn't perhaps try to do more.

You're critical of others, too, because you can't stand it when people don't do what they should do properly, and you don't understand how anyone could be so sloppy. You're not critical because you enjoy being difficult, but because nothing pleases you more than being able to deliver flawless execution on a project.

Sometimes you worry a lot about what could go wrong, and often will not rest until you get feedback that says you did well. Also, you are a tad shy — and you can overcome this by simply voicing your thoughts. You are, after all, more intelligent than most.

As a Virgo at work, you are a hard worker, and you solve problems. You're amazing to work with, especially when you allow yourself to be generous and kind. No matter the job, you're an invaluable asset to the team, always.

The Virgo at a Party

Virgos and parties are a tricky thing. Now and then, you'll let your hair down and have fun, but usually, that's only after a few drinks have loosened you up. This doesn't mean you're not social; you'd rather hang out with people one-on-one or in small groups.

You're probably the person who sits at the party with a drink, enjoying watching other people dancing and being goofy. It's not that you're a party pooper, and it's not that you're not having a good time. You just love to observe.

When you do get in on the "madness," you have a great time! You leave everyone's jaw hanging, whether it's you belting out the tunes to a Christina Aguilera song with particularly high notes, or dancing like the love child of Ciara and the late great Michael Jackson.

But, when the alcohol wears off, you are more than happy to take a seat — or leave. One thing you could never be accused of is being that *one friend* who doesn't know when the party's over. Speaking of firewater, when you notice you've had way more than you should have, you're the first one to head right home. You have incredible self-control and will only let yourself sway from side to side and crumble into a puddle on the floor when you're in the relative safety of your home or with people you love and trust.

The Virgo at Home

As a Virgo, nothing matters to you more than a home that is neat and tidy. You may not be religious, but you definitely take the phrase "Cleanliness is next to godliness" to heart. You live by it. Your home must be in order. You care little for clutter and will declutter often and regularly. You've probably had your friends and family raise eyebrows at you when you say stuff like, "I need to clear this place out," because from where they're standing, there's nothing that needs clearing!

You love it when your home has lots of space and lots of light. So, creating this space, you live and breathe the idea that everything has its space. It's not just that you're stubborn about this need for an order for nothing; it's that you really need the order to function. Without it, you can't help feeling off and not at peace.

With home decor, you choose minimalism. This doesn't mean a lack of taste by any stretch of the imagination. You pay attention to color, style, materials, craftsmanship, and every other element in every room of your home. You love to have beautiful items that increase your home's elegance but are also functional and practical.

If anyone wants to get to know you, they'll find the real you in the comfort of your home. Where outside, you might be accused of being a tad too straightlaced and having resting rhymes-with-witch face, at home, you let loose totally. You might break into a silly song and dance routine just because you're about to have an amazing pizza, or, well, *just because.*

Since the home is where you are okay with being vulnerable, you are mindful of who you let into your space. Even when they're with you, you're mindful of how long they stay there — unless they're part of those you consider near and dear.

Chapter Two: Virgo Strengths and Weaknesses

In this chapter, we will take a quick look at the Virgo's strengths and weaknesses when they are a friend or family member. So, let's begin!

The Virgo's Strengths

Of all the traits you or your friend have as a Virgo, the most admirable one is conscientiousness. You make a point of doing a good job at whatever responsibility has been assigned to you, and inevitably this leads you to greener pastures and higher ranks, whatever your field is.

As enigmatic as you seem, the real action goes on beneath your calm, cool exterior. Inside, you're restless, eager to be making the most of your time. You're intense in a controlled and focused way, and you direct that intensity to things you think will improve your life.

You're really not the kind to just binge on Netflix all day in your pajamas, and chances are on the rare occasions you do give in to that urge, you're still going to make sure you at least did one thing you saw as productive before you hit the hay. As far as you're concerned, there's always a chance to be better and do better, and you snatch every second to work on being a better version of yourself.

It's not a random turn of events that you're so obsessed with needing to do stuff. After all, your ruling planet is Mercury! That means you love the constant activity, whether it's learning to become a stock trader or figuring out how to become a better gardener. You are driven to make things happen and make them happen as perfectly as possible.

The Virgo absolutely sucks at procrastinating. You're incredibly organized most of the time, and you're all about making things happen. While the rest of the world dreams, you do.

As a Virgo, you are open to love, but you need a lot more than love to be happy and at peace with yourself. For you, it's not enough to have a lover, or friends, or kids, or a home. You want to be sure that you mean something; that your existence is contributing to bettering the whole.

You are full of ambition, and for you, it's not just about raking in dollars. It's about wanting to grow in knowledge and wisdom and to apply all that you've learned in a way that benefits you and everyone around you.

No one has as pure a purpose as you do. In fact, this is the thing that the Virgo stands for. You're not living your life to exploit people. You aspire to much higher ideals, and nothing appeals to you more than the chance to be of service.

Long ago, Virgo symbolized the harvest. Recall the image of the Virgin, with a sheaf of wheat in her hand? This represents that those under the Sun sign Virgo will always take the skills, knowledge, wisdom, and information they have, plant it, and then harvest the fruits to enjoy and share the benefits of all that they have sown. You, dear Virgo, are a nourisher.

If there's one thing no one can accuse you of, it's not being unintelligent. Your memory is sharp, your mind crisp and capable of analyzing as no one else can, and you can cut through the haze and arrive at clear answers thanks to your mental faculties.

Another thing you're incredibly great at is figuring out why people really do what they do, no matter what they claim their reasons are. You are most likely the one your friends and family check-in with before they do major or important stuff because you are often great at fishing out the weak links in their plans.

Logic is your playground, so you have no issues with ripping apart a problem and reconstructing it into its solution. You're excellent at coming up with answers and putting an end to disagreements.

It's not like you to make a decision before you have all the facts that you need. You thrive in the world of facts and turn your nose up at such things as psychics and crystal balls and whatnot. You're not swift to make judgments based on emotions, and you don't particularly like it when people do that either.

The Virgo's Weaknesses and How to Navigate Them

As great as always being rational is, consider making room for such concepts as faith, spirituality, and synchronicity. Since you are a fact loving Virgo, here's a fact you will definitely love more and more while you ponder it: Things happen and we meet people for a reason. It's not random. This is the challenge you face as a Virgo: To be willing to accept and allow for such things as faith.

Your ruling planet Mercury is all about thought and assumptions, and these things are what form the reality you experience. To assume the worst and always think the worst will inevitably lead to the worst experiences for you.

You need to know your tendency to avoid your true emotions because you'd rather indulge in denial. You might insist you're not mad at something, or that you're all right with the way things have turned out when someone else gets the guy or the girl or gets the cushy job or promotion you wanted. All this does is keep the ugly feelings hidden within you.

Another thing you want to be mindful of is your tendency to be focused on one thing to the exclusion of the big picture. You have amazing talent in organization and being precise, but sometimes that makes it hard to notice if anything else that matters is going on.

Because you trust logic explicitly, it makes it hard for you to be imaginative, and inspiration doesn't strike you as often as you could let it. You tend to fall back on what you already know works, rather than look to the new. It matters to you to learn why things work the way they do and how they work. The good thing is you're a mutable Sun sign, so you can make changes as needed so you can incorporate the new into the old.

You might make too much of a habit of turning molehills into mountains. You take a small, simple problem and blow it out of proportion by complicating it. What you might want to learn to do is not be so analytical of things; sometimes things really are as they seem, and there's nothing more to them than that.

As a Virgo, you're naturally reserved, maybe even a little shy. You don't make small talk a habit as it's anything but relaxing for you to shoot the breeze with strangers about such mundane things as the weather or your choice in nail polish. You'd rather deal with people on deeper things that actually matter; it is in this situation where you thrive, and your laser-like wits and intellect shine through. In your one-on-one interactions, you allow people to see just how full of wit, insight, charm, perception, and wisdom you are.

You don't kid yourself by saying, "Money doesn't matter." You know of its importance, and you're an expert at handling your finances, even if you don't like to toot your own horn. You're not the kind to shell out money on needless things or snake oil. This doesn't mean that you're a cheapskate; you're just adept at getting incredible value for a steal.

Because you're very clear about what you accept and don't accept, you can get just a tad too critical. You're not okay with the status quo, and you'll do all you can to make things better. You'll push people to give better than their best.

Sometimes, because you're so aware of all the ways things could be better, you let this knowledge get the best of you, and you get unhappy. However, you do the best you can to avoid being in situations where others can criticize what you're doing wrong — unless you're the unique kind of Virgo who can handle criticism and is okay with admitting they don't always get it right.

As far as your health goes, you want nothing short of the best for yourself. You never need a call from your doctor asking you to come in for a checkup because you show up all on your own, like clockwork. You take your vitamins, and you move your body as often and as well as you can. This is great, but you need to beware of your tendency to worry too much about your health. When you worry like this, you become tense and nervous, which naturally predisposes you to fall ill. Also, be mindful of giving in to hypochondria, where you assume you're sick even though you're fine.

There's nothing as amazing as being in the right relationship, where there is much warmth and love. You're a naturally loving, giving, loyal, devoted, and kind soul, being born under the Sun sign of Virgo. Whenever someone is fortunate enough to win your love, you do all that you can to serve them and keep them happy.

Who You Really Are

There's no one as dedicated and strong-willed as you are, and you'll go to any lengths to make sure you see something through to the end, and it's all perfect. The reason you're this way is simple: You can't stand the thought of being a failure at something, and you lean toward being a little too hard on yourself. As "critical" as people think you are, you dial your criticism up to the hundreds when you aim it at yourself.

If anyone thinks they can figure you out, they need to think again. You're a puzzle, bound up in mystery, shrouded in an enigma. When you're dealing with people you don't know too well; you'll often hold back. Even those you know and love will still describe you as reserved. As cool as you seem on the outside, there's a gushing torrent of emotions on the inside where no one else can see. No one is as intense as the Virgo, and not only that, but you are also given to sensitivity at extreme levels — something no one you don't want to know will ever know about.

You enjoy being able to take care of people around you, whether that means providing materially or giving much needed useful advice. However, you like when you're shown appreciation for your acts. It matters to you that the people you help actively demonstrate that you're not wasting your time and that they are thankful for what you offer them. For you, it matters that you serve a purpose, that you provide assistance because people do matter to you.

Who Others See You As

People think of you as someone who is an achiever. You are the epitome of the go-getter. As such, you're often assigned a lot of responsibility, and people trust you to handle whatever they throw your way. They know that you can deal with any problem you face because of your incomparable skills.

Your friends and family will often come to you so you can help them understand why they act the way they do, or why they feel how they do about their career, loved ones, or whatever else is bothering them.

You are incredibly skilled at prioritizing and finding the order in the midst of the madness. Where everyone is losing their heads, you're the one keeping things rock steady.

Because you're picky (in a good way), people will always look at your recommendations on everything from cuisine, to fashion, to books and movies. You never, ever let anyone in so easily. Your heart may be *wherever,* but it is most definitely never going to be on your sleeve. For this reason, some people erroneously assume that you're cold and unfeeling. If only they knew just how deeply you feel for and care about them!

The Virgo in the Family

If you could change the way a few of your relatives acted, would you do it? Be honest. Think about that one creepy uncle, or that nitpicking sibling, or your overbearing mum. Sometimes we wish we could change the people fate threw us with, but since we don't have a wand or a magic spell to fix them, the only other choice we have left is to run away... Okay, that may be a tad dramatic. Perhaps we could try understanding them a little better instead. This is where astrology can prove quite helpful! Looking at the stars, you can figure out what exactly makes the Virgo tick.

With astrology, you must consider other things besides the Zodiac signs and where they're placed, as these things also play an important function in your unique family dynamics. I'm referring to the modalities we spoke about earlier — mutable, cardinal, and fixed — and the elements — Earth, fire, water, and air.

The Virgo belongs to the Earth element, so you'll find them having qualities reminiscent of Earth. For one thing, you'll find that they're the most down-to-Earth family member of yours. They're modest about the things they've accomplished and are capable of, and they're also incredibly grounded.

Virgo is the most pragmatic person you know at home. You'll notice that they can be a wee bit conservative sometimes, and that's okay. They love to have a routine, as it gives them a sense of order and stability, and makes them feel safe and at ease.

You'll notice your Virgo relative loves to analyze things and makes a point of being practical, thinking through every angle before they make a decision or a move. The thing about Earth: it is *rock steady,* unlike air and fire. The Virgo is not a big fan of surprises. A surefire way to incur their wrath or make them feel uncomfortable would be to put them on the spot. But ... if the Virgo has learned to embrace her mutable trait, then she will handle whatever you throw at her — while letting you know after your little stunt that what you did was not cool with her!

Just like it's not so easy to change a rock into something else, the Virgo is not entirely open to change. They're an organized lot, you see, and they'd rather do something they're familiar and comfortable with than risk rocking the boat. This might seem like a terrible thing, but it isn't. You'll find that the calmest, most patient, and most steadfast head at home is the Virgo. You can rely on them to get the job done. You can trust that if they said they're going to start doing something, it's going to get done.

In the midst of confusion, panic, or a heated argument, you can draw upon your Virgo relative's infinite well of reason. The next time there's a crisis, look around the room, and you'll notice that the Virgo is the most poised person there. The only problem with them being so steadfast, poised, and stable is that you might find it hard to tell what they're feeling or thinking. Not that this is a problem. If you want to know what's running around in their heads, just ask. Don't be pushy about it; in their own time and in their own way, they will give you an answer.

Earth is an element all about materialism. This doesn't mean your Virgo relative is materialistic by any stretch of the imagination – at least, not in a superficial way. Do they have high sophistication in taste? They do. But they're not big on an ostentatious display of their possessions, or anyone else's, for that matter.

For the Virgo, what matters the most is emotional dependability and stability. They find that just as important as being on a financial stable ground. Speaking of money, the Virgo does their best to make sure it's never a problem so they can live life without ever having to worry about cash.

Another interesting thing about this Earth sign is that they love to touch, and they have sensuality in spades. You might not think them all sugar and spice and everything nice, but they're affectionate, sentimental, and genuine in all their feelings.

Earth Meets Water

If you consider nature, you'll notice that water and Earth have a relationship that benefits each other. This is the same thing with the Earth Virgo and any other water signs in the family. If you're a water sign yourself, and you have a Virgo relative, you've probably noticed that you have good vibes with each other. Earth and water bind, deeply, unshakably, and effortlessly.

Being of the Earth, the Virgo has all the patience they need to deal with the complex nature and moods of water signs. At the same time, Water signs are great at emotionally supporting the Virgo and creating a comfortable and safe space for the Virgo to get into their feelings. Sure, the Pisces might think of the Virgo as being wound up too tight, but there's really nothing but love there. The Water sign will often push the Virgo to be a lot more compassionate and perceptive emotionally, while the Earth will give Water calm and stability.

Earth Meets Air

The Virgo and air signs all share a similar sense of humor: Droll. They have the same sensibilities as well: Delicate. And what about their views on drama? Distasteful. That being said, because of the Virgo's practical nature, they might have a problem with how frenetic and unpredictable air signs tend to be. On the flip side, if you're an Air sign, you probably think the Virgo is just unyielding, way too rigid, and too darned measured in every step they take.

While the air sign is all about ideas, the Virgo, being of the Earth, prefers the tangible and practical. If you're the parent of a Virgo and a Libra, for instance, don't be upset by your child taking issue with you when you're indecisive. Don't despair, though; your Virgo can teach you why it's worth it to commit to a decision, and you can teach them how to let loose and be a little more spontaneous.

Earth Meets Fire

You'd be hard-pressed to find more opposite elements... Okay, there's fire and water, but we're talking about the Virgo here. Fire signs tend to be spontaneous, and this is the opposite of the cautious Virgo. If you're a Virgo parent, this is the reason your Sagittarius kid finds you a little too stifling. That doesn't mean there's no upside to this tricky dance between Earth and Fire.

Virgo could stand to gain a lot from the fire sign's love for life and living, learning to be okay with experiencing the new or unfamiliar and making peace with the unknown. On the flip side, the Virgo can help their fire sign relatives by giving them stable footing and teaching the value of focus, consistency, and patience.

The Mutable Virgo in the Family

Since the Virgo is mutable, that means they're incredibly flexible and versatile; they can learn to deal with change. Almost like a chameleon, they adjust to whatever environment or situation they find themselves in.

No one is as accommodating, compromising, and obliging as the mutable Virgo. Ironically, as organized and practical as the Virgo is, and as deeply in love as they are with their routines, they'll go with the flow whenever the circumstances dictate they should.

The mutable Virgo deliberately takes the least resistant path. They're the best team player you could have. They're not keen on leading, but they can light the path when it comes to teaching the rest of the family to be at peace with new developments and be willing to settle in.

Being mutable means the Virgo is not a fan of conflict in the family. They will do their best to see things from everyone's perspectives, and it's this quality of theirs that makes them excellent mediators, helping people sort out their differences and getting things back to normal.

Chapter Three: The Virgo Child

The Virgo baby is a sensitive and touching child. They get startled by all sounds, prefer to be touched only by familiar people, and cry when a voice around them doesn't sound tender enough.

The Virgo babies distinguish between strangers and family early in life, and they are uncomfortable with being left alone with unfamiliar faces. They are prone to restlessness caused by uncomfortable cribs, sharp sounds, wet diapers, and bright light.

While the Virgo baby won't cry severely, they will surely throw tantrums. They will whimper and keep their faces wrinkled until their comfort is restored. These guys need a constant stream of love and encouragement; otherwise, they feel helpless and unprotected.

Virgo children lean toward dealing with insecurities even at that young age, and this keeps them from participating in children's groups and any unfamiliar event or communicating with strangers. But don't be fooled; they are self-confident and fearless little ones, but only in the company of loving, familiar faces.

Virgo children are typically curious about their surrounding space and are attracted to everything unknown despite being hesitant and cautious. They will never jump headfirst into a strange situation, and no steps will be taken without the guidance of a familiar adult. Even then, they will continually look to the adult for approval or reaction while moving ahead. The adult is tasked to supply praise, self-confidence, and explanations.

The minute they learn to speak, everything speeds up! Virgo babies will ask about anything and everything, especially the names of things. They seem to have a knack for that. Reading becomes one of their favorite things to do. They recall all the poems and stories, repeating them happily as often as they feel the need to.

They prefer completely harmless toys like dolls, cubes, or teddy bears. They are also enthusiastic about plot games, taking on the role of doctor, teacher, parent, and so on. These little ones are completely taken with animals and will deeply appreciate owning a pet like a puppy, parrot, hamster, kitten, and so on. This helps them develop discipline and a sense of responsibility early in life because they are quick to figure out how to take care of their tiny animal friend.

The minute they can move around comfortably, little Virgos become great helpers. They will jump at opportunities to participate in chores around the house like washing dishes, cleaning the floor, or at least trying to, especially when they receive any praise and encouragement. This habit sticks because they quickly learn to clean up their toys, stay neat, and ensure that their rooms are in order as best as they can for a little human. Mostly, this behavior extends well into adulthood, especially if they received praise and encouragement from their parents or guardians during the formative years.

As a preschooler, they might prefer to spend most of their time playing alone, drawing or figuring out their toys. For learning, the Virgo preschooler commits! But often, there is one thing that causes problems for these kids: communication with fellow children. This can go unnoticed until it is time to play team sports or any activity that involves teamwork.

Virgo children are usually found alone, preferring to observe and engage from a distance. Without guidance from parents or teachers, they might become so isolated that they begin to think they are not like others, sometimes leading to an inferiority complex.

As I mentioned earlier, Virgo children place a lot of importance on neatness. They must maintain that purity internally and externally. They are trustworthy, especially with finances, being the kind to spend their school money on meals or anything that seems practical and useful. They are eerily calm, making one wonder what goes on in their tiny heads.

Expressing emotion doesn't come easily to them because of their intense levels of restraint and quietness. Everything they say is thoroughly thought through more times than you can imagine. This is a double-edged sword as it can be a blessing to have a calm and collected child or a problem when you need to know what issues they might be going through.

The Male Virgo Child

All Virgos are deep thinkers. The Earth is a grounding force for those born under this sign, unlike the daredevils of the fire signs. This is the reason the young male Virgo is drawn more to mental activities than the physical ones. The Virgo boy thinks through as many possibilities as he can and plan for each one. If you have a Virgo boy, you've likely noticed how infrequently you need to remind him to take caution because he always does! He isn't prone to the use of brute force, militancy, or bravado. Instead, he leans towards attentiveness, foresight, and intelligence.

This does not mean that every little detail in the Virgo boy's mind is placed in compartments. There are moments when he experiences anxiety – even when he shouldn't. This is the price to pay for constantly absorbing information, as knowledge can prevent one from acting without a care in the world.

For instance, he may be excessively concerned about little things and hold himself back from experiences he would have otherwise enjoyed had he not been riddled with worry.

The Virgo boy does not like compromises. This can annoy others who don't see through the Virgo lens, which enhances the content and standard of everything around. A Virgo boy can easily be perceived as picky and petty when, in reality, he is just observant and alert.

The Female Virgo Child

The little girls in this category possess a strong wish to know and understand things in life. Where they're not nurtured in a warm, loving environment, this desire to understand everything can morph into an ugly need to manipulate — which isn't their fault if they aren't raised by the best of parents.

Keen observation and the ability to choose are characteristic of the Virgo girl at an early age. She's a good communicator and an even better listener. During her moments of silence, her eyes constantly see the world, noting the words and actions of those around her. She'll spend a lot of time analyzing the world around her in her head.

Because the Virgo girl requires perfection, she is prone to an inferiority complex. Outside of the right support systems, she can be her own worst critic because she creates unrealistic expectations of herself in her head. These expectations make her wrongly assume that she will never be enough as she is. This is why she needs a proper foundation of love and care, and would stand to gain a lot from being with people who *do* see her efforts and acknowledge them while letting her know she's fine just as she is. Most important, she needs to know that it is okay to make mistakes. This is especially important because the less she sets impossible standards for herself, the more she'll be able to enjoy a rich, fulfilling life.

The Virgo girl's inner voice tells her to do her best to make a good impression on the surrounding people. This can be a good or bad thing. This is a great thing sometimes because it means she'll make sure that she can connect with the people around her and create a comfortable space for one and all.

On the flip side, it could mean she gets bent all out of shape because she's trying to adhere to other people's standards for her life while neglecting her own joy — and some of those standards are actually based on her assumptions of what she thinks is required of her, not what the others in her life explicitly ask for.

Health of the Virgo Child

The intestines and stomach are the Virgo child's vulnerabilities, and they can be particularly prone to poisoning. You need to be careful when selecting meals for the Virgo baby. Just because something works great for other babies doesn't mean it's just as good for your Virgo child.

Remember that your Virgo child is susceptible to nervous disorders, and they tend to withhold their emotions from people they do not trust. Even when you — their loving and trusted parent — need to know how they're feeling, let them understand they can let you know anything, and be sure not to condemn or judge them for what they feel.

Virgo children tend to develop lung disease, but gastrointestinal problems are more common. Don't worry if your Virgo child is skinny growing up. Whatever you do, don't force-feed them! Their digestive system is finely tuned, and they're in touch with it. If they don't wish to eat something, or they don't want to eat anymore, trust that it's for a good reason — even if they don't know the fancy medical jargon to explain it to you. If you're worried that they don't have enough of an appetite, you can always consult with your medical doctor rather than take matters into your own hands.

Virgos eat the exact food that they need, and if that means they are a little smaller than the other kids, no problem. They have great intuition for selecting what works for them and what doesn't. This isn't synonymous with ignoring your Virgo child if they are underweight, so get help if that is the case.

Hobbies of the Virgo Child

One of the first things you'll notice about a Virgo child is that they tend to finish whatever they start. They are overly self-critical and can spot their own shortcomings and mistakes before you do, so don't bother pointing them out.

The Virgo child already knows where they went wrong with whatever they're doing. If you think you're offering assistance by showing them their mistakes, you're not. You will only completely demoralize them. They thrive in intense concentration, so don't be surprised if they throw a fit because you invaded their personal space to offer your "recommendations."

The Virgo child is drawn to any activity that requires intense concentration. They love to read, write, draw, paint, play instruments, or do whatever else they can with their hands if they're so inclined. They have an incredible eye for detail, so you can expect that whatever they're doing will be hands-down amazing.

Whatever your Virgo child is attracted to, you can count on one thing: they will be deeply focused on it. Sometimes, you might struggle to get them to drop what they're doing to come and have a bath or dinner. Don't take this to heart and don't force them to leave either. Just let them know they have a few more minutes to wrap up, and then they can come back to their hobby when they're done taking care of their tummies or bodies.

The Virgo Child at School

Virgo children are almost always the ideal student at school. They have a lot of fun learning, which is the whole point of school, anyway. They love books, be they full of stories or intriguing concepts about life. Your Virgo will never be one to cheat in exams. Often, the other kids want to cheat off of them. They're the students you'll see scribbling away and probably needing an extra sheet because they want to get down every thought they have about what they've learned so far.

Parental Advice

Show your Virgo child as much as you can of the world through books, travel, documentaries, or whatever. This is important because it opens them up to the possible ways they can express themselves. You'll be taking advantage of the mutability of their sign by allowing them to have an array of different ways they can structure their life.

Do not try even for a second to insinuate that there's anything wrong with your child's need for order and structure. Encourage them! But as you do, let them know that not everyone is as neat and orderly as they are, that it's okay, and that they can be accommodating of other people's messes within reason.

When you need to offer criticism to your Virgo child, you must make sure it is constructive, meaning you build them up rather than tear them down. Share your criticisms with them as a friend. Use persuasion and influence, not punishments and force. Rather than say, "You should have done it this way," encourage them to come around to your way of thinking by asking, "What if you tried it this way? What do you think about that?" If they offer you reasons, they don't think it could work, then gently coax them by asking, "Well, what else do you think we could try doing that might be even better than what we did before?"

You never need to raise your voice at your Virgo kid to make a point, because they actually are logical and get you anyway. Yelling does only makes them clam up and make sure you'll never learn what they think or feel about anything ever again. Your Virgo child doesn't care for violence, anger, or confrontation — especially when they're the recipient.

Give them access to books - *many* books - be they storybooks, encyclopedias, travel books, etc. It is from these books that the child can form their own world view. This doesn't mean your child doesn't care for toys and gadgets, so please get them those as well. Whatever hobbies they have, it is your job as their parent to create an environment that allows them to engage in them as passionately as their little hearts want to.

Just as important as letting your Virgo child explore her natural proclivities is helping them learn how to interact with others and come out of their shell. Show her it's okay to work with others by having her join children in groups — preferably ones centered on her interests. When she becomes okay with the concept of spending time with others, she'll be open to exploring activities outside her comfort zone, knowing she now has the tools to interact with others around her.

The Virgo child drifts away from his parents or guardians if he feels misunderstood, so it is important to build and cement the trust between you two in the child's formative years. Talk to him with an air of calmness, without judgment or reproach. Genuinely be happy with and for him.

Chapter Four: Virgo and Love

Here's an interesting fact about Virgos: They tend to take extra time falling in love. It's not that they're incapable of love, or not given to being all dreamy and romantic, but for them, whoever they will give their heart to has got to be worth it.

The Virgo does not care for silly, meaningless flings; they want depth, they want the truth, and they want dependability. No matter how many butterflies they feel in their stomach when you pass by or when they smell something that reminds them of you, they'll still keep their heart firmly where it belongs unless (and until) they can be certain you are here for the long haul.

The Virgo: The True Sapiosexual

Virgos are the sexy nerds of the zodiac. As a Virgo, you consider the mind the sexiest aspect of a person. You're a sucker for amazing conversations, witty banter, and even double entendres. There's nothing you love more than conversation tennis, where the other person can give back as good as they get.

For you, a surefire way for someone on Tinder to go from matched to unmatched in .0000001 milliseconds is when they only ever throw you one-liners... or even worse, one-word replies where they can't even be bothered to spell it all out!

The Virgo: Anything BUT Cold

If you're a Virgo, and you've ever read a book or article that says something to the effect of "Virgos can come off as a tad too cold," then you've probably kicked and screamed against that a million and one times because you know it's not true. Sure, you seem that way sometimes, but usually only with strangers, people you're not comfortable with yet, or people who crossed you.

For being in an intimate relationship, whoever is lucky enough to have you had better be well prepared for the white-hot heat that is your love. When you're sure about someone, you give them yourself one hundred percent. You let them in. You let them dive deep, and there they can see your emotions run deep and true.

Support for Your Virgo

Virgos are their own worst critics, valuing perfection in themselves above all else. Having a partner who showers you with unconditional love, support, and encouragement leads to a healthier and happier Virgo. People should tread carefully and softly with you during conflicts, or they might risk weakening the bond instead of strengthening it.

The Virgo prefers a mature partner, and for a good reason. You need a partner who can be trusted not to overreact to every little crisis, one who can stay focused on the facts of whatever issue you're dealing with in the now, rather than hear only what they want to hear and dredge up irrelevant things.

Best Matches for Virgo

Let's consider the signs that make the best matches for the Virgo. These are signs that bring out the best qualities of the Virgo and can provide a balance for the not-so-great qualities.

Scorpio

The Virgo and The Scorpio are the most amazing match -one of the strongest pairings in the Zodiac. The Scorpio is wild and intense, while the Virgo is down-to-earth, and this makes them work beautifully together.

You both care. A lot. The Scorpio can always be trusted, and they value trust as one of the most important things in any relationship. They're not the best at opening up, but as soon as you work your way into their hearts, they are more than happy to love you with an intensity you could never have imagined possible.

The Virgo is about taking care of other people's needs before they consider themselves, and so often they criticize themselves for not giving even much more than they already do — which is funny because the Virgo gives and gives and gives. As a Virgo, it just feels good to be giving.

Now, you and the Scorpio feel things deeply. Your Scorpio might not be obvious about it, but they're emotional. They'll put up a huge wall so that no one sees that, and they can stay safe. That's right... your Scorpio worries about being vulnerable, so they stay sealed until someone worthy (that's you, Virgo) comes around and breaks them open.

When the Virgo and the Scorpio get together, sparks fly. Things get intense and deep. You each know you can depend on each other. Even as friends, your loyalty knows no limits. You both learn from each other and grow together. The depth of understanding you both share needs no words — not even for you, dear Virgo. You know your Scorpio through and through, and you're unafraid to be just as naked with them in your heart.

Capricorn

Capricorn makes an amazing partner for Virgo. Being both Earth signs, you are both realistic and prefer to be focused on worldly materials. You both excel in various fields and possess a deep intuition about each other's needs. If a Capricorn-Virgo couple is spotted, they probably met at a work-related occasion and hit it off immediately.

You two have a great sense of humor that keeps you constantly laughing together. It is a good way for you two to relax and unwind, especially to get into a sensuous mood.

Despite all the similarities, you both have distinct traits that allow a balance in your relationship. The Capricorn is usually drowning in work, with their eyes zeroed in on the future, can tend to neglect their health and other important factors in life.

But the Virgo is more focused on the details than any other zodiac sign; still, they are prone to losing focus and getting off track. As a Virgo, you can make sure that your Capricorn lover remembers important details like self-care while your Capricorn can help you maintain focus.

Taurus

This is another wonderful match for you. You are both Earth signs, so you are bound to share the same realistic views of the world. The Taurus is one of the domestic signs of the zodiac while you are the most organized. These qualities are the highlight of your successful relationship.

Like Capricorn, you two also have notable differences that enable you to balance each other. The Taurus is chill and likes to enjoy the pleasures of living. You have no choice but to relax and savor the pleasures of life with them. The Taurus can also be the anchor you need to feel grounded. What you bring to the table as a Virgo is a motivation, among other things.

The Taurus' calmness can easily transition into overindulgence and laziness. You will make sure that Taurus does what needs to be done when it needs to be done, or even sooner because that's just who you are.

Cancer

The Cancer might seem like an odd match for you as a Virgo, but you two score high on the compatibility chart. You deeply understand each other in ways that other signs do not. You also tend to worry and fuss about everything, and this can be annoying to other signs. This similarity fosters tolerance in the relationship because you both get it!

This difference, though, is that despite your tendency to fuss over everything, you fuss about different things. Your perfectionist nature makes you worry about the little imperfections. The nurturing nature of Cancer makes them worry about the needs and safety of others. Cancer is a water sign, so their imagination is as boundless as the ocean. This causes them to exaggerate the threat before them or its potential, making them worry when they don't even need to.

But your different targets of worry create the perfect balance in your relationship. Cancer will soothe you, letting go of the little imperfections while you can bring clarity to the mind of Cancer in the face of imagined threats. This balance will be reinforced if you ever have children because you make the *best parents.*

Pisces

Pisces is your polar opposite. Theoretically, opposite signs score high on the compatibility chart, but only a few opposites are highly compatible in reality. This match is one of the few.

Opposite signs are expected to be the best partners for each other because opposites equal polarity and polarity brings about balance. The polarity between these two signs can't be explained concretely, but it can be observed in practice. While Pisces is focused on the emotional and spiritual side of things (you know, the bigger picture), you are more concerned about the details, the logical and material side of life.

You are both service-oriented and modest, but this is manifested in different ways. Pisces offers compassion and spiritual support while you offer hands-on assistance. This way, they are a match made in heaven. Pisces works to soothe and calm you while you keep Pisces grounded in the real world.

Worst Matches for Virgo

Time to look at the matches that score low on the compatibility chart. This doesn't mean these signs are terrible people; they simply don't go so well together. *Think of ice-cream and fish.*

Aquarius

As intellectual as Aquarius is, they are one of the worst matches for the equally intellectual Virgo. Despite the intense brainiac energy emanating from you two, you think differently.

You enjoy analysis and practicality, and you like to categorize stuff. Aquarius gets their kicks from thinking *outside* of the box. You both speak different languages, but you have immense intellectual respect for each other even with these differences.

Besides that, there isn't much else going on between you two, especially romantically. To Aquarius, you are overly critical and fussy, while you are constantly annoyed by Aquarius' disregard for rules.

You both don't have a connecting factor or anything to attract you to each other, so it is likely that you will never even consider a relationship with each other. You may end up as work colleagues or just friends interested in a shared hobby.

Leo

Leo also has few common interests with Virgo. Unlike you and Aquarius, where you simply feel nothing for each other, the match between you and Leo will annoy the signs. Ironically, this sometimes works to form a bond between you.

Leo enjoys being the center of positive attention and admiration while you would rather stay backstage working the strings. Leo thinks that you are critical and petty, while you think the Leo is arrogant and pompous.

Like Aquarius and Virgo, it is unlikely for a romantic connection to be established between Leo and Virgo. It is possible for you to go on dates once or twice, but they yield nothing substantial. You are not bad people as individuals; you just don't fit romantically.

Sagittarius

Sagittarius and Virgo are 90 degrees apart on the zodiac wheel. This type of relationship is called a square. Theoretically, this indicates incompatibility, but in reality, square signs form better relationships than signs with no feature at all. The tension produced by their position on the zodiac wheel can bring about a great amount of sexual chemistry between the parties.

Despite the sizzling sexual tension between you two, you are highly incompatible. Things might be blazing in the bedroom, but outside of that, you find it hard to connect or move forward on the same foot.

Physical chemistry and romantic feelings might be enough to attract you, but if the relationship is to survive, the two of you must be able to function together outside of sex.

The problem is, when you even attempt a non-sexual activity together, Sagittarius quickly becomes bored and frustrated with your over-analysis and attention to detail. Meanwhile, you get wracked with anxiety and nervousness over Sagittarius' enthusiasm for cutting corners.

Quick Recap

Romantic compatibility is high with you and Capricorn, Pisces, Taurus, and Cancer. They understand your personality and provide stability and balance to your sign. But your literal match made in heaven is the Scorpio.

You have almost nothing in common with Leo and Aquarius. This lack of a common denominator is the reason for your inability to become romantically involved with one another. There is sizzling sexual tension, but between Sagittarius and you. While this is great, you cannot accomplish any task together outside of sex.

When looking to zodiac compatibility for guidance, always remember that a successful relationship requires much more. Compatibility will tell you which signs are the best together, but the success of a relationship depends also on dedication and commitment.

With adequate dedication and commitment, even the most incompatible signs can experience a beautiful relationship. Without these qualities, even the best pairs become incompatible.

As for Virgo, you are a pretty straightforward sign. You are not a player. Think back to your first time at the beach as a kid when you were cautious, testing the water. You took it slowly, didn't you? That was the Virgo in you. You are logical and methodical. You avoid emotional exposure, so you take their time to make sure that the person is worth the emotional risk and effort.

The Teen Virgo and Relationships

It can get difficult to know when a Virgo is developing feelings for you, especially when they haven't crossed that boundary into adulthood just yet. The males have a tendency to always move with a wingman. It's nothing serious; they just like to know that they won't be rejected when they make their move.

The teen takes his time to observe his potential love interest, keeping an eye out for any red flags. When he is completely convinced, he has no problems moving in fast to get the girl.

Virgo teens, in general, are overwhelmed by the newness of love initially, but beneath all that is a lover that is prepared to protect, adore, spoil and lavish you with gifts and attention.

Thinking Long-Term with The Virgo

Every relationship has a honeymoon phase, usually initially – when things are great – and you two seem completely smitten with each other. For some, this phase continues throughout the relationship. For others, things go downhill.

If you're with a Virgo, you might notice them becoming critical of things you do, and becoming even more of a perfectionist. None of this comes from a place of contempt, so don't read it the wrong way. Often, if your Virgo is letting you know things they aren't comfortable with, guess what? The only reason they're doing that is that they've grown to love you that much more. They trust that you'll see what they're saying as coming from a place of wanting you to be the best version of yourself.

To the Virgo, the way you express yourself with these criticisms matters. Speak with your partner as your deepest, truest friend — which, knowing you, they are. You want to be gentle and easy with them.

If you come from a place of love, then each time you and your partner discuss your issues, you'll make progress. Tap into your sensitive side as you speak with them. Put yourself in their shoes and let your words wash over you too. This way, you'll know exactly how to communicate with your lover so it is productive, healthy, and uplifting for you both. While you're at it, hear them out too!

Diving Deep into the Emotions of the Virgo

You are sometimes perceived as an introvert because you don't express your emotions as often or as quickly as other signs. Expressing emotions can seem like a threat to your outward image of calmness and control, so you'd usually rather not indulge — except for when you're in love. You will be emotional because you trust your partner enough to know they will not use that vulnerability against you.

Committing to a Virgo

Signs that are compatible usually hold similar ideals and seek balance in life. Virgos want a romantic partner they will mate to for life, but that rarely happens at the first attempt. The variability of character and the expression of the traits particular to this sign depend also largely on any additional astrological signs and their individual natal charts' positions. When trying to understand what makes your Virgo tick, you must consider any energies and nuances on his chart that can either disrupt or enhance his Virgo energies.

Quick Facts About Virgos

- They like things in a particular way.
- They are extremely logical.
- They know what they want.
- They are a total planner.
- They can solve almost any problem.
- They might seem judgmental, but they're just trying to help.
- They value loyalty.
- They can be perfectionists.
- They can be hard-headed sometimes.
- They are independent.

Obstacles that Arise When Dating a Virgo

- They might be a little too quiet.
- They might worry a lot, but usually for a good reason.
- They might criticize you a lot, but not with mean-spirited intent.
- They are even harder on themselves than on anyone else.
- They have a tendency to obsess over things.

Quick Guide to Dating A Virgo

- Choose honesty every time.
- You should care about your appearance and your smell.
- Don't be a drama queen.
- Don't keep your opinions to yourself either.
- Find their heart through their stomach.
- Be orderly.
- Trust them to lead.

Attracting the Virgo Man

If you are interested in seducing the Virgo man, you must begin with respect for his order and cleanliness. Usually, he would be slow to enter romance because he takes his time to get to know people. But, when he does know you, you must maintain a certain amount of consistency, or it will be over before it starts. This doesn't mean there will be no space for personal growth with a Virgo. All I'm saying is that you cannot pretend long with this sign.

The Virgo man puts up a cool exterior, but don't be fooled; his sensual and emotional needs run deep. You must be patient with his habit of over-analysis to reach his warm depths. Hard work and dedication must win any sign over, but even more so for the Virgo man.

Do you want to sweep him off his feet? Inspire him. He likes to be reminded of his own talents. In the search for a partner, honesty, patience, and order are prioritized. Have these, and you're already on the right track to winning his heart.

Attracting the Virgo Woman

A Virgo is typically a combination of close attention to detail, commitment, common sense, and intelligence. A female Virgo is nothing less, being unsurprisingly smart, capable, and modest.

Like the Virgo male, she values cleanliness. So, you'd better not just look good; you must be neat as well — at least within reason. She gets that not everyone is as orderly as she is, but you must make an effort. Also, your smell matters. A lot. That doesn't mean you should drown yourself in a vat of Axe, though.

Any attempts to woo this woman might seem daunting initially because she will probably wear a mask of indifference. The truth is, she is far from cold and impractical. She simply likes to be cautious and realistic about her new relationships. There is no way this woman will give herself to you without a complete scan of your personality, its pros, and cons. She feels deeply and loves unconditionally.

She is not to be pegged as materialistic or spoiled under any circumstances. She is an Earth sign so expect her to appreciate the luxuries of the world, like travel, art, the fine things of life. You're not obligated to get her these things, as she's always going to seek them out and make them happen for herself, with or without you. She also enjoys practical, thoughtful gifts.

Chapter Five: The Social Virgo

Are you that friend who always seems to have every situation all figured out? Are you discerning yet sociable? Hardworking but modest? Never arrogant but well-informed? You are a Virgo to your core, and everyone needs at least one Virgo friend.

Why The Virgo is An Amazing Friend

You are extremely organized. You have the title for the most practical and methodical sign in the zodiac. It doesn't matter if you're organizing a cocktail party or planning for a presentation at work; you are always relied on to deliver your A-game and make sure the activity goes as smoothly as silk.

I bet if your friend were to look through your phone, they'd probably find a variety of apps that help you maintain the order of things in your life. You love lists, filing systems, office stationery, and helpful apps.

You are the one friend who is as punctual as life allows. You always remember important birthdays and the solution to virtually every life problem, which always comes in handy. Your capacity to stay calm under pressure is unprecedented. Then there's that thing you do when you whip out a contingency plan when it is most needed and unexpected.

You are a knowledgeable and great conversationalist. You enjoy a stimulating conversation, a good book, and a healthy banter. You aren't the type to lean back and say, "I don't know," unless you do not know, which makes you genuinely eager to know. You're not a know-it-all; you simply like to KNOW.

You are also concerned about the thoughts and feelings of those around you, so even if you're not very vocal about it, you do your best to remain polite and inclusive.

You enjoy acquiring knowledge. But most people get surprised and unsure when you ask your thousand questions about something you don't know. You don't like this, but you get it.

Your aversion to adventure contradicts your constant thirst for knowledge, but your desire for routine and order justifies it. You may not want to go on that hike in those devilish mountains, but that doesn't stop you from encouraging a friend who actually wants to go.

Your memory is epic. You have mastered the art of recalling the little details. People catch themselves, saying, "How in the world did you recall that? We had that conversation ages ago!" Your memory is a blessing and a curse.

You always carry yourself with an air of dignity and class. Have you seen Divergent, the movie? The Erudite sector pretty much sums up the Virgo personality. There are few signs as self-respecting as your sun sign. You pride yourself on your ability to stay calm during a storm, stay away from meaningless arguments, and consider all your options before taking a stand instead of cutting corners. You have impeccable manners and always seem dressed for the occasion.

At first sight, it is easy to assume that you are incapable of letting your hair down and having fun, especially if you're caught working. Unfortunately for first impressions, they don't always matter because you can get your groove on around people you are comfortable with. Initially being reserved never hurt anyone.

You don't like to feel embarrassment because it is one of the feelings that seems to linger with you for quite a time. I know you remember all the embarrassing stuff that has made you cringe a little too often, and you've resolved never to let that happen again.

You are very perceptive and highly ambitious in every aspect of your life.

Everyone knows that your standards are higher than Ru Paul's heels, so they feel flattered when admitted into your inner circle. You like mature, intelligent, and high-achieving friends, not because you are a snob, but because you always want to get better, and you understand the influence of friends on the matter.

You rarely stay friends with people who have no sense of direction, but you stay to motivate and inspire the few times you do. If you have friends at work, trust they know how ambitious and uncompromising you are.

Despite your ambitious streak, you avoid atrocious power grabs. You prefer the long game, putting your career plan together, sticking to the schedule, and challenging the challenges. You are patient and diplomatic, which is why your schemes yield results most of the time. You don't mind the long wait.

You are always open to working on your friendships. You are a firm believer in the power of hard work. If you commit to an idea or project, you are prepared to see it through to the end. Some people might even find you a little single-minded and intense when you are zeroed in on a cause or problem. This is a handy trait for friendships.

You take no aspect of your friendship for granted, knowing that all relationships are still under development. If there is an argument, you are less likely to brush it under the rug. You'd rather tackle any problems immediately, further strengthening the friendship. You may not have a bunch of friends, but you prioritize those you do. You make one of the best friends anyone could have. Your practicality, knowledge, order, and encouragement of others are among the prized traits in healthy friendships.

You may be drawn to people with similar interests and intellect, but now and then, get with that one friend or group of friends who pull you out of your shell and throw you over the edge of a yacht. Basically, friends that make you try new things.

Virgo Friendship Compatibility with Other Signs

1. **The Virgin and the Ram:** You and Aries in a friendship? How did that even happen? Aries probably started it, being obsessed with challenges and all. You are generally a reserved person, but Aries likely interpreted that to be a sign of discernment. Winning your acceptance adds another colorful feather to their cap — and there's a lot of space on that cap. True, you are very picky with people you let into your life, but you approved of Aries because of their warmth and enthusiasm. They are generous with hugs, kisses, and encouragement. Aries admires your dedication and hard work. You don't like their "Me first" way of life, and they don't like your picky attitude.

2. **The Virgin and the Bull:** You and Taurus are naturally drawn to each other. You find great comfort in the Bull's loving and loyal nature while they appreciate your readiness to help or pitch in when they need you to. Maybe you think that Taurus can be a little complacent, and they think that you can be delusional, but if you stopped dragging the bull to territories

that they'd rather not visit, maybe your friend wouldn't sigh so often. You are likely to share similar interests.

3. **The Virgin and the Twins:** You are ruled by Mercury, which is the planet for sharp intellects. Unfortunately, that's about the extent of your similarities. While you are grounded and serious, Gemini has their head in the clouds. You are more comfortable working with concrete, logical concepts, while Gemini would rather deal with ambiguous ones. You are very cautious and secretive, while your friend would rather bare it all. Ironically, you are attracted to your differences. You also appreciate Gemini's cleverness while they appreciate your ability to fix issues.

4. **The Virgin and the Crab:** You can birth a relationship that can last for decades. As you both prefer the warmth of home, you'd rather have a quiet, cozy night by the fire than be out at the local bar, even with friends. You love Cancer for their ability to calm your burned out nerves while they love your attention to detail, how you always remember birthdays, or their best color. Your friend has the habit of hoarding, which pisses you off to no end because you thrive in order and simplicity. Your friend isn't too happy either about your frequent refusal to indulge their flights of fancy. But besides these, you two are great friends!

5. **The Virgin and the Lion:** You need a lot of courage to befriend domineering Leo. It is understandable, but considering the love and warmth oozing out of the lion. Still, it can get very exhausting, massaging Leo's ego, especially for a person as modest as you are. Leo also tires of your constant worry of impending doom. If you can focus on their many wonderful qualities like capability, intelligence, and loyalty, you can give them space and opportunity to appreciate your reliability and efficiency. You both are animal lovers, so that's a great conversation starter!

6. **The Virgin and the Virgin:** It must be lovely having a fellow Virgo as a friend. At least, you won't be worried about them placing a wet glass down on the antique table you purchased last fall or walking all over your recently polished floor with muddy shoes. Also, the Virgo is a beautiful conversationalist so you can depend on this friend to bring you all the juicy gossip and give you a full summary of the week's best-seller without dropping spoilers. The major downside to this is that you two have a habit of feeding each other's insecurities instead of offering encouragement. You both are filled with talent and need to be open to riskier opportunities than you allow yourselves experience. You both enjoy the natural scenery, so consider long bike rides or a walk in the park.

7. **The Virgin and the Scales**: You find Libra's intelligence so satisfying. But certain things about your pal are a little hard for you to understand. For instance, Libra's avoidance of any discomfort. You prefer to deal with problems head-on before they become too much to handle. You also struggle with your friend's inability to concentrate on one subject or person for long. They also have a few issues with you. They don't appreciate advice they didn't ask for. They also don't like to manage money and be scolded for their impulsive spending.

8. **The Virgin and the Scorpion:** The mystery of the scorpion makes them a hard nut to crack, but if anyone can do it, it's you. Scorpio has an affinity for you, probably because you are always willing to assist others. You value authenticity in

yourself and others. If you made a promise to help at an event, you'd be at the location thirty minutes early with anything you feel will be needed. This dedication grants you a soft spot with Scorpio. Despite the time it takes for you to build a friendship, you soon learn of the scorpion's many wonderful qualities like sensitivity, loyalty, and persistence.

9. **The Virgin and the Archer:** Sagittarius, while being full of spontaneity, is an exhausting friend for you. You both share a deep love for knowledge; but you can't seem to understand why they just won't settle down. Sagittarius, on the other hand, is fascinated by your desire to over-analyze everything, from the cashier's hairstyle to the cat's preference for dry food. If you find a way to handle each other's mannerisms, a lot of strength can be drawn from this friendship. Allow the archer to push the boundaries of your experiences. Travel together or try out exotic cuisine. In return, your advice to get organized and become more efficient will be appreciated by the archer.

10. **The Virgin and the Sea-Goat:** It is never a surprise to see you two become fast friends. Being Earth signs, you and Capricorn have shared values. You both don't shy away from hard work and feel the happiest when doing something productive. You two also have a deep respect for family traditions and routines. There is no sign more excited about the holidays than you two. The preparations start weeks in advance, and while Capricorn can get a little domineering, you two are quick to sort out your issues and move past. They don't like it when you are overly critical of their faults, but the similarities between you two are enough to overlook any unpleasantness. The pros outweigh the cons here.

11. **The Virgin and the Water Bearer:** Nobody brings chaos to your life as much as Aquarius does, so why are you so attracted to this unconventional friend? I'll tell you why. Deep down, you are yearning for excitement. You are at your best with regularity and order, and you derive pleasure from organizing chaotic environments. But, when you feel a little bored, that's when Aquarius storms the show, proposing a nude sprint later at midnight or skinny midnight dipping in a nearby lake. Will your wild friend ever convince you to switch sides? Very unlikely, but you live vicariously through them, enjoying the show from a distance. Aquarius is one of the smartest signs of the zodiac, so I'm sure you two will get along swimmingly and may even share a love for sci-fi.

12. **The Virgin and the Fish:** Despite you two being polar opposites, the two of you become fast friends. Chaotic Pisces is grateful for the order you provide, while you enjoy their short stories. Sure, you hate it when the fish shows up an hour late to the restaurant, but you do know that your endless worrying can make you difficult. When the fish tests your patience, because they will, comfort yourself with the fact that you will never find someone who listens as perfectly. Similarly, the fish appreciates your ability to turn dreams into reality.

The Virgo at a Party

To you, people exaggerate parties. Parties are great, but overrated. People think that attendance somehow reflects their value as a person. Especially birthdays. People make a huge production out of the event, throwing all kinds of emotional tantrums if anyone as much as disregards it.

Birthdays are a huge deal, parties too. But Virgos are very low key about social events. They aren't as hung up on parties as other zodiac signs. This does not mean that they never attend parties. Sometimes, they willingly enjoy the baby shower of a loved one, a wedding party of a friend, and so on, or unwillingly enjoy a rave at the club or a frat house party.

You are usually in tune with your inner world and what you want out of life. This results in you being more concerned with what truly exists than extrinsic experiences. You are more likely to concentrate on the core symbolism of the person's birthday other than the outward displays and extras. To put it more simply, you would prefer to focus on what is in a gift box than fuss about how beautifully it was packaged. This is the reason you don't go crazy about your own birthday; you prefer to enjoy the day with people who are special to you.

"Stop trying to take me to random parties!" This is one thing you wish your friends understood. To impress a Virgo, this is not really how to go, and you may transmit the wrong message to them.

If you intend to throw a party or are to organize an event, then ironically, the Virgo is perfect at planning. They'll give you nothing less than perfection at the end. This doesn't mean they want to get down on the floor — you might need to hand them a drink or two for that.

How Virgos Make Friends

When you feel comfortable enough in an environment, you are an excellent communicator. It isn't uncommon for you to be reserved among strangers at the start, but when you've established a baseline for everyone and the environment, you're perfectly comfortable matching everyone else. In other words, you like to read the room and read people, so you know the best way to connect with them.

If You Have a Virgo Friend, Pay Attention to This.

Virgos may get the "forgive and forget" memo, but they will take out their favorite red gel pen and cross out the forget part into oblivion — especially if you continue to hurt them again and again.

Your Virgo friend will give you a shoulder to cry on when you need it, but be prepared to get a lot more than that. They will help you get back on your feet by doing all they can to remind you of why you're awesome and capable — even if it means they must physically, literally drag you out of your funk.

If you notice your Virgo friend is intensely focused on something, for the love of everything holy, that is the exact time to *not* bother them about something trivial like your hunger for Lebanese shawarma. They'll snap out of whatever they're working on if you really need their attention for something, but please make it something important.

The Virgo needs order. If you're messy, it's not going to work for them. Even if you have a room in their home to yourself, if you're messy, it's not enough for your Virgo that they *cannot see* the mess; they *know* it's there. And eventually, they will make you clean up, so you don't wind up bringing roaches, or a bad smell, or whatever it is they'd hate to their home. They also know where they put what and hate when you move it. Even when the Virgo makes a "mess," leave it as it is. There is an order that only the Virgo understands in that chaos.

If your Virgo friend spends the day lounging and doing nothing, very few miracles can draw them out. Let them have it. No one works as hard as they do.

Loyalty is everything to the Virgo. Their huge hearts that radiate so much warmth despite their ability to heavily strike anyone who tries to hurt you is only one among many reasons they are loved by all who know and understand them.

Chapter Six: Shades of Virgo

Decanate and *cusps* are astrological terms that split your sun sign into different categories. These categories further emphasize and define certain traits and qualities particular to your sun sign.

Every birth date falls within a specific decanate of a sun sign while only certain birth dates are within a cusp. Basically, every cusp is a decanate, but not all decanates are cusps.

Everyone is born within a particular decanate of a sign, and people may also be born on the cusp. In this chapter, I hope to clarify the meaning of decanates and cusps in your life.

Decans or Decanates

Each astrological sign is divided into three categories. Each is called a decan or decanate. This term originates from a Greek word *dekanoi*, which means "separated by ten days." This term was taken from the Egyptians, who had a calendar that divided each year into 360 days. The Egyptian annual calendar had twelve months per year, each containing thirty days. Every month is further split into three sections, each containing ten days. These ten-day subdivisions were called dekanoi.

Astrology still splits each zodiac into decans. Imagine the entire zodiac to be a circle. A circle measures 360 degrees, and one decan is only a 10-degree part of that circle, each one ten days long. The sun passes through the zodiac circle (all the signs), at roughly the rate of one degree a day. Note that this isn't accurate because not every month is exactly 30 days, but the math is the same.

Now, the decan of a zodiac sign doesn't alter the fundamental characteristics of the sign. Instead, it only refines and personalizes the zodiac's general traits. For instance, imagine you were born into the third decan of Aries. You are still very much an Aries; but you have now been distinguished from the Aries in the first and second decans. You are special and different from them while they are special and different from you.

Each decan is represented by a constellation in the sky. The constellations' special spiritual translation also contributes to the uniqueness and quality of individuals born under different decans.

Finally, each decan is ruled by a planet, also known as a sub ruler, because it doesn't dethrone the sign's overall ruling planet. This sub ruler, kind of like a Vice President, only works to add to or enhance the special qualities of that particular decanate.

Decans of Virgo

- Decan: First
- Date: 22nd August - 1st September
- Keyword: Analyze
- Constellation: The goblet, crater, or cup of Apollo. It represents emotional generosity.
- Sub-ruling planet: Mercury

Mercury is the planet of mental activity. It is both sub-ruler and ruler for this decan, granting you an intellect to be reckoned with. You tackle problems with rationality, always seeking the reason for everything, and then applying that knowledge to the search for a solution. More than a few times, your insightful contributions have been considered as prophetic, when they are simply results of acute observation.

You radiate a great amount of warmth and wit that attracts admirers and acquaintances. But not everyone gets a ticket into the inner chambers because you expect nothing less than decorum and intelligence in the people you call friends.

When you fall in love, you morph into a devoted, hopeless romantic who is extremely sensitive to their lover. Your calm exterior does well to hide nervous energy brewing beneath. You are prone to secretly worrying and fussing over little problems.

- Decanate: Second
- Date: 2nd September - 12th September
- Keyword: Efficient
- Constellation: Hercules, the powerful demigod who wins a victory over evil
- Sub-ruling planet: Saturn

Saturn is the planet of tenacity. This, combined with your ruling planet, gives a special edge to your personality. You are focused on the details and prefer to plan in advance to avoid mistakes.

You are usually perceived as focused and persistent when, in truth, you are mutable and versatile. Your goal is the constant demand for perfection in yourself and the determination to always outdo yourself. You are the kind of perfectionist that suffers unnecessarily when you fall short of your own expectations.

In love, you are the most sympathetic and gentle soul. You are willing to cross oceans to please your partner, who is a fast disappearing quality today. You are relatively easy to live with as long as nobody awakens your stubborn nature.

- Decanate: Third
- Date: 13th September - 22nd September
- Keyword: Discriminate
- Constellation: The bear driver or the old herdsman. The symbol of using wisdom
- Sub-ruling planet: Venus

Venus is the planet of pleasure. The outgoing and welcoming qualities of this sub-ruler combined with Mercury signifies that you have a way of winning people over. Approval is your major motivator. You are a connoisseur of expression, using written and spoken words. You are simply charming with an air of creativity and perfect use of color represented in your appearance or surroundings.

Your sense of style is always properly interpreted, and this projects a powerful personal image of who you are. Confidence and carriage are your major assets in the work environment, and you are recognized for your diplomacy and sensitivity.

You find no joy living under limitations, so you are attracted to creative adventures where you have free creative control. When you fall in love, you are generous and warm, despite your almost incessant demand for attention.

Cusps

Have you ever, at any point, felt like you were a mixture of two zodiac signs? Like you may be a Pisces, but also something else? It's like having one leg in two nearby countries, and it is called a cusp. Every zodiac sign has its cusps, a combination of two zodiac signs. It is common to find people who are Scorpios but have Sagittarius qualities. Many people were born at the end or the start of a zodiac sign, which can lead to confusion when trying to determine their place in astrology.

When a person's birth date falls within a few days of the sun's transition from one sign to the next, it means that the person was born on a cusp and their personality can be affected by the two distinct zodiac signs.

A cusp is an invisible barrier that separates a pair of zodiac signs next to each other. With this sun's disc being roughly half a degree wide, it is possible for the sun to create a cusp as it moves through all the signs. This movement causes the solar disc to be halfway into the next zodiac, with the rest remaining in the present one.

Place a red cup and a blue cup side by side on the ground, with an inch between them. Draw a line in the middle and slowly move a matchbox from one side to the other. During movement, observe the period when half of the box is on the red side while the other is on the blue side. That, my dear, is a cusp!

The Significance of a Cusp

Birthdate on a cusp makes you a hybrid of the two signs. The energies emanating from the two signs may not get along, or they might... either way, every individual born on a cusp acquires certain qualities, based on the cusp you were born into:

1. Power cusp: 16th - 22nd April
2. Energy cusp: 17th - 23rd May
3. Magic cusp: 17th - 23rd June
4. Oscillation cusp: 19th - 25th July
5. Exposure cusp: 19th - 25th August
6. Beauty cusp: 19th -25th September
7. Revolution cusp: 18th - 24th December
8. Prophecy cusp: 18th - 24th December
9. Mystery cusp: 16th - 23rd January
10. Sensitivity cusp: 15th - 21st February
11. Rebirth cusp: 17th - 23rd March

Virgo Cusps

Cusp: Virgo-Leo
Date: 23rd - 27th August.

You are Virgo with a dash of Leo. Your reliability, generosity, and graciousness attract people to you like a moth to a flame. You are also known for your creative streak and a great sense of fashion. You are noticeably witty, optimistic, and fascinating. Undertaken projects almost always turn out to be a success because of your keen attention to detail and quick thinking. It isn't uncommon to see you in charge of events because your organizational skills are legendary among the zodiac signs. This can make you a little impatient with others who are not as quick-witted as you are, but that usually inspires your colleagues' responsibility and creativity. Social settings bring out your best qualities. When in love, you are unreserved, fiercely loyal, and warm.

Cusp: Virgo-Libra
Date: 18th - 22nd September

You have Virgo and a little Libra in you. You are perceptive, intelligent, and in love with ideas! You are naturally outgoing and have a way of getting through to people on a psychological level. Your mind is always buzzing with ideas or information, and that makes you always in the mood for stimulating conversations. Your social skills are most valuable in a work environment. You are a lover of beauty and aesthetics, making you prone to becoming a collector of rare and beautiful items or engaging in creative adventures.

Chapter Seven: The Professional Virgo

There's that one employee who does things the right way to a fault at every workplace; they show up a half-hour earlier than most workers and drive everyone nuts with their perfectionist and detail-oriented attitude to work. That person is most likely a Virgo.

Everyone knows how particular and neat you are, with your million to-do lists and properly organized notes. You are a good enough team player, but you prefer your own creative space to just do what you do best. You wish someone would just hand you that autonomy you desire so much.

As expected, you thrive in work environments where rules sustain the profession's untainted reputation. As much as anyone can do almost any job with proper training and dedication, certain professions are better suited to your unique talents, Virgo.

1. **A Writer:** Since you have a great many thoughts flowing through your mind at any point, and you love to have your own space to work, then you would excel as a writer. You love being on your own. The only other thing you might enjoy more than cracking open a good book is penning one down yourself, or at least challenging yourself to do just that.

2. **An Accountant:** I have mentioned your keen attention to detail often now because it's one of your most popular and most prized qualities because it always comes in handy. Combined with your understanding of numbers and critical attitude, you almost seem like the perfect candidate for this job. This career path allows you to satisfy your need to go over things as many times as you need to be certain. It's challenging to handle another person's money, but your discipline ensures that your moral compass stays facing the right direction. Similar careers include bookkeeper, auditor, hedge fund manager, and coder.

3. **A Nutritionist:** You want to make the world a better place, and one way to do that is to teach people better ways of taking better care of themselves through their eating habits. Add that to your existing fascination with nutrition and health, and you are all set for a satisfying profession. Everyone knows that Virgo enjoys practicing what they preach. Chances are, they already practiced it a thousand times before the preaching started. You'd rather teach from experience, am I right? Similar career paths include masseuse, life coach, and dietician.

4. **An Acupuncturist:** You already have an interest in natural healing methods and health, so this would be a satisfying path for you to tread. You enjoy testing out herbs, health hacks, vitamins, etc. Studying the science behind this practice is a common practice for members of your sun sign. Similar career paths include yoga instructor, holistic healer, reiki healer, and natural pathologist.

5. **A Professional Housekeeper:** If your daily life is a nonstop swirl of laundry, organizing, straightening, and housework, turning this natural sense of order and aesthetics into a job will fully maximize the perfectionist in you. Similar

career paths include personal assistant, home stager, wedding planner, and professional organizer.

6. **An Executive Assistant:** No one is quite as organized as you are. Combine this with your eagle focus, attention to detail, and efficiency, and you become the perfect executive assistant. These are the perfect traits to possess when organizing schedules for yourself and others, especially if the other person is a celebrity or a company's CEO. You are excellent at organizing schedules, meetings, functions, and trips, and will not make a fuss if your boss adds a few tasks like house-sitting, miscellaneous duties, and shopping. You will organize things either way, why not get a paycheck to boot?

7. **A Statistician:** Your obsession with details makes this an excellent career for you. It isn't the easiest job to do, but an opportunity to collect and analyze statistics for a company or the government will surely put your best skills on display. Similar career paths include geologist, auditor, research analyst, consultant, and forest ranger.

8. **An Archivist:** This is another career that will exalt your penchant for categorizing and sorting. This job demands attention to detail, which is not only your forte but also a part of yourself that can't be ignored. You will find this satisfying. Similar career paths include art historian, archeologist, museum director, bookkeeper, and so on.

9. **A Computer Engineer:** When there's a fault with systems workflow or information output, you are the ideal person for the job (with proper training, of course). You are infinitely patient, a necessity when dealing with faulty technology. No sign will take their time like you will, to find and erase all the duplicate files and junk information, rebuilding the system, and ensuring they run as smoothly as possible. Similar paths include electricians, town planners, and systems analysts.

10. **A Laboratory Technician:** Your unique talents make you perfectly suited for this job. Gathering data, keeping records, sorting information, and compiling reports is the perfect activity to keep you mentally engaged and give you the satisfaction you derive from orderliness. Your thoroughness, focus, and ability to create results are legendary. You might drive your colleagues nuts with the amount of time you take to work or your occasional need to take "one last look" at the material, but they know that you always deliver impeccably. Similar career paths include scientists, data analysts, biochemists, and surveyors.

11. **A Welder:** This work requires a high level of concentration, a steady hand, and accuracy. One wrong move and the project could develop uneven edges or cracks. Even worse, the whole structure could collapse, but not on your watch. You make sure that every weld is performed with utmost accuracy to the standard of the industry. Similar career paths include craftsman, architect, sculptor, furniture designer, and ceramicist.

The Virgo as an Employee

You are an idealist to your core. Your idealism is an asset in the workplace, and people know it. When given a task, you throw yourself into its center and remain submerged until it is done. While Aries and Capricorn are like you in this way, what separates you from the bunch is your determination to do the job to the highest quality in your rulebook. You do this not because you like to be better than others, but because you believe that a thing worth doing should be done well.

You don't appreciate inferior performances or a job that wasn't done whole heartedly, which is why everyone you work with knows that any project you embark on will be completed with utmost precision and care. A Virgo is an excellent worker.

You function meticulously. This is another trait that closely follows the unyielding need for perfection. When given a task, you dive into the heart of the issue and analyze it, leaving no stones unturned. If there is a high-profile assignment or project that requires utmost attention and thoroughness, they most likely have your number on speed dial. You are not like Gemini, whose attention is fleeting, taking them from one incomplete task to another. Or Aquarius, who is a master at envisioning abstract ideas. You can't help but lavish attention on the job at hand, considering every clarification and clause. This alone is enough reason for you to excel in fields like fashion, banking, law, and others that demand an acute eye for detail and an unwavering concentration.

You are not afraid to dish out criticism. As a Virgo employee, you will gladly point out any flaws in the system — even if you're the reason the flaws exist. You're not afraid to own your mistakes. If the boss caused the problem, that doesn't exempt them from your criticism either, especially when you deem it necessary. This is because you exalt perfection over the sacredness of titles and positions.

If you're an intern or a fresh recruit, keep your criticisms in check for the time being, until you get the lay of the land and understand the power dynamics at play. Usually, this should take you about three months. Don't just jump in with your stick, poking bears willy-nilly.

That said, it would be a lot easier if your coworkers can try to remember that as a Virgo, your overly critical behavior doesn't come from a place of hatred or malice, but a desire to see everyone do better. You're not in the habit of tolerating work that is less than standard, and you are willing to do whatever it takes to get quality.

You are grounded. (No, not that kind of ground.) As a Virgo, your primary element is Earth, and this is consistent with your grounded, practical, down-to-earth personality. You are practical and only concern yourself with activities that seem to have a promising outcome. You are blessed with a discriminating eye and sensible mind, which draws you only to pursuits that can reach a logical end.

You are not like dreamy Pisces whose imagination seems to flow in whatever direction they please or like Gemini, who has an airy brilliance about them. So, you are the ideal choice for positions that entail an incessant focus and strong analytical skills.

Another professional field where your intrinsic skills come in handy is the service sector like charity, health, banking and finance, entertainment (think writing, directing, continuity, and so on), education, hospitality, and much more. These and similar fields put you in your element because of your constant readiness to help others, another key trait of your Sun sign.

You are all too willing to bury yourself underneath a ton of commitment and hard work if you know that you are making life better for someone somewhere. This is probably because of your ruling planet Mercury, who was depicted in ancient Roman mythology as an impossibly busy god, who was always found in a race against time to deliver messages to and from divine entities.

You may become a workaholic if you aren't one already. The major disadvantage of your highly industrious and meticulous persona is that you are prone to becoming a workaholic. You display symptoms of the no *play- just work* syndrome. Five in every seven Virgos are workaholics, and you may just be in the majority. You are a firm believer in service first and leisure later.

Everyone you work with appreciates your workaholic nature, even you, considering it skyrockets you up the professional ladder. But it also comes with an added unhealthy lifestyle. Think of a buy-one-get-one-free situation. When a person, no matter the zodiac, is cooped up inside almost every time, focused on work with so much nervous intensity, they become prone to a variety of health concerns.

However, if you have Virgo employees, give them a break when they feel under the weather because it's rare, actualized Virgo who will take one themselves. If you are a Virgo employee, make the most of your weekend — and not by working incessantly. Don't worry about a dive in your productivity because there's no doubt about your ability to get the job done. I mean, it is you, after all.

Your zodiac has a significant impact on your personality, which makes you, a Virgo, an asset to your field. This isn't simply because of your meticulous and dedicated attitude to work and everything. It is also because you are one of the few employees that thrive with or without supervision.

Granted, sometimes you work really slowly because of the amount of caution you exert when performing a task. But you can be trusted to work alone because your mind runs a lot of miles per minute, and you have a strong sense of responsibility and work ethic.

The Virgo Boss

As a boss, you enjoy blending into the background while remaining present and keeping your eye on your workplace. You like to stay involved in everything happening around you while still giving your employees enough space to do their work.

Being in a position of power doesn't affect your willingness to get your hands dirty when necessary. You like having a personal but professional relationship with the people that work for you. As mentioned earlier, you like to be present and in touch with the work environment, employees included.

You request team meetings, reports on everything and anything being done right now and soon. You like to know because you are not fond of unwelcome surprises, especially at work. Everything must be organized from start to finish.

You also want to be in touch with those who work for you. You'll have team meetings, want reports on everything being done, what's happening next, and the whole plan of execution from start to finish.

At your best, you can be a kindhearted, soft, and trusted adviser who is excellent at analysis and decision making. You give specific instructions on how to do what needs to be done and sometimes lend a hand when you think is necessary.

At your worst: You become a fussy micromanager who judges and criticizes without sympathy. You not only watch everyone like a hawk, but you also waste no time pointing out every flaw and every wrong move. You become insatiable. So, what's the fix?

The Introverted Style of Leadership

This kind of leadership is ideal in any productive work environment. Here, you should exhibit a quietness and tenderness that commands respect while still leaving you approachable. Listen more than you speak and render advice more than you complain, instead of commanding everyone's attention and interrupting discussions.

This style of leadership will leave you flexible and receptive to daring projects and new ideas. This will encourage constructive criticism and suggestions from your employees, which you should carefully pay attention to, leaving your mind open to new information. This creates a better work environment with employees who feel heard and valued, which increases motivation, proactivity, and productivity.

If Your Boss is Virgo...

The most vital thing to remember when working for a Virgo boss is this: know exactly what you're trying to say! This means having all your figures, details, and facts on hand when interacting with them. They think through every single word you speak, so say what you mean. It is relatively easy to work under a Virgo boss. All you need to do is:

1. Be proactive and be hardworking.

2. Obey all company policies and follow necessary procedures.

3. Know your job and avoid making mistakes.

4. Prepare to support your suggestions with logic and feasible evidence.

5. Make sure that you and your work area are neat and tidy.

6. Dress modestly and neatly.

7. Keep emotions and sentiments off the work unless sentiment is required to do your job, like with service providers.

8. This might seem irrelevant but don't gossip, especially behind your boss' back.

9. Take responsibility for your mistakes and immediately act to correct any damage you've done.

Once you have made the necessary adjustments to your boss' calm, professional, and perfectionist attitude, you will see her best qualities bursting through the seams. Let's run through these qualities.

Tender, just, and helpful: Your Virgo boss may drop many criticizing remarks about the project you are working on, but she will also show you a way out of your dilemma and request the corrections repeatedly to be sure that you are on the right track. She will make sure that everything you need to do a stellar job is provided to leave no room for excuses. She may even offer her help sometimes. Her kindness is not limited to professional issues. If you need a break or an off day for important personal matters or an illness, she will understand.

Trustworthy: Trust is a huge deal for the Virgo boss. But you will uncover just how unbiased, kind and helpful he is when you have his trust. Don't forget that the Virgo is more sensitive than he seems on the outside, and would like to be assured that her help isn't taken for granted. Most bosses are grateful for a thank you note, but the Virgo boss will be really impressed by one. He will feel more appreciative and touched by your gratitude than most.

Zero small talks: Have you noticed that your Virgo boss isn't into any kind of small talk? She is not the type to engage in conversations at the workplace unrelated to work unless you two have a personal relationship outside of work. If not, expect no kind of chit chat. She maintains openness and clarity when communicating about work-related issues and is a pro at giving positive feedback if it is deserved. She has no problems making her employees feel appreciated and seen. Negative thoughts she might want to share about your work will usually be done in private, to preserve your dignity and reputation in the work environment.

Calm and lenient: despite his desire for perfection and his discerning eye, he is a relaxed and open-minded person to work for. These attributes make the work environment less tense, comfortable, and more productive. Think of him as a boss who might seem bossy but really isn't. He is modest in professional behavior, interpersonal relationships, and appearance.

Obstacles the Virgo Faces at Work

Your keen sense of observation: While one of your prized traits in the work environment, it is also the culprit behind your anxiety. You tend to look back to a problem you experienced so many years ago and cringe at the thought. You couldn't believe it happened, and you blame yourself. This leads to self-doubt and excessive, unnecessary worrying.

Life struggles are real, and it isn't easy for you to be overwhelmed with so much natural optimism, but you can counteract this by consciously deciding to always see the good in situations and people. Focus on the times when you were simply badass. You did it before, so you can do it again. Be grateful for all that you are and have.

Your tendency to critique others: You are great at critical thinking, but you are also popular for how much criticism you give to others. It is understandable to want to help others, but you need to remember that not everyone appreciates unsolicited opinions.

You also need to water down your criticisms before sharing them, because some people are more sensitive than others, and you don't want to go around hurting people's feelings, do you? The end doesn't always justify the means, remember that.

Your stubbornness: When you imagine an idea or a thing you want, you whip out your imaginary ear lids and call it a day. You can sometimes be averse to opinions, even the good ones. You can be defiant, but don't have to be. It is okay to have preferences and want things to go a certain way.

But leave room for suggestions and growth. Unexpected situations and factors can be helpful. You may not believe this, but everything happens for a reason, and it is absolutely impossible to control everything. Leave room for flexibility.

Your tendency to worry too much: You enjoy knowing that everyone around you is happy, and even more so if you are the reason for this happiness. This can mean pushing yourself to extremely uncomfortable lengths to please people, especially at work. You need to remember to choose yourself sometimes. Your needs, health, and happiness matter too. If you need to call in sick, do it. If you cannot take on a project for personal reasons, that's okay too.

Your tendency to get frustrated easily: As a perfectionist, you can be your own worst critic. You do not allow yourself to be anything less than the perfect image of yourself in your head. You will literally ruin an entire project because you don't think you did it perfectly. First, breathe. Nobody is perfect. It is okay to make mistakes. It is okay to do your best and leave the rest.

Your penchant for overthinking: You just love to overthink everything, don't you? This can be a good thing and a bad thing. Go over facts, ideas, and situations thoroughly before deciding. But overthinking can also make you see things that aren't there. Again, breathe. Trust your gut, forgive yourself for past mistakes, and let things go.

Your unwavering demand for independence: You like to do this by yourself, and that is admirable. I am a firm believer of "if you want something done right, do it yourself." But it is okay to ask for help when you need it. You may not be comfortable bothering people, but there are those who will readily help you because they love you or they are being paid to. Either way, take it!

Your inclination to be choosy: You are precise, and that is a quality that makes you excel among your peers. But make space in your life for new and different experiences. You never know where they'll take you or what you will learn.

Chapter Eight: Virgo Sexual Compatibility

Knowing all your sun sign qualities, you know that you make an attentive and patient lover. This can be infuriating for people looking for a quick rump. You prefer to concentrate on your lover's preferences, possessing almost biological knowledge of their erogenous zones. This makes you one of the most sensual and desirable lovers of the zodiac.

But you tend to give yourself too much of yourself to others to the detriment of your own sexual needs. You need to allow yourself to be pleasured as intensely as you do others. Remember, sex need not be perfect or neat. It is more enjoyable when mutual and packed with spontaneity. We all know you're great in bed, but let's see how great in bed you are with other signs.

Virgo and Aries

This is definitely a hot match. Aries is more than capable of sweeping you off your feet before you even blink. This is very exciting if you are in the market for fast, furious, and nasty. But you are likely to catch yourself stopping everything in its tracks by saying something like, "You won't even take me to dinner at least?" Everyone on the block knows that Aries doesn't like to beat about the bush, especially with sex. But you kind of like information about who you're swapping body juices with.

In the bedroom, kitchen, or car, Aries is effortlessly passionate and sexy, but not the most considerate. This might irk you unless you somehow decide to make it your goal to fix it. You could enjoy yourself while allowing Aries to fall right into your plans to become an all-knowing parent. You don't even have to bother about looking for complex ways to seduce this person because many Aries people go about their day in an almost perpetual state of arousal.

Surprisingly, a lot of Aries folk know their need for the guidance and help you will gladly provide. In gratitude to you for the tips on sex positions and simple table etiquette, Aries will bathe you in adoration. They are the kind to barge into your office to inform you that you will be carted off to a fancy adventure sure to end with two of you tangled up in the sheets.

Aries is strong and highly active, with almost no tolerance for many things. So, if you are searching for a person who will drag you out of your hole, be responsive to and be grateful for your grounding influences, Aries is the one for you! This will finally teach you to allow yourself to go and be sexy.

Virgo and Taurus

This reasonable and logical person will tickle your senses from day one. The many similarities between you two will guarantee a quick friendship. Taurus will be capable of acquiring all the material possessions you consider being of value, but cannot survive with anything less than the highest amount of luxury. You might also find aspects of this sign's preferences baffling, like why a person believes in the necessity of a solid gold key holder.

But, when sex is brought to the table, you might see the light in Taurus' desire to just lay in luxury. Taurus's planetary ruler is Venus, the planet of desire, and this usually brings a sensual touch to this Earthy sign. Instead of your reaction to things you feel and see in terms of what you can gain or learn from it, Taurus usually just does it because it feels good. Snap! Like that.

This means you must let go of a lot of thoughts while sex is happening, and just connect with your instincts. Taurus will pretty much respond to anything you do, so don't overthink it. Over time, you both will get along more easily than you did at first, but certain adjustments might need to be made to keep the sexual fire burning. This will reduce your overthinking a little and simply allow yourself to indulge yourself now and then.

Virgo and Gemini

You and that chatterbox sign are naturally drawn to each other. This is because you both share the same planetary ruler, Mercury. Gemini manifests the daytime energy of Mercury, smoky mirrors and tricks, while you are the planet's nighttime side. You think through everything that you feel through your senses and try to categorize them. You have developed a method of seeing the order in everything.

Chaotic Gemini will like this about you and will need your help. You might notice this before sex, but everything becomes crystal clear when you do. While you're setting the mood, Gemini talks the entire time, so you might have to think of ways to relax them.

When the verbal part of your time with each other ends, you are likely to experience a very satisfying connection with Gemini. Your vast knowledge of human anatomy and its pleasures will astound them because they probably didn't know about this much sexual information! They will also do everything in their power to please you. But you must remember to be vocal and clear when telling Gemini what you like. This experience will teach you there is always something new to learn from everyone, despite how people look. Gemini's many notes and observations will fascinate you for quite a time.

Virgo and Cancer

This moody, messy and sensitive sign will draw you in because it feels like you have found a true companion. You both are very concerned about caring for others and rendering services to people who need them. The difference between your acts of service is that Cancer would rather get in there and do things for people, while you take more of a life coach approach. This manifests most beautifully in bed.

You will instinctively know the Cancer's needs because you just have a weird way of knowing what will benefit people. You two might experience the wrong kind of friction if you get trapped in a loop of unwillingness to be pleased. Cancer is quick to figure out what you want and will go to great lengths to please you. They also expect you to appreciate the good loving you're getting.

You will also need to take great care in handling Cancer's fragile feelings. They might not appreciate your subtle suggestions and hints. Eventually, there could be a possibility you both become exhausted from trying to outdo each other sexually. This is a great match if you're looking for a quick affair. The lesson to learn here should be obvious now. Forget everything you have internalized about receiving sexual pleasure. It can be just as fun as giving.

Virgo and Leo

This sign is flashy, very sexy, and dashing. They will capture your attention without even breaking a sweat. You might notice a few flaws here and there, like a tiny, creased part of their shirt, but quickly, you'll be accepting of this fabulously wrapped package that oozes undeniable style.

Don't even think of suggesting the sexual activity because this spirited sign would rather be the one to get the ball rolling. Once the majestic lion is finally finished sweeping you off your feet, you'll see that their roar is not even as scary as a nibble. The lion is a huge stuffed bear that gets cozy in your arms and takes all the love that can be given.

Despite Leo's tendency to be domineering and demanding in daily life, this sign is one of the most generous signs of the zodiac. They are generous souls that get a kick from pleasing you. That said, the Leo gets their ego stroked by the number of times they can make you lose it. Leo can be very noisy, with a voracious appetite. If you two decide to go further than a quick tangle, you may need to tame their pride a little. If you succeed, you are guaranteed a lover forever.

Virgo and Virgo

Meeting a Virgo like yourself can be quite a rewarding experience for the two of you. Not only will there be countless similarities like ideas, ethics, and tastes, but the sexual pull between you will also be approved of by both parties. Now that you have met someone as reserved as you are, it could be awhile before a move is made in the sensual direction, but that's cool. Just imagine the things that get your engine going, like the fact that there's finally someone to care for you.

When you both get tangled up, it's easy for you both to know where the major buttons are. There might be an initial struggle or competition to outdo each other, but things will be smooth sailing from there when you find your rhythm. There is a lot of potential for this to develop into a long-term relationship. Unlike the pairing between you and a few other signs, there is no competition for attention between you two. If a relationship stems from this passionate affair, you both could become too comfortable with each other.

Do your best to keep things interesting between you. Throw variety into the mix by going on short getaways occasionally; just don't spend every single second together. Here, the quote, "Absence makes the heart grow fonder," has never been more fitting. Being apart for a little time will grant you two the opportunity to see why you want to get together again. The lesson you will learn from this is to remain open to the possibility of finding someone as thoughtful, generous, and almost as perfect as you are.

Virgo and Libra

Libra's enticing exterior will pull you in, especially because of how hard it will be for you to point out a crack in their shell. The Libra is almost always as beautiful as they come. Their taste, eye for beauty, and uncanny intelligence are also something you find very impressive.

You may be completely aware of the tangible sexual tension between the two of you that is like an invisible string connecting your bodies. But it will still be a challenge getting Libra to even seem affected by your sexual advances. Libra is a hopeless romantic with high expectations of the perfect fairytale romance. These expectations can be a little unrealistic, even for you. But you enjoy a challenging experience and will jump right in.

Look forward to a little negotiation before you can finally take them to bed. Libra will be comfortable knowing you are worthy of the amount of romantic devotion they can give to their lover. Libra brings their delicate touch and old fashioned sensuality to the bedroom, which impresses you. In return, you do exactly what they want, how they want it, almost effortlessly.

But tread carefully because they tend to be all too willing to let you please every physical need without returning the favor. This will definitely work against the sustenance of a long-term relationship if you ever begin one. Put up solid boundaries and layout your expectations.

Whether you're interested in much more than a one-night stand or not, you will learn a valuable lesson from this experience. Spending time around incredibly beautiful people like Libras will make you feel closer to that perfection you've always yearned for.

Virgo and Scorpio

Getting to know Scorpio can be a daunting experience for you. At first, you might feel like a deer caught in headlights or like a character in Dorothy's squad when they finally met the wizard of Oz. Scorpio will ooze the energy of a guru, resolute but quiet. They are naturally confident people, and this can make them seem very intimidating. Don't overthink it, though; your efforts to always improve their experience with you will earn you points.

The Scorpio will quickly take to the bedroom to get you thinking about sex in a whole new light. Once they have their arms around and on you, you may feel your soul literally taking breaks from your body. Scorpio is here to take you to the edges of pleasure and give you a hard shove, making your whole body ache as your first orgasm rips through you.

The Scorpio will be very impressed with your knowledge and ability to hold your own. Regardless of their reputation for being manipulative and possessive, Scorpio prefers the company of those who can stand their ground. They admire those who avoid being overwhelmed by the sheer euphoria that accompanies the experience of sex with a master. If you are thinking toward a long term relationship, you may succeed.

While you are on the receiving end of their love and loyalty, you provide suggestions and helpful hints for dealing with tiny details they are usually too busy to tend to. Here you will learn that sex is full of magic and mysticism.

Virgo and Sagittarius

This gregarious and carefree Sagittarius is very appealing, as you will see on the first date. The both of you will have no problems getting along because you are both capable of adapting to varying situations without letting a little wind throw you off course.

Sagittarius does not need that much of an incentive to walk into a lair prepared strictly for sexual stimulation. The only issue is your inability to keep them from wandering around. A Sagittarius requires enough space to exercise the beast that lives within. You can interpret this either metaphorically or literally, but it is wise to remove any delicate items or values from the scene or scenes of action.

The spirited Sagittarius causes minor but costly accidents when overly excited, especially when they get a taste of what you're capable of in bed. They are almost incapable of staying in touch with their humanity during sex, but this can be a good thing as you'll probably get your kicks from their enthusiastic reactions to your techniques.

If this experience stretches into the long term, you both might have to figure out a way around your different schedules. While you like being informed of any plans in advance, your lover is not only always geared up for the next adventure; they live in anticipation of exciting new places to visit every day. Indulge your Sagittarius sometimes. Here you'll learn that things can just float where they will, trusting that everything will return to normal when you're ready.

Virgo and Capricorn

This seemingly conservative person will pique your curiosity right away. Finally, a person you consider worthy of the type of service you enjoy providing. Meanwhile, Capricorn would rather bite their own tongue than tell you they appreciate your willingness to deal with the tiny details. You might expect a basic night of passion with this one, but you couldn't be more wrong.

Your skills and vast experience with the human body will not be a novelty to Capricorn. The sea-goat doesn't climb down the ladder of success to mingle with the rest of us for no reason. This sign, which seems like an serious workaholic, can suddenly transform into a fun and spontaneous personality. You are both Earth signs, so trust the Capricorn knows how to get freaky and dirty too.

If you are uncomfortable with any fetish or even a straightforward attack, you better watch out. Capricorn will show you different shades of horny! You'll enjoy the show, of course, as long as Capricorn is trustworthy enough to let what happened in Vegas stay in Vegas. Capricorn is also big on trust, so you can rest assured that the events of the night don't see the light of day.

It is possible to form a long-term relationship with this sign if you avoid taking on the role of constant warden. When Capricorn transforms back into the role of a cold-hearted executive, you might feel put off. The lesson you will learn from this is that it is sometimes necessary to submerge yourself in the depths of sexual sensations.

Virgo and Aquarius

Aquarius is popular for their eccentric behavior and ability to stay detached, but once you spend more time with this spirited person, you forgive a few quirks. Aquarius somehow always has a story to tell, and you enjoy good stories even though you spend more time poking holes than listening.

Really take this relationship to the physical stage immediately because the journey to similar mental levels will not be a natural one. If you must understand this water bearer, you need to recognize and respect people who not only reason outside the box but also live there.

You'll quickly realize how this comes in handy in the bedroom. Aquarius is most receptive when they are fully convinced that you agree with them on a lot of things. Their tendency to form boundaries based on political and social viewpoints is a part of what makes them such great visionaries.

Aquarius might have a hard time forgetting the exact quality of your sheets, but if you hit them in all their right places, the size of the carbon footprint you just made will not matter in the slightest. There's a slim chance that you see eye to eye with Aquarius, so it may not be possible to have a serious relationship with this sign. Whether you both hit it and quit it or you're in for the long term, you can learn a lesson from this. Acceptance is a valid precedent of love, and it should always be mutual.

Virgo and Pisces

It makes little sense that this absent-minded and seemingly incapable Pisces is the perfect match for you, but that's what it is! You'll see why once you begin to drown in their eyes. While you have views and ideas basically set in stone, Pisces exists in an entirely different world. Actually, when you talk to the fish, you may notice that the bridge between what many people term *reality* and where the fish goes is small. This will awaken a great amount of desire to care for your fish. The Pisces will become interested once they realize that you know how to transform their lives from unbearable to exciting.

Your willingness to meet each other halfway will reveal an adventure that heals the many emotional wounds you may have. Visiting the dreamy world through experience in Pisces' bed now and then is the ideal cure for your sometimes-rigid way of life. You will be completely unaware of what hit you, but that trip to ecstasy that is sex with Pisces will be worth it. The experience is a transformative one, so it will be difficult for you to avoid having a serious relationship with this sign. The lesson to take home from this is that the perfect way to deal with all your worries is to relax and allow the Fish to love you until you completely let go.

Chapter Nine: The Moon Sign

The moon's location in your horoscope is the second most important astrological factor after the sun's location. Your sun sign influences the aspect of your personality that is most clear on the surface. It is the factor that influences how others perceive you. On the other hand, the moon sign is the aspect of your personality that exists within you. It is the factor that influences how you see *yourself.*

In the world of astrology, the moon signifies instincts, feelings, and the unconscious, while your sun sign reflects your will, your moon sign reflects your instinctive responses. The most popular astrologer of the early 20th century, Evangeline Adams, stated that a person's sun sign represented their individuality while their moon sign represented personality.

Over the years, different astrologers have defined the sun's effect to be a vital force, while the moon's effect is deemed an inherent force. In simple terms, the moon is responsible for the part of you that responds before you even take time to think.

The differences between the sun's impact and the moon in astrology are the predecessor of the theory of the *Id* and the *Ego* by Sigmund Freud. Sigmund's theory states that the ego is human consciousness, represented by the sun in astrology, and the Id is the human instinct, represented by the moon.

Your moon persona is the part you hide from everyone else. Humans have a tendency to condemn instinctive behavior, calling it primitive, brutish, and uncivilized. This is why your moon persona is that aspect of your that you consider unsettling. It is who you really are at your core, that part of you that freely entertains feelings of jealousy and hate, fear and uncertainty, even desires that you are too ashamed to admit to yourself. This is surely not the entire picture of the moon's impact on your identity.

Your moon sign is also responsible for the part of you that acts on spontaneity. It is the part of you that shows true pleasure and happiness, the part responsible for your response to emotional stimuli. The moon heavily influences the side of you that finds pleasure in the little passions of life, like the sweet scent of flowers, the smell of the Earth after a heavy rain, the joy that comes after a long soak in the tub. The moon is inseparably connected to your responses to your immediate environment. This is because the moon has dominion over the five physical senses; hearing, touch, sight, taste, and smell.

In the world of astrology, the symbolism of the moon can be complicated or even cryptic. It also represents your responses from infancy to childhood. It symbolizes your memories, your past, and your dreams. These can be said to form your inner psyche.

Landis Knight Green, a well-known astrologer, said that the moon is the beginning of the subconscious. Your moon identity is most expressed in dreams, the daydreams you ignore while you continue with your daily activities, and the sleeping dreams that plague your mind in your waking moments.

The moon's power over human emotion is the reason for its influence in your openness to others and their feelings about you. This obviously means that the moon has a major influence on romantic relationships. A solid and sustainable emotional connection is usually indicated by the woman having her moon in the same position as the man's sun. For instance, if he is a Cancer sun sign and her moon is in Cancer, they have an amazing chance of experiencing a long and happy relationship because they will both have a deep comprehension of one another.

You must have wondered, at least once, how two people born under the same sun sign can have such different personalities. This usually leads to a question, "What are their moon signs?" I'll explain this using two popular entertainers with their sun in Sagittarius. Bette Midler and Woody Allen.

The two share the same birthday and month, being 1st December, but not the same year. Allen was born in 1935, while Midler was born in 1944. The two people express powerful Sagittarian traits like frankness, humor, autonomy, and true freedom of expression.

Woody Allen is an intelligent, humorous man with barbed humor appealing to intellectuals. Being an auteur, he is a screenwriter, producer, and director who even acts in his own movies created outside the studio.

Bette Midler's career started as unconventional comedy performances in the bathhouses found in lower Manhattan. Her audiences were mostly homosexuals. But she moved on to major performances on stage and television, in movies, as a comedian and singer. She is famous for her dramatic performances, always portraying characters that are a tad too outrageous, dauntless, and wacky.

These are two entertainers who have spent years in the entertainment industry, growing and eventually breaking free of limitations to express their unorthodox ideas using their senses of humor. Let's probe deeper.

Woody Allen's moon is in Aquarius. This is responsible for his displays of rebellion. His moon sign is expressed in his free-thinking attitude of a typical Aquarius-moon personality in complete control of his life. In his private life, workplace and politics, he is progressive, unorthodox, and radical. He also portrays the emotional detachment long associated with Aquarius. His roles in films are not full of passion; his characters communicate incisively about life and its conditions, but not so it captures his audience's emotions. Rather, they intellectually stimulate in a typical Aquarius fashion and make people laugh.

People born when the moon is in Aquarius have no problem with ending a relationship (and even doing it coldly). The public has seen this in the continuous private soap operas featuring Woody Allen and the women in his life.

Bette Midler was born with her moon in Cancer, and there is a certain emotional quality that can be perceived in her. She communicates an intense amount of emotion in her work. The characters she portrays display a vulnerability usually associated with Cancer. She takes the roles of brave, lovable, and adorable women who reach out to others and care for them.

As a musical artist, Bette released hit songs that contained a deep emotional significance like The Wind Beneath My Wings, which was about a supportive partner, another Cancer value. Her personal life is very private, a major characteristic of Cancer. She is blessed with a stable and lasting union with children.

Throughout history, people have feared, worshipped, and studied the moon. From the information obtained from relics about the ancient civilizations, say that the Moon entity, usually female, always ruled beside the Sun. Certain religions even considered the Moon to be stronger than the sun because it was the seat of spiritual knowledge and wisdom.

There is a day set aside by the Romans to celebrate the Moon. This name has stood the test of time, even until today. It is now called Monday, instead of the Moon day. Scientists have been studying the power of the moon over tides, fertility, plant life, menstruation, crime, emotion, and biorhythms. Astrologers keep discovering subtle, new ways the moon's influence is felt in our daily lives. The position of the moon in your horoscopes enhances your sun sign. It contributes to new forces, elements, and motivations to the personality of your sun sign.

The bond between your moon sign and sun sign personalities is like a marriage. They are in perfect harmony, sometimes. Like a marriage, they have differences that can foster a stronger connection to build a sustainable partnership, with each personality putting their best foot forward. But, like all marriages, the conflict will arise when contrasting traits collide against each other.

If you ever feel like you are in a perpetual battle with yourself, if you ever think that you have dual personalities inside you constantly at war with each other, you can find peace in astrology. Study your moon and sun signs. Discover the negative and positive aspects of these signs and try to identify these special elements in your own personality. You will realize that a better understanding of the factors that motivate you will enable you to be more compassionate with yourself. You will also finally reconcile what has always seemed to a complicated swirl of contradictions.

Meanwhile, if your moon and sun sign are the same, you will discover that the sign traits are manifested twice as strong in your personality.

Know thyself. That is the inscription carved by the ancient Greeks on the temple walls at Delphi. It is a phenomenon that has baffled humans for more than a thousand years. Astrology is the key.

The Virgo Moon

Having the moon in Virgo influences your sun sign in two ways:

On the plus side, you are meticulous, determined, intelligent, resourceful, and responsible. The downside is, you can be a hypochondriac, judgmental, overly critical, cold, argumentative, and high strung.

The Virgo sign stabilizes the shifting outcome of the moon. Virgo, being the sign of logic and intelligence, gives an acute analytical bend to the moon's impact. If you have your moon in Virgo, your mind is refined and discriminating. You don't seek knowledge for knowledge's sake; there must be a use or relevance of the knowledge you aim to acquire.

Your instinctive response to the sensory information you receive from your environment is to analyze everything you see and hear. You like to take as much as you need to go through the information while questioning everything you obtain. You are such a skeptical personality that you tend to disapprove of things, even if they are right in front of you. You enjoy discussing ideas and digging deep into other opinions, even though external notions do not easily influence you.

You are not a stubborn person per se; you are simply very attached to a theory until proved wrong by facts. You like to seek the truth, being a firm believer that truth is the only remains after the exposure of falsehoods. You're definitely not the person who views life through wine-colored glasses. This doesn't make you pessimistic or sour; you simply address life as it is. This practicality and realism is the reason you are so great with money and business. You see, the big picture rather than the momentary satisfaction, and you worry more about security and providing for your old age.

Having your moon in Virgo is the reason that extra sprinkle of professionalism and perfectionism in every task you engage in. You prefer to take a methodical approach to issues, figuring out the exact solution, and dealing with the problem one step at a time. But your tendency to worry, fuss over every possible negative outcome, and waste time thinking up many contingencies is a little frustrating. You are of the belief that too much productive effort can be destroyed by the absence of the last tiny effort, so you are extremely hard on yourself and others.

You live a life of complete discipline, which can be suffocating. You are the person who would leave their shirt buttoned all the way to the very top, even if it's very uncomfortable but looks perfect! You have a problem understanding scatterbrained or illogical minds, somewhat weird considering how drawn you are to Pisces. Anyway, believe that such people are straight out of a Disney cartoon. You are not only very picky with your choice of friends, but you are also the same way about the cultural activities you participate in.

Your moon sign is responsible for that judgmental quality that follows you almost everywhere. You never miss an opportunity to learn from experience. Women born under this moon sign are sometimes perceived to be unfeminine because they exhibit certain qualities that many don't see as feminine - thoroughness, efficiency, and orderliness.

All Virgo moon people are reserved despite their gender. They also shy away from unnecessary gushiness and sentimentality and are usually considered standoff-ish. The truth is it's the uncivilized Virgo who displays stingy pettiness, picks people apart, and is standoff-ish.

Generally, people with their moon in Virgo show their generosity and care through practical means. You can always rely on them. The sign of service is Virgo, and moon Virgos are just itching to be useful.

Regardless of what your sun sign might be, the lunar Virgo qualities of seriousness and caution manifest in your personality. Your industrious and practical nature is even twice reinforced if your sun sign is one of the Earth signs. You also have a healthy relationship with money.

If you have your sun in a fire sign, the lunar moon manifests endurance and strength to assist your unreserved creativity. This combination is great for politicians and performers. If you have your sun in an air sign, the lunar moon grants you an even more acute intellect and a flair for authenticity. If you have your sun in a water sign, you are bestowed with a more expansive dimension to your emotional personality because you are gifted with a rare mix of hardheaded realism and psychic truth. No matter what your sun sign is, your moon in Virgo grants your acute mental abilities and an intellectual and practical approach to situations.

Celebrities with their Moon in Virgo

1. Amy Adams (American actress)
2. Alice Dellal (Brazilian model)
3. Anna Paquin (Canadian actress)
4. Elizabeth Moss (American Actress)
5. Madonna (Singer and songwriter)
6. Bella Hadid (American model)
7. Blake Lively (American actress)
8. Donatella Versace (Italian fashion designer)
9. Dolly Parton (Singer)
10. Jodie Foster (American actress)
11. Gal Gadot (Israeli actress)

12. J. K. Rowling (British writer)
13. Chelsea Handler (American comedian)
14. Kate Bosworth (American actress)
15. Nicki Minaj (Singer and songwriter)
16. Barbara Stanwyck
17. Serena Williams (American tennis player)
18. Linda Evangelista (Fashion model)
19. Elle Fanning (American actress)
20. Natalie Portman (American actress)
21. The Olsen Twins (Fashion designers)
22. Carey Mulligan (American actress)
23. Michelle Williams (American actress)
24. Jada Pinkett Smith (African-American actress)
25. Joss Stone (Singer and songwriter)

Chapter Ten: Virgo and the Planets

We all know about the solar system. We go to bed at night with the certainty that morning will come again, same time tomorrow. This trustworthy pattern is not only responsible for our day; it also marks our seasons, years, and even our lives. Our adherence to these universal laws allows us to determine the planets' past, present, and future positions at any given time.

Each celestial body in our solar system moves at a different rate and velocity in its own orbit or path. This makes it possible to have an endless supply of unique combinations of planet placements in the sky. The moment you were born, the sun, moon, and all the planets were in specific positions, creating a specific arrangement in the sky. This particular combination will not be seen again for at least four million years. There will not be another human with an identical horoscope as yours seen on Earth for four million years. That person will not be the same as you because of the varying environmental and genetic factors.

How about multiple births, you might wonder? They should have the exact same solar combination, right? Wrong. The ascendant moves by a degree every four minutes. Technically, twins born with as little time as four minutes between them will have their ascendants in two very different zodiacs if one twin broke through during the ending of ascendant and the other at the start of a new one. Even a difference as insignificant as a degree, right in the same Ascendant, will manifest different qualities in the two babies. The minute the Ascendant moves, it produces a different birth chart.

What about people born on the same day and at the same second, maybe even at the same location? These people are called time-twins or astral twins. A lot of time is now being funneled into research on the life-patterns of astral-twins. The results so far are mind-blowing. It has been recorded that time-twins have eerily similar life patterns. There are many cases of them getting married on the same day, having the same mobile number, and even the same genders of children. There are those that are even known to have traveled, relocated, quit jobs, and divorced simultaneously. A few even die simultaneously and with the same cause of death.

Clearly, astral-twins are extremely rare. The distinctive position of the sun, moon, and all the planets in your birth chart is most likely particular to only you. You might have your Sun in Scorpio or Leo, but you differ completely from any other Scorpio or Leo. Imagine how many distinctive fingerprints exist in the world. That's about how many individual horoscopes there are as well. Suppose you intend to obtain more information on the influences of the planets in your life. In that case, you must know the various positions of the planets and their individual influences before applying this knowledge to your personalized birth chart.

Every planet can influence astrology in very specific ways. Each planet rules over a particular aspect of your personality or outlook on life. For instance, Mercury oversees your mental outlook, while Venus is ruler over all things desire.

The manifestations of these different aspects of your personality depend on the placement of these celestial bodies. If the placement of your Mercury is Gemini, you are likely to be quick-witted and talkative. If your Mercury happened to be in Capricorn, your efficiency when handling a project's details or carefully plotting plans beforehand would be legendary.

If your Venus is placed in Leo, you will not be content until you are showered with more attention than you can ever need from a partner. If your Venus falls into Aquarius, you will be of the belief that the freedom to express oneself is one of the most important building blocks of a romantic relationship.

Virgo Ascendant/Rising

At the exact moment you were born, there was a point on the eastern horizon called your Rising sign or Ascendant. The Sun is responsible for your conscious actions and reactions, and the Moon handles the past and your subconscious tendencies.

But the Ascendant is responsible for your instinctive response to your environment, particularly if there are new elements involved. It is concerned with the way you interact with the outside world by merging all the energies in your sun and moon signs, and the rest of your natal chart. Everything that happens is filtered through your Rising sign, indicating the core function of your soul.

People with Virgo Ascendant are usually a little too modest in their appearance and personal mannerisms, although much depends on the placement of their ruling planet, Mercury, on their birth chart. There is a generally reserved but intelligent aura about them that is impossible to miss. These somewhat shy individuals need time to analyze as many elements in their environment as they are comfortable with, before warming up to new people and circumstances. This trait can be perceived as exactly that or as judgmental and standoffish.

This position comes with heightened physical awareness. People born in Virgo rising are acutely aware of their body and its responses to any external and internal stimuli. They pick up on these signals faster than any other Ascendant. Several them are especially fascinated by and interested in physical health. They have a tendency to find comfort and peace in mind-body consciousness exercises like yoga. They are also very passionate about food, although they can be very nitpicky about what to eat and where because they devote a good amount of attention to what they put on and in their bodies.

As is typical with Virgo, these natives have a penchant for worry, especially when facing new territory, situations, and people. They are drawn to people in need of help — or is it the other way around? Therefore, their relationships may have an air of confusion at first, especially due to the Virgo's aversion for messiness... and what is messier than emotions?

Many people with Virgo Ascendants are known for their quiet charm. But, once they've been given the necessary space and time to warm up to their environment, you will realize how much they bring to the table. They make incredibly loyal friends who will go several miles out of their way to help you. It is normal to feel surprised by the modesty hidden beneath a distant and critical first appearance.

The rising sign or Ascendant is usually called the mask we wear when we're exposed to new information and people. More accurately put, it is the instinctive response to our immediate environment. Our Ascendant reveals our natural security and day-to-day coping mechanisms.

As mentioned above, the Virgo Rising natives' traits are also influenced and modified by the location of the planetary ruler of the Ruling sign. For instance, if you were born with a Pisces Ascendant, with Venus, the planetary ruler, in Gemini, you will react to your environment differently from a person with Pisces Ascendant with Venus in Scorpio.

More on Virgo Rising

With your Ascendant in Virgo, you strive to perform every task skillfully with precision, caution, attention to detail, a perfect sense of craftsmanship, and perfectionism. You have a keen sense of observation and have a sharp sensitivity to every single element in your immediate environment. This ensures that you tend to little things that might seem negligible to someone with a different Ascendant. You notice everything, no matter how subtle. You see into the fine grains of life.

Your only desire stronger than your need for perfection is your desire to be of service and assist as many people as you humanly can, most likely in a modest, understated, pedestrian fashion. You are interested in charity for truly helping others rather than for glory or personal recognition. Your basic yearning to be of use and service, your readiness to participate in ongoing practices aimed at improving those lives around you, your readiness to change, or adapt to your circumstances all enable you to always make a positive impact wherever you go.

Also, whenever you feel physically out of balance, you obsess and worry about your health, which only works to worsen your issues. Anyway, all these are simply general characteristics associated with the Virgo Ascendant.

Virgo Ascendant with Mercury in the Signs

Mercury in Aries and Virgo Rising: Mercury is your ruling planet, and it is in Aries. This is an indication of an acute intellect combined with an intuitive handle on situations and the capacity to stand your ground. Your mind is creative and always buzzes with authentic plans and ideas. You can be very impatient, and it shows during conversations with people of duller and slower wits.

You also have a tendency to be aggressive and too argumentative if you are sure that you are right. You are usually found dominating conversations, with little or no receptivity. You are also not very good at listening. Remember that this interpretation is independent of the other factors in your natal chart, which might suggest receptivity to other opinions. You are usually sought as a symbol of authority in your field of expertise.

Mercury in Taurus and Virgo Rising: Your planetary ruler, Mercury, is in the very humble, grounded, and sympathetic sign of Taurus. This indicates that you would rather provide practical service than an emotional one. You ooze efficiency and orderliness, only thinking in very pragmatic, realistic, and logical terms. You have a thing for math or finding a solution to issues with definite, straightforward answers instead of abstract, intangible, and open-ended ones. You are drawn to simplicity, common-sense, and logic as opposed to abstract and complicated.

You are one of the most patient people in the world, with the ability to handle mundane, repetitive, or stressful tasks. If other factors in your natal chart suggest imagination or creativity, you will still have a hard time ignoring the solid or Earthly side of things. If any part of you leans towards art, it is usually the utilitarian, practical, and functional kind of artwork. Concrete data, information, and facts are your specialty.

Mercury in Gemini and Virgo Rising: Your planetary ruler, Mercury, is in the spirited, quick and lively sign of Gemini. This indicates high levels of intellect and mental activity. It is safe to say that you are excited about everything. You absorb new ideas at once and react quickly to changing circumstances and needs. You enjoy organizing information and ideas or simplifying communication for better understanding. This could be an important area of your career or the services you give.

There's a good chance of you becoming a librarian, writer, editor, manager of a fast-paced work environment, or computer scientist. You suffer from nervous stress when you engage in excess mental activity. It would benefit you to pump the breaks a little to calm your nervous system and preserve your health. You also have a fast metabolism. Lucky you!

Mercury in Cancer and Virgo Rising: Your planetary ruler, Mercury, is in the subjective and sympathetic sign of Cancer. This indicates an interest in the healing arts, specifically children's and women's health. You are also passionate about food and nutrition, teaching, and human psychology. You have a tendency to overthink situations, leading to unnecessary worry and anxiety. You are long overdue for a meditation lesson, which will help you release all that pent up tension and anxiety.

You also have a penchant for criticizing the people you care about, especially if you think it is for their benefit. Your specialty lies in the domestic arts, especially because they are also your way of contributing to society.

Mercury in Leo and Virgo Rising: Your planetary ruler, Mercury, found its way into the self-expressive and creative sign of Leo. It indicates frequent use of your creativity, ability to communicate kindly, dramatically, and even colorfully. All these are important aspects of your primary function. You have a tendency to edit and censor the childlike, spirited, and artistic areas of your personality. This will only hide your light, and you were born to shine as brightly as you can.

Mercury in Virgo and Virgo Rising: Your planetary ruler, Mercury, is also in Virgo. This indicates a stable mind with an inclination for apparent logical analysis, classification, and designation. You have a penchant for developing specialized techniques and abilities in a practical field. But, unless other factors in your natal chart indicate an inkling of understanding or vision, you have a tendency to forget everything else in hot pursuit of the tiniest detail. You usually find yourself lost in an abundance of facts and data, which usually renders you incapable of perceiving the overall meaning or direction of things.

Mercury in Libra and Virgo Rising: Your planetary ruler, Mercury, has found itself in the unbiased, judicious sign of Libra. This is a strong indication of diplomacy and the ability to communicate your criticisms, logic, and observations as tactfully as possible.

You are very humble and impartial, with an uncanny ability to see things from an objective viewpoint and give unbiased feedback. This gives you a reputation for a good arbitrator or mediator. You find the logical, practical, and rational nature of science very appealing. You are also an ardent lover of aesthetics, form, and beauty.

Mercury in Scorpio and Virgo Rising: Your planetary ruler, Mercury, is in intellectual Scorpio. This is an indicator you have sharp and powerful perceptions and a strong capacity for research, probing analysis, and detection. You value discretion and are good at keeping secrets. You lean towards barbed-wit, negative criticism, and bitter or dark humor.

Mercury in Sagittarius and Virgo Rising: Your planetary ruler, Mercury, has landed in Sagittarius, the sign of idealism. This means you have solid beliefs, opinions, convictions, and philosophical ideas you keep to your heart. These ideas are the building blocks of your view of life.

You are of the notion you know what is best for everybody, which leads to criticism, usually unsolicited, and frustration. You set the bar impossibly high for yourself, which can lead to bouts of anger and disappointment.

Your sensitive and highly strung nervous system is responsible for the regular holistic habits that calm you and, in turn, others around you.

Mercury in Capricorn and Virgo Rising: Mercury, your planetary ruler, is in Capricorn, the sign of detachment. This makes you a symbol of objectivity, clarity, discrimination, and even-mindedness. Your detached persona gives you an outlook on life is devoid of passion, and while this might sound like a bad thing, it grants you focus like nothing else.

You are not the easiest to flatter or be swayed by flamboyant acts of courtship. Your specialty is discernment and realism. You are drawn to simplicity, order, and structure, as they are the values that guide your entire life.

Mercury in Aquarius and Virgo Rising: Mercury, your planetary ruler, has found its way into the innovative and inventive sign of Aquarius. This indicates your willing to help and serves others, which may be manifested in suggestions of new ideas and concepts.

Your ability to think outside the box is one of your most prized and defining qualities. You are usually fascinated by the unconventional areas like unorthodox health care or methods or healing.

Mercury in Pisces and Virgo Rising: Mercury, your ruling planet, is in Pisces, the sign of receptivity and sensitivity. This indicates your ability to pay attention deeply and truly, be empathetic, compassionate, and serving. You have a poetic imagination and a readiness to be inspired, and this balances your technique and keen attention to detail. Here, you become the technician and the artist.

Conclusion

"My best can surely be better."

Dearest Virgo, these are words by which you live. Your graceful, albeit obsessive, and harmonious nature makes you one of the most admired signs of the Zodiac. You are a firm believer that anything good can be transformed into something great, and these qualities push you even higher than your standards. Your wit and intensity is unmatched, which is why it isn't surprising to find your friends running to you, their walking encyclopedia.

You, Virgo, are famous for your grace and ability to negotiate your way out of the stickiest situations. But your unyielding wish for perfection makes you one of the most challenging personalities yet.

It is completely understandable to demand excellence, but it is also necessary to apply a touch of compassion. Go with the wind sometimes because there's a good chance of ending up somewhere extremely exciting! Always remember that.

Now we've come to the end of this book; I hope you've been able to see yourself for who you truly are. I hope that somehow, you know what to do to work on your messy bits — and there's nothing wrong with messy bits, dear Virgo! We all have them. It's part of the human experience, and the mess isn't going anywhere.

On that note, understand that you are flawed, and that is perfectly fine. Love yourself more. Be more open and accept that you are really amazing as you are. You are special. You are loved. Even with your flaws, you are perfect.

Part 7: Libra
The Ultimate Guide to an Amazing Zodiac Sign in Astrology

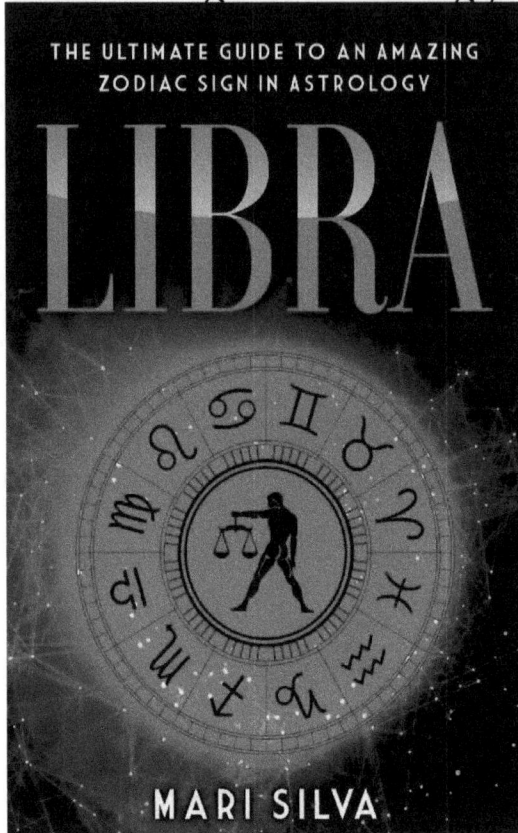

Introduction

Most people in the western world are familiar with the concept of zodiac signs and horoscopes, even though they may take them only at face value. This very fact begs the question, "Why in this information overloaded society, do people still like to read their horoscopes?" Is it for fun, out of curiosity, or in the genuine belief that horoscopes matter?

This little guidebook introduces readers to the fascinating world of astrology and to the Libra, in particular. In doing so, you will gain a deeper understanding of signs and what lies within the messages you read in your daily newspaper. Each chapter delves into the traits, strengths, weaknesses, career paths, relationships, and Libra tendencies. Armed with this information, Libra can interact and communicate at a deeper level with other Libras.

What is Astrology?

Astrology is known as a pseudoscience. This means the study of Astrology is based on beliefs asserted to be both factual and scientific but do not conform to scientific methodology. Thus, Astrology is perceived as biased as it cannot be proven in a scientific manner, but moving on from this modern perception, remarkably, Astrology has been around since the second millennium BCE. Its roots can be found in divine communication, meaning that ancient societies interpreted terrestrial events and human relationships in terms of celestial cycles and their belief systems.

Many societies have imbued these divine communications and have incorporated them into their cultures. Hindu and Chinese culture still predict earthly events from celestial events. In the western world, astrology's roots can be traced back to Mesopotamia during the 19-17th century BCE. From there, it found its way to Ancient Rome and Greece, and to the Arab world, where it eventually spread to Central and Western Europe.

Many scientists are adamant there is no basis for the belief in Astrology and the horoscopes. Astrologists beg to differ. So, which is correct? Again, there is no real answer, as both beliefs can be said to be correct. Astrology was perceived as the only "science" in Western history and was associated with alchemy, meteorology, and astronomy.

When scientific discovery rose to the surface in the 18th, and 19th-century scientists professionalized medicine and scientific methodology, pushing Astrology out to the fringes of knowledge. Thus, it lost its status in the academic world, but notwithstanding the above, polls have shown that almost a quarter of British, Canadians and American people still maintain that the trust and belief that the stars determine their lives and fortunes. A survey conducted by the National Science Foundation revealed that nearly 50 percent of those surveyed believed that astrology was scientific or "sort of scientific" (Baird, 2013)

The belief that the planets and the stars can affect a person's personality and mood and even their environment is based on when a person was born. Horoscopes printed in newspapers do exactly that. They predict what a person's day will be like based on when they were born: what star sign they were born under. They are intended to advise people on how to conduct their day and what to expect. Though scoffed at by many commentators, it is certainly the case that the seasons are created relative to where the sun's orientation around the earth and is the planet's energy source. Also, as most of us are aware, the moon impacts the ocean's tides. But is this weather, not astrology?

Another question is: Does astrology influence people and their lives? The simple answer is yes. If nothing else, it makes us feel better when we read our horoscope, and it promises good things or tells us something good might come into our lives. It is a very human response. Seasonal change affects how we feel and sometimes how we act. Gray skies make us feel moody, and low, clear sunny days make us feel energized.

For those of us who value astrology and use it in our everyday lives, reading astrological signs is like seeing what is beyond the universe and understanding how the planets and stars move in ways that relate to human lives. The study of astrology provides information that tells us where we are in the universe and how our lives are intrinsically linked to nature and the universe.

Signs of the Zodiac

It is useful in this introduction to acquaint you with all the Zodiac signs before we delve further into the sign of Libra. You can refer to this when comparing the sign of Libra with other zodiac signs.

- Aquarius - the Water sign - (January 20th - February 18th)
- Pisces - the Fish - (February 19th - March 20th)
- Aries - the Ram - (March 21st - April 19th)
- Taurus - the Bull - (April 20th - May 20th)
- Gemini - the Twins - (May 21st - June 20th)
- Cancer - the Crab - (June 21st - July 22nd)
- Leo - the Lion - (July 23rd to August 22nd)
- Virgo - the Maiden - (August 23rd - September 22nd)
- Libra - the Scales - (September 23rd - October 22nd)
- Scorpio - the Scorpion - (October 23rd - November 21st)
- Sagittarius - the Archer - (November 22nd - December 21st)
- Capricorn - the Goat - (December 22nd to January 19th)

What You Will Learn

The chapters of this book are divided into eleven parts. Each chapter will provide you with a deeper understanding of the Libra. The first chapter introduces you to the basics of astrology for the zodiac, including houses, elements, ascendent signs, and more. The second chapter will introduce you to the Libra to create a profile you can relate to yourself or Libra's you may know. The third chapter considers Libra's strengths and weaknesses and is a useful guide to understanding yourself and other Libra's you may work with or spend your life with.

In Chapter 4, the Libra female is explored. What makes the Libra woman tick? How does she approach her world? Chapter 5 compares the Libra man and contrasts him with Libra woman. Chapter 6 considers the Libra child. What should the Libra child grow and to thrive successfully? Chapter 7 is the central chapter and examines the Libra in love. This chapter discusses compatibility with other zodiac signs and explores how Libra people work towards making their relationships flourish.

Chapter 8 and 9 journeys further abroad and delves into the Libra personality at work and in social settings. Chapter 10 celebrates the Libra and discusses how some people born under this sign have changed the world. Completing our investigation, the book will close with a summary of what Librans need to flourish in all aspects of their lives.

Chapter 1: Astrology for the Zodiac

Before we dive into Libra, it would help to give you information on important elements to help you understand astrology better, especially where Libra is concerned. We'll start with the four elements.

The Four Elements

There are 12 zodiac signs, and these are split into three groups of four. Each group is an element – Fire, Water, Air and Earth – and each has its own traits. Put together, these groups are the natural world, so not surprisingly, they depend all on one another.

Fire – Aries, Leo, Sagittarius

Earth – Taurus, Virgo, Capricorn

Air – Gemini, Libra, Aquarius

Water – Cancer, Scorpio, Pisces

Fire

Unsurprisingly, this is a dynamic, passionate and temperamental element. Fire can do two things – keep you warm or destroy anything in its path. And, although it quickly burns out, its ashes can refuel its power. Fire signs need to be carefully managed and nurtured as one spark can wreak destruction.

Air

Air signs are about motion, ideas and action, the "winds of change" if you like. Sure, some are airheads, but others possess a gravity-defying powerful G-force personality. Air signs bring a certain freshness with them, and you should be prepared to be swept up by one sign.

Earth

These are the grounded signs, the ones that keep it real and bring everyone else back down to earth. They are stable and loyal, sticking with their friends and family no matter what. They are practical people but can be somewhat materialistic, focusing on the surface and not what's beneath.

Water

Water signs are sensitive, emotional and intuitive. They are deep, sometimes refreshing, sometimes drowning you in their depths. They often dream intensively and some experience and intuition that borders on the psychic. One of the most important things to them is security. Take it away and they will dry up.

Astrology Qualities

The only way to understand the zodiac signs is to understand the three astrology qualities:

- **Cardinal** – initiators
- **Fixed** – doers
- **Mutable** – finishers

Each has its own defining strengths, weaknesses, and features that exert influence over their respective signs.

There are four zodiac signs to each quality, and each sign is allocated to a zodiac quadrant. The qualities combine with just one sign from each element so, for example, there be one fixed water, earth, air and fire sign.

As the elements group specific signs together, indicating traits and behavior, the qualities also group specific signs, highlighting the common traits and behaviors they share. Every person has a role to play in life – some are starters, some put the hard work in, and some are the finishers. Knowing the relationship between the signs and the qualities helps you identify what role you play in life.

On the Western zodiac wheel, signs opposite one another share a quality. So, while these signs may be the opposites of one another, there are certain characteristics they share.

Cardinal Signs – Aries, Cancer, Libra, Capricorn

Cardinals are the initiators, the ones to get things moving. This quality represents new beginnings and energy, and these signs are natural born leaders, with the brains to come up with fantastic ideas. They are competitive, usually the first to come up with a trend, and they highlight the route that everyone else follows.

Fixed Signs – Taurus, Leo, Scorpio, Aquarius

Fixed signs are society's foundations, the builders. They take the ideas the Cardinal signs come up with and run with them, creating something from the idea. They are reliable, they do what must be done, are creative and see everything through to the very end.

Mutable Signs – Gemini, Virgo, Sagittarius, Pisces

The mutable signs are the finishers, the ones who finish what the cardinal and fixed signs start. They are adaptors, going with the flow, analyzing a situation before deciding their course of action. They are thrivers, regardless of the situation, and are open-minded. Mutable signs are adventurous and selfless, adapting to the qualities of those around them.

The 12 Houses

If you know anything about astrology and start signs, you've heard of the Houses. Each asteroid, planet or celestial point lies within a specific House, indicating valuable information about your personality, your past, present and your future. As the planets make their journey across these domains, they trigger emotional and tangible events. It is these Houses that make astrology so amazing.

What Are The 12 Houses?

Everyone's birth chart is divided into 12 sections – the 12 Houses, but the Houses differ from the zodiac wheel in that the latter is based on the yearly rotation of the sun while the former is based on the 24-hour rotation of the Earth around its axis.

Because the Houses are rotating on a 24-hour basis, it is critical that your birth chart be calculated using your exact time of birth. Every four minutes, the Houses also move, so even if you were born on the same day as your best friend, you will both have very different charts – unless you were born within four minutes of each other, of course.

The 1st House

The first House is the defining House of Self. It is your defining House, representing your body, your appearance and your temperament. It focuses on your mental capabilities, your stamina, strength and so on. It is often overlooked, but it is the House responsibility for an individual's weaknesses.

The 2nd House

This House deals with the needs that arise from the 1st House. It represents wealth, personal finance, the concept of value and material possessions. These, as many would agree, are the primary needs of most people in modern and olden times.

The 3rd House

This House governs communication, community and transportation. Where Houses 1 and 2 deal specifically with the body, this House focuses on the mind,

The 4th House

The 4th House revolves around home, family, and everything that ties a person to one place. It is the House that focuses on belonging, instilling a sense of that in each person. It may be with his or her real home or somewhere they see as their home.

The 5th House

We are all children inside and some of us like to let our inner child out more than others. The 5th House focuses on that inner child, on any activities we find pleasurable, including those that we remember and love from we were children.

The 6th House

This is the House responsible for our health and well-being. That includes the mind and the body, and the focus is on satisfaction and nutrition. This House also deals with daily schedules and management, helping us deal with structure, organization, and schedule-setting.

The 7th House

The 7th House is all about the external matters in our lives, the concept of perspective. This is about things outside of our control and things that happen because of something someone else did. Because this means observing your actions and yourself embodying the external world, it also covers relationships and marriage – it is sometimes called The Marriage House and its motto can be translated to The Spouse.

The 8th House

Just about every zodiac sign hates this House. Why? Because it represents everything we want to run from, to avoid. This includes life limitations, taboos we should otherwise be able to enjoy, fears that hold us back from achieving our goals. It is also known as the Haunted House, representing sex, death and transformation, and a penchant for the supernatural and the occult.

The 9th House

The motto for this House is translated as Journeys and that makes it the House of travel, exploration, opinion and perspective. This House is responsible for every question we have ever asked, every philosophy in life, because it allows our mind to wander, to question everything and ask questions never asked before.

The 10th House

This House represents everything we cannot stop talking about. Often, when we talk about our lives with others, we are hung up on the same things – the weather, work, what we succeeded or failed at, home life, and so on. That is all down to the 10th House. It is responsible for public image, achievements, and professional aspirations.

The 11th House

The 11th House is the House of Friendship, but it also lets us go deeper to interfere with and try to befriend our inner selves. This helps us come to terms with our existence and helps us move forward. This is also a House where innovation and technology live, often resulting in revolutionary ideas being born.

The 12th House

The final house is called the House of Self-Undoing. It governs everything that has no physical form – secrets, dreams, and emotions. It is a House that can turn your life into nothing more than a prison, a House that throws down the hurdles we must overcome on the path we choose through life.

Astrology and Ascendant

The ascendant, or rising sun, is one of the most critical elements of our charts as it indicates which sign rose on the Eastern horizon at the time we were born. It uncovers the impressions you give people, what they get from you depending on your behavior. It also provides you with everything you need to learn how you should behave to make the most of what your astrological sign gives you.

Your ascendant will ensure that you know what others think of you and how they see you. That means you will also know how to behave and how you should communicate with others.

Your astrological sign is also known as your solar or Sun sign. This indicates where the Sun was at your birth time, and this sign will reveal your deepest traits in terms of personality. On the other side of the coin is your Moon sign, indicating where the moon was during your birth. It is much deeper than your Sun sign as it reveals the real you inside, the person you know yourself to be. Your Moon sign reflects your inner fears, your longings and emotions, and all the obsessions bubbling away beneath the surface of the persona your Sun sign provides. It's about your anxieties and motivations and it has a significant impact on your relationships, how you bond with others and how you feel about anything and everything.

Libra Decans

Do you ever wonder why two people who share the same zodiac sign are so different from one another? We all know of another person who shares our zodiac sign but is the opposite of what we are but, while it may be a simple question, the answer is a little more complex. Zodiac signs alone do not dictate a person's nature. That requires the entire birth chart.

Ancient astrologers knew this, and they divided each zodiac sign, while modern astrology has gone several steps further. The zodiac signs are divided by their qualities, elements, negative expression (feminine), and positive expression (masculine.) Another method used for dividing signs and determining rulership is using the Triplicities in a division known as the decanates.

Should we know what these are, though? Are they important? Sometimes, yes, they are because they can tell you the whole story. To understand more about a particular zodiac sign, understanding the rulers and decans is important and effective with predictive astrology.

The rising Sun's decan is ruled, and that ruler influences the entire life, for the given time, especially if the planet is in a strong position I the natal chart and any life aspects are governed by that ruler. That made sense, didn't it?

Every zodiac sign governs a part of the natal chart, 30 degrees, to be precise. We have 12 zodiac signs, each governing 30 degrees, making up the entire 360-degree natal chart. Each zodiac sign is further divided into three more divisions, each one 10 degrees. There are three decans for each sign, one for each 10-degree division, and each decan has its own ruler. That ruler becomes the sub or co-ruler of the sign. Once you understand the Triplicities - fire, earth, air, and water - you can determine each decans sub-ruler.

Each sign's decan shares a Triplicity with the zodiac sign in the same order they appear in the Zodiac. So, for example, Aries first decan is Aries and Mars rules it. Leo is the second decan, and the Sun rules it. That means the Sun rules the second Aries decan. Here, to help you, are the three decans for Libra:

Libra of First Decan - September 23rd to October 3rd. 0° to 10°. Ruler - Venus.

The first decan, ruled by Venus, produces the peace-lovers of the entire zodiac. These are people that need the finer things in life and know of any relationship imaginable between them and their fellow women and men. But, despite being very You-Oriented, they can be quarrelsome and unbalanced, and one of their biggest dilemmas is the lengths to which they rely on others and how much they should go it alone.

Libra of Second Decan - October 4th to 13th. 10° to 20°. Ruler - Uranus

The second Libra decan is Aquarius and, with rays from both Saturn and Uranus, are often called the "deepest Libras." They immerse themselves in how the human mind works and love to watch social interaction themes. In an abstract way, they may often err towards higher learning and, in a romantic sense, they may be somewhat paradoxical. They want the perfect relationship where both parties share everything, but they need more solitude and space than they might have realized.

Libra of Third Decan - October 14th to 23rd. 10° to 30°. Ruler - Mercury

This decan has rays from Mercury and is the restless Libran. Their natural polarity and ambivalence, particularly in terms of romance, are brought to the fore here. These Librans may spend their entire lives looking for the perfect relationship. They are good with people, logical and intuitive, making this a versatile decan. Charming people comes easily to them, and they want communication more than any other sign.

Libra Cusps

Aside from wondering why two people from one sign may act differently, some people also feel as though their traits are a combination of two Zodiac signs. Some signs are born on the cusp with traits from two signs, for example, you may have been born as a Libran but feel you have Scorpio traits too. When you are born at the end or start of a sign, it's confusing to know where you fit in.

When a person is born within a few days of the Sun moving from one sign to the next, they are classed as being born on the cusp and their traits are influenced by both signs. But to avoid any confusion about what zodiac sign you are, you can be born only under one Sun sign - your official Zodiac sign. So, if you were born in the last few days of one sign, that is your zodiac - you cannot be a Libra and a Scorpio, for example.

While cusp is somewhat confusing, it is no bad thing. Sure, it can feel like a burden to have traits from two sun signs, but it can also be a blessing. While you can inherit negative traits from your second sign, you can also benefit from the positives, and that opens a whole new world of possibilities for you.

There are two possible Libra cusps – Virgo-Libra and Libra-Scorpio – here's what it can mean for your characteristics and personality traits.

Virgo-Libra

Dates: September 19th - September 25th

Name: Cusp of Beauty

If your birthdate is between September 19th and 25th, you are one of the Virgo-Libra cusps. From your Libran side, you still have that indecisive nature while you inherit a closed-off nature from Virgo, and this combination makes it difficult to settle into a steady relationship. But Virgo's analytical nature combines with the caring nature of a Libran, ensuring that, when you do settle, you do not need words to know what your partner wants or needs.

Libra-Scorpio

Dates: October 19th - October 25th

Name: Cusp of Drama

Those born between October 19th and 25th are Libra-Scorpio cusps. Normally, the indecisive nature of Libra would stop you from making any quick decisions but add the Scorpio's ability to be very precise, and that is no longer an issue. The Libran charm is retained, but you must juggle that with the typically cynical nature of the Scorpio.

Chapter 2: An Introduction to Libra

The zodiac sign for Libra is the Scales (meaning balance). The scales symbol has its roots in the Scales of Justice, which Themis, the Greek Goddess of divine law, held aloft as a symbol of justice. Thus, even today, the image of Lady Justice can be seen wherever the rule of law and customs is served. Found in the constellation of Libra, its element is Air. Ruled by Venus, the quality of Libra is Cardinal. This means that Libra belongs to the four most important signs (Capricorn, Libra, Aries, and Cancer). They are important because they stand at the turning point of mild seasonal change. As the seventh astrological sign represented in the Zodiac, the sun's transition across this sign occurs around the September equinox (23rd) and 22nd of October. Unlike the other eleven zodiac constellations, which are represented by mythological characters and animals, Libra is represented by the scales, an inanimate object.

The Libra Symbol: The sign of the scales represents harmony and balance. Those born under the sign of Libra are said to have traits such as fairness and equality. Libra is associated with romance, with Venus as its ruler. Venus in mythology is the Goddess of love. Each sign in the zodiac has a standard design recognized by most people who either follow their horoscopes or study astrology, but as with the other eleven signs, the Libra symbol is modified and re-imagined by whoever recreates the image. Sometimes, the scales are portrayed as a glyph (a line drawing) on other occasions, the scales are represented as elaborate scales of justice.

Libra, the Air Sign: Libra, Aquarius, and Gemini are all air signs. People born under these three signs can be thought of as having the capacity to be detached when dealing with most situations, being rational and calm when coping with difficult circumstances. While in Greek mythology, Themis is associated with the scales of justice, in Roman mythology, this honor belongs to the Goddess Justitia. Marcus Manilius, a poet and resident of ancient Rome, suggested that Roman judges were born under the zodiac sign of Libra. Ancient Rome has many associations with Libra. For example, it was believed that when Rome was founded, the moon was in Libra. This meant that Rome was founded in righteousness and balance. The Romans explained this by noting that the night hours matched the day's hours, demonstrating balance. In Ancient Greece, it was believed that Scorpio, Virgo, and Libra were intrinsically linked and that they make a "claw" in the sky, which can be identified as the stars that make up the constellation of Libra.

Ruling Planet: Venus: Venus, the goddess of love, rules Libra and is known as the planet of beauty. Venus also rules Taurus. In ancient mythology, the planet Venus is the strongest influence of all the celestial bodies. Those born under the influence of Venus are seekers of justice, strive for harmony in their social and intimate relationships, and possess charm and beauty. Venus is also the influencer of art, literature, and music. Those born under the sign of Libra will have a love of music and art. Venus dominated people will seek comfort in their surroundings and those whom they care for. Happy in domesticity, Libra's are loyal, and friendships tend to last a lifetime, but on the negative side, because Venus influences harmony: Libra shies away from conflict rather than resolving it. Overly emotional, Libra's can get hurt by even the smallest slight and brood over past arguments.

Libra's are complex people simply because of their quest for balance in their lives. Prone to lethargy one minute and hyper-action the next, Libra's can be viewed as paradoxical. It is true that Libra's value physical attributes over what a person is like inside, but once committed to a friendship or loving relationship, Libran's will stay true, if not a tad possessive. Don't depend too much on Librans in an emergency, though. They dither, even in the face of real danger. Libra's ruling planet Venus dominates the decision-making processes. Even when facing imminent danger, Libra's will attempt to weigh the possibilities when the need to act is staring them in the face.

Being born under the influence of the planet Venus makes Libra's lovers of luxury living. They have superior tastes and adore public functions and elegant parties. Some say that Libras hate being alone but is surrounded by nice, comfortable, and luxurious things, such as décor and fine food, they are happy. Venus is not a boastful planet, so Librans rarely boast or act superior to others. This is because Venus represents sensuality and femininity, which makes Libra attractive to others. In Greek mythology, this planet is also associated with the Goddess Aphrodite. Venus, too, is probably the oldest known planet in the universe. It is the brightest, except for the moon and sun, sometimes called the Jewel in the Sky.

Colors: The Libra colors are pale blue and light pink: airy colors that bring calm to the Libran soul. Symbolic of cool softness, these colors represent balance and clarity, reminiscent of Libra's charm, sweetness, and likable nature. Never a person for gaudiness, Libra prefers harmony in their colors, so look for hues such as pink, tan, and white when matching décor and fashion. Bold colors tend not to impress the Libra, but do approve of black as a classically elegant look. When power is required, Libra's reach for pink every time as an energy boost pink does the trick.

When the Libran needs to show dominance and power, such as in the workplace or when attracting a partner on a first date, pink provides the energy needed. For good luck, Libra will turn to blue. While the Libra preference is for soft blues, any shade of blue brings good luck to the wearer. So, blue is the "go-to" shade when looking for a promotion or going after a job. Those who know Libra's well, will know that white is also a hue often used by them in fashion and décor.

If you are a Libra, try these colors and watch how they work for you. For example, try wearing a white outfit. Though not always a practical color, white makes a bold statement and worn in the right way, the virgin aspects of this color can be eliminated. A white bathing suit or skinny white jeans boost Libra's energy. Try white décor in the home, teamed with pinks or blues with perhaps a bold darker cerise or navy blue for surrounding that match your Libran personality. To stimulate concentration, Libra uses blue to provide calmness, clarity, and bravery when required. Think in terms of "blue sky" thinking, with no barriers or borders, endless sky, and vast room areas of creative thinking. Blue is also a useful color when emptying the mind after a long day at work. Meditation gurus suggest thinking of endless blue sky when meditating.

Gemstones

- **Opal:** For the Libra, gemstones and crystals are often an important aspect of their lives. Opal is considered the Libra birthstone. Opal provides the Libra with inspiration and creativity, synchronizing their relationships and their everyday lives to promote harmony and balance. Wearing opal or having these gemstones around ward off negativity and prevents nightmares, a common occurrence for Libra's who struggle with justice and balance issues. A good luck gem, opal provides courage when needed.

• **Tiger's Eye:** This gemstone is also associated with Libra. This gemstone provides stamina, and if you are a Libra, you will know that trying to accommodate everyone's needs, and putting them before your own, is tiring and drains your energy. Keeping this gemstone close helps you maintain balance and provides the internal and external boost you need. When life is challenging. Citrine can be added here too because it helps Libra to navigate difficult situations and rise to challenges that may need decisive action.

• **Rose Quartz:** This gemstone is said to represent unconditional love. Pink has particular significance for the Libra and is the moonstone that provides self-love and is supportive of loving relationships. Many of Libra's feel incomplete when living alone. Libra's are often heard saying that they want romance in their lives: a loving partner's romance. For some Libra's, the restless feeling they sometimes get for no apparent reason is often the result of the unspoken desire for a romantic relationship. Rose quartz inspires see one's own worth and that loving oneself foremost, is the greatest of all gifts. Astrologists believe that Rose quartz can attract a love interest in the Libra's life. To enhance your feelings of self-love, use rose quartz around the home, in the bedroom, and in your bath.

• **Lapis Lazuli:** This beautiful blue gemstone brings deeper reflection and intuition into Libra's life. It enables the air element to permeate the Libra environment to centering the emotions. Libra's are not overly fond of conflict and either placate or turn away from such challenges. The Lapis Lazuli helps the Libra to express themselves more assertively. Libra's are known for their diplomacy, and the gemstone reinforces this trait. If you are a Libra, carrying this gemstone in your purse or in your pocket will enable you to feel confident and less in difficult situations. It provides positive energy when needed.

• **Aquamarine**: This is a favorite birthstone for Libra. This holds immense energy. Keeping this stone close provides the Libra with tolerance and open-mindedness. Used when meditating, Aquamarine offers the possibility of reaching a deeper level of intuition.

• **Bloodstone:** This gemstone provides bravery and courage for the Libra. It is a green stone flecked with red. If you are Libra, you must add this to your gemstone collection. It has powerful properties for keeping you grounded. Most Libra's know they can be perceived as being unreliable and unfocused. This is because the Libra does find it difficult sometimes to stay in the here and now and often see problems when they are not even there, but this is not a fair perception of the Libra, who are in a general well focused and always interested in what is going on around them and in the lives of those they care about.

Famous Libra's

Not surprisingly, many famous people are Libra's as the sign favors those born under the sign with traits such as creativity, love of art, music, and design. Who was born on your birthday? I think you will all agree these are beautiful, creative, ambitious, and artistic people. These celebrities have many traits in common, whether it's music, theater, movies, writing, or design.

- Bruce Springsteen – Sept 23rd – Personality – a born leader
- Will Smith – Sept 25th – Personality - Ambitious
- Catherine Zeta-Jones and Michael Douglas – yes, both have the same birthday Sept 25th
- Catherine Zeta-Jones – Personality – Creative/Resilient
- Michael Douglas – Personality - Entrepreneurial
- Barbara Walters – Sept 25th - Personality - Entrepreneurial
- Olivia Newton-John – Sept 26th - Personality – Creative/resilient
- Serena Williams – Sept 26th – Personality – Compassionate
- Gwyneth Paltrow – Sept 27th – Born leader
- Jerry Lee Lewis – Sept 29th – Sensitive/passionate
- Ian McShane – Sept 29th - Humanitarian
- Julie Andrews – Oct 1st – Perceptive/passionate
- Susan Sarandon – Oct 4th – Lone wolf
- Kate Winslet – Oct 5th – Entrepreneurial
- Matt Damon – Oct 8th – Full of energy/constant motion

Life with the Libra

Knowledge of how the Libra emanates their character traits and personalities can be useful when trying to understand or get to know a Libra. It is also useful for the Libra themselves, as having a deeper understanding of how you might react under certain circumstances can enhance your lived experience. Here, I summarize the Libra at home, at work, and out and about. These topics will be covered in more depth in future chapters.

The Libra at Home

The Libra's home may not always be calm and harmonious, but this is what the Libra will strive for in their personal lives at home. Being creative, Libra will usually have a well-designed home filled with artistic touches in décor and wall art. If you are a Libra, then you will possess many interpersonal skills, and your desire to create a harmonious home will urge you forward in this quest, but the need to create balance in your family life may create problems, especially when having to make decisions. What school should the children go to, what décor looks best in what room, what hobbies do you want to pursue? These are all questions you, as a Libra, will constantly go backward and forwards on.

For settling disputes in the family, things get even more tense as you try to negotiate conflicts so the outcomes are fair for everyone. Your whole motivation in your home life will be for calm, harmony, and creativity. Your Air sign means you will strive to master the core principles of honesty, equality, and justice. You will work hard to imbue these principles in your children and your partner. However, these characteristics may be interpreted as indecisiveness and reluctance to come down from the fence on important family decisions. A trait of the Libra is to see themselves through others' eyes, which will make you highly sensitive to unthinking remarks by family members. But as a Libra, you will provide the rock on which the foundations of your family life exist. Your diplomacy and ability to compromise pour oil on troubled waters, making you shine brightly as a parent and as an intimate partner.

The Libra at Work

Libra is a great person to work with because compromise is their middle name. If you are Libra, you will already know this. You will love to work in a team and thrive on group activities. Because you like to see the whole picture, the details don't bother you too much. This can make other employees unappreciative of you, particularly when you are indecisive. Being too laid back at work can create ill feelings, particularly if those around you are impulsive or operate mostly on adrenaline. Male Libra prefer to work with people they like. Simmering conflicts and unfriendly environments will distress them, as Libra's are quick to feel the surrounding tension. Toxic work environments suit no one, but the Libra male will feel particularly depressed in unhealthy work environments.

As a boss, the Libra male will find it difficult if employees are unhappy and prefer to have conflict out in the open, even though he may be indecisive about what action to take due to getting to the truth. When issues are not resolved, the Libra man and woman will fall into a moody silence, and this affects work. To outsiders, the Libra, usually so conciliatory and entrepreneurial, will seem lazy and apathetic because when equilibrium is not balanced, neither is the Libra.

The woman employee born under the sign of Libra can seem like an enigma. On the surface, she will appear sweetness itself to those who work with her. Prepared to compromise and take on board other people's suggestions and ideas, Libra woman will be mild-mannered and softly spoken. Not every Libra woman fits this description, and if you are a Libra, you may not either. Generally, women born under the sign of Venus are not tough cookies and rarely display their sexuality in public, but don't be fooled by this congenial sugar icing look. Beneath this show of soft freshness is a sharp ambitious mind and a fierce drive that makes the Libra woman and man born leaders.

Don't be fooled either when Libra woman bows to the requests of others. If the scales are not balanced, they beware. The Libra woman will not be happy and will have no qualms in saying so. Libra woman upset in the workplace will throw the whole place into chaos until she can restore harmony and balance back into her life. This makes Libra women and men born leaders and ambitious workers. The dichotomy between the laid-back employee or boss and the lazy disgruntled employee/boss combines to make leadership dynamic and inevitable.

The Libra in Social Settings

Getting ready for a night out on the town, then be prepared for the Libra to keep you waiting. Libra's are very conscious about how they look and can be quite vain. So, you may have to drag them from the mirror to get out on time. But if you know a Libra, you will know that they are gracious, good-humored, and fun to be with. Libra also can attract people to them, so if you are out on the town looking for new friends, they take your Libra friend with you.

If you are a Libra, then you will know that you are attractive. You will love the social side of your life, even though you may sometimes be a loner. Not that you don't like company, it is rather that you can deal with being on your own, but when the invitations come in, you need no encouragement, but beware, Libra's want things to go right, so a social occasion that goes wrong does not go down well. They especially don't like being rushed and, when pressured, tend to walk away. In relation to friendship and intimate relationships, Libra's are romantic and strive for the perfect match, whether in a companion or an intimate partner.

Libra's are dreamers, so they like the company of fellow dreamers, although this easy-going match may not in the end amount to anything. Again, if you are a Libra reading this, you will also know that Libra's like to be spontaneous and happy to go off on an adventure at the drop of a hat, so finding someone with the same spontaneity is a Libra dream. Socializing is a favorite occupation of the Libra, and they like nothing more than spending time pampering themselves. This is true for the Libra male and the female. So, spa days and champagne evenings, not forgetting the chocolate, is just pure heaven for the Libra. Libra's usually have a small but loyal circle of friends. They take the lead when dispute breakout and are always ready to offer advice: maybe too ready occasionally, and this is where your Libra friends may appear to be too pushy. But Libra people, while generally wanting to have fun, are clever and articulate and make loyal, charming friends.

Chapter 3: Libra Strengths

As with other signs of the zodiac, Libras have strengths and weaknesses. Libra's strengths are indeed formidable, and this is what makes those born under this sign so attractive to others, but they also have weaknesses, and if you know a Libra or are a Libra yourself, you will have no problems relating to some of the best and worst things about Libra. It is not surprising given their star sign that Libras care very deeply about right and wrong, and the symbol of the scales plays a dominant role in how they conduct their lives. Injustices played out on the world stage unsettle them greatly, and are not averse to voicing their opinions, whether it is politically or at a societal level. At a personal level, they stand up to injustice when manifested among friends, work for colleagues or family. This is the reason Libras are good to have on the side. While they may be mediators and peacemakers, they will challenge injustice and are prepared to sacrifice their own freedoms for others.

On a more negative level, the Libra is not as direct as some star signs, and this can be troubling Libra friends and family. So keen are Libra's to keep the peace and it can be difficult to accept their word. This is because they tend to choose their words very carefully, especially if they think their words may upset. If you are Libra, you know that you will probably say anything to avoid conflict or hurt others' feelings. So, while the Libra will fight for justice, at the same time, they are likely to avoid confrontations, instead preferring to use diplomacy and conciliation than harsh words. This makes the Libra rather like an unexploded bomb. They will be passively aggressive but may explode in rage at the slightest thing that goes wrong.

If you know a Libra, then you will not be surprised to know that one of the most negative aspects of their personality is their fear of being direct about how they feel. Libras can easily be taken advantage of by domineering partners because of their indecisiveness and evasive tactics when dealing with conflict. So, let's look at Libra's strengths and weaknesses in more detail.

Strengths

• Innate Elegance

If you are a Libra, you will have an innate elegance. Whatever the fashion or trends at any given moment, and you may wear the latest fashion, whether it's grunge or smart casual, you will instinctively be drawn to elegance. How often have you been out with a friend and lingered over the Jewelry displays in the windows of high-end stores? It's not the flashy ruby-red necklaces or huge diamond rings that catch your eye, but the single pearl droplet earrings elegantly mounted in delicate silver shaped claws. The elegant understatement is the hallmark of the Libra.

When it comes to décor, whether male or female, Libra, your home will be tasteful and coordinated. If you have a penchant for twinkly lights, these two will be elegantly displayed to bring out the best of your surroundings. This elegance is a strength. You can rely on your Libra friend to make the best choices when it comes to arranging furniture, picking out elegant clothes, or just behaving in an elegant manner when out socializing.

• Romantic

The most well-known trait of the Libra is their romanticism. Whether it is in literature, art, music, or love interests. The Libra is drawn to the romantic. If you have a Libra partner, then romantic candle-lit dinners should be on your agenda. But even a cozy night in by the fireside should be romantic: the wine nicely cooled, the lights down low, and romantic music playing in the background. How many Libras like nothing better than curling up with a romantic book or listening to love songs on a vintage record player?

Many artists are Libras, and this is no surprise. This side of their personality comes out in your work. The Libra shies away from dark thoughts and shady corners. If you have a Libra partner, then you will recognize this romantic side of their nature as a strength. They will always present the best possible view of the world and will always see the beauty in the smallest object, flower, or sentiment. Treasure the Libra for their ability to look for the best in people.

• Adaptable

Libra's strength is its adaptability. Even when times get tough, they rise to the challenge and adapt to most situations. This does make Libras useful allies. Libras are more likely to survive messy divorces, house moves, and job changes. They may not like it, but something inside them kicks into action when knocked down and they stand up, ready to try again. This is a particular strength if you are looking for work, whether it's in show business or retail. Libra's don't give up once they get the bit between their teeth. If you know a Libra, you will have heard them say many times, "Oh well, we/I will just have to make the best of it", or "I know I can make this new situation work for me." Being adaptable makes the Libra calm and balanced when chaos reigns around them. Yes, they may be unsettled by the tilt of the scales when things change, but the Libra drive for balance will soon restore equilibrium.

• Fine Aesthetic Tastes

The libra tends to have good taste and intellectual judgment, so it is quite likely to recognize something that has aesthetic beauty. Good taste is something that is understood through the senses, such as hearing, touching, tasting, seeing, and so forth. The notion of fine aesthetic taste aligns beautifully with Libra's innate sense of elegance and, of course, romance. It could be argued that aesthetic taste is the cornerstone of the Libra personality. They will tend to shy away from the rough or untidy elements of everyday life unless these elements are used to explore deeper meanings, such as in poetry and art. Libra musicians and filmmakers have a tendency to explore the murkier sides of the soul when crafting their art.

Your Libra friend is likely to enjoy good food and the feel of soft fabrics. Watch your Libra friend walking through a store selling soft linens and fleecy robes, they just cannot resist touching them as they pass. If you are Libra, how many pairs of fleecy bed socks do you own? Fine dining and fine art and literature capture the Libra imagination, so if you have a Libra partner, choosing them, Christmas gifts should be no problem at all. Libras make good teachers, so if you want to learn the finer things in life, ask the Libra.

• Fair/Righteous

This is an obvious strength of the Libra. Fairness and justice, doing what is right even if it creates problems, are intrinsic in the Libra makeup. The Libra will find selfish acts abhorrent, and this can make them unpopular at times. If someone in your friendship group is not prepared to dish the dirt on another member of the group, saying "this is wrong, they are not here to defend themselves," then more than likely, that person is a Libra.

Many politicians begin their careers because they see injustice in the world, and they want to help put things right. It is not surprising that some were born under the sign of Libra. Alexandria Ocasio-Cortez and Kamala Harris are both Libras. Libra's are drawn to professions that fight for social justice. Of course, no one is a saint, and sometimes people behave badly, and Libra's are no different from anyone else in this respect, but if you are a Libra, you will probably admit that when you behave badly towards another person, it upsets your equilibrium for a very long time. This tends to make you depressed until you can restore balance.

• Leadership Skills

Libra are born leaders, so make brilliant bosses. Since being fair is intrinsic in their nature, they tend to do what is morally right, so Libra bosses generally have loyal employees. If you work for a Libra boss, there is a likelihood that you work with a happy band of people. Libra's do not do well in atmospheres that are heavy with tension. If employees are disrespectful or combative, you will see the Libra temperament show, and communication is likely to break down very quickly.

Your Libra boss will probably want to keep the peace and will be open to honest discussions about how you feel about certain aspects of work. Being confrontational will not work with your Libra boss. If you are a Libra, then you might want to consider jobs or activities in which you can show your leadership skills to your best advantage. Bruce Springsteen is a Libra, and while it's fun to know that he is known as the "Boss," it's no surprise that he was not just "born to run" but born to lead his band to success too.

• Diplomatic

The Libra is diplomatic. They will do anything not to upset the balance in their own and other people's lives. How many times have you, like Libra, been called in to negotiate and keep the peace? Libra parents are especially good at being diplomatic with their children. When faced with difficult family disagreements, the Libra is the one who usually calms the situation because they tend to look at all sides of an argument. When someone is clearly wrong about something, the Libra will employ tact and diplomacy to correct wrong opinions and actions.

Libras are analytical, and this can be frustrating for their family and friends, but it is one of Libras strengths because they are often the ones who present all points of view in a diplomatic way so that grievances that could have escalated into downright conflict are settled in a manner that suits all parties.

• Loyal

Your Libra friend will love you forever, unless, of course, you upset their equilibrium, then they will anguish long and hard about whether to maintain your friendship. Loyalty is a strong characteristic of Libra. Your Libra friend or love interest will expect loyalty from you too. Their commitments are strong. The most abiding strength of a Libra is that they will stick by you through almost any crisis or upset. Betrayal is not in their playbook. If your intimate partner is Libra, then feel free to tell them how much you love them and remember that just as they will stand by you, they expect no less from you.

The Libra will always prioritize your happiness. They love making people happy because it makes for harmony in their lives. Ever ready to help people in times of need, the Libra will go beyond what is expected of them. Easily taken advantage of the Libra will do anything to make you happy. If you want a favor from them, you won't have to ask twice. Remember, too, that because Libra's are hopeless romantics, they will pull out all the stops to show their loyalty to you, whether it's ordered a table at a nice restaurant or the best seats to see your favorite band.

Chapter 4: Libra Weaknesses

People born under Libra's sign are complex beings that do not hide their "inner feelings." They are captivating, diplomatic, fair, and intensely loyal. Many people agree that Libra is a beautiful person, inside and out, but just as they cannot hide their personalities' positive aspects, they cannot hide their weaknesses either. If you are a Libra or have Libra friends, you will recognize some weaknesses below.

• Hesitant and Indecisive

Yes, this is probably one of the most noticeable Libra weaknesses. They just cannot decide, and if they do, they are likely to change it again. Being hesitant and indecisive plagues the Libra. Shall they take that job or stay where they are? What if things go wrong? Should I tell that person I don't want to see them again, or will I regret it? It must be admitted that in a crisis, it must be admitted that Libras are hopeless. While they are born leaders, they must have a steady, balanced environment.

If you have a Libra friend, you can help them overcome their hesitancy and indecisiveness by calling on their strengths. Libras are very adaptable, point out to them that deciding even it turns out to be the wrong decision, is not the end of the world, that they can make things work unless you need to get them out of a burning building! Libra's indecisive nature is mostly due to their ability to see both sides of an issue. For the Libra, doing the right thing is their ultimate quest. Libra's often envy and admire friends and family members who are decisive, but unfortunately, their own hesitancy makes them appear weak in the eyes of more assertive people.

• Afraid of Being Offensive

Don't ask the Libra to be cruel or heartless to people because they can't do it. Even when they have been hurt, the Libra cannot find it in their nature to knowing to offend people. If they inadvertently upset people, they are profoundly unhappy. This weakness prevents Libras from defending themselves when it is necessary. It also makes them look weak in front of others.

If you are a Libra, you may have experienced being hurt by other people's remarks, even when you are never cruel or hurtful yourself. This is because some people around you recognize that you will not give as good as you get, so it's almost like you are giving them license to be offensive. Take a page out of one of your more assertive friends' books, if you offend someone, it is probably because they deserve it. If a libra friend is reluctant to offend where necessary, appeal to their better nature by suggesting that their acquiescence will only make that person offensive to even more people.

• Demanding of Justice

Sometimes the Libra can be infuriating when it comes to the subject of justice. Their demands for justice can border on the extreme. For example, because Libras are generally highly intelligent people, they like to debate to the extent that they can wear people out. When the Libra thinks that justice has not been served, they will stop at nothing to make sure that people know about it. This can be infuriating for those around them. But having said this, if you have a Libra friend or live with a

Libra, you will know that they are complex beings that don't easily fit into a nice, neat frame. They are like butterflies, flitting from one characteristic to another. Their inconsistency is never clearer than when demanding justice.

The Libra can be extremely sulky when their views are not taken seriously, or worse when they are not listened to. This appears to be someone at odds when arguing that justice needs to be served when manipulating a situation to bring you onto their side. The Libra is not averse to weighing the scales in their own favor to convince people that something is unfair. Libra inconsistently can often be thought of as a weakness, particularly when arguing for fairness, but for the Libra, the scales are not balanced easily, they require careful adjustment to come into alignment. For others to see both sides of an argument, the Libra will be seen to dip from one characteristic to another, becoming indolent excessive, and moody one minute and balanced the next. Those who don't understand this are often startled by the contrasts in this supposedly level-headed Libran.

• Inadvertently Seductive

Can a person be inadvertently seductive? Well, of course they can. The Libra is an intelligent being, and this can be extremely seductive. When trying to attract a Libra, you will notice they like to talk about deep and meaningful topics, so often, it is hard to get their attention onto what you have in mind. This aesthetic aspect of their personality and they're seemingly "unaware that you find me attractive" demeanor can be very seductive and can be inadvertently so. Libras have the power to attract from across a crowded room, but don't imagine that they know this. That "come on" look may not be all that it seems. Libras can be put off by clumsy coarse approaches.

If you know that the person you want to flirt with is a Libra, you will have a head start. Libra responds to the elegant conversation, and as you might guess, a good debate. But do not be confrontational, this approach turns off the Libra. If you have the intention to get your Libra date into bed, there are one or two things you might like to consider. Generally, the Libra will prefer lovemaking in a bed rather than seemingly spontaneous romps in the back seat of a car. One of the great weaknesses of the Libra personality is their reluctance to be earthy and dirty. Remember, elegant Libra

• Narcissistic

Even given the weaknesses above, the Libra is often thought of as the most beautiful and loving zodiac sign. But beware, some Libras have a dark side to their personality, and this is their narcissistic tendencies. As a Libra, you may well admit that what takes up considerable your time is focusing on yourself. This is because you like to please others, so this entails looking your best, feeling appreciated, and being admired. This affords the Libra the balance they strive for in their lives.

While narcissism is a weakness in the Libra character, they are narcissistic with good intentions, but this personality trait, shown to the world as self-confidence and egotistical, may often hide a tortured soul that craves recognition. This makes the Libra sensitive to criticism. If you know a Libra, you will easily recognize this trait. They hate criticism of themselves but are comfortable criticizing others. The charming Libra can quickly turn petulant and aggressive. To get along with a Libra, but discover they are narcissistic, then you need to accept there are limits to their charm and goodwill. Explain to a narcissistic person, whatever their star sign, that you will not be a foil for their inflated ego.

• Weak-Willed

The weak-willed Libra can be frustrating at times, but this negative perception of the Libra can be contentious and over-stated. Indecisive Libra can collapse when required to decide and then abide by it, but it is not necessarily the case that the Libra is superficial. Lying on the bed of moderation is a tough call. The Libra appears to be weak-willed because their overriding goal is balance and harmony. They will always try to do what is best to keep the peace. If you are a Libra, do not dwell on this negative perception of yourself. You want what is best for those around you, and you strive for fairness and justice in your own life and the lives of others. Yes, your hesitancy can appear to be weak, but you have a strong sense of justice, so use your diplomacy in an assertive manner and ensure that you support your decisions will clear messaging. For example, "I am not prepared to go along with this until I have thought it through" and then stick to it.

If you have Libra friends and partners, you know how tough it is when decisions must be made, and those decisions must be adhered to. You know maybe your Libra may change his or her mind, but this being weak, it's cautious. If you care for your Libra, then recognize this and confront it together. Since the Libra can be easily influenced, perhaps a serious conversation is all that must help Libra decide and abide by it.

In family situations, the Libra parent may find it difficult not to give in to demanding children. They may administer punishment for misdemeanors, such as taking away favorite technology devices, but quickly relent when the child cries or makes a fuss. If you have a partner who is a little weak-willed when it comes to disciplining the children, then perhaps you need to help them to be more assertive, but this needs to be done within the framework of a balanced discussion rather than a confrontation.

• Adopts Palliative Solutions

The Libra will most often reach for a palliative solution to problems. Perhaps this is a deeply inherent characteristic of the Libra. but it can also be perceived as a weakness. For example, the need to paper over the cracks, using a band-aid when something more substantial is required.

The therapeutic nature of the Libra can be seen often. If you are a Libra, how often have you be accused of not seeing things how they are. Palliative solutions to problems can sometimes work, and there are many occasions when the sledge-hammer approach does not work, but this approach to problem-solving does not always work and can be seen by observers as turning a blind eye to the real issues. If you are a Libra parent, you may wish to sit a child down and discuss their bad behavior and offer solutions that do not address why the child is misbehaving. If so, you must draw on your nature's intellectual side and face the problem head-on. Otherwise, you are not teaching your child to address serious behavioral problems.

Often the Libra looks on the bright side when a more realistic response would be more effective. Looking for solutions that do not address the real issues can be difficult for the Libra. They require a sensitive discussion to enable them to see that, sometimes, a palliative solution will not always restore balance and harmony in their lives.

• Lazy

If you know a Libra, how often have you heard from describing themselves as have the capacity to be incredibly active or supremely lazy. This dichotomy is essentially reminiscent of the scales, either they are balanced, or they are not, but this can be said of other star signs too, so this lazy aspect of the Libra needs to be viewed with caution as Libra laziness is a complex notion, particularly as it is an alliteration easily ceased upon people writing horoscopes. If you are a Libra, or you know a Libra, you will know that one weakness of the Libra personality is that they cannot sit still. They are restless souls looking for balance in their lives and so energetically strive for harmony in their lives, which is hard work, so the notion that the Libra is lazy needs to be tempered with the idea that activity and laziness are counterbalances and work well for Libra equilibrium. If you don't know the Libra too well, this indolent behavior be a weakness rather than a strength.

Because the Libra is aesthetic in nature, they will search out relaxing activities such as sitting in a deep comfortable armchair reading a book, or relaxing on a spa day with friends, doing nothing at all except pampering themselves. But remember that the Libra probably work hard to achieve this balance in their lives. Those born under the sign of Libra make good travel writers, combining hard work with the luxury of exploring romantic locations and Mediterranean sunsets. So, do not be fooled by this "weakness" in the Libra personality, striving for a time when you can simply do nothing without guilt or being irresponsible takes planning and hard work.

In Summary

Having explored the strengths and weaknesses of the Libra personality, it should be remembered that environmental influences also affect the way people behave. While the above do not pretend to define the Libra, these traits are common in those born under this zodiac sign.

This chapter ends with a positive look at the Libra personality and the most common traits. The Libra is a loving, caring soul, and if you are lucky enough to have a mother, sister, or intimate partner who is Libra, then you are lucky. If you are looking for a friend or someone to spend your life with, then Libras are the most desirable people in the zodiac. They will remain constant and true and work hard to provide you everything you need to make your life comfortable and happy. Libra always looks for balance both in relationships and at work.

So, if you have a Libra as a partner, a word of advice - hold on to them because you will miss their love, inner beauty, and affection should they leave you.

Chapter 5: The Libra Woman

Lover

Having read the first two chapters of this guidebook, the Libra is influenced by Venus and has the scales to symbolize fairness and justice. Renowned for being the most beautiful of the zodiac signs, it is little wonder that people are drawn to them. Many people find themselves captivated by the Libra woman, not least because she will constantly challenge your assumptions about her: one minute, demur, and compliant, the next outspoken and erratic. Though not open to criticism, the Libra woman is only too ready to admit when she is wrong. In love, the Libra woman strives for harmony and balance. She loves being loved and thrives on attention. Once in love, a Libra woman will remain devoted, but she will expect only honesty from her partner and does not fare well with mind games. Being fair in love is paramount for Libra woman.

In love, Libra woman will be passionate and flirtatious. When showered with affection, she will flourish. This does not mean she is high maintenance. But she can look after herself and is not averse to spending time on her own. What Libra woman wants is someone she can rely on when she feels vulnerable. So, dependability is high on her agenda. But typical of the Libra, she will expect her independence to be respected. Thus, Libra woman can swing from being dependent to independent depending on what situations are occurring. Since Libras are not happy dealing with conflict, they will rather talk out arguments and rarely explode into anger. This desire to talk things through can be disconcerting for their male partner since many men prefer not to discuss their innermost emotions. The Libra woman can appear intrusive and whinny when turning a hot-tempered argument into a "let's sit down and discuss this" discussion. A partner's refusal to have a deep and meaningful discussion can leave Libra woman feeling moody and depressed.

As an air sign, Libra woman is likely to intellectualize sex. She will consider her partner's needs and her own and then try to encapsulate that bedroom fun. Libra woman is seductive and enjoys lots of foreplay since sensual pleasure is important when making love: touch, scent, and loving words all contribute to the Libra woman's sexual activities. Partners of Libras women are lucky in the bedroom because sex must be as giving as it is loving. Having said this, Libra woman is no siren in the bedroom. She can be coy in the bedroom until she trusts her partner. Her indecision can also make it hard for her to open up about what she wants in bed, but when she trusts you, the Libra woman will be everything you want her to be and more. You need to be sensitive to Libra woman's needs in the bedroom. If she wants to talk, then you let her talk. Respect and honesty are as visible in the bedroom as they are in everyday life.

Compatibility

• **Libra and Virgo:** At first blush, this sexual combination seems not to match. Virgo is an earth sign, while Libra is Air. Ruled by Mercury, Virgos are rather shy with bedroom fun. Libras, while being a little coy, will want more sexual adventure, which will quickly develop into spiritual love with deeper meanings. But as the Virgo personality gets to know the Libra at an intimate level, it really can be opposites attract with each bringing their own unique personalities into playmaking for a deep, rewarding love attachment.

• **Libra and Capricorn:** The first thing to note is that sex is extremely important to both these zodiac signs. And yet you wouldn't believe this because both signs like to take things slow and easy. Often Capricorn and Libra are not initially attracted to each other and do not pursue a deeper relationship, but, if something ignites the spark, then watch out because they can make sweet music together in a loving relationship. Friendship is important to both these signs, so friendship is a key factor in their relationship if they do fall for each other. Timing is important so for Libra and Capricorn, so when they feel the time is right, then their standard sexual attraction heats up, and the barriers fall.

Try Another Match

First Dates

So, it is your first date, and you have discovered your date is a Libra. What should you know so your date goes swingingly? First, know that Libra woman likes a good time, and she will not be passive in this expectation. She will work hard to ensure that you have a good time too. Even if this will be your first and last date with your Libra woman, she will make the best of things and not waste your evening out. No matter where you take her, Libra woman will show an interest. Her natural curiosity and intellectual approach to life will ensure this.

Libra woman will not make you feel awkward, and she will not make fun of you, no matter how nervous you might be on this first date. She may tease and even be a little flirty, but she will not make you feel bad. This is due to the Libra penchant for being indecisive. She will be happy for you to decide about where to go and even what to eat. She won't complain even it's not her cup of tea. So, don't get nervous or wrapped up in what she will think of the evening, she will happily go along with it, and in some respects, this is a little disconcerting because you may come away from your date unsure about how the evening went.

Libra woman likes to talk, so don't be surprised when she guides you into a meaningful discussion from anything from philosophical discussion to local politics. If you have romance and love-making on your mind, probably visiting a museum or a movie theatre is possibly not the best choice of revenue, because she will want to discuss, in-depth, the ins and outs of the museum pieces or the complicated ending to the movie. Your Libra date will likely respond to intellectual chat. She likes reading and the arts and likes discussions peppered with romantic references.

Your Libra date is likely to turn up a little late as she will take an age to decide what to wear. She likes her clothes to match the venue and her mood and will have probably changed clothes a dozen times before she walks into the restaurant to sit down opposite you. She will be critical of what you wear, too, although she won't remark on it. Don't turn up casually dressed unless the venue calls for it. Make an effort. Libra woman likes style and elegance. Remember this, too, when you choose the venue for your first date. A warning of caution, too, when dating a Libra woman for the first time. Try not to ask her to decide where to meet. She will be indecisive and probably text you a dozen times with a change of venue. She may still be undecided even after you meet up, getting distracted about whether she has made the best choice. So, unless you are a Libra too (it's possible you will never decide where to meet), you take the lead and suggest a venue. She won't argue.

Compatibility

- **Libra/Libra**: When meeting someone for the first time, it doesn't matter whether you are compatible or not. There is more to a love match than just what star sign you are born under, but some star signs get along well on the first date, even if it does not lead to anything permanent. Libra woman will respond to someone who puts their heart and soul into caring for them. This is the reason Libra and Libra have a good time on a first date. Both being Air signs, they will immediately look for a romantic opening to their first date. Candlelight, soft music, and a nice fine wine will probably be on the menu.

- **Libra/Aquarius**: This is a good match for a first date. The Aquarian won't go out of their way to find fault with their first date any more than the Libra will. Thus, they will happily settle down to getting to know each other. They will also be interested in what the other has to say. Libra and Aquarius are a good match in general, with each finding inspiration in the other. This love match tends to work permanently, too, with each allowing the other the room to be themselves, but resolving problems together: Aquarius is just what the Libra woman needs when problem-solving, and she will take her lead from this more decisive star sign.

Hobbies

If you have read the previous chapter in this guide, you will not be surprised to learn that Libra woman has many hobbies and often flits from one activity to another when she gets restless or bored. Her main hobby is keeping everything balanced, and this takes up a considerable amount of time and planning.

- **Home Décor:** The Libra woman likes home décor, which takes time and no small amount of energy, which she can easily tire of if things are not going well. While she will days, weeks, maybe designing the décor for a particular room in the house, she is just as likely to buy something on impulse she has noticed in a shop window and then completely re-model the room based on that one impulse buy. This is what makes home decorating so absorbing for the Libra woman. Everything must be in perfect harmony. Because Libra woman comprises yin/yang (counterbalance), visitors to a Libra home will find funky inexpensive items sharing space expensive, elegant items making for an interesting but calming home atmosphere.

- **Shopping:** While shopping is a popular hobby will Libra woman, it rarely includes shopping for food unless it is in high-end food emporiums and delicatessens that offer exotic or selective foods. Supermarket shopping bores the Libra woman, so she is likely to drift down the aisles, dropping anything into the basket that resembles an evening meal, but window shopping, clothes shopping, and shopping for furniture take up considerable time on the Libra calendar. When shopping for clothes, Libra will be very indecisive, so usually has trusted friends or family when engaging in clothes shopping.

- **Hill Walking/Trekking:** This is the perfect hobby for Libra woman. She adores the outdoors, especially hill walking and treks that offer spectacular scenery. A nature lover at heart Libra woman will find perfect peace and tranquility sitting at the top of a mountain, taking photographs, or just quietly meditating. The perfect symmetry of nature, whether rugged or softly undulating, provide inspiration. Libra woman has restless feet, so walking and taking long treks in the outdoors satisfies her need to be moving. Also, Libra likes nothing better than doing nothing. Hill walking, perversely, meets that need in Libra. Having nothing to do but put one foot in front of the other while being at one with nature is the ultimate pastime.

• **Gardening:** Given the time and where possible, Libra woman will spend time gardening to relieve stress. Gardening also allows her to be creative. Drawn to natural colors and shapes, gardening fulfills the creative need in Libra. Libra may prefer to lie in a hammock reading in the garden rather than moving the grass or weeding. For the better off Libra, a gardener will take care of the mundane tasks while she spends time pouring over seed catalogs and gardening magazines in the quest to find the balanced garden. Libras make excellent gardeners as their creativity and search for harmony result in gardens that are welcoming, tranquil, and in sync with nature.

Compatibility

• **Libra/Virgo:** Sharing hobbies can be extremely rewarding, but things can go terribly wrong if two people are not compatible, and this is never truer than with creative hobbies. The Libra woman will look for activities that require balance and synchronization. A hobby buddy needs to be of the same mind, or the Libra woman will walk away. Virgos make good hobby buddies as they are more assertive but look for inspiration in other people. They will happily contribute to hobbies that require challenges such as hill walking or trekking and will find enjoyment in shopping for the unusual or elegant.

• **Libra/Aquarius/Gemini:** This is an excellent combination of signs. These signs are inspired by seeking inspirational activities such as walking and traveling. Like Libra woman, Aquarians and Geminis are searching for harmony. They have no wish for the drama that surrounds activities such as extreme sports and dicey travel destinations. Libra/Taurus: This makes a wonderful combination with each star sign looking for beauty in their surroundings and in the food they eat. Together the Libra woman and her Taurus hobby buddy will enjoy long discussions about how to search for the best foods and finest wines and will spend endless hours looking for just the right fabric or piece of furniture to decorate a room.

Money

Money is the bane of Libra woman's life, whether she has a lot of money or no money. Often, she is wondering if she will ever be worry-free with her finances. Interestingly, this zodiac sign is going through a new disruptive planetary phrase, and so Libras, both women, and men, need to address their financial circumstances before the turn of the 21st century. If they do, they will find that any money issues they have experienced will all disappear. There are several reasons the Libra woman is not good when handling money. First, she finds it hard to save for a rainy day: that trip to a foreign country or that elegant chair taking center stage in the store window beckon her to spend her money.

If you are a Libra, you will know that you also love buying gifts for family and friends as you always want to show your love and affection. If you know a Libra, you are fortunate to be on the receiving end of Libra's generosity, but it is also your duty to show you care for her, too, by loving and accepting her generous traits. This might mean being there for her when she is broke.

Many Libra women believe that they are cursed by ill-fortune when it comes to money. Of course, they are not, and once Libra woman saves instead of spending, she will recognize how much more balanced her scales of fortune are, and this will keep her equilibrium steady and true. Being intuitive means you, as a Libra woman, will have the acumen to write down how your finances are progressing and recognize where you need to save for future occurrences.

Libra women can be lazy with bookkeeping, which must be worked on if financial circumstances are to improve. The Libra woman will not scrimp and save if she can get away with it. This means she will probably spend too much money on heating the home, filling the freezer, or stocking up the wine cabinet. Spending time on financial accounts will reveal to the Libra woman she must balance the books first for a balanced life.

While the desire to seek luxury and elegance is an inherent trait in Libra woman, it is also what might keep her short of money. If you recognize this trait in you, as a Libra woman, then it is time to take stock. You can make your home elegant with your eye for beautiful things without breaking the bank. Try new Feng Shui designs in your home with a view to spending little or no money. Use your creative instincts to create harmony and style by being intuitive and spiritual.

Before going any further about the subject of money, it is useful to point out that money does make the world go around. We all need to support ourselves and our families: we need to eat and feed ourselves and if we are lucky, have enough left over to treat ourselves occasionally. Libra women are generous to a fault and often give to others while going without themselves. Libra woman will spend a considerable amount, if they earn it, on charity donations. They are often likely to give money to homeless people and give generously to food banks and homeless centers. Libra woman is a spiritual being and often believes that harmony in the universe is found by being generous with their money.

Compatibility

• **Libra/Cancer:** This is a match that can cause both parties being better off financially. People whose star sign is Cancer have the tendency to be careful with their money. Saving for the future is almost second nature to many Cancers. For example, if a Cancer has experienced hardship in their younger years, they tend to want to avoid poverty by saving for a rainy day. This may be challenging if they have a Libra woman partner, but it is not insurmountable, and both will learn from each other. The Libra woman comes into her own when her Cancer partner is influenced by getting rich quick schemes. Because of Libra indecision, they are likely to dissuade Cancer to part with their money based on false promises. Thus, this partnership is the best of both worlds, the capacity to save money on the Cancer side, and the ability to analyze doubtful money schemes on the Libra side.

• **Libra/Leo:** For people born under this zodiac sign, there is a tendency for them to be lucky in money matters. They can make good financial decisions based on little information. Leos have a nose for sniffing out a good financial opportunity. Unfortunately, they also have a liking for luxury lifestyles, and this can be disastrous for the Libra woman who may go along with dubious financial schemes.

• **Libra/Virgo:** Being one of the hardest working star signs means this is a good financial match for the Libra woman, who can offer creative ideas to make money but may not have the stamina to carry them through. Virgo enjoys material wealth, which on the one hand, does not bode well for a Libra who may need to save money for the things she desires, and Virgo may be hard-pressed to throw money around on what they believe is not a good investment, but with careful balancing, which Libra is adept at, the Libra/Virgo combination can lead to a very good financial outcome.

Chapter 6: The Libra Male

Lover

If you want someone to love, then find yourself a Libra male. They are sensational to love, especially as his ruling planet is Venus. Responsive, wickedly charming, and sensitive to boot, what is there not to like. Well, some might say there is plenty, but we will get to that later. The Libra male exudes confidence, so with him at your side, you will glide smoothly through social occasions, noted as you go that many eyes are on your attractive partner. The Libra man is drawn to women who are clever and feminine. He admires an elegant woman and is naturally attractive to women who are creative and artistic.

There are people who may find Libra males a little demanding as a love interest because once they fall in love, they want to be around you all the time. While this may seem a tad overbearing, they will stay forever faithful. On the surface of things, the Libra male may appear a little flirty, but this is mostly directed at their lucky partner. Partners are appreciated and loved however flirty they may appear towards people they find interesting.

The Libra male is sensitive to how others see him, so he will always try to good when he stands at your side. He takes a lot of time getting ready to go out, so get used to fighting over the bathroom mirror. Like Libra women, the Libra male is very fond of looking at his own reflection. This might seem vain, but the truth is Libra male worries about what others think about him, so much of the preening is to do with how his love interest sees him. If you do not show respect or even admiration for him, you will quickly see a darker side to his personality.

Libra male is an adept manipulator, especially socially. He will never miss an opportunity to show you off for his own ends rather than because he is proud of you. His flirty overtures to those around him are usually an attempt to be included in the elite circles he so admires, but if his love interest shares the same aims in life, which are usually such things as fine dining and luxury vacations, then his love match may be made in heaven. Libra male is romantic, and he never fails in this trait. He sees romance in everything. He desires sophisticated people who are also open to romantic evenings by the fire with champagne and fine food.

Libra man oozes sexuality, and this is part of his charm. He likes his love interest to be adventurous in bed but sensual too. Mystery drives Libra man wild. He is a patient lover. He wants his partner to feel secure, and trust in a sexual relationship is important to Libra male. The Libra man can be hard to snare. He likes his freedom and being an Air sign, he doesn't particularly relish the idea of being tied down, but once you have him, the probability is you will have him for life.

Compatibility

• **Aries/Libra**: Aside from a Libra/Libra partnership, Aries/Libra is a match made in heaven. They are primal opposites with Libra under the ruling house of Venus and Aries under Mars. Interestingly, while their passion burns brightly, to begin with, they tend to settle down into a more passive/aggressive relationship, so if things go wrong, they will go all out to hurt each other. This love match can be volatile, so beware. Together, both these star signs must work on their relationships because once they have settled down and Aries' energy joins with the indecision manifested by the Libra, they are likely to mate for life.

• **Taurus/Libra:** This is an interesting love match. Each sign is ruled by Venus, but their personalities are opposite. Libra male will want everything to look good. They are sensitive to attractive scents and beautiful fabrics. Taurus, as a partner, will want comfort over good looks. They want to feel substance beneath their touch rather than style. Libra male is looking for sexual pleasure in his relationships. While this may be the same for the Taurus partner, they will express this desire in a different way, and this can sometimes hinder what could be a very solid intimate relationship.

First Dates

As with the Libra woman, Libra male likes to be in settings creating inspiration, such as museums and art galleries. If you know your date's star sign and it happens to be Libra, then arranging a first date to a theatre or art gallery will immediately gain Libra males' interest. Be aware that what you wear on your first date with a Libra male needs to be appropriate and stylish for the occasion. Your first impression with your Libra date needs to be a good one. If you are a woman, think a black dress with clean, sophisticated lines. As a touch of wickedness, wear a splash of red: a stylish red beret or red high-heeled shoes. This will wow your Libra date.

If you are into star signs, you will know that your Libra date will be sociable, so he will be looking for a beautiful genuine smile. Show him off if you are confident and pleasant. The Libra male is not particularly taken with shy people, particularly on a first date. That's not to say he wants a date that he can jump into bed with on first acquaintance, quite the contrary. He will be looking for someone who can stimulate him mentally. He will want a challenge. He will want to woo you, so he can use all his romantic charm. Expect the first date with a Libra male to be conversational. So, pay attention because he will want you to tell him lots about yourself. If you are kind and caring and love doing things for charity or engaging in voluntary work, he is likely to be smitten, and a second date is on the cards. Remember, his fairness and sense of justice defines the Libra male. If you are involved in good causes, he will want to know all about them.

Compatibility

• **Libra Male/Aries Woman**: Most astrologers would agree that Libra and Aries can be deeply attracted to each other. At first blush, they appear to have nothing in common because those born under Aries's sign can be jealous and possessive. She will want to be the dominant partner, and because Libra male is more passive, then trouble could be brewing if there is a second and third date. Aries is passionate and fun to be with, so if Libra man is a little undecided about suggesting sex on a first date, his Aries date might just be the one to decide for him. The night may be a night to remember, but perhaps it might be the last date too. Libra men like to get to know their love interest before making a commitment.

• **Libra/Gemini:** This is a good match for a first date. Both Gemini and Libra are observers and are people watchers, so they will have lots to talk about. Geminis are articulate, funny, and witty. Libra male will warm to a Gemini immediately, matching his date's conversational tone. Libra may be undecided about a second date, but Gemini's warm and intellectual personality will win him over in the end.

Hobbies

The kind of hobby someone has us a lot about that person. Astrology is uncannily correct for matching hobbies against star signs. Libra male pursues many of the hobbies that Libra woman enjoys. He enjoys the great outdoors, so Libra male will look for someone who can share this love with him.

• **Hiking:** Hiking is a passion for many Libra males, and he will not be amused if he is prevented from striding off into the wilds. Travel and adventurous are top of the hobbies list for Libras. With his romantic traits and his love of elegance, his pursuits are varied and often opposite. For example, Libra will love hill climbing, and hiking, not just for the challenge but for the beautiful scenery only climbers experience as they stand at the top of a mountain range.

• **Cultural Tourism:** Conversely, a Libra male, can be seen gazing into the sunset on a beautiful exotic island, the blue sea glittering against the crystal champagne glass in his hand. Libra man can be seen wandering around busy street markets in Italy with a guidebook in hand or sitting at a street café in Paris people watching. Libra man needs a companion at his side who will share these journeys of discovery.

• **Reading:** As much as Libra man likes movie nights with his partner, he probably will have a novel tucked behind the cushions that he will dive into if the movie does not keep his attention, and this is quite often. Libra man is restless, so staying home can be quite a chore. Books are likely to be a passion of the Libra male. He will enjoy browsing through bookstores and libraries. His taste is wide, from natural history to American Literature.

• **Decorating:** Watch out for the Libra male. He loves home decorating, and if he is a bachelor, his home will be smart and stylish. Libra male likes to buy fabrics that are sleek and symmetrical. Black and white are favorite design colors for Libra male. Because technology also appeals to Libra make, he will purchase much of his décor online. Physical shopping expeditions are not his cup of tea.

Compatibility

• **Leo/Libra:** This is an interesting match as Leo likes to be energetic. They are also willing to try new hobbies that challenge them. These traits particularly appeal to Libra man. Leo is a good hobby buddy because Libra man likes to be stimulated, so he will be dragged along to challenging activities, such as hang gliding or surfing. Libra males' love of music and art can find him and his Leo buddy learning to play a musical instrument or attend art classes.

• **Libra/Aries:** As usual, a partnership with an Aries seems to be inevitable for Libra males. Neither sign like inactivity. Staying home watching TV is not their cup of tea. Neither do they like spectator sports, preferring to engage in sports rather than passively watch, so a pairing of Libra males with an Aries, whether male or female, will find them in pursuit of hobbies that expend their energy. Aries people prefer energetic hobbies, so a Libra may find himself off for the weekend cycling or running a marathon.

Money

The Libra man is not all together careful with his money. At times, he can be downright over-indulgent when it comes to spending his money. Not one to think in practical terms, Libra man will often buy on impulse, most likely something that he wants rather than something he needs. Having said this, do not mistakenly think that Libra has no respect for money because he has. Often Libra males will use his logic to make what others may think is a frivolous investment and turn it into a long-term stable investment.

Since Libra male enjoys living a stylish life, Libra man will ensure that his bank account is stable and balanced so he can indulge himself in a life of travel and adventure. As with most Libras, this is done with a flourish and goodwill. He enjoys the luxury of seeing his bank balance grow, but for the less well-off Libra male, money may always be tight because his generosity towards himself and others means he cannot save towards future stability.

Because Libra male is logical and intellectual, it is likely that if he can afford it, Libra man will employ someone else to take care of his finances. If you are married to a Libra male, the person utilized to do this might be you. So, beware, your Libra spouse's finances could keep you awake at night. When his bank account is stable, Libra male will feel that the scales are balanced, and he is more likely to feel secure and happy with his lot.

If you are a Libra male, then you need to focus your attention on your finances and work out ways to live the way you wish on a budget. This may be an anathema to you but working out how you can travel to an exotic destination for your vacation without breaking the bank requires that you draw on your logic and intellectual. Living on a budget can be done in style if you put your mind to it. If your partner is Libra male, then you should guide your man in the right direction by telling him that a stable bank balance will make for a harmonious life – which the Libra male craves.

Compatibility

• **Aries/Libra:** Once again, the Aries Libra match comes into play. Both these star signs are much in sync, so both need to be quite careful when it comes to saving money. Aries is bold when it comes to making investments and sending money on the things he or she desires. Aries is fearless, where Libra male is indecisive. However, one thing you both have in common is that you both strive for challenging careers, so you probably can afford the lavish lifestyle you desire so much. But neither Aries nor Libra finds budgeting easy, so a challenge that may be difficult to overcome is ensuring that your bank accounts are stable, which Libra males may find very unsettling. Aries can be impulsive people, so paired with the Libra male who is more cautious, Aries attraction to dubious financial ventures can be nipped in the bud before they create too much damage.

• **Virgo/Libra:** The Virgo/Libra combination can be good financially, but it can also lead to fireworks if not careful. The Virgo is down-to-earth and practical and therefore is not always willing to take chances, which in many respects is good for the Libra male who sees life in more colorful terms. Virgo instinctively knows how to budget, which is why the Virgo/Libra match can be so dynamic. With Virgo's ability to use money carefully and Libra males' creative tendencies, much can be made from little. Together Virgo and Libra make a good partnership, and if this partnership is a financial one rather than an intimate one, these two can go far in relation to business ventures in creative industries such as photography, movie-making, and publishing.

Chapter 7: The Libra Child

This chapter turns our attention to the Libra child. Never is astrology more fruitful than when we consider our children or nieces and nephews' traits, for example. How often have we compared our own children with our friends and families' children? Is it merely different environments, is it more to do with gender differences? If we conclude that children are born with particular kinds of traits that either hinder or help them as they grow, then studies of these traits through the prism of astrological can be although useful fun.

The Libra Child at Home

No one suggests that your Libra child is a mini-Libra adult. Added to their personality traits are social conditioning and environmental conditioning. As they grow, primary and secondary conditioning plays a huge part in how the child matures into adulthood. However, if we can identify inherent traits in our children and encourage positive personality traits, we can contribute to making our children thrive.

The Libra child is social and is likely to talk early, even if his or her language only makes sense to themselves. Libra child likes the company, so is also likely to cry when left alone at times such as bedtimes, or as a young infant when they can't see the care giver. They love to play games that involve interaction with others. For example, playing visits to doctors or shopping expeditions. Libra child also lives tea parties and usually surrounds themselves with lots of toys to who he or she will play host to.

Pleasing others is a trait you will see in your own or other Libra children. They smile a great deal and are chatty, keen to tell you what they have been doing with their day, and generally involving themselves in adult conversations that sometimes appear to be an attempt to attract attention. This is not the case; they just want to join in and be sociable and are quick to learn social niceties such as greeting people politely and shaking hands if encouraged to do so. For this reason, Libra children should be gently discouraged from speaking to strangers. Their desire from an early age to please others needs to be managed, so when they are old enough to understand, they should be taught to be cautious when around strangers.

Your delightful tiny Libra child will enchant you with their desperate attempts to form words. They will study your facial expressions and try to emulate them, and they will respond ecstatically to cooing sounds and adult laughter. Talking to your Libra child is vital in enabling them to develop because communication, whether in speech, body language or drawings, forms a major component of the Libra personality. With mealtimes, parents realize that while their Libra child is not particularly a fussy eater, they have a hard time deciding what they want to eat. If you have watched a child um and ah over whether they want apple juice or orange juice, with the parent running backward and forwards with a choice of offerings, then that child will probably be a Libra. Not that they are awkward or spoiled; it's that the indecisive side of their personality is beginning to show, and they genuinely cannot decide which to choose. In all probability, if they choose apple juice and the rest of the family choose orange, they will probably suspect they have made the wrong choice and demand to have the same juice as everyone else.

Even as a quite young child, Libra's independence is easily recognized. They are likely to get frustrated easily because they have lots of thoughts tumbling around in their heads, and they struggle to act upon them. As stated earlier in the chapter, you should not see your child as a mini-Libra adult or a "mini-me," which is quite a common trend. But you will note that the ability to be analytical, which is a strong Libra personality trait, is evident in a Libra child from an early age. They are fast learners and are sensitive to what they see as unfairness in their young eyes.

If your Libra child has siblings, then make no mistake, this is the child who will insist that candies and other snacks are shared out equally. Otherwise, you will have a war room situation on your hands whereby you will be having to explain yourself and negotiating new terms based on fairness and equality. You may have friends or relatives who have laughed with you about such issues and joke around about having to measure slices of apple and count out raisins when delivering snacks to their Libra children.

Many children like to show off and demonstrate new skills they have learned, whether it be dancing, singing, or playing a musical instrument. Libra child's desire to be sociable, combined with their easy-going, fun-loving personality, makes them love being the center of attention. So, if you are visiting a friend or relative with a Libra child, expect to be regaled with the latest rendition in the child's repertoire, whether it's a song newly learned, a new dance step, or a letter written to Santa. As the parent of a Libra "wannabe celebrity" child, it is often necessary to take the child in hand and encourage them to cool their enthusiasm and let the grownups chat.

The Libra Child at School

As the Libra child grows, she or he will articulate their thoughts better, and their personalities will begin better formed. With the secondary influence of school, Libra child has more social material to work with and more decisions to make about how they respond to life in general. For example, by school-age Libra, children have likely gotten over their capacity to cry or sulk when left to their own devices. They have learned to like the periods they are left to play on their own because it provides them opportunities to be creative. Still chatty children, it is likely the first thing a schoolteacher may notice about their young student. Libra children will respond well to class-room environments because they are colorful and creative activities will be encouraged. However, by temperament, the Libra child tends to be a little suspicious of other children, to begin with. Sensitive by nature, they may be upset by even the slightest teasing from another child.

Classroom environments need to be orderly but warm for the Libra child to thrive. They like their own space, which they keep neat and tidy. However, they are likely to want toys and books around them as companions in their daily activities. The Libra child's orderly, balanced environment extends to fairness in the classroom. As shown earlier, the Libra child does not respond well to what they perceive as injustice. While they are chatty and articulate from an early age, they are likely as a child to withdraw from perceived unfairness and internalize their distress rather than discuss it.

As a parent, caregiver, or teacher, you must allow the Libra child to express themselves otherwise, this sense of justice remains with them for a long time. For example, most parents and teachers know that if a child is not chosen to be the main character in a school play, their disappointment often results in them accusing the teacher of being unfair. If this scenario is played out with a Libra child, their sense of injustice is not easily forgotten, even though the accusation rarely is based on truth. Libra children dwell on a perceived injustice and encouraging the child to discuss these emotions provides the opportunity for the child to evaluate the situation, and since they are good at this, much oil can be poured on troubled waters.

On justice and fairness, Libra school children will expect the truth, and their analytical minds will ponder such stories as the tooth fairy and Santa Claus from an early age, so if your Libra child, it is likely to be he or she that breaks the terrible news to their siblings that Santa doesn't exist. At school, the Libra child will probably be the one who asks lots of questions when the teacher reads to the class and is disruptive when bored. Often Libra's child is already familiar with the stories presented to them in class and can recite the storyline almost verbatim.

As Libra children get older, they may struggle with some classes that do not meet their learning needs. For example, math will probably not be a popular class for them, and they will best thrive in classes that are creative with numbers in colorful and active ways. Also, math is too formulaic for the small Libra mind that prefers to flit from one creative process to another. They will be avid readers, and as they grow, they will begin to demonstrate fierce independence in their learning. They want to read everything, no matter what genre. Teachers and parents know that Libra children will also want to share their knowledge with them, for, according to the Libra mind, what is the point of knowing stuff if you can't talk about it with other people?

As the Libra child develops further, the Libra schoolgirl/boy will demonstrate their negotiating skills. Libra children, like their adult counterparts, do not like conflict or being around confrontational people. Their friendship peer groups will have the same qualities. While not responding well to conflict, Libra's child can be a bit of a gossip and will enjoy discussing others behind their backs, even though they will feel abject remorse having done so. Libra's child's chatty disposition leads them to stray into awkward situations such as whispering in corners that can quickly lead to trouble.

The sense of injustice only comes about when the Libra child feels that a friend has betrayed their trust by repeating what has been discussed with the unfortunate victim. Thus, Libra children can find themselves in conflicts of their own making simply because they find it hard to keep a secret or keep their thoughts to themselves.

The Teenager

First things first; teenagers *are teenagers.* They behave the way they do because they make new neurons in their developing brains, which causes them many problems: one a rebel without a cause and the next all sweetness and light. Astrology is useful because knowing a teenagers' zodiac sign and the ruling planet can help you understand their confusions a little better. You can also teach them to recognize their traits so they can develop the positive aspects of their personalities. Molly Hall (2020) suggests that Libra teenagers are especially creative and have big dreams and aspirations.

If you are a Libra teen reading this, you will know that your social life is important. You are prepared to defend your best friends until death – so long as they don't betray you. Like all teenagers, the opposite sex takes up much of their brain space, and Libra teens are more so because of their romantic personalities. Venus is your ruling planet Libra teens, so what can you expect? However, if you are a boy and interested in a Libra girlfriend, then expect to tow the courtship line. Libra girls want the romantic walks in the park and the rom-com movie nights. Sounds good, doesn't it?

Libra teen is attracted to people who are cool and fashionable. Libra friends are likely to be cool kids at high school, intelligent but not nerdy. Often, Libra teen will have one close friend who they will converse with most the time, cell phones are never out of the Libra teen hands, and texting best buddy is a regular occurrence that causes much consternation at home. If you are Libra, then you know that your share every waking thought with your bestie. In relation to studies, it will be with your buddy who you study with. Since Libra teen likes sports, you will likely choose activities that two can play, such as tennis, badminton, and for the more intellectual pursuits, checkers.

Never underestimate the Libra teen or take them for granted. If you are a parent of a Libra teen, you know how bored they get when they are not challenged. You may be surprised to discover that not only does your Libra teen spend copious amounts of time in the bathroom preening and goodness knows what, they are also open to suggestions that involve visiting museums and even the opera. Many Libra teens are attracted to the arts, especially the theatre, so encourage them to develop their intellectual side.

At school, the Libra teen will probably be in the drama group and debating society. Not that they are particularly energetic; the Libra teen is the epitome of laziness when they get the chance, but it has more to do with their drive to do something different. They are always on the lookout for something different, which often leads them into deep waters. They are not as tenacious as other star signs, but they are more easily led. A classic example of how this presents itself is when a classmate wishes to work on a presentation with someone else so they can get out of doing the work themselves. Libra teen is a sucker for flattery, and since they crave friendship and conversation, they often fall for this and end up doing all the work while their sneaky teammate goes off to pursue their own interests, and because teen Libra doesn't like conflict, they will say nothing.

At the end of the day, the Libra teen is popular because they are calm, friendly, and balanced in their approach to life. This, at a time when life appears chaotic and confusing for many teens. Because of their negotiating skills, the Libra teen will be sought after to settle disputes and to ease difficult situations. They are good at this because they will do anything to avoid confrontation. So, if you are looking for someone to fight your corner, it's not likely to be a Libra friend. But if you feel you have been treated unfairly, the Libra teen has your back. Teen Libras' can argue a case for justice. This is the reason teen Libras are often on school committees. They are clear-headed and can settle disputes and articulate student concerns to school authorities/governors.

The Libra teen will probably walk the other way when confronting disputes among other students. Unless they are approached to help settle a dispute. However, if you are a teen reading this or a parent of a Libra teen, acknowledge that life is not always calm and harmonious. Confronting problems, and people making problems sometimes need to be tackled. If you are a Libra, you know this already, because you are nothing if not true to yourself. Having integrity is important to you, not least because when peace is restored, you are at your best.

What Libra Kids Need to Thrive

Bringing up a baby can be a daunting task for parents, especially when dealing with some of the more difficult traits inherent in your child. However, most of us survive being practiced when we were children, and there is plenty of advice for new parents. By studying the astrological sign under which your child is born, you are gaining some knowledge about how your Libra child might respond in any circumstance. There are many things that children need to develop and thrive so that as little kids, they grow to be sometimes kids so big you will be looking up to them. Below is a list of what the Libra child needs so they thrive throughout their childhood, adolescence, and teenage years.

• Libra is an Air sign, so they are sociable little things. This sociability will last throughout their developing years if they are encouraged to express themselves. They should be read to from quite an early age as they are likely to be early talkers.

• Your Libra child will be adaptable and will not mind sudden changes in routine if it is explained to them what is happening. Libra's sign is Cardinal, so they are more than happy to experience new things.

• Libra teens are often attractive youngsters who can attract the wrong sort of friends. It is important to recognize that the Libra teen can be a little gullible, so ensure that they feel at ease discussing their personal life with you and know that you will not judge them. The Libra teen hates confrontation, so when the unsuitable friend arrives on the scene, you need to ensure you don't make a scene. This will likely be perceived as unfair by the Libra teen so tread carefully around the subject of unsuitable boy/girlfriends.

• Ensure that your Libra child is given the opportunity to thrive in activities that utilize their creativity. Encourage dance classes for Libra boys and girls. Get to them to take an interest in educational pursuits outside of schools such as nature walks and stargazing. Young Libras have curious minds. Make sure they have an intellectual stimulus.

• Maybe you think your Libra child in vain, and this is not an altogether positive aspect of the Libra personality. Educate your young Libra in recognizing that too much introspection is not always a good thing. They need to be also taught that beauty is not everything. Your teenage daughter, for example, maybe obsessed with her body weight. As a parent, you need to discuss this aspect of your daughter's personality. Since the Libra is open to a critical evaluation, a grownup discussion about how this obsession does not make for a calm and harmonious life may be all that is required.

• Libra children will rarely be found on the supermarket floor, screaming for candies they are denied. They are calm and bidding. This can be a burden for them as they grow up. Inoffensive children are often offended easily by an inadvertent remark or a perceived slight. Watch out for this as Libra children can stumble in their confidence building if they carry around others' criticisms. They are not good at dealing with criticism, especially as their aim in life is to make others happy. Encourage your Libra child to be open with about their feelings. This will help you to point them in the right direction and take away unnecessary anxiety.

• Begin early when teaching you Libra child about money. Even as children, they squander their pocket money on bright and pretty items, they assure you they desperately need. The money will burn a hole in their wallets, so pocket money issues must be handled carefully so the child develops respect for the money they are given. You should teach your Libra child about money because as they grow, you will notice they are more interested in the beauty in the world, like a fresh flower or a beautiful painting. With minds like butterflies, they will dart from one lovely thing to another. Money is unimportant to them, so teenagers are likely to squander hard-earned dollars they make from their part-time jobs on music and clothes and forget to save for the future.

Chapter 8: The Libra in Love

Libra and Aries

Air and Fire are powerful elements when that come together. There are sparks – combustion. This relationship will be passionate and intense. On the one hand this elemental chemistry can create a fire that burns intensely forever. But it can burn itself out. This is the same whether Libra is a man and Aries the woman, or vice versa. Whether this love match will survive is written in the stars. If it survives, the differences between their two personalities it will be a match made in heaven.

Libra and Taurus

This is an important match to notice. The Libra and Taurus are looking for the right person to share their lives with and when they find that person, love with grow and likely will be "til death do us part". Both signs are easy going and both strive for harmony in their lives. Both star signs are ruled by Venus so love will be deep and lasting. Taurus is stubborn so complements Libra indecisiveness.

Both instinctively seek tranquility in their lives, but Taurus may find Libra's breezy attitude to life a little irritating as the Bull sign is determined and steady. As a love match, they are near enough perfect. So long as they work out their small differences, and they will be small. Libra and Taurus are likely to live happily ever after.

Libra and Gemini

Both Libra and Gemini have intellectual personalities. Libra (the scales) is honest and true which balances some insecurities in Gemini. Initial attraction from the viewpoint of the Libra is the clever repartee of the Gemini. Libra will fall for wit every time. Both these signs have defined personalities that tend not to change much throughout their lives. One of these personality traits is their capacity to go with the flow and adapt to change when necessary or desired.

Both signs can lead and neither shows much concern about which one does the leading. A sticking point in this love match might be that Libra's indecisiveness starkly contrasts with Gemini's trait of staying with a decision once it is made. However, Libra's adaptability will likely override this, and should they remain together, they will make a formidable twosome that no one can out asunder.

Libra and Cancer

Cancer and Libra are often attracted to each other immediately. Both signs are looking for love and romance. For the Cancer, finding a romantic partner is sometimes awkward since they are a little insecure when it comes to turning on the charm. However, Libra has enough charm for the two on them. While not as out-going and sociable as Libra: Cancer men and women are rather shy, Libra, being astute and analytical will determine the difference between being shy and standoffish and will guide the relationship in the way both parties want it to go. Libra and Cancer will openly demonstrate affection for each other.

Both signs adore having attention lavished upon them by each other, so relationship bonds will become very secure. The challenge within this pairing is that neither sign responds well to conflict: Libra being indecisive when angry, and Cancer unable contain their anger. Thus, a simple conflict can turn into an "all out" war. Providing both signs can adjust and iron out their differences the bonds of love will remain forever close.

Libra and Leo

Cancer and Libra are often attracted to each other immediately. Both signs are looking for love and romance. For the Cancer, finding a romantic partner is sometimes awkward since they tend to be a little insecure when it comes to turning on the charm. However, Libra has enough charm for the two on them. While not as out-going and sociable as Libra: Cancer men and women tend to be rather shy, Libra, being astute and analytical will determine the difference between being shy and standoffish and will guide the relationship in the way both parties want it to go. Libra and Cancer will openly demonstrate affection for each other.

Both signs adore having attention lavished upon them by each other, so relationship bonds will become very secure. The challenge within this pairing is that neither sign responds well to conflict: Libra being indecisive when angry, and Cancer unable contain their anger. Thus, a simple conflict can turn into an "all out" war. Providing both signs can adjust and iron out their differences the bonds of love will remain forever close.

Libra and Virgo

Virtually living next door to each other, these two signs can't really fail when they decide to form a love match. They are compatible. Libra is Air and Virgo is earth – the perfect balance. However, there is a whole lot of sky between and this is the space in which differences occur. Both signs hate confrontation and so tend to run-away from simmering resentment rather than facing it. However, since neither wishes to pursue arguments, fights usually end with a kiss and make-up and both are prepared to move on with their lives: sweeping disagreement under the carpet. When Earth and Air mingle, magic happens, especially in bed. Love making is essential in this love match with each knowing what the other wants.

However, both signs have a rather lazy demeanor at times, and this is no good for either of them. It can be concluded that while Libra and Virgo will be attracted to one another, they do not always bring the best out in each other.

Libra and Libra

Not surprisingly Libra and Libra will have much in common and share the same personality traits. But does this make them compatible in love? Well, because of their caring natures, and the desire to make those around them happy then this is indeed a good love match because they will care for each other.

Both signs tend to have impeccable behavior traits with sexual compatibility and will learn from each other what makes for a loving intimate relationship, each knowing the boundaries and personal protocols of the other. Chatting into the early hours of the morning, snuggled up in bed is one of Libra/Libra's favorite pastimes. This love match will demonstrate great love for each other and hold each other in great esteem. Will this love match last forever? It is hard to guess with this pairing because while they are made for each other, they have one major flaw reflected between the two.

Libra must be able to trust the people they are with. If that is broken, whether perceived or real the relationship may become broken forever. Provided that trust issues can be put to bed, this pairing has the potential to last forever.

Libra and Scorpio

This is not a love match that usually works well. It does have great potential providing that each is prepared to discuss issues and agree to disagree. Generally, this love match is grounded in respect rather than chemistry. Scorpio has defined individualistic personality traits compared to Libra's more easy-going approach to life. But Libra and Scorpio can make a formidable two-some Libra's balanced approach to life compliments Scorpio's more insecure aspects of their personality. Libra brings stability into Scorpio's life and what cements this relationship is their mutual love expressions of love in the bedroom. This love match make great lovers, contributes to an enduring match.

Outside of the bedroom it may be a different story with both signs wanting to control the way their lives are progressing. Each may find the other a little too controlling and over-bearing. Scorpio is a little insecure and this makes for the potential to be jealous. Libra will not tolerate jealous and dominating behavior so for the match to work, it maybe that Scorpio must be guided by the balance that Libra offers.

Libra and Sagittarius

The chances of forming a lasting relation is high when this pair get together. Libra (Air) and Sagittarius (Fire) means this is a love match based on passion hard to extinguish once ignited. These two signs have a lot in common, but their differences are valanced out which suits both Libra and Sagittarius. Libra is deeply attracted to star signs caring and who love to around people. Sagittarius has these traits in abundance.

The Archer recognizes the need for justice in the world so will live by the scales of justice, making a love match one that will endure. Being next door neighbors on the Zodiac chart Libra and Sagittarius have much in common, the latter responding well to Libra's laid-back attitude to life. Sagittarius likes excitement and is a mini hurricane, so having Libra to calm the eye of the storm makes good sense. Sagittarius loves to live in the moment, can be impulsive and even reckless. Libra does not respond well to this as they desire stability in their love match.

Sagittarius can also be thoughtless in their criticisms, testing Libra's equilibrium. This two-some should take things slow to begin with before committing to a long-term relationship. They need to get to know their partner first, otherwise they could be in for a bumpy ride.

Libra and Capricorn

If you know a Capricorn, or you are one yourself, then you will know that people born under this sign are full of energy and drive. They waste no time in striving for what they want from work, love, and marriage. Libra will fall for these traits big time and will invest huge amounts of time in cultivating the relationship. This may not be reciprocated by the goat who tends to be more focused on their own needs.

However, once in a loving relationship Capricorn will likely support his or her Libra partner, providing stability and loyalty. Tis love match have a natural infinity towards each other and in public they present themselves as a hardworking focused two-some. Capricorn is a solid sign that responds to the material things in life. Libra – on the other hand – is aesthetic. This difference can be an irritation in this love match with Capricorn tiring easily of the airy way that Libra breezes through their life.

Sexually, this love match works well, with each sign understanding the other's needs. A critical aspect of this match is that both signs care a great deal about what they themselves look like and how they might look to others. This can make this two-some become distant over time, taking each for granted and focusing their attention on themselves or others. Not renowned for a successful long-haul, these two signs must work hard at making life sweet and its possible, neither sign has the stamina for it.

Libra and Aquarius

This love match will be steady and true. Neither sign wants to rush headlong into relationships and neither sign is impulsive when deciding. Aquarius will fall for Libra for his or her intellect and capacity to have deep and meaningful conversations. Libra will be drawn to Aquarius for the same reasons.

This love match has the potential to be nothing short of beautiful because both signs will desire it to be so. Their home will be artful and beautiful, their love lives balanced and their professional lives intertwined with their leisure activities. Libra and Aquarius are like pieces in a jigsaw that fit. Like in any relationship things don't always fit together perfectly, especially to begin with. Both signs may feel they have met their soul mate, but Libra's penchant for being indecisive and indolent can be a real irritant for Aquarius who is more impulsive and energetic when deciding. Aquarians are fiercely independent signs and are not always happy about Libra's desire for steadiness in their lives.

For this love match to work, and it is worth making the effort, these wrinkles must be ironed out. When it works, this love match will endure because the water carriers' impulsiveness is balanced by the scales careful balancing.

Libra and Pisces

If you are looking for a steady, laid-back, easy love match then this is the ideal pairing. Neither likes confrontations and, so avoid conflict like the plague. Romance is high on the agenda when these two signs find themselves. Each will cherish the love they feel for each other. It is notable that children raised by Libra and Pisces parents will be clam and loving, whatever their star sign.

Pisces lovers are loyal and will shower devotion on their chosen soul mate. Trust forms the cornerstone of an enduring relationship. This easy-going romantic attitude is likely to flourish as time goes by, but as will all pairings there are always irritants that have the potential to blow up the relationship. Both signs are idealistic so when either sign falls below expectations trouble starts. Libra's constant indecisiveness, a strong personality trait in Libra can wear Pisces out.

Those born under the sign of Pisces tend to wallow in self-pity at times and this aspect of their personality will rise when they feel worn down by the breezy way that Libra floats through life. For this love match to flourish, both signs must work hard to mend the fissures bound to appear when balance is disrupted. Both signs will dwell more on perceived slights than on the romance that blossomed when they first met. Both signs must build trust between them if they want their love match to last.

The Teenager in Love

The Libra teen, as discussed in a previous chapter, is complex. On the one hand, Libra teen is vulnerable and easily influenced. But they are indecisive and a little lazy. When exploring first relationships, all these traits come into play. Libra teen sends a great deal of time thinking about love and the opposite sex and may even have a very unrealistic view of what their first relationship will look like.

If you are a Libra teen taking your first steps on the exploration of relationships, the steady indecisive side of your nature must prevail. Your ideal version of love and romance may be hard to find. You are young and on the brink of discovering the adult world. You have old-fashioned ideas about chivalry and loyalty. For the moment, stick with these ideals and they will keep you safe from people who want to take advantage of your loving nature. As you explore new relationships and experience the first pangs of love, you will find life enchanting. Walks in the park, Autumn leaves blowing in the breeze are exciting, hold onto your passions, the landscape may be perfect, but the partner may not be. Use your intellect and logic to make decisions based on sexual attraction and romance.

Adult Relationships

Ruled by Venus, Libra is never happier than when they are in love. Libra loves being in a relationship with all that that entails. When the Libra falls in love, the stars twinkle more brightly, the world is awash with color. Meeting who they believe is their soul mate for the first time in a meeting indelibly written on their hearts. For the Libra man or woman, meeting a new love interest usually occurs at a social gathering such as weddings, night clubs, or festivals. Libra may even strike up relationships in museums or art galleries, meeting someone who is like-minded. Flirty Libra, if they are out to snare, the love of their life will be flirty with people they find attractive, but flirty in a sensual, elegant manner, and this is how Libra uses his or her charms to get who she or he wants.

If a Libra man or woman finds someone they can relate to, they quickly fall in love. This may come as a surprise to the lucky recipient of Libra's love and attention. Depending on what star sign they were born under, it could mean it scares them away, or they are equally attracted and willing to surrender to the love and attention they are receiving from the romantic Libra.

A Libra woman may be indecisive, but, she wants romance and intellectual stimulation. If she gets this, she is likely to be adaptable to the demands of her lover. If you are a woman falling in love with a Libra man, there are things you need to know to take a new relationship to the next level. The Libra man is looking for balance in a relationship, so don't go for the Sandra Bullock zany personality look. Go more for the Jessica Rabbit look immortalized by Kathleen Turner in Who Killed Roger Rabbit? Libra, a man, may well try to change you as that you fit his perfect ideal of harmony and balance.

There is little doubt you will fall for Libra man, and if this is your first real love affair, you will fall big time. He is charming and attentive. Many Libra men and women possess charismatic charm, so two Libras' experiencing first love may proclaim all the old love cliches such as "I knew a first glance he was for me" or "Our eyes met across a crowded room." The list is endless, and the Libra experiences first love will repeat these cliches to anyone who is prepared to hand around long enough to listen.

Libra in marriage/long-term relationships and how their traits influence the relationship.

The compatibility chart above indicates, in brief, which star signs are likely to develop into long-lasting relationships. While Aries and Libra make a good love match on the surface, this pairing is not likely to last, especially if it is a Libra man and Aries woman. This is because Aries partners like to tackle issues as they arise, addressing the nub of the problem immediately and forcibly. Libra hates conflict, so both partners will find these situations, serious or not so serious, unbearable.

Based on their personality traits, Libra men and women make good marriage partners because they will avoid petty disputes, and while they like to lead and take control of situations, they are happy to go along with whatever their partner wants if it keeps them happy. Earlier in this guide, you learned that Libra partners are loyal and very caring, lavishing love and affection on their partners if they, too, are loyal and loving. Libra women often marry Taurus men or Libra men. Libra/Libra combinations are more likely to stay in their relationships for the long haul. Libra women can be manipulating using their charm to get what they want, and this threatens some marriages as partners with more assertive characteristics such as Leo and Taurus will not fall for this tactic for long.

A Quick Guide to Dating a Libra

• Turn up on time for your date. Libra does not like to be left wondering what whether you will turn up or not

• Always dress appropriately. Libra likes stylish clothes and will be affronted by the casual dress on a date

• Court your Libra date romantically. Use the flowers and champagne strategy. If this is beyond your budget, plan a romantic walk along the river or a park. If it is Autumn, she will be smitten.

• Take your Libra date to inspirational venues. Museums, art galleries, and cultural festivals appeal to intellectual Libra.

• Be prepared to engage in deep and meaningful conversations. Libra's date likes conversation.

• When attempting to take your relationship to another level, romance your date elegantly. Libra's date does not go for rough and ready sex.

A Quick Guide for Navigating Relationships

• Remember to hold onto the qualities that first attracted your partner to you. You are loving, caring, intellectual, and your desire to make people happy should not be influenced by people who are toxic or do not have your interests at heart.

• Be open to the personality traits inherent in your partner. They can collide with your lesser positive traits. For example, you do tend to be a little indolent at times, do not let like a like-minded partner reinforce this negative aspect of your character, or you may find you become bored with your passive lifestyles and become bored with each other.

• Be open and honest about your desire for harmony and balance. Most people like this in their partners. But you must also show your partner you easily adapt to change. While they may be afraid to upset your equilibrium because they know this unsettles you, let them know that you are ready to go on that travel adventure he or she always wanted to do, or you are willing to move house if his or her job demands it.

• Don't be obsessive about where things go in your home, because this can be a killer for a relationship if your partner is less than tidy or does not value elegant furnishing as much as you do. Sometimes it doesn't matter if the less than elegant gift his or her mother bought for looks out of place on the window ledge. Just be your usual generous self. Making people happy is your strength.

• Don't be indecisive when it comes to deciding whether your relationship is working or not. If the relationship is not working, then muster up your courage, confront the issue, and end it. This can be particularly difficult for the Libra to do, particularly if your partner is kind and considerate. Use your excellent communication skills to end the relationship. It is not your style to storm out of the house. Confront your demons, tackle the difficult conversation, and leave a broken relationship gracefully.

Chapter 9: The Socializing Libra

The Libra is a social being, always ready to join in with conversations and thrives in the company. So, what is Libra like as a friend? This chapter brings together some of the character traits discussed in previous chapters. For a quick guide to compatibility, see below how Libra interacts with other zodiac signs.

- **Libra/Aries** - Astrological opposites, but Aries are always willing to put up with Libra keeping them waiting because they can't decide what to wear.

- **Libra/Taurus** - This match enjoys traveling together and spending time listening to music.

- **Libra/Gemini** - Great companionship between these star signs, both being conversationalists.

- **Libra/Cancer** - Two different personalities but Libra friend always supportive of Cancer friend's insecurities.

- **Libra/Leo** - Two immensely attractive and glamourous friends who share lots of outdoor pursuits.

- **Libra/Virgo** - Virgo friend's clever mind and organizational qualities compliment Libra friend, especially those people on the cusp, virtually living in the same house, so to speak, because they share many traits in common.

- **Libra/Libra** - This is a chummy relationship that may have been formed as children together. They share the same traits and love all things elegant and graceful.

- **Libra/Scorpio** - Libra loves their devil may care Scorpio friend as it compliments Libra's more cautious outlook on life.

- **Libra/Sagittarius** - Libra will happily accept the more raucous, jokey characteristics because they are fun to be with.

- **Libra/Capricorn** - This makes for a rather difficult friendship but will enjoy traveling together to exotic locations and cultural adventures.

- **Libra/Aquarius** - This is a friendship based on Libra talking and Aquarius listening. It is a friendship based on companionship.

- **Libra/Pisces** - Pisces intuition suits Libra temperament, as Pisces friend always willing to listen to Libra's ideas.

Party Time for Libras

There are few Libras who refuse an invitation to go to a party, whether it is a girl's night out, a family or friend's wedding, or a night out that turns into a party. And what about those parties you and your friends gate crash? How Libra party girls or boys interact socially is usually based on their character traits, both positive and negative, which have been discussed in previous chapters.

- **Birthday Parties**

    Who doesn't like a birthday party? Well, there are some, but not the Libra, who is Mr. or Miss Sociability. If you are Libra, you will relate to this scenario. First things first. What gift should you buy for your best friend's birthday party. Oh, decisions, decisions. Libra man may just go to the nearest jewelry store and pick out an elegant bracelet or watch. The decision may come from whether it is a watch or a bracelet.

For Libra girl, this is a different story. What to buy your best friend. She loves funky ornaments, but has she got too many of these. On the other hand, should you buy her something to wear? You know her well enough to choose something she will like. Choosing gifts for friends and family is not one of Libra's strong points. Being indecisive can mean you buy something on impulse and pray it will be ok in the end.

Then there is what to wear. You have been considering this for weeks, maybe months. You are not one to wear the same thing twice, so although you have a closet full of beautiful party wear, you need something special. Usually, your friends know this dilemma you put yourself through, so they will always be willing to go shopping with you. But they do so secretly hoping they can force you into buying something, anything, so you will stop talking about it.

Libra girl is a little vain, so it will likely be one of the last to arrive at the party. However, if you know a Libra girl, you will know that she will turn up elegant and eye-catching. Libra girls like to wear dramatic outfits for parties. Cool symmetrical lines are the trademark look for a Libra. Black and white is a favored look for Libra, which she knows will always turn heads. Those who may be attracted to Libra girls may find themselves up for a challenge in a party environment. Getting this girl's attention for long enough to express your interest will be hard.

Libra girls at a party will gravitate to people engaged in conversations. If you are Libra, you will relate to the scenario in which they always appear to be an interesting conversation going on in another room, usually the kitchen, so you are often torn between dancing and drinking and moving into the kitchen to join in the conversation.

Never a shrinking violet, Libra will surround herself with people ready to chat, dance, or generally delve into other people's conversations, invited or otherwise. As the Libra girl is usually the last to arrive at a party, she will generally be the last to leave. Afraid she might miss some interesting conversation, she will linger in the kitchen to help with the cleanup. Only then will she turn her attention to the opposite sex, one or two of whom may have been hanging around waiting for Libra girl to come up for air. Do not be fooled by this air of distraction, because Libra girl probably has had you in her sights all evening.

• The Wedding Guest

Libra girl is fabulous at wedding parties. If you are a friend or lover, you can trust them to behave impeccably on such a formal occasion. She will expect her escort to be impeccably dressed as she herself will be. The rules of engagement for buying the wedding gift is much the same as above. If you are Libra, you will know the feeling of relief when the bride or groom presents you with a present wedding list. What to wear is another story altogether. However, friends of Libra girls who are also invited to the wedding know that she will arrange shopping expeditions so they can decide what to wear.

Libras are desirable guests at weddings, especially if they are close friends of the bride or groom. He or she will be called upon the calm the nerves of the anxious star of the show. As a Libra yourself, you may have experienced having to calm the ruffled feathers of the bride when she decides that, she doesn't love her husband-to-be, so the wedding is off. This is where Libra girl comes into her own. A skilled negotiator and diplomat, Libra girl, can cajole the nervous bride, make her laugh with funny anecdotes about their adventures together, and altogether restore harmony. Libras enjoy weddings. They like the opportunity to dress elegantly and the love the pomp and circumstance.

Libras particularly enjoy an outdoor wedding because they appeal to Libra's sense of harmony with nature. The balance seems to the right for the occasion: joining two people on the cusp of a new life. Surrounded by swathes of flowers, music, and fine wines, what more could Libra ask for. Sharing romantic occasions such as this with another libra is just the perfect way to socialize.

- **Party All Night**

From an early age, Libras have been social animals. They will have a large circle of friends whom they go out and about. Girly nights in and out are a favored leisure activity for Libra girls. Usually surrounding themselves with like-minded souls, Libra girls are not so much interested in cruising around town looking for a date, but they are more interested in socializing with their friends. While they are romantic love dinners and elegant cocktail events, Libra likes to share her passion for witty conversations, intellectual discussion, and trying out fancy restaurants. But a Libra girl is adaptable. This may be a challenge for her friends, especially those born under the sign of Cancer who may feel unsettled with their Libra friend's penchant for being undecided about how to spend the evening.

Friends of the Libra will not be surprised when arrangements are changed at the last minute or when the venue morphs into something different. Even given that Libra may have taken ages to dress appropriately for dinner at a fancy restaurant with friends, he or she is just as likely to be influenced into moving on from the restaurant to join other friends at a karaoke party, whether she is in formal wear or not. The prospect of listening to music and even singing herself is attractive to the sociable Libra, who feels at home in large groups of friends.

Having a Libra friend can be frustrating and perplexing. This gracious, elegant, socialite Libra, can easily become embroiled in a less than salubrious situation because she has been attracted to the charm of an admirer. Fortunately, loyal friends from all every zodiac sign who are more than willing to take care of the person who usually takes care of them.

Libra's as Friends

Libra people make friends easily. While being a little undecided at first, once Libra feels comfortable with his or her companion, friendship is bound to follow. Libra friends are also loyal and will likely be the one who keeps a friendship alive. He or she will maintain the friendship by texting, staying in contact on social media, and working out arrangements to meet up with friends. The Libra will keep their concerns to themselves about how much of the friendship is down to their commitment rather than their friend's. Ever striving for balance and harmony, Libra will strive to keep friendships alive.

Many people are attracted to Libra's personality. Libra has friends from all walks of life and will generally forgive most weaknesses in their close friends. The Libra girl will make friends by being attentive and at ease with new acquaintances. She is drawn to grace and dignity, so she will avoid more raucous personalities. Friendship groups are often formed from within the social activities Libra is attracted to, such as hiking clubs, art classes, and book clubs. Libra is not fond of being alone for long lengths of time, so she will actively look for opportunities to socialize, even though she may take forever to choose the right outfit for her hiking trip or visit a music festival.

Libra makes friends easily because she is extrovert by nature and will make new acquaintances feel at ease. Always willing to try new adventures, Libra will be exciting to be with and fun at formal and informal parties. If you have a Libra friend, you will know that it is she who will introduce to new experiences: the hike along the Appalachian Trail, ride, or the camper across America. She is just as likely to introduce you to a new movie or the latest bestselling novel. She only wants to make you happy. Once you realize this, then you can trust your Libra friend to be there for you for the long haul. Libra is a curious being, open-minded to a fault, always ready for a new adventure that should embark on with elegance and style.

When making new friends, Libra will look for open-minded people who are trustworthy and real. Libra hates superficiality. She doesn't trust it, and this makes people a little wary of Libra. Her intellect always comes to them when she meets people for the first time. She will be curious about your background, your likes and dislikes, and what your values amount to. For some star signs such as Capricorn, this may be just too much to handle. Not renowned for conversational skills, Capricorn dislikes this inquiry if it seems too intrusive.

A diplomacy is often a tool that Libra uses when making new friends. They are good listeners even though they like to talk about themselves a lot. They can see both sides of the coin, and this makes for interesting conversations. People who meet Libras for the first time are usually attracted to this characteristic because it indicates that the Libra is listening to them. Thus, men are often attracted to Libra women without knowing why. Diplomacy also comes into play when Libra socializes in a group. She wants to keep everyone happy, so she will steer conversations away from contentious issues that might create tension in the group. Again, this is a characteristic that draws people to them, and which makes it easier for the Libra to strike up new friendships.

How to Sustain a Libra Friendship

A social butterfly, Libra is always happy when her friends surround her. Don't try to tie your Libra friend down to an exclusive friendship, as this greatly upsets her equilibrium. Libra may have a small circle of friends or a wide friendship group, but she will favor them all equally and would never be happy when a friend tries to come between her and her other friends. Libra's quest for harmony and justice will ensure that all her friends are treated with respect and loyalty.

Remember that your Libra friend will all take the high road in debates and on issues important to her. She will always think things through before making decisions, and while this can be irritating for some star signs, Aries friends cope very well with this trait in their Libra friend. This indecision is not a weakness, although it is seen by many as being just that. It's just a desire to ensure that justice is served, and she has arrived at a fair conclusion.

Libra loves to debate, so if you want to foster your friendship with a Libra, remember there is never a simple answer to a Libra and the likelihood you must sit down and listen to a lecture on something that is dear to Libra heart is ever-present. Libra is also generous with her time, money, and knowledge with her friends. She or he has a huge heart, and if you are a friend, then she sees you as a worthy friend.

Libra girl will turn to you when she wants to share news, recipes, clothes, and plans. She won't share her boyfriend with you, but she will share most everything else. This is Libra's Achilles heel. Often Libra's generosity makes her vulnerable to those who would take advantage of her kind nature. Just as she is prepared to fight your corner, you must be prepared to fight hers. Being a friend to a Libra is a rewarding experience and one likely to last a lifetime.

Chapter 10: Libra at Work

Careers

There is no shortage of professions suitable for the Libra intellect and temperament. A look at seasonal changes and celestial movement suggests that the yearly cycle influences how a Libra will fare in their professional journey. As always, the Libra looks for balance in their lives, and starting a new job at the beginning of the year makes good sense to them. In some respects, this is a typical response because the new year (January 1st) suggests resolution, and this is something that Libras are a little short of. Indecision can lose Libra's many job opportunities. Always ready to make fundamental changes in their life as with a change in job, the Libra will want to take every opportunity to find balance.

A new job, a new year resolution, a new opportunity with the chance to make new friends and experience something different. Another important aspect of changing jobs at the beginning of the year is that if things don't go well, there is plenty of opportunities to find something else. January, February, and March are very productive months and tend to be when businesses look at staffing issues. Professions begin to take stock of their human resources, and new businesses make a dramatic entrance. This is the reason "startups" are around the first three months of the new year. As a Libra, instinctively recognize this cycle of events, so don't be indecisive. If the opportunity arises for a change of job, then follow your instincts and go for it.

April, May, and June should see your creative job or business begin to take root. It is spring. The seeds you planted in January should now be breaking through. It's time to take a break and assess how the first half of the year has worked out for you. Being a creative person, you are likely to keep a professional journal. The springtime is the best time to go back over the past six months and decide what works for you and what doesn't.

Libra has an analytical mind, so this will probably be a natural part of your professional life. If you are in a caring profession, keeping a professional development journal will be like second nature. Reflection is a big part of Libra's overall character. Makes people assume this that Libra's are indecisive. Reflecting on the first part of your year, whether in a new job or not, is crucial for Libra equilibrium. They will want to balance the year out and they will want to ensure that the decisions they made earlier in the year, as difficult as some were, will bear fruit. Keeping a journal will also indicate to you where there are opportunities to enhance your career, whether through promotion or taking on more clients. Around this time is a good time to consider the expansion of premises or a reduction in staff. Libra will want to keep all staffers happy and feeling secure, so regular assessments are important.

July, August, and September are complicated months for many Libra professionals. It is a Vacation period for many, and school is out for summer. For those in the caring professions such as medicine or nursing, the Libra experience differs from Libras in teaching professions, for example. The wide-open spaces may call the adventurous Libra, but work will come first for some, which can be frustrating. Just when you need to recharge your batteries and evaluate your progress, the summer period can be exhausting and stressful, with seasonal weather changing people's attitudes and affecting character traits.

For many Libras it is the silly season when distractions abound, and your butterfly instincts upset your equilibrium. This is the time to recognize your ruling planet's impact and how the equinox can impact decision making. Whether your work steps up during these months or not, it is time to stake stock and to draw on your positive characteristics. It is tiring to ensure that your staff/students (fill in the blank) are achieving their goals and are happy. By September, be doing things to make yourself happy too.

By the time October, November, and December arrive, Libra working woman and man will feel charitable. If things have not gone well this year, Libra will look on the bright side. Using their logical and evaluative skills, Libra's generosity will manifest itself in giving to local causes and charitable organizations. Because Libra is a little indecisive, Libra professionals will be looking to organize holiday vacations for themselves and their workers. Everyone loves Libra bosses and Libra colleagues in November and December as Libra natural good surfaces to ensure the holiday season is happy for everyone. Libra's open-handed generosity is never more evident than at Christmas time when the time of giving balances out the scales is providing harmony and goodwill.

Libra Career Paths

- **Doctor** - Doctors take the Hippocratic oath to care for people and do them no harm

- **Psychologist** - Skilled communicators with an evaluative mind

- **Architect** - Perfect choice for Libra who appreciates designs that tell a story and blend in with the environment

- **Nurse** - The caring profession is perfect for the Libra

- **Fashion Designer** - Good design and impeccable taste is a dominant Libra trait

- **Engineering** - The Libra intellect and logic makes engineering a perfect choice

- **Veterinarian** - Caring is the name of the game here, whether animal or human.

- **Lawyer** - Diplomacy and a strong sense of justice is symbolic of Libra

- **Scientist** – The Libras curious mind and analytical skills make science professions a perfect match

- **Doctor of Philosophy** - Forever curious about the world, whether religion, politics, history or literature, this profession draws in many Libras

- **Musician** - Libras adore music and to choose it as a profession is every musical Libra's dream.

- **Teacher** - Libra likes nothing better than sharing their knowledge and experience.

- **Artist** - Whether as an amateur or professional, this is a popular choice for Libras

- **Writer** - Creativity is a dominant feature of the Libra personality, so whether, writer or poet, Libras find their home in this profession.

8 Professionals and Their Star Signs

Name	Profession	Strengths
Bruce Springsteen	Musician	Dedication, creative storytelling
Oscar Wilde	Writer	Aesthetic, artistic, communicator
Christopher Wren- British Architect (1832 – 1723) Also astronomer and anatomist	Architect	Logical, intellectual, curios mind
James Lind - Scottish doctor who discovered that citrus fruit cures scurvy (1716 – 1794)	Doctor	Analytical, caring, curious
Alfred Nobel - Swedish (1801 - 1872) Invented dynamite - Nobel Prize named after him	Scientist	Passivist, Inventor, logical curious mind
Ralph Lauren	Fashion Designer	Artistic, ambitious, leader, creative
Michel Foucault (1926 0 1984)	Philosopher	Curious, intellectual, hard- working, stylish
Sunny Hostin (Senior legal correspondent for ABC News	Lawyer	Ambitious, hard-working, intellectual, strong sense of Justice

Libra in the Workplace

Not unexpectedly, the Libra worker is calm and works best when there is harmony in the workplace. Their stable temperament means they will rarely get into arguments at work. Neither will they be drawn into industrial disputes unless there is a clear case of injustice and then they will be prepared to lead a revolt. In the everyday affairs of the organization, Libra will not make waves. Unlike their Cancer colleges, they will not burst into tears at the slightest criticism, but they will feel it deeply and dwell on criticism silently for a long period.

Within the organization itself, the Libra will have to take positions such as front-of-house or service and complaints counters. They are clear-headed and diplomatic, so customer complaints services are good roles for Libra employees. Libras make good receptionists and are loyal workers to their bosses. Libras shine at jobs such as doctor's receptionists and appointment secretaries where a cool head and diplomacy are crucial. Libras invariably know the right things to say and do when tempers get heated, so they are often relied upon to deal with awkward or angry customers. Friendly and approachable Libra can be an asset in an office environment or in a role where they are representing the firm. In public relations roles, they are superb. Employers tend to recognize Libra tact and diplomacy when they see it and usually use them to organize events and business meetings with VIPs.

Libra is bipartisan at work and does not favor one person over another. They are open and friendly to everyone. This makes them a little bit of a bad bet if someone is looking for an ally at work. Balance forms the basis of the Libra personality in the workplace, and they will likely be instrumental in pouring oil on troubled waters when tempers get heated at work. The Libra desk will be organized and beautified. Tasteful, personal items will be on display on the Libra desk, with artful prints lining office walls if the Libra has an office or workstation to themselves. This makes an interesting comparison to the Leo worker, who is likely to be more over the top with office décor. But both Libra and Leo enjoy luxury, so they will probably share ideas about home and office décor.

The Libra Employee

The Libra hates gossip, so it will not be found gossiping in the photocopying room or the around the water-cooler. It is not so much that Libra is not curious about the people he or she works with. When occasionally they fall prey to the influence of a gossipy co-worker, the sense of secret camaraderie is appealing to them. However, gossip makes Libra feel uncomfortable. Sneaking around discussing other people behind their backs disturbs their equilibrium and does not appeal to their sense of fair play.

Libra's strength in the workplace is their ability to organize events. This is where you will likely find Libra, busy organizing venues, and collecting donations from co-workers to pay for the little extras that will add style and luxury to the event. Libra enjoys the challenge of organizing social events, partly because they are extrovert social butterflies themselves, but also because it allows them to spread a little happiness among the workforces. It is possible, too, that indecisive Libra will wander around different venues for weeks ahead of the event simply because they can't decide which venue might be most appropriate.

While Libra is a social being, they are comfortable in their own company when working. However, unfortunately, for Libra, they are easily distracted when spending long periods working alone. Homeworking is not the most welcome job for the Libra, because they like the busy office or workplace's social aspects. Therefore, Libra can be easily seduced away from their desk with promises of lunch with co-workers or pleas for help with other workers' projects. This aspect of Libra's personality can make Libra seem lazy because they sometimes miss deadlines because other things have captured their attention. However, in general, Libra is likely to work hard to meet deadlines because an agreement is an agreement and should be taken seriously.

Libra fits into a busy working environment very easily. Because they are adaptable, you will likely find the Libra engaged in multi-tasking in different office jobs. Quite at home talking to clients, they are equally happy running errands for busy co-workers. Where you will not find the Libra is in the manager's office complaining. Libra will turn a blind eye to petty disputes in the office and is likely not to complain to the boss. Instead, Libra is apt to dwell on conflict and internalize perceived slights, which can cause them stress.

Notwithstanding their desire for harmony and calm in their surroundings, Libra can be found in the union office if they believe that injustice exists in the workplace. Libra's strong sense of justice and fair play overrides their distaste for confrontation. Libra can be found in unio meetings and demonstrations. Prepared to risk imbalance in their lives, Libra's caring nature comes to the fore when supporting those facing injustice.

Libra can also be found in the workplace restroom, not simply to eat lunch or take a break but to co-workers. Colleagues need to distinguish between gossip and simulating conversation when they spend time with the Libra. Libra is sociable, and even at work, will look for ways to spend time chatting. This can be a weakness in the Libra make-up. Libra will often rush back work, having been distracted by friends or colleagues over lunch.

Timekeeping is not something that Libra is good at. Getting ready for work will take Libra ages because this star sign pays particular attention to what they look like. Taking a few extra minutes looking in the mirror when they are already late for work is a big fault of Libras. People born under the sign of the scales, while appearing bright and breezy, with a carefree attitude, spend quite a lot of time rushing from one place to another because they are late.

Challenges in the Workplace

Timekeeping is not the only challenge that Libra faces in the workplace. Numerous obstacles can make Libra scales tip in the wrong direction. Libra is impulsive. This can cause problems in workplace relationships, especially if the Libra is in a management role.

For example, impulsive behavior can be dashing off emails without thinking things through first. Ironically, thinking through things is a Libra strength much sought after in the workplace, but unfortunately, impulsive behavior is also balanced against this strength. Libra is yin/yang, and this is evident in Libra's capacity to be impulsive. Deciding based on impulse may not be a regular occurrence for Libras in the workplace, but true to Libra extrovert nature, when it happens, it can be unsettling for everyone involved.

Libra indecision is a dominant trait in the Libra character. Ina busy workplace being indecisive can be a huge disadvantage. This inability to make quiet or timely decisions is not based on Libra's ability to act quickly, but it is more to do with needing to think about how an action could have an undesirable outcome for colleagues or the company. Close work colleagues will accept that Libra will be undecided about things, but, patience can be tested when a decision is needed immediately. Libra will hesitate, and this can be worrisome. Libras will not be attracted to jobs in which decisions rest upon their shoulders because Libra is nothing if not logical. They will be aware that certain roles will not suit them, so they tend to accept that they will not make good brokers and could never see themselves working on the stock market.

Libra chattiness is one of their most endearing attributes. No one has to ability to make people feel comfortable and accepted than sociable Libra. However, this can be a huge obstacle in the workplace. Libra finds it hard not to be talkative. Both men and women Libras are great conversationalists and will endeavor to discuss anything they are curious about or have ideas about. Time stands still for the Libra when they deep in conversation, and this is a weakness in a busy workplace. Never one to say two words when fifty will do, colleagues, are often faced with long emails and conversations they cannot extricate themselves from. Time wasting for the Libra usually entails having too many long conversations or chats with colleagues.

Boredom is a weakness of Libra. The workplace is an obvious environment for boredom to manifest in Libra's day. Restless for stimulation, Libra will become easily distracted when bored and will find it easy to drift off into a world of their own. Libra likes to be stimulated most of the time. They will look for ways to relieve boredom at work. Often, they will listen to music on earphones or browse the internet. This makes Libra look lazy. In many respects, it can be said that a characteristic weakness of the Libra is indolence. Again. This is the complexity of Libra and balancing scales. Libra is hardworking, creative, and productive, but when there is little to stimulate their intellect, they become bored and lazy. This is a challenge for Libra in the work environment, and they are often caught out losing concentration and not focusing on the work at hand.

Tips for the Libra Worker

Recognizing one's character traits is a desirable attribute. When we recognize our strengths and weaknesses, we can better achieve success in our lives. This is important in the workplace because by developing our strengths and addressing our weaknesses, we become better workers and are more likely to be promoted or given more responsibility and thus more pay. Successful people play to their strengths, and the previous chapters have demonstrated how those born under the sign of Libra can recognize their strengths and develop them. In the workplace, Libra can strengthen the positive aspects of their characters by reflecting on their weakness and addressing them. Below are useful tips to improve Libra's work experiences and improve their earning power.

• Daily Routine

Libra requires stability in the workplace. Developing a productive routine will help Libra to feel in control. Employ your leadership skills to delegate tedious and repetitive jobs if that is possible. Overwork or disorderly routines will distract you from your work and inhibit your creativity. Get up early to begin your daily work routine. Ensure that you allow plenty of time to get ready and arrive at work on time. Try to get work clothes ready the evening before to avoid indecision about what to wear if you do not have to wear a uniform. Take regular breaks when you can get so you do not get distracted or bored. Routine, once accomplished, will ensure that you have a balanced work-life that is creative and productive.

• Communication Techniques

Libras do not lack in communication skills, but these skills should be used in a productive manner. As a good communicator and listener, you will have a head start in perfecting these skills. Do not get distracted when you converse with colleagues. Stick to the topic and do not allow others to steer you away from the matters at hand.

As a Libra, you are easily influenced by other people's opinions, and this makes you indecisive. Stay focused and make proper time for important conversations. Keep emails strictly to the point. Workers rarely have the time or the energy to wade through long emails. Because of your natural ability to write, you can get carried away when writing emails or speaking on the telephone. For a more productive working day, reduce the time spent on lengthy emails and wandering conversations.

• Creative Outlets

Use your creative instincts in the workplace. Evaluate how creative applications can improve your environment and make the working environment more pleasant for yourself and your co-workers. When working on projects, allow your natural creative instincts to come to the foreground. Many Libras work in creative industries, so their passion for art and writing or music can be utilized to their best advantage.

In an environment where creativity is lacking, think about how you can improve your space. If you share space with other people, discuss how you can bring a little more harmony and beauty into your environment. This can be done by getting rid of discarded items that clutter the workspace and replacing it with a more attractive classical objects easy on the eye and appeal to your sense of balance. Libra workers are renowned for bringing a little tranquility into a chaotic work environment.

Chapter 11: What Does the Libra Need to Live a Rewarding Life?

Over the course of this guidebook, you have been introduced to the world of Libra and his and er characteristics. Bringing all the Libra traits together and using a series of bullet points, this chapter discusses what Libra needs to be happy and productive.

- **Romance**

Into every Libra, life must fall a little tenderness and romance. Libra women and men thrive when they are loved and admired. The Libra needs to know they are loved and cherished. Thus, Libra woman needs a partner who will wine and dine her and smoother her with love and attention. Just watch the Libra woman grow in confidence when she feels secure and happy.

The Libra will find romance not just in a loving partner but in the books she or he reads, in the music she listens to, and in the cities she visits. As the saying goes, love is everywhere, and Libra knows this. For those people who know and love a Libra, never underestimate their need for attention. What Libra needs after a hard day at work is stimulating conversation, a loving kiss, and maybe romantic fun in the bedroom.

Friends are an important part of the romance that Libras seek. Watching romantic films together, wandering around romantic locations may be taking photographs or just watching the sun go down. For the Libra, friends are as important as lovers in bringing beauty and inspiration into their orbit. With Venus as Libra's ruling planet, love and affection extended to friends, family, and lovers.

- **Stability**

Libra was born under the sign of the scales, and stability is an important need. When the scales are balanced, and everything is weighted evenly, then Libra is settled and calm. Libra will seek stability in relationships and in the workplace. Unable to deal with confrontation, Libra will walk away from volatile relationships. Conflict is not part of their make-up. Even as children, Libras will require order and stability and will not take kindly to harsh words. In the Libras world, all things are equal, or they should be.

If you are a Libra's friend, you need to be a steady friend and not blow hot and cold. Libra needs to know that you can be relied upon when she needs your support. Many Libras have friends they have known since childhood, and they are ones who they will turn to for companionship. Stable friendships contribute to a Libras equilibrium. You know as a Libra friend he or she will not expect you to be at their beck and call. They are independent beings and want you to be too. However, they do expect you to be steady in your friendship.

If you are a Libra lover, he or she is looking for a stable lifestyle set for the long-haul. Stability for the Libra means she knows where stands and what is expected of her. She also understands that her indecisive butterfly whims and fancies are part of her make-up, and she doesn't want to be changed into something that you want rather than what she wants.

• Adventure

Libra is always looking for adventure. Impulsive and intuitive, Libra recognizes the need to brush the dust off her heels and see the world. No bedroom slippers for the Libra. The great outdoors attracts both Libra men and women. As an Air sign, Libra has a great love of the beautiful outdoors. Libras need to be free to roam, to meet new friends, and see new places.

Libra has a great sense of adventure, whether it's in far-away countries or in their own back yard. The need to explore does not just relate to the physical world, either. Libra needs to explore the abstract world too. Both Libra women and men have curious minds that find them exploring philosophy and literature. Walking through a museum can hold fascinating insights into the adventures of the past. Libra needs to type of stimulus to thrive and make the most of their world. Exploring relationships is an adventure, too, and other star signs are attracted to Libra simply because they can see the light of curiosity in their eyes when they are first introduced. To know a Libra is to be introduced to many adventures, of the mind, soul, and the natural world. It is abundantly clear to those who know a Libra they need to be inspired, and they need to be stimulated.

If you have a Libra child, you will already know that your little Libra will want to explore the world around them. What adventures lie beyond the pantry door, who lives in the apple tree in the yard, and where do shoes come from? These questions are quaint and often funny. They can even be a little irritating, with the word why constantly on Libra's child's lips. This curiosity needs to be nurtured because the Libra adult will continue to see life as an adventure, to be explored and questioned.

• Friendship

As with other signs of the Zodiac, without friendship, Libras will not thrive. They need companionship like a fish needs water. While they can spend time alone and do so often as they bury themselves in hobbies such as art, literature, and music, sharing life experiences with friends is a particular joy for Libra. Friendship holds a special place in the life of a Libra. This is because Venus influences how a Libra perceives companionship. Love is experienced when loving a friend or an intimate partner. Life is reflected through the eyes of a special friend or lover. Libra will maintain friendships for most of their lives, and this nurtures their souls.

If you have a Libra friend, you will know that you will be included in their lives, but what can be a little disconcerting is that Libra, while valuing friendship highly, is likely to treat all their friends equally and will not play one off against another.

If you are a best friend, then you will have known your Libra for a long time, and a breaking of trust between you would be devastating for you both. Friendships may be a natural, normal occurrence in most people's lives, but for some, friendship is not a priority: family may come first, or a person may prefer their own company. The world does not end because you have few if any, personal friends. This is not the case for Libra. Friends enrich Libra's life, and without them, they will not thrive.

• Loyalty

Astrology informs us that Libras are fiercely loyal. There is nothing superficial about Libra's loyalty, and they need loyalty in return. Libra requires confirmation they have your loyalty, and they expect commitment because if they invest their time, energy, and love in you, they expect it returned in the same measure. This is how Libra balances the scales. Libra will always fight your corner and will never betray your trust. As much as Libra is a social being and loves being around other people, once they have committed to you, it is for keeps.

Libra is not likely to stray from a relationship, and they expect no less from their partner. Libra's flirty nature can be, and often is perceived as disloyalty by jealous partners. This is not the case. Both Libra men and women have an inadvertent sensuality that is part of their charm.

They are not selfish people and love to be liked and admired, but their loyalty to their friends and their partner is without question. Libra has a big heart, and loyalty is a huge slice of how Libra loves. When Libra is betrayed, it is devasting, and they take a long time to recover their equilibrium, so Libras never do. Go gently with Libra, as they are easily hurt. Once in a secure relationship, Libra will remain a loyal partner and go the extra mile to ensure that they are happy. In some respects, it is easy to be loyal to Libra because of their sunny disposition and loving nature.

Conclusion

A Check List

• Libra was born under the sign of the scales, which means they believe in justice and equality and will use their intellectual prowess to fight for fairness in society. Their element is Air, and their ruling planet is Venus. The gemstone that represents their birth is the Opal. Libra's most common traits are honesty, fairness, love of beauty, and a desire for elegance and style in their everyday lives.

• Because of their easy-going nature Libra gets on with most zodiac signs, but Gemini and Aquarius are the most compatible.

• Libra gets on well with people at work but is a chatterbox, often struggling with deadlines.

• Libra is a party animal and a great conversationalist. Libra woman will often turn up late for parties since she is vain and will spend far too much time in front of the mirror getting ready.

• The Libra home is usually well organized and aesthetically pleasing. Libra enjoys decorating and has a love of luxury and style. Libra's furniture will be carefully arranged to achieve balance and harmony.

• Libra strengths: innate elegance, romantic nature, adaptability, aesthetic taste, their adherence to fairness and justice, diplomacy, and loyalty. These strengths make Libra an ideal friend, work colleague, and intimate partner.

• Libra weaknesses: Hesitant and indecisive, afraid of offending people, inadvertently seductive, narcissistic, and weak-willed. Friends, family, and work colleagues will find these weaknesses frustrating and will often lose patience.

• Libra woman is loving, vulnerable, and easily influenced. Her innate elegance and style, making her attractive to both men and women. Libra women will have a creative profession or an intellectual job that requires diplomacy.

• Libra man is a catch for any woman. He is charming, thoughtful, and romantic. Expect the flowers and champagne first date and a devoted husband and father for the long-haul.

• Libra child is sociable and chatty but hates to be left alone to play. Libra child speaks early and enjoys reading and drawing.

• Libra in love is a gift from the gods. They will devote their life to making you happy. They are loyal and committed to a stable relationship.

• Libra is an extrovert so enjoys parties and get-togethers. No matter what the party occasion, Libra will be sociable, and party guests will naturally gravitate towards them.

• Suitable professions for Libra men and women include doctors, scientists, writers, musicians, philosophers, and lawyers. Many famous celebrities bear out the Libra mark of creativity, diplomacy, and leadership.

• Libra needs to be needed. Both Libra men and women thrive on love and attention. Love is the cornerstone of Libra's temperament. They are big-hearted and spend their lives making other people happy.

Part 8: Scorpio

The Ultimate Guide to an Amazing Zodiac Sign in Astrology

Introduction

Astrology is important, and it's amazing how much insight you can find about your life from studying the way the stars affect your day-to-day choices. It has helped many people figure out why they act the way they do and what to do about it. I should know — I've enjoyed the benefit of understanding astrology for most of my life.

With astrology, you can finally get to know and understand the people around you - not just yourself. It is vital to have this level of understanding about life, allowing us to be more compassionate, loving, and accepting of the people around us at their best and at their worst. The second you become aware of where you stand among the stars, you can no longer go back to how you used to be. It's radically life-changing!

Within the field of astrology, you'll find so many terms that, while poetic, serve to flesh out every bit of the unique individual you are. You get to discover things about yourself you never even noticed about the one person you thought you knew the most: YOU!

In this book, you will discover what it means to be a Scorpio. You'll learn about your strengths, your weaknesses, and how you can take charge and overcome them so that you can be the best Scorpio you can. It might seem weird to most people to think of their lives as patterned after the stars, but the fact is that you are made of star-stuff! The essence of you is the essence of the cosmos. You're a walking, talking, breathing universe all on your own!

You see, astrology goes way beyond just putting all 7 billion-plus people on the planet into 12 boxes and calling it a day. It's so much more than that. Through astrology, you can learn how every single individual has unique needs, while at the same time being almost like everyone else. In other words, astrology can help you discover how we're all different *and the same.*

Since the beginning of time, humans have looked to the stars for wisdom and guidance in their affairs. So, you could say that the practice of astrology is as old as humans. Don't let its age fool you into thinking it is a field of study that is static – or dying because of unchanging ideologies. Often seen in Vedic, Chinese and even Western astrology, this continues evolve and provide new and profound insight as the years go by.

This book is all about the Scorpio zodiac sign of Western astrology. There are many levels to this sign, and as needed, we will veer off into discussing other zodiac signs as they tie in with the Scorpio.

That you're reading this says you're very interested in learning about the mysterious, magnetic Scorpio, because you are one yourself or you have a Scorpio in your life that you'd love to understand better. Well, you're in luck! With this book, you have all you need to know about this wonderful sun sign. Have fun peeling back the Scorpio's many layers!

One last thing: Astrology does not imply in any way, shape, or form that your life is locked in, predestined to be one way, and no way else. It doesn't suggest you are fated or doomed to live out your life on one track, never veering left or right. What astrology is about is helping you discover your strengths and weaknesses, so you can become a much better version of who you are. I'll wrap up this intro with the wise words of Sir Francis Bacon: "The stars do not compel; they impel."

Chapter One: An Introduction to the Scorpio

More often than not, when you hear someone say, "She's a Scorpio," they're talking about the Sun sign. The Sun sign is basically whatever point the Sun is at as it makes its way around the Earth each year, moving through all 12 signs of the zodiac.

In astrology, the Sun is a planet within its own right. It's the most powerful one, and for a good reason: All horoscopes have the Sun as the most influential star when it comes to how you live your life and how people see you. It influences your choices, your motivations, and your reasons for striving to achieve whatever desires you've set for yourself.

The Sun sign gives you the blueprint of who you are as an individual. It's the very foundation of your personality. Everything else that's stacked upon it may make one Scorpio somewhat different from another, but in the end, it gives a dependable picture of who you are. So, if you're hoping to understand your Scorpio lover, or friend, or family member, then you're doing a great job by looking into their Sun sign.

Maybe you've studied Scorpio astrology in the past and thought, "Hold on now, that is so not true! I'm not like that!" Well, that's usually because the Sun sign only gives you the basic outline of who you are. To get the full picture, you must look at your Moon sign and other factors. If you looked at your birth chart, you might learn that while the Sun was in Scorpio when you were born, the Moon was somewhere else.

Every planet on your birth chart can be at a different sign than others. This is precisely why you feel misunderstood when you read those horoscopes. It's the reason you're so unique and intricately complex. If all Scorpios in the world were the same, life wouldn't be near as fun!

To have a much more accurate picture of yourself, you must consider your birth chart in its entirety. Even after that, you must allow for the fact that you're human. You're very capable of breaking the mold that your Scorpio zodiac sign has assigned you if you want to.

While the stars may guide you, at the end of the day, you determine what you become. You're in charge, always! With that out of the way, know what your tendencies are as a Scorpio so you can have a better relationship with yourself. If you're not a Scorpio and just looking to understand this sign, you will find yourself better able to relate with them.

Sun Signs and Their Divisions

It is vital that we consider the ways in which the zodiac signs are grouped. So, let's get into it.

Dualities

As far as dualities go, every zodiac sign is feminine or masculine. There are six signs in each division. Each division is called duality. You might understand what it means to be feminine or masculine, but no matter what they are, neither is better than the other; they are simply neutral in respect to "better" or "worse."

Feminine signs are receptive, alluring, and magnetic. You'd think feminine signs are passive, weak, or bad, but that is not the case. Masculine signs are direct and energetic. Again, I must clarify that the masculine isn't better than the feminine or vice versa.

Think of feminine signs as possessing a vast ocean of quiet strength, being very self-constrained, and full of powerful inner resolve. But masculine signs portray strength by directing all-action outwards.

The feminine signs are Pisces, Taurus, Capricorn, Cancer, Virgo, and last but most definitely not least, Scorpio. The masculine signs are Gemini, Leo, Sagittarius, Libra, Aries, and Aquarius.

Triplicities

You can further classify each zodiac sign into groups of four. Since there are 12 signs, there will be three in each group. Therefore, they are called triplicities. Each triplicity is a representation of one of the four elements: Water, Earth, Fire, and Air. These are the elements that form the basic traits of the zodiac signs.

The Water signs — Scorpio, Cancer, and Pisces — are in tune with their emotions and their intuition. The Earth signs — Virgo, Capricorn, and Taurus — are some of the most practical and stable people you'll ever meet. The Fire signs — Leo, Sagittarius, and Aries — have a robust enthusiasm for life and are the most active signs. The Air signs — Aquarius, Libra, and Gemini — are very intellectual and adept communicators.

Quadruplicities

The 12 zodiac signs are also divided into three groups, with four signs per group. These groups are called quadruplicities. Each quadruplicity represents a specific quality:

- Fixed
- Mutable
- Cardinal

The fixed signs — Scorpio, Aquarius, Leo, and Taurus — are not particularly welcoming when it comes to change. That's actually a good thing, as it means they may not start things, but when they do, they set their minds squarely on the goal they need to accomplish and will not stop until they finish and perfect it.

The mutable signs — Virgo, Sagittarius, Pisces, and Gemini — are the most versatile of the lot. They can be flexible, and they're willing to bend and weave no matter what circumstances life throws at them. They're okay with adapting as needed.

The cardinal signs - Aries, Cancer, Capricorn, and Libra — are often the outgoing ones. They're very enterprising and love to start things.

Realize that no two zodiac signs are precisely the same combo of dualities, triplicities, quadruplicities, elements, and qualities. Each zodiac sign is unique and expresses itself in different ways from others.

Polarities

There are six polarities with two zodiac signs per group. The polarities consist of signs considered opposite to each other in terms of their traits and characteristics. Let's see what they are:

- Aquarius have grand hopes and ideals, while Leo is all about expressing their unique creativity and creating their own fun.
- Cancer is passionate about home life, while Capricorn cares about their public life.

- Aries is fully about self, while Libra focuses on creating partnerships.
- Gemini longs for self-expression, while Sagittarius is about processing higher thought and philosophy.
- Virgo is passionate about work and self-improvement, while Pisces is dreamy and self-delusional.
- Taurus prizes their personal possessions, while Scorpio is all about sharing their possessions and building grand legacies.

Every zodiac sign has special numbers and days, unique plants and colors, metals, places, jewels, and so on. Each sign also has good traits and challenges. Regarding colors, you need not live your life only wearing colors native to your sign. You can wear colors that aren't tied to the Scorpio, and you can take meetings on other days besides your lucky one. The world will not end, as you've probably already noticed. Having said that, you might be pleasantly delighted if you tried to incorporate these things which you're about to learn in your life. Now we've got the basics about groupings out of the way; we can turn our attention fully on the Scorpio, a magnificent, mysterious, magnetic sign.

The Scorpio (October 23 — November 21)

Here's a quick guide on everything you need to know about what it means to be a Scorpio.

- Your duality is feminine
- Your triplicity is Water
- Your quadruplicity or quality is fixed. You are very passionate, very emotional, and just as imaginative. You have persistence in spades. Passionate and emotional as you are, you can be subtle. You also are pretty unyielding and obstinate, sometimes.
- Your ruling planet is Pluto. This is the ancient god of the dead and the netherworld. According to astrology, Pluto oversees regeneration, and directs the beginning and ending of all phases of life.
- Your symbol is the Scorpion. This creature is deadly and can poison all enemies with a single, fatal sting.
- Your glyph or written symbol depicts the Scorpion's stinger connected to a symbol for human reproductive organs — the part of the body ruled by Scorpio. This symbol represented the phoenix in ancient times. The phoenix symbolizes regeneration and immortality. The curved lines and arrow in the Scorpio's glyph symbolize strong emotions grounded in practicality and directed at a higher consciousness.
- Your dominant key phrase is *I Desire.*
- Your polarity is Taurus. Scorpio is focused on legacies and inheritance. You feel the call of destiny and a sense of purpose. You are happiest when you share your life-force with others. The Taurus, on the other hand, is about owning and possessing. Those who are born under the Taurus sign have a desire to have, take, possess, and collect. They have a hard time letting go of anything that they deem theirs.
- The body parts ruled by Scorpio are the genitals. Scorpios are prone to infections of the urinary system and venereal diseases. Because of their rather volatile emotions, they are also prone to ill health - or plain exhaustion.
- Your lucky day is Tuesday.

- Your lucky numbers are 2 and 4.
- Your magical birthstone is Topaz. This stone brings calm and serenity to your mind and keeps you safe from illness and enemies. It also helps you release your innate occult powers.
- Your special colors are maroon, burgundy, and crimson. These colors signify a deep, burning passion.
- Your cities are Liverpool, Newcastle, Washington, D.C., and New Orleans.
- Your countries are Morocco, Norway, Tahiti, and Algeria.
- Your flowers are Rhododendron and Chrysanthemum.
- Your trees are bushy trees and Blackthorn.
- Your metal is Plutonium.
- Your animals are crustaceans and insects.
- Your challenge: As a Scorpio, you tend to make other people angry because of how jealous and secretive you can get sometimes. With a temper that stings, you can make others so angry they become violent.

Famous Scorpios

1. Sylvia Plath
2. Charles Manson
3. Whoopie Goldberg
4. Julia Roberts
5. Hilary Rodham Clinton
6. Calvin Cline
7. Pablo Picasso
8. Marie Curie

The Scorpio at Work

When it comes to working, you'd be hard-pressed to find anyone as passionate as the Scorpio — except maybe the Virgo. The Scorpio is generally very zealous no matter what they are working on at the time. As a Scorpio, you are motivated to give 110 percent because you have a deep fear of failure, you're very loyal, and you bring a unique perspective to whatever challenges need to be solved at work.

You're very charming and have a strong will. You're magnetic — but of course, you already know that. With a personality like yours, you pull in your coworkers. Ironically, you like to operate alone. You like to take the lead on projects, but you're also comfortable following someone else's lead — as long as "someone else" knows what they're doing and is clear on what they want you to do. You love to go after your goals with all you've got, but you'd rather be left alone while you do so.

While you may have a strong fear of failure, you're different from others in that where that fear might paralyze them, you use it as fuel to propel you relentlessly toward success — and succeed you do.

If you've got a Scorpio as one of your team members, you will find them an invaluable asset. They are strong team players, though they'd rather handle the parts of the project that require no one else but them to get done. This could be somewhat of a challenge, but it's one that the Scorpio can easily handle with a little compromise. They have only to allocate time to work on group tasks and their personal tasks.

The Scorpio at a Party

At first blush, you might presume the Scorpio is way above mixing with the rest of boring humanity at your party, but that's not the case. As a Scorpio, you're not exactly a social butterfly. Some Scorpios can flutter about and be the life of the party, but those aren't the typical ones, and those guys and gals probably have some Air element influence, anyway. Mostly, a Scorpio couldn't care less about social cues or the right way to act at a party. What does that even mean, "right way?"

You're not a fan of chit-chat and small talk about nothing. You're to the point and have no trouble saying whatever "politically incorrect" thing you want to. It almost sounds like you're antisocial, but that is not true! What you are is *socially selective*.

You see, the thing about Scorpios is that they love nothing more than to vibe with their own tribe. With their tribe, they can socialize without a care in the world, morphing from that reserved person at the party to a carefree social butterfly. There's a very interesting thing about that tribe: It might not have more than ten people in it, assuming it's even more than three to begin with.

So, if you want the Scorpio to have a good time at your party, you'd better be a part of the tribe or let them bring along their own tribe. Then you're sure to have a good time. Other than that, you will simply have to allow the Scorpio time to figure out what everyone's about before they let loose.

The Scorpio at Home

The Scorpio is a water sign, and this means they're very calm. They're also just as versatile and passionate about everything. While some people might think the Scorpio's propensity for mystery and drama isn't so great, it's actually a good thing! Also, we'd all do well to remember there is no one as profoundly devoted and loyal as the Scorpio is.

Now when it comes to Scorpio's home, you can rest assured that they've channeled this level of devotion to making it somewhere they always want to come back to at the end of the day. As a Scorpio, your home has a very personal touch, with your own very dynamic, functional, and stunning installations, and your added nuances.

As much as you enjoy socializing with your tribe, you crave balance. For this reason, you need a space you can retreat to so you can recharge and be by yourself, somewhere away from life's constant hustle and bustle. You'd rather live somewhere that's far from the noise of the city.

Because of your mysterious air, you love strong and dark tones that ooze opulence. You aren't exactly a fan of white or pastel shades. You'd rather have rich blue, noble black, elegant grays (the darker, the better) and powerful wine-red tones, which you can contrast with one another.

Your home is your sanctuary, furnished with only the best materials. You will settle for nothing less than the finest, and you love that air of understated elegance and luxury. So, opt for metal, marble, leather, and the rarest of woods. You also enjoy having all that luxury graced with a touch of coziness, functionality, and comfort.

Chapter Two: Scorpio Strengths and Weaknesses

In this chapter, we'll be focusing on the Scorpio's strengths and weaknesses, whether they're your colleague, friend, family, or lover. Let's get right into it!

The Scorpio's Strengths

One of the most lovable traits of the Scorpio is that of idealism. This zodiac sign is all about extremes. You've probably heard of people born under this sign as weak yet powerful; cold, yet passionate; clinging, yet independent. As a Scorpio, you're a beautiful bundle of contradictions! You have both sides of the spectrum of human nature within you.

You're never one to do things halfway. Others find it easy to depend on you to get the job done. If you make a promise, you will definitely stand by it, unlike a sign like the flaky Pisces, for instance.

You're emotional, very magnetic and alluring, and you're very forceful in situations that call for a show of strength. Speaking of strength, you draw yours from deep reserves within you as a water sign, and you pull through most things that would have others caving easily. With you, the water element is fixed; you're like a deep and bottomless well, or an iceberg, if you prefer. It may seem to those who do not know you well enough that you're quite difficult to approach and pretty impassive, but beneath the surface, you have so much passion turbulently roiling, invisible to all but whoever you'll get close enough to see.

You may seem calm on the surface, giving a smile as needed, but you're very persistent about whatever you set your heart on, and you're very strong-willed as well. That you're strong-willed doesn't mean you're not willing to bend and weave a little in terms of finding solutions. Whenever things don't go your way, you're not the kind to bow your head in defeat. You spring right back up to your feet and try something new, again. No one is as adept or agile at you for spotting trouble or obstacles and elegantly getting around it all. You don't just find a way; you find a score of ways to get your goal. It is this flexible nature of yours that allows you to remain in control.

Your mind is very philosophical, and you might have a keen interest in religion – as well as the occult. You have an uncanny way of knowing what's going to happen before it does. Somehow, you also understand what it means to be human more than others, and without being consciously taught, you know of the deepest secrets of life.

Water signs are psychic, but with you, Scorpio, you can dive even deeper into the psychic world, deeper than most others. Where others would chicken out and run away, you run eagerly into the rabbit hole, eager to explore more of what is your natural playground. It's no coincidence you're this way. The Scorpio is a sign that reigns supreme over birth, death, sex, and regeneration. These are all aspects of human life we must all confront and which we all know next to nothing about. Most Scorpios are incredible surgeons, scientists, doctors, and spiritual leaders.

You're not the kind who is willing to just be okay with what appears on the surface. You're a deep diver, willing, longing to go deep beneath the surface. It doesn't matter what it is you're doing. You could be learning how to make cosmetics, or learning to levitate, or reading something just for fun. Even then, you pierce way beyond the surface of things, to see that which others would miss. It's just how you are.

You're so flexible and adaptable that it's nothing for you to take your very formidable drive and zeal and channel all of it into new endeavors. You're not afraid to dive into completely new careers or projects that you've never had to deal with. When disaster strikes, you will marshal every resource at your command to make sure it all ends successfully. No one is as shrewd and practical as you are. You are a champion at setting immediate goals that are real and tangible and making them happen. Your single-mindedness and amazing concentration will often get you success.

With money, you're clever. You're a conservative spender. Amassing wealth is easy for you. With business, you are the sort who will first do things and then announce you've done them. Your opponents could never keep up with you because you're always light years ahead of them.

It's a sad situation that a lot of astrologers do not ever mention just how kind, loving, loyal, generous, and gentle a Scorpio is. A lot of idealists in life follow the highest and most noble principles – and they are Scorpios. These people have been a wonderful force for positive change in the world and continue to be that way.

As a Scorpio, no other sign feels things as intensely as you do. Emotion rules the day with you. Whether love, work, hobbies, relationships, or causes, you're very passionate about it all.

The Scorpio's Weaknesses and How to Navigate Them

It's a travesty that you're so misunderstood compared to the other signs. You usually have your own agenda, and no one besides whoever you reveal them to will know anything. You have so much brilliance, and there is so much depth to you.

You may seem very much at ease, but no matter how relaxed you seem, there's a lot going on in your head. You're always trying to work out what to do next and strategizing your life. The reason you're this way is you need to be in control. If you're ever not in control, you interpret that to be putting yourself in danger, psychically. There's nothing you hate more than the thought of being out of control or relinquishing control to forces outside of you. For you, control equals safety.

You can use this control so it works well for you, by bringing sanity back in times of chaos, or by helping others to make a dream of theirs come true by teaching them to control themselves, or setting up your workspace and home space so you can perform at your best.

When the Scorpio isn't evolved, they often try to manipulate and control other people and situations for their own gain or greed. With this Scorpio, the tug of war between light and dark in their psyche is very real and very turbulent.

As a Scorpio, you can and should use that same fervor whenever you have a goal and put it into relationships that feed all parties involved. Invest this energy in personal projects that mean a lot to you. If you're not mindful, you might expend energy, time, and resources on things and people that do not deserve you. When you do this, it's inevitable that your efforts are wasted, and upon realizing it's all been for nothing, you focus inwards as you wallow in a sea of regret and loathing; this can easily cause you to become destructive to yourself and others.

Being very emotional, you avoid giving of yourself to causes and other people who aren't worthy. This is great when it's all good emotions, but when negative, the resentment, jealousy, and vengefulness you can unleash upon the world are beyond legendary. The only thing just as legendary is your ability to endure, your drive, and energy. So, seek to find meaning in your life. You will be best served by finding your deepest calling and following that with reckless abandon.

In relationships, your best and worst traits show up in full strength, and this can make your relationships a bit complicated - perhaps more than "a bit." It may seem odd, but you're the kind who can be affectionate, kind, and yet unpredictable and violent. Even when you're the happiest, there's still the possibility that your mood will swing the other way with the force of a thousand waves.

While you're very loyal to those who you consider your tribe, you can also be possessive and jealous. For you, it's not okay that anyone you care about or love might feel something for someone else besides you. It's because of your all-or-nothing nature that you're this way. Here is a list of words you often wonder what use they could serve in language: Casual, restraint, and moderation. You love fully and live it fully. There is no in-between.

You're the kind of person who absolutely will never forget when someone has been good to you, and you will do your best to pay back doubly. On the flip side, you never forgive a wrong, and you are more than willing to wait years at a time to attack back with vengeance. If you're not a Scorpio and are simply trying to understand the people born under this sign, then know this: You'd better never cross them. If you do, you will have crafted yourself the worst enemy in the world, one so subtle and so deadly, willing to burrow in the sands of time to await the perfect opportunity to strike you down with relish... much like the actual scorpion in the desert.

The Scorpio is fiercely competitive, although you'd never guess it just by watching them. As a Scorpio, you will save every valuable piece of information you come across, and when the right opportunity comes around, you will use it as needed. If a rival shows a hint of weakness, you'll be there posed and ready to move in for the kill.

You can get very obsessive about your goals or whatever drives you, and this can make you difficult to reason with. You'd rather control and dominate anyone who will give you even an inch to do so. You get very suspicious, and you're slow to let people in or trust them with your heart. The good thing is when you do let them in, you love them, truly and deeply. Learn to be more open to the world. Forget what the news says; not everything and everyone is out to get you. Open up, and you'd be surprised at the wonder and the gift that is humanity.

Who You Really Are

Dear Scorpio, you are a person of incredible willpower, strength, and determination. Sure, you might do a good job of seeming calm and unflappable on the outside, but deep down, you are a raging sea of emotions, which you do a good job of keeping under wraps by focusing it into activities you deem useful.

You're a very high achiever. You just "get it" with no effort — thanks to your psychic abilities, which you have come to know and trust during your life. You listen to your gut as it tells you to strive for more and greater, and you will not let yourself slack on that front.

When you see an opportunity for greatness, you are the person who goes over it with a microscope and a fine-tooth comb before you jump right in. You're a warrior with a lot of energy to fight for all you believe in. Your one ongoing lesson is to continue to channel your energy toward positive goals and ideals. As you do this, you will become one of the greatest people in life, always winning all the time. Sure, sometimes, it feels like you're a warrior all by yourself. You feel too complex to be understood, and you don't have the words to express what you feel. In those times, it remains perpetually clear that what you know what you want, you want it badly, and you will not stop until you've made it happen.

Who Others See You As

Because of how incredibly secretive you can be, people are so desperate to discover what makes you tick. In a group, you're likely the wise one people turn to for answers because you have an uncanny way of knowing how the future will go. You have deep insight when it comes to why others do the things they do.

One thing people know about you is how sensual you are. It's not unusual for them to fantasize about you making love to them, maybe forever. Some see you as being too ambitious, too controlling, and very hungry for power, but even with all of that, they see you as someone they can trust because you never make a promise you don't intend to keep.

The Scorpio in the Family

With family, no one loves as hard or as deep as the Scorpio. In the family, if you need help with a project or a problem, or you just need solid advice, the Scorpio is the best person you could count on to be there for you. There is no length they will not go to for you to see you smile!

However, if you ever cross a Scorpio, they're fine with cutting you off, blood or no. They will take a moment to feel terrible about the fact that you messed things up so badly between you two, but only just a moment. The next minute, they will not hesitate to cut you off. You might as well be dead to them — figuratively and literally.

It might seem a little too over the top, but remember this is a sign with whom there is no such thing as a middle ground. They don't do half measures, ever. So, if you value your relationship with your Scorpio, then you'd better never betray them. If you do, you can expect that they will not let up until they've had their revenge or until you've shown that you're truly and deeply sorry and are committed to changing your ways.

The Scorpio often falls back on their emotions and instincts, and because of this, they're the one in the family who feels other people's pain the most. Your Scorpio sibling or parent or child will often just get you, without you having to over-explain how you feel or what you're thinking. They are completely sympathetic and will go above and beyond to make you happy. In fact, the Scorpio regularly will ignore her own needs to focus on everyone else's in the family — especially if she's a parent.

Being a water sign, your Scorpio very well knows what human nature is like, so if you ever try to hide something from them, just know that it's pointless. If you think you succeeded at hiding it, then know that they're only choosing to ignore it and let you off the hook until you're ready to come to clean yourself.

The Scorpio mom is amazing because she knows her kids inside out. She knows when there's something wrong. It's the same thing with the youngest Scorpio in the house; they're very adept at being able to discern when something is off when there's tension or trouble. Without being taught, they just know how to show a lot more affection and to be gentler when they notice a sibling or a parent isn't feeling so great.

If you need the best advice, an ear to whine to, or support, then you can count on the Scorpio. However, there's nothing more irritating to the Scorpio than when people aren't even aware that they have needed to or that they aren't happy. Since the Scorpio is very subtle in how they express their very intense emotions, it can take a fair bit to learn how to read your Scorpio and realize they're not okay with something. That being said, taking the time to read their subtle cues is well worth the investment. You'll learn that while they can be moody at the most unpredictable of times, they are also the most fun, loving, affectionate, and playful people you'll ever meet.

Water Meets Earth

Water and Earth are elements that go together naturally, offering mutual benefits to each other. If you're an Earth sign, you and your Scorpio will get along fabulously well. Others will often envy this bond between you.

The Scorpio can offer the emotional support that Earth signs need so they can comfortably share their feelings. As for the Earth sign, they have more than enough patience to deal with the Scorpio's moodiness and complex nature. They are of the Earth; and like the Earth, they will always be there.

Water Meets Fire

Put Water and Fire together, and what do you get? A lot of steam! The Scorpio is a passionate sign on its own, and people born under this sign are volatile, acting out erratically. The same thing goes for the Fire signs as well — but that's about where it ends with their similarities.

Fire is often left scratching her head for figuring out the mystery and enigma that is the Scorpio. The Scorpio might be exhausted by Fire signs because of their ultra-grand, larger-than-life aura.

Fire signs are great at giving the Scorpio a lift in their mood because of their playfulness, and they help the Scorpio be more confident about expressing their feelings. The Scorpio gives back to the fire signs by teaching them how to mellow out, be less selfish, and more empathetic.

Water Meets Air

Believe it or not, Water and Air are opposites - at least, astrologically. Where the Air signs are okay with being vocal and logical, Scorpio is more emotive and intuitive, so the connection between these two will require a lot of effort for it to work.

For example, a Scorpio parent may get very frustrated with constant chatter from their Gemini kid. Although, it is still possible for these family members to be of benefit and balance each other out. The Scorpio can learn how to live life without being so grounded in emotions from the Gemini. Meanwhile, the Scorpio can show the Air signs that there's nothing wrong with expressing their emotions, rather than trying to rationalize everything.

Water Meets Water

The thing about other water signs and the Scorpio is there is a LOT of emotion. Maybe even too much. Sure, the Scorpio can understand all the other water signs, and they can figure out what the other person needs without them saying a word, but these signs together are likely to have standoffs full of pouting and sulking when they don't see eye to eye. For instance, the Scorpio can easily become impatient with the Pisces because the latter can be a tad too insensitive, and a Cancer will have issues with how intense the Scorpio is and their unwillingness to communicate.

The Fixed Scorpio in the Family

Fixed signs are set on doing things the way they intend to, and they're also consistent. This can be a good thing in that you can count on the Scorpio. On the other hand, this could be bad because they can get really stubborn and refuse to listen to advice no matter how well it could serve them.

As a Scorpio, you're not a big fan of taking risks without knowing what you're getting into first. Your fear of failure keeps you from being reckless, and so you're often in the family to sound a note of caution when someone's about to fall for a scam or something.

You're incredibly patient, and you persevere no matter how bad things get, so often, you might find yourself being the one everyone at home relies on — unless there's another Scorpio or fixed sign in the house that the family can lean on too.

Your family recognizes the resilience, strength of character, and stamina you have, and so they know they can count on you to pull them through rough times, down to the very end. Your family knows that you're dependable, loyal, diligent, and dedicated. They trust you, and you give them lots of reasons. Because of you, the family has a sense of stability.

Chapter Three: The Scorpio Child

Scorpio children are just as fascinating as adults are. We're going to dive into what you need to know so you can raise your Scorpio child right. Let's get right to it!

The Scorpio child is secretive. As you no doubt know by now, Scorpios love their secrets. The little Scorpio is no exception, as they keep many things bottled up within themselves. There's nothing they want more than a lot of quiet, alone time, as well as privacy so they can be themselves.

You should not think for even one second you could ever hide anything from this bright and intuitive kid! Your Scorpio child is an incredible master of perception and knows the second something's off. More likely than not, he's the one who will figure out all the family secrets. You could try to discourage her from making you bare your soul, but there's very little power you wield when she sets her intense gaze upon you.

The Scorpio child is really, sensitive. Sure, your kid might seem very calm and at ease to the ordinary eye, but your little one has the wildest emotional roller coaster within him. It goes super-fast, has crazy twists, and turns — and you can bet the speed and twists are even more intense the more silent your child is, whether he's silent because he's giving the silent treatment or just super quiet.

As a parent, you have one job only: You need to get him to come out with whatever is bugging him when you feel there's something he's not okay with. It's important that you begin from a young age to encourage him to share his feelings. You see, Scorpio kiddos are just as extreme in their emotions as adults. They can go from the longest pout you've ever seen to the cutest, warmest smile in a matter of seconds.

For the Scorpio child, you must always reassure them. You'd be hard-pressed to find a stronger kid! When they are feeling intimidated, they will not admit that to you or anyone else. The Scorpio child is bold, brave, and ready to take on any challenge or unfamiliar situation. However, they are often full of insecurities and fear.

For this reason, you've simply got to reassure your Scorpio child. They need you to let them know that everything's really, truly, okay. Dishonesty doesn't work; just let them know despite whatever's going on, things will be all right. Give this kid lots of affection the way she wants it. You could hug her, hold her, or if she's a toddler, you could cuddle with her. Only do this until she is comfortable again and then release her.

Your Scorpio kid loves mystery and intrigue. Your Scorpio kid is just like the scorpion in the sense they love two things: Darkness and hiding. Your little one loves games like hiding and seek and any other game that means he gets to pull a vanishing act.

There's nothing the Scorpio child loves more than fantasy, magic, and mystery. They're probably the one kid you have whose love for Harry Potter runs super deep. If you're looking for something and can't find it, best believe the Scorpio will sniff it out for you. They love when things are hidden and need to be found. You've got a little Sherlock on your hands!

No other kid is as strong-willed as your Scorpio kid. From the day she's born, your Scorpio baby owns you and everyone around you with her eyes. They can be unnerving, seeming to pierce through your soul and strip you down to who you *really* are. She also has energy for days and days!

Your Scorpio child will take every chance she gets to test boundaries and challenge whatever rules you've set for her. Being fiercely competitive, you can rest assured she will not stop until she wins. It doesn't matter what your little Scorpio is doing at the moment; you can bet that she's the best at it and will beat everyone else hands down.

Whatever you do, you must be gentle but firm when disciplining your wee Scorpio. Don't ever assume, "Oh, they're a kid, they won't remember anything." They do! They have the most amazing memories. Add to that their high propensity for vengeance and vindictiveness, and you don't want to cross them — no matter how little they are! No one can cook up schemes for revenge like the little Scorpio. No one can hold a grudge as long as they can either.

Your Scorpio is pretty intense. But you already knew that, didn't you? The Scorpio child is intriguing, magnetic, you could say. Whether they want to, they always draw a following — which is funny because your little Scorpio is probably an introvert, being born under this sign.

With the people who matter the most to the Scorpio — family and close friends — they are the most loyal little ones ever. They will fight for you if they love you. However, with strangers, the Scorpio kid is not necessarily the most caring. At best, they can be indifferent to people they don't know. At worst, they can be impolite, and sometimes they even get cruel — especially if your Scorpio child gets even a hint of weakness from whoever it is. It is up to you to teach them how to be gentle with other people's feelings.

Your little Scorpio is possessive. She might not necessarily be okay with having to share snacks or toys with the other kids. It's just a Scorpio thing, really, but there's nothing you need to worry about. She can grow out of it with loving guidance from you. You need only to praise her whenever you notice her sharing with her siblings or with her friends.

Another thing you want to do is to make sure you give your little Scorpio a lot of your time. You want to make sure you spend time with your Scorpio one on one and make sure you do that on a schedule. If you don't, she might start to feel jealous, and those intense feelings will sooner or later come bursting out and scaring everyone. You know what they say: Hell hath no fury than a Scorpio baby ignored? Something like that.

The Male Scorpio Child

There's nothing your Scorpio son loves better than to dominate at home. Your child is very strong. He's got good health in spades and can be a tad aggressive, so you'll need to tame that trait in him. Your job is to be there as a sterling example to the male Scorpio, teaching him to respect authority and how to have a healthy attitude about losing to someone else. If you will teach your Scorpio son this, then you've simply got to make sure you and your spouse continue to show him these values in different ways so your Scorpio son can grow up a good guy.

Because your Scorpio son is of Water, you must learn how to balance, showing him affection by giving him structure. When you don't do this, your Scorpio son will simply retreat deeper and deeper into his shell. On the flip side, when you give him with lots of love and lots of structure, your Scorpio son will come out of his shell and will be very eager to share his feelings and thoughts with you, frankly and honestly.

When your Scorpio son hits his teens, he becomes territorial. If he needs a moment to sort through his thoughts, he will retreat to his bedroom and do just that at some point; that is his sacred space. You do not want to go in there uninvited. Do not desecrate it by barging in; respect your teenager's need for space. Think of it as the cave your young scorpion retreats into and decompresses from the sensory overload they've had to experience.

Like Scorpio daughters, your Scorpio son wants nothing more than the truth from you at every point. This also means he expects that if you make a promise, you keep it. If you ever have to break your word to your Scorpio, son, then you'd better have a very, very good reason. Otherwise, it's better to stick to it or be like your Scorpio son: Simply never make promises you do not intend to move heaven and earth to fulfill.

When your Scorpio son becomes a young man, you'll notice that he's attractive to many people. It's important that you prepare for this stage by teaching him the importance of taking responsibility for his sexual prowess. You've also got to teach him that his partners are not trophies for him to brag about having, but actual human beings with feelings he would do well to respect.

The Female Scorpio Child

Your Scorpio girl is full of drive, with her eyes squarely on the future. You'll notice that your daughter will have strong desires to take on a certain career when she's much older. So, it's your job as a parent of this amazing child to give her every tool she could want or need to make her dreams happen.

Yes, over time, there will be changes to that dream. She might decide she no longer wants to be a magician and would rather be a violinist. Whatever the case, her passion and determination for her goals remain just as fiery, and you should always nurture her dreams. Never try to insist that she focus on one thing. Give her room to discover herself.

You'll notice that your Scorpio daughter tends to be very private, and this can make it tough to communicate with her. Sometimes, you need to lay all your cards on the table because this is the only way to encourage her to allow you to get a peek into her stormy head. She's got a knack for hiding things; it's no coincidence that she loves to play, hide, and seek! Another great thing about your very private Scorpio daughter is that she is the absolute best at keeping your secrets. She loves it when you share them with her because that says to her you trust her. She will keep your secret until the end of time.

Chances are you've noticed your Scorpio daughter loves the night. Being a night owl, you've got to give her structure with her bedtime routine. Your Scorpio child loves the dark. With all her heart, he believes there is a lot of magic in the darkness. So, don't be weirded out if you go to check on her during the night and find her little eyes are wide open!

As your Scorpio daughter grows, her love for the dark becomes a need to explore life and ask lots of questions. Do not, by any stretch of the imagination, think these questions are your run-of-the-mill silly questions either. They'll be deep and insightful and could even cause you to do some soul searching yourself. Here's a helpful hint: If she asks you something you don't have the answer to, please don't make one up. Explain to her you don't have the answer, but you will discover and let her know. If you don't, you will have her mind spinning in constant circles, and she'll retreat until she has an answer that works.

Your Scorpio daughter is sensitive, even more than you think. It's not unlike her to hold on to things that have hurt her badly, all while doing her best not to let it show. You must do what you can to help her let go of those troubling, painful emotions, especially as she becomes a teenager.

You can expect that as your Scorpio daughter becomes a teenager and then a woman, she will have many people interested in dating her because she's so very mysterious and alluring. Seriously, her magnetism is so strong that even if you're the toughest of parents, you will have a hard time keeping them away from her. What you should do instead is to instruct your daughter she deserves the best in a partner and show her that it's important to respect the other person's feelings.

Scorpio Child Health

Your Scorpio child could never be accused of not having energy. Still, your Scorpio child may be susceptible to illness, which often comes at the most unexpected of times. You want to be very aware of your Scorpio's diet, making sure it's got all the nutrients they need to stay strong and healthy.

As your Scorpio child gets older, they become susceptible to issues affecting their reproductive organs. They can get cystitis, eruptions, venereal infections, and urinary tract diseases. So, as soon as it is reasonable, you want to teach them about the importance of being clean and staying safe.

Another thing you want to know: your Scorpio child could become ill because of these difficult emotions. As they grow older, this could mean falling ill because of them being too stressed out or overstimulated. It's important that you teach them such helpful practices as mindfulness meditation, so you can help them stay on top of their feelings and decompress as needed.

A Scorpio has calcium sulfate as its cell salt. This is the salt that helps with repairing damaged tissues and keeping infectious diseases at bay. It's incredibly helpful for keeping the mouth, nose, throat, esophagus, intestinal pathways, and reproductive organs functioning in tiptop condition. When your Scorpio is deficient in this sale, they become more susceptible to sinus infections and colds that never go away, infertility, and skin eruptions that refuse to heal.

You want to make sure your Scorpio gets foods rich in calcium sulfate, like radishes, cauliflower, figs, onions, black cherries, tomatoes, and coconut. It's also vital that they get food that's loaded with calcium, like yogurt, cottage cheese, and milk. A high protein diet would serve them immensely. You also want to make sure they get their fruits and veggies, and if they must have bread, make it whole grain. Fish (and seafood in general), almonds, green salads, lentils, beet, betties, bananas, citrus fruits, walnuts, and pineapples are great for them.

Whatever you do, do not give your Scorpio large meals. Whatever they have in the evening needs to be light. Give them spring water, not tap water. Being a Water sign, it's important that your Scorpio stays hydrated. Also, the fact that your Scorpio is of Water means it's easy for them to pick up other people's negative emotions. This causes them to become moody, brood a lot, and blow problems out of proportion in their minds. Inevitably, this leads to health problems. Again, mindfulness meditation will help your Scorpio here.

Hobbies of Scorpio Kids

You can put your Scorpio kid in a class for whatever will need them to be dedicated to and patient with whatever is being taught. While the Scorpio son is very interested in joining the military or becoming a private eye, the Scorpio daughter is amazing at sports.

Scorpio kids will often grow up to become journalists or doctors. They have a great intuition and often know where to go for the hottest scoop, or how to treat a peculiar case. When it comes to picking their university, please don't pressure them. Let your Scorpio's intuition guide them. Also, don't pressure them into a profession — not even medicine or journalism. There are other things that the Scorpio excels at, you know. This is a very creative sign, and they can excel as actors, writers, craftsmen, whatever! Just allow them to follow their passion.

The Scorpio Child at School

With school, your child may dominate others in his class. However, your Scorpio kid is a fast learner. They're very astute, intelligent, and have a great work ethic even at such a young age. It's important that your Scorpio child always has something interesting and useful to keep him occupied so that his energy is always productively used.

If your Scorpio kid doesn't like something, best believe she will not be interested in learning it, no matter what you do. You've got to let her decide what topics she's most interested in. Often, she'll pick things that will prove useful to her over time.

Parenting Your Scorpio

When your Scorpio child is among her peers, she's easy to pick out. She's the one who's busy brooding, her eyes soulful, her head filled with so many thoughts. What's really going on is that she's observing everything around her carefully. She has mastered the art of observation without seeming like she's observing. With group activities, she joins in with her closest friends, with whom she shares a bond of loyalty and trust.

You'll notice that your Scorpio daughter or son has powerful emotions. It's these emotions that they use to explore their world. Sometimes, they get so intense that other kids are simply overpowered by it all. Even you can be overwhelmed by them! What you need to do as a parent is to let your Scorpio experience their emotions fully. Let them know it's okay to talk about how they feel and let it out in a healthy way.

When your Scorpio kid has an outburst, it's only because he's been holding on to it for so long, doing his best not to let things get to him. It's because he's finally reached the end of his rope. So, whatever you do, please do not treat these outbursts as though they were nothing more than just temper tantrums. Your Scorpio kid genuinely needs your help. Help them understand why they feel as deeply as they do, whereas other kids are more happy-go-lucky.

You can help your Scorpio release her emotions by encouraging her to explore creative activities, like writing, painting, music, gardening, photography, or any other art form. The Scorpio child is ridiculously talented. You'll find you don't even need to give them any formal lessons to learn to play an instrument or mold something. They're just naturals, thanks to their Water element, which puts them in touch with their intuition and gives them a natural appreciation for art and working with their hands.

Encourage your Scorpio child's psychic abilities. Teach them to rely on their intuition, as they're naturally intuitive. You can play a game of telepathy with them. You or your child acts as the sender, and the other person acts as the receiver. Whoever is playing the sender needs to think of a number or color or shape (whatever you want, really) and visualize it as clearly as you can. The receiver needs to sit with their eyes shut and their mind empty and then say the first thing that pops into their mind. You'll be amazed at the results!

Chapter Four: Scorpio and Love

Of all the zodiac signs, Scorpio is the most mysterious and most profound. When they're in love, a Scorpio is very intense and very devoted. Like the Cher song goes, this sign is all or nothing!

I should point out that you, dear Scorpio, when you have someone in your sights; you can get a bit melodramatic because of the conflicting emotions and complexities that plague you.

It's okay that you're this way. You're a Water sign. This means you'll push the Air away, wear down the earth, and put out the fire. Does this mean love is a tragedy for you? A thousand times, no! When you do let go completely and trust someone else with your heart, there's only one way to describe that relationship: magical.

The Scorpio: Love so Deep

Because of the Water influence, you will often feel your love for your partner deeply. You can become introspective and are driven by your emotions. Since the primary emotion in your relationship is love, you will climb mountains for this lucky person.

Since your quadruplicity is fixed, this means that your love runs deep. When you decide you've found the person you want to spend the rest of your life with, you decide. There are no ifs, ands, or buts. You're going to hang on. You will fight for your relationship. Giving up is not in your vocabulary.

When you fall in love, it is unmistakable. You can feel it in your soul. For reasons beyond your comprehension, you want to be with this person. Sometimes you have the wish to control them, but consider keeping that in check.

As a Scorpio, you want to feel it all. You want the hours and the lows, the love, and the pain. You love how you feel, and you want more and more. You're fine with totally losing yourself in love, seeking, and allowing yourself to be radically changed by it.

The reason you're so intensely passionate, possessive, protective, and downright loyal as a lover is because of your fixed quadruplicity and the element of Water.

Creative in Love

As a Scorpio, you're unusually creative, and this same love for creativity comes to play when you're in love with someone. You dedicate the same passion you use in learning a piano piece or crafting a hedge fund strategy to loving this person.

You literally invest yourself in loving your partner. You want to follow this feeling until you're old, gray, and gone. You often will write poetry or song lyrics about the passion you feel. As a Scorpio, you consider your partner to be fortunate to have a lover as devoted and true as you. Light or dark as it may be, you find catharsis in expressing everything you feel in art. Small wonder then that a lot of Scorpios create great works of art inspired by love!

The Jealous Scorpio

You feel everything deeply. So, as deep as your love is, it can be a terrifying thing when you become jealous. Your jealousy is just as boundless as your love is. This can be a terrible thing if left unchecked.

Your water-driven and fixed nature, which mean you express and feel jealousy just as deeply as you do love. When you're jealous, you can become downright vengeful. You become very unforgiving. Whatever happens next, only the man in the sky could save your lover or whoever from you.

Whenever you have been spurned by a lover, you feel it like deep inside your soul. It feels like death — and no, that's not you being dramatic. It truly feels that way. It's only natural too because you're not like the Fire signs, which can be optimistic in the wake of a broken heart, or like the Earth signs, which can still find a way to be stable when love has left them, or like the Air signs who can nearly rationalize their pain away. You're a Scorpio, through and through. That means you feel. You're emotional, and extremely so.

The Dependable Scorpio

Sure, being with a Scorpio can be a rollercoaster ride for navigating the highs and lows of their emotions, but one thing you can count on for sure is that they are loyal and committed to you and only you.

Scorpio is very dependable. They'll ride out the highs and lows with you. If you give them the same faithfulness and loyalty, they will up the ante. Remember, this is a sign that makes a point of repaying everyone generously. Give good; you get a lot of good. Give bad... Well, you have only yourself to blame for whatever happens next.

Best Matches

Now let's take a quick look at the signs that are most compatible with the amazing Scorpio.

Virgo

Scorpio and Virgo are literally a match made in heaven, as they are one of the best pairings ever as far as astrology is concerned. You, Scorpio, are a wild one. You're intense. But the Virgo is one of the more practical and stable signs, and this makes you both a wonderful pairing, Water and Earth, fixed and mutable.

You both care a lot about whoever you're with. Virgo's nurture other people's needs before their own, and they will often be hard on themselves, simply because they feel like they're not giving enough of themselves or doing enough for their partner.

As for you, Scorpio, you're very trustworthy. You consider trust to be very important, right up there with loyalty, if you're going to make your relationship work. When a Virgo worms her way into your heart, you're very happy to lavish your love on her with an intensity that might scare off other signs, but *not the Virgo*.

Just like you, the Virgo feels deeply. You might not be as obvious about your deep emotions, but they're there. You worry a lot about your softness and vulnerability being out there for the world to see, so you keep it all under wraps until a Virgo makes you her last bus stop and breaks down your walls.

There is so much compatibility between you two, intellectually, and in the bedroom. Virgo is very willing to let you take the lead, and with your need for the control, you're more than happy to. The Virgo finds your confidence super attractive, and you, in turn, love that he can be trusting enough to let you be in control and not challenge you.

In a funny twist, the Virgo's willingness to let you be in charge brings out your softer, gentler side. Since the Virgo is of earth, rock steady, and calming, they can influence you to relax and put you at ease. The result is that you both have a very stable relationship, not plagued by volatility. Another thing that helps is that you both love your me-time and respect it when the other person needs their space. You're both good with finances and never have to worry about the other person overspending.

Scorpio and Cancer

These two have a lot of similarities, the most obvious being they're both water signs. The best part is that even their differences complement each other. Cancer and Scorpio enjoy a lot of intensity with emotions, which binds them together.

Both signs love their privacy, value loyalty, and are very in touch with their intuition, which makes things beautiful in the bedroom. You both know what the other person wants.

Because of the nurturing qualities of the Cancer, your insecurities are put at ease. While Cancer is as emotional as you are, they have fewer hang-ups about expressing how they feel. This is a good thing for you since they can show you it's okay to let it out. Also, the fact that Cancer is flexible will make for a great relationship between you two, since as a Scorpio, you're not too big on making compromises.

Scorpio and Pisces

You're an excellent match. The Pisces is gentle and loyal, and that works great for you, Scorpio, since you're not so quick to trust. This match works well because as a Scorpio you want to lead, and a Pisces is happy to follow in your footsteps. They'll let you take the reins and adjust to accommodate whatever you need. Sex is also amazing and passionate for this same reason, and it sure does help that both signs are full of emotion.

The Fish and The Scorpion both have a tendency for very dramatic mood swings, switching from high to low and back. This is great because they understand that about each other. However, the intensity of the highs and lows can cause a fair bit of drama.

Worst Matches

Scorpio and Sagittarius

These two signs have a lot of qualities that contrast and will often lead to lots of conflicts. You, Scorpio, are private and mysterious. The Sagittarius, however, is very blunt and open. You may not be so quick to show your hand, but Sagittarius is okay with sharing her entire history with people she met only two seconds ago.

Where you tend to be deep and intense, the Sagittarius would rather keep things light and airy. You don't quite enjoy their tendency to not take things seriously.

The Sagittarius is a huge fan of debate, whereas the Scorpio is really not into being challenged. Add to the Sagittarius tending to be insensitive in their openness and bluntness, and it just makes a relationship between you two darn near impossible. You're emotional, and you hate it when people are insensitive.

The final nail in the coffin is that here you're very prudent about your money; the Sagittarius is very reckless and an impulsive spender. Other signs might think them generous or spontaneous, but you just consider them wasteful.

Scorpio and Gemini

Gemini doesn't hold a candle to Scorpio when it comes to emotional depth. They simply cannot relate, which is why it could never work. Add in the Gemini being a social butterfly at heart, while the Scorpio is not terribly social, and you've got a recipe for heartbreak. Plus, Geminis love to be around people. For you, Scorpio, who needs her space, this could be a nightmare.

Whenever there is conflict, the Gemini falls back on teasing you. Other signs may enjoy this, but you find it very irritating as a Scorpio. In the end, you both could never work because the Gemini considers you a wet blanket, while you find them the most superficial person ever.

Scorpio and Aquarius

The problem with the Aquarius as far as you're concerned is that they're a tad too distant and emotionally shallow. If you've ever been in a relationship with one, you may have had to constantly go into battle with them. Your emotional needs were always challenged by their constant intellectual analysis and rationalization.

Like the Sagittarius, the Aquarius can be blunt when making his points. Sometimes, he pushes this bluntness to the point of harshness, which means they will inevitably say something that you would never forgive or forget, being the Scorpio you are.

You do have some compatibility in the bedroom. You're both very open to trying new and adventurous things. Also, make-up sex between you is explosive. Like a drug, you keep coming back for more, even though you know sooner or later this relationship must end.

The Scorpio with Other Signs

Scorpio and Taurus

If anyone understands your jealousy, it's the Taurus. In fact, they're even flattered by it. What you both have in common is that you're thrifty, loyal, and very ambitious.

Where the Taurus can be relaxed and chill, you are a tad too intense for them. However, the one thing that makes you both incompatible is this: You're both super stubborn, and you have terrible tempers. You'll need to work on this if you want to have lasting love with each other.

Scorpio and Libra

In so many ways, you're both opposites. You're emotional, but Libra is very analytical. You have an intimate circle of friends and love deep connections, but the Libra loves to have a lot of light banter with many people. You're super intense, but the Libra keeps it casual. You can make this relationship work if you are both willing to compromise.

Scorpio and Aries

Oh, how you love the passionate Aries! You love their fire, but one thing keeps you both from working seamlessly: you can't quite get Aries to commit. This is not a problem if you're not interested in settling down. Because of your shared passions, you can both have mind-blowing sex.

Aries is a whimsical person, while you're very practical compared to them. There's only one way to make this work: You must not get too jealous when you see Aries doing their thing, and Aries must settle down and commit to you.

Scorpio and Leo

You both have very strong personalities. You both love control. You're both loyal, although Scorpio strongly doubts that Leo even knows the meaning of the word "loyal," and for a good reason: Leo is a born flirt. All that is flirting will only make the Scorpio jealous and stark raving mad.

However, there is an upside: You both are incredible in the bedroom together. The chemistry is unparalleled! But if you're looking for something more than a roll in the sheets, you'll notice you both have an issue with letting the other take control, especially with the Scorpion's wish to take charge in the face of Lion's pride.

Scorpio and Capricorn

You're both ambitious, diligent about what you do, and loyal. Capricorn is nowhere near as emotional as you are, Scorpio, but you can get them to be more romantic and emotional. You love that the Capricorn is dependable and down to earth, while the Capricorn can't get enough of your passion. It's not a bad match!

Scorpio and Scorpio

This relationship is amazing, since you feel like you've finally found a lover who gets you completely. You both love that you're emotional and loyal to each other. However, there can be struggle with this relationship because you are way too alike. You might also find that you're not so excited because mysterious as you both are on your own, together, there's no mystery. Add in the fact that you don't quite like the negative traits inherent in people born under the same sign as you, and, well, this might not last.

The Teen Scorpio and Relationships

The teen Scorpio in love has an active imagination and the same intense feelings common to all Scorpios. When any other teen falls for a Scorpio teen, the pull is simply powerful. It's super tempting to check your brain at the door as you walk into the teen Scorpio's world.

The teen Scorpio can be very affectionate, more so because they've probably not yet had any experiences to feel jaded about love. Since the relationship is new to them, the teen gives their all and holds nothing back. Intense is the only word to describe any relationship the Scorpio teen is in.

However, the Scorpio teen is very given to melodrama, drumming up crises where none exists. They strongly need to oversee everything and everyone around them, and exert their influence on whoever they're with. In other words, the Scorpio teen is willful, often to the point of being bossy in their relationships.

Remember that your Scorpio teen thinks about sex more than most, is intense, and super obsessive. Despite - or because of all this - the Scorpio remains very powerful and intriguing. Once the Scorpio teen has someone in their sights, their single-minded focus alone is enough to make other teens go weak in the knees. Your Scorpio teen might never say it aloud, but they enjoy having others under their control.

In a relationship with the Scorpio teen, it would be unwise of their better half to tag them on a social media post without their permission. They're not a big fan of public displays of affection. Just because they let you take that intimate picture doesn't mean they want you to post it for the whole world to see.

The partner of a Scorpio teen in a relationship would be wise to take time to win over the Scorpio. Let them reveal themselves to you when they're ready and the way they want to.

Thinking Long-term with the Scorpio

When you finally win over the Scorpio, you must do everything you can to never betray them. They have incredibly high standards and will not be so willing or able to forgive you or forget what you did.

If you're a Scorpio, then you treasure loyalty, trust, and love. You give these things freely to those who have shown you they are worthy of them. However, when your lover crosses you, you make a point of having them earn back your love, assuming you don't decide to just call it quits.

You're always to the point and very focused. You don't do half measures, and the same thing goes with relationships. So, when you're with someone, you're not with them in the meantime. You're with them for the long haul.

If you're in a relationship with a Scorpio, expect to enjoy more love than you've ever imagined possible. Also, the fact that they're the most amazing conversationalists and are articulate makes them absolutely alluring to you.

One likelihood you can have with a Scorpio is that they will do their best to figure you out on every level. Something about the Scorpio's eyes makes you feel you have nothing to hide, and you'd better not try either. When you choose to lay yourself bare before them, being honest about who you are, you will simply make them fall even deeper for you.

Quick Facts about Scorpios

- They're awesome at leading, inspiring, and encouraging others.

- You don't want to hinder their personal growth, or they will ruin you.

- They're not fans of people who are fake or superficial. They prefer deep connections with people who are driven and passionate.

- They do okay with long-distance relationships, staying deeply loyal no matter what.

- They are very particular about their words. They mean what they say and say what they mean.

- They are deathly afraid of being betrayed. Scorpio's find it particularly difficult to deal with betrayal at any stage in the relationship.

- They treasure honesty from those they care about.

- They love to be right — but this isn't a bad thing! They simply need self-assurance that they're on the right path.

- There's nothing they love more than being understood.

- They can be incredibly stubborn, just like the Taurus. Still, they can be open to doing things differently when coaxed the right way.

- Cross a Scorpio and get the full impact of their wrath.

- They never give up on projects that matter to them.

- The Scorpio is the multi-tasker extraordinaire.

- They're super resourceful and very driven.

- They can be incredibly loving and so peaceful, but can be filled with intense loathing and start World War III on the other end of the spectrum.
- They're tough to read, but they're well aware of their emotions.
- No one will have your back as a Scorpio does.
- They're super fun and very creative. It's never a dull moment with this sign!
- They love sentimental gifts from people who matter.
- Let them down once, and you might never get another shot.
- The Scorpio isn't a fan of quitters.
- Who loves to go to the most far-flung locations in the world for a vacation? This sign.
- They detest unfair judgments.
- Your Scorpio can be your partner, lover, or friend for life.

Obstacles that Arise when Dating a Scorpio

It isn't easy loving a Scorpio, but if you can work with these facts about them, you'll find it's totally worth it:

- They take a fair bit of time before they open up.
- They can get a little moody sometimes.
- They will need alone time, and that's okay.
- There's never a moment they're not ready and raring to go with sex. If you have a high sex drive, then this shouldn't be a problem for you.

Quick Guide to Dating a Scorpio

Dressing seductively will score you a lot of points. With lust, the Scorpio reigns supreme above other signs. Looking good is worth it, but of course, you need to do more than look good.

Before they say yes to a date with you, chances are they've gone all detective on your case. They'll do more than look you up on Google. They have ways and means to figure out what you're really about and see if they want to explore you more in person.

The Scorpio is slow about love. They aren't the sort to fall in love at first sight, and even if they do, they will take things slow and steady. They love it when seduction is subtle and are not fans of a direct, vulgar, or brutish advance. Just because they love sex does not mean they do not have standards and dignity... And just because they have standards and dignity doesn't mean they are not masters in the bedroom. That thing you heard about Scorpios? It's true.

Expect that the Scorpio will ask you lots of questions, allowing you to reveal yourself while being very adept at giving you only enough information to make you feel like you've got enough information. If you're lucky enough for them to pursue things further with you, you'll realize how little you know — and it will be such a delight to you!

Pick a spot for your date that seems to be secret, one that not everyone goes to or knows of is good for the Scorpio. Pay attention to them. Sincerely, share your passions with them. If you're going to see a movie, make sure it's one that has some mystery that needs to be unraveled — and make it a complex one.

It is imperative you show yourself to be confident — not by faking it, but by being okay in your own skin. You can be supportive of the Scorpio, but for goodness sake, don't be cloying with your sympathy, and don't be patronizing in your "support."

Pay attention to the Scorpio so you can give them the most thoughtful gifts they want, and they will appreciate that. Organize a getaway for you both; go somewhere; no one knows who you both are, and somewhere no one you both know can find you. They'll appreciate that.

Whatever you do, don't tell lies to the Scorpio, not even to impress them. They'll know it, or they'll find out one way or another, and then it's over between you two. The Scorpio loves a challenge and loves to be in control. You may indulge them, but do so without giving your power away; otherwise, you will lose their respect.

You must consider your motive for dating them. If you're thinking of using the Scorpio, then you'd better rethink it. Attempting to boss your Scorpio around is pointless. One way or another, the Scorpio will get their way. Don't bother trying to compete with them.

The last thing you want to do is to be so mired in your insecurity or self-pity around them. They won't stand for it. It's unattractive and is bound to push them away. Also, don't be too desperate and assume that you two are now an item when the Scorpio hasn't expressly said so or acknowledged the same thing.

You must be respectful of the Scorpio's need for privacy, and that means you should share nothing intimate about your relationship with your friends, whether in person or on social media. Again, never tag them in anything without asking them if it's okay.

Attracting the Scorpio Woman

To attract the Scorpio woman, realize that she loves to wield her sexual power, and so you mustn't come on to her too soon or too strong. She needs her space. You can allow for a touch here, a look there. This is not the time to be impulsive.

You must respect her. She needs to know you will not flake out on them when things get intense because she gives herself completely when she falls in love. So, you'd be better off with a slow build so she has time to know who you are. She's more about your actions, not your words. She values devotion over-sentimentality or just being "cute."

If you're just a braggart with nothing to offer when it comes to actual experiences, she can spot that from a mile away. She knows her strengths and knows her weaknesses just as well. You'd be wise to be very upfront about yours, without being overconfident or having a woe-is-me attitude.

You want to be the sort of person who watches her back, doesn't tease her when she's dealing with serious issues and shows respect for her innermost needs. The Scorpio woman is very pragmatic and all about taking action. They may have psychic abilities and be in touch with their intuition, but they're also aware of reality. They love it when their partner is productive and determined to make something of themselves.

Finally, you must be steady and consistent. The Scorpio woman is not looking for someone going to "hit it and quit it." She wants someone to be there for the long haul.

Attracting the Scorpio Man

He is full of secrets, and they will not come spilling out of him any time soon. You would be better off questioning him about things like what he's interested in and other safe subjects. Be very clear that you're not interested in invading his privacy, and he will come to respect you more. You can be sure that as you relate, he's feeling you out on a gut level.

The last thing you want to do is tell all on your first date. The Scorpio man is not a fan of someone who spills their guts way too early. If you notice you talk too much after a drink or two, maybe you should tone down the drinking.

There's nothing the Scorpio man loves more than someone who is in complete control of their life. To turn him off, show yourself to be the exact opposite. If you have no confidence in who you are, you might find the Scorpio man's every judging eyes to be intimidating and too much to bear. Hang in there, and when he warms up to you, you will find it was worth the discomfort.

With conversations, you can't go wrong talking about dark mysteries, hauntings, and weird things about the human psyche. He thrives and revels in that kind of talk.

Be mindful that it might be hard to tell what he feels about you at first blush. However, if he calls you and asks for another meeting, then you know he's serious. His attention, like his sign, is fixed — on you! If you treat him casually or like he doesn't matter, prepare for a nasty reaction. Remember that the Scorpio man doesn't trust easily, so it's possible for things to not work out for reasons best known to him and out of your control.

One thing about the Scorpio man is that his sensuality is unparalleled, but you'd never guess it because he keeps it under wraps, carefully hidden by his immense ability to control himself. Don't be fooled, though. His basic element is Water, which only means one thing: He is deeply emotional, and acts based on how he feels.

The Scorpio man loves to be subtly seduced, so give him just a bit here, a bit there, so you have him dreaming about what more there is to come. He is fine with drawing out the pleasure and stacking block after block of sexual tension before finally giving in. Also, he loves discretion when in public, as it gives a lot of time for the tension between you both to build. You want to make sure you can save him something for when it's just you two alone.

Chapter Five: The Social Scorpio

As a Scorpio, you're probably sick and tired of being called antisocial. Again, you are anything but antisocial; you're simply very selective of who you spend time with. The only way people can get to know this about you is if they become a part of your tribe — the only people who ever see the warm, witty, loving side of you when you're not self-conscious and you're carefree.

Why The Scorpio is an Amazing Friend

Scorpios connect deeply with their tribe. When you're a Scorpio, and you're with the people you connect with deeply, you can be very charismatic, charming, and engaging. You're the kind of person who engages others emotionally and makes them feel okay to share their feelings.

When dealing with people outside of the tribe, you're not bothered to pretend as you care about them. Even if they're your mother's nearest and dearest friend, you won't act all warm and cuddly if you don't feel like it; you don't see what the big deal is. You might be cordial, but that's about it.

You're not mean; you're simply selective because you love your tribe with a passion. Anyone who thinks you're mean has read you wrong. You're a Scorpio, which means you're very much about conserving your energy. You don't give it out to random strangers. You like to be mindful of where your time, passion, and interest goes. You're not a fan of random people or large crowds. When you're with your tribe, you can be the most adorable and lovable person on Earth!

As a Scorpio, you prefer deep, meaningful bonds with people. Inevitably, that means you will only be able to bond with a finite amount of people so you don't drain all of your energy. You're particular about who you spend time and swap ideas with, and you want to make sure that you don't waste any of it all on connections that are barely there or superficial. That might be okay with Aquarius since they don't discriminate and can share their emotions and affections all over the place, albeit thinly, but that doesn't work for you.

When you have the attention of a Scorpio, they're validating you. They salute who you are. It's a gift that you should treasure because it's very rare for them to give such lavish attention to anyone like that. It's not something they give all the time or a gesture that you can dismiss as lacking in substance. The Scorpio differs greatly from other signs in this regard.

Scorpio's are very shallow and often believe everything is about them. They reserve their attentiveness and emotions for a specific few. If you're one of these special people, you can rest assured you're getting the ultimate insight, kindness, charm and affection. They love to share with anyone who becomes a part of their tribe.

Because of how strong their love and devotion are, it's important that the Scorpio disregards anyone who isn't part of his tribe. He's not keen on socializing. She cares little for chatting. They don't care much for any social prompts they might get.

If you're not in the Scorpio's tribe, you must learn not to take it personally because odds are it has nothing to do with you. And no, they're not being cold or arrogant or playing games with you either.

They're just very selective about who they spend time with because they need to be able to preserve and protect their energy since, for the most part, they will often give others energy at their very own expense. It's a matter of survival, not snobbery.

Why Tribes Matter to Scorpios

The Scorpio holds her tribe in high esteem because this is a sign that's all about intimacy, not just in romance but in every form. Sure, the Scorpio is a very individualistic person. You might even be tempted to tag them, loners, since they don't feel a need to socialize or partner up with someone all day every day like the Gemini, Libra, or Pisces. That said, they can hop out of the loner bus now and then and spend a lot of their time and space with best buds.

Here's a Curious Fact About the Scorpio: Give them a romantic partner that's a great match, and they'll be fine. That's their primary need. There, they have no need for a platonic tribe, but they can still have one and love them as deeply and fiercely as they love their partner. Go figure.

Joining the Scorpio's Tribe

First, you must prove yourself to be trustworthy. When it comes to friendship with a Scorpio, you cannot afford to make a promise and not keep it! You must show loyalty and show that you're willing and able to communicate emotionally with them. Having said all this, this alone doesn't get you into the tribe.

You see, the Scorpio lives by its instincts. The Scorpio, you know, places a lot of value on the cosmic and the intangible. Picking their tribe can involve a lot of factors totally out of your control, and you could even say out of *their* control as well.

For instance, do you have chemistry? If you don't, how do you create it? You can't. It either is there for you both or isn't. Do you both have the feeling that you've known each other a lot longer than you really have? Do you fall seamlessly into conversations or just plain communion together? Do you feel comfortable together even when no one's saying anything? Do you experience a sense of synchronicity between you two when you talk, or joke, sing, dance, or cook together? It doesn't end there, though.

Part of these intangibles is that soul level call and response between two people who instantly get each other, so when one of you needs the other around, they're there and meeting the exact need every time. Also, do you know what it means to speak without words? Maybe you do, but does that happen between you and the Scorpio? Are you able to tell just from intuition how they're feeling or what they're thinking? Are you comfortable sharing your emotions even more than society would consider okay or normal, and if so, does the Scorpio sense that you're the kind of person willing to take that risk?

Also, consider if you're the type of person who can create changes in the Scorpio's life or set off a chain of events that rocks them but in a good way. Is this you? Are you able to keep secrets and take whatever is told to you right down to the grave? It might sound dramatic to you, but not to the Scorpio. Do you solemnly vow to be there for the Scorpio, to nurture the friendship just like you would a relationship? Again, you might think this is over the top, but that's not the case. If you still think so, then the Scorpio definitely doesn't intend to be your cup of tea. At best, you'll be an acquaintance, but never part of the tribe.

The First Rule of the Scorpio's Tribe: Don't Talk About the Tribe

Okay, not to be so dramatic, but if you're not a part of the Scorpio's tribe, you won't even know that they have one to begin with. You might never know who their people are, let alone their names. You might wrongly assume that the Scorpio is without friends. It's possible to even for the Scorpio's own family to be completely unaware of the fact that they have a whole freaking tribe of their own.

Within just moments of meeting someone else, you can tell as a Scorpio whether you want this person to be a part of your tribe. This feeling should not be compared to the sexual desire you may have had for this person, even those who have shared your bed in the past may not be let into your clan.

So, who makes up the tribe? Usually, you have Water signs as friends, especially fellow scorpions. You may also have people born under the Eighth house, and those with very intense Pluto influences. However, your tribe really comes down to your personal needs, your birth chart, what you like, and the energies you have in spades versus those you lack. There's no telling what it is that will draw you to someone else, so it's possible that your tribe is made up of several other signs.

The Scorpio's High Social IQ

Sure, to the untrained eye, it might seem that you have no form of social aptitude when dealing with the public. However, you have a lot of traits that show you to be socially intelligent, more so than most, and more than you're often willing to let on.

As a clear instance, your very astute observation skills, sharp and intense stares, and your ability to probe deeply into the psyche of whoever you're with is beyond amazon. You know how to read moods excellently. You read faces and places with just as much ease.

Someone uninformed might dismiss the Scorpio as a sociopath, but even they cannot deny that when you flip the switch, you're magnetic, and you ooze charm. It's the whole reason everyone wants you, or wants to be you, or wants to be around you. Some Scorpios can turn their magnetism and charm off and on as needed. There are others who will draw a crowd no matter what they do, even though they would rather go unnoticed.

The Most Socially Engaged Sign

We've already discussed the Scorpio's tendency to become disengaged, but this doesn't mean you're socially detached. It really means that you're engaged *socially.* In other words, you connect with whatever environment you find yourself in so deeply and intensely that you need to take a moment to keep yourself in check. You feel the need to repress the feelings inside of you, so you do your best to look unphased by them. On the inside, though, your reactions are off the charts because you're so in tune with the moment! This is another sign of your very high social IQ as a Scorpio.

You've simply got to continue to sort through all the frustrations around, so you know what or who deserves the intensity of your reactions, whether it's the outsider, a wallflower or someone who doesn't fit the mold. Then, of course, there are times when you very well know beneath all the seeming normalcy of things, something's not quite right, and perhaps even dangerous.

When you're a sensitive Scorpio, you find that some places have you so reactive that you can't stand to be there — ditto for some people, too. You can't stand to be in the same room as they are... Unless it's a part of your plan to get revenge or something of the sort. While other signs are fine with socially playing nice or ignoring whoever they've labeled "enemy," you feel the negative emotion so strongly that if you didn't get out of there yesterday, you're going to explode (or implode.)

When you're one of the stronger Scorpios, you have no issues totally shutting down and raising walls against all incoming stimuli so that it's just you in your own world, much like the Scorpio child does, so well to where parents and teachers often wrongly assume their child is autistic. This strategy, however, takes a lot out of you because it requires truckloads of concentration.

To wrap this all up: The Scorpio's ability to remain socially reserved is because of a very impressive level of discipline, all in the attempt to stop yourself from giving in to the temptation to use your Scorpio traits for ill instead of for good. You're very wise to be socially reserved. As any Scorpio who demonstrates "social promiscuity" can tell you — especially if they are young — there's a tendency to give in to such ungraceful behavior like manipulation, backstabbing, cattiness and gossip. They do this a lot more than any other zodiac sign. So, let no one make you feel like crap for being deliberate about how you socialize!

Scorpio Friendship Compatibility

Scorpio and Taurus: The bull is your astrological opposite. Yet, you know you know that all your secrets are safe with them, and you value that. While the bull may care little about your feelings sometimes, you don't pay as much attention to their wish to be comfortable. Still, Taurus has an amazing sense of humor and helps you find laughter even in sad or annoying things. What you offer to the Taurus is your uncannily accurate intuition, which keeps them from making rave mistakes they'll regret, especially with matters of the heart.

Scorpio and Aries: With this friendship, occasionally there will be flying sparks. That's one of the reasons you enjoy the Aries. They're not afraid to argue with you, and you relish every chance you get for some good sparring. It doesn't matter how much your views differ with politics and religion; you love that the ram has some fire going on! It's quite nearly as bright and as hot as your zest for life. How to maintain this wonderful friendship is to remember that the Aries never holds grudges, or at least they rarely ever do. Whenever you and your friend argue, they likely would have forgotten about it half an hour later. So, don't hold grudges against them, no matter how tempted you are to do so.

Scorpio and Cancer: Well, it's only natural for you water signs to get along! You love that the Cancer is incredibly affectionate. You'll never tell them this, but you enjoy it when they make you your favorite meal or get you your favorite drink. As for the crab, they love how you're able to tell what they're feeling without them having to say a word. They love you would never ever tease them for feeling the way they do and that you respect how sensitive they are. You both enjoy the water and probably love water sports like boating and swimming. You also both enjoy all activities that require using your hands — stuff like baking, sculpting, gardening, and so on. At the end of the day, no matter how boring or mundane what you're doing is, as long as you're doing it together, you both have the time of your lives.

Scorpio and Gemini: Gemini is really upbeat, and this contrasts with your own personality. This is one reason you enjoy being in their company. You love how they're able to send your blues running for the hills, thanks to their youthful spirit and their constant optimism. They help you remember that you should look on the bright side, no matter what. However, you can sometimes have an issue with their non-stop chatter, and in the same vein, they don't enjoy it when you get all moody and silent as usual. Still, you both are very fascinated with life, and you love to figure out the unanswered questions together. You both enjoy the mystery! This binds you both together.

Scorpio and Leo: Another optimistic sign, Leo, boggles your mind with how they always passionately pursue reasons to remain upbeat. You love it, and it captivates you to no end. When you're with Leo, everything just seems brighter. You find it hilarious when they try to establish control over you, and you wonder how they could ever assume that they can get the upper hand as far as your friendship goes. The lion is innocent. You know this. They are too pure to beat a lifelong strategist like yourself. Still, occasionally you should stroke the lion's ego. It's only fair since they're supportive when it comes to your talents.

Scorpio and Libra: Oh, the Libra. So charming. So impossible to resist. You love how beautiful and graceful they are. You're a complete sucker for their wit. You're a lot more emotional than they are since they're very light-hearted. For this reason, you both can have misunderstandings now and then. You might think that their casual statement was them being caustically chastising you. You're not the kind to be vocal about your displeasures, and so when they say something that rubs you wrong, it's way too easy to ruin your friendship. Here's a tip for keeping this friendship going: If they say something or do something that gets to you, then you should speak up about it right away rather than sit and stew. After all, you can trust the scales to weigh and address your complaints in a balanced way.

Scorpio and Sagittarius: The Sagittarius loves to have fun. You? Not always. That said, you still have a lot to gain from this upbeat friend, while they could take a page or two from you by learning to be sober when needed. The archer is the person who helps you open your mind so that you're willing to meet new people, have new experiences, and come up with new, brilliant ideas. You get to show them how it can be dangerous not to be discerning and discriminatory when needed. This friendship works for you both in that regard. Now, you may not care for their bluntness, which is legendary, but admit that your penchant for keeping secrets drives the Sagittarius up the wall! Still, these are just minor issues to be concerned about when you're both doing things you love to do together.

Scorpio and Aquarius: No one is as unpredictable as Aquarius. As good as you are at reading people, this sign is a challenge. You can't find a single logical thing about the way they act — and oddly enough, this is why you are full of admiration for the water bearer. You love that they have the most unorthodox ideas. They keep you entertained. Sure, you might find that Aquarius is, well, all over the place with the things they're interested in. Still, you love how loyal they are. For you, their loyalty is all that counts. For Aquarius, they absolutely cannot resist your charms. Each day, they continue to be shocked at how well you can deduce things that lurk beneath the surface, unnoticed by others. If you're okay with how forgetful they are, then they can make peace with how jealous you get, and you can both be great pals.

Scorpio and Capricorn: You love how stable Capricorn is, and they love how passionate you are. When things get a bit too much for you, the goat will always be there with their stabilizing influence. They have the most practical advice, which you will find to be amazing. They'll keep you clear-headed and still, no matter how stormy things get. You are great at helping Capricorn find their inner spark whenever they become overwhelmed by the world and its issues. You may not like how pushy Capricorn gets, and they may not like that you're never willing to just let things go, but at your core, you both share the depth and a lot of similar interests.

Scorpio and Pisces: Your bond with Pisces is soul deep. This is one person who is okay with you and all your faults and warts. Chances are, they were drawn to you because of your faults, to begin with. They just love when people have flaws because, to them, it makes people more human and relatable, and this is why you guys have a good thing going on. They love spiritual issues, just like you do. Like you, they desire intellectual conversations about the law of attraction, religion or philosophy. You might be irritated by their tendency to hop from opinion to opinion, but this isn't a big deal because there's so much you love about hanging out with them. In any case, you're not perfect either. The fish is not a fan of your intense obsession over a love interest.

Scorpio and Virgo: There's not a better friend to have by your side than the Virgo. Because they're so down-to-earth, they will give you the perspective you need on anything. If you feel like you need someone to give you a reality check or tell you the truth without sugarcoating it, then the Virgo is your pal. When the Virgo analyzes whatever you share with them carefully, they'll let you know what they think is the most honest yet tactful way possible, respecting your feelings. Your Virgo friend is full of admiration for you, just as much as you love the gifts they share with you. The level of your intensity continues to be an inspiration to the Virgo, who's a tad shy about sharing how they feel. Thanks to you, they can learn to turn their love for writing, reading, or anything else into an actual passion. Now, the Virgo is prone to nitpicking, and this can irk you sometimes. But your habit of holding grudges will drive them nuts with impatience. After all is said and done, a little understanding from both of you will go a long way towards building a lifelong friendship.

Scorpio and Scorpio: When you're friends with another scorpion, it's an exquisite pleasure and exquisite pain! You love them because, finally, here's someone who understands your intense passion for life. As for the pain, it's because you're both experts at going down to the very depths of hopeless despair. Still, there's an upside to being friends with another Scorpio: You both have a deliciously dark sense of humor, which proves useful when things get tough for either or both of you. You'll get mad at each other and explode; there's no avoiding that when it's two scorpions in a friendship. Still, you'll wind up finding each other again and again because there's nothing more amazing than the empathy you both share, which creates an allure too intense to resist.

Chapter Six: Shades of Scorpio

Your sun sign is split into cusps and decanates, or decans, if you will. These are basically categories that help you further define yourself as the person you are, rather than just a simple focus on your sun sign all by itself. Everyone's birthday falls under a certain decan and cusp of their sign. We're going to look at each one in detail below.

Decans

All zodiac signs are split into three unique categories, with each called a *decan*. This term comes from the Greek word *dekanoi*, which translates to "separated by ten days." Originally, the Egyptians had this term. They had a calendar which assigned 360 days to a year. Another interesting thing about the Egyptian calendar was that each year had 12 months, each made up of thirty days — and that meant no one born on the 29th of February ever had to worry about celebrating every four years, which is a good thing. Now, each month of their calendar was split into three parts, with each part comprising ten days. These ten days were known as dekanoi.

To date, astrology still divides the zodiac into decans. Think of a circle that is 360 degrees as a whole; one decan would be no more than a 10-degree part of that circle, which lasts for just ten days before the next decan takes over. Each day, the sun goes through this zodiac circle by just one degree. Yes, this is not entirely accurate since we now work with a calendar where some months are over 30 days and one month has a day that ghosts us all every four years, but you get the idea.

I want to clarify that a sign's decan does not radically change the traits of that sign. It does improve the connection that the person has to their sign. If you're a Scorpio born in the fifth decan, you can expect to differ greatly from another Scorpio born in the second decan.

Each decan is assigned to a constellation. Every constellation has its own spiritual implications, which lend themselves further to making you unique. And each decan is ruled by a planet, often called a *sub ruler*. Think of the sub ruler like the second in command or vice president. It simply enhances your unique qualities within your decan.

The Three Decans of Scorpio

As you're a water sign, here are the three decans you need to know about as a Scorpio. You'll learn which one you are soon enough.

The First Decan — Intensity: October 23 and November 2

Being born under the first decan means you are Scorpio/Scorpio. Your ruling planets are Mars and Pluto. You're the purest of Scorpios, and your Scorpio energy is enhanced in good and bad ways.

You can remain calm even in the face of danger or the toughest of situations, thanks to Mars and Pluto, when they offer you strong support. However, when the planets are challenged, maybe you can have extreme fears. Still, it doesn't matter because you're always more than prepared for the worst.

You're the most sensual of the Scorpios, and your libido is unparalleled. You have obsessive tendencies, strong desires, and are beyond driven. As much as you love pleasure, you are also open to grief, loss, sorrow, and suffering. You don't think things come easy; still, you have a bulldog-like tenacity for getting what you want. You have the willpower and courage you need to overcome the odds, and you are amazing at rebounding when things don't work out, and at starting anew.

You're a loner for the most part, and you're very secretive about your personal business. You're not the kind who's super talkative or friendly at first blush. Your eyes can be rather intimidating to those not bold enough to meet fire with fire. You might also seem unapproachable or cold, or sometimes even cruel.

According to evolutionary astrologists, you're the one just learning how to make use of your energies as a Scorpio, and you might make a few mistakes you need to learn from during your life.

In tarot, the Scorpio's first decan is represented by the Five of Cups. The keywords of this decan are grief, loss, and anger.

The Second Decan — Transmutation: November 2 to November 11

You're a Scorpio/Pisces. Just as driven as any other Scorpio, but also possessing the Pisces energy and the rulers Jupiter and Neptune, all of which moderate your drive. The most common themes in the lives of those born under this decan are death and resurrection.

If this is you, you feel as though you have a much higher purpose than most. You'll go through a lot of transmutation in the process of figuring out what that purpose could be. When Jupiter and Neptune are properly placed in your chart, it's possible and easy for you to figure out your talents and gifts. If these planets aren't well placed, you might find you don't have as much faith in yourself as you should, and you don't trust others as much as you should, which could lead to you being needlessly scared of failing or being betrayed.

As a Scorpio/Pisces, you seek wisdom. You love it when you deal with smoke and mirrors, hidden meanings, and elusive hints. You crave mystery and are not afraid of taking a walk on the dark side. You care about the occult, the mystical, the esoteric. You are always looking for what is real and true, and as such, you will sacrifice whatever you must find it.

Your magnetism is beautifully raw. It never wavers, and it is extremely seductive. You might find yourself as a healer, always willing to sacrifice yourself. You might have a bit of a God complex, adept in the art of manipulation, unparalleled when it comes to your cunning, which you use to gain control over other people. Your mysterious aura draws people to you.

In the tarot, Scorpio's second decan is represented by the Six of Cups. Your keywords are peace, forgiveness, and harmony.

The Third Decan — Manifestation: November 12 to November 22

As a Scorpio/Cancer, your Scorpio energy is tempered by Cancer and the Moon. You have emotional integrity, and you're comfortable trusting your feelings. You're not the sort who would ever give in to compromise.

You tend to sacrifice yourself and take care of the people nearest and dearest to you, but you're also sensitive, and so you get hurt easily. You'll never show the pain openly, of course, but you never forget what caused it to begin with. When time and chance present themselves, you will exact revenge, and do so generously.

You have deep and dark emotions running through you as a Scorpio/Cancer. When the Moon is challenged on your chart, you could easily just bury everything you're feeling while feeling lonely, lost, and abandoned. When your Moon is properly placed, you are better at dealing with your painful emotions. It's easier for you to observe them, and as such, you can be forgiving of yourself and others and to be more accepting.

Your willpower is a Scorpio/Cancer is unparalleled, as is your self-confidence. You have it in you to always do good and sensitive. You can be a compelling writer or speaker who moves people forcefully thanks to your eloquence and compassion. Your charm also makes it, so you always get results when you work with a group, or you're going after something that you believe in heart and soul.

The Scorpio's third decan in the tarot is the Seven of Cups. Your keywords are finding where you fit in, soul searching, and self-examination.

Cusps

Now let's talk about cusps. If you've ever bothered to read material on various zodiac signs, chances are you've thought to yourself, "Well, why do I feel like Scorpio and Libra wrapped in one?" You wonder if there's any truth in astrology and you wonder if it's not just a bunch of people writing many things about people born in each month and hoping some of it sticks. Well, there's an explanation for that.

Every zodiac sign has something called a cusp, which is basically like the boundary between one sign and the next. Say your birthday is right when the sun is moving from one zodiac sign to the next; that would mean you were born on a cusp, and you would express yourself not as one sign but two! Sometimes both energies blend beautifully, while other times, it's a bumpy ride. Still, depending on the cusp you're born into, you take on certain qualities:

- Aries/Taurus — the power cusp: April 16 — 22
- Taurus/Gemini — the energy cusp: May 17 — 23
- Gemini/Cancer — the magic cusp: June 17 — 23
- Cancer/Leo — the oscillation cusp: July 19 — 25
- Leo/Virgo — the exposure cusp: August 19 — 25
- Virgo/Libra — the beauty cusp: September 19 — 25
- Libra/Scorpio — the drama cusp: October 19 — 25
- Scorpio/Sagittarius — the revolution cusp: November 18 — 24
- Sagittarius/Capricorn — the prophecy cusp: December 18 — 24
- Capricorn/Aquarius — the mystery cusp: January 16 — 23
- Aquarius/Pisces — the sensitivity cusp: February 15 — 21
- Pisces/Aries — the rebirth cusp: March 17 — 23

Scorpio Cusps

The Drama Cusp, Libra/Scorpio: If this is your cusp, then you're ruled by Pluto and Venus. You're the type of person who is quick to let people know exactly what you're thinking, even if it will be painful to hear. It would be best if no one asks you a question that could lead to a hurtful, blistering truth unless they're ready for it. It's a great trait to have for work and at home, but if you are not mindful of how you drop your truth bombs, you might bruise a lot of heart.

You can be critical. You can be tenacious. And you can be oh so seductive. Because you're very willing and able to tell the truth, you have the upper hand when it comes to your social interactions with others. You're brimming with charisma because you have tons of sexual energy, pure and raw, and you're also charming in a very detached way. You can get sarcastic sometimes and even bossy, but in all of that, your honesty makes you the object of admiration.

With relationships as someone born on the cusp of Libra and Scorpio, you're super loyal and romantic. The problem is, your loyalty is so intense that you can get jealous sometimes, and that jealousy can wreck your love life if you don't watch it. Fortunately, you've got a very dogged tenacity about you, so if you want to do your best to keep your jealousy in check, you will find a way to do just that.

Your ability to stay determined and single-minded about your goals is great with work, as you often make your big goals happen. You can have a bit of ego, though, so you want to pause and think through things when you feel unwilling or unable to change something.

An important thing to do all the time is a check-in with yourself about your ego. You want to know if it's in the way of you becoming the best version of yourself. While you do this, you need to apply the same honesty you dish out to everyone to yourself as well and be just as brutal. Cut off anything you don't need that's getting in your way, whether it's a habit or a person who drains you every time you meet.

A final note for those born on the Libra-Scorpio cusp: Jealousy is something you want to quash. It will do nothing good for you. You want to learn to trust yourself and the people around you. Sure, you don't like the sound of this advice (or any advice, for that matter, since you'd rather people minded their own business and left you alone), but it will help you to take it in the long run.

The Revolution Cusp, Scorpio/Sagittarius: This is quite the combination, with the Scorpio, intense and dark, and the Sagittarius, active and bold. You're ruled by Mars, Pluto, and Jupiter. Your whole life is about going against conventions. If you learn that something should be done a certain way, you'll seek additional ways to do the same thing. You're the type of person who becomes an expert at anything easily, by teaching yourself. You love to learn by doing an activity and getting your hands dirty. Astrologers consider you to be the zodiac's wild child and a rebel at heart as a child.

When you do grow up, you can be contrarian, rebellious, and revolutionary. You're a true leader, with no fear whatsoever. You take everything you've ever learned during your many adventures and apply that towards becoming the best of authority figures. It's possible for you to become a truly powerful person, ever progressive, but here's the thing: You need to learn to always be objective and never let your emotions cloud your judgment. If you give in to knee-jerk reactions, that could be your undoing.

When you're born on this cusp and the Scorpio energy is stronger than the Sagittarius, you'll notice that jealousy is your weak point and could cause your possible downfall. You're possessive when you're in a relationship, but on the flip side, you're loving, romantic, and kind. You are competitive, often competing against yourself, allowing you to achieve great success. You have a drive that makes you see things through to the end, and never, not once, do you not complete something you set out to achieve.

Being a Scorpio/Sagittarius means you will be at loggerheads with authority, so ditch the thought of a 9 to 5 job and consider becoming your own boss. Chances are, you already know this, and you've already set things up, so you never have to answer to anyone that isn't you. If this is you, be mindful: Always be kind and generous with your professional life.

Something to remember as a Scorpio/Sagittarius is that you can get pessimistic, adopting a dreary, been-there-done-that frame of mind. For this reason, you tend to feel left out of things. However, you've got a lust for life unmatched by any other, and that makes you a super amazing person!

Chapter Seven: The Professional Scorpio

That people are very drawn to you, dear Scorpio, can be very useful in your career. You're one of the most ambitious and determined of workers, and you know without a shadow of a doubt what it is you want to achieve professionally.

You're determined to make your dreams come true, and you know just how to strategize your way to success. It also helps that you're able to keep a level head when everyone's losing theirs because of a chaotic event. You're more patient than most, and you can endure the highs and lows of whatever your professional life throws at you.

You're not a fan of taking orders, and you'd rather work on your own. You're the best at giving orders, though — quite literally. You'd do excellently well in the military. Despite this, you're not the type of person who likes to be in the limelight, professionally. For you, it's all about pulling strings behind the scenes because, as far as you're concerned, that is where true power lies. You could make a wonderful tax inspector, or a detective, police officer, or even a spy.

You have an innate ability to lead, heal, investigate, create, and touch people with your talent and your mind. That you're very curious about everything and you're passionate about the mystical things in life means you could also do well with pathology, psychology, and research.

Science is a field you should consider, as scorpions are great physicians, and usually the best of surgeons. You could also excel in art, journalism, and literature if you consider those professions.

You're the type of person who instinctively knows the difference between right and wrong, even when others can't really see it. Therefore, you will be excellent in the business, as long as you work independently and don't feel like you're confined. You are the woman with the words that flow like honey. It's not unusual for your presence to be requested at things like TED talks because you're a powerful orator, and you write as powerfully as well. Consider a career in marketing, or maybe even politics.

So, you have a rough idea of the kinds of jobs you can handle. Let's really get into a few that you just might find to be a perfect fit and why you should consider making a career change if you're not already doing something you would naturally find fulfilling.

Scorpio Jobs

As a Scorpio, you're magnificent in terms of jobs. You work hard, and your powers of perception are extraordinary. You love when your work has zero distractions, and don't be so accessible to everyone. You love it when you can do things the way you want to. However, here are some positions you should consider:

Detective: You're infinitely curious, and you love to discover secrets while holding on to your own. So, you'd be really good at figuring out all the stuff people do their best to keep under wraps. You're amazing at going undercover, silently watching everyone like a hawk while they remain blissfully unaware that they're giving themselves away. You're the best of researchers, and you never stop until you've uncovered everything. It also helps that you have a thing for revenge. You could also be a life coach, a private investigator, or a journalist.

Chemist: You love work that is scientific in nature. Through your curiosity, you'll be able to come up with new reactions or even challenge the status quo in your field. Your hands are steady, and your love for research will serve you well in this profession. For these reasons, you should also consider these professions: biologist, coroner, oncologist.

Pharmacist: You're very hardworking and ambitious, but more than that, you are the type of person who is enduring and has lots of fortitude. These traits make you very suited to being a pharmacist. Sure, there's a lot of education involved, and you've got to be as precise as possible, but you'd really shine here, combining your science know-how with your people skills all well-being left alone to do quality work. You could also be a surgeon.

Psychiatrist: Of course, this job has you all over it! You get to hear all sorts of salacious secrets — all while helping your clients to figure out the messes in their lives and feel better. You're amazing at mapping out the human psyche and looking closely at details, and this line of work will keep you very engaged. You'll also be immensely successful at it. Other professions like this for you to consider are therapist, guidance counselor, biographer, memoirist, anthropologist.

Surgeon: You're driven, intense, and have endurance in spades. You're also plagued by a need for excellence in all you do, and you always get said excellence. It's for this reason that you would do fabulously well as a Surgeon. Your tenacity and deep reserves of inner strength allow you to continue what you're doing, even when others have lost hope. Other professions you should consider are EMT, tradesperson, electrician.

Researcher: You can find a fair number of scorpions in scientific labs, deeply immersed in research for the government or private agencies. You love nothing more than to consider a problem and then figure out how to deal with it. You're great at evaluating conundrums and coming up with results. You need to be the best at everything that makes you more likely to be the researcher who comes up with the answer to eradicating the common cold and cancer or coming up with an amazing weight loss fix. Consider these other professions as well: marketing executive, consultant, analyst.

Auditor: Your keen eye for details, precision, tenacity, and endurance will ensure your success in this field. You have no issues sifting through all sorts of data for hours on end. You're very effective at communicating and just as dependable, which means you're the kind who can make critical decisions. Also consider these professions: data analyst, accountant, researcher.

Human Resources: You would have no problems going over the most convoluted of health plans and working out all 401ks. You're good at remaining on top of things when it comes to employee records, as well as figuring out their very complicated needs. You know how to manage several things at once, and you know how to prioritize effectively. You'd be amazing at this profession, but you could also consider these: systems engineer, cultural architect, chief operating officer.

Hypnotist: You love to be in control, and you're enamored with the human mind — the unconscious where all sorts of dark wonders lie in wait for you to discover. You can work with clients trying to break terrible habits or get over phobias. You'd have to suggest things to them while they're under hypnosis to help them with these issues or help them remember things they've buried and tucked away from their conscious mind, or even help them recall their past lives. You are the go-to sign for all things hidden and secret. Also consider these professions: astrologist, medium, psychic.

Sex Therapist: If anyone has issues in the bedroom that need fixing, you're the best person for the job. Imagine it: You get to hear all sorts of fascinating secrets, learn about people's sexual fantasies and all other embarrassing things people would rather not share — and none of that phases you. You're Scorpio, after all! Nothing could shock you, and you have a knack for getting right to the heart of the issue. You, better than anyone else, can help your clients to work through their bedroom problems. You should also consider these occupations: life coach, occupational therapist, urologist, OB-GYN.

The Scorpio Employee

You're highly determined to get things done. You're never confused about the things you want to achieve or the means you need to make them happen. You're the type of person who moves with a sense of purpose, remaining steadfast to your goals. When you've been assigned a task, your boss knows that it's already a done deal. You're going to make sure they get what they want, no matter what.

You've got a very analytical mind. You've got one of the most perceptive and sharpest minds of all the signs, while also being aware of your true nature. You are the employee who understands what other people are thinking and feeling without them having to say a word.

You know what drives your colleagues — or what would drive them to action if they're not moving as hard or as fast as you'd like. You know their weaknesses and their strengths, and you use this knowledge to get them to pull their own weight, whether it's about completing a task, demanding better pay, or anything else.

You're extremely confident in yourself and your abilities, for a good reason. The Taurus and Capricorn may know a thing or two about being determined, but something sets you besides these signs: You know darned well what you're good at, and you trust yourself implicitly to handle whatever needs to be done.

You're not the sort who deludes themselves, and you'd never lie to yourself about your weaknesses, strengths, and motivations. You've got this quiet self-assurance that has nothing to do with an ego like it would with Aries or with self-aggrandizement like it would with Leo. You're self-assured because you know yourself objectively. You're not the kind of employee who would blame other workers for what you know is your own fault. Instead, you set about fixing things and coming out on top!

You crave power. Usually, this motivates you. It's the reason you do all you do. It's not about needing to feel secure, like the Taurus, and it's not about wanting to put amazing ideas into action like the Aquarian employee. For you, you're about the power, which means your position, your influence over others, and all the trappings that come with being the head honcho or the one who moves and shakes things.

Your need for power will shape your relationships with your coworkers. You're the person who will try again and again, despite constantly being told "no." You are unflappable in the face of rejection because you believe that you will have your way sooner or later. You're not fazed by tantrums either, and you're happy to allow people to have their way because you know in your heart that you're the one who really is central to their success.

As a Scorpio employee, you know very well that the way to get power is through your boss, and so you will do everything your boss asks. If a coworker were to rub you the wrong way, they should watch their back. You are legendary when it comes to revenge and vindictiveness, using your fatal sting on all who you believe deserve it. You're not likely to forgive a wrong, no matter how much time has passed or how many times you've gotten an apology. When the time is right, that coworker will regret not leaving the company the day you took on the job.

It would be wise for your boss to treat you with dignity and caution, no matter how accommodating you are. You will find a way to match their position or surpass them. The last thing they need is to be on your bad side.

You are super secretive. You're reserved and cautious. You don't engage in social relationships at work because you love your privacy, and you don't think it's necessary. You'd rather have lunch on your own, not chat it up at the water cooler. You won't be caught dead trying to organize the Christmas party, that's for sure. If anyone wants to get along with you well at work, then it would be wise for them not to go poking and prodding about your social or personal life.

You are calm on the outside, yet you feel things intensely. With working, you only ever allow just a glimpse of your strong emotions to come through, often in a quick flash of anger or annoyance or in a warm look of appreciation. You're a pro at hiding how you feel, and your emotions will remain hidden.

In the end, you're an employee with your own business to run: Becoming number one. Your steely tenacity, sharp mind, and unswerving courage mean that wherever you work, you're that company's most valuable asset.

The Scorpio Boss

You're very determined. As a Scorpio boss, you're courageous and tenacious, and these are the qualities that have landed you where you are. You're not afraid to take risks, even in the face of insurmountable difficulties. You're going to start, and you're going to finish what you start. You're not the type of person who opts out of things you've gotten yourself into, no matter what happens. This is why you're the best at leading others, and you're the best at dealing with crises in the company.

Because of your courage and dogged determination, you expect others to give you the same energy. Never are you indecisive or squeamish about making tough decisions. You march on in confidence well-founded in your abilities. For you, it's not a popularity contest. You will put your employees through whatever you believe is necessary to get the best out of them.

You're extremely temperamental. You oscillate between extreme emotions. You're better at keeping your emotions in check at work than in love, but sometimes you show these emotions by being very critical of an employee who messed up while being full of praise moments later. You're not like the Libra, who maintains balance and poise. You're the type of boss who doesn't mind playing head games with your employees if you sincerely believe it will get them to do their best work.

You're cautious and hold on to your secrets. You're not like the Cancer or Libra boss who gets chatty with the employees about their family. You will never give them even an inkling about what you're thinking. There's no point in your employees trying to know your business because they'll get nothing out of you and will only annoy the heck out of you.

You seem very calm and collected, yet you are full of all sorts of very intense emotions. Your passion knows no bounds — and it's the whole reason you choose to be secretive to protect yourself from those who would exploit these emotions. You're never going to bare it all for everyone to see because you believe it would lead to disaster, hurt, and disappointment.

You're extremely perceptive. Your powers of perception are unparalleled, and they help you keep control of your employees. You're able to tell what people are all about with mind-boggling accuracy. You can get right to other people's core and understand what makes them tick. Therefore, you have a natural bent for the occult and the psychic, especially if you're female. Anyone who wants to impress you had better be honest about themselves, as with your eyes alone, you can cut through deception like a hot knife through butter — and you detest dishonesty deeply.

You're possessive and jealous. With the people you care about, you're *very* possessive. How does this translate to work? Well, your employee had better mind themselves when it comes to moonlighting or their allegiances to whoever you consider "the enemy," which could be a rival company or brand or someone else who is vying for their seat.

A Libran boss may be able to demonstrate equanimity, but no one should expect you, the Scorpio boss, to understand that the only reason you were just face-timing the head of a department in a rival company is that they're your brother's wife. Either the employee deals with you and your company alone, or they resign.

If an employee ever tries to put one over you, then they have better just clear their desk. You're the type of boss who will exact vengeance if you feel you've been betrayed or cheated, and there is no length you will not go to teach the offending employee a lesson.

It could be a tad daunting working for a boss like you, but your employees are thankful because they can borrow a leaf from your determination and drive as they observe you working. They need only to be honest, hardworking, and loyal, and they'll have a swell time at the office with you!

Obstacles the Scorpio Faces at Work

Your vindictiveness can be a problem. Because of your vindictive nature, you may run into some problems at work. This same vindictiveness could very well hold you back from true greatness. You really should learn to let go of grievances. You can't always have everything you want, and you need to make peace with that fact.

Also, you'll want to get a grip on the underlying aggression which hides beneath your calm and collected exterior because occasionally it could break out — and it could mean the difference between advancing in your career or remaining stuck where you are.

You're not a team player. If you work in a solitary environment, this is okay, but when you work with others, your ambition combined with your secretive nature is detrimental. You might consider your coworkers to be your competition and wall yourself off from them. You want to dial back your intensity and give cooperation a chance. You might like it! Or not. That's okay.

You must resist the urge to play dirty. Let's not sugarcoat this fact: No one's a better, more cunning, diabolical schemer than you are. You have dirty tricks that *have dirty tricks* for days up to your many, many sleeves. This is great when you're on the battlefield, and you're a general going up against a formidable enemy, perhaps, but you need to dial that back for working.

For one thing, you're wasting all that amazing mind power on trying to get even and ruin someone else. You need to realize, in the end, it's not worth it. It will not change what happened, and all you'll achieve is making everyone else too cautious about dealing with you — so much so they'll just keep their distance. This is not particularly the best or most productive work environment to be in.

For another, you need to be mindful of becoming so lost in the constant scheming that you forget about what matters to you the most: Securing a much better position for yourself at work. At the end of the day, you need people to be able to put in a good word for you, and if all you do is cause trouble, then you might as well kiss your dreams of success goodbye.

Be mindful of your jealousy. Sometimes, things aren't what you think, despite how astute you are at judging things and people. It won't help to assume an all or nothing stance for dealing with your colleagues and bosses.

You've got to understand that humans are all different and complicated, and they won't fit neatly into the boxes you've assigned to them. They will have many motivations, relationships, friendships, and connections — and there's nothing wrong with that! Just because someone is friends with another person in a different department or company, or they're friends with someone you deeply despise, doesn't mean they could be out to get you or have betrayed you.

Learn to be at peace with the fact that you will not always be number one in the life of every member of your tribe, whether that tribe is a personal or a professional one. We all have lots of other obligations — including you! Resist the temptation to undo these other connections you don't approve of, because eventually you'll also alienate the very people you're trying to keep all to yourself. Worst-case scenario, your company will give you the boot when they learn how toxic you've been, or if you're the boss, your employees might decide there's not enough money in the world that could tempt them into staying with you.

The next time you see a colleague you value "fraternizing with the enemy," just stop, take a moment, shut your eyes, take a deep breath, exhale slowly and tell yourself it will be okay. When the people around you notice how accommodating you are, who knows? You might discover some amazing individuals you might never have known if you remained jealous.

Chapter Eight: Scorpio Sexual Compatibility

Scorpios are simply hypnotic. They brim with pure sensual and sexual magnetism. They're the one sign that has you falling in love faster than usual, with their ability to see through you, right to your very core, and that uncanny hold they have over you sexually. You may fall easy for the Scorpio, but they don't fall that easily for you — and that is by design.

The thing about being Scorpio is that it's difficult for you to trust. It's going to take a lot to get you to drop your guard and just let someone in. This is ironically part of your allure and what gives you that mysterious aura everyone is so drawn to. Nothing's sexier than the mystery you exude! People are drawn to you because they want to know what lies beneath your seemingly cool and collected exterior.

People assume that you're the type of person who's just cold, always scheming and calculating. This is far from true. You just don't want to get hurt because you feel things deeply and profoundly.

Your sexual prowess and stamina is the stuff of legends. Anyone who's been in bed with a Scorpio knows that nothing and no one else will ever compare or be as good as you. You take sex seriously; in fact, you could even say sex is sacred to you. It means surrendering to ecstasy as one, and you don't take that lightly. Also, it's how you're able to release and express the emotion you don't let out easily, which is why most Scorpios need to have lots and lots of sex.

When you're in love, you're one hundred percent committed to the other person. You're very devoted and very loyal. As far as you're concerned, this is your last stop, and you will be with them forever. Your love can border on obsession, and the more insecure you are (often because of being betrayed in the past), the more you will need to be in control, and the more you'll allow jealousy to take over you.

The Scorpio and Fidelity

You're not into being unfaithful to whoever you're with. You desire security, and so you value permanence and commitment in your relationships. The only time you ever stray was when your partner went fishing at a different lake already. You're not going to forgive or forget that without payback.

Scorpio and Aries

You both have a lot in common. You just have different styles of battle. Where Aries is quick to go in for the kill, you prefer to go for the slow burn. You'd think you both couldn't work because Aries is fire and you're water, but it's not that bad. You both have an incredibly high libido, and that can make for a lot of passion between the sheets! You'll both experience a tussle for control on account of being ruled by Mars, and you might not be willing to surrender to each other. You also will have a lot of mutual jealousy.

Scorpio and Cancer

You're well-matched with the Cancer since you're both aware of what the other person needs on a gut level. Your connection can be profound and intense. You're both very passionate, which is great because it means you'll be very intimate and loving with each other.

However, the second jealousy or sexual insecurity arises, things can be blown out of proportion.

Scorpio and Libra

You're not likely to click in the beginning. The Libra keeps a cool head most of the time, and so they may not be able to relate with the Scorpio's intense passion and jealousy. Being with the Libra means you will get jealous a lot because they can be a tad indecisive when it comes to committing sexually. You love a healthy spar, but the Libra doesn't care for confrontation, and so you'll find their never-ending niceness to be disingenuous and irritating. However, once you both have a sexual relationship that is steady, you can get pretty intimate and close with each other. This is because you both value togetherness, and you put a relationship that absorbs you both above all else.

Scorpio and Capricorn

You both have a lot in common because neither of you commits to a relationship easily. You'd both rather go slow and steady. Capricorn might find your sexual passion a little too hot to handle sometimes. You, on the other hand, might think the goat a tad too distant and cold, especially in the bedroom. However, you are both very serious about love, and with some work, you can easily get through your issues.

Scorpio and Taurus

You're an amazing match! You both have a yin yang balance going on, which makes you a wonderful whole. The Taurus will need to be a bit more sensitive, and you, the Scorpio, will need to be a bit less sensitive. Also, you both need to learn to get a handle on your jealousy and sexual insecurities. However, you're both committed and loyal to one another, and you can make this work.

Scorpio and Leo

You both have high libidos. This can make things amazing in the bedroom. No one could ever accuse your love life of being dull. However, you both have a tendency to want to control the other, and you don't find it easy to give yourself fully to the other. What results is a constant battle or power struggle that can develop into full-on aggression. You're both prone to jealousy when it comes to sex, and you, in particular, Scorpio, can get very suspicious and distrustful.

Scorpio and Scorpio

Sexually, there's no denying that you're a perfect match. You're both aware of what each other wants and needs, and your souls are intertwined in an inexplicably amazing way. You're both passionate, and this means a lot of chemistry in the bedroom! The only trouble is when you both get possessive or feel sexually insecure; then issues get all out of hand. You both want to be in charge, and neither of you is interested in surrendering to the other. Your minds are ever suspicious, your egos ever vulnerable, and you can play a lot of power games when it comes to sex.

Scorpio and Aquarius

Sexually, you're both really mismatched at the start. The water bearer has a take-it-or-leave-it viewpoint and is not a fan of being tied down. This is precisely what makes you grow jealous and even resent them. For the Aquarius, you're a tad too manipulative, and they wish you would let them be rather than be so possessive. The only way things can work for you both is if you lighten up, Scorpio. Also, the water bearer must learn to be a lot more sensitive to your vulnerability and sensitivity, both of which run deep.

Scorpio and Gemini

You're both not really a match. The Gemini is quite the flirt. They can be a tad inconsistent and fickle with love. You already know without a doubt this means you will get jealous more times than you care to, and you will resent them for making you feel that way. As for the Gemini, they think you're too controlling and too possessive sexually. How to make things work between you two is simple: The Gemini needs to understand that you are a deeply passionate person, and you don't do half measures, so they need to be respectful of your feelings. On your end, Scorpio, you can try to be a little less intense. A tricky proposition, but if you set your mind to it, you can make it happen.

Scorpio and Virgo

You have a lot in common with this Earth sign. You both take your relationship seriously, and you both value security and privacy. This is great! Sure, the Virgo can find your emotional intensity a tad too overwhelming, and you might think the Scorpio way too much of an aloof, clinical prude, but because you're both willing to make a good go of your sex life, there's no problem you can't resolve together.

Scorpio and Sagittarius

This is not a perfect match by any stretch of the imagination. First, the Sagittarius has a bad case of wanderlust. They can be flirtatious with just about anyone, and this will naturally cause a Scorpio to get jealous and possessive. The only way things can work with you two is if the Sagittarius makes a conscious, continuous attempt at curbing their enthusiasm for being so flirty to respect your sensitive feelings, while you try to understand that if they love you, no matter who they flirt with, their heart is yours and yours alone.

Scorpio and Pisces

You're a great match! You're both aware instinctively of what the other is afraid of and what makes them insecure. You both connect on a very deep, incredibly tender emotional level. More than the Pisces, you'll value the physical aspect of sex. For the Pisces, what they want is more romance. They want more of your soft side. It can be a problem when you look at your Pisces as nothing more than an easy lay; you can bully into doing your bidding whenever. However, as gentle as the fish is, they're slippery, and you will have a tough time pinning them down.

Chapter Nine: The Moon Sign

Other than your Sun sign, your moon sign is just as important in astrology, as it basically affects the bits of your personality intrinsic to you. It influences the way you look at yourself. The Moon is all about feeling, instinct, and the unconscious. Contrast this to the Sun, which is all about your will. According to Evangeline Adams, where your Sun sign shows your individuality, your Moon sign shows your personality.

For astrologers, your Sun is a vital force, while your Moon is an inherent force. The Moon oversees the aspects of you, which react before you even take time to think about your reaction.

You're the only one who sees your Moon persona or instinctive behavior, which we've been socialized to keep under wraps on account of it being "uncivilized" or "brutish" or "primitive." So, your Moon persona is the part of your personality you and others would consider rather disturbing. It's the part that gives in to negative emotions and thoughts with reckless abandon. It's the part of us that we're not willing to admit exists.

The moon is also responsible for your spontaneous behavior. It's the part of you that is honest in its happiness and pleasure, and the part that always answers to emotional stimuli. It influences the part of you that wants to play in the rain, roll down a hill, pluck an apple off a tree and eat it there and then. The Moon dominates all things sensual, as in your five physical senses.

The symbolism of the Moon in astrology is a tad cryptic. It is all about your reactions and instincts from when you were a wee baby to a little child. It's a representation of your dreams, past, and memories, all of which come together to create your inner psyche.

According to astrologer Landis Knight Green, the Moon is basically an expression of your subconscious. You're in touch with your Moon sign in your daydreams and your sleeping dreams as well. It has power over your emotions, which means it governs your romantic relationships. If you're a woman with your moon in the same spot as your man's sun, you will have a well-balanced relationship. Your Moon sign is yet another reason you're different from other Scorpios.

The Scorpio Moon

Being born with your Moon in Scorpio, you're the type of person who is well in touch with the darker bits of the human psyche. You're aware of the things that are hidden from others, but this gift can be a heavy burden to bear.

As a Scorpio Moon, you're all too aware of the words left unsaid. No one does subtext better than you. No one could trick you, and as passionate as you are, you're incredibly grounded in reality.

You're secretive, and you never want to get too close to anyone, especially if you've had bad luck in love before. The anxiety you feel could be considered life and death. This is the reason you're not so keen on plunging into love with all of you.

When you're a Scorpio Moon, it can be hard for you to be as intense as the Scorpio Sun in day-to-day life. Because of this, people fear you. And because of that, you keep all your emotions locked up.

When you can't express how you feel, you're emotionally blocked, and this block will show up in your body. You get ill; often, it's a stomach-related illness since the Moon oversees the stomach.

For the Scorpio Moon, nothing less than total engagement on a soul-deep level will do in life. Yet, they always get involved in love affairs that are as passionate as they are dramatic. They need to find that same passion in other aspects of life.

You're very sensitive to everyone around you, taking on their moods, both good, bad, and neutral. You're vulnerable to dark environments where it's stagnant, heavy, toxic, and of low spiritual energy. It's important for you to find time to purge the negative emotions you feel throughout the day. With time and practice, you'll learn how to rely on your instincts with people and circumstances.

The Stillest and Deepest of Waters

When your moon is in Scorpio, you often try to seem like you've got everything under control and like it's all cool. However, a lot of brooding intensity lurk underneath that facade. You feel too deeply, and you're deathly frightened of anyone knowing that. Your friends and family know not to prove you too much.

You're secretive, and you get lost in all the emotions you feel. When you're not self-aware, you can become swallowed up by the force of emotions within you. You can get lost in revenge, jealousy, and resentment. You're a bit of a conundrum, having to repress your feelings, which only makes them way too powerful to keep locked up within. You'll learn if you haven't already that the best way to tame your inner aggression is to let the feelings out.

You're the one who totally understands everything about the human condition, and so you make an amazing criminal detective or dramatist. You would thrive in any career where your piercing insight is needed. Also, you'd be successful.

With romance and work, you must have all the avenues you can to express your many intense feelings from the depth of your emotional reservoir. Winning your trust could take years and lots of attempts to break down your walls.

Because you are a fixed sign, you don't let go of people you value easily. You hold on tight to the trusted few that have become part of your tribe. You know of how to connect with people on a deeply emotional level, and you know that you need the connections you make to feel safe and secure in your emotions.

As a Scorpio Moon, you love people willing to explore life with you deeply. You love to help them see the truth about themselves. For you, truth matters above all else. You'd rather face an ugly truth than try to dress it up so no one gets hurt because you understand that being dishonest only leads to more pain and hurt than honesty could cause in the long run.

Your sexuality is powerful. Everyone can feel it. Sometimes, desires can get very primal and make it very difficult to hold on to emotional fidelity. However, being in a relationship with you is amazing because you provide trust and sensuality in spades. You can be vengeful, moody, secretive, and resentful, but on the flip side, you're full of ambition, intense, sensual, intuitive, and imaginative.

Some folks are not happy with how you are with emotions. You might feel like no one gets you. You might detach from the circumstances you find yourself in or trying to control others, but it's only because you don't want to be hurt because you're very vulnerable. A less self-aware Scorpio will find themselves lashing out at the people around them or getting resentful and jealous. If this is you, then you need to take time out to contemplate. You need to find healthy ways to release your intense emotions. The only way you can be truly at peace is to let yourself be emotionally open.

You've got a loving heart, and you're loyal. You're in touch with other people on a psychic level. People are drawn to you; they come to you with their pain and darkest secrets. As a great friend, you offer them whatever you sense; they really need to feel better emotionally. You deal with crises better than anyone else.

Celebrities with their Moon in Scorpio

1. Thandie Newton
2. Nia Long
3. Bob Marley
4. James Dean
5. Alfred Hitchcock
6. Jason Momoa
7. Katy Perry
8. Mila Kunis
9. Eddie Murphy
10. Snoop Dog
11. Francis Ford Coppola
12. Beyonce
13. MIA
14. Alexa Chung

Chapter Ten: Scorpio Rising

The more people discuss astrology, the more they advance beyond their sun signs to understand themselves better. They look at their moon signs, check out their birth charts, and more. However, not everyone knows what a rising sign is, so we will dive into that right now.

All About Rising Signs

The Sun will typically be in each sign for 30 days, while the Moon spends only two-and-a-half days in each one. The rising sign got its name meaning, just on the horizon when you are born. You'll need to know your precise time of birth instead of an estimate to have a proper birth chart.

Where the Sun shows your deepest self, and the Moon shows your internal emotions, the ascendant or rising sign is the way you view the world, or first impression people get when they meet you. The more people get to know you, the more they see the rest of who you are. This happens over time.

Think of your rising sign as a mask you wear or a hallway with many rooms. This rising sign also defines your ruling planet, which is what fuels the energy of your sign. When astrologers consider houses, signs, and planets, they also consider the ruler of each house, sign, or planet. There's so much more to just your moon, sun, and rising sign. So, when you cannot identify with any Sun sign, remember there are other things to consider.

Finding Your Rising Sign

Again, the only way to know your rising sign is to know the precise time you were born. That means you must get your long-form birth certificate to know when that was.

When you have it, you can head on over to Astro.com, where you can get an accurate calculation of your moon, sun, and rising signs. You'll also be able to do this with apps on your phone, like TimePassages and Costar.

You need to remember that there's a lot of nuances involved in astrology. So, you might not quite agree with the description of your rising sign, but that's only because there are so many other moving parts to consider. You must think of which house your ruling planet occupies, among other factors like where the planets were relative to one another when you were born. There are so many combos and possibilities.

Scorpio Rising

As a Scorpio rising, you're alluring, quiet, and mysterious. You're charming, but it's not always sexual charm. There's always a lot going on beneath the surface, and people would love to know what gives. You're intense for good reasons. There are things you've been through that cause you to put up walls, particularly if there are other Scorpio factors influencing you, so it takes a while for you to open up enough for others to get to know you.

You have very astute and keen animal instincts. You are passionate, and you have forces within you that you can channel towards regeneration and healing, as needed by you or other people or society. Your will is strong, powerful, yet quiet and understated. You are undoubtedly a force not to be messed with. You know people's pain intuitively, and you're great at healing — or wounding, if they ever cross you. Trust your instincts, and you will achieve the greatest heights. Your ruling planets are Pluto and Mars.

Scorpio Rising and Mars in Aries: Mars is in the sign of Aries, which is courageous, motivated, and independent. You lead and blaze trails for others to follow. You're bold and original. You're a warrior, fierce in competition, possessing killer instincts which you should temper with kindness even when you mean well. Your shadow side is selfish, ruthless, and uses extreme force.

Scorpio Rising and Mars in Taurus: Mars is in Taurus, which is productive, sensual, and fertile. You're all about sensuality, satisfying your desires and appetites. You love to enjoy life like a great feast, but the best way to experience happiness is for you to not give yourself over to your cravings or overindulge. You're steady in your will, very determined, and possess the stamina you need to make your dreams happen. You're highly successful. Being obstinate and not being willing to change or let go can be problematic for you, so beware of that.

Scorpio Rising and Mars in Gemini: Mars is in Gemini, which is dexterous, clever, and skillful. You're great with your hands and possess the sharpest of reflexes. You're good with language, and it plays an important part in your destiny. Your shadow self is scheming, crafty, shrewd, and self-serving. You are gifted with words, and you can use them to heal.

Scorpio Rising and Mars in Cancer: Mars is in Cancer, which is emotional and full of soul. Your sensitivity is deep. You're very protective of animals, children, and life in general. You are naturally empathic and can connect with your surroundings on an emotional level. You're passionate, and you're very sensuous. You won't find it easy to communicate, understand, or articulate your feelings so it makes sense intellectually or rationally. You find it easiest to communicate using music.

Scorpio Rising and Mars in Leo: Mars is in the confident, proud, and ever radiant Leo. You have a lot of willpower, and you would make a great leader, able to influence people by the thousands because of your magnetism. You have a strong, intense, vital force, which along with your consistent focus, helps you to carry out your noble ideals. You must make use of your personal power the right way. Your shadow self can be tyrannical.

Scorpio Rising and Mars in Virgo: Mars in Virgo means you're about special skills, service, technical know-how, and knowledge in general. You're interested in health sciences, medicine, chemistry, and biology. You are very astute in your observations, and you analyze things well. Your work is ever efficient and thorough, mostly because of your obsession. When you're not balanced, you get overly worried and critical of yourself and the world. You're usually the force behind a king or acting as a shrewd advisor.

Scorpio Rising and Mars in Libra: You have a desire to cooperate with others. You love to work in reams, and you always find a way to balance everyone's needs, including your own. Your actions are because of your need for connection, beauty, and harmony. You need to be wary of suppressing your desires and not acting for your own sake, as this can lead to conflict and hidden anger. Remain honest in all you do, and whatever you do, and don't try to make your goals happen secretly or by using others. Bring them together and choose to always be fair.

Scorpio Rising and Mars in Scorpio: You're at one with nature's primal forces. You need to remain connected to nature in an uncivilized, raw, and wild way. You give off the energies of death and birth, destructiveness, and creativeness, and you get why both ends of the spectrum are essential. Your physical presence is palpable, and you're full of passion and vitality, which you could use for good or bad. Learn your power and learn what it means to have it and use it. It can be your strength, and it can heal you and others. For you, what matters more is how intense experience is, and not its permanence.

Scorpio Rising and Mars in Sagittarius: You're adventurous, expansive, and spirited. You're all about the future. You're drawn to risk, and you love challenges. The more dangerous the pursuit, the better. You're very philosophical and idealistic, using your convictions and need for fairness to check your instincts. You're all about passion and zeal. When you're not balanced, you get self-righteous, zealous, and reckless. When you're at your best, you love to explore, and you inspire others. For you, there is much joy in adventure and exploring life.

Scorpio Rising and Mars in Capricorn: You're ambitious, practical, and earthy. You love goals that are tangible and material accomplishments. You get the way the world works, and you always calculate before you get going on making your goal happen. You have a great work ethic, self-discipline, and self-sacrifice. You can become a workaholic. For you, your ambition in terms of career is more important than anything else. You can also be in a place of authority if you desire.

Scorpio Rising and Mars in Aquarius: You're about the collective. You're unconventional and a free thinker. You are interested in regenerating society as we know it. You know of the problems plaguing mankind, and you know how to create solutions that are most innovative, either on your own or with others. You're at your best playing a group leader, a dissident, or a reformer.

Scorpio Rising and Mars in Pisces: Visionary, dreamy, and imaginative describe you. You're open spiritually, which means you can easily connect with other realms or enter altered states of consciousness. You use art or visualization to heal yourself and others. You're not great with intoxicants like alcohol, as they make you feel powerless and confused. You have amazing psychic abilities, which can become even more pronounced if you want them to be.

Scorpio Rising and Pluto in Aries: You've got a passion for being a hero and a person all on your own. You're free. You're a daredevil. You're bold, and you've got arrogant confidence, which could be your undoing if you're not careful.

Scorpio Rising and Pluto in Taurus: You're stubborn, willful, inflexible. You are obsessed with economics, wealth, and money. This could dictate your destiny.

Scorpio Rising and Pluto in Gemini: You need to understand everyone and everything. You value education and intellect. You're driven to use your head.

Scorpio Rising and Pluto in Cancer: You need to let go of all old conditioning and the familiar ruts you're in. You need to let go of all the loads the old world has placed upon your shoulders so you can regenerate and use your powers for good.

Scorpio Rising and Pluto in Leo: You've got to let go of your desire to fawn over those who are charismatic. You need to stop loving power so much. You get into self-glorification, use a lot of self-will, and pay attention to just you and your desires. You need to deal with this if you are to attain your greatest ideals.

Scorpio Rising and Pluto in Virgo: You desire perfection. You feel you must purify yourself, and this need can become a tad obsessive. You feel guilt over a lot of things, whether the wrongs are real or in your head. You are great at perfection, technical expertise, and analyzing everything in-depth. Your work is ever so precise.

Scorpio Rising and Pluto in Libra: You crave equality, justice, and fairness. You want to balance. You see corruption and injustice, and you desire to bring this to light so it can end. You're also concerned about how the balance of power plays out in your personal relationships.

Scorpio Rising and Pluto in Scorpio: You can go to the darkest depths just to give the world some light, consciousness, and healing. When you use your powers for selfish gain, you feel like you're all alone, and you become your worst adversary. You know of rapture, depth, and things that are horrific. You could be the best of healers, perhaps even a Shaman, if your heart is in the right place.

Scorpio Rising and Pluto in Sagittarius: You need to revise, to cleanse, and to take your beliefs about how life works even further. You need to get rid of your inherent dogmatism and overzealousness, and your biased convictions, so you can attain the highest of heights.

Scorpio Rising and Pluto in Capricorn: You can breakdown and buildup society, from businesses all the way to the government. You need to get rid of hypocrisy, corruption, and greed, and there is no one better suited to this work than you are. You have a very strong will, and you need to tamp that down with kindness and humility.

Conclusion

Dear Scorpio, you're amazing! Know that. You're the one sign in the zodiac that is often misunderstood, so my sincerest hope is that I've been able to help you and others understand what you're really like. No one could possibly match the intensity of feelings in your heart, and this is a great thing when you're at your most loving, willing to allow yourself to be vulnerable and open.

Love everything about who you are and never have to apologize for it. This is not a pass for you to be a crappy person when you're at your worst. I simply mean that when you do feel low, you need to remember your best qualities and aspire to "strengthen your strengths," so to speak.

Learn to be more trusting of people. The fact is that people can and will continue to disappoint. After all, we're humans, and there's no such thing as the perfect Sun sign, Moon sign, house, or decan or what have you. So be willing to trust because the more you trust, the better your intuition gets at discovering who's right for your tribe and who isn't.

We've finally come to the end of this book, and with any luck, you now have a deeper, clearer understanding of who you really are. There's nothing wrong with you, dearest Scorpio! You're amazing, so own it!

Part 9: Sagittarius
The Ultimate Guide to an Amazing Zodiac Sign in Astrology

THE ULTIMATE GUIDE TO AN AMAZING
ZODIAC SIGN IN ASTROLOGY

SAGITTARIUS

MARI SILVA

Introduction

The mysteries of the zodiac are all around us, but deep within the core of our personalities, our sun signs connect us with the universe. If you are a Sagittarius or know one, you can dive deep into the passionate fire sign with this guide. Our complete guide explores what it means to be a Sagittarius, how the planetary movements affect you, and what challenges you'll meet throughout life. You'll have the opportunity to understand more about Ophiuchus, the evasive sign residing within your house and explore the context of being born to the Ninth House of the zodiac and being ruled under Jupiter.

As a Sagittarius, you might have noticed key strengths and weaknesses. Learn more about what those mean for you in daily life, and how you can address them head-on. Sagittarians love to explore, wander, learn, and speak their mind. You can live your best life and feed into these aspects of your core personality. Sagittarians have the chance to rule the world and lead a strong group of diverse friends forward through life as a guide and mentor. As a natural leader with a deep passion for freedom, you'll find that people come to Sagittarians for a variety of reasons. With enhanced knowledge about yourself or the Sagittarius native in your life, you will adapt your approach to various life obstacles and use your strengths to keep you moving toward the future with the classic Sagittarian positive mindset.

Chapter 1: Sagittarius in the Zodiac

Over 4,000 years ago, a combination of overarching beliefs came together. Romans, Egyptians, and ancient Babylonians had independently charred the heavens into the same findings. When Rome and ancient Egypt came together, they combined their findings to chart the stars with a mathematical and scientific foundation. This was the birth of astronomy. These civilizations brought together their mythologies and understanding of the heavens to deliver the zodiac we know today. Through many thousand years of research and tracking planetary movements, and personality traits and changes, astrology eventually split from astronomy.

All three civilizations identified the 12 houses and the 12 constellations that would rule the zodiac in the thousands of years to come. This is the same zodiac we know and use today. Astrology plays a large part in our lives, regardless of how much people do or don't believe it. We're all in the universe together, and those who understand and acknowledge the widespread network of connection can understand their strengths, overcome weaknesses, and plan their daily lives for the best possible outcomes.

Astrology has waxed and waned through the centuries, but it has always been present in our societies. Even when belief was at an all-time low, the zodiac and the time of year we're born impact our personalities and our daily lives.

In this book, you'll can explore the Sagittarius zodiac sign and what it means to live as a Sagittarian. This book isn't exclusively for those born to the sign. It can help anyone better understand a Sagittarian friend, sibling, child, parent, romantic partner, or even coworker.

Here you will have access to not only an in-depth look at Sagittarius but the impact of the movements of the planets, and moon signs, rising signs, as well as the two forms of Sagittarian cusps.

Mythological Origins of Sagittarius

Sagittarius's mythical origins vary from Babylonian belief, Roman belief, Greek belief, and Sumerian mythology. It is easy to see a connection between each story and how it may have adapted over the years. There are also clear similarities that play into the beliefs behind the Sagittarius personality, although each civilization had a different angle when the personality was reviewed.

Among Babylonian mythology, Sagittarius was acknowledged as the *centauresque* God Nergal. Sagittarius among the Babylonians had a horse-like body, human-like torso, wings, the scorpion of a Stinger poised above the horse's tail, and two heads, one human and one panther. Nergal often is shown representing war and scorched earth.

Romans had a different approach to Sagittarius. They used the root of the word the Sagitta, which means arrow. Initially enroll, many observers identified a teapot among the constellation, but eventually, The Archer's bow and arrow won out, and the constellation was declared Sagittarius.

Eratosthenes, one of history's best-known astronomers, pushed that the constellation was a satyr rather than a Centaur. This was another term for Sagittarius because it was through storytelling that the center motif we know now came to form. The legend of Sagittarius among

Roman mythology is that Crotus was the son of Pan, and he lived atop Mount Helicon and invented archery. Eventually, Sagittarius was placed among the stars when the muses requested it of Zeus.

The connection between the muses and Sagittarius appears again in Greek mythology. Sagittarius is still shown as a centaur or as a half-human and half-horse creature. But in Greek mythology, the centaur was a nurse to the muses, and played careful watchman to guard them. Sagittarius is identified as aiming his arrow towards the heart of Scorpio. This story is like the beliefs among Sumerian mythology.

Basics of Being a Sagittarius

What makes a Sagittarius? Sagittarians are born between November 22nd and December 21st. They are the 9th sign within the zodiac circle, and they're symbolized through the Archer, who is aiming his bow at the higher realms of life.

To offer a clear overview, here are the most present and forceful elements within Sagittarius:

- Fire sign
- Mutable modality
- Assertive duality
- Ninth house of the zodiac
- Ruled under Jupiter
- The power colors are blue and purple
- Represents potential health risks within the liver, hips, and thighs
- Represented as the carnation
- Stones include turquoise, blue zircon, topaz, and citrine

Overall, Sagittarians are the most curious and energetic personalities among the zodiac's personas. They are also known for their love of travel, open-mindedness, and strong philosophical opinions. They are the people who ask the big questions. They want to know the meaning of life and explore their purpose.

Of course, that is the big picture image of a Sagittarius. On a personal level, they are often extroverted, enthusiastic, easy to excite, optimistic, and they enjoy change. Their mutable modality tied with their fire element make them extremely passionate about what lies ahead for them.

The mutable modality is what makes them so excited about the change. At the same time, the fire element gives them that drive to seek it out rather than the other elements with the same modality. Sagittarius is not a war between any of its present factors, such as its modality, element, planet, or house. These all come together nicely for Sagittarius, so it's likely that they'll feel at peace within themselves most of the time, but they may have a hard couple of years as a teenager while they're still figuring this out.

As a final note for the overview of Sagittarius, they value freedom above all other things. That love of freedom is best shown through famous Sagittarian John Jay. Jay is among the twelve most well-known founding fathers of the United States, the first United States Chief of Justice of the Supreme Court. He helped lead the changes that formed America following the Revolutionary War, and in 1799, he proved he was an advocate of widespread change by freeing all slaves within New York. John Jay is one example, but history has countless figures who stand out as those who put their highest value on freedom, honesty, and change.

Born to Jupiter

One of Sagittarians' most defining aspects is that they're born under Jupiter and how closely that connects with their fire element. The planet Jupiter is the largest of the celestial bodies, excluding the sun. Many in astrology idealize Jupiter for its benevolent and beneficial nature. This planet brings a lot of hope into Sagittarians.

Jupiter represents growth, expansion, healing, miracles, good fortune, and higher education. For Sagittarians, this planet marks the core of their personality, and it often means they see the world through those classic rose-colored glasses. Jupiter is the reason so many Sagittarians experience such high levels of enthusiasm and optimism.

The Mutable of the Fire Signs

Mutable signs come in the time of year when change is imminent. Of course, fire is the element of passion, and after fall, there is a passion for change to enter the season of quiet, death, and rebirth. Sagittarians aren't afraid of facing hardship or rough times. They will still charge ahead and stay the course, knowing that change is the only thing that will end the hardship in front of them.

This deep desire and the acceptance that change comes in many ways contributes to the Sagittarian optimism. Sagittarians do look forward to the winter and see it as a season of purpose. They aren't looking at winter as the season of hardship but are looking to it as the bridge to reach springtime, birth, and revitalization.

Sagittarius: the Final Fire Sign

Each element presents a trio of zodiac signs, and where the signs fall within that trio indicates how that element impacts that sign. Sagittarius is the last of the fire signs. It's preceded by Aries and Leo. To give context, areas as the first fire sign is like the ignition of a fire or that slow crackle that happens with kindling. Leo often represents fire in a full blaze in its purest form.

Sagittarius is the final fire sign that presents something uplifting, it is the slow burn, and it's through this that Sagittarians can often carry out monumental feats. They train themselves to have long stretches of energy rather than short bursts of energy or moderate energy levels and rest that come with Leo. Of the three fire signs, they are known for their generosity, and outshine both Leo and Aries when it comes to being generous and working with good intentions.

As a fire sign, they are often more compassionate and hold a deeper understanding of the human condition. They are often compelled to give more than they can and struggle between the desire to be more generous and their ability to do so.

The Sagittarius level of generosity is often a surprise to other signs. Sagittarians often give much more than people see, and unlike Aries and Leo, they aren't quick to jump for recognition for their generosity. They may even seem hesitant to make commitments or go through with plans, and that's because they've overwhelmed themselves with obligations wanting to volunteer their time and energy. There's also the widespread idea that Sagittarius is our flighty or non-committal. Their flightiness is their wish for change, and their non-committal attitude often exposes their underlying feelings or opinions about this person. If a Sagittarius can provide their time, energy, or money, then their flightiness and their level of commitment can drastically change.

Sagittarian Men and Women

Fire signs have larger differences between men and women than the other elements. With earth signs, you can guarantee that both sexes are pretty much grounded. Fire signs burn in different ways.

First, Sagittarius men are classically idealistic and opportunistic. They exude this innocence and can come across as annoying or childish. They often work in blind faith and trust just about anyone, which can cause a lot of unfortunate outcomes, especially when dealing with romance and business. Male Sagittarius are less in tune with Jupiter's logic element, but are more aligned with Jupiter's spark of curiosity.

Sagittarius men also receive the upper hand in Jupiter's gift of luck. They may go through long stretches of unluckiness, and that is typically a lesson they need. This lesson allows them to learn that they can't rely on good things to come their way. And they have no tolerance for dishonesty or inconsistent behavior. This is exceptionally noticeable when they are children. They need parents who are consistent in expectations and discipline.

The other side of Sagittarius men is their sense of humor and their ability to make friends. They quick to make friends, whether they want them or not. They have these magnetic personalities which just pull people in, but all Sagittarians are also prone to the foot-in-mouth syndrome. They often say things too bluntly or are too forthcoming with their opinions when they don't have knowledge on the subject. Sagittarius men are often blessed with the gift of humor and can deliver these overly blunt opinions or insight through the mode of comedy. This gift allows them to keep many more friends than Sagittarius women may experience.

On the downside, men under this sign are also prone to thoughtlessness and scattered thinking. They may have big dreams and want to help cultivate long-lasting change, but unless they have someone to guide them through those changes or help them achieve that goal, it may take much longer than it should. These men need a guiding light and constant reminders of why they're working on a particular project.

Sagittarius women, on the other hand, apply logic ruthlessly and are more prone to accept the general structure of an organization than Sagittarius men. These are the women who know what needs to be done to accomplish the big goals and achieve big change. The struggle they face boils down to communication.

As mentioned earlier, Sagittarians often struggle with being too blunt and too straightforward. This challenge is even more difficult for these women. A Sagittarius woman is the one who will ask embarrassing questions in Group settings, speak inappropriately often, and be disarmingly honest, but many make this a strength rather than a challenge. They use their honesty and frankness to catch others off-guard. One particular Sagittarian celebrity has made a reputation of this, Chrissy Teigen is well known for expressing her opinion unapologetically an all matter of the public forum. The trick here for these ladies is to decide whether this is a challenge you must overcome or a strength you will embody in everyday life.

Women under this sign are extraordinarily independent. Not necessarily that they live alone or are abject to family life, but they see themselves as individuals who contribute to various groups rather than a person subjected to labels and roles.

Understanding Sagittarian Cusps

Every person on a cusp has a bit of a different twist when it comes to their zodiac signs and what you might expect from their core personality. Sagittarius cusps struggle because one is a water-fire combination, and the other is an air-fire combination.

The Scorpio to Sagittarius cusp combines water and fire. Although these two normally contradict, their level of intensity is what makes the Scorpio-Sagittarius cusp widely successful. Traditionally, Scorpio was ruled under Mars and known for action, although the modern zodiac shows Scorpio represented through Pluto with a deep psychic connection and ties to death. When you take that and bring it together with Sagittarius, you have someone who is very open and receptive to change while also prone to take the necessary action to achieve their goals.

Those born on the Scorpio to Sagittarius cusp are more likely to see widespread success, but they may have difficulty in keeping friends. They will make friends quickly like all other Sagittarius is, but will probably lose them a little faster because of their matter-of-fact way of telling things and that extra dose of anger they get from their Scorpio side.

When it comes to downsides, the Scorpio-Sagittarius cusp often brings quite a bit of a know-it-all attitude, and these people can quickly become overly self-righteous. They may deliver truth bombs when inappropriate and obsessively dive into the research to make sure that they are right about something long after the conversation or argument has ended.

On the other side of the sign is the Sagittarius-Capricorn cusp, which ranges from December 18th to the 24th. These visionaries have a strong grasp on prophecy and how to propel change and control the direction of change to accomplish that prophecy. Capricorns are known for their intense determination and stubborn or headstrong nature. Inherently, this seems to contradict the Sagittarian's want for change and a go with the flow approach to life. It's possible that a Sagittarius-Capricorn cusp could get the best of both worlds. They could understand limits and lessons which come from Capricorn's planetary rulers of Saturn and support that curiosity and need for change associated with Jupiter and their modality. The trouble is that it is *just as likely* they will receive the worst of both worlds. Then they could be stubborn and overly blunt with their opinions. They may be intensely determined to prove others wrong and drive away many friends.

Those born in the Sagittarius-Capricorn cusp range are often carrying, loyal, and reasonable. They apologize frequently but also answering questions and giving advice.

Being Sagittarius

The elements that play a role in being a Sagittarius make up specific portions of your core personality. As a whole, Sagittarians are friendly, curious, adventurous, and fun people.

As you read your way through this book, you'll see how the different elements of being a Sagittarius play into different aspects of your life, such as childhood, romance, career pathways, and more. But your element, modality, and the sign itself don't independently determine your personality. Sagittarius is your sun sign and the essence of yourself. But other planetary movements and planetary presences within your natal can affect you too. How the universe impacts your path always comes to viewing and experiencing life through the lens of a Sagittarius.

Chapter 2: Who are Sagittarians?

Sagittarians don't hide who they are, and they're unapologetic in almost every aspect of their life. Those born to Sagittarius have a purpose in life, and they know that drive to explore and defy boundaries defines who they are through all stages of life. They don't adhere to standard conventions, and they actively seek information that may contradict a few of society's core beliefs. They are the people who ask questions; they want to know why and why not. Sagittarians are the truth-seekers of the Zodiac.

They need for knowledge, curiosity, and exploration all comes down to their ruling planet Jupiter. Jupiter's flow of energy focuses on the higher mind, expansion, and good fortune. You'll have the opportunity to learn a bit more about Jupiter, but it's key to mention that right initially because of what an important role it plays in their life.

There's also the need to mention the modality of Sagittarius. As a mutable sign, they often go with the flow and have a good-humored or jovial nature about them. These are just a few of the many strengths or benefits that come with being a Sagittarius. In this chapter, you'll have an introduction to those strengths, a handful of the challenges they face, and the overall view or big picture of who Sagittarians are in life.

What Does it Mean to be a Sagittarius?

At first sight, it looks as though being a Sagittarius just means you were born between November 22nd and December 21st, but those familiar with the sign will know that Sagittarians are fiercely independent, good-humored, charming, and occasionally, annoyingly optimistic. Sagittarius born also tend to be sent mental and quick to anger. At their worst times, they may seem inconsiderate or overreact too small events.

Many of the most remarkable traits found with Sagittarius natives are their ability to be blunt, philosophical, and extraordinarily independent. Those born to this sign are more than a little outspoken. They will often lead conversations in the direction they want to put out their ideas and opinions. And Sagittarius people often find themselves in friendly debates. The keyword is friendly. Because of their open-mindedness, Sagittarians are widely accepting of differing opinions and views. Part of the underlying element with this bluntness and this outspokenness is the Sagittarian's drive for truth and learning. They take a "truth hurts" approach to philosophical, political, and social subjects. Those born to Sagittarius don't consider her brothers anyone out there who can't handle the truth. They believe everyone needs to hear it and will do everything possible to spread the word.

What often causes a conflict for Sagittarians is their need for picking apart abstract views and philosophical ideas. They like the concept of aspects of life not having clear answers, but they hate not finding the one answer. This contradiction helps them continue growing and is often why Sagittarians are lifelong learners.

All the elements of Sagittarius we've addressed above stem from two key factors of this sign. Their ruling planet of Jupiter, and their element of fire, but it's their modality that presents the final element of the over-arching Sagittarius personality. When people look at Sagittarius on a surface level, they often see extreme independence or outright restlessness. Sagittarians need personal freedom like we all need air, and it's because of their mutable quality.

The mutable modality is what drives the need for change, and it happened when seasons change. Sagittarius marks the end of fall and the beginning of winter. Those born under Sagittarius are looking to the forthcoming, and when they're tied down, they think that the future will only hold the same thing that they've been experiencing. Sagittarians are not necessarily averse to long-term relationships, and they cultivate long-term friendships well. The trouble is that when things stop changing and being new, the Sagittarian checks out. For those born to Sagittarius, they see it as a "been there, done that" situation.

For example, if a Sagittarius has had a friend for a long time, and they've seen that friend frequently go in and out of the same bad relationship, they might end their friendship. In this example, the Sagittarius will not have much patience for hearing about the same problems again and again. They won't be very accepting of their friends, being incapable of moving forward. Because of this low tolerance for repetition and their drive to live without restraint, it looks as though Sagittarius men and women have trouble cultivating relationships.

These elements of a Sagittarius personality are tied into the Sagittarius element, modality, ruling planet, and Association with planetary movements. Although astrology is not widely accepted as a science, there is more astronomy that plays a role in understanding your sun sign and its impact on your day-to-day life. It is easy to say that Sagittarius natives are usually dependable and open-minded. Those observations are surface level. Throughout this book, and starting in this chapter, you'll have the opportunity to look at the in-depth analysis necessary to understand planetary movements, sun signs, moon signs, and how the universe affects you.

Understand Your Different Signs

To start things out, being a Sagittarius is your core personality or your sun sign, but you have other signs to consider, and they can direct what type of Sagittarius you are and how you present yourself to the world. There are sun signs, the most well-known among the Zodiac, moon signs, and rising signs or ascending signs.

The sun signs are the most known within western astrology, and when people refer to the Zodiac, they're referring specifically to sun signs. Most people only know their sun signs and haven't explored a Natal chart or birth chart, which reveals where their planets were in various houses during their birth. Most horoscopes you find online or receive through apps on your phone are only based on sun signs and don't account for other factors of your birth chart. This is often because of convenience. It is easy to calculate your sun sign because you only need to know your birthdate.

Sun signs play a key role in astrology and understanding the Zodiac for a few reasons. First, the Sun is the center of our solar system and is seen as the root of life. Second, as a planetary force it symbolizes the core self or ego. Finally, the Sun represents centeredness, life, and illumination. If you're looking to learn more about yourself, then you should learn about your sign.

Your sun sign is what you are; Sagittarius is the representation of core aspects of your identity that are unchangeable. Understanding this can help you become your best self by acknowledging and understanding common challenges while playing to your personality strengths. Those who focus on walking a path that aligns with their energy and their individual sign will often see greater successes in life and greater connection to planetary changes and vibrations.

Sagittarius as a Rising Sign or Ascendant

Rising signs are often called your ascendant, and this is how you present yourself to the world. Your chart begins with your rising sign, the first house of your chart. This will often unveil how you begin things in life and your alignment between spirit and body. Imagine if all the elements of your life were spanned across the sky. This is the horizon of that sky where the Sun rises.

It's unfortunate that people don't pay much attention to their rising or ascendant sign because it can help them understand how other people view them. While your sun sign is learning about yourself, your ascendant sign is learning about how you present yourself to others. When people find inconsistencies with their personality and their sun sign, their rising sign is often responsible.

For example, a Sagittarius born with their rising sign in Capricorn may initially appear reserved, hardworking, and quiet. Although Sagittarians are known for their ability to work diligently, they're rarely reserved or quiet. Most common is that the Sagittarius may initially seem shy or meek, and once they get to know the person or feel comfortable in the environment, their inner Sagittarians come out.

The ascendant sign changes depending on where you were born and the time of your birth. It is a bit more complicated than calculating your sun sign. Raising signs change every couple of hours, but you can find online calculators that can help you find your rising sign if you know the place and time of your birth.

Learning more about your rising sign gives you more self-awareness. You will better understand how you adapt to new surroundings and how that rising sign interacts with your sun sign. Rising signs do not inherently carry the same traits as sun signs. There are significant differences between both signs.

You will need to calculate or find an online calculator to find your ascending sign. To offer a bit of insight, here's a quick overview of Sagittarius ascending.

Sagittarius rising signs often rely heavily on intuition and are often found to be very confident with themselves in every situation. These are the people who will own every room they walk into, and if they don't know what's going on, they'll fake it. People with a Sagittarius rising sign are clever enough to get away with "faking it" through many situations and are very optimistic, which puts everyone else in a good mood.

Sagittarius as a Moon Sign

Your moon sign is an indicator of your inner self or the parts of yourself which you hide from other people, even those close to you. This is your innermost, emotional side, the areas of your personality you safeguard. Moon signs can also support the kind of parent you are, how you process emotions, and how you feel about your memories.

Lunar energy tends to manifest in different ways based on the element. For example, water moons are often extraordinarily empathetic and place a high value on emotion. Earth moons focus on creating stability in their finances and work life. Air and fire moons usually seek ways to cultivate their sun sign and to bring out their core personality without added responsibility.

A Sagittarius as a moon sign would drastically magnify the Sagittarian's drive for freedom. They may feel an extreme aversion to connecting to relationship ties or settling down. Those born with Sagittarius as their Moon sign are gypsy types with a need to wander and roam. They engage and emotions on two ends of the gamut. Moon

Sagittarians desire alone time and independence to assess and evaluate their emotions. On the other end of the spectrum, moon Sagittarians seek new experiences and interactions with new people. They gain emotional benefits from watching other people process their feelings without having a relationship with that person.

Those with the moon in Sagittarius are also problem solvers. Because they look so critically at their inner self and separate themselves from relationships, they have a unique opportunity to analyze their feelings objectively.

Understanding Your Signs and How they Function Together

It's highly unlikely that you'll have Sagittarius as all three of your major signs. Before proceeding through the remaining chapters, you might quickly evaluate your natal chart online. Through an online chart creator, you can see your ascendant and moon sign. Those can both help you explore different areas of how you understand and express your core personality.

Get to know a bit about these other two signs. It can be very helpful to understand the elements of these signs and their ruling house. For example, anyone with a Cancerian moon sign might have greater receptivity to understanding emotions and processing emotions of those around them. This astrological superpower is because the moon is Cancer's ruling planet making it exceptionally strong. Just the same, a Leo ascendant radiates magnetic energy and pulls people toward them. They're self-aware and present their sun sign proudly because Leo is ruled under the Sun.

Then there's the matter of your signs working together, or often, against each other. A fire sign such as Sagittarius or Leo with a water sign Ascendant might seem shy, reserved, and laid back. A fire sign with a ground sign Ascendant might seem overly focused and headstrong.

Understanding how your various signs work together can navigate through your core self with greater confidence. If you know how you present yourself to others and how you process or hold on to emotions, you can identify how they fit into your individual personality. You can also use these factors within your whole personality to build a life that emphasizes your individual self's positive values and helps you overcome common challenges throughout life.

Chapter 3: Impact of Planetary Movements on a Sagittarius

Planetary movement or transits impact all our lives and mildly different ways. How the planets move is consistent for everyone. That is beyond our power, but how those movements impact us largely depends on our sun sign and how our houses appear on our natal chart. In the last chapter, we discussed the Natal chart or birth chart, and it's important in understanding astrology. There are a few takeaways you can grab from the planetary changes based on your sun sign alone. In this chapter, we will be looking at how these movements affect those born under the Sagittarius sign.

Remember that planetary bodies, which include Pluto, the sun, and the moon, are all in continuous motion. There's also the earth element, which means that understanding how these planets interact and move is a bit of a complex matter. As we work our way further away from the sun, we see larger orbits and fewer opportunities for these planets to enter your specific sign.

What Elements of the Universe Affect Sagittarius?

Virtually everything in the heavens can impact each person in a way consistent with their core personality or their sun signs. Planetary bodies within astrology include planets, stars, moons, and planetoids. Sometimes there is specific significance tied to certain signs where a planetoid or star may affect those signs and not others.

Sagittarius is one of these signs with Kaus Borealis and Kaus Australis found within its constellation. The presence of these two prominent stars can bring out key personality traits when their brightest and when Sagittarius is present. Kaus Borealis is associated with strength and flexibility, while Kaus Australia enhances goal setting and aiming high.

The impact of Sagittarius' stars will be greatest when Sagittarius is present. For those in the Northern Hemisphere, that is from early June to late August or early September.

Planetary Movements

The heavenly bodies and their movements are in constant flux; you can still use basic information about each body to plan ahead. Those who follow astrology may be familiar with terms like Mercury in retrograde, and this is where those terms come into action.

Astrologist's look years into the future to help map out when planets will enter certain houses and signs. This element of astrology is where it becomes more science than anything else. These planets and other celestial bodies move on predetermined tracks. These reliable movements caused ancient civilizations to use the movements of the planets and stars as the basis for their calendars and the calendars we use today.

Mercury in Sagittarius

Mercury appears in two primary formats. First, the planet can simply be in Sagittarius, or it can be in retrograde through Sagittarius. When Mercury interacts with Sagittarius, it promotes freedom of thought and open communication. The downside is that most of this communication starts quite optimistic and then takes a turn. Sagittarians should be especially careful to use whatever tech they have when they begin conversations because these discussions can quickly become arguments.

When Mercury is in Sagittarius, you may notice other signs taking on Sagittarius means of communicating. Other people may be less inclined to keep opinions to themselves or stay quiet about what they think during a conversation. Mercury is the house of communication, and it often prompts people to explore new ways to communicate. Unfortunately, so many people living mild amounts of fear of Mercury because of information problems.

There's another element that comes with Mercury being in Sagittarius. Organization. Sagittarians are never great at organization anyway, but they may feel the need to declutter when Sagittarius enters Mercury. For those born to Sagittarius, Mercury entering your sign often brings about the feeling of having too much stuff and the need for open space. It does, though your demand for personal freedom is manifesting in your immediate living space.

Mercury can remain in Sagittarius between 14 and 30 days. That doesn't offer a large window, but it does offer quick relief if that stretch of Mercury in Sagittarius isn't working out well.

Venus in Sagittarius

Venus is the planet of love and still rules relationships to this day. When Venus enters Sagittarius, people are more prone to see the good in each other. Other signs may put on those rose-colored glasses that Sagittarians wear daily. Additionally, Sagittarius natives and many other signs will perceive the need to learn new things about their partner and have new experiences together.

Venus can go on in Sagittarius for anywhere from 23 to about 60 days, and that can be *good news* for many relationships. Sagittarius natives feel the effect of Venus directly when it's in this sign. They may idolize their lover and appreciate their ideas and beliefs rather than engage in friendly debates and arguments. Sagittarians also become more serious when Venus is in their sign and may even consider settling down.

The great news is that when Venus is in Sagittarius, many people are generally more open to experiences and ideas. But if Venus is in Sagittarius for an extended amount of time, it may feel like an emotional overload. After about 20 days, Sagittarians are ready to move on from Venus, but they have a bit of a checklist. They typically aim to experience something new and build up their relationships before exiting Venus. Sagittarians should know that they don't demand to be perfect during this time. They can still be themselves and not overwhelm themselves with emotion. There isn't any desire to be perfect for their partner, parents, children, or friends. When in Venus, Sagittarius natives are easily pleased but can feel as though they're stuck in a rut or not contributing enough to their relationships.

Mars in Sagittarius

Mars is in Sagittarius for about one and a half months or six weeks. During that time, watch out. Sagittarians already have trouble keeping conversations from taking an unfortunate turn. When Mars is in Sagittarius, those born in Sagittarius have an exceptionally difficult time with patience, keeping their anger in control and restlessness during a conversation. Although Mars has nothing to do with communication, it has a lot to do with anger as the God of War rules it.

Sagittarians may offset a little of this by choosing text-based communication and taking measures to reduce the time spent waiting on a message. For example, instead of angrily waiting for your partner to text back while you're trying to cultivate an argument, turn your phone off for 10 minutes or leave it in the other room, forget about it for and then return to it. You might also try to set restrictions on your phone during work hours, or times you want to yourself so you won't be bothered with conversations that might distract you. Of course, this isn't a permanent solution. Sagittarians love social interaction, but sometimes for the sake of their friendships and other relationships, they might need to step back a little to avoid arguments and fights.

People with Mars in their Sagittarius on their natal chart do face peculiar issues for Sagittarians. If you are Sagittarius and Mars is in Sagittarius on your birth chart, you may have noticed a distinct problem with follow-through. Mars often embodies chaos, and when that mixes with the Sagittarian's gusto for life, it means big dreams and little action. If this is your case, carefully assess which projects you want to pursue and how much time you dedicate to that project. That way, you can reduce the number of half-done projects lying around the house or sitting on your desk.

Saturn in Sagittarius

Saturn and Sagittarius have quite a few things in common. They are both deeply entrenched in ethics, spirituality, and a higher mind, but Saturn and Sagittarius differ because Sagittarius is about restrictions and rules. Sagittarians, ruled under Jupiter, is about limitless possibilities and extraordinarily high aspirations. So, when Saturn enters Sagittarius and as it transits through, Sagittarians have this insane ability to carry out a lot of the projects they've started.

Sagittarians aren't known to set down a project, but they are known to take their time when Saturn is in Sagittarius. They have this acceptance period, where they acknowledge what they need to do and get it done. First Sagittarians, this is also a great opportunity to achieve a little inner reflection. Many Sagittarius natives use this time to evaluate how in tune they are with themselves and if they're giving their higher calling in life enough attention. It's an excuse to do a bit of moral inventory.

Uranus in Sagittarius

Uranus hasn't entered Sagittarius since 1988, and no one should expect it to circle around again anytime soon. When Uranus is in Sagittarius, there's a fair amount of rebellion. There are a lot of pushbacks against taboos, education, and belief systems. This is fairly consistent with what was experienced in the late 1980s and early 1990s. Uranus left Sagittarius in 1995.

The Ruling Planet of Sagittarius—Jupiter

Here is the planet that rules Sagittarius, Guardian to the abstract and higher mind, the yen for curiosity and ideas. There's really no way to downplay Jupiter. It's such a force.

Jupiter is the planet of luck, and promotes the formulation of ideology, operates within the spirit realm, and rules directly over religion and philosophy. These are all things that tie to the higher mind. That connection is what leads Sagittarians in their lifelong quest for learning and new experiences. It often leads many deep into the spiritual realm, and even when Sagittarians aren't necessarily religious, they may be interested in understanding religion and spirituality.

Let's explore that luck side for just a moment. We know that Jupiter is in your natal chart in the most important position, your sun sign. Jupiter has two streaks of luck. The first is plain luck. Good fortune just seems to come to them, and they often receive what they need at just the right moment. But there is also the stroke of the judge and jury element of luck. Sagittarians will often learn lessons the hard way when it feels like their good luck has run out, and then at the last moment, there could be leniency. Luck, at least with Jupiter, is not always about getting help when you need it. It can often simply be the lesser of other consequences.

Jupiter, in Roman mythology, was the God of both the Sky and nature. He was also called the father of both gods and men. In Greek mythology, this represents Zeus, who overthrew Saturn, or Kronos, father of Zeus. As part of this mythology, Jupiter serves as a bit of rebellion, but these stories mark the significance of ideology and religion as Zeus and Jupiter both overthrew gods who ruled through chaos and fear.

Mercury in Retrogrades Effect on Sagittarians

Mercury often retrogrades. On average, it will retrograde three or four times per year, and when it does, it brings trouble. Not all retrogrades are bad, but the impact of Mercury's stranglehold on communication often causes trouble for many signs. Sagittarius feels these impacts even more painfully than other signs because of their blunt way of communicating.

Although Sagittarians don't worry about what others think, especially if it's about something they said, this retrograde poses specific challenges. Sagittarians should expect to have frequent disagreements and feel constantly undermined in conversations when Mercury is in retrograde.

To counteract this, Sagittarius natives can focus not on the conversation itself but on the activity that comes from it. Especially at work, Sagittarians can focus on the affairs and good activity that happens because of other people sticking up for their opinions. Remember that your opinions and ideas often overwhelm those around you. The trouble is they see your passion as aggression, and they may not stand up to you to voice their own opinion. Most of the other signs don't realize that you're opinionated but also open-minded. Mercury in retrograde can be frustrating, but it can also present the opportunity you've wanted to get into deep and complex subjects with people who normally avoid conversation.

Sagittarius in Different Houses

There are 12 houses in the zodiac, and each houses a zodiac sign, but they are different. Instead, the house reflects the earth's reflection on its axis since the zodiac represents the movement of the earth around the sun. Of the 12 houses, it's common for people to have a closer tie to the house of their sun sign, but each house will affect your life.

When you have your birth chart or natal chart, you can find any planetary bodies in your different houses. This presents the opportunity to assess each facet of your personality and daily life, keeping the houses and planets in mind. This element sees both the trees and the forest; you're looking at the big picture with the small pieces in mind. The houses vary for each person as a small piece of their personality. Someone can have multiple planets or zero planetary bodies in any house, but you can use this quick guide to navigate the different houses through the Sagittarius personality's eyes.

1st House – House of First Impressions, Leadership, and Appearance – Ruled by Aries

The first house is ruled over by Aries and is larger than life. Sagittarians often feel deep within their first house, and that's where they get their sense of humor. Sagittarians with Sagittarius in their first house are certainly quick with smart remarks, but temper that off with a bit of goofy humor.

Even when Sagittarius is not in the first house, you strongly connect with leadership and first impressions. That can cause a strong connection.

2nd House–House of Environments, Senses, and Money–Ruled by Taurus

Sagittarians aren't always deeply rooted in their second house, it's ruled by the earth sign Taurus, and a lot of it has to do with travel. The difference between second house travel and Sagittarian travel is that Sagittarius natives have nomadic tendencies to learn and witness ideologies or spirituality in different countries. With the second house, this is the house of environments and senses, which often pulls more toward static environments.

3rd House–House of Communication, Travel, and Community–Ruled by Gemini

The third house is one of communication, travel, and community. When looking at your birth chart, consider how deeply connected you are to your community. Those with a fire sign in their third house will often feel a deeper understanding of obligation to those around them. If Sagittarius is in the third house, a person might feel torn between a need to get away and the need to stay.

What most Sagittarius get from their third house is a deep sense of community and communication. Sagittarius natives already have a solid foundation for travel, and they need not pull from another house to feed that need. Instead, this house can help Sagittarius understand how they interact with communities and how they communicate with strangers or people they've just met.

4th House–House of Home, Family, Privacy, and Foundation–Ruled by Cancer

This house represents home, family, and essentially starting a family of your own. It closely links to the moon, and your moon sign, and your sun sign, can play a part in your fourth house. The sign in your fourth house during your birth has the most monumental impact, and that is your moon sign. But, as different signs enter the fourth house, you'll feel subtle changes in your ideals around family and home.

5th House–House of Self-Expression, Creativity, Attention, and Fun–Ruled by Leo

The fifth house is about pleasure and satisfaction. Sagittarians often find great fun in travel or exploring other cultures. If you don't feel the wanderlust, then consider watching foreign sports teams, romance movies in different languages, or learning a new language yourself.

6th House–House of Health, Service, Routine, and Helpfulness–Ruled by Virgo

The sixth house is the house of health. Sagittarians notoriously have trouble with their hips and liver. They're prone to sciatica, but a Sagittarius may feel better as a few signs move through the sixth house. Of course, it's best to take responsibility for overall health. Stars or no stars, stay active, cultivate healthy routines, and maintain good diet habits.

7th House–House of Relationships, Both Business and Personal–Ruled by Libra

Libra sees over the seventh house, but as different signs move through it, there are fluctuations in daily events regarding relationships. The seventh house is largely responsible for personal and business, but it's typically called the house of marriage.

8th House-House of Birth, Death, Transformation, and Energy-Ruled by Scorpio

The house of birth and death often feeds carnal desires such as energy and sex, but it can also manifest in hatred and anger. If you're harboring anger, then watch out as Sagittarius enters the eight house. When you're watching your star chart, pay careful attention to this house, it's a great opportunity to approach sex, and redefine your energy.

9th House-House of the Higher Mind, Religion, and Education-Ruled by Sagittarius

This is your house, the house of the higher mind and education. Explore and learn everything you can as long as it's fun and engaging. If something becomes "work" and not mandatory to your career path, drop it. Your ninth house can help you build a great wealth of knowledge if it doesn't weigh you down. This will heavily affect your career.

10th House-House of Structure, Tradition, Career, and Image-Ruled by Capricorn

This house is how we feel about the rest of the world. It brings us to assess and accept our obligations, plan out for big projects, and to know when to accept personal responsibility. Capricorn is largely a responsible and organized sign, so not surprisingly, this is its house, but the overwhelming trouble is that Sagittarians have almost a natural allergy to planning and feel compelled to follow obligations. It's likely that you'll struggle to identify with this house throughout your life.

11th House-House of Friendships, Technology, and Future-Ruled by Aquarius

Sagittarius natives know all about friendship and often have the most tumultuous and rewarding experiences in friendship, but this house also rules over technology and what lays ahead. Any Sagittarian may feel a strong pull toward the changes that the eleventh house brings.

12th House-House of Endings, Tying Loose Ends, and the Afterlife-Ruled by Pisces

The twelfth house is reasonably the house of endings and the one that can also result in undoing. Sagittarius people need to be exceptionally careful and aware of their twelfth house as it can lead to a fair amount of self-sabotage. This drives people into secret affairs to destroy a stable and loving relationship. Or where you might continually put off a big work project because it's easier to fail and risk getting fired than to face the challenge of moving up.

All these houses impact your daily life, and with an active star chart, you can plot exactly which houses you must face with the most attention on any day.

Chapter 4: Strengths of Sagittarians

Sagittarian natives have unique superpowers in the world of the zodiac. They see the good, the light, and act with the assumption that the best is yet to come. Manifesting and working towards the positive outcomes are what set Sagittarians apart from the rest of the signs and leads to all their strengths. They're often applauded as the best-natured of the fire signs and most fun-loving of the entire zodiac.

Those born under Sagittarius love life and are optimistic about all the wonderful things to come. They see no point in dwelling over the past or obsessing over things that might go wrong. Sagittarius' natives fixate on the intangible word in those situations. They see the "might" and "possibly" and the "could" as unlikely events they shouldn't worry about. Typically, Sagittarians don't focus on their misfortunes either, often because they know that good luck or a turn for the better is near.

Their ability to look toward the future enables them to play towards the strengths regularly. We're going to cover weaknesses and common Sagittarian challenges in the next chapter, but you'll see here that it's often a matter of these challenges being of a similar nature to their strengths. When a Sagittarian goes overboard, there can be a few drawbacks. But, for now, we'll focus on how these strengths often allow Sagittarius natives to live their best lives with generally little effort.

As the cherry on top, Sagittarius natives tend to have the most direct and straightforward personalities, which make them focused on their strengths. They don't prefer to get muddled by all the other little things in life. Most of the time, Sagittarians find out what they're good at and spend their lives improving in those areas or using those strengths to learn and explore other areas of life.

Loyalty

Loyalty is a frequent presence among fire signs. Unlike other elements, fire signs are most notably loyal. Although Sagittarians are free spirits and don't like getting trapped into a clique, they'll still be devoted to various people in their lives.

The usual or typical setup for this style of loyalty in a Sagittarius' life is that they'll often connect with a few friends scattered across a few different friend groups. Using standard high school cliques as an example, a Sagittarius might have one close jock friend, another close preppy friend, and another close punk friend. None of these friends independently will understand how they all came to be friends with the Sagittarius or why they all found such good friends in one person, but Sagittarius' can often bring unexpected people together, and when that happens, it's magical. They not only deliver outstanding loyalty, but they cultivate it in other people.

One character example Sagittarian is Rachel Green from Friends. A Sagittarian who clearly is the glue among the oddball assortment of companions in the group. They don't find themselves in cliques, but instead are found giving their loyalty to independent friends, or extracting the best from each clique to build a group of friends.

Sagittarians also hate prejudices, and they actively work to cultivate friends from all backgrounds. They want to be friends with the world, but they know that it can lead to trouble. As Sagittarius natives make friends easily, it can seem as though they'd have problems devoting their loyalties to only a few people. That couldn't be further from the case. A Sagittarius native might find this easy, but they only have a handful of best friends. In that sense, they offer unmatched loyalty, and they can easily rank their loyalty to specific friends.

If you are a friend, family member, or romantic partner to a Sagittarius, you may have witnessed this loyalty firsthand. Those who put ultimatums to Sagittarius born people such as, "it's them or me" the person proposing the ultimatum will lose. If they ask them to choose between their relationship or their friends, the friends will win.

As a friend to a Sagittarius, you're lucky beyond belief. But be careful not to ask too much from your Sagittarian friend because they're loyal and generous enough to give more than they can.

As a family member to a Sagittarian, tread carefully. Sagittarius born are loyal, but unlike Cancer, Leo, or Pisces, they don't inherently value family members above friends. Aim to cultivate a friendship as they enter adulthood and accommodate their needs as best you can without groveling for their friendship. Sagittarians hate groveling.

As a Sagittarian's romantic partner, there's much opportunity for lifelong loyalty, but also the risk of losing it all quickly. Sagittarians are notoriously hard to pin down, so if you're in a relationship, you've cleared the biggest hurdle. But, if it ever becomes a matter between you and the others in their life, they'll likely choose those who they've known for years over a lover.

Sagittarians are supportive of those individuals in their life, and they want to see them succeed. They also prefer to see people in good relationships and to cultivate relationships and friendships that stand the test of time.

Where a Sagittarius can falter in this strength is sentimentality. There's one overwhelming element in Sagittarius: they speak their mind. They are the friend who will always be honest and forthcoming. Unfortunately, many people can't handle that, and they will often leave. That's okay, though, because Sagittarius natives don't enjoy the sentimentality of fragile or overly emotional people. They don't give their loyalty in exchange for anything. It's free. They only expect to not be taken advantage of, used, or exploited.

Naturally Athletic and Adventurous

Sagittarians are athletes, whether they particularly aim towards athletic excellence or not. Their athletic nature helps to build up their adventurous strength. Sagittarius want to get out into the world; walking through the many wonders and traveling deep into foreign countries or new towns. Typically, Sagittarians take long strides and swing their arms when they walk. It's very purposeful.

And they might enjoy athletic activities that deliver a thrill, things like spelunking, mountain climbing, bike riding, CrossFit, or even yoga. If it can take you to new places or deliver unique experiences, then it's worth the Sagittarian's time.

The strength lies in the fact that this culminates in a larger collection of planetary impact. First, you have the ruling planet Jupiter, God of Gods. Second, you have the energy and passion of the Fire element and finally, you have the change accepting factor of the modality. They exude a vitality for life, and they spread it. They energize other people with this strong internal energy.

The best way to keep up this strength is to do more of it. Exercise, explore, or be active often in life. When you're taking a break at work, take a walk around the building or the area. Even if it's only to the parking lot and back, it will boost your energy for the rest of the day. Better yet, you'll likely find that many people will go with you. People naturally prefer to be around you, especially when you're active. That's because they unknowingly have a magnetic attraction to your high level of adventure and athleticism, and they want to share in that vitality for life.

Sagittarius natives must know they shouldn't be shut in for too long. You might need to get out of the house or the office building, so you don't feel closed in and separated from this natural strength of yours. Better yet, you may pursue a career or hobby that enables you to build on these strengths regularly.

Curious

Curiosity killed the cat, but the Archer is safe in this scenario. Sagittarians often let their curiosity lead them through life. They are the toddler or child who constantly asks, "What's this?" or "Why?" and they want full answers. This reigns because of Jupiter. As the planet of higher mind that Sagittarians have a natural pull toward learning.

But Sagittarius natives will reach a point where they have the control to direct their curiosity. As children, Sagittarians show interest in everything from art to math and even deep into music and the outdoors. They're the children that are extremely demanding when it comes to their parents having enough energy to keep up. But, as they reach their mid or late-twenties, they know what they're generally good at and can direct their curiosity toward that field and related subjects.

For example, two famous Sagittarius authors include Mark Twain and C. S. Lewis. Although both wrote extensively in fiction, both also explored multiple genres and wrote observational non-fiction for the time's politics and ethics. They used their skill in writing to explore other interests they held. It's also worth noting here that these two Sagittarians were extremely strong in the pursuit of knowledge. Although only C. S. Lewis received a formal education, Mark Twain was a passionate lifelong learner. Twain used his love of language and printed material to explore other elements that weren't taught in school. While working at a printing press, he used that time and access to materials to learn about botany, history, and government.

Positive to a Fault

In the opening of this chapter, we couldn't get enough of Sagittarian's positive attitude, and it's true. You probably won't find a more positive person in life than a Sagittarius. They're also willing to spread that positivity.

The result of this high level of positivity is often a great sense of humor, willingness to crack a joke, and an extroverted personality. They're extremely direct people and spend little time worrying about the possible consequences of their behavior.

In the best of times, this means that the Sagittarian can devote plenty of time to manifesting their best life. They walk into situations believing that the best outcome isn't just possible. It's the most likely outcome. They're happy, and simply being happy often drives many people to treat them well, and give them what they want. Sagittarians also, unintentionally, provoke a lot of romantic relationships with this positivity.

All of this comes from fire's radiant energy and Jupiter's innate luck. They bring their own light into the world, and they don't rely on anybody else for their happiness. With eccentric optimism, they tend towards impatience and be a little too easy to excite. As children, they can be demanding and occasionally annoying because of their high energy, while as adults, they might seem self-centered or too energetic for many people. That's fine because, again, Sagittarius natives don't need anyone else to be happy; so as far as they're concerned, this is not their problem.

Independent

Sagittarians value independence highly; they hold on to it with a vice grip. They want the opportunity to release their passions, seek all the knowledge of the universe, and live with reckless abandon. Looking for independence and unquestioned freedom.

This seems like a weakness to everyone else, as though they can't be tied down and never have meaningful roots in any specific place or with any person. But the Sagittarius would never be bothered or influenced by other people. The Capricorn-Sagittarius cusp may exude this to an even higher degree.

They are also very straightforward, and with the cusps of this sign, that can easily mean a lot of angry outbursts, but Sagittarians are usually laid back, and understanding Scorpios and Capricorns are not.

How is this a strength for Sagittarius natives? Their high level of independence gives them the freedom to seek whatever they want from life. These people think far outside of the box and are exceptionally skilled with creative problem solvers because they aren't tied to other people. And they handle internal struggles easily because they've learned early in life they need not rely on anyone else.

Understanding the Overall Personality of the Strong Sagittarian

As a whole, few things seem like contradictions but work together to create such a strong force behind their personality strengths.

First, they are both loyal and independent. But most of the time, people confuse the two as the opposite when they're just different. Sagittarians don't rely on other people for anything, and that means they can give a different loyalty than what most people experience from other signs. They want nothing for their loyalty, and they may seem like a distanced friend, but true friends of a Sagittarius native know how important their independence is to them.

Second, they are hyper curious and athletic. People have adopted this "brains or brawn" mentality, and it looks like a person can't be both. That's evidently not true, and not every Sagittarius is brawny per se, but many enjoys adventure. Usually, adventure requires physical prowess, but many Sagittarians have found another way to create adventure. C. S. Lewis, the creator of The Chronicles of Narnia and much other fantasy and Sci-Fi novels, cultivated his own adventures. He didn't need to venture out into the wilderness; he made his own world with his curiosity and his intellect.

Finally, a Sagittarius may seem blunt, brazen, and oddly... exceptionally positive. It seems like bluntness and insensitivity would seem like a negative person's trait, but these all come from a positive person. They will say what they want with little regard for anyone else because of their high value for independence, but their positivity often means this is coming from a good place. If a Sagittarian says, "Your diet can't be going too well if you keep inviting me out for pizza," they aren't saying that the other person is fat. They're pointing out that their friend isn't meeting the expectations that they set for themselves. This Sagittarius is offering support through the only way they know-how; they don't doubt they can meet their goals – *they're just trying to help reach the standard they want to achieve.*

Overall, Sagittarians are something different. They can seem like a bonkers assortment of personalities, but they have it together, and when they don't, it doesn't bother them.

Chapter 5: Common Sagittarius Challenges

Sagittarians may ride their independently created high for most of their life, but everyone faces challenges. While they are ruled under Jupiter, which has a huge role in their life, and it's the largest body in the solar system besides the sun, they always are on the cusp of excellence and expansion. These are the people who explore and want to know absolutely everything about the world around them. That is where they experience most of their challenges.

If you've lived around a Sagittarius, you might have noticed these demands tie directly into their core personality, and sometimes they don't even notice. For Sagittarius natives, reading through these challenges may be truly eye-opening. Unlike other facets of the Zodiac, those well-versed in planetary movement and the sun signs, this won't be a moment where you can sit back and nod your head in agreement. Many Sagittarians may outright argue that these aren't challenges. Many could even push that they're positive elements of their personality!

Those who know a Sagittarius native will easily see these challenges or weaknesses common among those born to the ninth house.

Impatience

A Sagittarius native cannot and will not wait patiently for anything. Sagittarians are among the children of the Zodiac and embody this style of forever-young mental state. This stems directly from their modality and their wish for ultimate flexibility and constant movement, but that need for constant movement is the same thing as outright restlessness.

The mutable element encouraged them to accept change and seek constant change. In an instance where a Sagittarius may be told to wait six months for a promotion, that person is more likely to leave their job and to find a different position with another company. Even if that doesn't result in a promotion, it's something different, and Sagittarians crave that.

In terms of school, many Sagittarians are checked out by the time they hit high school. They may manage this in one of two ways. They may see high school as a necessary evil and simply do enough to get by and rebel completely. Or, they will excel and stay among the top of their class to have the most options available to them after graduation. Sagittarians are big goal-oriented, and others of them can think of their long game, but many tend to focus on the short game and can't be patient enough to reap the full rewards of their hard work.

In the workforce, the Sagittarian's need for change usually leads to impatience, and that impatience is worn right on their sleeve. A Sagittarius won't appreciate being stuck in a dead-end position, and they won't like being overly committed to a company. They may even quit a job to prove how much freedom they have.

With love, the need to change and move forward rarely drives them in the direction that people would expect. They don't rush into marriage, and they are not impatient to settle down and start a family. If anything, they are impatient to reignite that steamy romance that fuels the beginning of a relationship. They love the honeymoon phase, and for them, the need for change is rushing toward that honeymoon phase again, even with a new person.

Intolerance

Two primary factors contribute to this weakness, and this is one challenge that Sagittarians might count as a superpower period. But watch out because they may be falling for their own foolishness. Sagittarians receive a gift from the ruling planet Jupiter and the 9th house being the higher mind's house. Sagittarians can read people and assess deeper elements of a person at face value.

Arrange their exceptionally intuitive nature allows them to pick up on a person's character quickly. On its own, it is a gift, but when you combine that with their overwhelming honesty and their want to have an entire society of non-conformists, Sagittarians simply can't stand individuals who wear a mask in public. If a Sagittarius can tell that someone is different in private than they are when around other people, they will reject them from their lives. These are not people to be polite for the sake of being polite. They don't deal out "BS", or put up with it either.

There are two other personality factors that Sagittarians absolutely cannot stand. A Sagittarius native will not tolerate someone being selfish. This is where Sagittarians do differ from other fire signs. Although both generous, Aries and Leo put their needs above the needs of others. They would weigh out both sets of needs separately and decide which was the most logical course of action before simply putting their demands first.

Afraid of Commitment

This issue is not necessarily a weakness or a downfall, but is instead a matter of misinterpretation. It's a challenge that Sagittarians experience because of what everyone else thinks. But Sagittarius natives don't care what anyone else thinks, or their level or ability to commit. They realize that they're freedom seekers, and that they won't be forced into any relationship.

Sagittarians often view romantic situations in a negative light as a situation of one adult controlling or holding back another adult. That's not the case, and it can take Sagittarians a lifetime to figure out that good relationships don't involve anyone controlling or manipulating the other person.

Now, Sagittarius natives don't like feeling fenced in, and relationships can certainly cause that, but they aren't afraid to commit. They fear committing to the wrong person. A Sagittarius will rarely give this much consideration to the possibility of something going wrong. They are naturally positive people and don't think about things going wrong, but with relationships, they will spend a lot of time dwelling on all the things that could work out the wrong way.

To put it simply, if someone shows even the slightest inclination of:

- Complicated drama (including family drama)
- Perpetual selfishness
- Need for constant approval
- Judgmental nature

A Sagittarian native truly craves that deep soulmate connection, but they know that it's a once-in-a-lifetime shot. They aren't in any hurry to rush into a relationship or a commitment with anyone who might not fit the bill. Instead, they're likely to have many relationships while on the search for someone that will help bring out the best in them so they can return the favor.

Sagittarians need someone who can keep up with their high energy or enjoy sitting out occasionally. Letting the Sagittarius native have freedom is important, and they typically believe that freedom and independence should foster the relationships even during marriage.

One of the primary challenges that a Sagittarius will experience is that others feel they're afraid of commitment. Others will try to push the Sagittarius native to commit or move on and become impatient, which can mean they experience the end of many relationships. This challenge is that they will believe it is a "not my problem" situation, but if they don't communicate what they expect from the relationship, it will quickly become their problem.

Bluntness

With communication, Sagittarians don't hesitate to "tell it like it is." They say exactly what they mean, and they say it whenever they feel like letting the words loose into the world. Overall, it's an utter lack of discipline and tact, but they're just speaking the truth from the Sagittarian viewpoint, and everyone deserves to hear it.

This particular challenge comes up whenever they are unhappy. You may notice in many other sun signs that people might clam up, retreat, or silently brew over words they want to say but know aren't right. A Sagittarius just won't do that, and it comes down to the factors of their ruling planet Jupiter and their fire element. These two combined mean they are passionately on the quest for truth and knowledge and want everyone else to experience it. When the Sagittarius native is hurt, they'll take to very public forums to ensure that everyone knows how they were wronged and what they think about it.

In the workplace, this causes significant issues and challenges. A Sagittarian may struggle to move up within a company or stay on any team for very long, not only because they lack patience but also because they just have no tact. It's likely that someone in the company or on the team will get tired of listening to the Sagittarius complaining about the same thing or worse, dropping "truth bombs" in important meets or emails.

For Sagittarians, you might try a few of these tactics to overcome this struggle:

> • Practice active listening where it may be inappropriate to voice an opinion. For example, when another person is leading a meeting.

> • Don't address large groups on matters which involve specific individuals. For example, don't respond to the entire company in an email when the matter involves only one or two people.

> • When feeling like you need to educate those around you on how things "really are", give yourself a break and step away. Your fire side may spur a craze of anger and leave everyone feeling bad about the situation.

Careless and Often Bored

It would be a grave mistake to say that a famous Sagittarian such as Winston Churchill was careless, but he certainly had his moments and was often bored. In fact, he was notorious for walking away from things that didn't keep his attention or wouldn't result in action. He had no time for people who were all talk, and when he grew bored with something, he let others handle it. For carelessness, there are key moments in history that mark this leader's often forgotten challenge. The Great Fog incident in which many people died because of the government not taking measures to protect the people is possibly the most notable. Churchill brushed off this danger as "mere fog" and could not be bothered to give it any more attention.

Sagittarians want to live a happy life and to do that. They put all their focus on the present. That is why many great leaders are the great leaders we know them as they looked at the present and made the best possible decisions for the time, but daily, this can present problems.

They may leave multiple projects unfinished for long periods and be inconsistent for handling elements within their work life. Anytime there's a matter involving someone counting on them, they might have trouble keeping tabs on why something is important when it is also boring.

To avoid boredom:

> • Connect regularly with those who value the task as critical or vital for frequent reminders of why these boring tasks are necessary.

> • Devote a limited amount of time to boring tasks, so it is manageable and does not overtake your life.

> • Determine how much time it is fair to give to boring projects or tasks, so they don't feel like they are taking forever.

To avoid carelessness:

> • Ask a friend or coworker to go over your work.

> • Create a checklist at the beginning of the task when you're still very focused and then use it at when you are close to completion of the task to make sure you didn't cut corners.

> • Enjoy the learning process; focus on what you're experiencing and learning rather than how much you want the project closed.

To help a Sagittarian overcome this challenge:

> • Create extrinsic rewards for milestone completions.

> • Offer the ability to learn and investigate new factors of the project or task whenever possible.

> • Take advantage of their bluntness to determine when a task or milestone isn't necessary or doesn't serve a purpose.

Special Challenges for Cusps

As mentioned before, many Sagittarius natives fall right on the cusp lines for Scorpio or Capricorn, and these two signs often aren't reasonable or easy-to-handle cusps. Scorpio comes with a slew of complications in communication, emotion processing, and the opposing planet's matter. Where a Sagittarius always looks to the future and thrives for positivity, Scorpio is quite the contrary.

Scorpio-Sagittarius Cusp

Battle of emotions, the Sagittarius with their big emotions and the Scorpio that hides their emotions under a thick shell, is a recipe for explosive arguments after long brooding periods. They're also more prone to feel unappreciated and not say anything. They may work through long periods of boring work with no reward and feel slighted or disengaged with nothing else to show for it. They will hate this and often take it out on their loved ones instead of those in their workplace.

These cusps should speak up more and take responsibility for putting their complaints with the right person. Seek someone that can help your situation rather than those around you.

Sagittarius-Capricorn Cusp

With Capricorns, there's the matter of both the Capricorn and Sagittarian side loving others to be wrong. Now, from the Sagittarius point, they love to debate and learn and argue. They don't want the other person to feel wrong. They just want to win the argument while Capricorn wants to make someone feel like they never might win an argument against them when they're mad.

Sagittarius-Capricorn cusps should pay careful attention to how they speak to people. These communication downfalls can cause a lot of lost friendships so important to Sagittarians.

Chapter 6: Sagittarius Through Childhood

Sagittarians are among those within the forever children of the zodiac. They would be the lost boys of Neverland, as they simply don't seem to get older, but their childhood experiences will dramatically shape the adult Sagittarian, more so than other signs. For example, a Sagittarius who received a lot of praise as a child will probably seek a rewarding career with frequent praise. Although Sagittarians don't exceptionally care for what others think, they will associate that frequent praise with the comfort of home.

But there is a more common situation that Sagittarians face. Hating their childhood, or having an extreme dislike for it. One of the primary weaknesses of a Sagittarius is their inability to deal with certain types of people. Suppose they grew up with someone they saw as extremely needy or someone who seemed to victimize themselves perpetually. There, they would likely have an even harder time being around those who do this later in life. They may forsake their family, even though they are exceptionally loyal.

The wrongs and good deeds that Sagittarians experienced as children will act as their north star throughout life. They will use it to guide themselves toward what they believe is best for themselves and help to expose how they can improve and learn from their early childhood experiences.

What to Expect from Sagittarian Children

A Sagittarius child will display at high levels of activity almost around the Clock. Expect these children to stop taking naps early into their toddler years, and waver between independent and needy. Sagittarius child is exploring their need for freedom, but they want to do so with the safety net. They may attach more to one parent than the other at various points, and that could be to test the waters of what each parent will let them get away with doing.

A Sagittarius child might be very happy playing on their own or with siblings through the early years, but it's not likely that they will form a very strong bond with the siblings unless they are close in age. During the toddler years, they may be easy to help reach milestones. Sagittarius children typically learn toilet training faster, are more helpful with household chores, and take pride in completing a project, whether that is for preschool or an art project of their own creation. These are all factors of their budding personality. They are valuable in home, and they pick up on these early age milestones so quickly because they already foster that need for independence—their wish to participate in projects and play with groups fuels their growing extraversion.

It is possible during childhood that Sagittarians males and females differ the most. Women will spend this time exploring different facets of their identity, and by the time they reach their teenage years, they'll have most of their core personality solidified and ready for adulthood. Sagittarian males use early childhood as playtime and then figure out their identity during their teen years and eventually solidify into their core in their 20s or even 30s.

Sagittarius Girls

Sagittarius girls are a pleasure to raise. They have extraordinarily disarming charms about them. They use their inquisitive nature to prompt others into engaging with them on a deeper level than most children can prompt from an adult. They're also quick to let any thoughts they have rush out of their mouth, which makes for a complete lifetime of "Kids Say the Darndest Things."

They startle and surprise most people with their intellect, their curiosity, in their bluntness. These are the kids who ask where babies come from at a very young age, and they're the ones who will ask why it's essential to get good grades or why it's necessary to want to be something when they become adults. And they want real answers. They won't take fluffy answers. They will keep digging until an adult gives them a quantifiable answer they can sit right with.

Unfortunately, a lot of parents of Sagittarius girls will frequently apologize for the things their child says. These parents should also be careful not to say anything they don't want repeated. You would not want to joke about the desire to kick a (mean) family dog in front of the young Sagittarius girl, who will find her aunt and report the statement promptly.

You see, Sagittarius girls are always listening. They need to know exactly who is around them, and who supports them into adulthood. They will quickly form very strong bonds with the people in their family they feel are most suitable for raising them. These young girls may attach to an aunt or cousin with more devotion than they would to their siblings.

But Sagittarian girls come out with one of the most redeeming qualities in children. They are hopelessly devoted to the truth, and you should never expect your Sagittarius native little girl to lie. These young children are also optimistic. The Sagittarius girls are a bit more suspicious about the ebb and flow of life than Sagittarius males are, but you'll notice that most Sagittarius girls persevere through life with a can-do attitude.

Sagittarius Boys

Sagittarius boys will give anyone a run for their money. These boys need to be born to another high strung fire sign that can keep up with their energy. When Aries or Leos have Sagittarian boys, they can thrive together and cultivate a lifelong relationship that naturally progresses is from parent to child to an adult friendship based on mutual respect.

These little boys are at venturers. They need to get outside and play in the dirt and not come in until the sun is down. If they are prone to video games, then they want adventure-based games with lots of action and big worlds to explore. Sagittarius boys show many of the most prominent challenges in their early years. These boys will outright rebel against any sign of routine, and they will outright hate normalcy.

As toddlers, this can be extremely difficult for any parent; what almost makes it worse is that the young boy is simply having fun, and hopefully, the parent can show they shouldn't shut that down every time. Yes, sometimes, you do need to adhere to a schedule or meet certain milestones but parents of Sagittarius boys should remember that they are very young children, and especially as toddlers, playtime is often more important than following a schedule or routine. This child uses playtime to explore the world around them and better understand how the surrounding adults are acting.

Although Sagittarius girls may be much more mature than boys in childhood, one thing that boys do is to *reenact through imagination.* Through imaginative play, you may notice that Sagittarius boys will often act out things that seem far out of the realm of normal, but they're exploring conversation and deep concepts. They may be playing Pirates, but what they're doing is exploring the idea of right and wrong, theft and redemption, slang, and formal speech.

One of the biggest differences between Sagittarius natives in their younger years is that boys are a bit more charming. Sagittarius girls will use their bluntness and curiosity to spurn adults into specific behavior, while boys are sweet and welcoming. They want to be around you, and they don't want your undivided attention. They simply want your presence. Most boys won't begin to explore that wish for freedom until their teenage years. They might also reserve more their curiosity until they're teenagers.

Early Social Butterflies

Even at young ages, Sagittarians are just social butterflies. They can't help but make acquaintances, and their high energy is perfect for leading childhood games.

Even as babies, they might enjoy being held by a multitude of people, not just their parents. When they enter toddler years, they relate to others with ease and find friends in almost any environment. They are the kid who happily waves bye to mom or dad as they run off into the preschool room while other kids are crying that their parents are leaving.

Parents of Sagittarius natives might have to work a little harder to instill the idea of "stranger danger" - or untrustworthy people. They need to prove who has certain responsibilities with them and when things are or are not right. For example, if parents are separated, you may work to explain who will pick them up after school or which bus they should be taking home. There is also a high risk of carelessness when it comes to social situations. A Sagittarius child may not be aware of how late it has gotten or that their friends have moved on to something else or another activity.

Require Constant Entertainment

One element of a common struggle for Sagittarians children is that they need constant entertainment and stimulation until they learn to engage in imaginative play at about the ages of four to six. They need someone to walk them through how to play with certain toys and how to engage with other children. Although Sagittarius children make fast friends, they desire someone to show them how to participate in that play at an early age.

Sagittarius kids do love exploring the world and will happily bring you a mountain of rocks, sticks, or acorns they collect or turn into projects. They prefer to do these things with someone, they don't want to be sent out into the backyard alone, and the parent will quickly be notified about their opinion on that situation.

There are a few challenges with entertaining young Sagittarians in a public space. Sagittarius natives love the hustle and bustle, but taking a Sagittarius child into a grocery store or out for a shopping trip may seem like a chore because they want to get into everything. From pulling things off shelves to loading up the cart with random items, they will find ways to stay entertained if the adult in the situation isn't providing them an outlet.

Now, if you have a child like this, you can make this game. Remember that Sagittarians love the idea of responsibility even at a young age, and they understand that it helps foster their independence in later years. Even as a toddler, they can help pick out items off the shelf and dutifully placed them in the cart. Make sure that if you're taking them out for an errand, you give them a job and make them feel like they're an important part of the task at hand.

Understanding Your Childhood

Now, this is not inherently a Sagittarius problem. Many people struggle to understand their childhood and the lens that crafted their view of the world. As this sign you might feel drawn to this troublesome issue because of your connection to the planet of the higher mind and your deep-set curiosity.

Perhaps the first step is to review your parent's actions with a little of compassion. Sagittarius natives are quick to evaluate people in a harsh light and make judgments they stick with for long periods of time. As an adult, you might consider that your parents were in a much different situation than you understood as a teenager or as a child. Even just by reading this chapter, you could notice certain patterns that your caregivers had to struggle with as you developed your independence and your personality.

High-energy children often report they did not feel as though they had enough attention or engagement as a young child. Now, if the parent in the picture was also working full time, then it's likely that the Sagittarius child spent more time in school or with babysitters. As an adult, you can understand a lot more about the situation surrounding your childhood, but that doesn't explain away your feelings.

As a fire sign, you have a tendency to be more logical in how you view the world, even with those Sagittarius rose-colored glasses giving you that optimistic framing. This would be the moment to assess your childhood analytically and see what positives you could take away from the experience. Many Sagittarius natives don't feel a deep connection to their family, even if they have loyalty towards them. Allow yourself to consider the factors around your childhood and explore what may have happened that was beyond your reach.

What a Sagittarius Child Needs

Now, a Sagittarius child demands a lot. They need a great deal of attention, creative outlets, engagement and energy; but when a parent can deliver this, it's an exceptional experience. These are the children who will ask questions that make you smile and generally make observations that seem like they come from an adult's mind.

They are ready and happy to learn about the world around them, and they already have an optimistic view of life. Even at early toddler ages, they often think in the frame of the best-case scenario is likely to happen.

The parent to a child of this sign should not expect the child to sit for long periods of time or undergo confinement in playpens. It may initially seem that the Sagittarius child is impatient and high energy; when the adult tries to engage them and run out that energy, they can compromise and set up routines if they understand that their needs are met through those routines.

Chapter 7: Sagittarians, "The Best Friend"

The ninth sign of the zodiac combines personality traits that prime them for a best friend position in nearly anyone's circle. They're extraordinarily open-minded, and they tend to surround themselves with diverse individuals. They will generally bring an eclectic collection of acquaintances that could thrive together, depending on their signs and aspects of their personality. They are looking for the widest variety of people possible, and it's easy to think that they might have a checklist of sorts for keeping friends around.

Sagittarians are always on the lookout for the chance of meeting new individuals. It's not just that they're outgoing. They're genuinely interested in learning about various life experiences. They're out for the opportunity to hear about other ways of going through life and assessing relationships and personality elements. A Sagittarian will rarely pass up the excuse to sincerely converse with someone about their opinions, views, or experiences. Sagittarius natives make friends extraordinarily fast, and often the other person feels as though they've made a friend for life, but that is for them to decide.

Although Sagittarians make friends quickly, they usually only have a small circle of people they consider close. Within that circle, they are the truest form of their "self" and it's when they're with their friends that they're happiest. If you're the trusted close friend of a Sagittarian, then you have something truly special, and you should be sure to feed or bolster that friendship frequently.

Friends of Sagittarians and the Sagittarius native themselves have difficulty with maintaining relationships. While they are always approachable, they have trouble feeling trapped or overly committed. It may seem like they've made a new best friend only to drop them or move on to another person a few weeks or months later.

As an overview of the Sagittarius as a friend, they are open, sincere, loving, and loyal. They will genuinely show interest in their friend's drama and anything they have to say, making nearly every other sign feel good about themselves. Fire signs most notably have a deep connection to character and self. As the last fire sign, Sagittarians love helping others boost their ego while getting a little surge of ego themselves.

Who is Sagittarius as a Friend?

A Sagittarius is the best of friends, they're the life of the party, and they're the ones who always want to have a bit of fun. To give a few pop culture references, Aang from Avatar: The Last Airbender, Gina from Brooklyn Nine-Nine, and Penny from The Big Bang Theory are all Sagittarians and fierce friends. The other element of this friendship you can easily see in these examples is how they are all unapologetically themselves around each other. That is one trait in a friendship that makes them such good people and draws others in so closely.

Sagittarians will rarely put on a mask for anyone. They don't need to impress society or anyone individually, but this isn't an *"I do what I want to stick it to everyone else"* issue. They genuinely don't think that what anyone else thinks matters. Jupiter rules over this sign, and through the many mythological tales of Jupiter or Zeus, they just have no one to impress. They are the God of Gods and the defeater of Gods. This ties into the relationship because this raw authenticity is something that nearly every other person in existence envies or desires to achieve. So many people live behind masks or do things to appease others, and when they see Sagittarians not even considering that as an option, they want in on it. They want to experience that love of self and life in the raw how Sagittarians do; it is through friendship that happens.

Now, Sagittarians love a good party, and that doesn't align with everyone. For enough people, it hits home, and a Sagittarius isn't always looking for the house-rocking, party-hopping, have-the-cops-called-for-being-too-loud type of party. Sometimes they're truly happy at a small kickback or backyard bar-b-que. They bring to each gathering, no matter how big or small, their raw and uncontainable personality and energy.

As a friend, you can count on this sign to connect people and with people. Will you spend a lot of time alone with them? Probably not. Those under this sign are a few of the most extroverted that you may ever meet, and unlike other hot and fiery signs like Leos, they want little solitary time to recharge. Unlike Aries, they don't get overly aggressive and need to waste time putting the pieces of every relationship back together every couple of weeks. Now, a Sagittarius can have a bad day or streak where they're too blunt, too forthcoming with their opinions, and too "in everyone's business", but that's usually to blame on a planetary movement rather than their core personality.

They want to be around people, and they don't feel bad for saying what needs to be said, but when they fly off the handle, which happens most often when mercury is in retrograde or in their house, they know they need to fix things with certain characters.

As a friend of a Sagittarius, someone might experience one of these situations:

> • Flawless friends with the occasional disagreement of opinions

> • Unbroken friendship with a few big fights a year when the planets are causing trouble.

> • Solid friendship with no quarrels, but you know you're not their "best" friend.

> • Close friendship that often feels as though they're at risk of losing friends who will eventually clutch too tight and drive the Sagittarius away.

The pattern is that the Sagittarius will often fix their conflicts or overcome disagreements with their closest friends only. Suppose one of their acquaintances has a disagreement. There, the Sagittarius will usually not see it as an investment to recover the friendship if the other person doesn't want to work for it. Essentially, they know what they bring to the table and how great of a friend they are, so they expect people to put in the effort too.

On another level, Sagittarians have a great sense of humor, and they're always good for a laugh. Famous comedian and Sagittarian Richard Pryor is absolute proof, but other comedians include Tiffany Haddish, Patrice O'Neal, and Ron White. They get people to laugh without trying, and they often prompt other individuals to explore their talents with humor too. They often have that perfect sense of timing for joking around, even though they don't understand that when it happens to regular conversation, but they approach all things in life with the thought of fun and comedy.

A lot of their comedy is for their friends. Sagittarians want to make their companions laugh, and they want to see people have a good time around them. They'll be outlandish and say the things that everyone is thinking but doesn't want to say. It's that approach to comedy and humor that makes so many people want to be buddies with a Sagittarius.

Sometimes, a Sagittarius friend might seem a little overwhelming or overbearing. Sagittarians want to fix everything, and sometimes they'll crack jokes in inappropriate situations when it is clearly not the moment. They do that because, in their mind, it's a way to work out the situation, to make it less sad or less frustrating. Sagittarius natives also don't understand that they need not fix every problem for their allies.

Often, a person may only need the Sagittarius to listen. They could take a note here and spend more time listening in to their friends rather than jumping straight into the action. Meanwhile, their companions might be a little more direct when they don't need help but just a listening ear.

Sagittarius Friendship Compatibility

Like all other signs, when it comes to compatibility, they're widely compatible and get along with many more individuals than other signs. Here is a complete guide to a Sagittarius' relationships with other types.

Aries

Fire signs burn bright together, and although they may not be lifelong friends, they can have a great time partying. These two will match each other in terms of energy and a love for fun. A Sagittarius and Aries will connect when adventuring and going through everything with little planning and zero care for what else is happening in the world.

They are excellent friends but may go long periods of time without seeing each other. The only trouble is that the Aries may not enjoy the eclipse of power that happens with these two.

Taurus

Taurus and Sagittarius are usually not a good mix. Scorched earth is the best way to describe what happens when this earth sign and fire sign get together. The Taurus thrives in familiarity and material possessions. Whereas the Sagittarius sees material items as a chain to any particular space, it's an anchor, and they hate that. And the Taurus is exceptionally stubborn, and that gets under the Sagittarian's skin. Overall, very low compatibility.

Gemini

The Gemini sign is astrologically opposite from Sagittarius, and in a true opposites-attract moment, they do rather well together. A Gemini will complement the Sagittarian traits. You both seek what the others has. The Gemini wants the Sagittarian openness and humor, while the Sagittarian wants the Gemini's skill mastery and focus.

Cancer

Cancers are the whirlwind of emotions and compassion, which is everything the Sagittarius isn't. Sagittarians aren't slow-moving. They have little connection to the moon and can't stand sensitive people. That is everything that a Cancerian embodies. There is hope for this combination. Cancer might be that lone best friend that a Sagittarian has for their emotional needs and because Sagittarians can often help this sign.

Both signs love food, and they prefer the serenity of the outdoors. When these two get together, they can talk about the deep things in life, such as human nature, religion, and concepts that go beyond the physical plane.

If you have a Cancer friend, know that a Cancerian needs space the same way you do. Being too needy will often result in trouble as a Cancer wants time alone the same way that you want freedom.

Leo

To describe this powerhouse couple, we need only look at a few of the most infamous fictional or real-life couples. Think of Thelma and Louis, or Bonnie and Clyde, and that would accurately depict these two together. They brim with energy, they want to party, they're outgoing, and they're fierce friends. They could be best friends if the Leo of the group can stop themselves from becoming possessive. Leos want their friends around all the time, and for a Sagittarius, that might be too much quality time.

Virgo

A Virgo is a cautious planner, they want to know exactly what is going, and a Sagittarius just can't deliver that. But a Virgo is one of the very few who can appreciate the unfiltered opinion and insight that a Sagittarius provides. They are equally honest and forthcoming and understand that it's honesty, not abrasiveness.

Libra

Libras are dependable and aren't quick to jump to conclusions. There's a mutual agreement in this friendship that you can be good friends for a long time through honesty. Is this your best friend? Not really. Libras are notoriously low energy. They don't want to go on crazy adventures, or go out partying all the time. And there could be trouble with the Libras tendency to embarrassment.

Scorpio

Where Sagittarians always see the good in life and the possibilities of what could come, Scorpios are the opposite. You're Piglet, and they're Eeyore. So, can you two get along with each other? In many ways, yes. You are both prone to fighting, but you also both enjoy proving the other person wrong, so it could be a shared passion. The act of irritating others and each other could cause monstrous fights where one will eventually come around, and then they can start all over.

Sagittarius

Even better together! Sagittarius pairs will continuously push each other to do better, go bigger, and adventure more. Two Sagittarius natives together are unstoppable.

Capricorn

Capricorns find comfort in having their possessions nearby, and that stick to proven methods. Sagittarians love the novel and new, so they don't mix well with Capricorns, although they can rely on a Capricorn for useful insight on how to make the most of their strengths. Capricorns are good advisors to Sagittarians, although the Sagittarius native may not always want to hear what they have to say.

Aquarius

A fire sign and an air sign can make a fire tornado, and this mix is a great match. As friends, they're often adventurous together, and the Aquarius will usually present the planning and management that Sagittarians lack. They can put together travel plans and make sure they both have the right documents and budgeting to enjoy their trip. These two will push each other to explore, and the Sagittarian will help the Aquarian forget others' judgments.

Pisces

A true water sign that likes to put a flame out, Pisces can't take Sagittarian-level honesty, and they want nothing to do with crazy adventures. They party and they do have deep spiritual ties, which is where these two can connect. It's likely that this will be a passing harmony rather than a lifelong affair.

When Friends Fight

Sagittarians make good friends, even the best of partners, and it's common that they'll have many people happy to jump into friendship quickly, but there's always the chance of a fight. Sagittarians love to prove people wrong, and it's not even that they like being "right". They love the thrill of aiming to show someone exactly how they're wrong. They do fight often, and sometimes it's because they've taken a joke too far.

Being a Friend as a Sagittarius

- Understand that others aren't as open with communication – both receiving and giving

- Know that you need a diverse collection of friends to ensure that you're not alienating a few or overwhelming others.

Being a Friend to a Sagittarius

- Take the blunt honesty as an act of love, they love you and want you to succeed or thrive, and they think they're helping.

- Take a break when you can't keep up. It will only cause problems.

- Absorb the little things that Sagittarians do, like their generosity or optimism.

But when a Sagittarius fights with someone they care for, they are quick to make up and resolve the issue. Fire signs work with optimism and are often the ones who will work to make something right, even if they don't necessarily think they were wrong. A fire sign can acknowledge they were too aggressive or pushed too far. To them, a great friend is always worth a bit of humbleness or an apology.

On a final note, don't take their jokes too seriously, and give them space to support their freedom. You will lose a Sagittarius as a friend in two ways. You could be too clingy or dependent, or you could be too sensitive. If you find their jokes offensive, then it might not be a good match because the Sagittarius will not be pushed into stopping what comes so naturally to them. Sagittarians will always be their true self, so they won't do much to adapt to their friends' needs.

Chapter 8: Sagittarius in Love

A Sagittarius is notorious in love, perhaps for all the wrong reasons. It is not what it appears on the surface. Let's take a quick glance at what a relationship with a Sagittarius looks like from the outside and to the other person involved in the relationship.

The beginning of the affair is a whirlwind. The other person may not have even realized how fast and how hard they've fallen in love, or at least fallen into enthusiasm. Sagittarian's energy can suck in just about anyone, and they make people feel special. Who doesn't love that? Then, things slow down because the other individual needs a rest, and it seems like this is the settling of the water. It looks like you're done with the rapids and into the smooth and steady side of the river. And then it happens, they grow distant, and they break up with the person. What happened? From the outside, no one knows. It sounds like Sagittarius natives are just bad at romantic relationships because they're great friends, so just their lovers suffer this terrible fate.

From the inside of that relationship, it's a drastically different experience. If more people spent time looking at the Sagittarius in love rather than the lucky soul they've fallen in love with, they would see in an aggressive, fun, and confident person at the beginning of a relationship but once that honeymoon phase tapers off and the challenge is gone, the Sagittarius starts to see all the other qualities of their partner. They started to see that maybe they don't bring out the best in this other, and maybe this person isn't outgoing and extroverted but is instead a little reserved. That is when the Sagittarius distances themselves, and eventually, they leave.

When a Sagittarius is in a relationship or is flirting with someone and getting ready to enter a love union, they make their zest for life contagious. It's almost impossible to avoid the feeling of loving life and adventure when a Sagittarius falls for you. Sagittarians also enjoy spoiling their partners, and they do so with big gestures and a lot of generosity. Like most fire signs, Sagittarians love passion, but they won't stay in a relationship where either person must compromise any part of themselves.

It's that unwillingness to negotiate that makes Sagittarians seem so flighty. They are the ones holding out for that absolute perfect match, and they're fine waiting well into their later years to find it. If a partner starts pressuring them to enter an affair or to take their relationship to the next level, it's almost always the end of that part of their life.

Sagittarius Compatibility in Romance

Unsurprisingly, Sagittarians are highly compatible with many signs for short periods of time. But they link up with key signs for long moments of time, and that is what a Sagittarius should look for in a partner.

Aries

These relationships are fire, and these two will have a lot of fun spending weeks or months playing hard to get for each other. Neither takes anything personally, and they both need a lot of independence. Aries and Sagittarius are fairly compatible if Aries can control their jealousy, and Sagittarius doesn't ask too much of their partner.

Taurus

These two are great hookup buddies, but nothing beyond that. Venus and Jupiter align happily on sexual terms, but outside of that, this earth sign spells disaster for Sagittarius. While Taurus is often concerned with what other people think, Sagittarians don't care. These two will be nitpicking at each other quickly in a relationship.

Gemini

A relationship between a Sagittarius and Gemini is all about the mental connection. These two signs both have deep roots in spiritual affiliation and higher thinking, and that is where they find joy together. This is one of the few relationships where a Sagittarius native might spend more time conversing with their partner rather than having fun with a group of people.

Cancer

The trouble between Cancer and Sagittarius is that the Cancer would have to let go of a lot when it comes to emotional needs and expectations. A Sagittarius would not ask that of their partner, and so these two rarely work out very well. Basically, Cancerians look for supportive and nurturing environments, and they create routines that establish security. These drive a Sagittarius native out of their mind.

Leo

These two fire signs really can help each other utilize all their strengths and overcome common challenges for both signs. They are both outgoing, they both love to entertain and host parties, and they both enjoy doing new things. Of course, Leos tend to have a lazy side, but their need for alone time often means that they don't mind when the Sagittarius goes out and has fun without them.

For Sagittarians, Leo is the almost perfect match. If you find you may enjoy a long term relationship where neither of you has exceptionally high expectations of the other, and neither of you wants the other person to change. It's everything that a Sagittarius look for in a relationship.

Virgo

Virgos can match the quick wit of a Sagittarius, and they have a bit of humor so they can play off and enjoy banter together. The difference is that Virgos are more objective and analytical, and they might not give in to all of Sagittarians big thinking or breaking apart deep concepts. Otherwise, great conversations can quickly turn into a full out fight because the Virgo is asking "where's the proof" and the Sagittarius is playing the "what if" game.

Many people discount Sagittarius and Virgo's ability to click on a long-term level, specifically because many people observe that Virgos are reserved and tend to be quiet. The trouble is that usually they are composed and quiet in new situations, and once they

Libra

There are a few key issues with relationships between Libras and Sagittarians. First is the trouble of appearance. Sagittarians don't pay attention to what other individuals think about them, and they will often do whatever they please. Libra's care very much about what other individuals think of them and worry about their appearance, and how to handle themselves in public situations. They might be easily embarrassed by their Sagittarians partner, no matter how much they love them and enjoy their company.

The second issue is money. Dating a Libra can quickly become expensive, and Sagittarians don't have that much of a connection with material possessions. They may see the libra's shopping habits and spending habits as frivolous and that they are missing out on the finer things in life experienced because of material goods.

Scorpio

There is a deep sexual connection, but the novelty wears away over the first few months. This is a classic situation for Sagittarians. Scorpios are mysterious and stimulating and want to have deep conversations, but they don't have the energy or the outgoing nature that Sagittarians do. The Scorpio gets sucked into the Sagittarius vortex of vitality and optimism, and then eventually, the Sagittarius sees that the Scorpio is essentially the opposite of them. They don't want the Scorpio to compromise, and they are not willing to bargain, so the relationship ends.

Sagittarius

A Sagittarius dating a Sagittarius could be the start of a good joke. You're both a little flighty, neither one of you is great at commitment, neither one of you cared very much for money, and neither of you is very practical. It sounds like a recipe for disaster, but an underlying element could change the states for Sagittarius and Sagittarius relationship: moon signs.

Sagittarians don't deeply connect with their moon signs as they are not highly emotional people, but relationships are always emotion-driven, and when a Sagittarius and Sagittarius get together, their moon signs become more prominent in determining compatibility.

Capricorn

Capricorns and Sagittarius are the perfect setups of how opposites attract. Capricorns are careful, they plan, they analyze, and they look closely at risk. Sagittarians run headlong toward risk, and they don't care about analyzing or planning or being careful. But these two sides are deeply rooted in learning and experiencing new vantage points through the human experience. They love to learn from each other, and they love to see how the other one is often immovable in what they need from the relationship.

This is perhaps the highest compatibility that a Sagittarius could have except for Leo, and it's because Capricorns are dependable, ambitious, and committed. They return the loyalty, accountability, and honesty that Sagittarians provide. One famous Sagittarius-Capricorn couple is Chrissy Teigen and John Legend.

Aquarius

Aquarius is just as intense as you are, they are just as independent and adventurous, but they're passionate about different things. Most Aquarians are deeply rooted in family, and they aren't willing to budge in terms of managing their life around what they want to carry out. A relationship between an Aquarius and a Sagittarius could often result in a "ships passing in the night" situation.

Pisces

Philosophical, which can lead to interesting conversations, but these two don't click because Sagittarians are extremely self-confident, and Pisces are the opposite. They need reassurance, comfort, and support. A Sagittarian will not provide that for long.

Don't Misinterpret Commitment Signals

Sagittarians love to rush into things, but they are slow to commit. They're sometimes famously slow by being lifelong bachelors or bachelorettes. They're holding out for the best option. They are the kid at the candy store that could have any piece of candy, but they want that one that is going to hit the spot and leave them satisfied for a long time.

They also need someone who will fit in with their friend group and who won't feel alienated by being around friends often. Many signs associate romantic partnerships with privacy, but the partnership should just be an ever-present factor of their life to a Sagittarius. If they go out with friends, then their partners more than welcome to come. If their romantic partner doesn't want to spend time around their friends, then there is a problem because they're never going to see them.

Slightly Insecure and Needy

There is trouble that comes up in a romantic relationship that doesn't appear in any other element of a Sagittarius life. Insecurity. Sagittarians are always confident, and they have no problem jumping into unknown situations with bravado. But, after a couple of failed partnerships, it's common that Sagittarians get a little insecure.

After a few failed relationships, it's likely that the Sagittarius will begin to panic as soon as they feel that the honeymoon phase is ending. They'll dwell on whether they invested too much of themselves and the possibility that the other person got bored with them.

They'll wonder if they should end the relationship now to save on heartache later. Why aren't they calling, texting, or doing exciting things the way they used to? These are the questions that will invade a Sagittarian's mind when they see the honeymoon is done, and time to build a life together.

The only cure for this is to understand that your past relationships didn't work out because you were resistant to compromise, and you were unwilling to let someone else compromise for you. That is a very noble reason to let relationships go, and it's better to have let them slip by if it means finding that one great love of your life later.

If you feel like you're becoming too needy because of this insecurity, communicate it with your partner. Explain that you don't know where the relationship is going, but that you feel the need to spend more time around them, and you want to keep that honeymoon phase going. The honeymoon phase can't last forever, but you certainly can work with your partner to keep things new and interesting.

What Sagittarians Need in a Relationship

More than anything else, a Sagittarian needs a commitment rooted in trust. They cannot have someone frequently asking them where they're going and what they're doing. They will not put up with that for long and will bail on the relationship quickly; that said, Sagittarians aren't necessarily one for open relationships. They want to live independently alongside one other person. They need to bring out the best in that other person while also being the best version of themselves, and it's difficult to find that with one person, so why would they try it with multiple people?

A Sagittarius native will also require clear and blunt communication throughout the entirety of their relationship. This will help aid the level of independence they need, as both parties will understand exactly what the other needs. Finally, when it comes to communicating love, Sagittarians crave physical comfort and small reminders. They don't need grand gestures, and they rarely look for the other individual to go out of their way. They want the kiss at the door before someone leaves the house and the nice text message halfway through the day just to know that the other person was thinking of them.

Chapter 9: Sagittarius, the Life of the Party

Sagittarians know that high-energy activities, spontaneity, and a zeal for life come naturally to them. From the outside, other signs might see Sagittarius natives as simple party animals. Their high intensity and their overzealous personalities make them the spotlight of most parties and well-known in many party circles. These are the people who will know where the celebration is and who is going to be there. The level of electricity is hard for anyone else to match except for in the party scene. At these events Sagittarius natives find their equals in terms of intensity and presence.

Sagittarius born is the OG party animal, the ones who want to jump onto a table, riding the mechanical bull, start the dancing at a big party, or dare the rest into getting into the party mood. Overall, other signs have little chance of slowing down a Sagittarius. They're simply too much of a force. They're unstoppable, much like the Archer. If they want to achieve something, they will certainly do it.

Those born to the Sagittarius sign know that partying brings out the essence of their soul, and they need everyone else to operate on their level. Sagittarians are often the first to suggest a party or gathering, even a calm one. They want everyone together, and to vibe off the collection of high-energy and good moods that come together at a celebration.

Sagittarians Thrive in the "Party" Scene

Those under the Sagittarius sign don't just love parties. It's where they thrive. If you could work through your early years hosting or planning events or slinging drinks at a bar, those might be a few of your fondest memories.

What should other signs expect from Sagittarius party scenes? Think underground New York or West Hollywood. Now, Sagittarians don't need to "fit" the scene to make an appearance. If they hear there's a party, then they're heading out. For example, they may often head out to a rave without even liking Electric Dance Music.

Besides thriving in the party scene, they have an odd approach to the scene's seedy underside. Sagittarius are natural thrill-seekers and gamblers, but they aren't exceptionally prone to habit-forming addictions because they don't like feeling dependent on anything. Although a Sagittarius might repeatedly try or experiment with drugs or drink to excess, they will often identify when they must reel in that behavior.

It may be difficult for Sagittarius natives to understand that more is not always more. They are prone to get hooked into a variety of behaviors, so it's important to be aware of that challenge.

Alternatively, if they have fallen into addiction, their loyalty to those closest to them will often spur them to correct the behavior before too long. Sagittarians and their friends or family should keep an eye out for the early signs of addiction or dangerous activity with experimenting in the party scene.

Always the Ones to Go Out but Don't Expect a Routine

Without a doubt, Sagittarius is the wild child in the group in the zodiac. They hit the party scene regularly, but not in any routine way. Sagittarius' hate routine in every element of their life and that happens with partying too. They won't hit the same clubs on the same nights, and they won't make a habit of doing the same things repeatedly. Instead, they prefer all their free-time unscheduled so they can do what they want.

This works out exceptionally well for their friends because it means they can always count on a good time, but never know what's in store. Sagittarians are also laid back, so if someone else does want to do something specific, they can usually go with the flow and accept the unexpected plans.

Routines are among Sagittarius' top dislikes. They hate routine and will avoid it at all costs. About going to parties: it means that they're the ones who shake things up and bring people out of their routines to make sure that everyone, including themselves, has a good time.

Sagittarians also dislike people who think they need to please others, so any "plastic people" present in the group will quickly be called out or dismissed. They make it easy for everyone to enjoy themselves as long as they're not judging anyone else.

Sagittarians Bring the Party

Sagittarians make parties and "make" parties. They don't have a problem for handling, organizing, and hosting a party. Sagittarians often enjoy planning and hosting. They are among the best hosts in the zodiac with close contenders of Pisces and Leo, but they can make another's event a hit. They are explorers of new experiences and can often think up new games or conversation starters on the spot. If they walk into a party that was just getting started or that hasn't yet gained momentum, then it will certainly reach its full swing shortly after a Sagittarius shows up!

They're the ones who encourage other people to try new things too. Sagittarius natives will get people on the dance floor, having deep and engaging conversations, and interacted in party games that are fun.

Be Wary of Philosophical and Political Conversation

Sagittarius natives are exceptionally prone to getting into deep conversations. Unfortunately, they're not the savvy conversationalist for these kinds of topics. They have strong opinions and rarely take much consideration into other's opinions. Political conversations rarely go well for Sagittarians, which is unfortunate because even though they don't listen well during these exchanges, they are genuinely interested in learning.

With this matter, Sagittarians may not realize that they're bringing the conversation down or becoming aggressive. That is, until they're in a full-blown argument where they've lost complete control of themselves and killed the party vibe. They are a huge risk when around others with strong political or philosophical views. Now, when not at a party, these people can get along great and dive deeply into conversations that make a lot of other people uncomfortable, but these topics aren't for all types of events. Many people just want to have a good time and get a break from deep or political conversations. But their blunt and abrasive way of carrying conversations usually means these conversations will kill the mood.

How to Help a Sagittarius with a Party

Because Sagittarians are so good at celebrations, it is a common occurrence that they'll plan something, or someone will ask them to plan their event. Many signs that see their prowess for this will want to jump in and support, but how can you help without diminishing the Sagittarian charm that makes this party so great?

The best way to help a Sagittarius with a party is to ask directly. Say, "What can I do to help with the party planning?" As Sagittarius is so direct with their communication, you can be sure to get a direct answer. You must communicate as directly as the Sagittarius, from food to the invite list. They might want updates or check-in to see if you need help. That's not because they don't trust you; it's because they have so much energy they probably planned to do everything themselves and are surprised that things are moving so quickly.

Another way to help is to show your support. Never has there been a fire sign that didn't soak up the occasional compliment. Sagittarians don't care what others think, but they do acknowledge it when other people appreciate them.

A genuine compliment can help the Sagittarius buck up on any sore feelings that might have happened in the planning process. Many elements of party planning are sure to go wrong. For example, if they were planning a gathering and told everyone it was a potluck, then it's sure that someone won't bring something, or two people will bring highly competing dishes. The Sagittarian, in this example, might feel as though it's not so difficult to follow directions. They might feel that their guests should be able to follow the simple directions of bringing a dish, or even get a little heated about it. A compliment from a friend can heal that wound and bring down the desire to lash out. When they feel wronged, they'll stop at nothing to take action or get revenge against them. But as a close friend, you have the power to bring them down, to get them back into the partying mood, and move on from the hurt feelings.

When Should Sagittarians Avoid a Party?

Sometimes, a Sagittarius should just avoid the party altogether, but when is that? A Virgo, Aquarius, and a Taurus throw a party, and the Sagittarius stayed home. They should consider who will be at the celebration before they go. If they know that someone will be there who they can't stand, they should sit this one out. They shouldn't try to force a good time, and the middle of a party is not the time to make amends or sort out why you two don't get along.

Sagittarians should also avoid parties that primarily have introverts or homebodies. If these people don't like going out and actively avoid it, then you won't have much fun. That party will shut down early, and you might be left with a night that has no plans, and it's too late to go on an adventure.

Sagittarians need not be at every celebration, even though they want to be. If they have addiction issues, they may need to separate themselves from the scene, and find another outlet to be around people in good spirits without a lot of opportunity for substance or alcohol presence.

The thing is that Sagittarius natives don't need substances or alcohol to have a good time. They do it for themselves, but they can fall into these habits, and it can be a hard struggle to face.

Key Sagittarius Partying Take-Aways

Overall, the Sagittarians party often and party hard. They turn it up to eleven, they dance all night, and their energy really gives a positive surge to everyone around them but they should watch out for the possibility of getting too attached to the party lifestyle because it can put a damper on other life areas.

There is also the risk these abrasive and blunt individuals will turn conversations sour at a party. It happens occasionally, and usually, there's no saving the event after that. They simply will feel like they stuck their foot in their mouth, and then they might feel bad throughout the rest of the party. And they could get the urge to prove that other attendees wrong and just blatantly attack the other person with their intellect and opinions, which is unfair in the best of times. Other signs simply aren't prepared for that battle, but a Sagittarius is always ready to dominate a conversation on politics or philosophy.

Sagittarians should go out often for their mental health. They need to be around many people in good spirits where they can expel their energy. As they do this, they'll feel more in line with the rawest version of themselves. Sagittarius natives will do best when they're surrounded by many friends.

Chapter 10: Sagittarian Career Paths

The Centaur has countless career paths that could suit them well, but which is really the right one? You need the opportunity to think freely, constantly improve, and seek out rewarding changes. But what career can deliver that? Where can you travel, have adventures, and explore the need to learn and dive into the higher mind elements?

Your sign is that of the traveler who aims for big goals and often succeeds. Sitting still is possibly your biggest challenge in the workplace. Many Sagittarians find comfort in being an entrepreneur and may even open businesses with the express plan of selling them for a profit within a few years so as not to get tied down. As a visionary, you're often the one who comes up with solutions to problems that seem like a dead end and the ideas for new products or services that truly meet the customers' needs.

Sagittarius has a distinctive association with career and money. In general, they don't have much of a mind for it—usually, they are drawn to careers involving long-term plans and cooperating with other people. Sagittarians make excellent friends, but whether they make great coworkers or employees is yet to be seen.

Sagittarius with Career and Money

Sagittarius natives have key factors within their core personality that directly impact their career paths and their relationship with money. The most significant factor is their inability to concentrate on one single interest. Again, these factors circle back to Jupiter, the ruling planet, and the ties to learning as much as they can. Many Sagittarians feel as though they have a very limited measure of time to learn all the universe's secrets. Because of that feeling, they'll pick up hobbies left and right, and their interests will build up quickly. It's important that a Sagittarius learn to focus on two or three primary interests that can tie in with many smaller hobbies. For example, most Sagittarius' love to travel, and they can do this through a career that involves frequent travel. They can enjoy local food and getting to know the local customs during their travels.

One book that directly addresses a lot of what Sagittarians need in a career is called Doing Work You Love. It calls for that inner passion for coming out and focuses on how Sagittarians feel the need to flee from job to job because they are not satisfied.

As the sign which represents higher education and the stronger mind, it's likely that a Sagittarius will feel more rewarded and more complete in a position where they can learn. Working as a teacher, religious official, or in a cutting edge industry such as gaming or technology will allow you to learn new things all the time. It may even demand it. There is the ongoing belief that Sagittarians thrive in publishing, but the industry has changed dramatically over the last 100 years. Now publishing often involves sitting at a desk for many hours a day and making phone calls. It is not the over- the-top getting the paper out on time environment that it once was.

But Sagittarians are known as wordsmiths, and famous Sagittarian wordsmiths include Mark Twain, Jay-Z, Taylor Swift, and Winston Churchill. With public speaking, Sagittarians truly *thrive*, and they often are happy to set out on performance because, in truth, they're just themselves.

With specific projects, Sagittarius natives excel with projects with many small goals. Sagittarians would be well suited as a project manager with various construction companies or companies that are expanding quickly. Your follow-through skills may not be ideal for project management opportunities, but your ability to work closely with people and to negotiate compromise makes your talent to perform exceptional.

Sagittarius natives reap the benefits of Jupiter's good luck with money. They care little for money, and they aren't extraordinarily interested in physical products or possessions. They usually buy what they need – and occasionally buy something they like. Like other fire signs, they have a very generous nature and likely enjoy shopping for others more than for themselves. That relationship with money plays into their career path because many Sagittarians aren't connected to their job or career on a monetary basis. They may leave one job for a job that pays less but offers more intrinsic rewards such as exploring new topics or leading a team.

Perhaps it is because they care so little about money is that they consistently seem to have it. Sagittarians would much rather spend cash on adventures such as camping, traveling, going out with friends, and once in a lifetime experiences like bungee jumping. Sagittarius natives always seem to have enough money to do what they want and be generous, but if it's the choice between changing jobs and not being able to travel as often, it's a clear choice. For the situation of staying with a job where they don't have as much freedom as they would like and having money, they would leave the job and have less capital rather than reduced freedom.

Who is the Sagittarius in the Workplace?

As an employee, the Sagittarius is the wild card. These will put together the absolute best holiday parties and remember things like Administrative Appreciation Day or Food Service Appreciation Week. It's likely that it's a Sagittarius in charge of putting together who decorates a desk or car for a birthday or an anniversary. Sagittarians love to celebrate and make people around them excited to be doing what they're doing. Having a Sagittarius as a coworker is absolutely amazing unless they are ready to leave.

When Sagittarius is disgruntled, they are usually biding their time, and it might be because of how loyal they are to their coworkers. Sagittarians are loyal almost to a fault, and they may spend time in a position they don't like or under a manager they can't stand because they feel like they are serving as a buffer for the rest of their coworkers. If they see that a boss is around pushing their coworker, they'll be the first ones to stand up and defend them. Additionally, if they know that a good manager isn't getting the respect or appreciation they deserve, they will be the first one to say something to the team.

For managers, this bluntness and unpredictability cause quite a bit of trouble. Sagittarians aren't motivated by money, so supervisors usually know they can't buy these people off with a raise. Additionally, there might be motivation towards accepting a promotion, but you can never tell with a Sagittarius. If they are happy with their position and think a promotion would restrict their freedom, then they'll take a pass and won't accept it.

Managers are often left wondering exactly what's continuing to happen when they go into a meeting because they don't know how that Sagittarian will react. But the Sagittarius native will have a lot to say, and they will not hold back. The best way to manage a Sagittarius is to provide intrinsic rewards. Let them hold a party, have more freedom, have a little more time at the water cooler. They are likely providing you with superior work, so it is well deserved that they get a little extra here in there.

Particular Challenges That Can Direct Career Paths

We have come back to the particular demands that plague Sagittarius natives throughout their lives. First, they are restless. Second, they need to excel and move forward, but they don't wish to be tied to any one company or entity, and finally, they are impatient. What are the Sagittarius to do?

Initially, they should prioritize what they value most in their personality and what type of jobs they could find to benefit that personality aspect.

Here's an example that lists many of the most common values that Sagittarius natives look for in a job or career:

- Ability to work outdoors
- Travel frequently
- Freedom to change schedules as needed
- Ability to help people
- Ability to learn new things
- Variety in daily work
- Big goals

When Sagittarians can list the things they are looking for in a career, they can focus on what's most important to them and eliminate the noise. For example, the person may be interested in landscaping work, working as a Park Ranger, providing tours of a local attraction or natural feature, or even doing work with the local government such as waterworks.

Now, if the list above looked more like:

- Helping people
- Learning
- Traveling
- Working outdoors
- Big goals

A list like this one might guide a Sagittarian into teaching, specifically teaching abroad. Many Sagittarius natives do religious work, which constantly delivers a lot of traveling opportunities, the chances to help communities, and a lifelong learning experience.

The core element here is to take what is most important and then assess the different career paths that are most closely aligned with your sun sign.

Hating Routines and Overly Organized Elements of Life

Usually, the driving factor of whether a Sagittarian can make a job a career is how much routine is in place. If the job involves the same morning routine, that might be fine. But the same routine throughout the whole day will quickly drive away a Sagittarius, even if they love the job. They hate the overly organized environment and simply can't stand working for "Type-A" people.

The trouble with this is that the Sagittarius native will feel confined within their job, and that's the majority of where adults spend their time. If they can't have freedom in their workplace, then they might feel as though their entire life is planned out, and they've reached the end of their freedom streak before they've hit thirty. Sagittarians have a knack for exploding situations way out of proportion.

Make Your Own Way

One exceptionally famous Sagittarian has shown the tried and tested method that would work for nearly any Sagittarius... Walt Disney. He not only made a name for himself, but engaged in public speaking often. He was creative, had complete freedom in his work schedule, and controlled every aspect of his business. He worked with people he chose and found joy in connecting with others through storytelling. Walt Disney embodied nearly every career element that a Sagittarius could want. It's well-known that once Disneyland was established, he would often walk the grounds and spend time outside.

Another famous Sagittarian who forged that same path is Andrew Carnegie. He was not only one of America's most noteworthy industrialists who revolutionized the steel industry, but he was also one of the leading philanthropists of his time. He worked several jobs before finding his love for the steel industry. Those jobs included working as a telegraph operator and Railroad Superintendent.

Top Jobs for Sagittarius

These really spell out the basics of what a Sagittarius need in a job. A Sagittarian may thrive in any of these positions, but your personal interests and passions should direct you toward a career you can love for life.

Architects

Sagittarians are exceptionally creative souls with problem-solving. Architects often work far beyond the building's standard structure and often work alongside those implementing the "nuts and bolts" of the building. They're looking for ways to make these buildings visually appealing while also unbelievably useful. They fit into design-based roles, but they have trouble because design jobs often mean small amounts of travel, and it means sitting behind a desk. Those are two things that Sagittarian's hate.

On the other hand, an architect will also be on the scene during construction and oversee many project elements. Similar to a project manager, this gives the architect a leadership-type position while also allowing them to be on a construction-site at irregular intervals.

Then there's the final element that the architecture and building industry design is constantly changing. The design elements that are trendy or popular are constantly changing, and that's something that Sagittarians truly enjoy.

Grade School Teacher

As a grade-school teacher, you could control each day and make sure that your routines embrace your need for freedom, and you get to share that with the children. Having the ability to get creative and bring excitement into a classroom can fit in with many Sagittarians. Additionally, teachers usually have a lot of freedom for taking their classes outside for science and art projects.

As a teacher, you could explore your passion for learning every day and help kids build that excitement as well.

Theology Based Careers

Those born under Jupiter connect deeply with theology, and you might feel inclined to explore religious or theological careers. Working within a church or within the studies of religion can, surprisingly, come with a lot of travel. Additionally, you can affect the lives of countless people, even if you're only looking to validate information or spread the word.

This career path is common among Sagittarians, as it allows them to immerse themselves in communities. They don't even have to work in association with a church, but through theological research, a Sagittarius could easily connect with and help many people in need.

Sports Coach, Life Coach, or Personal Trainer

Sagittarians love helping people be their best "self", and you can carry out just that as a coach. As a life coach, sports coach, or personal trainer, you can connect directly with someone who needs a boost, and give them what they need. You can teach others how to build new skills and devote themselves to bettering their life. This career path can also keep you outside a lot and often comes with freedom with your schedule.

A Combination for Interests for a Career, Not Just a Job

Sagittarius loves humanitarian work or doing good for others, and they can find many jobs where this is an ever-present element, but that doesn't mean that you'll be happy with the first non-profit job that comes along. Instead, look for a job that allows you to do good while still exploring the many elements of life that interest you. Just because you're a Sagittarian doesn't mean that you must sign up for missionary work. If you're not very religious, then it's not likely a good fit. But you can find several organizations that allow you to travel and help others with good pay, and no travel expenses.

Ideally, you'll can have a lot of paths to follow. Sagittarius natives love the ability to keep their options open. Don't over commit to one company. Instead, devote yourself to an industry or something you're passionate about rather than one enterprise, or one institution.

Chapter 11: The Great Zodiac Shift and Ophiuchus

Way back in the 1970s, people discussed a 13th sign. Then in about 2014, NASA stepped in and put their foot in it. The great Zodiac shift impacts Sagittarians more than almost any other sign in the zodiac because this 13th sign is present through most of the Sagittarius in range.

Are there 13 signs in the zodiac? There are many reasons the ancient civilizations responsible for astrology's foundation omitted the 13th sign. There is an overwhelming mathematical balance in having 12 signs rather than 13. With 12 signs, there are four primary elements, and each element has three signs. And there are three modalities, and each modality has four signs. Each sign is represented by a planetary body in our immediate solar system, as there are 12 heavenly bodies in the solar system if you include the sun and the moon. Ancient civilizations also used 12 signs for the zodiac as it accurately represented the 12-month calendar they used during that period of time. This is true among Babylonians, Egyptians, Greeks, and Romans.

So why is everyone still talking about this 13th sign? Each time the 13th sign, Ophiuchus, is brought up, it becomes about whether ancient civilizations knew about this sign. The answer is yes, Ophiuchus has historical roots, the constellation is historically acknowledged, and it has a presence in the universal set up for astrology.

In 2014, NASA underwent more scrutiny and publicity when it announced that the zodiac was done wrong. The statement was not made to undermine astrology, which NASA doesn't acknowledge as a science, anyway. The message was more of a fun historical fact segment, and they didn't mean to cause the stir that happened. They saw it as a fun insight into history, and many within the astrological community took it as a personal offense.

Part of the problem with the 2014 report is what happened in the 1970s. The idea was present it to the public as though it was new; as if these ancient civilizations were not aware of this 13th sign and had accidentally omitted it.

Ophiuchus has always been present in the heavens, and its position along the ecliptic was well-documented among ancient civilizations. It simply wasn't selected among early astrologers. Ironically, it is one of the classic arguments against astrology where astrology lists and non-believers can agree. This sign was not chosen with a purpose, and even 4,000 years ago, astrology and astronomy were different things. Today, astronomy is a very scientific and mathematically driven field. Although they are the foundations of science and mathematics in astrology, historical presence and information give us a different view of the same heavenly bodies. Astronomists classify planets and consider the various aspects of life and the environment. Astrologists look at how the universe affects *people* directly.

Many people have a ton of questions about Ophiuchus, and it's well worth exploring how exactly this constellation and its movement can affect a Sagittarius native.

Did NASA Really Change the Zodiac?

No, NASA came out and stated that they didn't change the zodiac. They were just making an observation. The space agency came out and announced that it wouldn't change astrology because it doesn't deal with astrology. Their business is astronomy, and they felt it was a thought-provoking and fun experience. All the same, they cultivate quite a lot of talk.

The zodiac and the universe are not accurately represented on a flat piece of paper. The ancients did the best they could with the tools and resources they had. For 4,000 years, each new generation refined and improved the zodiac's visual representation until about the 1600s, which delivered the modern model of the zodiac with the circle that shows the elements, modalities, the symbols of each sun sign.

What is Ophiuchus?

The sign Ophiuchus falls from November 29th to December 18th and three additional cusp dates on either side. Most Sagittarius natives are inadvertently affected by Ophiuchus in one way or another, even though the zodiac hasn't changed.

Ophiuchus is not like any other sign within the zodiac, mostly because it's not a sun sign. But, moving aside from that, the constellation illustrates an actual person that historians can prove to have existed. The sign also represents a humanoid figure, which aside from Aquarius, makes it the only other sign to do so.

Ophiuchus is directly associated with and represents Imhotep, the royal vizier. Imhotep was well-documented as an astrologer, architect, sage, and the second King within Egypt's third dynasty. After his death around 2600 BCE, he was worshipped as a god of medicine in Egypt and Greece. Ophiuchus was the illegitimate child of Apollo or a demi-God who would sail the seas bringing life through legend.

The sign Ophiuchus differs dramatically from other sun signs because it has no element and does not belong to a common modality. Additionally, it doesn't have an opposing sign. In Greece, it was known not directly as Ophiuchus but instead as Serpentarius, the Serpent Bearer.

The imbalance of this thirteenth sign breaks away from many of the structured elements of the zodiac.

Ophiuchus Personality Traits

Ophiuchus is the rare sign to depict an actual man; even Aquarius, as the water bearer, only represents the idea of a man. This has led many to become jealous of Ophiuchus because they are believed to possess Ophiuchus's wisdom, specifically with matters of medicine and science. If that sounds familiar, then you're on the right track as Sagittarians already have an innate curiosity, and much of that could be attributed to Ophiuchus.

Typically, one should expect an Ophiuchus native to have an insatiable knowledge for wisdom and learning. That lines up directly with Sagittarian traits. Other common elements among this sign are a good sense of humor, a touch of jealousy, and an openness to change, but they take on a few Scorpio traits, including an explosive temper and a high inclination toward an inflated ego.

Overall, they often show:

- Curiosity and a desire to obtain new wisdom
- Great family connections

- Good luck
- Visionary problem-solving skills
- Innate ability to interpret dreams.

Strange Elements of the Ophiuchus Sign

Ophiuchus is both passionate and smart, but there are plenty of odd traits about them, which mark them as different from all the rest. We've mentioned that they have no element, and they have no modality, although they seem to fit within the mutable modality along most accurately with Sagittarius.

Their element-less nature can make them seem like exceptionally bland people. Not just at first, many people report that Ophiuchus natives might just be less interesting than those who are purely Sagittarian. Taylor Swift falls square into the Ophiuchus dates, and many people wonder who she is behind the red lipstick. It's well-known that she's not responsible for all or most of her songs and has led a very secretive life off-stage. Even she reports that she's not very interesting.

In that same nod, you have Ozzy Osbourne, which is alarmingly interesting. Why are there drastically different results from the same factors? Many bring it down to their lack of element.

To give this context, water signs are notoriously emotional in both good and bad ways. Scorpio, Pisces, and Cancer are the water signs, and they are all either internally emotionally high strung or an external ball of emotion. Air signs, including Gemini, Libra, and Aquarius, spend most of their time thinking. They're logical and communicate well, but their intelligence leads them into complicated conundrums often. Fire signs, including Aries, Leo, and Sagittarius, are passionate, loyal, and a bit fiery. Whereas earth signs, including Taurus, Virgo, and Capricorn, are rooted in the physical world, things they can see, and accomplishments they can prove. They're often extremely productive and work-oriented.

Given the nature of those born to the Ophiuchus sign, many people assume that they belong to the fire collection. They tend to be passionate, but not in any static way. You can't say that Ophiuchus is passionate about family and luxury how Leos are, or passionate about fairness how Aries are, or they share the same passion for independence and freedom how Sagittarians do.

Could This Explain Sagittarius' Eccentric and Unpredictable Nature?

Absolutely. Not having an element means that there's nothing grounding them together, but it certainly explains how Sagittarians can have such a drastically wider scale when it comes to personalities than other signs. Other signs were affected by the zodiac shift, but remember, there wasn't much of an actual shift. In fact, many of those who are Pisces now would have been Pisces back in the 1600s – or even the 800s.

The difference with Sagittarius and the other sun signs is that Sagittarius, for the most part, involves Ophiuchus. Ophiuchus naturally falls within the date range that ancients laid out for the sun signs.

What to do if You're a Sagittarius-Ophiuchus?

If you find that you're a Sagittarius also born within the Ophiuchus dates, there are things you can do to curb the negative elements of this under-examined sign. First, put jealousy aside because it's the trait most associated with Ophiuchus that isn't already in your wheelhouse. Second, carefully consider your interests. If you've spent a life dedicated to science and medicine, then you might have more in tune with this planet-less and element-less sign than your fellow Sagittarians.

Finally, you might dedicate a particular time to exploring this sign on your own. Remember that it's possible to interact with Ophiuchus in your moon sign and your ascending sign. Overall, we know that Ophiuchus natives spend a lot of time independently and alone. They appreciate their privacy and show very focused interests rather than the Sagittarius sign's fleeting interests. There are many opportunities for those of the Ophiuchus sign, as they are often extremely concentrated and accomplish goals easily.

Chapter 12: Thriving Sagittarians

Sagittarians represent the growth of the human spirit and the development of belief. They cultivate liberation and optimism wherever they go. They're the sunflowers that turn their face to the sun, and they help everyone around them do the same. A Sagittarius will refuse to sell themselves short or meet social norms if it doesn't naturally fit in with who they are. They see the bigger picture and value themselves, but they understand and can align it with everyday situations and people.

A Sagittarius will use their philosophical mind to help solve problems in social situations. They'll also turn to their good humor to that relieve tension in many cases. Sometimes this can go too far and get them in a bit of trouble, but Jupiter's gift of luck and the fire element's gift of charisma helps them out of many sticky situations.

Overall, they wish to encourage others to see the good in things and strive to live their best lives. That's all they want to see in life is everyone exploring their highest selves. They want no one to wear a mask in public or change their behavior based on another person's opinion, and they would love for everyone to chase their dreams and go on wild adventures. They do have trouble when it comes to encouraging others to do things they think they should do. Even with this minor setback, Sagittarians make good friends because of their optimistic and inspiring nature.

Sagittarians rarely have any problem thriving wherever they are until they feel trapped. They may feel caged in and a need to run. It's the horse aspect of their centaur symbol. They need wide open spaces, lots of freedom, and little rules or restrictions in life.

Time to Play and Lots of Freedom

The first thing that a Sagittarius needs to thrive is the opportunity to play a lot. They want to have fun, and that usually happens in social settings. A Sagittarius native may have fun online gaming with a ton of friends, or even on a server where they can meet new people and have in-depth conversations while enjoying themselves.

They will enjoy a lot of time outdoors. Things like Geo-caching and hiking are classic hobbies for a Sagittarian to get outdoors, spend time with like-minded people, and connect with the elements. Sagittarius natives hate habit, so if it means doing the same thing every Saturday, they'll quickly abandon it and move on to another hobby.

The second thing that Sagittarians need is a good party; regularly, but not scheduled, Sagittarians should go have fun. These events can range from a kickback, bar-b-que, or meet up at a local brewery. They might also include wild nights in the New York party scene, raves in the desert, or barn parties. There's no limit to how often this sun sign can go out, and there are no restrictions on how that fun should happen. They know how to relax, and they know how to have fun.

Parties are a great way for Sagittarians to boost their friends. They help break people out of their shell, and those who would normally stand on the side of the dancefloor looking sheepish are quick to follow a Sagittarian out and do several well-loved dances. Unlike other fire signs, Sagittarians don't consume people with their ego or their intellect; instead, it provokes it in others.

But they need a lot of freedom. If anything feels scheduled or regular, they reject it. They are rebels in the most fundamental way of rebellion. They don't feel the need to do something because someone else said they needed to. However, they don't seek freedom out because of rebellion. It's their nature. Jupiter is the planet of the higher mind. They are in the modality of change and under the element of passionate fire. They passionately love change, so they can grow mentally and develop their understanding of the world.

A Relationship Founded on Trust and Sustained Through Fun

There is a lot of misinformation and mis-attributed belief about Sagittarians when it comes to relationships. Are these characters flighty? Yes. Are they quick to get out of a relationship? Yes. Does it take them a long time to get into a relationship? Usually. Are they more prone to short affairs rather than that one lifelong love? Yes.

But people fail to see the bigger picture. A Sagittarius is loyal, loving, and open. It is often their negative qualities that pull the relationship down, but it is typically the Sagittarius that leaves the relationship, and here is why.

A Sagittarius cannot be anything but themselves, they cannot mask their personality, and they won't try. They are unashamedly who they are, and the world can take it or leave it. So, when they're in a relationship, they're giving what they must give. They offer that loyalty, openness, and love. When they see that their need for freedom, high-energy, and strongly held opinions affect the relationship, they may begin to think it's time to move on. This challenge creates a domino effect where the other person will clutch to the relationship even tighter and become more insecure about their stance. The Sagittarius will often leave because of their needs, and because they know that they aren't helping other person thrive either.

Ultimately, a Sagittarius will find their best match in either a Leo, Aries, or Aquarius. Leo and Aries are obvious choices as they allow for a relationship to grow on the foundation of trust and fun. These other fire signs realize what it means to need space, and they tend to not worry too much about their romantic partner wandering or doing their own thing. Additionally, these signs can both be high energy, and when they're not, they won't mind when the Sagittarius goes off to do something fun without them.

Aquarius is unique. Clearly, it's not a fire sign, but it does have many things in common with a Sagittarius that makes for a great romantic relationship. Foremost, they're both highly independent, and neither will be likely to tell the other what they want to do. Second, Aquarius is also deeply entrenched in the need to explore philosophy and the concepts that drive human belief. These two will have a lot of fun together and not make unreasonable demands of the other person.

Typically, in a relationship, you can expect the Sagittarian to be high energy and to question everything. They crave to know why you love your hobbies or what led you into your career. They're also not impressed with boring answers such as, "well, it's good money" because they need the full story. Additionally, they will want to wander. They may not be unfaithful because Sagittarians are loyal, but they will crave to meet new people and have lively conversations. Sagittarius natives don't have time to put up with jealousy and don't want someone tracking their every move.

Getting down to the biggest issue that people bring up with Sagittarians and relationships: settling down. When do they do it? Usually, when they find the one who lets them be themselves. That sounds cliché, but it's true Sagittarians don't settle down until they've found "the one" who doesn't ask them to negotiate and won't compromise their values or needs either.

The spouse or significant other should expect constant change and fun plans almost non-stop. They should also expect to be open with how trusting they are, and that trust is the relationship's foundation.

Sagittarians thrive when they have a solid partner by their side and when they support each other.

A Career Path That Works on Multiple Levels

Sagittarians need to find satisfaction through their employment, or they'll jump around often. A Sagittarius native will rely on the duality of their zodiac sign to easily move in and out of different environments, and they thrive in the challenge of learning a new position.

Now, a Sagittarius native might need a little push in the right direction from people they respect and trust. Most Sagittarians will find nothing satisfying in entry-level positions, but they experience particular troubles in obtaining all the information necessary and putting in the time to move upward in any specific industry. The struggle they face is that they want to learn everything they can, and they usually do so before they can advance into the next reasonable position.

They need a career where they can be around people who matter and help others improve themselves. Ideally, they will work where each day will bring something new. Even when there is structure, they thrive in high-energy and unpredictable industries that offer a lot of opportunities for problem-solving.

Additionally, a Sagittarius will probably face unique issues with their coworkers. They say what is on their mind, and that can prevent them from moving forward in their career. It may even be an issue of energy where the Sagittarian high intensity is just too much for another coworker, and it can cause conflict.

Countless career paths can put a Sagittarius on the right path with all the right opportunities. But even then, it's likely that the Sagittarius will change careers more often than other signs would during their lifetime.

Make a Plan to Continue Learning

A Sagittarius can't thrive or be happy if they aren't learning in one way or another. One Sagittarius spoken to during the creation of this book pointed out they didn't need to learn anything tangible, only accept new information. So, he avidly listens to audiobooks and podcasts since the radio holds little appeal for him. Another pointed out that they would use the *Great Courses Plus* and take classes on anything that caught their interest.

As the philosopher and the adventurer within the zodiac, there are many times when they don't need a formal plan for book-provided or information-driven education. They will learn through experience, so they choose field trips and cultural programs or opportunities. A Sagittarius would see traveling as the greatest lesson and may make frequent trips to local museums or art centers.

Reel in Those Emotions

Sagittarians are fast to anger as a fire sign, but their modality for change and their Ninth house of the higher mind draw their focus away from that desire to snap. Then, there's the Sagittarian's sudden jump into melancholy if they aren't doing things that align with their core self. If they are stuck in a dead-end job, can't party, don't have fun, and feel caged in by their family or relationship, then they are outright unhappy in every form of the word.

The concern isn't that Sagittarius natives have the opportunity for such big emotions. It's that they have trouble changing speed. They get stuck in one gear, and although they want to change, it can feel as though they're fixed in a rut. This rut could be a lesson given from the planet Jupiter about making your own luck or forcing your own way into a better situation. Remember that both representatives of Jupiter, being Jupiter (Roman God) and Zeus (Greek God), both had to fight to take down their father and become the God of Gods.

These big emotions can feel alarmingly unstable and even make the Sagittarius feel as though their emotions imprison them. When they get mad, they get petty. They will unfriend people on social media and outright ignore those who slighted them. Then, when they are sad, they become emotionally tired and try to flee anything. They may quit their job, refuse to eat, hide in their bedroom for days, or bolt and leave without a word to anyone.

To keep these big emotions from controlling you, you should have a regimen of actions that feed your inner Archer. At least one fun thing, at least one way to connect with new people, and one way to express your humor allowing you to joke with others.

Keep Your Emotions in Check with These Tips

- Do little things that make you happy
- Understand your moon sign – It has a deeper connection with your inner emotions than your sun sign.
- Distance yourself from bystanders when you're at your worst. You lash out, so take the innocent ones out of the picture. Turn to reliable friends, or just get time alone to recharge.

Feel Your Sagittarian Strengths

The best way to ensure that you're living your best life is to move forward with a clear vision and a focus on taking on both physical and intellectual challenges. It's far too common that Sagittarius natives fall to their weakness of poor planning, and because of that, they often don't meet the big goals they have for themselves. Sagittarians thrive when they face big challenges and can push themselves to be even better. They want to see their hard work turn into something useful, and that is the reward. They don't put so much weight into gathering material possessions, so don't overly focus on what you have, but instead, on what you accomplish.

Those born in the Ninth House have a strong ego and are stubborn. If you're the friend, family member, or romantic partner of a Sagittarius, they can be challenging to understand. Their fiercely loyal nature makes it seem as though you should give them more attention, but they want independence and freedom. Their inclination to help others improve themselves makes it appear that they don't need that same support. That is what you can give a Sagittarius to help them thrive. Communicate how clearly you understand that they can accomplish their goals and take on big demands.

With a mindset towards forwarding momentum and an emphasis on big demands and rewards of the higher mind, a Sagittarian can lead one of the best lives possible. They are not so easily affected by their environment and can truly thrive anywhere as they welcome change and new challenges. Sagittarius is among the noblest signs, and it will affect those in their life, often in a positive way. All they crave in return is the freedom to be themselves with a bit of humor in their life.

Conclusion

We hope this book has helped you discover yourself or the Sagittarius native in your life. Sagittarians are complex individuals that put themselves out there for all the world to see. It appears they would be a "what you see is what you get" group but they unknowingly face many challenges in their life they don't understand. Typically, a Sagittarius will flit through life with one passion, one career, one lover after another.

Throughout this guide, we've discovered that the demands they face are often the difficulties of the other person involved in their life. The Sagittarius themselves don't care for what anyone else might think, and often take pride in doing things their own way. With an unmatched desire for freedom and independence, not surprisingly, a few of the world's most notorious political and public figures are Sagittarians. They exude confidence, have magnetic personalities, and, as you've seen here, always approach life with the best-case scenario in mind.

Thank you for reading our guide, and we hope that you have found this helpful in your day-to-day life.

Part 10: Capricorn
The Ultimate Guide to an Amazing Zodiac Sign in Astrology

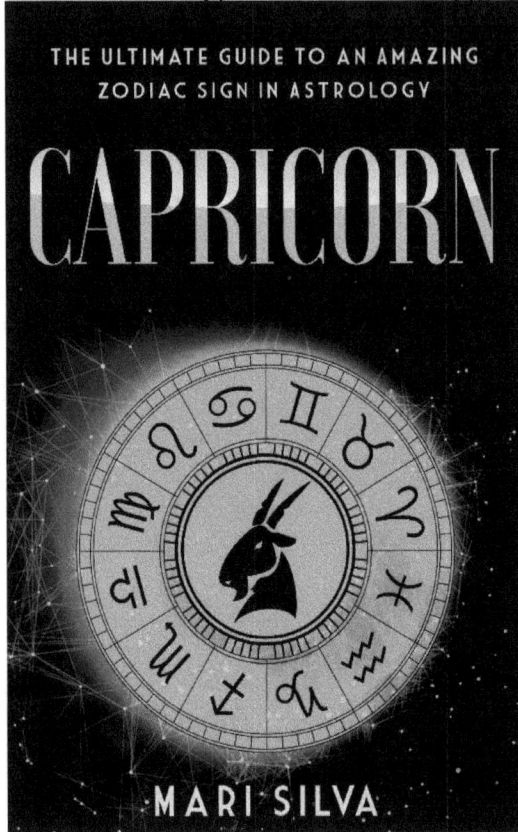

THE ULTIMATE GUIDE TO AN AMAZING
ZODIAC SIGN IN ASTROLOGY

CAPRICORN

MARI SILVA

Introduction

The stars and planets have always played a significant role in our lives, and this has been true since the beginning of time. Each of us is born with our own destiny, with no exceptions. Even though we are each just a small part of the universe, we have our own cosmic significance.

In ancient times, there were a lot of stories or myths created around such things. They gave the stars and the planets a lot of importance. Stars and planets acted as a guide and divinity for people. While there are a lot of skeptics now, there are also many believers. There are also those who are curious and want to learn more. Whatever the reason may be, astrological and astronomical factors are an inescapable part of the world.

When we are born, we have a certain blueprint created uniquely for us. It is a combination of genetics and characteristics related to the astrological time at which we are born. The extent and exact details can never be predicted, but the horoscope is something that people have looked to for centuries. We find a lot of information about our destinies and ourselves through our sun signs.

One of the earliest mentions of the zodiac is found in Babylonian astrology. Their concept was further influenced later by Hellenistic culture. It is believed that the sun signs represent many characteristics of the people they are related to.

This is why people have always been interested in learning about the zodiac; it helps them learn about themselves and the surrounding people. In this book, we will focus specifically on one particular sign in the zodiac – Capricorn. You will learn about the traits unique to people belonging to the sign of the Sea-goat. This book will reveal the secrets behind the mind and heart of a Capricorn at every stage in their lives.

You will understand what their strengths and weaknesses are, along with what they seek in life. While each individual on Earth is unique in their own way, learning about their zodiac signs can help us learn about them. So whether or not you are a Capricorn or if your friend, spouse, family, co-worker, or child is one, this book can be immensely useful as a guide to figuring out this sign.

The ancient art of astrology has been regaining popularity over recent years. Learning about your zodiac sign and horoscope can act as a reference point in your life. It will give you guidance and more valuable insight.

A broad range of topics has been covered, from Capricorn as a child and adult to Capricorn's compatibility with other signs in love or at work. Being in tune with your zodiac sign or learning about the Capricorn in your life will increase the potential of leading a happier life.

As you read this book, remember to keep an open mind. This will help you discover a lot about Capricorns as well as the other zodiac signs.

Chapter One: An Introduction to the Capricorn

Capricorn is the last earth sign among the twelve zodiac signs. It is also considered one of the cardinal signs and is a negative earth sign. The ruling planet of this house is Saturn, and the origin is from the horned goat constellation of Capricornus.

You have probably seen it being represented by a goat figure when you check your horoscope or read about zodiacs anywhere. This symbol is a sea-goat, a mythological creature with the tail of a fish and a goat's upper body. There is also a relation to Enki, who was the god of wisdom and water for Sumerians. In the mythology of Babylonians and Akkadians, he was later called Ea and was considered the god of intelligence, magic, creation, and water. The equivalent of Capricorn in Hindu mythology is Makara, and the crocodile represents the sign.

- Date: If you are born between December 22 and January 19, you are a Capricorn.

- Symbol: The sea-goat.

- Element: The element is Earth.

- Polarity: Negative.

- Ruling house: Tenth.

- Quality: Cardinal.

- Tarot card: The Devil.

- Favorable Colors: Brown, Khaki, Black, and Purple.

- Colors to avoid: Yellow and Red.

- Famous Capricorn celebrities: Michelle Obama, Kate Middleton, Liam Hemsworth, Dolly Parton, Diane Sawyer, Kit Harington, Denzel Washington.

Symbolism and Myths Associated with Capricorn

The mythology associated with the sea-goat representing Capricorn can be traced back to the Bronze Age. For the Babylonians, Ea was a protective god of creation, water, and knowledge. The sea goat also has other associations in Greek mythology. It is linked to Amalthea, the goat that nursed Zeus when he escaped his father's wrath as a baby. Another tale depicts how the broken horn of Amalthea became Cornucopia. Cornucopia was the horn filled with earthly bounties.

This zodiac sign is also linked to Pricus, who was the father of sea goats. Pricus tried to protect the sea goats by turning back time when they wandered onto dry land and lost their ability to think and speak, but he had to give his children up to the wild. Pricus then made the constellation of Capricorn and gained an immortal home in heaven. Pricus' tale is considered the reason why the melancholic and sad stereotype is associated with most Capricorns.

Season

The season of Capricorn begins on 21 December in the western zodiac. This is when the winter solstice starts in the northern hemisphere. The light and heat from the sun are at their lowest during this time of the year. The length of the night is somewhat greater than that of the day. From the winter solstice, the days start a slow ascent towards the spring equinox as they lengthen. The spring equinox will represent the last and fourth season of the year. The activities of a winter mirror the affinity of a Capricorn for preparedness and resourcefulness. Conservation and hibernation take place for most creatures in this season.

Mode

Capricorn is one of the cardinal signs in the zodiac. It holds the elemental energy of leadership and initiation. The beginning of winter marks the Capricorn season when energy and light levels are at their highest. The root of the strong cardinal authority of a Capricorn and their nature is the season's definitive quality.

Element

The element associated with Capricorn is earth. It is the most solid and heavy element. Ancient astrologers considered the earth to be the densest form of all matter. This element represents everything that nature is built of and upon. Without it, there is nothing that could take material form. The affinity of a Capricorn to lead, administrate, and wield material power are all linked to the earth element and its tangibility.

Planetary Rulership

Domicile of Saturn: According to classical astrology, Capricorn and Aquarius were both ruled by the planet Saturn. They considered Capricorn the nocturnal resident of this planet. This disciplined and ambitious earth sign allows the expression and enactment of Saturn's most authoritative and stern functions. Being organizational, productive, and practical are all abilities thus granted to a Capricorn.

If you are born with Saturn in Capricorn, these abilities will usually come naturally to you. Such folks tend to have an innate sense of responsibility and duty. They use it to bring order and structure to their world. Capricorns are born with a deep sense of awareness of any adversity around them. They also accept that they were built to weather the hard times they would encounter.

The Detriment of the Moon

This zodiac is in polarity with Cancer, which is a cardinal water sign. Since the moon rules Cancer, people of this sign are emotionally nurturing, protective, and sensitive. They are comfortable being vulnerable and innately intuitive. This contrasts with Capricorn folks, who are a lot more serious.

Capricorns have a stronger work ethic and want to achieve more so others acknowledge them. The moon in Saturn compensates for this detriment. Someone born in this placement tends to have a protective barrier around them and their emotions. It takes a Capricorn a long time to open up to someone completely and show vulnerability. There can be a Saturnian effect due to this placement and cause these natives to have bouts of depression or sadness.

If they are wounded emotionally, they are prone to become cynical. Such experiences make it difficult for a Capricorn to trust people again. Folks with the moon in Capricorn take a long time to admit a need for emotional support. They always pride themselves on their self-reliance and independence instead.

Exaltation of Mars

Mars is the planet of war, drive, and combat. It has a specially exalted place in the sign of Capricorn. Mars's power and propulsion will blend uniquely with the single-minded and steady work ethic of a Capricorn. This placement allows the creation of people good at martial arts and other sports. They also have strategic and tactical minds.

Such people work towards their goals helped by their strengths and endurance in an orderly manner. This placement helps to subdue the rash qualities of Mars and allows its energy to be stabilized so its natives can persevere and endure well.

Fall of Jupiter

According to classical astrologers, Jupiter was exalted in Cancer, and there he expressed his knowledge, benevolence, and expansion in an auspicious way, but some say that Jupiter had his fall in Capricorn, which is the opposite sign. A detriment is more of an adaptive challenge compared to this, but it still causes discomfort to the planetary force.

Capricorn is an earth sign that is cool and dry. The archetype is reserved and cautious, while Jupiter promotes optimism and faith. This is why the energy of Jupiter cannot flow freely. Instead, natives develop cautious optimism where they find it difficult to believe that the universe is working in their favor or that they have good fortune. But Jupiter's enthusiastic qualities may still shine through and allow these natives to survive the adversities they face in life.

House Rulership

Tenth House

The Twelve Letter Alphabet is a modern astrology system. Here, every zodiac sign rules a certain house amongst the twelve in the birth chart. Psychological astrologers created this innovation to help match the related house topics to the sign affinities. The tenth house of career and public status was assigned to the Capricorn zodiac. This happened due to the ambitious and earthy pursuits of a Capricorn that align with the tenth house's concerns. Time and patience tend to rule Capricorn, which is why Saturn's analytical sub-signature is invited to this house.

Twelfth House

According to traditional astrology, Saturn is the planetary ruler of Capricorn. Some say that the twelfth house is where Saturn finds its joy. The twelfth house is one of confinement, isolation, and solitude in the birth chart. Classical astrologers also called this house the house of a bad spirit. This meant that the twelfth house was connected to themes of anxiety and shadows which can cause mental anguish.

It is this relation to Saturn which is responsible for the biggest trials and tests that a person faces. It manifests as a feeling of being burdened with many concerns and responsibilities. This is why Saturn is better able to express itself in the twelfth house, but this placement can be considered good despite its difficulties because it is also linked to the theme of persevering until the defeat of all hurdles.

Characteristics of a Capricorn

Personality

The personality traits of people in this zodiac are derived from yin qualities that are receptive and feminine. This is why Capricorns are engaged with their inner awareness and oriented towards contemplation. Regardless of gender, a Capricorn will be disciplined, determined, and masterful. This is at the core of a Capricorn man or woman's personality. It displays their resourcefulness and resilience in the face of the cold season they are born in.

Capricorn is a cardinal zodiac sign and thus has the qualities of a builder, climber, and achiever. They can set lofty goals and achieve them by taking one step at a time. People born with this sign are reliable, consistent, and determined. You can also see them often deliver a lot more than they promised. Those with the sign of the sea-goat take their reputation and honor a lot more seriously than others.

Chapter Two: Capricorn Cusp Profiles

While learning about a Capricorn's characteristics, you also need to consider those who come into the cusp category. A cusp is when a person's birthday falls right between two zodiac dates. You are considered as on a cusp if you are born within the three days before or after the transition from one zodiac to the other. For Capricorns, there are two such cusp profiles.

One is the Capricorn and Aquarius cusp, while the other is the Capricorn and Sagittarius cusp. The first is at the end of the Capricorn period, while the other is at the beginning of the Capricorn period. Such people tend to have characteristics from both of the houses they fall on the cusp of. This is why inner conflict is a real issue in their personalities. Such people have difficulty making decisions because their different traits are always clashing with each other. As you read more about the two Capricorn cusp profiles, you will better understand this.

The Capricorn-Aquarius Cusp

If you were born between January 17 and January 23, then you were born on the Capricorn-Aquarius cusp. A person born in the Capricorn-Aquarius cusp tends to possess polarized and contrasting energies, making them unique individuals. You tend to be a hardworking idealist, and in the tarot world, you are considered an amalgamation of the Cusp of Mystery and Imagination.

If you look at the two signs separately, they differ greatly from each other. Yet, this combination allows these individuals to look at the world with an unconventional perspective in unparalleled ways. The ruling planet of Capricorn is Saturn, also known as the planet of lessons and limitations. This encourages Capricorns to have a very practical outlook on life and focus on their real-world responsibilities.

But the Aquarius sign's ruling planet is Uranus, which pushes people to develop radical and unconventional thoughts and gives them the ability to open the minds of people around them. When these two stark personalities come together, it can create a powerfully brilliant, creative, and ambitious individual.

Since the Capricorn-Aquarius cusp is a contrast of personalities and perspectives, which are the elements capable of influence, you can also create a complex contradiction as well. The Capricorn side, or the *earth* side, is extremely grounded and determined, while the Aquarius side, the *air* side, has a strong affection for spontaneity and variety. This can be a challenge considering that you have to feed both these halves of your personality, but if you can channel these energies in a healthy and productive fashion, you can grow and succeed no matter what life may throw your way.

A person born on the Cusp of Imagination and Mystery tends to have a lot of internal excitement. You may find your mind constantly churning out interesting thoughts and creative ideas, and you have a chance of experiencing more epiphanies and breakthrough moments than most people, but this constant output of dreams and ambitions flowing through your psyche can make you seem uninterested and detached from most people and situations you might be in.

A person born on the Capricorn-Aquarius cusp can stimulate conversations, making them look like a wiz while conversing with other people. You can see the world for what it really is, and you are drawn to discuss its problems and find ways to fix it. While this gives you the ability to have intriguing and fascinating conversations, it can be isolating and intimidating when it comes to connecting with your close ones, such as your friends and family.

Your mind is teeming with wisdom and unconventional opinions about different issues pertaining to you and the world, but this might keep you from checking on your friends and family, and it can lead to estrangement and strain your personal relationships. Although it may be a very noble endeavor to think about the bigger picture, you should not forget to take a breather now and then and check on your loved ones and nurture your personal relationships.

If you are born on the Capricorn-Aquarius cusp, you can be certain that your life will not be dull. While you are not grinding and working tirelessly on your creative ideas as well as the social connections you have, you are filling your life with excitement and purpose. As a unique individual, you can become a powerful leader and inspire meaningful changes if you will put effort into it, but be mindful that even the most profound ideas need the support of the surrounding people; do not neglect to put effort into connecting with the people in your life and making them feel appreciated.

Strengths

Self-determination, creativity, wit, empathy, and idealistic thought processes are just a few of the many strengths that people on the Capricorn cusp possess. Being born on the Capricorn-Aquarius cusp, you are naturally blessed with a strong drive for success and creativity while formulating your thoughts.

Although these contrasting character traits might clash, these differences allow you to envision meaningful and positive changes and have bigger ambitions and ideas. You can empathize with others and put yourself in their shoes, allowing you to look at the world from different perspectives. This makes you a great friend and a kind and generous soul, if you take the time to have conversations and listen.

Weaknesses

When they aren't at their best, detachment, chaos, selfishness, critical thinking, and prejudice are the vices common with the Capricorn-Aquarius cusp. Because you have to be so involved with creativity and imagination to keep yourself motivated and busy, you may inadvertently close yourself off in your own world, and you may feel like you do not need the company of other people to add meaning to your life.

You become more comfortable being alone with your own thoughts, and this can unintentionally leave your loved ones feeling unloved and unappreciated. This can become counterproductive and have a negative impact on your personal relationships, which is a shame because these people also happen to be some of your greatest supporters.

Suppose you are born on the Capricorn-Aquarius cusp. In that case, you need to remember the importance of a strong support system and put effort into your personal relationships now and then, or they may become a hindrance and affect you in negative ways.

Compatibility

If you are born on the Capricorn-Aquarius cusp, freedom and self-sufficiency are extremely important to you. You tend to thrive on your own, and more than often, you may feel like commitment and codependent relationships are not your cup of tea, but you also require the support and companionship that a lover has to offer. It may take time before you settle into the idea of having a partner, but once you do, you will find that a good companion helps to keep life fun and light.

Fire signs tend to be more compatible with the Capricorn-Aquarius cusp; they will be drawn to your creativity and your work ethic, and they readily offer their support and easily get behind your unconventional and radical ideas. Air signs such as Aquarius, Libra, and Gemini also make good companions for the Capricorn-Aquarius cusp. They can keep up with you intellectually and understand your not-so-emotional personality better than the other signs.

Key Takeaways

Develop the habit of self-assessing and reflecting on your emotions sometimes. Although it may be easy to get lost in your own head and keep yourself occupied, you also need to keep yourself grounded and keep one foot in the real world. You do not want to miss out on the small but meaningful conversations happening around you.

Try to listen to others while they are talking to you and keep your prejudices and preconceptions in check. Everyone cannot be as quick and creative as you are. If you maintain self-awareness and put in the effort, don't forget to enjoy your life and have fun; this will keep the sense of possibilities and imagination alive for you in the long run.

The Sagittarius-Capricorn Cusp

People born between December 18 and December 24 are a part of the Sagittarius-Capricorn cusp. You will become a true visionary, and you have a capacity for tremendous success. The Sagittarius-Capricorn cusp is also known as the Cusp of Prophecy, and your inherently strong willpower and determination will help you achieve anything that you set your mind to.

Jupiter, as the planet of expansion, rules Sagittarius, while Saturn, as the planet of limits and lessons, rules Capricorn. This means that you have the best of both since they are not so contrasting as compared to the Capricorn-Aquarius cusp. This unique combination of sensibility and inspiration gives you the ability to be not only a great visionary but also a practical realist who can inspire real changes.

As a Sagittarius-Capricorn cusp, you are fueled with a strong passion characteristic of a Fire sign (Sagittarius) as well as the strong willpower and determination of an Earth sign (Capricorn). This helps you make your way through life with a fierce tenacity that most people lack. Your fire sign helps you stay positive and excited to face life, but that alone can die out quickly if not supplemented by the consistency and willpower of the Earth element. Learning to balance these two elements of your personality can help you achieve a lot more than you might think.

People born on the Sagittarius-Capricorn cusp tend to be loyal, caring, and socially active. People who love and admire them and have a genuine interest in the things they have to say constantly surround them. Being reasonable and enlightened as you might be, people will constantly turn to you for advice and support, and you will find yourself providing guidance to the people that are a part of your life. Just remember to be empathetic and gentler to the people who come to you looking for advice. You can be a powerful leader and teacher to those who need it as long as you are patient and don't get aggressive with people; after all, not everyone learns at the same pace.

The concoction that is the Sagittarius-Capricorn cusp can create brave and hardworking individuals who are ready to grind and put in the work that success demands. You will be a motivated individual who is eager to climb the hierarchy and create your own meaningful space in society, but this strong drive and focus can create a rift between you and the people around you if you let it go unchecked. Your uncompromising attitude and independent personality have the potential to change the world, but it might also leave you feeling a little lonely now and then.

Being born on the Cusp of Prophecy, you will have all the potential right at your disposal. While you should be grateful and humble for this natural energy and determination within you, you need to channel it and let it out through positive outlets. You have the potential to make a genuine difference for others as long as you have a definitive plan. If you can be empathetic towards others and have a fun journey to the top, you will become the great teacher and leader that you were destined to be.

Strengths

Those born on the Sagittarius-Capricorn cusp are responsible individuals with a strong drive for success. You also have the ability to be outgoing and friendly towards other people because of your fair and humorous nature. Your strong desire to expand your knowledge allows you to experience and learn from everything that life has to offer.

When this is coupled with your fiery drive and undying determination, it can give you the ability to create a positive impact in your life as well as on those who are a part of your circle. You can delve deep into complex ideas while also being organized enough to pave your way slowly and steadily towards success. Strategic problem solving is your strong suit, and if you can consistently keep your positive attitude, you can become a powerful leader.

Weaknesses

When a Sagittarius-Capricorn cusp is not at their best, they become moody and closed off. They can be intense with their interactions, and when things go badly, they can become selfish and impatient. People can interpret that in a negative way and make you seem like an isolated individual. With all the hard work and passion that you put into your work, you might have no time for the people who are a part of your life. Although you are extremely helpful and loyal to the people in your circle, you might lack the emotional balance that a true friendship or companionship really needs.

Compatibility

Being a part of the Sagittarius-Capricorn cusp or the Cusp of Prophecy means that you have strong leadership qualities, often teaching others and being occupied with your talents and the things that interest you. To be able to develop a strong romantic relationship, you should seek someone who is a good listener and is willing to learn from you and understand you as a person. Fire signs will encourage your hard work and drive, encouraging you to become better and more capable. Earth signs will also help you keep a foot in the real world and appreciate your reliability.

Key Takeaways

Isolation can happen inadvertently, so try not to cut off the people in your life, even though that may seem very tempting in certain scenarios. Professionally, you are a capable worker who can come up with brilliant ideas that can help you become highly successful in the workplace. Small talk is not something that you will be very fond of, and you need fun and philosophical conversations to inspire you to live up to your potential. Focus on your friendships and personal relationships, and you will feel extremely satisfied with all aspects of your life.

Chapter Three: Capricorn Strengths and Weaknesses

In this section, we will delve into the Capricorn's key traits, both positive and "challenging." If you have a Capricorn in your inner circle, you may notice that they tend to do things that you definitely dislike or like. And if you are a Capricorn yourself, you may relate to the things mentioned here.

For instance, the Capricorn has no trouble approaching strangers at parties and is comfortable chatting away to the staff at a store. They'll say yes when you propose to go out and don't have that "I just want to stay home" default other signs have.

Now let us look at the positive as well as negative traits of the Capricorn personality.

Strengths of Capricorn

Hardworking

This is one of the most positive traits of a Capricorn personality. They are more diligent and serious than any other sign in the zodiac. People from this sign persistently work at any task they take up. If they are given homework at school, they make sure to get it done properly. If they have a test coming up, they work hard so they can get the best score possible. If they are given a project at work, they spend a lot of time ensuring it is carried out efficiently.

That a Capricorn never gives up is one of the most admirable things about them. Even if they are not naturally talented at something, their persistence gives them the chance to do well at it. Their can-do attitude is enough for them to succeed in life. Capricorn individuals are always willing to learn something new if they think that it will bring them closer to their goals. This is why it is important not to underestimate the tenacity that Capricorns have.

Ambitious

People from this zodiac sign tend to have very lofty goals and are ambitious in life. They set goals they make sure they can achieve. They know that hard work and persistent effort will get them where they need to be. This sign is always driven to improve. They want to do better than they did yesterday, and they want to do better than those around them. This competitive ambitiousness keeps them going on the toughest days.

Even if they have to put in a lot of long and exhausting hours, they will do so to get what they want. They expect material rewards for their hard work, and this could be in the form of anything from money to fame. A Capricorn is one of the best partners to have with you on a school or work project.

Responsible

A Capricorn is also a very responsible person. They tend to be a lot more mature than other signs of the same age. They approach things in a disciplined and pragmatic way. Capricorns like staying organized and tend to follow the rules. They like taking the straight path even while working endlessly towards their goals. If a Capricorn makes a mistake, they are quick to learn from it and own up as well. They accept their mistakes and thus surpass these hurdles quicker than most. They are also very reliable for remembering important details like passwords.

Honest

Capricorn individuals don't see the need to lie. It is rare to see them be dishonest about anything. If they ever do lie, they will own up to it just as quickly. This positive trait in a Capricorn is one reason their relationships are stronger. They make it easy for their spouse or friends to trust them, and they make sure to keep their trust. This is not a sign that will cheat or lie to you.

Calm

It is great to have a Capricorn on your side during an argument. They always keep their cool and are good at handling pressure. Their calm and analytical nature makes it difficult for someone to win an argument with them. They can always counter fiercely with facts that no opponent can deny. They are good at protecting themselves as well as those around them by keeping a cool head in difficult situations. This is why they are also good at giving advice to others who are more emotional.

Weaknesses of Capricorn

Pessimistic

While being grounded and realistic is a good thing most of the time, it has to stop at a certain limit. If you are pessimistic, it will only make you focus on all the negative things in life instead of the positive. This is why pessimism is one weakness of a Capricorn. Their no-nonsense attitude often makes them miss out on good things. It leaves them feeling unhappy and dissatisfied in life.

Capricorns seem to get stuck in a negative cycle when they focus more on how things look instead of how they feel. Their constant need to succeed and come out on top leaves them very disappointed when they fail at something. Their need for perfectionism applies to everything in their life. They adopt a negative view of their future when they have to face any failures or feel like things are not perfect. This dejectedness and pessimism also have a negative effect on the surrounding people.

Workaholic

Being hardworking is a positive trait in Capricorn, but they take it too far and become workaholics. For a life to be well-lived, there has to be a balance between work and pleasure. Capricorns tend to push themselves to the point of complete exhaustion. They are too obsessed with perfectionism and success, and they miss out on a lot in between. They forget to take time off and relax as they single-mindedly pursue their dreams. Working hard is a great quality, but becoming a workaholic works far more against them than for them. They are too hard on themselves and compromise their mental and physical wellbeing.

Stubborn

Capricorn is a sign that is known to be extremely stubborn and set in their ways. While this sign thrives on diligence and ambition, it is hard for them to understand that not everyone feels the same way. This is why they often hold other people to their own impossibly high standards.

Capricorns are strict and value tradition to the point where it is difficult for them to accept any new changes. They struggle with opening their minds to new things. They find it difficult to look beyond themselves since they are always focused on what is practical and realistic. This sign's stubborn mindset makes it very difficult for people from other signs to get along with them.

Guarded

It takes time for a Capricorn to open up to someone. They are very guarded and self-preserving. They don't give in as easily to emotions as the other signs, and this can be difficult for their partner to deal with. Capricorns take time to trust others and talk freely with them. They only become expressive towards their partner once they are completely sure of the relationship. This can often backfire and push away someone who might have had good intentions. Being this guarded can even leave them with no one to talk to, which can lead to depression over the years.

While these are generalized traits of a Capricorn, there are always exceptions to the rule, but these points can help you understand most Capricorn individuals better. Capricorn's great thing is that they are always willing to work on improving their weaknesses if they feel like it will benefit them or make them better.

Chapter Four: The Capricorn Child

Every sun sign has a certain set of personality traits associated with it. This is not only limited to grown-ups but applies to children as well. Learning about your child's traits based on their sun sign can make parenting a lot easier for you. It would help you in understanding and predicting their behavior. It would also make it easier for you to deal with different situations. Your child would belong to the tenth zodiac if they were born between 21 December and 21 January.

Reading a little about your Capricorn baby will definitely be helpful in their younger years. Even if you don't have a child yourself, it will help you understand and deal with any Capricorn child in your life. It could be your niece, nephew, or even your friend's children.

Traits of Capricorn Children

Here are traits that most Capricorn children tend to possess:

Adaptable

While you might expect most children to have difficulty adapting to certain situations, it does not apply to a Capricorn child. They have an amazing ability to adapt to different situations, and this takes a lot of pressure off their parents. Taking them to new places, meeting new people, weaning them off liquids and onto solids are all simple processes. You won't have trouble with potty training or teaching them table manners either. Getting them to build good habits like doing their homework regularly will be a piece of cake. You might find that they don't accept things right at once because of their strong personality, but they take little time to adapt.

Persistent

Capricorn children are often mistaken as underdogs. People get surprised by what a Capricorn child can accomplish once he sets his mind to it. You might expect something to be out of their league, but if they want it, they will chase after their dream until they achieve it. They don't give up on things that genuinely interest them or are important to them. Another great quality is that they stick to their principles but don't preach to others about it. They don't compromise on things they consider important.

Ambitious

Capricorn children hold their dreams close to their hearts. Even if it seems to be an unachievable dream, you cannot shake them off it. They are ambitious, and their persistence helps them achieve their dreams most of the time, but they don't share their dreams or ambitions with many people. Only those they trust or are close to will know of it. These children will do a lot to achieve their goals.

Old Souls

A Capricorn child is not known to throw tantrums or act up. They are usually quiet and appear to be well behaved. You will see that they behave a lot more maturely than other kids of their age. This is why they are called old souls in a young body. Parents with Capricorn children will barely face any issues during the growing years. These children are calm and collected. They are also great at adapting to changes and are not easily shaken by unpredictable situations.

Perfectionists

Children of this zodiac like perfection. You will see they always finish their homework on time and that they keep their books and belongings in place. They like having their room clean and well kept. If you go about it smartly, you can take advantage of this perfectionist trait in your child, but if they learn of your intentions, they might want to rebel.

Predictable

As you spend more time with your child, you will notice patterns in their habits and behavior. It is easy to predict what a Capricorn child will do in most situations. If they trust you and can confide in you, they will share their thoughts with you, but if you can't build trust, it can be difficult to guess what is going on in their mind.

They Follow Rules

This is another reason it is easier to bring up a Capricorn child. They seem to have inborn respect for rules. Once you teach them what is right and wrong, they will follow these norms. They also have good intuition in judging what is right. Their deep regard for rules often makes them come across as conservative when they grow into adults, but they sometimes break the rules if the situation calls for it. If your child seems to break a rule, you should ask for an explanation. They usually have a very good reason for doing so. If you still feel like they were at fault, you can make them understand by using good reasoning and logic. This will help you get the point across to these little adults.

They Need Respect

Even as children, Capricorn children have a major need for respect. They dislike being treated disrespectfully. They also tend to think that they have to prove themselves so they can earn respect and love. This is why they try their best to follow the rules and work hard, but you need to tell your child that they deserve love and respect even if they don't always come out on top. Show them that you respect their goals and thoughts, but you also need to let these emotional beings know that they are loved despite everything.

Capricorn Kids at Home

As I've already mentioned, Capricorn children are wise beyond their years. This is why you need to treat them a little differently than other average children. They are serious, even at a very young age. You will notice that they ask deep questions that are more suited to adults. They are also quite sensitive to a deviation in their regular routine. It is better not to leave your Capricorn child with an adult with which they are unfamiliar. It is usually a little beyond their comfort zone. You can help them with this one step at a time. Another thing to notice is that Capricorn children usually dislike loud noises. It is advised to avoid subjecting them to such noises or leaving them with strangers too often as a toddler.

Once a Capricorn child gets interested in something, they can be a little obsessive about it. If they like to play with trains, they will probably want to read every book or watch every show related to trains. If they like dinosaurs, they will soon learn the names of every species. Don't be surprised if they often beg you to take them to the museum instead of wanting to go to the amusement park.

When you see your child take this much of an interest in something, encourage them. Express your interest and support for the things they love. This is one of the best ways to help them learn more as a child. Learning always begins at home.

When they grow into their teens, you might see that they are often critical of you or others at home, but this is only because they have a strong sense of what is right and social justice. They are not shy about expressing differences in opinions over such matters. As a parent, you have to learn not to take it personally. Instead, you can contact them by showing interest in their hobbies or by trying to initiate activities together.

For instance, if your teen likes to read, you can read the same book and have a discussion over it. If they like certain movies, you can show an interest and ask them for recommendations. These are easy ways to connect with Capricorn children. They are a lot less likely to want to talk about serious feelings or thoughts at this point in their life. So you need to work on building bridges.

While they act like little adults, they also have a silly streak. Try to draw it out much when they are children. Encourage them to play often and to do things they enjoy instead of focusing solely on schoolwork. While academics are important, they also need to learn other things. Instead of signing them up for competitive activities or events all the time, help them participate in collaborative ones.

They should learn to communicate and socialize with other children. Most Capricorn children prefer sticking their nose in a book instead of running around with other kids. If you don't help them participate in group activities, they may get lonesome. As a Capricorn parent, you have to give them room to grow and encourage all their interests. Express appreciation for the small things and not just for the big wins. This will help them grow into confident adults. Be expressive with your love and watch them grow into a caring and empathetic Capricorn.

Capricorn Kids at School

You will see that your child finds it easy to adapt when they start school. While it is normal for them to feel a little uncomfortable in the first few days, they soon get used to it. It will not be difficult for you or their teachers to help build good study habits in them. You will see they like keeping their books neatly and they mostly have good handwriting. You won't have to clean up after them since they like keeping their desk and room well maintained.

Capricorn children are ambitious and work hard for their goals. These go-getters can be competitive, so it will be difficult to console them when things don't work in their favor. They hate seeing an 'F' on their report cards, and they don't like coming in last in anything. You have to explain a lot and help them understand that it is okay to fail at times.

Mostly, they do well in school. If they show an interest in a particular subject, encourage them to pursue it. They may even take it up as a career once they grow older. Once they set a goal, it is nearly impossible to change their mind. They persistently pursue their interests as far as they can.

Capricorn children like having tasks to do and often get listless when they are free or bored for too long. Help them stay engaged with schoolwork, games, and other activities often. This will help them learn more and will also make it easier for you to keep them happy.

What a Capricorn Kid Needs to Thrive and be Comfortable

Capricorn children are not very troublesome to raise, but you should understand them and help them feel loved and comfortable. As a parent, it is your responsibility to learn how to help your child thrive in their environment.

Consistency is important for Capricorn children. While you have to teach them to adapt to changes, you also need to avoid exposing them to more than what they would be comfortable with. Try not to change their schools too often. It can be hard for them to leave behind friends and make new ones. This applies to changing homes as well. They like a routine they are familiar with. Continuity comforts them. Capricorn children are better at sticking to schedules than their parents usually.

Help your child grow up with a lot of nature around them. Capricorns have an inborn affinity towards nature. If you let your child out in the yard or in a park, they can easily spend hours amusing themselves. Nature is nurturing for them. It is also the place they like to retreat to and think.

These children are ambitious and practical but love being rewarded. When they do well, remember to reward their achievements. Also, remember to be kind and console them when they fail. Praise their little achievements the same as you do their big ones. Also teach them the value of things with little examples. Give them a piggy bank to store away any pocket money they receive. Teach them to spend only on things they need or want instead of splurging on useless things. They will pick up these habits as a child and do better as an adult this way.

You also should teach your child to be flexible. Capricorn children can be stubborn, and it would not benefit them to see things only in one way as they grow up. Help them understand the importance of looking at situations from different perspectives. Teach them how to act appropriately in various situations. Being one-tracked all the time may inhibit their growth.

Understanding a Capricorn child according to their gender:

Capricorn Girls

If you have a Capricorn daughter, it is easy to notice how they seem to act and talk like adults from a very young age. She never seems like a child. Even as a toddler, you will find her obstinate. These girl goats can charge head-on when challenged. You will also learn there are two sides to these children.

A Capricorn girl is usually carefree and happy, but it can be quite sad to see them in their melancholic moods. They lose all their fighting spirit when they are low. You have to give them a lot of extra attention and shower them with love in such moments. This melancholic side of your Capricorn daughter may be a little hard to deal with at times, but this is one of the rare hitches in her personality. These children are not high maintenance, and they are not very peevish. You won't have to deal with tantrums over dinner or the clothes you bought them. They will eat whatever they are served and wear anything you give them. They also love to organize, so get the toys that help her play in the way she likes.

As a Capricorn, your daughter needs to feel in control. You have to give her tasks to do so she can fulfill this need. She will appreciate having an established routine to follow. Give her a few simple chores, even as she grows. The love for continuity causes Capricorn children to get off balance when there is a disruption in their routine. But you have to help them overcome it so they can adapt well as adults.

You will also notice that your mature daughter prefers playing with older children a lot more than those her age. She likes having conversations with or hanging around adults. Her communication level is usually above other children her age if they are of a different sun sign. Once your daughter finds a friend she likes, she will hold her/him dearly for life.

While playing, you will see that your daughter prefers games with a purpose. Instead of playing tag, she would rather dig into your garden. Instead of playing in the sand, she would rather read a book. A game that helps her build or create something would be better suited for her.

While Capricorn children do well in school, you might see she misses deadlines at times. This is because a Capricorn child likes doing things in their own time and with their own approach. As a perfectionist, she might take a lot longer to complete her tasks. She will also be averse to any nagging or constant reminders to do things. You have to teach her to follow deadlines, but it will be easier to get things done if you just let her do it her own way.

With manners, Capricorn girls are very well behaved. They act respectfully and kindly towards others. They don't have a tendency to display arrogance, no matter how much they achieve. They are trustworthy and dependable. You might see that she takes time to warm up to new people, but she will open up completely once she does.

Capricorn Boys

If you have a Capricorn son, you must remember that they need security. They do not like being disrespected even at a young age. As parents, you have to show authority in a respectful yet firm way for them to receive it well. Since they are more mature than other children their age, you should have a conversation that makes them feel like you are treating them like adults. If you make the conversation simple, it will only be taken in a negative way.

Just like a Capricorn girl, your boy is also an old soul. He will spend a lot of time and thought in figuring out his personal goals instead of wasting time. While a Capricorn boy is ambitious and goal-oriented, he also pays equal attention to his family. You will see that he can reach his goals a lot faster than most of his peers because of his sure-footedness.

Even while facing new challenges he will stay calm and composed, but he hates being ridiculed or misinterpreted. This shakes the balance for a Capricorn boy. It can often affect him for weeks on end, so it is important for parents to help in regaining balance again. Showing appreciation and attention at such times is essential to helping them.

A Capricorn boy child is quite well mannered. He pays attention to etiquette and good behavior. He always tries to present himself neatly. But even while they dress well, you might sense a certain degree of uncertainty in them. You must praise them a little to restore their wavering confidence. Show your appreciation for his appearance whenever you see him put in that extra effort.

You will also notice that these boys like keeping their room or things neatly. Unlike most other children, they won't leave their socks or toys lying around. They like making their bed and keeping everything in its place. They have their own sense of order, so avoid fiddling with their things. Allow them to create their own comfort zone. Keeping these things in mind will help you raise a happy Capricorn boy in their younger years.

Activities Well-Suited For Capricorn Children

A Capricorn child is wise beyond his/her years, and this is why they enjoy hanging around adults. Your child will appreciate having conversations with you. They also like feeling helpful to their parents, so don't shy away from assigning simple chores even at a young age. While they may seem like homebodies, you must encourage them to play with children their age.

If you take them to the playground, you will often see that they hang back instead of rushing to play with the others. As a parent, you must help them come out of their shell. Encourage open-ended games as a group. Also, avoid too many competitive games. A Capricorn child is competitive by nature, and it will often end in tears or sulking if they don't win at such games. Instead, encourage games that allow everyone to mingle and enjoy without being pitted against each other.

Capricorn children are easily drawn to books, so do your best to encourage the habit of reading. Don't let them spend too many hours doing this since it can make them grow into loners. But allow them to appreciate the joys of reading at a young age. It will help them learn a lot over the years. When they are toddlers or quite young, choose books that will help them learn good morals. This will help in building a foundation for their values. You can then allow them to explore other books of their liking as they grow older.

Chapter Five: Capricorn in Love

Now we get to the part many readers look for, the Capricorn in love and relationships.

If you are looking for a long-term relationship, Capricorns are the wisest choice. They are committed, reliable, and faithful. Even if the relationship is difficult, they are determined to make it work. If you are Capricorn or are in a relationship with one, it can be helpful to learn more about a Capricorn in love. This makes it easier to work on the relationship and make it stronger with time.

The Conventional Lover

Prudent and Loyal

They tread slowly and are rarely willing to jump right into a relationship. They take their time to observe the situation and only get involved if they think it looks right. They like having control over everything all the time. If they feel like they can't trust someone, they will never enter a relationship with them. But once they do, they are loyal and trust their partner wholeheartedly.

Financially Savvy

This is great for someone looking for a financially stable partner. This sign knows how to handle their money well and are skilled with finances. This is why they are also attracted to others who are wise with money and work hard to earn it. A lot of Capricorns choose to work at banks, as accountants or as managers. They like being friends or lovers with others who are similarly smart when it comes to financial matters.

Giving and Protective

They do their best to protect the things that they hold close to their heart. This applies to their material possessions and to the people they love. Being in a relationship with a Capricorn is great since they want to do their best to keep stability and protect their partner even if it is at great personal cost. They are giving by nature and don't hesitate when it comes to their significant other, but their protective nature can get a little possessive, and not every partner can deal with it. Individuals who are carefree and treasure their freedom will find Capricorns too restrictive and feel smothered. But people who want a reliable partner will appreciate this possessiveness in their Capricorn partner.

Controlling

This sign is a natural leader, and it is not because they consciously want to be dominant or get attention. They just like having control so they can do things the right way. This controlling trait can be a drawback in a relationship with people who are more spontaneous, but if their partner is a perfectionist, Capricorns find it easier to navigate things.

Passionate About their Relationship

It takes them time to relax and feel free with their partner, but their love is made clear once they do. But you cannot confuse emotion with passion. This sign is never a naturally emotional one. They consciously avoid any dramatic emotions and refuse to let emotions rule over them. It can be frustrating for their partners, who usually have to coerce the

Capricorn into sharing their feelings. But if Capricorn is paired with a similarly practical partner, the relationship can be very strong.

How to tell if a Capricorn is in Love?

Capricorns are rarely a flirty type of personality. In fact, they find flirts unattractive. Their approach to romance is a lot more traditional, and they have a more authoritative bearing. If you are interested in a Capricorn, you will usually have to make the first move. If the Capricorn is interested as well, they will let you know directly, but if they are not as direct, there are other ways to tell if they are interested in you.

- They will try to take every chance possible to get close to you.
- They are always generous with you.
- They make plans around you and will change their schedule for you.
- They try their best to impress you.
- They try making themselves indispensable to you.

Not every Capricorn is forthcoming about letting their interest show. They do it through their actions and wait patiently to see if the other person is interested as well.

Strengths of a Capricorn in a Relationship

Capricorns know what they want, and they also know how to get it. They go through their lives at their own controlled pace and move step by step. Capricorns listen to their head more than their heart, and this is not always a good thing in relationships. Even though a Capricorn's practicality is not very exciting, it helps them get things done. They are traditional and take the well-worn path. This sign is trustworthy and reliable. They are the ones you can go to for advice.

Capricorns get uncomfortable when they feel emotions running too deeply in their relationship. This is why they start distancing themselves a little to avoid attachment, but they are considerate and good lovers despite being on the tame side. They take their time making love just like they do everything else.

Challenges of a Capricorn in a Relationship

One challenge that most Capricorns face in a relationship is that they find it difficult to express affection to their partner. They think there is a time and place for everything, and this applies to love as well. They dislike any public displays of affection, but this could be something their partner needs.

Capricorns need to be flexible and consider what their partner needs to feel valued. This sign can only overcome all their inhibitions when they find the perfect partner. They need someone who will help them get better at handling emotions and opening up more.

Capricorns also tend to hold on to a grudge for a long time, and this is something that none of their partners will appreciate. They must learn to forgive and forget. Forgiveness is an important aspect of a good relationship. If the Capricorn remains stubborn about everything and refuses to relent in any argument, it's difficult to sustain a happy relationship.

Dating a Capricorn

Do you have a crush on a Capricorn or are you in a relationship with one? It is completely understandable why someone would be attracted to this sign. They have beauty with brains and are the most ambitious and hard-working sign in the zodiac roster, but Capricorns can be elusive when it comes to matters of love. You need to know this if you want to date a Capricorn.

This planet was named after the titan who tried remaining a ruler by eating his offspring, and this is why Saturn is linked to daddy issues quite often. But on a more serious note, the 29.5-year orbit of Saturn signifies true adulthood for a Capricorn in their late twenties. This is the point where Saturn comes to the same position it was during the time of a Capricorn's birth.

Saturn's return is when you become your true self and gain control of your life. It gives you all the tough love that comes hand in hand with adulthood. But the intensity of Saturn is not known for Capricorn. This is why people from this sign feel obligated to work very hard from a very young age. They think that they must be responsible at every point in life. This helps them develop a great work ethic, and you can see this displayed in many prominent personalities like Michelle Obama and Greta Thunberg.

The resilience of a Capricorn is often what defines them. The sign of the Sea-Goat that can navigate land and water can overcome any hurdle in their life. Capricorns live their life with the big picture in mind, and they never let anything, or anyone gets in their way. To date this sign, you have to remember this. Even if they have the same feelings as you do, their practicality will make them choose what is better for their goals.

Capricorns are naturally great at navigating work relationships, but this does not apply to their personal relationships. They choose partners who appear to be perfect instead of taking time to see if they are really the right fit. They also use their business strategies to navigate their relationships. Capricorns have a premeditated view about who would be the perfect partner for them, and this leaves them disappointed in the end.

Someone who looks good and earns well is not necessarily the right partner if you just choose them based on these credentials, but Capricorn will learn this the hard way. Once they do find the right partner, Capricorns can access true emotional intimacy.

When a Capricorn is in a relationship, they are completely committed to it. Capricorns don't commit to someone unless they are serious about it. They change their schedule to accommodate their partner and expect the same from them. Capricorns tend to have a very tangible and physical connection with their partner. In a relationship, they need quality time together. Capricorns are very work-oriented, and they want someone they can rely on. They need a partner who can give them stability and reassurance.

If you date a Capricorn, you also have to remember that they have great memory power. If you say something once to a Capricorn, they will always remember it. Even if it was an offhand comment, it leaves a deep impression on them. This quality has drawbacks as well as positives. It means that they are great at remembering birthdays or anniversaries. But it also means that they will remember anything hurtful you say to them.

This earth sign has very high standards and is never willing to settle for less than what they consider the best. Capricorns are attracted to people who are ambitious and resilient like them. They are also attracted to those with skills that they themselves are lacking. So if you want to pursue a Capricorn, put your skills blatantly on display for them to notice. They love a challenge and appreciate the best in others. But no matter what you do, try never to let a Capricorn down.

Don't make a promise and break it. Don't under-deliver on what you say to them. Even if you intend to do something, set the bar higher and surprise them by doing more than you said you would.

Compatibility

Capricorn is not a very romantic sign and is better known for being loyal, honest, and serious. They tend to be very focused on business and don't pay a lot of attention to pleasure, but if they find the right partner, Capricorns can be very devoted and dedicated to the relationship.

When it comes to compatibility, you have to understand that people from this sign will always consider practicalities even if they fall in love with someone. Some say that their placements impact relationships with different signs in the wheel of the zodiac. While Capricorn compatibility is explained further in the next section, let's learn a little about the best and worst matches for this sign.

Best Matches for Capricorn

These signs are highly compatible for a Capricorn partner:

Taurus

Capricorn is well suited for Taurus since they are both down to earth and practical. These earth signs place equal importance on materialistic wellbeing and can thus understand each other. They are a well-balanced couple with similarities and differences. Their similarities make the relationship easy for them while their differences help balance each other.

Capricorn is hardworking and ambitious and often forgoes pleasure for work. Taurus is a lot better at enjoying life and can often get lazy. While a Taurus helps a Capricorn relax a little, Capricorn motivates Taurus to work harder. Taurus is also adept at bringing out the sensuality of a Capricorn when they are in a relationship.

Virgo

This is another excellent sign for Capricorn to pair up with. Virgo is also an earth sign like Capricorn. The sharing of the same element between these signs allows their relationship to be harmonious. Technically, the relationship between Virgo and Capricorn should be just as pleasant as that with Taurus, but this particular pair can have a little more tension between them since Virgo has more nervous energy. In a relationship with Taurus, the latter takes on a stabilizing role for Capricorn. But with Virgo, Capricorn is the stabilizing partner.

Despite this, Capricorn and Virgo can be supportive of each other and balance things out. While Capricorn sees the bigger picture and sets long-term goals, Virgo is better at dealing with short-term tasks and taking care of details. This pair has a great romantic relationship, but they will also succeed if they work in business together.

Scorpio

Capricorn and Scorpio are similar in certain ways. Both are quite serious and are good strategists, but neither like making small talk and both prioritize work over pleasure. They can seem very much alike for someone looking in from the outside. In a business partnership, this pair can be quite formidable.

One aspect of this match-up is that they both are completely comfortable with each other. This is not just because their relationship is great; it is, and their differences only balance them out. The deeply passionate Scorpio is paired well with the seemingly unfeeling and pragmatic Capricorn. Capricorn provides stability to the relationship, while Scorpio helps soften Capricorn down.

Cancer

Pisces has, technically, better compatibility with Capricorn than Cancer, but by nature, these opposite signs are great partners for each other. The value they place on family life is one reason this opposite pair works well together. The entire family should take part in getting chores done at home, and they should all interact adequately with people outside their little world. Capricorn and Cancer symbolize this polarity. These concepts are known as Agora and Hestia in Greek philosophy.

In most cultures, they are tied to specific gender roles. Even though it is changing a lot in recent times, gender roles are deeply rooted in traditional society. This is why the marriage between a Capricorn man and a Cancer woman is quite traditional by nature. But for a Cancer man and Capricorn woman, there will be a natural reversal of roles. This particular pairing will succeed only if both are comfortable navigating through the social consequences.

Worst Matches for Capricorn

Now let's look at the least compatible signs:

Leo

A relationship with a Leo will be the most difficult one for a Capricorn. There will always be a sense of competitiveness in the relationship, as both want to be leaders and are extremely different from each other. Leo is a royal sign regardless of any social status or background. A person from this sign will always crave admiration and attention. Their primary motive as a leader is just to shine; they don't just want to be in charge of getting things done.

Capricorns like being a leader because they need things to be accomplished. They don't have the same flair as a Leo and may even find it unattractive. Leo, on the other hand, may find Capricorn boring and dull. It is rare to see a relationship between the two since they seldom get attracted to each other.

Aries

Similarly, there is the issue of a power struggle with a Capricorn and an Aries as well, but a Capricorn can still find an Aries attractive, unlike their general view of Leos. There is a square aspect between Aries and Capricorn that causes friction, but this square also leads to a lot of sexual tension between the two. When you hear a story about two people who hate each other at first but wind up together, it is usually one where this square is present.

Aries and Capricorn both want to be in charge of the relationship. Both signs like getting things done but have different ways of going about it. Aries don't think much before leaping into a project. They have a lot of energy at the beginning of the project but can rarely sustain it throughout. Capricorns like taking their time and always think first before doing something. Once they start a project, they will want to see it through. These are the kinds of differences that make their relationship volatile.

Libra

Capricorn is also in a square relationship with Libra, but it is a comparatively less volatile relationship. This is because Libra likes avoiding conflict as much as possible. Partners from these two signs will be attracted to each other but constantly be annoyed as well. A Libra does not compete with a Capricorn like they would a Leo or Aries, but they do not like giving up control, even though it may not seem like it at first.

People from this sign are good at getting what they want without displaying an outward need for control. Their social graces charm people from most other signs, but this does not work on a Capricorn. Their indirect approach will only annoy a Capricorn, and the directness of the latter is frustrating for a Libra to deal with.

In the next section, you will learn more about Capricorn's compatibility with other signs in the zodiac.

Chapter Six: Compatibility of Capricorn with other Zodiac Signs

Compatibility is another detail to keep in mind when dealing with different zodiac signs. This is especially important for love relationships. Understanding the compatibility of a Capricorn with other signs will help you in many ways. You can use this knowledge to avoid relationships with certain people whose personalities and thoughts will utterly clash with yours.

You can also use it to foresee the odds that your relationship with a certain person will positively influence your life. The dynamics between a Capricorn and every other zodiac sign is unique in its own way. As you read on, you can think about your relationship with someone of a certain zodiac sign and infer whether you see the truth in what is given here.

Capricorn and Aries

Sex and Intimacy Compatibility

When it comes to sexual compatibility, things are difficult for this combination of zodiac signs. The ruler of Aries is Mars, while that of Capricorn is Saturn. These planets are usually considered archetypal opposites and karmic enemies. The contact of Mars with Saturn can result in a lot of objective and physical obstacles for a healthy sexual relationship. Saturn will put a lot of pressure on Mars and draw away its energy.

The relationship between a Capricorn and Aries couple will lack sexual desire. It will lead to feelings of incompetence and may even cause impotence in one or both parties. A relationship between Aries and Capricorn is often triggered by an unconscious need to be sexually restricted or held back, but as with most things related to a Capricorn, the Aries individual could, in time, achieve some sort of balance. Despite the difficulties in their relationship, they might be able to find sexual satisfaction to a certain degree, but by the time this happens, the Capricorn partner may lose their need and energy to take part in such intimate relations.

This is why such relationships tend to come to an end. The combination of these signs is not easy or light in any way and is especially difficult in matters regarding intimacy. Separation is the best way for them to find balance again. A couple with this zodiac combination may be attracted to each other but should usually stay at a safe distance due to their differences.

In the best-case scenario, the Capricorn partner can control their passion and support the libido of the Arian. The Aries partner could learn a lot about their body and its needs from their Capricorn partner, but this balance is rarely achieved, and these two personalities inevitably clash in one way or another.

Trust

Aries and Capricorn individuals are both "all or nothing" types. Trusting each other will come easy to them. Even if they have a lot of difficulties and misunderstandings in other aspects of their relationship, neither will betray the other's trust. But they also tend to take this trust for granted. They can lose sight of the things that they should treasure in their relationship. This is why one partner should always remind the other about the qualities in their bond that should be appreciated.

Communication and Intellect

Capricorn exalts the ruler of Aries, Mars. This is why Capricorns and Aries should stick to conversations about work, career goals, physical activities, or achievements. Other than these topics, these two zodiacs have no common ground. A Capricorn partner will rarely allow their impulsive Aries partner to form their own opinions. They don't consider their opinions practical or useful. They usually consider the behavior of their Aries partner quite unacceptable even though they respect the energy spent.

Capricorn individuals are well-grounded and thus can measure situations rationally. This rationality causes them to hold on to their opinion about the tactlessness or idiocy of the Aries partner, but this can be extremely difficult for the Aries partner to deal with since they have a strong need to be respected and to have certain boundaries.

Aries, on the other hand, lack patience with their Capricorn partner. It seems like they only want people who will be useful in their life and are otherwise boring. They also seem to lack emotions and compassion. In one way or another, both the partners will always be wrong. They will be stuck in an endless battle of egos and be unable to understand what they really need from their partner; but it can be difficult for them to come out of this relationship, despite the chances of better relationships to be found elsewhere.

Understanding

Capricorn and Aries will always have difficulty in understanding each other. Initially, both partners will look at each other as a goal they set for themselves. They will think that their partner can change and grow if they put in the effort, but the problem with individuals of both these zodiacs is that they have no desire to change.

Despite their unrealistic expectations from the other, they hold on to the image of the person they think their partner could become. This is why there is an apparent lack of understanding between these individuals. They are only in love with the false image of their partner they have created. They waste their energy and efforts in pursuing the change they want to see. There is an emotional disability in the relationship between these Saturn and Mars zodiac signs, but the problem is not really about lack of emotions. Instead, the real issue is a lack of acceptance and understanding. They have their own opinion of what is right and perfect and are too narrow-minded to expand these conceptual horizons. This is why they can't accept their partner as they already are, but want to see changes.

Values

Capricorn and Aries both value clarity, honesty, and independence. This is why their values are never an issue that causes trouble in their relationship. When it comes to how they view people outside their relationship, they are mostly in sync. They may have trouble with their own relationship because they don't share certain values. Even though an Arian may value endurance and persistence in another, they don't necessarily want to develop these qualities in themselves. They also don't want to be controlled by someone with such characteristics.

Similarly, Capricorns may value their partner's focus and speed, but it is not necessarily something they want in themselves. These qualities would hinder their ability to pay attention to detail or cause psychological needs to be left unattended.

Shared Activities

Aries individuals tend to love waking up early and exercising, but Capricorns will never be able to understand this need to run at five o'clock in the morning. Capricorns, on the other hand, can spend their whole night doing something boring, but Aries can never understand the value of this thoroughness. Being studious is only of value to the Capricorn individual, while Aries love the results of physical exertion in their routine.

The latter is quite impulsive, while the former needs to weigh things before acting. Both have difficulty in understanding the other's values, but they can both find activities they could enjoy participating in together. Both individuals appreciate the value of routine and keeping their body fit. This means that they can figure out a time of day that would be suitable for both of them to work out, together. It would be motivating and uplifting for both partners to do such activities together in their day. Indulging in such shared activities can be very helpful in improving their relationship with each other. It would also allow them to understand each other better.

A relationship between Capricorn and Aries will never be easy. They will always compete with each other, and there is no telling who will come out on top. Separation is the only time they will find relief, but if they stay together out of stubbornness, they will spend their lives banging their heads against the wall. Their relationship can only be a success if both are willing to respect each other unconditionally and stop trying to change what they don't like. If they decide to pay attention to what is already good in their partner instead of highlighting their flaws, they can truly complement each other. Unfortunately, their rulers have a malefic nature that will prevent this accepting and positive relationship. If people with this zodiac combination ever get together, they should try their best to let their partner live the way they like and be accepting of their differences.

Capricorn and Taurus

Sex and Intimacy Compatibility

When it comes to sexual relations, Capricorn and Taurus can be quite frigid. This is why they would make the perfect couple. When they partner with other zodiacs, it is hard for them to open up. This is why they feel the need to experiment more. In such relationships, Capricorns display ingenuity in sex, but when a Capricorn partners with a Taurus, they are able to relax more. This couple can get to know each other better and thus can find comfort in their relationship.

Capricorn won't feel like they have to put in extra effort, and Taurus will stop fearing the chances of getting hurt. Identifying the source of the problem in this intimate relationship lies in the understanding of the moon. Taurus exalts the moon while Capricorn doesn't like it. If the Capricorn partner has trust issues or doesn't fall deeply in love with the Taurus, it can prevent an emotional connection between them. This problem will be further intensified by Taurus individuals having the need to be loved in an unconditional way. This can scare their Capricorn lover away.

The gap between individuals in this zodiac combination is caused by their different approaches to love and sexual instincts. Capricorn supports Mars and prefers physical strength with initiative. Taurus has trouble understanding Mars and does not like aggression or initiative. This can cause a lack of emotions for the Capricorn in their sex life and will lead to frustration for the Taurus. It can even cause impotence and lead to a lack of desire in their relationship. If they don't hold on to intimacy in their sexual relations, it can cause problems for this combination of zodiacs.

Trust

Capricorn individuals never indulge in lies or tolerate it from others. They find lies unnecessary but are not necessarily judgmental about it. When a Capricorn lies, it is usually just to see if the other person can catch their lie, but in relationships, Capricorns prefer complete honesty. They want things to be true and clean with their partner. This is something that their Taurus partner can sense, and it allows them to feel secure in the relationship.

While a Taurus can sometimes feel the need to lie to their partner to hide certain things, that is not the case when they partner with a Capricorn. Venus rules the zodiac of Taurus and is exalted in Pisces. This is why they understand that secrecy is important in relationships. But when they are with a Capricorn, they can stay true to their love and have a good relationship for a long time.

Communication and Intellect

Capricorn and Taurus are different by nature, but they are able to understand each other quite well. They also encourage their partner to grow in the way that they need to. While differences can cause trouble for some combinations, here it makes them the perfect couple. Taurus and Capricorn complement each other in a subtle yet pleasant way.

Taurus is blessed with a deep understanding of the moon, but this is something Capricorn lacks. Fearing emotions can cause neglect of emotional needs. Taurus makes it their mission to teach their Capricorn partner about the importance of being kind to oneself. Capricorn contributes to the relationship by teaching Taurus about responsibility and working towards goals without being distracted by emotions.

Understanding does not always come easy for this couple, but this can be overcome with compassion and empathy. If they put in a little effort, this couple can support each other better than any other combination of signs. They are both earth signs, and if they reconcile their differences, they can create magic together.

Emotions

Both these zodiacs tend to be careful in matters of love. This is why you cannot say with certainty if they can find emotional fulfillment together. If they begin a relationship, they must overcome this pattern. The Taurus may not feel like there is a good emotional connection in this relationship, but it will be the opposite for the Capricorn, who will appreciate their Taurus lover.

Once the Taurus can dig deep enough and reach the Capricorn's emotional core, they will experience immeasurable satisfaction. At this point, the two partners will never want to separate again. The Capricorn will feel like their heart has finally been touched, and they will try their best not to let go of their Taurus partner.

Values

Both signs value the material world and can go far together. Capricorns are good at leading the way to success and achieving financial security. Taurus is good at motivating and creating. Regardless of their goals, together they will find it easy to achieve them. The only hitch is their approach towards family and emotions. The different sides of personalities should be observed as complementary and not destructive. This will allow them to coexist peacefully together.

Shared Activities

Capricorns seem to never stop working, while a Taurus can seem lazy. Capricorn needs to rest more than any sign in the zodiac. Since they are highly ambitious, they tend to drain their own energy reserves, and Taurus helps restore this energy. They help their Capricorn partner eat and live well by taking a break from work. The striving nature of the Capricorn partner can also be motivating for the Taurus. It helps them overcome their tendency to be lazy and instead work at creating something. Together, this couple can achieve a lot. They just have to find a balance between work and rest.

The relationship between a Capricorn and Taurus can be very deep and almost unreachable for other signs in terms of creative power. They are complementary in a gentle way. While others might find them boring, they live exciting lives together outside the eyes of the outer world. The Taurus partner can motivate the Capricorn to persevere while the Capricorn can teach the Taurus ways to achieve what they want. They can work hard and raise a happy family together. This partnership can cause an unbreakable bond, especially if they can connect emotionally.

Capricorn and Gemini

Sex and Intimacy Compatibility

According to Capricorn, sex does not require many words. But a Gemini likes to explain every position and has knowledge of the Kamasutra. The latter also has a fondness for outdoor sex. When these two partners come together, it can sometimes be unbearable to watch. Their sexual philosophies differ completely from each other, and this makes it difficult to maneuver.

If you want a Capricorn to experiment with their sex life, you have to work at opening their mind and getting them relaxed. For the Capricorn, being with a Gemini is like caring for a child who will undoubtedly cause trouble. This is how it seems to the Capricorn even though it isn't always true. While Geminis don't think twice about indulging in sexual activities at any place or time, the traditional Capricorn feels a lot more responsible for their actions.

Capricorns and Gemini are rarely attracted to each other, but sexual relations are always possible. When it does occur, Gemini will always find the Capricorn too stiff and uncreative. The Capricorn will find the Gemini too unconventional. The relationship between these two zodiacs is funny because they both find each other boring. While most people find Geminis fun and interesting, their lack of deep emotions and focus is a turn- off for Capricorns. This is why sexual relations between the two are best avoided. If it does happen, they will have to set many boundaries and be creative to make it work.

Trust

Typically, it is not easy to trick a Capricorn. Gemini's are usually quite flirty and find it acceptable to partake in what they consider light adultery, but Capricorns, who never indulge in adultery, do not share this viewpoint. They need to be able to trust their partner completely and need clear boundaries for what is right and wrong. They will trust their Gemini partner because of the deep trust they award their partner anyway, but they will only trust their own interpretation of the truth.

Geminis do not put a lot of thought into their abilities, while Capricorns always go one step further. This is why it is easy for Capricorns to read a Gemini. They can easily tell when the Gemini is lying or discover what they have been up to. On the other hand, Gemini will find it extremely difficult to read a Capricorn or catch them at a lie because they trust them completely.

Communication and Intellect

A Gemini is great at communicating with others. They can resolve all kinds of issues by talking it out with people, but this ability of a Gemini holds little value for a Capricorn. They recognize that most of the things the Gemini talks about lack essence, but these partners can still hold conversations together since Geminis have their own serious side that resonates with a Capricorn's personality.

Even though Capricorn is the most difficult and strict type of sign to deal with, Gemini shares common things with them. The great thing about Geminis is they seem to be able to talk about everything under the sun. If a certain topic bores you, they will find something else to talk about. Capricorn individuals prefer talking about things that have a deeper meaning. They look for the hidden meaning in things and admire others who can discover this meaning. They are not as focused on details as a Virgo, but they may still spend their whole lives analyzing such things.

Capricorns like to figure out the logic behind the smallest things, and Gemini can give them a whole list of such things to analyze. As long as there is mutual respect, and the two individuals don't judge each other as someone boring or stupid, the relationship can help them understand the world better.

Gemini can benefit from the secure and steady nature of a Capricorn that will teach them to be better at organizing their thoughts and actions. A Capricorn will help a Gemini take their thoughts one step forward and get better at managing their time. Capricorns can benefit from the childish approach that a Gemini has towards life. The serious Capricorn can learn this quality from a Gemini to help them live a happier life.

Emotions

Both the signs are not very emotional since Saturn and Mercury rule them. The real problem is that these signs don't spark emotion in each other. When they come together, they seem to be immune to the other's charm, but if these signs partner with any other sign that is not too emotional, they will feel awakened. There is very little that connects a Capricorn with a Gemini. The main emotional connection between them lies in Gemini's dark thoughts and the emotional distance that a Capricorn has.

Values

Any information, regardless of its form or shape, is valuable to a Gemini. They appreciate a person's ability to be creative with their hands, to talk eloquently, and even how someone implements their various ideas. For a Capricorn, the things that hold value are punctuality, stability, and honesty. These signs' independence is attractive to both, but there is not much else that coincides in their world.

Shared Activities

The motives of a Gemini and Capricorn differ immensely. Capricorns appreciate useful things. This is why they only like participating in activities that are useful in some way. They don't enjoy a walk just for the sake of it. But if it means they will live healthier or if it will get them to a specific destination, they can walk for miles.

A Gemini can walk without a purpose. They don't need to know where they may end up. They are spontaneous and need not stick to a path. They might set out to buy groceries but end up at a movie. While Capricorn likes dedication and routine, Gemini loves to learn new things. This is where they both have a connection in problem-solving and constructive learning. Despite this, they usually walk in different directions in life.

Pairing a Capricorn with a Gemini would give you a strange fit. They both want the qualities that the other possesses, but they fail to recognize it in their partner when they are together. Gemini seeks a person who will keep them grounded and add depth to their lives. A Capricorn can do this, but the Gemini will only look at them as someone boring and unmovable. Capricorns seek someone who will help them relax a little and find joy in life.

Gemini can do this but come across as superficial and uncontrollable to the Capricorn. If they overcome their inhibitions and prejudice, this partnership could be valuable for both. Their differences can help them learn a lot from each other. It can allow them to achieve any goals they set for themselves. But this is only possible if they completely open up and learn to recognize the good in each other.

Capricorn and Cancer

Sex and Intimacy Compatibility

Capricorn and Cancer are a case of opposite signs that bring with them a strong attraction. Their passions are awakened when they come together, and they can be perfect lovers for each other. Cancer needs the patience that a Capricorn has, as it allows them to relax and feel sexy. Capricorns appreciate the fact that their Cancer doesn't take sexual relations lightly and acts true to their emotions.

Capricorn individuals may have had many partners throughout the years, but they only stay with someone who is emotional and family-oriented. The intimacy that a Capricorn lacks is exactly what Cancer brings to the table. The sign of Capricorn lacks home, love, and warmth. Cancer can be highly compassionate and heal Capricorn. This allows Cancer to thaw Capricorn's cold emotional state and thus improve their sexual and intimate relations.

Trust

Capricorns are trustworthy, but they are not very trusting. The way they think is influenced by the Pisces sign in their third house, and they tend to panic when it comes to intimate relations. When they are involved with someone, they know that the partner has a need for trust, and they show this to appease them, but they only truly trust their partner after a certain period of consistency or if other people corroborate their stories.

A Capricorn's relationship with Cancer works because Cancer rarely has any ugly secrets to hide. The exaltation of Jupiter in Cancer causes them to have high moral values. If Capricorns can show their devotion to Cancer, Cancer will trust them completely. But they are sensitive to the fact that Capricorn is not as trusting. Despite this, they choose to be understanding and pretend that they are not aware of this. The difficulty a Capricorn has with trust issues is endearing for Cancer instead of being repulsive.

Communication and Intellect

The strangest factor that Cancer and Capricorn have in common is genetics. This is obviously not to be taken literally. It just means that they have the same image of relationships that their ancestors had centuries ago. It is believed that our emotional bodies have information stored about the emotions our ancestors felt but couldn't act on or understand. Capricorn and Cancer connect at this point. When they meet, they feel as though they are long-lost friends or lovers and not just two people who just met. They have an instant affection for each other that is warm and familiar.

Even if their circumstances were completely different while growing up, they might feel as though they shared their childhood. This sense of familiarity helps these signs connect and talk about everything possible. There is an unexplainable closeness between a Capricorn and Cancer, but it is even more inexplicable how that emotional bond will come through in the beginning.

Capricorn is wary, and from the perspective of Cancer, this can be difficult to approach. Unless they can connect on a deep level, these partners will appear to have opposite goals in life. Cancer can be a lot more needy or clingy, while Capricorn is more independent and career-oriented. This is regardless of the gender of both signs. If they focus on this difference and see each other in a negative light, they cannot be happy together. But if they overcome it and reach out to each other, they will be complete.

Emotions

The love story between Cancer and Capricorn is an unfulfilled one left behind by their ancestors. This may lead to very strong emotions between the two and seem like a dream come true, but a karmic debt has to be paid before this couple can find happiness together. These two signs represent the axis of Jupiter's exaltation. Their expectations from the relationship and each other are closely linked to their emotional states.

Capricorn is considered one of the least emotional signs, while Cancer is considered a highly emotional one. One should focus on a career while the other should be focused on the family, but once these two signs lay eyes on each other, their emotions tend to run wild. Their primal differences can make it hard for them to come together, but this couple creates a stable and secure relationship with time. It is difficult to reach the emotional depth of a Capricorn, but a Cancer may take this as a challenge.

If a Cancer pairs with a Capricorn, it usually leads to marriage and a family together, but this earthly love only ends well if they accept each other as they are. Trying to change their partner will only cause trouble in the relationship. They can have a much better future together if they avoid this, and if not, they will only tire each other out.

Values

Both signs value practical sense and stability. They are opposite signs, but their values are quite similar. Cancer and Capricorn both seek stability in their life. They want a partner who will provide them with a sense of security. This will make these signs value each other. They will appreciate that they both never give up or quit even when things get tough.

Shared Activities

When it comes to Cancers, they have no preferences for what their partner indulges in. They will be happy to let the Capricorn spend their time as they please if it is not imposed on the Cancer as well. Capricorn is a lot more specific about how time should be spent and will plan activities in advance.

The advanced planning gives both partners the chance to change their minds and decide on something else if they suddenly realize it is not something they want to do. As long as this pair shows respect for each other's personalities, they won't have trouble agreeing on things. Cancer will rarely be up for sacrificing their sleep for work, and Capricorn won't tag along for shopping trips to buy decor. They have to find activities that both will enjoy. If they respect such boundaries, their time together can be satisfying.

The deep-rooted need in Capricorn and Cancer to mend their ancestors' broken relationship allows them to relive an ancient love story. These sun signs can quite handle any karmic debt that needs to be dealt with. Once they do this, they can choose each other as their partners for life. When this zodiac couple comes together, there is a high probability of them ending up together.

Capricorn and Leo

Sex and Intimacy Compatibility

Capricorn and Leo both have a deep awareness of self. This is the one thing these signs have in common. A Capricorn is much more likely to find a Leo attractive than it being the other way around. It is rare to see a Leo being attracted to a Capricorn. Even if they do develop sexual relations, this couple rarely envisions a future together. Capricorn individuals are practical and cool-headed for the most part. Leo, on the other hand, is passionate and warm.

Not that Leo is completely impractical or that Capricorn cannot be passionate. However, these signs will see no common ground. The story of the rulers of these two signs is that of fallen egos, and they represent an archetypal conflict in the zodiac. It could damage their self-esteem and cause them to doubt their attractiveness and beauty. This may be caused by the fact that Capricorn fears the freedom of sexual expression possessed by Leo, which leads to insecurity in them both. These signs can rarely meet the expectations of each other.

The sex life of this couple can become quite boring. However, they don't realize that they are similar. For them to have healthy sexual relations, they need to try new things and be warm towards each other. If they fall in a rut, they remain in it for a long time. This causes a lack of confidence and loss of libido in both partners. In the end, there is no sexual desire in either partner.

Trust

Neptune falls in the sign of Leo, and this is something Capricorn knows. This is why they can clearly see behind any act Leo puts up. The Leo partner questions their own personality and motives when they see the depth that their partner will go to. Any lie told in this relationship will come right back, and so it is futile to indulge in them. The light of Leo shines bright in the darkness of Capricorn. There is nothing this pair can hide from each other. If either tries to lie or be secretive, it leads to mistrust. However, this pair usually chooses to trust each other in every situation because they have no reason not to.

Communication and Intellect

Capricorn and Leo have their own priorities in life. They have very different personalities, and it is not easy for them to come together. They often waste a lot of time trying to prove themselves right in any situation or argument. They fail to understand that they have their own role and mission in life to fulfill.

Instead of trying to change the priorities of their partner, they should focus on their own. It is actually better for both of them to have their own separate goals in life. They just have to try to accept the differences they have and respect each other. If they do this, their relationship can be fulfilling and satisfying. Capricorn can help Leo add depth to their lives and be more intentional. Leo can help Capricorns have a more creative view and be more positive in life. If these signs can make use of each other's abilities, they can accomplish any plan.

Emotions

Capricorn and Leo can have a very emotionally challenging relationship. This is not because of a lack of love between the two. It is more because of the fact that they love each other. Leo has warm emotions that can be cooled and buried easily. If they can't express their love, it can get them depressed. Capricorns need more time for their emotions, but the fiery emotions of Leo can disrupt this. This can make the Capricorn feel that their Leo partner is not right for them, even if they find them attractive or smart.

The way that both these signs build up their emotions is a problem in the relationship. Having time and patience is crucial for making their relationship work. However, Leo does not possess these qualities, while they are the forte of Capricorn. Without patience, it is impossible to reach the heart of a Capricorn. They take time to warm up to someone and express their emotions. If either or both these signs have experienced difficult relationships in the past, it is even less likely that they will fall in love with each other.

Values

Both these signs appreciate plans, organization, and presentation. Capricorn is a lot more capable of making plans and setting goals than Leo. Leo values this in the Capricorn since they themselves tend to go with the flow in most situations. However, Capricorns look for a partner with a calm and sensitive emotional center but fail to find this in a Leo. This only happens in certain cases. Leo prefers people who are openhearted, direct, and free with their smiles. If they judge the Capricorn as not having these qualities, there is no future for them as a couple.

Shared Activities

The priorities that these partners have will determine the activities they want to participate in. When a Capricorn wants to feel energized and vigorous, they will partake in anything that Leo chooses. The Leo will be willing to take part in activities of the Capricorn's choice only when they want to settle down. Good timing is very important in this relationship. If it is lacking, both partners will stubbornly resist doing what the other wants.

If Leo and Capricorn meet at the right time, they can get along well. However, if they share different priorities in life, it can be a problem for their relationship. If Saturn can be reconciled with the Sun, it can bring a lot of benefits. However, this is easier said than done. Capricorn can provide more structure to Leo's life, while Leo can help inspire creativity in the Capricorn. Even if their relationship doesn't end well, this could help them achieve what they want in their lives. These signs are very different, but it is impossible to stop them from achieving it if they have a common goal.

Capricorn and Virgo

Sex and Intimacy Compatibility

If Capricorn and Virgo were not both strict and stiff about sex, they could have a great sexual connection. Their relationship always seems to fall short of a certain degree of pure emotion. However, not that they lack understanding or patience for each other; there is rarely any sexual activity between this couple because they have more reasons not to do it than to do it. However, if they reach some synchronicity, the beauty of their sexual intimacy shows the kind of depth both signs are capable of. This comes across in the form of deep emotions they express during intercourse.

Both these signs look for a partner who takes sex as a serious act, not something superficial, and who believes that it should be cherished. This is a common ground for Virgo and Capricorn. Both partners also tend to be a little shy, and this can create more attraction between them. However, this is only possible if they meet at a central point. If their partner is respectful and reliable, Virgo is always willing to try new things and bring excitement into their sex life. Capricorn is a great fit for them only if both partners open up a little more at the beginning of their relationship.

Trust

Capricorn is a trustworthy sign, and this is something that most other signs recognize. This earth sign is reliable, honest, and never deceitful towards others. Virgo tends to be a sign that can be trusted as well, but they may be unfaithful if they lack faith in their partner. If they feel like they can trust their partner, Virgo cannot control their emotions and be vengeful. However, Capricorns can bring out the best in their partner and help them stay in a faithful relationship. It may take some time for both signs to get used to each other and build trust. However, once they do this, neither will break their partner's trust and the sanctity of their relationship.

Communication and Intellect

Virgo and Capricorn's conversations can seem very boring to onlookers from the fire or air signs. Other zodiac signs can rarely bear the flow of conversation between two earth signs. However, for these two signs, it is a completely enjoyable experience. They both have deep thoughts that they can share and discuss with each other. Seeing a similar depth of mind in their partner is incredibly exciting for both Capricorn and Virgo. They like exchanging informative and interesting facts and enjoy a respectful debate between themselves. They find the perfect adversary in their partner. These signs can complete a conversation in a satisfying way.

Capricorn is good at deciding when a debate is resolved while Virgo tends to decide on the next topic of conversation. They have a perfect system going for them. It is like gears fitting well and working without a hitch. Their intellectual conversations are where their passions lie. They find it very stimulating, and it keeps them happy together. Their communication skills are great, and they know that they can always talk it out. If there is a problem, they know that they can resolve it.

Emotions

Virgo and Capricorn are usually not emotional individuals. Capricorn is the zodiac of the moon's detriment, while Virgo brings the fall of Venus. Both these signs have their own emotional issues. However, their issues differ from each other, and this allows them to understand and help their partner. Just like the trust between them, it will take time for their emotions to build towards each other.

Time is of the essence in this relationship. Both partners will become a lot more confident as the passion between them slowly and steadily rises. Once they are confident, they feel a lot more liberated with their partner. They are open to experimenting with their sex life as well as in other things. This adds quality to their relationship. This couple takes time to slowly understand and discover new things about each other. As they peel away the layers from their partner, they notice things they missed before. It becomes a fascinating process for them and is an incredible aspect of their relationship.

Values

Capricorns and Virgos appreciate calm, cool, and collected behavior. No matter how complicated or difficult a situation is, they prefer to deal with it in a rational way. Since both of these signs are able to do this, they bring peace to each other. They also value the depth that their partner has and are grateful that they need not pretend to be shallow as with others.

Both these signs are well-grounded and practical. They like rational and sound decisions with regard to finances. However, the difference between them is that Capricorn will go to extreme lengths to achieve their goals while a Virgo will not. Seeing the extent to which a Capricorn goes can be too much for the Virgo at times. Capricorn will also find it difficult to understand the lack of motivation and competitiveness in a Virgo.

Shared Activities

Virgo is more focused on moving forward in life while Capricorn is focused on moving up. This is where these two earth signs differ from each other. They will have the same energy in following where their partner goes, but they rarely agree on the destination. This applies to activities they do together as well. It is important for these signs to find activities that will help them feel positive. They need a routine to keep them happy in life. If not, Virgo can sometimes make too many sacrifices and eventually become depressed. Capricorn is not always willing to take responsibility for what their partner does and is less likely to fall into depression with their partner.

Since both Capricorn and Virgo belong to the earth element, they can walk at the same pace. While other signs may feel like this couple moves too slowly, it goes exactly as needed for Virgo and Capricorn. They take their own sweet time to build their relationship with love, trust, and respect for each other. If they give each other some time, they can find the perfect partner in each other. They are also great at listening to what their partner needs and being willing to meet their expectations. Since they are both not emotional, their relationship may become a little too strict. However, this hurdle can be overcome with time as they grow out of it, spending their lives together.

Capricorn and Libra

Sex and Intimacy Compatibility

Waiting is the first thing that relates to the sexual relationship between a Capricorn and Libra. It is similar to a wife waiting for her ship-bound husband to come back after years at sea. Both Libra and Capricorn think of sex as an important aspect of their lives. However, these signs ruled by Saturn and Venus may have very little sexual activity as a couple.

At first, there may be a complete lack of attraction between them. Once they form a relationship, they discover the lack of sexual chemistry in their relationship. Even if the lack of attraction is not a concern for these signs, there will always be something that comes between them. This pair will have to deal with many factors out of their control. They will usually feel too pressured in the relationship, which could negatively affect their self-esteem. However, Saturn's exaltation in the sign of Libra could build an understanding between the two. It helps the couple understand the importance of good timing. It will also prevent them from making mistakes by having unrealistic expectations.

If Libra and Capricorn can overcome all other obstacles to form a bond, their sexual relations can be routinely approached and conservative. It will only bring satisfaction if both signs let go of any rules and strict premises.

Trust

This unlikely couple has a strangely high amount of trust in each other. While Libra may have questionable motives at times, their Capricorn partner will make them feel guilty about the slightest hint of a lie. However, if the Capricorn partner is too strict with them at the beginning of the relationship, it makes them feel judged and inadequate. This could lead to dishonesty in the relationship, even if there is nothing there to hide. The Libra is just secretive because they want to protect their privacy and themselves.

Communication and Intellect

Libra is not normally a very stubborn sign. However, when paired with a Capricorn, they suddenly become impossible to talk to and very headstrong. Due to Saturn's exaltation, Libra will love Capricorn a lot. However, they express this love unusually and seem to speak out of spite most of the time. This can lead to a never-ending battle between the two, with no one coming out on top. These two signs just keep building up walls even though they don't know why they feel the need to do so. The elements that these signs belong to can cause an obstacle to their understanding of each other.

Earth and air are far apart, and these partners can't reach out to each other. No matter the issue, they fail to understand each other. However, both signs have certain prudence that might allow them to have some interesting conversations and motivate each other.

As long as they remain rational, they can enjoy things with each other that most other signs would not find joy in. Both Libra and Capricorn would find immense satisfaction in solving a serious problem. Doing this together is possible if Libra uses their words and Capricorn acts on them. Their egos would be at an all-time high if they can put in some effort to find a solution together.

Emotions

The way that a Capricorn and Libra approach their feelings is a difficult point for them to reconcile. Emotions come naturally to a Libra since Venus rules them. However, they are also serious by nature and tend to hold back their emotions because they fear judgment from others. Capricorn will be the judgmental force that can hold Libra down. This also feeds the ego of the Capricorn and makes them feel like they are always right. This takes them even further away from the point at which they can meet their partner.

For a Libra and Capricorn to make it work, they have to show that they love and respect each other. Since Capricorn is not very emotional by nature, it is difficult for most signs to reach out to them. However, for a Libra, this task is more difficult than it is for others. Libra will back off as soon as Capricorn dismisses their emotions. Finding a central point where they both show absolute acceptance and respect for each other is essential for this relationship to work. They have to let each other cry, get angry, break things, or even make scenes in public if it can help them be more expressive.

Values

Taking responsibility and valuing time is important for both Libra and Capricorn. These shared values help them overcome their opposing personalities and any differences. They know that they have certain responsibilities towards each other and will see it through. Being earth and air signs, they are set in their ways. They are very different in how they speak and what they do. Libra considers their mind of great value, and Capricorn doesn't care about words if they don't see results. Being with a Capricorn can help Libra put their words into action. However, the romantic relationship between the two will not be pleasant for either.

Shared Activities

Being boring to everyone else is the best thing that these signs can do together. It is likely that their relationship will make them work hard without being creative, and when they rest, they are lazy. It is important for them to create a routine that will help them go out together and do fun things. If not, their passion for each other will die.

The best way to describe a possible relationship between Capricorn and Libra is to say it is difficult. They may enjoy all the troubles that come with their coupling and even stay together for a long time.

However, this is the kind of bond that most other signs will want to avoid. The real challenge in this relationship is that they don't respect emotional value. Both partners must figure out a shared language to express their love and understand each other.

Capricorn and Scorpio

Sex and Intimacy Compatibility

A special bond exists between Capricorn and Scorpio when it comes to sexual relations. Mars is a ruler of Scorpio, and Capricorn exalts it, thus causing the signs to be sextile. Capricorn's physical nature grounds the sexual needs of a Scorpio. However, these signs are the fall and detriment of the moon. This can cause a problem for the couple. Agreeing not to be too emotional or sensitive takes away any real intimacy from the sex life between these signs. They might enjoy their physical relationship, but they become cold and distant towards each other.

Even if they think that the physical relationship is enough for them, it won't appease their hearts. They realize their need for intimacy only when other people show up and fulfill this need. These signs are attracted to people from their opposing signs, Cancer, and Taurus. Those two signs are highly emotional in contrast to this couple. This attraction explains the need that Capricorn and Scorpio have for genuine intimacy that goes beyond the physical. They will not be truly satisfied until physical pleasure comes with emotions and tenderness.

The conservativeness of Capricorn can be frustrating for Scorpio since it exalts Uranus. However, they can take some time to help the Capricorn overcome their inhibitions and relax enough to try new things with their Scorpio partner. This sexual excitement will be difficult for the Capricorn to let go of. In return, Scorpio will appreciate the patience of a Capricorn and the sense of security they provide.

Trust

The one sign in the zodiac that Scorpio can completely trust is Capricorn. Being honest and direct, Capricorn will make Scorpio feel no need to be dishonest. The lack of true intimacy is the only thing that could cause distrust in this partnership. If they don't have depth in connection, they can't be sure about trusting each other. However, if both signs work on overcoming their insecurities and put some emotional effort into the relationship, this problem can be resolved.

Communication and Intellect

Capricorn is earthly, stubborn, and set in their ways, while Scorpio is constantly changing and evolving. This can be difficult for the Capricorn to deal with. They can understand each other well since Capricorn is patient, and they have a similar pace at which they do things. However, a disagreement between the two could cause a fight that lasts years.

The conversations between these signs are never easy or light. They both acknowledge the depth of mind in their partners and have a similar view on karma. However, you will rarely see them dance, laugh, or enjoy together. While the pair may think they don't need these things, it is not true. Everyone needs some fun and laughs in their lives. It is easier for the couple if they have mutual friends or share some dark humor. Capricorn can help Scorpio develop long-lasting friendships if they respect their crowd. Having the same group of good friends can be great for this couple.

Emotions

The emotional contact between Capricorn and Scorpio poses the biggest issue in their relationship. Both signs have their own emotional issues but dismiss them. At the beginning of the relationship, both will show their partners they are grounded and strong. However, they will fail to notice this impression will make them feel like they always have to be the strong one in the relationship. They will try their best not to show any signs of weakness even if they could do with some support. Both signs will drift away from achieving their emotional balance goal if they don't work on developing a deeper emotional understanding of each other.

Values

The values shared by this couple are interesting to observe. Capricorn brings guilt into Scorpio, the sign of the detriment of Venus. This means that their values are based on guilt, and they always feel like nothing is good enough. Although this can help them stay motivated and work on themselves, it can be difficult to deal with in the long run. They both need a healthy relationship that helps them accept that they are more than good enough.

Shared Activities

Capricorn and Scorpio strive for greatness together. Their energy will be focused on constructive activities so they can achieve the goals they have set for themselves. This relationship will not be an easygoing and joyful place where it is all rainbows and cakes. However, it is a great partnership to promote personal growth, realism, and practicality. If they share their past with each other, they can help their partner heal. They both like digging into the truth of things, and this will help them stay together.

Capricorn and Scorpio can share an inspiring relationship. They like to dig up family trees, search for the truth, and deal with any debt or unresolved karma. Both signs are deep and never take things lightly. They appreciate this in each other, and it helps to build a strong foundation for them. However, this depth and these values can also make their relationship lack emotion and become a little too dark. It could lead to depression or sadness and may even make them look for the light in someone else.

Capricorn and Sagittarius

Sex and Intimacy Compatibility

The sexual contact between this pair is somehow unbearable. Even if Capricorn and Sagittarius are attracted to each other and have sex, they will soon feel like they don't belong together. This feeling has no logical explanation but exists nonetheless between this pair. They can handle the differences in their personality quite easily since Sagittarians are easy going while Capricorns tend to understand their partner's immaturity as their own fault.

Capricorn seeks depth and meaning in their physical relations since they are patient and realistic. However, this pace is not something Sagittarians can always understand. They don't understand the importance of being as realistic as Capricorn. This pair won't be able to see their incompatibility at the beginning of their relationship. However, with time, it becomes obvious. Their differences will taint their sexual relations and make them realize that they are not suited to each other. Capricorn and Sagittarius can only have a healthy sex life if Capricorn loosens up, and Sagittarius starts respecting the physical. The meeting point for these signs is pure emotion.

Trust

Sagittarius is an honest sign when it comes to relationships. However, they have a problem for being honest with themselves. Capricorns notice this flaw and recognize that it is something that does not change in a Sagittarius. The problem is that Jupiter rules Sagittarius, while Capricorn is the sign of Jupiter's fall. Capricorn cannot comprehend the magic of life or any beliefs of a certain kind. They only trust in rational thought, hard work, and real results. However, Sagittarians believe that their positive beliefs can help them gain a good outcome in life.

Communication and Intellect

A Sagittarius and Capricorn should avoid talking or arguing about their belief systems. If they can do this, these signs are mostly quite understanding of each other. The optimistic smile of a Sagittarius can always bring a smile to the serious face of a Capricorn. Capricorn's practical approach helps the creative and fiery Sagittarius feel grounded. As long as this couple is respectful towards each other, they can build a lot together. Their vision is similar to builders, and they can bring their vision to life successfully.

Intellectually, they are a compatible pair as long as they don't expect any major changes from one another. These signs have complimentary protective roles, and this is the most beautiful aspect of their relationship. Both Sagittarius and Capricorn represent protection. If this couple builds a functional core together, they will never allow any outsider to impact their relationship. This pairing is the best choice for both signs if they are searching for partners who won't allow other people to meddle, interfere, or disrespect their relationship.

Emotions

It is possible for these signs to share an emotional language. This is because Capricorn looks for someone who will complete them, and Sagittarius becomes that person since it is where Jupiter is exalted. The heart of a Sagittarius and Capricorn come together at this meeting point. They can fall deeply in love with each other with some faith and avoidance of unrealistic expectations. Capricorn usually needs a tender and mellow person as a partner, but Sagittarius is rarely of this temperament. However, by understanding differences and becoming close, this obstacle is easy for the pair to overcome.

Values

Another common ground for Capricorn and Sagittarius is that they value intelligence. Sagittarians focus on learning and philosophy as they seek unity and the universal truth. Capricorn is a sign that is able to use knowledge in a practical way. This makes them a good pair. They can have the same wavelength if they don't think of each other as stupid.

Accepting each other will allow them to see that they have a similar depth of thought and share certain values. This is not possible if they judge each other at first glance. However, most of their values are still quite different, and both signs have very different needs as well. One places more value on responsibility, practicality, and focus while the other values creativity, freedom, and width of scope.

Shared Activities

You might think that a Capricorn partner would be too boring for a Sagittarius, and this might cause the latter to run off. However, this is not what happens in most cases. Since their suns share no relationship, these signs are respectful towards each other. This is why Sagittarius finds Capricorn interesting despite their differences. Their differences make these signs curious about each other, and Sagittarius, in particular, is always up for trying new things.

Sagittarius partners tend to enjoy a lot of childish activities that a Capricorn will refuse to participate in. However, they like to talk their serious Capricorn partners into these things in a joyful and fun manner. Both signs are smart and are aware of the differences between them. This makes their partnership a lot more refreshing and exciting for them.

The coupling of a Sagittarius and Capricorn is not ideal, and they rarely choose each other as their life partners. However, their relationship can be enjoyable and refreshing since both accept and understand each other despite their differences. No matter how short the duration of their relationship, they will have a good time together. This relationship will only be stable if the Capricorn puts in the effort to help the cause. However, the Sagittarius partner will always be able to bring joy to the Capricorn and acts as the pillar in this pairing.

Capricorn and Capricorn

Sex and Intimacy Compatibility

It can be difficult to predict the sex life of this couple. Being of the same sign, they will both exalt Mars. This means that they have strong libidos and like following their instincts. However, Capricorn is a sign that tends to hold on to restrictions. This pair may prefer making rational decisions instead of giving in to their instincts and looking for satisfaction. It is difficult to pair sexuality with practicality.

Capricorn is a lot more sexually creative when they are in a relationship with other signs, and they are also able to form a more intimate bond. However, when a Capricorn is in a relationship with someone from the same sign, they rarely satisfy their sexual or emotional needs.

Capricorn is also a ruler of time, and this means that this couple can end up waiting for a long time for things to happen. Since they exalt Mars, they won't lack initiative. However, in matters of sex and taboos, these partners can't seem to actually get to the point of sexual contact. If two people from this sign come together, their relationship may be extreme in two different ways. They might need very few words to understand each other, or they may never be able to understand what their partner means or needs. There is no middle ground for them.

Trust

As a Capricorn, it is easy to trust someone from the same sun sign. However, there is also a need to compete even in this matter. Both partners will feel like they are better and more honest than the other. This can make it difficult for them to build trust in the relationship. Lies are never a real issue in the relationship between two Capricorns. The problem is the silence they leave between them. When they try to communicate, both partners tend to leave a tense atmosphere between them, and this makes them question each other. The silence makes it difficult for them to identify with their partner.

Communication and Intellect

Capricorn is an intellectual sign with a lot of depth. This means that two people from this sign will have a lot to talk about. However, these conversations will rarely last long. Being extremely competitive, they will always end up in a debate. Instead of a prolonged debate, it turns into a silent tournament that neither wins. This couple needs to be open and speak their mind with each other. If they choose to silently analyze each other, they will not get far but instead, lose respect for their partner.

Most of the time, Capricorn partners will not feel the need to talk. Both will be interested in their partner's lives and would have many things to say. However, they don't share much since they seem to constantly have a fence up. When they work on a project together, it gives them the chance to talk, and this is when they discover how much they have in common.

Working together is the best way for this couple to have meaningful conversations and communicate. Having similar minds, they will be a lot more efficient at solving issues together. They can enjoy their conversations if they continue doing this.

Emotions

The emotional contact between two people from this sign is quite interesting. Both lack the ability to be emotional most of the time, and they will always try to be rational, cold, or controlling. They will recognize the same traits in each other, and this will only annoy them further. However, the great thing about this partnership is that they share the same values and approach to relationships. They will take their time to get to know each other and open up. Once the pressure falls away, they will feel safe in the relationship and be better at expressing themselves.

If this pair falls in love, it will take time to say it out loud. This is because Capricorns tend to dread any emotional displays. They are not confident enough to do this in private or in public. If they show each other some understanding and boost each other confidence, it will be a lot easier to be emotionally expressive. However, this will not be easily achieved, even if they respect each other. This couple will be more comfortable in silence and by letting each other be. They can understand each other because they are similar, but it will cause a rift between them if they don't work on their emotional connection.

Values

You may think that members of Capricorn share all the same values, but it isn't so. Every Capricorn individual can have their own values, and these are set in stone for them. It can be difficult for two Capricorns to share these values. If certain behavior doesn't appeal to them or they consider it wrong, they won't accept it even in the case of their partner. All their rules and values apply to any individual they come across. This couple should avoid questioning their partner's different values and instead focus on the values that they do share. Judging each other on such differences will only cause a rift.

Shared Activities

Although both Capricorn partners can easily participate in an activity together, one or both will refuse to. Even if they have the time to do it, they seem to avoid participating in shared activities out of spite. There is no other logical explanation for it. You would think differently since this sign is usually quite responsible and loyal. However, at the beginning of the relationship and until they loosen up towards each other, it will be difficult to get them to do things together. Once they do, they can actually see that they like doing a lot of similar things and will enjoy doing it together.

However, Capricorns are not great at understanding what their partner from the same sign might need or want. They have to be close enough to achieve this, and if they drift apart, they lose any understanding of each other. When this happens, the couple might choose to separate and instead look for partners from different signs who are more mellow and compassionate.

It isn't ideal for a Capricorn to be with a partner from the same sign. Two negatives sometimes give a positive, but with Capricorns, it is far more likely to give another negative. When one dominant Capricorn comes together with another, the relationship is not very functional. Both want to come across as the superior one, which will eventually lead to their relationship ending.

If they really want to make it work, they have to focus their sense of superiority and competitiveness outside their relationship. This will help them maintain balance in the relationship. If they don't stop locking horns, they might end up with different partners.

Capricorn and Aquarius

Sex and Intimacy Compatibility

Aquarius is the opposite of Capricorn, which is restricting and traditional. However, the same planet rules over both signs, and this means they also have similarities. The problem in these partners' sex lives is that they have a different pace because of their different elements. Capricorn is a thorough and slow Earth sign. This partner will only jump into a relationship with someone they respect and are attracted to.

When they have sexual relations, Capricorn will try to give it their best. Aquarius is an unreliable and slightly flaky Air sign. This is despite the fact that the master of reliability rules them. Aquarians don't think too much before jumping into a relationship and are quite spontaneous. They like things to be relaxed and not too serious in the beginning. This sign is rarely patient enough to go at the same pace as Capricorn. Capricorns like taking their time and making a plan, so the spontaneity and casualness of Aquarius can be a turn-off for them.

Capricorns don't like having sex hastily, so they don't rush into it with someone. Both signs are very passionate with the right partner, but the beginning plays a big role in how the relationship will work out. It is difficult for these two to reconcile since their approach is so different. However, they can become good friends since they have respect for each other. They can even have a sexual relationship as friends if they communicate well with each other.

Trust

Lies are not a big issue between these signs. Capricorns are set in their convictions and hate being wrong or making mistakes. Aquarius does not fear confrontation and places value on truth. This is why neither sees any reason to lie to each other. However, they both have different ideas of trust. It can be hard for them to accept each other. They may believe that both are honest but not believe that their relationship will work out. They only lack trust in their relationship.

Communication and Intellect

If you belong to a sign like Cancer or Taurus, it can be difficult to bear the intellectual relationship between Aquarius and Capricorn. Both silently but distantly respect each other. However, they keep growing further apart as they try to maintain this respectful relationship. They don't want to see each other in a different way and would rather separate than change the way things are.

This means they are far more likely to be lasting good friends. But it is important to remember that these signs are very different. They find it difficult to understand the way their partner lives. Their relationship can only last if they have a mutual love for a serious bond and shared interests.

Emotions

Capricorn and Aquarius have a strange emotional side. Both signs are usually quite unemotional and stay detached from others they are not close to. But this closed nature is not the reason that their relationship lacks emotional connection. For Capricorn, emotions need to be expressed in a practical and physical way. This earth sign is often called selfish since they place their own needs first.

Spiritual signs tend to find it difficult to accept the earthly nature of Capricorn. They don't understand the need for anything material or even money. Being an air sign, Aquarius has ultimate faith in everything. Their faith is not focused on any rules or religions that man has created. They want a partner they can share their floaty ideas and heavenly love with. They don't have an attachment to food, money, and even sex. They want to dream and live carefree. For Aquarius and Capricorn to bond emotionally, they have to accept the difference in their partner's reality.

Values

Aquarius needs freedom, while Capricorn places value on boundaries. This is why it may seem difficult for them to be in a loving relationship. But Capricorn precedes Aquarius, and there has to be some pressure for them to feel liberated. These partners come together in a strange way, but they realize they value the same things if they get closer. Both want loyalty and consistency from their partners. They also tend to have the same requirements while looking for a partner. Both signs dislike being with someone who tries to control them. Their needs from a long-term partner are surprisingly similar.

Shared Activities

Neither sign lacks energy. Capricorn is good at knowing where they should spend their energy. Aquarius is unsure of what to do with all their energy. This couple may not want to do the same things often, but they can take time to find activities they will enjoy together. The Aquarius partner should avoid insisting or trying to force their Capricorn partner. The latter should avoid trying to deny, restrict, or inhibit their Aquarius partner.

Aquarius and Capricorn may not be instantly attracted to each other at first. Though Saturn rules them both, they have different roles in the zodiac. The emotional contact between the two signs is the most challenging aspect they have to deal with. To stay together, Capricorn needs to be a little less grounded while Aquarius has to be a little less flighty. Finding a middle ground can be beneficial for both. Aquarius can learn how to act on their ideas from a Capricorn while Capricorn will be able to learn something new and bring some changes into their life.

Capricorn and Pisces

Sex and Intimacy Compatibility

If a Capricorn really wants to be relaxed in their relationship, they need to find a partner from the Pisces sign. The sexual relations between these two can be great since both are powerful in their own way. Capricorn is rational and strict, while Pisces is emotional and flexible.

Despite being different, they both are confident about what they believe in. There is a strong attraction between these two signs. If you observe the characters of these two signs superficially, it can be difficult to explain their sex life. However, Pisces can emotionally connect to a Capricorn in a different way than Cancer. It is more about their deep inner truth rather than passion.

Even though Capricorn seems to be a cold sign, they do not completely lack emotions. Although it may seem that Pisces is lost in their emotions, they can be quite rational at times. These signs can bring out the best in each other. Their rational-emotional understanding allows them to share a deeply intimate bond.

The sexual relationship between these two signs can be very spontaneous. Pisces will inspire Capricorn to open up and let go of their inhibitions. Capricorn will help pieces act more grounded and show their affections in a physical way. Pisces will get more serious while Capricorn will loosen up a little during the course of this relationship. If they can stay together for a long time, their relationship will have trust, stability, and emotional excitement in the perfect amounts.

Trust

Capricorn and Pisces will usually steer clear of any dishonesty if they understand and respect each other. However, there is still a chance for them to hit some rough patches. The rough nature of Capricorn can make the Pisces partner feel the need to lie at times. But if the Capricorn acts unreachable and closed up, they will fail to understand each other. The approach to trust that these two signs have is what makes their relationship beautiful. Both are wary of opening up to the world, and their trust has to be earned day by day. This is how both slowly come to trust each other and connect over time.

Communication and Intellect

Pisces partners can be very inspiring for Capricorn. Both care about good communication in a relationship. They like to be the ones talking, but they learn to stop and listen in this relationship. Since both are shy to a certain level, they have to pay attention to each other if they want to learn more about their partner. Both will do this and are genuinely interested in getting to know their partner in depth. However, they face a problem when Capricorn acts rigidly over their beliefs or opinions.

While Jupiter rules Pisces, Capricorn brings this planet to its fall. They can endanger the relationship between these signs. The simple disbelief of the rational and strict Capricorn can greatly damage Pisces' faith in their own convictions. Pisces live for their belief system and rarely give it up. However, their Capricorn partner can make them question their convictions and feel lonely. If their Capricorn partner is too domineering, it can make Pisces lose their inspired and spontaneous nature.

Emotions

When these signs come together, they can build a deeply emotional bond over the years. They can bring out the best in each other and facilitate constant growth in their partner. They do this without making any major changes in their personality and just try to do the best they can in the relationship. While Pisces may seem unreliable and flaky, Capricorn can come across as grumpy. These signs can annoy each other if they remain too set in their opinions or views. When this happens, Pisces will disappoint their earthly Capricorn partner, and Capricorn will drain the magic out of Pisces.

Values

The way that these signs approach their values is consistent in a way. Surprisingly, Pisces value stable emotions when they are in a long-term relationship. Capricorn also places value on their partner's ability to be emotional and think positively. This goes against their very nature but is the way they approach their values in this relationship.

However, they have problems when they have to use these beliefs or emotions in their everyday life. Pisces will not be able to value the cool-headedness or rationality of Capricorn. Sometimes they can be too different since Capricorn thinks it is impossible to find the perfect love Pisces dreams of. It is not easy for either of them, but they can overcome these differences if they value each other enough.

Shared Activities

At the beginning of their relationship, both partners will spend all their time together. This is in spite of the fact that they usually have very different interests. Capricorn will want to enter the world of their Pisces partner, while Pisces will want to figure out the mind of their

Capricorn partner. As they spend more time together, they will start taking part in different activities.

Pisces will realize that the interests of Capricorn are boring, at least to them. Capricorn will find the hobbies of Pisces crazy since they are not useful or well-planned. However, they will spend time doing some things together because they value traditions. While Pisces has a romantic idea about tradition, Capricorn respects tradition itself. Despite the different approaches, they will want to have some shared activities.

Capricorn and Pisces have a love story that is all about inspiration. Pisces is the one sign that can pull Capricorn into an exciting and unpredictable love story. Capricorn is the sign that can bring stability and peace into the emotional rollercoaster of a Pisces' life. Their relationship will make Capricorn more optimistic and cheerful, while Pisces can act more practically and think realistically. However, their love for Jupiter can cause some challenges. The different approaches that these signs have towards faith and religion can make it difficult for them to reconcile at times. This is why it is important that they each ask themselves if their own belief system works and if that of their partner does too. They just have to find a way to accept and respect each other's Jupiter.

I hope you can use this information to learn more about your partner or choose a partner from the sign that is most compatible with you. There are always exceptions to the rules, so you cannot judge a person just by their sign. However, certain relationships will have an easy flow to them, while others will require a lot more work. You also need to ensure that your partner is dedicated enough to the relationship to work through those obstacles that come when certain signs blend. But with a little time and sincerity, you can use this information to understand your partner further and improve your relationship.

Chapter Seven: Capricorn Friendships

This section will cover friendships, social life, and how the Capricorn functions in the world around them.

Capricorn takes their friendships seriously, just like everything else in their lives. They are loyal and loving, all about the shared stories and inside jokes. They like taking care of their friends and making them dinner. They use their strengths to help their friends as best as they can.

Capricorns encourage and motivate their friends and help bring out the best in them. They also aren't shy about letting their friends know when they are disappointed in them. They don't ignore bad behavior and call out a friend if they notice something they consider wrong. Capricorns are not the life of the party and like being in bed on time. They are not a fun friend, but they are always the ones with the best gifts. They are dedicated to their friends and expect the same.

How to be Friends with a Capricorn

To get close to a Capricorn, you have to be persistent. This sign may seem distant, but they just want to see if it is worth it before they invest in it. Capricorns are very observant and take time to judge if a person is worthy of being part of their inner circle. Capricorns value good character since they are very honest themselves.

To be friends with a Capricorn, you have to be loyal, hard-working, and honest. This is what will impress them. Also, display your skills to them since they are attracted to such things. To spend time with a Capricorn, choose a useful activity like a class where they can learn something, or join them for a walk or hike just for the health of it. A coffee date or dinner will seem pointless to them most of the time.

To maintain a good friendship with a Capricorn, you have to make an effort to stay in touch with them. Keep their birthdays and important events in mind. Check in with them regularly and send gifts once in a while. Capricorns don't like short-term friends who disappear from their lives. They appreciate the ones who stay or keep in touch even if it is a long-distance friendship.

Capricorns love to reminisce about the old days and talk about shared stories. They may not seem like a sentimental sort, but they really are. They like saving photos and looking at them once in a while. Keeping a framed picture of your Capricorn friend will show them that you treasure their friendship.

Capricorns Make Good Friends

They are Loyal

They do their best to have your back and protect you. Even if they don't agree with your choices, they will try to stand by you. They are somewhat parental in nature and give lectures, but it is only in your best interest.

They Remember Important Things

If you visit your Capricorn friend, they will make your favorite food or have your favorite wine ready. They will remember your tastes and give you exactly what you want for your birthday. They will remember the details of every story you tell them and the names of every ex or family member you talk about. This friend will know you inside out.

They Appreciate Your Strengths and Accept Your Flaws

Capricorns are usually like a guidance counselor for their friends. They will help you make plans and put your goals into action. They know what you are good at and how you can use it to your benefit. They will also know your weaknesses and accept you despite them.

Capricorn Friendships with the Other 11 Zodiac Signs

Capricorn and Aries

It can be challenging for Capricorn to have an Aries friend. Although Capricorn is up for the challenge, their opposite personality will clash. Aries is hotheaded while Capricorn is coolheaded. While Capricorn likes to savor their life, Aries likes rushing through it. Both are very ambitious and can have a strong bond if they support each other's ambitions.

Capricorn and Taurus

A Capricorn will always treasure their great friendship with a Taurus. This sign is humorous, loving, and loyal. They will admire the qualities of their Capricorn friend just as the sea-goat admires their virtues. Taurus will constantly praise the drive, dependability, and sophistication of a Capricorn. Both signs want financial stability so they can retire early. These friends love talking about their dreams for the future and what they want to do once they have achieved their goals. Any minor issues will barely affect their friendship over the years.

Capricorn and Gemini

Capricorn finds it hard to understand their Gemini friend, but it is not from lack of trying. The Gemini is an unpredictable bunch, and you can never tell for sure what makes them tick. They could be interested in one thing today and another tomorrow. Their rash behavior is difficult for practical Capricorn to bear. Gemini, on the other hand, finds the reluctance of Capricorn to try new things annoying. But Gemini friends are willing to put up with Capricorns if the latter learns to deal with their unpredictability.

Capricorn and Cancer

Although Cancer is the astrological opposite of Capricorn, they can still be friends. Cancer friends are compassionate and caring, and this can make Capricorns warm up to them. The executive ability of a Capricorn is similar to that of Cancer, and the latter considers them a kindred spirit. However, Cancer is a lot more emotional and sentimental than Capricorns. Nonetheless, these signs can create a good balance for each other.

Capricorn and Leo

Having these signs as friends will always attract attention. This could be positive or negative, depending on some factors. Leo is an outgoing friend who makes it easier for the introverted Capricorn to meet new people. But the sunny personality of Leo can outshine the quiet Capricorn. These two should avoid competing for the same things if they want to remain friends. Leo will be better friends with someone who is humorous, while Capricorn will resonate with people who have dry humor.

Capricorn and Virgo

The friendship between these two signs is quite noteworthy. Both signs are cautious, but they seem to take an instant liking to each other. Once they start talking, they realize that they both like activities like gardening. However, they could go about it differently. Virgo appreciates the slow pace at which Capricorn enjoys things while Capricorn likes the modesty of a Virgo. These two will be friends forever if they can overlook each other's flaws.

Capricorn and Libra

The friendship between these two signs is only possible if both consciously overlook their differences. Libra is a very different sign from Capricorn, and it is usually difficult for them to get along. Capricorn is focused on facts while Libra plays with concepts. Capricorns are steady folks, while Libras are constantly changing.

Libra will find it difficult to understand Capricorn's serious nature while the latter will hate the inability of Libra to make decisions. The one thing these friends will have in common is their leadership ability. Capricorn is good at managing materials, while Libra is better at executing ideas. Combining both talents can be beneficial for these friends. When they work at building something together, it makes their friendship function well, too.

Capricorn and Scorpio

These signs find great comfort in their friendship. Scorpio will understand Capricorn's cautiousness, and the latter will sympathize with how Scorpio plays their cards close. This pair will be comfortable in their silences and don't mind that neither talks a lot. The only hitch is that Scorpio does not like bossy behavior, and Capricorn will be uncomfortable with the grudge-holding Scorpio. But for the most part, they are congenial together. These signs have similar humor and enjoy dark comedies.

Capricorn and Sagittarius

Capricorn admires the traits of Sagittarius like their humor and honesty. Sagittarius, on the other hand, admires the drive and determination of Capricorn. This is why these two signs will want to be friends with each other. Both will help each other out when needed.

Capricorn and Capricorn

Having a friend from the same zodiac sign can be nice for Capricorn. They know that their friend will never leave them hanging or act irresponsibly. They can depend on them to look after a pet when they are away or to stay by their side at a party. These friends don't like discussing their darkest secrets, but they can depend on each other when needed. Being similar, they know that they can trust each other to keep their secrets safe and to stay loyal.

Capricorn and Aquarius

The most obvious friend for Capricorn is not Aquarius, but it still works for this pair. The unpredictable behavior of Aquarius acts as a catharsis for Capricorn. This sign reminds Capricorn it helps to toss out the rules at times and follow your instinct. Capricorn teaches Aquarius friends the value of traditions. But Aquarius will usually accuse Capricorn of being boring and stuck up while the latter will tire of Aquarius's rebellious nature.

Capricorn and Pisces

Capricorn is always willing to act as a sanctuary for Pisces, who look for shelter in them. They know that Pisces will be there to comfort them in their time of need. While Capricorn is usually quite introverted, they openly shed their tears in front of their Pisces friend. However, the lack of punctuality in Pisces can be very annoying for the punctual Capricorn. But most of the time, these friends get along quite well.

Capricorn at a Party

It is rare to see Capricorns out on the town every day. However, they always show up to a party when it matters. If it is a birthday or an event for their closest friends or family, Capricorn will always make it. They never flake on such days even though they like being in bed early. Capricorns are also great at hosting a themed party for their friends once in a while.

If you invite your Capricorn friend to a holiday party, they will be there without fail. While this sign is not very extroverted, that is not the case when they are with their trusted ones. If they accompany a friend to a stranger's party, they act responsibly and stay with their friend all throughout. They will drink a few but never more than they can handle. If they know no one at a party, they will make polite conversation and try to leave when it is acceptable to do so. This sign may not be the life of the party, but they have fun in their own way with the people they genuinely like.

Chapter Eight: Capricorn at Work – Capricorn Career Paths

In this section, we will look at Capricorn at work. Certain types of professions are better suited for the personality of a Capricorn. They do better in their careers when they choose these. You will also learn about the compatibility of Capricorns with other signs at their workplace.

Best Career Choices For Capricorn

Capricorns are best suited for a career in which they are able to capitalize on the strengths associated with their zodiac sign. Capricorns are inherently hard working and love dedicating themselves to a particular task. A Capricorn has a strong suit for being organized and patient. They can follow routines well, and they have a strong work ethic which helps them to multitask and thrive in a corporate world. Considering these traits, here are some of the best-suited career options available for Capricorn men and women.

Teacher

Teaching requires you to have a lot of patience, along with strong organizational skills. This makes this particular career choice a good fit for Capricorns. Teachers need to be able to stay organized and be able to handle twenty or thirty students in a class setting.

Teachers also need to have a lot of patience for dealing with young children, who tend to have short attention spans. All these challenges make Capricorns a perfect fit for the teaching profession. However, also remember that many Capricorns cannot relate to young children. There are also plenty of Leos and Gemini in the teaching profession because of their rare ability to relate to other people, including young children.

Professional Manager/Organizer

A Capricorn's strong suit is for being organized and being able to handle different things simultaneously, making them great professional managers and organizers, and even home decorators; they can effectively help their clients organize their homes, commercial spaces, or offices.

Most people without a lot of the traits of the Earth sign in their personal horoscopes cannot lead organized lives, and they need a Capricorn's help to organize themselves. Organization is something that comes naturally to a Capricorn and capitalizing on it professionally can bring a lot of success.

Accounting/Financial Management

Accounting can be considered the perfect dream job for a Capricorn. Capricorns are excellent at managing finances. Their strong organizational skills help them prepare large financial statements, making them great at accounting and financial planning. They can carry out these tasks with ease and almost perfectly, with no mistakes. Accountancy and financial planning is not a job meant for everyone, and most people do not enjoy doing it, but for Capricorns, it is something that comes naturally to them.

Like an accountant, a financial planner's job also entails working with the same management of finances and numbers, bank statements, and fund investments that accounting requires. Capricorns are great at predicting when to move funds and finding better areas that yield higher profits. They are great at managing risks, and they can guide people and organizations to financial security. Capricorns are proficient at financial management; it's something that comes to them easily.

Business Executive

Most corporate heads and managers are Capricorns; this can be a tough role to fulfill for most people since it requires strong organizational skills and excellent problem-solving capabilities. Being an executive also requires a lot of patience for dealing with many different types of people. It is also the manager's job to decide who deserves a raise or a promotion depending upon their performance, and Capricorns are great at making decisions by detaching themselves from these situations emotionally.

Programming and Information Technology

Being a skilled computer programmer requires exceptional problem solving and organizational skills. Capricorns are naturals when it comes to computer programming, coding, and data management. Although most people may find this job to be boring, Capricorns are tenacious and can focus on problems and work at it until they come up with a solution.

Capricorn Work Compatibility

Capricorns are one of the most persevering zodiac signs. If you are a Capricorn, the chances are good that you leave your employers feeling impressed with your drive, determination, and practical solutions. While other zodiac signs such as Sagittarius and Libra are adept at handling the social aspects of being in a workplace, Capricorns have a different disposition and prefer keeping a low profile and focusing on doing their best work.

Capricorn and Aries

While Capricorn is able to admire and relate to The Ram's high energy and strong work ethic, there can be some friction due to their brash behavior. As a Capricorn, you are the type of person who prefers to cover your strong and independent core with a soft and approachable velvet cover. Aries tend to overlook these niceties, and their brash behavior may not sit well with you.

While their brutish behavior may make you wince, you cannot deny that they can achieve a lot and bring some great results. Instead of criticizing them for their shortcomings, try to channel their talents to help you in different situations. After all, there is no point in issuing futile rebukes to people who are set in their ways and unwilling to back down. Similarly, it is also best to be direct and question them if you feel like something doesn't sit well with you.

While an Aries can help you with handling the aggressive aspects of your business, you can take charge of the duties that require finesse and subtlety. Together, you can make a great duo and do some significant work in your own unique ways.

Capricorn and Taurus

A Taurus can make a wonderful colleague for Capricorns, mainly because they share the same core values. Both Capricorns and Taurus seek jobs that offer stability, profitability, and luxury. If a Capricorn and a Taurus decide to go into business together, they can use their unique skills to create and sustain profitable ventures such as five-star restaurants, luxury car dealerships, and other high-end businesses. A Capricorn and a Taurus can quickly rise up through the ranks by providing each other valuable help and support.

By being the person who sets a higher standard for this modest zodiac sign, you can help them unlock their full potential, and they will reward you with their undying loyalty. A Taurus is also great at reining you in when you're going too hard and are at the risk of burning out. You need a reminder sometimes to take a break so that you can do your best work.

Capricorn and Gemini

Geminis are not the easiest people to work with if you are a Capricorn. That does not mean that the two cannot coexist together peacefully. The important thing to remember is that Geminis are not the best at following a routine regularly. Therefore you need to be a little smart while assigning tasks to a Gemini. Assign them with fast-paced responsibilities such as handling the reception desk, answering phones, taking orders, and waiting on customers while you are focusing on the long-term goals such as making financial projections, meeting deadlines, and formulating marketing strategies.

Although a Gemini may seem flaky to you, you cannot deny that a Gemini's optimistic attitude can brighten the atmosphere and bring out the best in you as well. Try not to be too reprimanding because of their eager behavior; after all, they have only your best interests at heart. The two of you can create a very dynamic duo and make successful curators, auctioneers, and archivists.

Capricorn and Cancer

Although the Crab is your astrological opposite, the two of you can work very efficiently as a professional team. Most Capricorns are workaholics, and they need someone who can identify that and tell them to slow them down and take it easy to avoid burning out. Cancer is perfect for this job. Similarly, a sensitive zodiac sign like the Crab needs a lot of praise and encouragement for them to function at their best, which a Capricorn can provide in spades.

Yes, your colleague's sensitive and moody nature can get on your nerves at certain times, but your professional side and no-nonsense nature can cut a Cancer to the core. If you are able to overcome these differences and admire each other's strengths, you can be an effective and efficient duo. Both of you are blessed with leadership qualities, although a Cancer is more gifted at working with different kinds of people while a Capricorn is better suited for working with products.

If you are planning to enter into a business partnership with a Cancer, consider going into the investment banking sector or the shipping industry.

Capricorn and Leo

Leos can make stimulating but challenging colleagues for Capricorns. Both of you are capable of tremendous hard work and have strong work ethics, although you may hold very different needs and goals. The Lion seeks fame while a Capricorn's main goal is a fortune. Leos loves leading a glamorous lifestyle while a Capricorn enjoys understated elegance.

Leos are notorious for spending lavishly on their indulgences while a Capricorn saves obsessively. However, if you can manage to overcome these differences, the two of you can create a powerful partnership and build a profitable empire. You will find a lot of success in real estate and other marketing agencies. A Leo loves working with people and being in the limelight. while you can keep busy behind the scenes orchestrating the operation and making the important decisions. A Capricorn is good at handling finances, but it may serve you well to listen to a Leo and work on your presentation.

Capricorn and Virgo

Working with a Virgo is akin to having your prayers answered. You can never find a more hard-working and honest colleague. A Virgo will never stand in your way professionally, and they will actually try to make your journey a smoother one.

If you are patient with a Virgo and make your expectations clear, you will receive nothing less than a stellar performance from this zodiac sign. Be mindful and remember that this is one of the star signs that are extremely prone to stress and burning out due to stress. If you are working alongside a Virgo, you are better off letting your colleague handle the day-to-day operations while you focus on the long-term projects and the bigger picture. Together, the two of you can use your combined skill sets to get the best results.

Capricorn and Libra

As a Capricorn, you appreciate and admire professionalism, and Libras certainly make a good show of the fine work that they do. Yes, their attitude may seem shallow and frivolous at times, but that may only be prejudice as the result of your own serious approach to doing things.

The two of you will need to meet each other halfway and find a middle ground that will work for both of you. You cannot deny that this zodiac sign has a very intelligent head on their shoulders. They have very strong powers of analysis and are keen on learning new things. At the same time, you are an expert at spinning straw into gold and creating something out of nothing.

This is something that a Libra will very much appreciate and admire. If you are working with a Libra, let them be the face of the operation and handle the clientele while you handle the executive operations. Although both of you may be blessed with strong executive abilities, you are much better at making decisions for the long run.

Capricorn and Scorpio

A Scorpio and a Capricorn make a very productive duo since both are extremely hardworking. This is also because a Scorpio has no problem with you being at the helm of the operation. In fact, Scorpios prefer working behind the scenes while gathering an intellectual edge over competitors. While a Scorpio keeps busy building financial dossiers, you can be the face of the operation and impress your clientele with your professionalism, diligence, and hard work.

You can rely on the Scorpion when it comes to facts and figures, which can then be incorporated into reports and presentations to impress your clientele. Although you may have small spats and gripes with each other, there is nothing that the two of you can't work your way around and create a powerful and productive partnership professionally.

Capricorn and Sagittarius

A Sagittarius' laid-back attitude can prove to be a distraction for you sometimes since you are an extremely professional and goal-oriented person. Although a Capricorn and Sagittarius have very conflicting traits, the truth is that a Sagittarius can be extremely important for the sake of your success.

This zodiac sign can connect with people from different walks of life, and the two of you can create a very diverse and impressive clientele and carve out a unique niche for yourselves. Besides that, a Sagittarius is also extremely honest and will likely keep a check on you to avoid any bad decisions being made. Similarly, you can also lend a much-needed structure and regimen to a Sagittarius' laid-back nature to bring out the best in them.

Capricorn and Aquarius

An Aquarius may attempt to test your patience during certain situations, but that does not mean that it is impossible for the two of you to co-exist and work in a partnership. Although this zodiac sign is more known for its creativity, you cannot deny its strong problem-solving skills. Similarly, an Aquarius will admire your strong work ethic and your ability to tackle big responsibilities without even letting out a hint of a complaint.

Work is one aspect of their life that Capricorns will always do well in as long as they love what they do.

Chapter Nine: What Does a Capricorn Need?

By now, you know a lot about the distinctive traits of Capricorn and what makes them different from other zodiac signs. For a Capricorn to succeed in their life, they have to remember some things.

An individual from this zodiac sign should be more confident about their decisions, whether at work or at home. Especially at the workplace, they have to learn to value their own decisions and thus gain respect from their colleagues at work.

While at work, this sign should work at looking more interested in their work. It is often seen that they are in a rush to leave when they get their work done even if colleagues are still at their desks. Changing this habit can be helpful and will make people notice their dedication.

Capricorns should try to choose things they love or are well suited for them instead of following the crowd. While they like the comfort and security in following others, they could achieve a lot more success if they walk the path less taken.

It is better for a Capricorn not to work with their spouse or even at the same place as them. This sign is very competitive and controlling, so this can have a negative impact on their relationship. Having a separate workplace is highly recommended for Capricorns and their partners. This would allow them to have space for their personal growth without being influenced by each other.

Capricorns need to try something new sometimes. This will help them gain exposure, come out of their comfort zone, and become worldly.

The individuals from this sign also need to work on becoming better listeners. While they have strong opinions and like expressing themselves, they should also give others the chance to do so. Letting someone talk without interrupting is a skill this sign needs to acquire. It will help them learn from the people around them and make them better listeners.

Having some "me" time every day can also be beneficial for their wellbeing. It will help them feel better and have more control over their temper even on the worst of days.

Being realistic is an inborn characteristic of Capricorn. However, it is also important for them to learn to be more positive in life. It is okay to hope for the best, even if you feel like there is a chance for things to go wrong. Indulging in some flighty dreams at times can be good for them.

Capricorns also needs to stop criticizing themselves all the time. They should think about the things they tell themselves and decide if it were something they would ever tell someone they loved. Constant self-criticism will only bring down their self-confidence and affect their abilities.

These things are some simple points that a Capricorn should keep in mind.

Conclusion

By now, you know a lot about a Capricorn's personality, along with their strengths and weaknesses. You also know how their mind works most of the time, and this can help you understand this standoffish sign better.

For a Capricorn, it is crucial to find the right partner in love who will help balance out their weaknesses and bring out the best in them. It is also important for them to be with a person who will understand their need to work hard and take their time as they go about things.

Many things are unique and admirable about this zodiac sign. I hope you found the information in this book about Capricorn enlightening. You can even recommend it to other Capricorns or people with Capricorns in their lives.

Part 11: Aquarius
The Ultimate Guide to an Amazing Zodiac Sign in Astrology

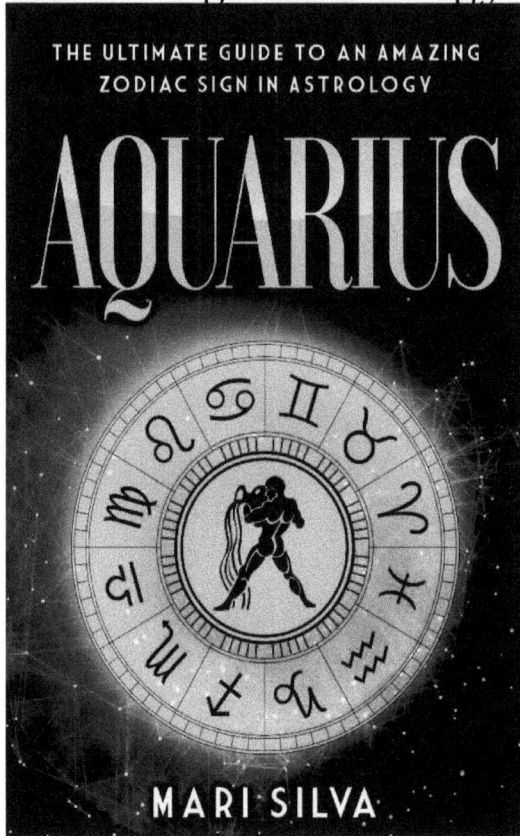

Introduction

People have been fascinated with the stars and the planets since ancient times. Before technology and the Internet became prevalent, the stars and planets acted as a guide to life and to the future. In the olden days, we had a much stronger connection with the celestial realm and the earth under our feet. Ancient stories and myths surround these celestial bodies, but the world we live in now is quite different.

Science is considered the real truth and everything else is questioned, but there is a little truth in everything, and this applies to the ancient art of astrology. Believing in zodiac signs and their relevance in our lives is something that many people have been opening up to again. It is not necessary to believe only in what you see or what is proven by science. You can also choose to believe in things that are beyond your understanding. This is why I encourage the exploration of zodiac signs.

Depending on the season and the day you were born, you will fall under one of the twelve zodiac signs. Learning about your own zodiac sign or that of the people around you can be immensely helpful. Most people know their zodiac sign, and a lot of them read their horoscope quite often as well.

In this book, we will specifically focus on Aquarius and endeavor to give you an in-depth understanding of any individual who belongs to this sign.

This book highlights the strengths, weaknesses, unique traits, and quirks of Aquarians. It will also give you a better idea about the compatibility in love, work, and friendship of an Aquarius individual with all the other signs.

The things you learn in this book might surprise you as you realize how much of it resonates with you or the Aquarius in your life. Essentially, this book should help any Aquarius understand themselves better, gain a better balance in life, and learn a lot about how great the impact of their zodiac sign is on their lives.

If you are ready to delve into the world of Aquarius, start reading!

Chapter One: An Introduction to Aquarius

Aquarius is one of the fascinating signs of the zodiac and is often considered "the alien sign." It is a quirky, unique, and a sometimes-bizarre sign that is full of heart and love. This chapter will help you understand the intricate details of this sign.

The astrological sign Aquarius appears eleventh in the Zodiac. It is a representation of the Aquarius constellation. The Sun enters this sign around January 21 and leaves on February 20 in the tropical zodiac. In the sidereal zodiac, the Sun enters this sign on February 15 and leaves on March 14. This factor is also affected by the leap year phenomenon.

The Aquarius Myth

The zodiac constellation of Aquarius is represented as a water bearer. This water bearer was Ganymede, a Phrygian youth from Greek mythology. He was the son of King Tros, the ruler of Troy. According to other sources, he may have been the son of Dardanus. One day Ganymede was tending the flock of sheep for his father when Zeus saw him and lost his heart to him. He assumed the form of a huge bird and bundled Ganymede away. From then on, Ganymede became the cupbearer of the gods. Orpheus sings this tale in the works of Ovid.

Constellation

The Aquarius constellation is a winter constellation situated next to Cetus and Pisces in the northern hemisphere. It is a fairly radiant constellation.

Symbol for Aquarius

As mentioned, Aquarius is usually represented as a water-bearer. This symbol is often depicted in other forms, such as a wise man, a young woman, or an old person. Sometimes only a pot filled with water is used to represent the sign. (The representation is merely conceptual and not a perfect definition of the sign.)

There are many ways for the symbol of Aquarius to be interpreted. For instance, one interpretation says that the collection of water represents the collection of wisdom. The Aquarius individual or soul is always in search of wisdom and is the bearer of the collective wisdom of humankind. It may sound quite lofty, but people who know Aquarian individuals will agree that this makes sense on a deep level.

Aquarian individuals believe in the essence of life and have tremendous healing capacity. They love to better their surroundings and community and perform acts of altruism. They like to improve the lives of people around them. They do these acts because they enjoy it, not for praise or credit. Aquarius dispenses kindness, wisdom, and serendipity through his pot.

In ancient times, the water bearer would walk many miles just to fetch fresh water for their community. Similarly, the Aquarius person is ready to travel through pain, difficulties, and struggle to search for truth, enlightening ideas, and wisdom. They would gladly walk the paths that others avoid.

The Aquarius Glyph and Its Meaning

To describe the zodiac signs in shorthand, astrologers all over the world use specific glyphs and signs. These are unique and different for each star sign and hold crucial meaning in representing the sign. The glyphs are simple, so anyone can emulate them with ease. The glyph for Aquarius, too, is simple, but it encompasses a deep meaning and represents the sign in the best way possible.

Many people get the Aquarius symbol as a tattoo. It is represented using choppy waters or a bolt of lightning. The choppy-waters glyph has two waves moving in parallel. This glyph showcases the deep hidden nature of the sign.

Aquarius is an intelligent sign blessed with the power of intuition. This allows them to know things, even if they do not understand the reason. The parallel-wave lines also depict an Aquarian desire for equality. You can notice these factors in any typical Aquarian person. They hate the disparity between classes, gender, etc. For them, everyone is equal. They have the desire to make and see the world in an equal light.

They believe that this can be done by bringing the great truths to light so that humankind can benefit from them. They are aware of the fact that this act can isolate or alienate them, but they gladly walk this difficult path with immense bravery.

Element

Each zodiac sign is ruled by one of the four elements: air, water, earth, or fire. The zodiac signs form four trios; therefore, you can see the overlapping of emotions, traits, and actions in signs belonging to the same trio.

Many beginners are often surprised to realize that the element of water does not rule Aquarius. The glyph has waves; the symbol of Aquarius is a water bearer; all these factors would seem to indicate that the sign has a close relationship with water, but it is governed by air.

Aquarians hate conventions and will never bow down to anyone's expectations; it is no wonder their ruling element shatters the expectations in this matter. The Air trio is comprised of Gemini, Aquarius, and Libra. All of these signs have a fast-moving outlook on life. They are witty, sharp, and intellectual. While the signs are similar in certain ways, Aquarius differs from the others because of particular characteristics.

The element of Air in the zodiac stands for ideas, thoughts, and intellectual reasoning. Aquarian individuals are often confused because they love humanity but do not understand emotions and feelings. This creates a constant sense of confusion. They are often unlucky in love, though it's no fault of theirs. As an Aquarian, the biggest issue that you may have to face is the difficult nature of heavy emotions such as sorrow, love, and grief.

Emotions such as these become immensely complicated when you try to approach them from an intellectual point of view, as would an Aquarius. When Aquarians do not have their reason to rely on, they get confused and frightened by their feelings. It is necessary to maintain your composure while dealing with a person of this sign.

These individuals often have profound and grand ideas, while eschewing shallow thoughts. They are artistic, distinct, and bold. They are provocative and enjoy humanity, and they help people with their combination of intuition and intelligence.

The heads of Aquarian individuals are full of ideas that move through their brains swiftly. They talk with passion and vividness. The sheer number of ideas often drives them in circles and throws them off towards tangential topics. As a friend of an Aquarius, be patient when they do this. Their mind moves in all directions with the speed of light. If they do not come back to the topic soon, you can nudge them in the right direction.

The Aquarius Planets

Each zodiac sign has particular elements or items that represent them. These include glyphs, symbols, elements, constellations, etc. Another factor that rules the zodiac signs is their planet; a particular "astrological planet", which generally correlates to one of the physical planets in our solar system, rules each sign.

According to astronomy, there are eight planets in the solar system, but in astrology there are more than eight. Some signs also share planets. Thanks to modern science, new planets have been discovered; over time, that has led to changes in the classical list of ruling planets. For instance, Mars once ruled the sign Scorpio, but Pluto (which incidentally is no longer a planet) rules it now. Certain other bodies of the Solar System also govern some zodiac signs; for instance, the Moon governs Cancer.

In the case of Aquarius, both Saturn and Uranus govern it. The interpretations of the traits and effects of both these planets differ a lot, but both work in tandem to bring the uniqueness of their personality to the forefront.

Saturn is a stern planet in the solar system, according to most interpretations. It is focused on self-discipline, order, and method. A code of conduct still governs even the most outlandish Aquarius people. This code of conduct is often personal and does not follow the code of conduct of other people.

Uranus is a planet that loves to do things of its own accord, just like the Aquarius individual who is unique and bold. Uranus rules higher learning, wisdom, new possibilities, freedom, and a passion for change. These traits are quite typical of the Aquarius person.

People are often scared and nervous about big changes, but Aquarius accepts them gladly and often enjoys them. They believe that life should always move forward, albeit in harmony and peace. They are full of wisdom and lofty ideals presented with total compassion.

House of Aquarius

Astrology is an infinite field, and a multitude of factors make it an intricate art. Even at the most basic level, there exists a lot of different concepts that make it difficult to understand for a beginner. For instance, along with the twelve zodiac signs, there are twelve houses. If you do not understand houses, you have most likely skipped over an integral aspect of astrology.

Astrological houses stand for the exact areas of a person's life that the horoscope talks about. Each house in astrology represents a unique factor. These houses stand for the places, people, situations, and circumstances that take place in life.

Each house is named after the zodiac signs, so they begin at Aries and end with Pisces. Each house has a particular feature, according to the zodiac wheel. To interpret the houses, you need to have a birth chart.

Eleventh House

The Eleventh House is the house of Aquarius. It is where you make your debut in society. It also stands for the reception or reaction that you get from society. It is considered to be the house of friends. It also includes other social circles such as colleagues and acquaintances. Like the sign, this house, too, is ruled by both Saturn and Uranus.

The Eleventh house shows whether you fit in or break away from your birth conditions and how you were raised. It sets the mood for these factors.

A person with a strong Eleventh House often ends in a tribe totally different from where he was born. Their original tribe may make them feel like an alien or an outsider. Other strong Eleventh House individuals may provoke the people around them and may break the traditions in which they were raised.

The ruler of this house is Saturn, along with Uranus. This house represents community, expression of the community, shared visions, collaborations, and togetherness.

House of Good Spirit

The ancient Greek astrologers looked at the Eleventh House as the house of aspirations. It is considered the house of good spirit and freedom, as it feels free after breaking the conventions of the society with no care for those involved. This provides its spaciousness that harkens to the guiding element of air. It allows it to be dreamy without any judgment.

The house is also known as the House of Divinity and is full of compassion. It allows the person to have a total big picture of humanity.

Many astrologers find it difficult or tricky to define the house, as it is full of contradictions, just like the sign itself. Both aspects allow for the simultaneous yet contradictory implications of individual aspirations, along with the potency of a group.

Colors for Aquarius

Aquarians are often considered the aliens of the zodiac system, as they are unique, think outside the box, and are way ahead of their time. They tend to look at the bigger picture and are thorough humanitarians. They strive hard to make the world a better place. They are often considered weird or slightly eccentric, but these factors make them even more endearing. This is why Aquarians have a lot of friends from various walks of life. This section will help you understand which colors are the best for Aquarians.

While Aquarius people dress and act in a way that makes them stand apart, there are certain colors that are genuinely good for the sign. Every zodiac sign has certain colors that are "suitable" for them.

Blue: a water bearer represents Aquarius, and not surprisingly, the power color for the sign is blue. Aquarians, like the water bearer, bear and bring knowledge and wisdom to the world. The color blue keeps them centered and calm. As Aquarians have the habit of going off tangents, the color blue can keep them grounded. It provides a calming aura that can keep them stable and focused.

Another color highly recommended for Aquarius is purple. The gemstone of Aquarius is amethyst, a bright purple crystal. It is a psychic stone that can enhance the wearer's intuition and other "psychic" abilities. Amethyst represents wisdom, compassion, and idealism, which are important traits of Aquarius. The overall persona of this sign is of intelligence and compassion.

Birthstone for Aquarius

According to astrology, Saturn is considered the toughest planet. This planet (along with Uranus) is supposed to rule Aquarius. Any Aquarian who can satisfy Saturn and make the planet happy will be a huge success in almost all walks of life. The favorite stone of this planet is Blue Sapphire. This is why Blue Sapphire is considered the birthstone of Aquarians. It is recommended to wear this stone on the middle finger in a ring made of gold. Wearing this on the right hand will improve the overall quality of your life.

Other Lucky Stones for the Aquarius

There are many other stones that are considered lucky and powerful for Aquarius. Some of these include garnet, amber, amethyst, opal, moss agate, sugilite, etc. The talismanic stone of Aquarius is jasper, while its planetary stone is turquoise. Let us have a look at this subject of stones, one by one.

Amber Stone

It is good for keeping negative energy at bay.

Amethyst

It is a healing stone that can help you get rid of past sorrows and guilt.

Garnet

It is another health stone that can help you achieve good health.

Hematite

It is a calming stone that takes away negative energy, pressure, and stress. It is good for self-confidence. It acts upon the Root Chakra and can convert the negative energy into positive vibrations.

Lucky Stone for Aquarius Woman

For Aquarian women, the following are the best stones:

- Agate
- Turquoise
- Garnet
- Amethyst

Lucky Stone for Aquarius Man

Aquarian men should wear these gems to bring about positive changes in their life:

- Jasper
- Garnet
- Amethyst

It is necessary to choose the right gemstone associated with your zodiac sign. If you choose an incorrect one, it may lead to the development of a variety of problems.

Characteristics of Aquarius

Aquarius individuals are generous and give with open hands, but they often get lost in their plans, ideas, questions, and creative solutions. They generally despise people breaking in on their thought process, but if you see an Aquarius friend being too lofty, it is your duty to bring them back to reality; otherwise, they might get too lost in thought.

It is also necessary to remember that, with their uniqueness, they are blessed with remarkable and powerful insight. Under their outlandish and sometimes strange outer appearance, they hide a pioneering approach towards the world, which can lead us all forward.

Aquarians have a set of characteristics found in most individuals belonging to this sign. These characteristics are positive ones as well as negative ones. It is recommended to enhance the positive characteristics and get rid of the negative ones to make your life more enjoyable.

Positive Aquarius Traits

Aquarians are often described as original, intelligent, and smart. They are future-oriented and are the visionaries of this world. Some of their positive traits are:

Vision

The most common and prominent trait of this sign is ambition and vision. They are highly ambitious about their personal and social future. Thanks to their humanitarian nature, Aquarians care for society's betterment and will put in a lot of effort to lead society towards a glorious future. They undertake various generous humanitarian causes such as fighting against world hunger, finding new ways to stop climate change, and tackling poverty and corruption.

Aquarians can be slightly dogmatic in their beliefs sometimes, but they will often do whatever they can to make the world a better place. They have a strong sense of justice and compassion. A combination of both guides their views and actions. They enjoy and love freedom and extend it to everyone.

Aquarians can change the world with their passion, humanitarian will, and unique perspectives.

Intelligent

One of the most cerebral signs, Aquarians tend to be highly intelligent but often get lost in analyzing things to find new solutions to a problem. Their intelligence is not limited to books alone, and it is possible to find Aquarians who are experts in various fields. They see possibilities in almost everything and love to analyze and dissect things. This makes them highly tolerant of a variety of viewpoints.

Aquarians tend to look at the big-picture, which makes them highly suited to solving problems. Their own ideas and constant bombardment of thoughts may distract them, but if and when focused, they can produce the best suggestions and well-researched, unbiased opinions regarding a question or an issue.

Original

People born under this sign are well known for their originality and uniqueness. They are surely one of the most unique people you will ever see, and they like to wear this fact on their sleeves.

They are innovative geniuses who love to think outside the box, especially with creative projects and finding solutions to problems. Often, Aquarians throw away the box and come up with something that can be revolutionary and path-breaking. Their penchant for revolution and novelty is also observed in their wish for a better world.

Originality and uniqueness mark the existence of all Aquarians. These factors also extend to their creative minds, so they often have various artistic tendencies. Aquarians love to use art as a medium of expression and take up media such as writing, painting, and composing.

In personal lives, Aquarians are often known as slightly (or in many cases very) eccentric, but almost all Aquarians enjoy this label. They would rather embrace their eccentricity and weirdness than lead a boring and inconsequential life.

Negative Aquarius Traits

Now that we have gone through the positive traits of Aquarius, it is time to have a look at the negative characteristics of the sign.

Cold

Aquarians may seem insensitive and cold. This is because they are less emotional and more pragmatic, which allows them a unique perspective on the world. They tend to over-analyze things, and that creates a sense of detachment from the regular world. This detached nature may make others around them feel uncomfortable. When this detachment is paired with their rigid ideas and thought processes, people often get put off.

They often run into problems due to their aloof and impersonal nature, especially when they are supposed to deal with a situation that calls for heavy emotions and sensitivity. When the situation is serious, you do not want to alienate people.

Condescending

Aquarians have a proclivity for deep thinking and ideas, which makes them one of the most intelligent signs, but this inclination also makes them susceptible to condescension. Aquarians are set in their ideas and often believe that they are correct, which automatically makes everyone else incorrect. They often fail to notice that they are talking down to a person, because they believe that their opinion is more than an opinion, i.e., it is a fact. Once an Aquarian makes up their mind, it can be downright impossible to have them change it again.

This trait can be the harbinger of the frustration of people around Aquarius, especially if they are trying to exchange ideas or propose solutions. The behavior of Aquarians can make others feel inferior.

Overly Idealistic

Aquarians are blessed with a vision that is an asset, but this asset can also turn into a curse if not handled properly. Aquarians tend to become too idealistic, which makes them chase things that are nothing less than perfect. Perfection is an impossible concept, but Aquarians may fail to realize this, which often leads to frustration, dissatisfaction, and in some cases, depression when they fail to reach the impossible and lofty standards.

Usually, their idealism can make the Aquarians slightly delusional and somewhat self-righteous.

Unpredictable

Aquarians love change and uniqueness. They often try to change for the better, but this quality can make them unpredictable. Aquarians often seem distant and emotionless; this is because they release their emotions, especially anger, in sudden, quick, and unpredictable bursts that seem to come out of nowhere.

Bad temper and anger management can be significant problems for Aquarians, especially the individuals who have to face a lot of pressure and stress. These individuals hate being emotionally vulnerable, so if something really grinds their nuts, they can lash out severely. This outburst may compensate for and include a lot of pent-up emotions.

Aquarius Characteristics in Common Situations

Sometimes Aquarians may appear to be insensitive as they face difficulty while dealing with their emotions and feelings. Their difficulty does not mean that they are not sympathetic or compassionate towards others. Aquarians can form close bonds with people (once they get comfortable with them). Here are some examples that show how Aquarians react in particular situations.

Aquarius in Love

They are all about mental and intellectual stimulation, and not surprisingly, an Aquarian person seeks the same qualities in a relationship, too. They need partners who can engage in interesting, complex, and intriguing conversations and who can tolerate their habit of going off on tangents all the time. As an Aquarian person, you can never feel romantically inclined towards a person unless they can provide you with some form of intellectual stimulation. This stimulation need not be about existentialism or the banality of evil; it can be about simple things such as video games.

Along with intellectual stimulation, Aquarians desire mental connection. They do not feel comfortable with a person unless they can form and enjoy a mental connection with them. Besides these two factors, an Aquarian also appreciates independence and honesty. An Aquarius person is incomplete without independence. They are hungry for freedom, even if it comes at the cost of being a loner. They need a sense of independence from their partner and will give the same to them. They always respect the boundaries of their partners and treat them as equals. If an Aquarius falls in love with someone, they will look at the relationship as a lifetime commitment. They won't be afraid of sacrificing to save and cherish their relationship.

If someone betrays or cheats on them, they experience anger like no other. They will most likely end the relationship immediately and move on. Aquarians don't forgive, and neither do they forget. We will discuss this in detail in an upcoming chapter.

Aquarius in Family and Friendship

Aquarians love their friends, family, and close ones. They cherish family life and enjoy people who are creative, honest, and intelligent. They are ready to make sacrifices and take risks for the sake of their family and dear ones.

As for friendship, Aquarians tend to be popular. They generally have a lot of acquaintances and are friends with many people. This is because they look at the world from a collaborative viewpoint. They possess a self-righteous and slightly condescending attitude which may make people uncomfortable, but generally, Aquarians are quirky, fun, and easy to hang around with.

Aquarians are bad with their emotions and despise being emotionally vulnerable. This may be a factor in their ineptitude at making close friends and forming personal bonds with people. They will always take time before they form a close relationship with someone. They will need ample time to process things and feel connected with someone on an intellectual and emotional level. Once you befriend an Aquarius, you will always be their most reliable friend. When someone breaks their trust, an Aquarius person goes haywire.

Aquarius Celebrities Who Espouse the Traits of the Sign

Aquarius people are known for being strong, original, and deep thinkers. They are humanitarians and are bold and dedicated.

There are a lot of advantages to being born in the Aquarius sign as it allows you to fight for causes that can change the world. They are uncompromising and can make difficult decisions. The only problem they have is they fail to express their emotions properly. Still, they can be highly empathetic towards the pains and pangs of others.

The element of air rules a lot of celebrities. Here is a list of some famous Aquarius celebrities that display many of the traits associated with the sign.

Ellen DeGeneres

Ellen has become an international star and is well known for her bold yet funny personality. She was born on January 28. She is a talk-show host, a comedienne, an actress, and a producer and is most known for her syndicated daytime talk show, The Ellen DeGeneres Show.

Along with her many Hollywood accolades, Ellen proudly displays the two remarkable Aquarius traits of philanthropy and humanitarianism. She is a staunch supporter of animal and LGBTQ rights and has started many charities. She regularly donates to various other causes, too. For her charity and related work, she has been awarded the Presidential Medal of Freedom.

Millie Bobby Brown

A young actress of considerable talent, well known for her path-breaking series, *Stranger Things*, Millie Bobby Brown is a true Aquarian. She strongly supports social justice and equality and uses her fame to make the world a better place.

She was born on February 19th and is the youngest-ever Goodwill Ambassador appointed by UNICEF. She has used her celebrity status to bring attention to the issues that plague the current generation of children and youth. Her humanitarian activities and disposition truly represent her Aquarian heart.

John McEnroe

Notorious for being the "bad boy of tennis," John McEnroe has all the Aquarius's classic traits. He was born on February 16, and is well known for his temper, on and off the court. He has had confrontations with his opponents, officials, and umpires. His "tantrums" or outbursts have made him famous with the press and social media, and these tantrums have been parodied multiple times, making him a pop culture sensation. He is an outspoken, independent, and strong-minded individual just like all other Aquarius people. He is ready to fight for the things that he believes in- literally and figuratively.

Elizabeth Banks

A progressive and talented actress, producer, and director born on February 10th, Elizabeth Banks has all the traits of an Aquarius person. She is a strong supporter and advocate of women's choice, rights, and autonomy over their own bodies. She has used her fame and power to influence people and ensure equal pay for the cast and crew irrespective of gender. She often inserts feminist and radical themes in her art pieces.

Her recent project was a reboot of *Charlie's Angels* featuring four strong female leads who bring down a corrupt organization. She drove people's attention towards women's empowerment in the film industry that has always been dominated by men.

Oprah Winfrey

One of the most recognized faces in the world, Oprah Winfrey (or just Oprah) is an embodiment of the Aquarius sign. She is an excellent listener and empathetic person. Her intuition and empathy have helped hundreds of celebrities and common individuals open up to her on her shows, such as The Oprah Winfrey Show and Super Soul Sunday. Her desire for equality allows her to look at her guests without an iota of prejudice and provide ample empathy and sympathy to them. She is empathetic towards their pain and plights. She was born on the January 29. Her other remarkable Aquarian trait is her penchant for charity.

Chapter Two: Aquarius Strengths and Weaknesses

Every person is blessed and cursed with a set of strengths and weaknesses. Individuals born under a particular zodiac sign tend to have certain similar common traits that they share. Some say that one man's food is another man's garbage. Similarly, something that is absolutely crucial for a zodiac sign can become outright trivial and despicable for another. It is necessary to understand your weaknesses and strengths that can help you lead your life in a better way. Aquarius is a contradictory sign; so, it is even more important to understand its strengths and weaknesses so that you can help yourself (or your Aquarian friend) to have a tantrum-free life.

Positive Traits

Here is a quick look at the positive traits of an Aquarius individual.

Unconventional

Aquarians are often fascinated by freedom, unconventional ideas, concepts, and technology. They are rebellious and are always in need of freedom. Their love for freedom does not mean that they do not appreciate people; rather, they like people and can appreciate innovative ideas. They love innovation and will appreciate an innovative idea, even if it is not plausible in real life.

Trendsetters

Aquarians are the trendsetters of the zodiac who love to interact with other people. The eleventh sign of the zodiac is known for its love for freedom. They may appear shy, but they can be quite lively and unconventional if the situation demands. They always focus on philosophical concepts, ideas, and feelings. This is possible due to their superior intellect, which they generally use to help others. They are not judgmental and tend to look at every side of the story before reaching a conclusion. They are adaptable, which makes them sociable, but they still prefer their solitude. They may need to go back and recharge their energy levels in solitude.

Stimulated Personality

The world is full of opportunities for all air signs, especially the Aquarius. Air signs use their minds thoroughly whenever they deal with new situations and people. Aquarians need mental stimulation; if they do not feel mentally stimulated, they get bored and lose all motivation.

Visionaries

Two planets, Saturn and Uranus, govern Aquarius. Uranus is well known for its visionary ideas and properties. These visionary ideas also make the people born under this planet visionary. This is why Aquarians are often highly intuitive and are blessed with the gift of precognition. This also makes them experts at planning things. They are versatile, powerful, bold, bright, and lovely. They are big thinkers, genuine humanitarians, and innovative workers.

Group Lovers

These people love to be alone, but they like to work in groups, which is why they often have a lot of colleagues around them.

Independence

They always strive for equality and independence. They do not like it when they are forced to stay under chains and hate it when their rights get stolen away from them. This often makes them seem detached and cold, but these two factors are just defense mechanisms against intimacy and brashness.

Charisma

They find it difficult to trust people initially, but once they learn how to do it, they can express themselves freely in a better and more guided way. This makes them highly charismatic, friendly, and sociable.

Popularity

People who belong to this sign are often popular, and they often try to make the world a better place. They do have their problems though; for instance, they may often indulge in concepts, ideas, and plans that can be unrealistic.

Communication Issues

If you are an Aquarian and find it difficult to talk to people sometimes, it is not your fault; it is your sign's personality trait. Aquarians often find it difficult to invest in emotions that make them run into communication problems. Learning how to establish connections with people and invest in emotions can help them learn more about others and improve communication dramatically.

Solitude

Their love for solitude can be taken as a negative as well as a positive concept. On the one hand, their solitude makes them seem distant and aloof, while on the other, it makes them focused, dedicated, and energized. Aquarians love to be alone sometimes, and if left to their own devices, they can bring forth new and exciting ideas.

If Aquarians are not given their space and solitude, they become cranky, and their clarity and precision of mind vanish. This often confuses their close ones as they fail to understand the reason behind this peculiar and unanticipated behavior. As an Aquarian, you must have noticed that you do not worry about giving explanations or reasons when you want to be left alone. This can startle your loved ones, and they may find it inexplicable. Avoid it.

Leadership

Aquarians are gifted with impeccable brains. They are remarkably charming, independent, and original. They pine for intellectual stimulation all the time and stay faithful to people who can provide it. These qualities make them a great team leader, despite being rebellious. Their non-conventionality makes them an inimitable leader as they come up with solutions that no one else can.

Attractive

Their charm, elucidation, boldness, and high intellect make them popular among prospective romantic partners, but surprisingly, Aquarians are more inclined towards friendship than romance. A problem that partners often face is that it is difficult to understand them. This can lead to frustration, especially if the partners do not get along with their enthusiasm and energy. Aquarians are careless when it comes to rules and norms, and that might seem distasteful to their partners.

Inventive and Active

They think continuously, which makes them active and inventive. They are always thinking of new ideas and finding new solutions to make the world a better place. They try to discover new ways to help others.

Love Changes

They not only desire change; they love it. They love to shake things just so that they can inspire others. They want to make everyone's life better, including their own.

Entertaining

They are strange, no doubts there, but this eccentric attitude makes them highly sought-after friends. They are never boring, and they generally possess a great sense of humor. They are good storytellers, and they will never bore you. They love to share their joy with others, which makes them popular with everyone.

Out-of-Box Thinkers

Their eccentricities also make them thinkers with rare precision and capabilities. They dare to imagine ideas that others simply cannot think of. They are often interested in philosophical discussions and possess an "outside the box" thinking. They often astonish others by providing simple yet effective solutions to complex problems.

Creative

They never sit idle; they always do one thing or another because they hate being bored. They are creative and individualistic.

Nice

They can seem aloof, but they are some of the nicest and caring people around.

Free Thinkers

They are great listeners and will often listen to others' opinions, but they rarely change their views about anything. They tend to stick to their beliefs and ideas, but this does not mean that they are unyielding.

Aquarius Negative Traits

It is clear from the previous section that Aquarians are blessed with a lot of positive traits that can help them change the world for good. These traits allow them to enjoy their lives thoroughly and with full dedication.

Not everything is great about Aquarians, though, as the sign also has negative characteristics. These negative traits are, in a way, a weakness for Aquarians, which often lead to problems. Getting rid of these weaknesses can make life easier for Aquarians. Here is a list of common weaknesses for the Aquarians.

Detached

They can be quite detached from the world and the people around them, which can often come off as disrespectful. As an Aquarian, it is necessary to learn how not to appear disrespectful as this trait may leave you being treated as an outcast.

Lack of Balance

This does not concern physical balance. Aquarians love taking care of their friends and family, along with other people. They are blessed with humanitarian instincts and tend to improve the atmosphere of their groups and teams. This can prove to be an asset for a team leader, but many Aquarians often forget that a team consists of separate individuals. While taking care of the team as a group is essential, it is also necessary to take care of the individuals as separate people. Each person has separate importance in your life and treating them as such will help you improve communication and relation with them. Finding the balance between the team and the individual is important.

Stubborn

They can be quite stubborn. They are dead-set on their views and opinions and do not change them no matter who tries to convince them and in what way. They will listen to the opinions of others but will strictly follow their own ideas.

Impatience

This is closely related to the previous point. Aquarians not only avoid changing their opinions or ideas, but they also tend to get impatient with people who try to change them. They hate it when people cannot understand their opinion or see their side of something.

Unpredictability

This is a pro as well as a con for the Aquarians. Unpredictability, combined with amity towards independence, may make Aquarians seem too impersonal and distant. Aquarians love their own thoughts and ideas that make them unpredictable and confusing for people who don't know them well.

The previous section covered the general traits of Aquarius. The next section will focus on specific key traits that are observed in Aquarian individuals of both male and female genders.

The Aquarius Woman: Key Traits

No sign is like Aquarius, not even other air signs. Aquarians are quite serious and connected to reality, yet they love indulging in philosophy and fantasy. Female Aquarians are powerful, almost like a force of nature, which can prove quite scary for people around her. Here are traits that can help you understand an Aquarian woman better.

Dominant Side

When you meet an Aquarian woman, let her dominant side come to the surface. This will help you understand her better. These women are generally wise, self-sufficient, and highly authentic. They tend to always be on the lookout for new ideas and freedom.

Humanitarianism

Like all other Aquarians, female Aquarians love helping others. They tend to interpret life in general in a surprisingly offbeat and out-of-the-box manner. They will amaze you with their interpretation of life. Some of the most famous Aquarian women include Rosa Parks, Virginia Woolf, Oprah Winfrey, Yoko Ono, Shakira, and Jennifer Aniston.

Independence and Mystery

A woman born under Aquarius is full of mystery, unconventionality, and passion. She loves independence. Aquarius is a fixed sign, so she doesn't like being controlled.

Helpful

They love helping others. Whenever you need advice or help, she will always be there for you. She loves caring for people and animals. She will always get involved in a cause if that can help to make the Earth and society a better place to live. She never backs down on a challenge or helping others.

Social Butterfly

An Aquarian woman loves socializing and will generally have friends from various cultures and places if her surroundings permit. She not only likes to make friends with various people, but she also tends to keep the friendships intact. She keeps her promises and is highly loyal. She is also loyal to ideas, concepts, and conditions. For instance, if she loves a restaurant or a place to eat, she will visit it frequently. In fact, she might even visit the same restaurant all the time. She is devoted and dedicated.

An Independent Lover

An Aquarian woman will be an independent lover. She loves the concept of love and may transform herself into various roles just to satisfy her significant other. She may play the sister, the mother, the provider, and even the father if the need arises.

While Aquarian women love the concept of love, they find it quite difficult to fall in love. They do not like getting attached to someone, even in love. The first few dates are used to establish trust only. Once trust is established, she may find interest in the person.

Love Hurts

Loving an Aquarius woman can be a difficult job. She is highly intelligent and independent. The partner needs to be mentally and psychologically prepared to deal with a force like her. An Aquarian woman puts a high price on communication. She is in touch with her feelings and emotions and filters them frequently to safeguard them. She is friendly, but she will never let anyone get to her with ease. As soon as an Aquarian woman falls in love with someone, she becomes the most dedicated person imaginable. It is difficult to predict her actions, which is why the other person may often feel shocked, surprised, and astonished in the relationship. For an Aquarian woman, lovemaking is cerebral, and she does not like any inhibitions; she likes to experiment a lot and will do a variety of new things in the bed.

Even in a relationship, an Aquarian woman will want and cherish her independence. She cannot tolerate a partner that does not respect her independence and self-reliance. Her ideal partner needs to be understanding, smart, and bold. They should understand the side of her that is rarely visible to anyone else.

Domesticity

An Aquarian woman is not very domestic. She needs her space and discretion in a partnership; otherwise, the relationship will die immediately. Aquarians hate tradition and an Aquarian woman will not be of the traditional type either. She will never do your laundry or cook your dinner. She is a rebel and will make her own path. The ideal partners for Aquarian women are Gemini, Libra, Sagittarius, and Aries.

Motherhood

While not all women love being a mother or want to be one, those who do can continue with this section. Aquarian mothers are full of love, but they need their own freedom. Their children often learn the importance of individuality early in their lives and know how to treat other people with respect and honor.

An Aquarian mother treats her children as equals and enjoys playing with them. She is always proud of her family and will talk about them with others quite often.

Friendly

An Aquarian woman is quite friendly and has many friends from various walks of life.

Reserved

An Aquarian woman enjoys her freedom thoroughly, which is why she may find it a bit difficult in the beginning to show her true feelings to other people. She prefers people who have the same views about freedom as her. Her group of friends generally consists of deep thinkers and intellectuals. She likes an intellectual challenge if she is comfortable with the person, otherwise, she may act reserved.

Diverse Person

They treat everyone equally, and it is no wonder that the group or social circle of an Aquarian woman will consist of people from many different walks of life. She will have all types of friends from a variety of social environments. All of them will generally have quite colorful and bold personalities. An Aquarian woman will always want a group of friends that is diverse and interesting, like her personality. For her, being multilateral is crucial. She values friendship and cherishes and celebrates her friends. She is reliable, devoted, and dedicated to her friends.

Money

They like having money, but it is just a means for achieving things, and not the goal. An Aquarian woman is not too focused on earning money; instead, she focuses more on whether she enjoys the work.

Independence and dedication allow Aquarian women to make a lot of money. She doesn't mind taking risks and is often open to a variety of new ideas. She is not mad after money, but she sure does know how to make it.

She is generous and will often donate generously to charity.

It is recommended for Aquarian women to hire accountants. Aquarians do not value money a lot and don't think of it too much. This may ruin their finances if not handled carefully.

Work

Aquarius is represented with a water bearer, i.e., the carrier of ideas; this makes the sign bold, intelligent, and creative. An Aquarian woman, too, is highly sought-after because she is imaginative and creative at her work. She knows how to make things happen and is good at being assertive and staying in control. This makes her a great boss and a brilliant leader of her people.

Colleagues and workers alike find her nice, inspiring, and dedicated. Her hard-working nature makes her a good psychologist, teacher, politician, musician, manager, social worker, etc.

Health

They are generally blessed with good health and do not indulge in exercise a lot. It is still recommended for them to follow an exercise routine to maintain their health. Aquarian women have their Achilles' heel in their heel. They should pay close attention to their ankles. She should pay attention to where she steps and should take care of her legs.

Trendsetter

They like to find and forge their own path, so you will rarely see an Aquarian woman in a regular mall buying simple clothes. She likes to buy unique pieces that look stunning and different. She doesn't like to follow trends; she would rather set her own trends. She works the clothes that she has, which is why her style is often described as interesting, courageous, and outside the box.

An Aquarian woman should wear emerald green, turquoise, and similar bright shades, as these colors are good for her. She tends to wear elegant clothes with minimal, discrete jewelry.

The Aquarius Man: Key Traits

The previous section covered details and key traits regarding Aquarian women; here is a small section covering Aquarian men's key traits.

Orders

Aquarian men hate to follow orders; don't expect them to do something just because you asked them to do it. Aquarian men are libertines, self-sufficient and highly independent. They are always looking for freedom in every situation.

Charming

Many people feel a bit overwhelmed after meeting an Aquarian for the first time. But if you give them enough time, you will be surprised by their intellect. It will charm you instantly, and you will be fascinated with his visionary, brilliant, and inventive solutions.

Unorthodox

An Aquarian man may seem slightly unorthodox initially or even later in the relationship, but this is normal. The unorthodox nature of an Aquarius man results from his unique perspective on the world. With time people learn to appreciate this uniqueness and take after him. He likes unusual things that many people are not aware of. He does not like to follow people, as he is a natural-born leader.

Innovation

An Aquarian man is blessed with extreme creativity and intellect. His ideas are often driven towards society's benefit and can bring in a change in the world if provided the proper opportunity. This superior intellect does not make him too cerebral, though, and he is more often quite down-to-earth. He will continue to be innovative and think deeply until you take away his liberty. Once you disrespect his freedom, values, and ideals, he may start to spiral downward.

Non-Conformity

An Aquarian man knows how the world works and can show you how it works if you permit him to. He will never take you to the usual places and will always try to find interesting places that sell unique things. The place will rarely have the regular and usual clientele. Aquarian men like to be non-conformists, and they will often have a curious lifestyle with a different and unusual career.

Famous Aquarius men include Thomas Edison, Bob Marley, James Dean, and Michael Jordan.

They Like Their Respect

To keep an Aquarian happy, it is necessary to respect his freedom but never overindulge it. An Aquarius man treats everything cheerfully, including love. He will generally be playful throughout the relationship and will be charming whenever necessary.

Aquarian men do not like displaying love in the usual old-fashioned ways. They may not even do the whole "I love you" routine when the time arises. This will be too conventional and normal for them. Aquarian men won't choose the usual gifts and regular dates, like flowers, chocolates, movies, etc. Expect going to old Chinese artists to get tattoos, having stars named after you, or going hiking and looking at caves.

Loyalty

An Aquarian man may be quite popular and have a lot of friends, but he is an incurable romantic under the guise of a rational person. He is an idealist, a loyal partner, and a true friend.

The large number of friends an Aquarius man has shows how popular and delightful he is. He is a diehard romantic, a rational person, a great friend, a trusted partner. He can be quite capricious, but ultimately, he is logical. His decisions may seem unusual, but they will be generally correct.

Freedom in Relationship

He prefers a relationship in which both partners respect and cherish freedom and independence. He prefers a relationship in which a partner is self-sufficient, much like him. This is often misinterpreted as a desire to have an open relationship, but this is false.

Hopeless Romantic

Aquarian men are truly passionate about their partners and will sacrifice everything, including themselves, for their loved ones. For him, great love stories such as Romeo and Juliet are fascinating. Not all Aquarian men act highly grandiose, but you will still receive unusual (often pleasant) surprises from them.

Mental Attraction and Intimacy

An Aquarian man is more interested in a person's mental and intellectual capabilities than their physical attributes. He should be able to communicate with the person and share mental intimacy. Without this, he cannot enjoy the relationship.

An Aquarius man is a true romantic who will love to show his affection from time to time.

In the Bedroom

An Aquarian man craves mental intimacy. He loves mental attraction and needs to form an intimate mental bond with the partner before anything else. He is not a laborious lover, but he will be innovative in the bedroom. He is governed by the element of Air. If you want to get to his erotic side, you will have to tap into his mental side. He loves to play mind games before anything else happens in the bedroom.

Challenges

The Aquarian man is bold and loves to try new things in and out of the bedroom. He may ask you to go with him on a marathon or jump from a plane. In the bedroom, too, he loves to try new things.

Commitment

They can be quiet, but they will always bring forth a new surprise once they trust you. It can be quite difficult to touch the core of a quiet Aquarian, but it is definitely worth the hard work. You will never regret being friends with an Aquarian.

They cherish their independence, and they will enjoy it forever. They will not commit to a person until they realize that the person is the one for them. Once he realizes that it is indeed the right person, he will commit immediately with total happiness. His partner should be understanding and intelligent.

Ideal Partner

An Aquarian wants a partner who sees life from his point of view. If he ever thinks that his independence is being threatened, he will disappear. He does not like it when things go badly, and he will show his unhappiness.

The best and most compatible signs for Aquarius are Gemini, Libra, Aries, and Sagittarius.

Visionary

An Aquarius man is intuitive and will always have solutions for problems, even if they seem unsolvable to others. An Aquarian man can be a great leader if he becomes more flexible. He is intelligent, logical, and smart, which makes careers such as a psychiatrist, engineer, financial consultant, investigator, or chemist perfect for him. He is a humanitarian at heart and desires to change the world, which means that he can be a good politician too.

Friendly

An Aquarian man has many friends and will always be interested in socializing with people. He is a social animal and quite popular with all kinds of people. While his friendliness makes him popular with a lot of people, not many of them understand him properly. He generally tends to hide his emotions and feelings and can react in a variety of ways in similar situations. He often tries to find the true feelings of his friends about him. It is recommended to indulge in this fantasy of his and see what he discovers.

Logic

An Aquarian man is driven by logic, and only logic controls his wallet. It is almost impossible to outsmart him, especially in business. He knows where and how to invest to earn the most profit. He always analyzes the risks involved in something and will invest once he understands the risks completely. He will always read the contracts before signing them.

Health

They are blessed with good health, as they are generally quite active. Excessive activity may bring problems related to the legs. An Aquarius man needs to take care of his legs.

Team Player

An Aquarius man is a team player and loves being in a team. He loves being a part of team sports and activities, as he likes to make new friends. The Aquarius man may have a lot of acquaintances, but he has only a few friends. He is a nice chap who is generally sure of himself. People may find it a bit confusing sometimes, as he tends to distance himself from others to maintain a proper relationship. He is a loyal person and appreciates and cherishes friendship.

Style

As far as style and fashion are concerned, the Aquarian man prefers clothes that portray his unique style and personality. He likes clothes that he feels look good on him and does not care about what others think. He often catches the eyes of other people with his interesting combination of clothes. If he ever wears jewelry, it is normally classy and rarely opulent.

Chapter Three: Cusps

Have you ever felt that you display the traits of two different zodiac signs? For instance, you may be born under Leo but you often show cancer traits or vice versa? You are not alone; this is a common condition known as being born on a cusp. People born on the cusp have two individual zodiac signs that work in various combinations. So, you may be born on the Leo-Cancer cusp, which means you will display related traits of both these signs.

When you are born under a particular zodiac sign, the sun is present in that constellation. The sun moves gradually between signs. If a person is born when this movement is taking place, it is said that they are born on the cusp. This allows both the neighboring zodiac signs to have an influence on the person.

The Sun's cusp period begins at 29 degrees and 30 minutes in the first sign and then goes through the next sign at 0 degrees and 30 minutes. You need to know the birth time of a person to calculate their natal chart accurately and to see whether they were born on the cusp. Due to the slight shift of astral bodies, the date varies from year to year. You can find out your natal Sun using any online sun sign calculator.

In astrology, a cusp is an imaginary line that divides two consecutive signs. The solar disc is around ½ a degree in diameter. This is convenient, as it allows the Sun to mount the cusp. The movement of the Sun allows it to be partially present on two sides simultaneously.

In simple terms, if a person is born three days before or three days after the change begins, they are born on the cusp and will display the traits of both the signs.

Cusp and Its Effects

Being born on a cusp can be quite a unique experience as it enables the person to have personality traits from both the signs, but often the energy of both the signs can compete with each other. This provides individuals with various qualities and problems. Aquarius, like all other zodiac signs, has two cusps. They are:

- Aquarius and Capricorn
- Aquarius and Pisces

Let us have a look at these two combinations.

Aquarius-Capricorn Cusp

Dates: January 16–22

The people born on a Capricorn-and-Aquarius cusp may show a lot of different sides of themselves to the public, but what matters the most is their personal and private life. Their waking dreams, inner fantasies, ideas, emotions, and feelings matter a lot to them. They are creative souls, and the workings of the inner mind matter most to them.

As their interior lives are so fascinating and rich, Capricorn-Aquarians may feel sad about or disappointed in their outside lives. They may find them constricting, dreary, dull, and lacking. They may feel a vague sense of ennui. This can lead to difficulties in their relationships. It is difficult to be with a person who loves to live in fantasy because real life can never live up to their desires.

A positive aspect of being highly imaginative is that it makes people born on this cusp quite creative. This creativity flows through them like a river.

People born on this cusp are great communicators. They love relationships based on lively intellectual discussions. This pairing of Uranus and Saturn can make for a person who is creative and emotional, but it can also lead to a desire for logic, context, and reasoning. Individuals born on this cusp are competitive and are driven by this paradox. This zeal for competitiveness combined with creativity can lead to great success if they can get past their fantasy life.

Most Capricorn-Aquarians have a lot of contradictions existing within them. They need a strong sense of security, but this desire is combined with a passion for freedom. They love learning but can feel overwhelmed by challenges. They want to change the world for the better but are often delusional regarding reality.

People born under this cusp can be quite critical, which may prove difficult for others. If you are a Capricorn-Aquarian whose critiques are usually poorly-received, try softening the blows.

Aquarius-Pisces Cusp

Dates: February 15–21

People born on this cusp are often thought to be the natural psychics of the zodiac.

They are tolerant, understanding, compassionate, and generally have extroverted personalities. They are quite sensitive. They like being around people as it can relieve stress, rejuvenate them, and offer a sense of purpose. They are often scared of being misunderstood.

People born on this cusp are goal-oriented, but they are also the biggest procrastinators. Procrastination can be built-in, which often disrupts the flow of things present in their minds. This can create a mess in their mind, but they rarely are worried about it. Their mind is as full of brilliant ideas as they are full of creative energy. This cusp is in touch with its emotional and compassionate side, which often inclines them to avoid their daily duties and chores, leading to problems later.

Neptune and Uranus rule people born on this cusp, so almost everyone loves them. They are brilliant, amazing, highly intelligent, and creative, though sometimes they feel that no one gets them. These individuals should always remember that it is not necessary for everyone to get you. The only thing that matters is that you understand them. Understanding someone can be the greatest strength a human can have.

The people born on this cusp have a brilliant mind that should be appreciated.

Capricorn-Aquarius Cusp Character Traits

The gender of the Capricorn-Aquarius cusp does not matter; they are all individuals who have been born to reform and change the world for good. They want to bring about ideal changes in the world that should have been made a long time ago. This combination of signs is quite vivid and strange, as, on the one hand, these people like to hold on to customs and traditions while on the other hand, they want to transform the world around them. The people born on this cusp tend to use their upbringing in a positive way and try to bring in changes using age-old traditions.

This cusp can be quite unpredictable because they are extremely smart and talented; in fact, their smartness can often border on insanity. They could still combine the cons with the pros and make them into "recharged pros" which can ultimately serve them better. Here is a list of positive and negative traits of this cusp.

The Positive Traits

- **Determined**: These individuals are highly determined and dedicated to goals, situations, and people.

- **Reformist:** They hate the status quo, and desire to bring changes to the world.

- **Practical:** They know how the world works, so they tend to avoid the idealistic outlook that is common with intelligent people.

- **Creative:** The elements of earth and air govern the people born on this cusp. This combination makes them quite creative and talented.

- **Visionary:** They possess an extraordinary vision and want to change the world using it. They believe that the world can be changed for the better and make it more comfortable for everyone.

- **Entertainer:** They enjoy fun and like to entertain others.

- **Disciplined:** They are highly disciplined about certain aspects of their life and tend to follow certain rules adamantly.

- **Vivid Dreamer:** Thanks to their immense creativity, they tend to look at things from a different point of view.

- **Traditional:** While they cherish a desire to change the world, they also indulge in traditions.

- **Responsible:** They are responsible and avoid pointless perceived problems.

- **Innovative:** They are innovative and can find quick solutions to difficult problems.

- **Enduring:** They have immense endurance and can work hard to achieve their dreams.

- **Multi-talented:** They are multi-talented and are interested in a wide range of topics.

- **Ambitious:** They harbor high ambitions, including how to change their environment for the better.

- **Loyal:** They are highly loyal towards their friends, family, and close ones.

Ultimately, this cusp yields a visionary, reformist, humanitarian, and philanthropist who values freedom and wants to help others achieve it. This sign is born to make a difference in society and is blessed with the qualities to do so.

This person is generally talkative and highly expressive, but he can also be reserved and shy. They have a private world full of vividness, fantasy, excitement, and eccentricity inside them. They are quite visual and love imagining things. This makes them creative and fun to be around.

They derive their inspiration less from reality than from the vivid dreams they tend to have often. This fuels their creativity and individual instinct that they convert into a medium of expression and communication. It also serves as a link between dreams and reality for them.

A lot of zodiac signs may tire of certain projects and let them go, but people born on this cusp like to fulfill every task they undertake. They possess an added supply of drive and motivation, which forces them to continue until they achieve their goal.

Perseverance is the biggest motivator for people born on this cusp. It allows them to gain power and authority. Being a fixed sign, it compels them to stay on the path towards the goal, even if the ultimate goal has no profit or gains. The Capricorn side of this cusp may ask to leave the project, but the Aquarius side will force the other half to continue for the sake of imagination and vision associated with the project.

Another trait, which is a blessing in disguise, is that the person born on this cusp has the qualities, abilities, and passion for transforming their dreams into reality. This cusp is an interesting combination of various traits including experimental, dreamer, realistic, and practical. They do not like following a well-trodden path; they would rather discover their own paths. They have curious minds and love to experiment with new ideas until they come up with something exceptionally rewarding and unique.

People born on this cusp are multi-talented. They can be a great scientist or a brilliant artist. This is why this cusp is also known as the Cusp of Genius. Their open-mindedness, combined with their radical viewpoint and creativity, makes them successful in most careers and fields.

Saturn rules both the signs present in this cusp. That planet is associated with hard work, and it is no wonder that the people born on the cusp of both these signs are dedicated and work hard.

People born on this cusp have the right amount of practicality, confidence, and caution. They have the desire to change the world, but they want to do so in a balanced and realistic way.

They are brilliant friends that never let their loved ones down. Their friends will never have a dull movement when they are around.

The Negative Traits

Here is a list of negative traits this cusp has.

- **Overcritical:** They can be overly critical of people and situations; that may alienate their friends.

- **Bossy:** They are smart, creative, and talented. These traits can often bring on judgment and bossiness.

- **Aloof:** They like solitude, which is often confused with being aloof.

- **Stubborn:** They can be quite stubborn, especially when asked to change their beliefs.

- **Secretive:** Their solitude can also make them seem secretive.

- **Harsh:** They do not mince their words, and let people know how things really are.

- **Narrow-Minded:** They do not like changing their ideas. Their love for tradition can make them a bit prudish and conservative.

- **Offbeat:** Some people may consider their uniqueness unappealing.

- **Rebellious:** They like to go against typical ideas and things.

- **Cold:** They are friendly, but they can also act cold at times, which often confuses their friends.

- **Unpredictable:** You can never predict what this person will say or do.

These individuals are determined and disciplined, which can make them quite bossy and critical towards people who are not disciplined. This demanding and overly critical attitude makes things difficult for them occasionally.

These individuals do not like being criticized. They cannot understand it when a person cannot see their point of view or share their vision. Their vision is perfect for them, and if people do not share it, they feel frustrated.

This cusp can be eccentric yet open-minded, but when their personal ideologies or beliefs are questioned, they can become narrow-minded quickly.

These individuals prefer high standards in almost everything in their life. They prefer to maintain higher standards in almost every aspect of their being. This is why they tend to be judgmental about people who do not live up to their standards and expectations.

This judgmental and overly critical nature makes it difficult to enjoy any relationship, as they always compare it with other situations.

Their offbeat and stubborn nature can be seen as rebellious, which may not sit well with a lot of people around them. They are extremely dedicated to their dreams and work towards them with a passion that makes them forget everything else. They are stubborn and do not know when and how to give up. They will leave no stone unturned to achieve something, even if it hurts them immensely.

They fear being misunderstood or not being understood at all. If they see this fear becoming a reality, they tend to enter a world of their own fantasy and diminish the reality. This is why they may often wander off into their inner world, which may make them seem harsh, cold, aloof, and secretive.

They are often said to be the life and soul of the party and enjoy social interactions a lot. But they only form good connections with people with the same intelligence quotient. This is why these individuals often find it impossible to keep personal relationships.

It is necessary for people belonging to this cusp to find a point of balance between reality and their dreams. If they do not seek this balance soon, they may become detached and depressed. This may seem quite a challenge initially, but with dedication, it can be done.

People born on this cusp are immensely interesting and fun to have around. They bring a sense of freshness wherever they go. They hate the monotony and mechanical nature of daily life and try to make it exciting and happy. They are friendly and social, but they also possess a sense of mystery around them. This is why this cusp is also known as the Cusp of Imagination and Mystery.

Aquarius-Pisces Personality Traits

People born on the Aquarius-Pisces cusp tend to be highly sensitive. They are more into their universal and personal space than world problems and concerns.

They prefer spending time with themselves to understand themselves better. It can be difficult for them to manage their day-to-day life, as it is quite a challenge to focus on mundane things for them.

These people desire experiences, but they fail to remain objective for a long time or find it difficult to do so. They are sensitive and finding a balance can be quite a task for them. For the best results, they need to learn how to put themselves out in the world and not hide in a shell. They need to learn how to feel comfortable and at ease with the world.

People born on the Aquarius-Pisces cusp are imaginative, compassionate, and sympathetic about others. They are disorganized and tend to procrastinate a lot. They may set goals frequently, but these two tendencies often result in them creating their own obstacles.

They are offbeat and eccentric, and they are unique and original. They want to change the world and are well suited to do so, as they are multi-talented. The only problem standing between them and a better world is their shy nature.

Sometimes these people are blessed with immense and incredible musical capabilities.

While they are often shy, they still love to socialize. They like to help others as the act relieves their anxiety and stress.

They are romantic and flirtatious and have genuine affection towards people. Their compassion encompasses everything. They look at the world from a unique viewpoint that others often fail to see.

People born under this sign are considered natural psychics. If they do not concentrate on these abilities right from their childhood, they may hide it and shut it down forever.

They avoid opening up to people, especially when they realize that others do not share their viewpoint and vision. They hate being ridiculed and cannot tolerate it.

This cusp is also known as the Cusp of Sensitivity. It is characterized by:

- **Sensitivity:** Those born under this cusp are quite sensitive to the emotional cues of others. They can understand what others seldom fail to realize. This sensitivity comes from their ability to see beyond the facades most of us put up.

- **Uniqueness:** The perfect amalgamation of air and water leads to a unique personality. Their ability to think and experience life is unique.

- **Tolerance:** The tolerance of this cusp is unlike any other. They are open-minded and welcome change with open arms. There is nothing even remotely narrow-minded about their thinking. This tolerance is often visible in all aspects of their lives.

- **Talent:** The Aquarius-Pisces cusps are extraordinarily creative and talented. Their tendency to let their imagination run wild is perhaps a leading reason for this.

- **Emotions:** Since this cusp is known for its sensitivity, they feel all emotions quite strongly. When surrounded by loved ones or in a happy environment, the positive vibes these individuals experience is magnified.

- **Artistic Merit:** One of the favorite artistic expressions of imagination this cusp is known for is painting or drawing. Most individuals born under this cusp have a natural inclination toward arts.

- **Dreaming:** This cusp is that of dreamers and inventors. They dream big dreams and aren't scared to chase those dreams.

- **Idealism:** This cusp is idealistic. They are strong proponents of the idea of "what should be" in all aspects of life.

- **Sensuality:** The combination of Aquarius and Pisces results in a cusp that's quite sensual. They are not only in touch with their inherent sensuality, but they aren't scared to display it.

- **Pride:** This cusp takes immense pride in their work and all other attributes of their life. Their pride doesn't translate into arrogance but shines through in everything they say and do.

- **Flirtatiousness:** The playful nature of Aquarius makes them good at flirting. The mischievous sparkle in their eyes while flirting is clear to anyone who pays attention. This desire to flirt, coupled with their sensuality, makes them skilled at flirting.

- **Loyalty:** Aquarians and Pisceans are both known for their loyalty. Unsurprisingly, the cusp of these zodiacs results in fierce loyalty. Once you have earned the trust of this cusp, they will stand by your side until you do something to break their trust.

- **Compassion:** This zodiac sign is sensitive to the emotions and feelings of those around them. So, they are naturally compassionate. They often try to do their bit to alleviate suffering and misery.

- **Practicality:** They are not just dreamers; their imagination, when tempered with a little pessimism, makes them practical.

The Negative Traits

Hypersensitivity: A similarity all those born under this cusp share is sensitivity. Even the slightest criticism is taken personally and magnified. Every comment becomes a barbed personal attack. This is one reason why this cusp is known to be quarrelsome.

- **Pessimism:** Thinking about the worst outcome in every situation might be termed as realism, but it is nothing more than pessimism. These individuals always have a "glass-half-empty" perspective toward life.

- **Secretiveness:** Playing your cards close to the chest seems to be the mantra for this cusp. They are incredibly personal and don't open up easily to others. What might seem like secretiveness to the untrained eye is merely their desire to keep things private.

- **Moodiness:** The cusp of the air and the water sign is known to be quite moody. One moment they can seem cheerful, open, and breezy, and the next, it looks like they are on another planet altogether.

- **Impatience:** This cusp is impatient. They want and expect quick results in all aspects of life.

- **Aloofness:** Aquarians are known for their aloofness. When this airy sign combines with the philosophical Piscean, the aloofness quotient increases, so don't be surprised if those born under this cusp seem too aloof.

- **Stubbornness:** It's difficult to imagine someone who shares water and air elements to be stubborn. These two elements are known to be free-flowing in nature, but the individuals with these signs have strong likes and dislike. They might not have many, but they will always stand by the ones they do have.

- **Escapism:** The active imagination of Aquarius, coupled with the dreamy side of Pisces, can result in escapism. These individuals are prone to escaping into their fantasy world or imagination instead of facing life's realities.

- **Quarrelsomeness:** Remember, the stubbornness that was mentioned? Well, the stubbornness essentially translates into strong opinions and ideas. If anyone disagrees with their ideas and opinions, be prepared for an argument. The sign is incredibly passionate about its views and will defend them vehemently.

- **Cold Personality:** The combination of air and water elements makes this zodiac cusp seem cold and distant. All this is usually the culmination of their inclination to escape the world's reality and their aloofness.

Peculiar Traits

This cusp can be quite peculiar. They love luxury, which is why they may stay in the real world just enough to enjoy this. They are very kind, and that often leads to problems as they strive hard to accommodate everyone. They do not like letting people down and tend to make many appointments simultaneously and ultimately fail to keep them all.

- They do not like talking about their failures but can exaggerate their successes and achievements.

- They love freedom and liberty. Their dreaminess, combined with their love of freedom, often drives them on the path of insight and spirituality.

- They are creatively gifted and can make stunning art.

- People love them and feel attracted to them.

If the situation is right, they may indulge in religion, science, and traveling.

Strengths

- This combination allows them to have a lot of compassion and a strikingly visionary nature.

- They can convince people to look at the world from a different point of view.

- They are not above breaking rules and can work around things just fine. This makes them the most understanding of people.

People born on this cusp tend to indulge in philosophical and spiritual matters more than real-life issues and chores. They would rather deal with their fantasies instead of keeping up daily real-world commitments; this is why they forget appointments, lose things, or show up late. They often stand people up because they cannot be bothered with real life trials and tribulations. The best advice to these individuals would be to focus on the real world more often.

Chapter Four: The Aquarius Child

Your zodiac affects you throughout your life, including your childhood. If you are an Aquarian who wants to relive their childhood and teenage years and analyze why you behaved in certain ways in particular situations, this chapter is for you. This chapter is also meant for parents or guardians of Aquarian kids and has many tips that can help you deal with them efficiently.

Like adults, Aquarian kids, too, are broad-minded and curious. They are free-spirited and are bound to create trouble for their parents.

A child born under this sign is like a loaded package. They are full of imagination, stamina, spontaneity, and stubbornness. They are sensitive and will get emotionally hurt easily. Their traits are extreme and keep on frequently changing, which is why it becomes difficult to label these kids.

Some key traits that most Aquarian kids share include:

• They are brilliant at coming up with original and unique ideas.

• They can be challenging to deal with, as they are irritable and sensitive.

• They have a lot of energy and stamina.

• They have a lot of friends and are generally sociable.

• Their future is generally bright.

An Aquarian kid can have a bright future if they are allowed to use and hone their natural talents carefully. It depends on how the parents raise these kids, as this forms the foundation of a person's character. Aquarius kids hate following orders, and you will be forced to struggle with their stubbornness in such situations. You will not be able to do anything and will get nowhere with them.

Like their adult counterparts, Aquarian kids are unique and follow their own rules and decisions. They have unpredictable personalities and tend to have a lot of mood swings. This can be quite a difficult situation for their parents. The best way to deal with an Aquarius child is by allowing them their space and time. Do not try to teach or order them in a pedantic or didactic manner. This will only increase your difficulties after you explain your point. The only way these kids will learn is with patience and freedom. Aquarius is a sign of "poles" i.e., it is composed of opposing extremes. You need to be patient if you want to get through to them.

Mood swings for adult Aquarians are commonplace, but they are even more severe in kids and teenagers due to their ever-changing bodies and brains. They can be quiet and peaceful at one moment, and the next moment, they may go berserk. They are generally intelligent kids, and sometimes they can be gifted. They have above-average comprehension skills and are full of rationality.

They are visionaries and idealists and try to set up and reach fantastic goals. They are friendly and full of empathy and compassion. This is why Aquarian kids are often the most popular kid in a social group.

They are unique and desire originality, which makes them stay away from commonplace objectives and the norm. Their personalities and goals will always be unique compared to other people. This desire for uniqueness is reflected in adulthood, too, and may play an important role in their careers.

Aquarian kids are practical, but they never forget their dreams. They might choose to be practical for a while, but they will surely circle back to their dream and try to fulfill it.

Kids love to daydream, and Aquarian kids are no different. In fact, Aquarian kids daydream more than other kids. This can prove to be problematic, especially at school. Parents of Aquarian kids often have to deal with complaints regarding lack of attention, but these complaints prove futile in view of their good grades and performance.

Aquarius is blessed with the power of intuition. Aquarian kids display a knack for clairvoyance or similar powers. They often reach a problem's solution or conclusion even before the problem is put in front of them.

Their thinking process is interesting and unique, but it can prove hectic for them if they overdo it. It may even turn out to be unhealthy and problematic.

Parents of an Aquarian kid need to help them learn how to organize their minds if they want them to develop into healthy adults. Parents need to let the genius of these kids shine among their peers. They should also focus on their physical side as the kids may avoid it altogether. Many Aquarian kids may just shy away from physical activity. Avoid allowing this.

Aquarian kids are in touch with their surroundings and are attuned to the nature around them.

Aquarian kids are sensitive, emotionally, and intellectually. They get affected by external factors with ease and are sensitive to negative criticism and comments. Negative criticism from anyone can affect their inner equilibrium severely.

Parents should be careful talking around Aquarius kids, especially when trying to help them. Do not let them feel obligated in any way, especially when you offer them any advice, as they will feel patronized. Forcing Aquarian kids to do something may lead to various long-term negative effects on these kids.

These kids are socially efficient and active, but they have difficulties in their love life and relationships. They overcome these difficulties with time; just provide them ample help and enough space and freedom to do so.

They sometimes have unrealistic visions and goals for the future. If you are worried about your kid having an impossible goal, stop worrying, as he may achieve the goal one day because of his dedication and passion.

Aquarian Baby

Parents might be surprised to see their Aquarian baby's intellect. Aquarians begin to show signs of high intelligence early in their life, which can seem quite remarkable to the people around them. Unfortunately, this high intellect is often accompanied by short temper and mood swings.

They are prone to tantrums and can easily go from zero to a hundred in a matter of seconds. Such impulsive behavior can be difficult to deal with, especially for new and first-time parents, but rest assured, the impulsiveness wanes considerably with time.

They are intelligent and keen, which will make their parents feel awesome, but it will also make other adults around them flabbergasted. Aquarian kids learn quickly and will generally succeed in most subjects. They are insightful, smart, and highly adaptable, which often surprises other people. These traits make Aquarian kids special.

An Aquarius kid's best friend and supporter is their mother. A mother can generally adapt and get on with a challenging kid. She can tolerate her child's ever-changing intellect and can teach them in many unusual ways.

It is necessary to challenge and engage an Aquarian boy constantly if you want them to reach their full potential.

The Girl

An Aquarian girl will generally be extremely interested in socializing. She is the center of gravity in all social interactions. She will be surrounded by new and old friends all the time, and they will keep on coming.

She will have many different friends over the years, but not all of them will stay with her forever. They will come and go frequently. As a parent, you need to keep a close eye on this and check the people she engages with.

Aquarian girls tend to have a daily schedule that they maintain religiously, thanks to their dedicated nature. Having a daily schedule allows her to keep a sense of stability and control, which she enjoys significantly.

She is a curious person, and her curiosity is her most dominant trait. This trait continues to be with her in her maturity too. Do pay attention to this trait, as she might explore unsuitable things at an early age.

Aquarians are born to be wild and free, and an Aquarian girl is no different. She loves adventure, and she will surely get into something that will broaden her horizons in the fields she likes. If she likes something, she will try to grow in the field.

Never take away her freedom from her, as it would be the worst punishment.

The Boy

An Aquarian boy will generally be full of energy, stamina, and a spirit of immense adventure. He will generally be hyperactive, and this will help him achieve his goals and fulfill his dreams.

Hyperactivity can also lead to chaos, which may make him a hectic and "crazy" individual. It is necessary to quell the fire inside him. He needs to learn how to control it early on. You can do this by allowing him to develop a daily schedule, which will give him a semblance of order and help him learn perseverance and patience.

Aquarians are unpredictable, and Aquarian boys are no different. They are unpredictable; they also have a lot of energy, making things difficult for their parents. Their intellect develops at a rapid pace, which is directly proportional to their curiosity about everything.

They are adventurous and may embark on surprise adventures occasionally. They will most likely not tell anyone, including their parents, about it. As a parent, it is necessary to keep a close eye on your Aquarian son lest he hurts himself.

Their personality might seem unique, strange, and downright alien to the outside world. Most of the time, they act even before they think as their mind keeps on changing continuously. This also reflects their adventurous nature.

Their adventurous nature will often lead to wanton behavior. They will break curfews multiple times. As parents, such behavior may bother you a lot, but avoid getting upset. They don't do it deliberately; they just forget to keep track of time when they are enjoying themselves.

Differences Between Aquarius Girls and Boys

There are many similarities between Aquarius boys and girls, but there are some key differences that parents should remember. Aquarius boys are smart, but they are also fickle and tend to get distracted easily. You need to help him in a non-didactic way to learn how to focus on his goals. This will keep him occupied and dedicated. Often, many Aquarius boys display symptoms of ADD or ADHD.

Aquarius girls love socializing and will focus a lot on social life. Dating and relationships can be difficult for an Aquarian girl as she can either fall heads over heels for someone or be totally distant.

Children in General

Aquarian children are highly gifted as far as team play is concerned. They are heavily into competitions and are often fierce competitors in sports that require teamwork.

They are bound to grow and flourish in most activities. They enjoy adventure and thrills of life thoroughly. They are often interested in fantasy and the supernatural, especially in animated shows, books, and movies.

They will love it if you teach them basic science tricks or magic illusions. They tend to pick things up almost instantaneously and will surprise everyone around them with their dedication and talent.

Their passion is off the charts, and they tend to forget everything while doing things that they love. They often get injured or incur bruises which they fail to notice, so keep a close eye on them.

Things That You Need To Know About an Aquarian Child

If babies could talk, the Aquarian baby would have been the philosopher/deep thinker of the lot. Aquarians are deep thinkers who can spend hours just thinking, and often overthinking things. It is an expression of their creativity. Once they do pick up some words, they will babble continuously about everything they find curious. This is just one of the many traits that Aquarian kids possess. Here is a small list of various traits you can find in Aquarius children.

They Are Quick Learners

Aquarian kids are naturally inquisitive. Their curiosity develops early on, and they are ready to learn new things. They inquire about anything and everything they do not understand and try to get to the core of everything they find in front of them. They disassemble things to learn how they function. If you ever see your kids breaking or dismantling their toys, don't worry; they are just fulfilling their natural instinct. Remember that great scientists like Thomas Edison and Galileo were Aquarians too.

They Are Empathetic

Empathy flows naturally in the veins of Aquarian children. While they are adventurous and energetic, you will never have to spend hours explaining a situation to your Aquarian kid. They are blessed with good listening skills and understand other people's feelings better than everyone else. They are brave enough to display their emotions and empathy. If you are scared or sad, your Aquarian kid will understand it immediately and try to help you get over it. They will always somehow understand what others are feeling.

They Are Fearless

Aquarian babies are adventurous and fearless. They are quick learners, but they also get bored easily and quickly. They generally look for exciting and new things constantly. They are not scared of trying new things; they seek novelty. They are open to new horizons and love to explore the unknown. This is how they make their life more interesting and enjoyable.

They Have Emotional Outbursts (Short-Lived)

Aquarians are born empathetic, but this empathy also makes them quite emotional. When they come face to face with challenges, they tend to lose their balance. Once they lose this balance, they may have significant emotional outbursts. These emotional outbursts can be scary, but they are almost always short-lived. Your kid will come back to their normal self in little to no time. This shift might surprise new parents as they will not understand the ultimate reason behind the outburst, but in most cases, your kid will let you know the reason on his own after some time.

People's Person

Aquarians love communicating and socializing with others, and Aquarian babies are no different. They are great at forming connections; that is why they tend to become friends with people quickly. They are always there to help a friend or a family member. They are friendly towards strangers too. An Aquarian kid will be exceptionally outgoing right from the start. Don't be shocked if they start smiling or talking to people right from a young age.

Aquarius Babies Are Full of Surprises

Parents of Aquarius babies are often surprised by seeing the traits of their babies. They are empathetic, social, fearless, and full of adventurous spirit. They often react in an unexpected manner and generally have wacky and bizarre answers for problems and their actions. Some people call them absent-minded while others call them dynamic, but ultimately, their brain works in a way that no one else can understand.

They Are Highly Energetic

The energy of an Aquarius kid knows no bounds. They are never tired of contemplating or thinking over a problem. Similarly, they do not tire of listening to their friends constantly blabbering about random stuff. Even after doing this, they will still have enough energy to play a sport or finish their homework. They are quick, and most people lag behind while they scoot ahead.

They Are Stubborn

Aquarius kids can be quite stubborn, which can cause a lot of problems for their parents. They don't let anything or anyone affect them, as they look at the world from a positive viewpoint. They are adventurous and free-spirited, which means they would rather do things of their own accord. They do not like being controlled and like being free all the time. If you want your Aquarius kid to do something, try to inculcate a sense of responsibility in them without being too pedantic or didactic. This will help them learn what is good for them. Never order or force an Aquarius kid to do something; they will not do it, and even if they do it, they will feel alienated and will begin to despise you.

They Are Strong-Willed Too

Aquarius kids are stubborn, and their stubbornness makes them highly strong-minded and strong-willed. They will focus on a goal with full dedication until they achieve it. This is one of the most important traits of an Aquarius baby as it generally drives them. They will not hesitate to give their best and put in every effort to achieve what they want.

They Know Their Likes and Dislikes

Aquarius babies know what they like and what they do not like. They not only know about their likes, but they are also serious about them. Aquarians are generally quite individualistic, and this trait is also present in the kids. It is almost impossible to persuade them differently once they make up their mind.

Interests and Hobbies

Aquarius kids are interested in almost anything that they can get their hands on. Their hobbies are varied and highly distinct, often borderline unique. They love all games and hobbies that allow them to play with other people and interact with them. They also enjoy activities that help them channel their creativity and learn new things. They develop an interest in new things almost instantaneously because they understand that the activity has some potential for entertainment.

One thing that binds all Aquarian children is "fun"; if an activity entertains them, they will love it, and if the activity bores them, they will get rid of it. This is why they have so many different hobbies and interests. Aquarius babies and kids get bored of things easily and move on to new ones quickly.

Making Friends

For Aquarian kids, making friends is not a big deal, as they tend to have good social and communication skills. They are highly sociable, and they like all kinds of friends. They will become friends with almost anyone, anywhere.

They are rarely worried about friends that are not like them, or about friends who do not meet them often; they will still try to be friends with them. Many Aquarians have made life-long friends in schools, but this does not mean they do not enjoy short-term friends as well.

At School

Aquarius is a sign blessed with immense intellect and smartness. Aquarius kids, too, are quite intelligent but what holds them back is their desire for freedom, and sometimes laziness.

Aquarius is a hardworking sign, especially if the person likes what they are doing. Aquarian kids do a lot of hard work, but most of the time they do not like to put effort into things that bore them, including homework. They will excel and achieve the highest grades in subjects that they find interesting, but they may even fail the classes they do not like or find boring. Often this may confuse the parents and frustrate them. A lot of times, due to ignorance, Aquarian kids are labeled as being apathetic or even dumb, but this not the case. These kids understand the subject matter of the classes they fail but they just don't want to put effort into studying for the tests or do the homework on the subject.

Independence

Aquarius kids are extremely independent. As soon as they learn to walk, they start getting away from their parents and everyone else to enjoy their freedom. They always want to do something on their own or with their good friends and close social circle. They love their parents, but they would rather enjoy things on their own. They do not like being dependent on their parents.

The older they get, the less they will depend on their parents. They would rather join clubs, school organizations, etc., and get on with their friends. They learn driving early on so they can move around on their own. They love leading their own lives and do not like others interfering in it.

What to Expect When Raising an Aquarian Child

Expect the Unexpected With an Aquarius

Always expect the unexpected while raising an Aquarian child. Your child will always keep you on your toes. They are full of intelligence, emotions, and energy, and love to be on the go all the time. They like meeting new people, visiting new places, trying new things, etc. They will mostly be busy and highly active all the time. They are fearless and adventurous. Always be ready for something new and exciting while raising an Aquarian kid.

They're a Little Absent-Minded

These kids can be quite absent-minded. Many parents often complain that their Aquarian kid does not hear them. They feel that the kids do this on purpose, but this is untrue. The kids may hear their parents but simply forget it, thanks to their absent-mindedness. Their brain moves at such a pace that they forget things frequently.

You may feel ignored while dealing with an Aquarius, but most of the time, their absent-mindedness is not deliberate. It is just too difficult for the kid to keep track of their thoughts all the time.

Aquarians Are Focused

Aquarian kids are dedicated, focused, and often stubborn. They do not give up until they can maneuver according to their desire. This stubbornness may often work against them; as a parent, try to control it subtly. Sometimes, let them be stubborn, as the experience will help them learn a lesson on their own, which will stay with them forever.

Roller Coaster Emotions

Aquarius is a sign full of contradictions, and Aquarius kids are no different. One moment they may be happy, laid-back, and carefree, but the next moment they may go berserk and spiral down hard. This is normal, as a lot of things can trigger their emotions. Everyone hates being exposed to the unexpected, but Aquarians tend to take things to the next level. They have extreme reactions. Most of these emotions disappear quickly.

Aquarians Are Empathetic

If you ever feel out of your element or feel depressed and are in need of kind words or a hug, your Aquarian kid will always be there for you. They will always be the first to understand what you are going through and to try to help you. They possess the almost uncanny ability to guess how others feel without needing to be explicitly told. This is why parents of Aquarian kids are advised to control their disciplinary methods, as your kids already probably know how upset or angry you are. Use gentle words to make them understand that their choices were troublesome and that they should learn how to make them better in the future.

Aquarius Love People

Aquarian kids are highly social because they are warm, charming, friendly, and engaging. They love all forms of positive attention and like to know the people around them. You can see how social your child will be right from an early age. Babies begin to smile at random people all the time from a young age.

Quick Learners

Aquarian kids are smart and quick, which can be a blessing and a curse for the parents. The kids can figure out a lot of things early on. They are not only book-smart, but most are also socially smart. They are generally the teachers' pets (if they find the subject interesting). Your Aquarian kid needs to feel challenged all the time; otherwise, they may grow lazy and stop caring.

Idiosyncratic

No one can figure out an Aquarian, not even their own parents. They will always march to the beat of their own drums and will always do the things they believe are the best. It can be difficult to understand the motive behind whatever they do, so it is necessary to keep communication open all the time. They will always be full of surprises and sometimes shocks. Always expect an enjoyable, wild, and rewarding ride while raising an Aquarius child.

Tips and Tricks

Toys for Aquarian Kids

While Aquarian kids will love to play with almost anything that they get their hands on, there are certain toys that they will enjoy much more than other objects. These include fairy wings, musical instruments, costumes, boxes, etc.

All these toys can help your Aquarian child to think and imagine new and exciting ideas. Aquarians love to make their own games, and these items will serve as props for their games.

Activities for Aquarian Kids

Aquarian kids are full of intelligence, imagination, and passion. They enjoy a variety of activities that tap into their creativity and thinking. Such activities include creating art and reading books. Aquarius kids all love to socialize and play with their friends on the playgrounds.

Aquarius kids love socializing, but they also enjoy the peace of solitude. This is why parents should try to provide the kids with ample time to recharge themselves. This includes solo time, playing by themselves, and allowing their imagination to take over the world when the adults are out of earshot. These activities will help the Aquarius kid grow and develop. Here are some activities that will help your Aquarian child enjoy their lives and grow.

Reading

Aquarius kids are artistic, intelligent, and imaginative, so not surprisingly, they are often fascinated with stories and tales. They generally enjoy stories with children from various parts of the world, fables, and fantasies. Aquarians like to identify the differences and similarities between their experiences and the experiences of other people. They like to imagine living in different countries and worlds and think about experiences that differ from their own. Some books that they will absolutely love include:

- Alice in Wonderland by Lewis Carol
- Dreamers by Yuvi Morales

All About the Aquarius Teenager

Aquarius teens, like Aquarian kids and adults, are unique, independent, and remarkable. They are also full of hormones and thus may drive the parents crazy in a new way every day. They don't mean to annoy parents deliberately, but they often get annoyed at people who don't tend to live up to their fullest potential. They can often misinterpret situations, sometimes without understanding the nuances thoroughly. For instance, if you come back from the office after a fairly busy day and complain about your office, they may think that you are not comfortable at the job and are selling out. They may not even look at all the positive reasons why you are doing the job, which obviously includes a paycheck.

Aquarius individuals are smart, but they tend to look at the world from a black-and-white perspective when they are teenagers. It is necessary to remind them occasionally that the world is not black and white; rather, most of it is gray. Aquarians are well known for their idealism, so don't shrug it away completely; instead, try to present the opportunities that can help them change themselves and the world around them. Allow them ample opportunities where they can volunteer to make a difference in the world. They will enjoy bringing about a change in the world.

Aquarian kids and teens have a strong sense of social justice, and they believe that the world can be changed for good. They do not like being talked down to. If you show you respect for them, they will respect you back.

Aquarius teens tend to have a lot of friends, just like their adult counterparts. They are smart and unique, but they need to have some structures and rules. Don't make the rules and lay them on them; aquarian teens will never follow rules that are forced on them. This will only lead to frustration for all those involved and may deteriorate the relationship between you. Instead, allow them to collaborate on making rules and setting up guidelines. These guidelines and rules should make sense to them, and they should feel they have put a lot of input into them. They are more likely to follow such rules without feeling angry or frustrated. Remember, Aquarians are autonomous and unique beings; the more you respect their autonomy, the more they will respect you.

Aquarius Teen's Likes

Aquarius teens are often polymaths, and they love a variety of things and fields. Some of the most highly-appreciated fields include:

Learning

An Aquarian teen will always enjoy learning new things and experiences; however, they may not feel comfortable with the school's rigidness. They like to learn on their own time and accord. They like reading books, enjoy making connections, and are passionate about figuring out new things and discovering new ideas.

Music

Every teenager loves music, but Aquarius teens love it with heartfelt passion. For them, music is life. They believe that songs and musical pieces can represent them in a much better way and can portray how they feel accurately.

Independence and Autonomy

For an Aquarius teen, their autonomy and independence are the most crucial objects. When they begin to learn that they are different from their parents and can make different life choices and enjoy different things, it provides them an almost surreal experience. Allow the teens to experiment as much as they want; encourage that behavior. Allow them to grow and let them find their own path with full passion.

An Aquarius Teen's Dislikes

Rules and Lack of Independence

An Aquarian teen abhors lack of independence. They will despise you if you use phrases such as "Because this is my house" or "Because I said so." They will never follow a rule that is forced on them. If you want them to follow the rules, allow them to collaborate on the process.

Cliques

Aquarians love to make a lot of friends, but they are ultimately lone wolves. They do not like being associated with a specific group and like to enjoy their freedom and independence. Instead of aligning with any one group, they prefer to float between different people and cliques. This makes them popular with almost everyone.

Privacy

Aquarian teens tend to be messy (all teenagers do) but never trespass on an Aquarian's privacy, or they will hate you forever. Entering the private space of an Aquarian is an invasion of their privacy. They will find it frustrating and annoying. Always seek their permission if you want to enter their private life or space. Respect their boundaries.

Chapter Five: Aquarius and Friendship

Aquarians are extroverts and are ready to make friends. They love adventure and always want to try something new with their friends. An Aquarian's social circle is filled with people who love their loyalty and charm. Most people are drawn to them since they exude a feeling of compatibility. Sometimes, people may wonder if an Aquarian is interested in them or cares for them, since Aquarians can seem disinterested and detached.

Aquarians As Friends

The Aquarius zodiac sign is the eleventh zodiac sign, and it is a sign found in the natural zone of social activity and friendship. It is easy for Aquarians to make new friends, and they are ideal friends. They are good at conversing with anybody around them, but they have only a few friends close to their hearts. Aquarians are amazing people, but they have many positive characteristics that people want to have in their companions or friends.

Aquarians are Loyal

If you have an Aquarian as a friend, you already know how lucky you are because they are the most loyal friends. An Aquarian is very supportive, and he ensures that you push yourself to meet your goals. If an Aquarian knows how passionate you are about achieving your goals, then he will do everything in his power to help you achieve them. They are never jealous of the people around them. Aquarians are good at cheering people up if they are having a bad day.

Love to Make Conversation

An Aquarian is great at conversing with people around them. If you meet an Aquarian at a party, you may talk to them for hours, and you may never know what got you started. Aquarians have the most interesting things to say to the people around them. They also ask the right questions because they want to learn more about people. Some may find Aquarians overbearing, and some Aquarians do not listen or cheer you up. There are others who may not want to help the people around them. Aquarians may want to take matters into their own hands whether or not someone asked them for help. What they fail to understand is that not everybody may want this help.

Love Fun

Since Aquarians love adventure, they are often unpredictable. You may think you know what an Aquarian wants or loves, but then they may say or do something that shocks you. They may seem a little crazy because of their spontaneity, and they love doing anything thrilling, adventurous, and interesting.

Idealists and Rebels

Aquarians are not traditionalists, and they hate following conventions. They accept no situation or explanation blindly. They always look for loopholes in the system and are not pushy people, unlike Aries and Leos. Their mantra is to live and let live. Aquarians are exceptionally kind, and this characteristic attracts people to them. They have humanitarian beliefs, and they are concerned about people's welfare. They rarely get too involved in relationships since they do not want to lose their freedom or independence.

Unconventional

Aquarians are unconventional and free spirits. Their habits and attitudes make them the most eccentric people. They are known for thinking outside the box and constantly looking for something new to do in life. They hate being bored. The combination of their kindness, love, and original thoughts makes them the best leaders. Their free spirit is as contagious as their positivity. If you hate your routine and want to spice up your life, you need to find an Aquarian friend.

Aquarius and Friendship

Aquarius and Aries

An Aquarian can communicate with an Aries easily. Aries are impulsive individuals, and this works in an Aquarian's favor since the latter loves adventure. An Aquarian and Aries can embark on long adventures together, especially those that involve dangerous activities such as bungee jumping, cliff diving, parasailing, and more. An Aquarian may tire of an Aries because the latter put themselves above everybody else. When they spend time away from each other, they understand how much they need each other.

Aquarius and Taurus

An Aquarian is in awe of a Taurean because the latter is loyal above everything else. Taureans are as true as they can be. An Aquarian and Taurean are both devoted to their friends and loved ones, and they will do their best to maintain a relationship. An Aquarian and Taurean will stick together through thick and thin. While Aquarians love crowds and noise, a Taurean is materialistic. They have a lot of fun when they spend time together, especially when they are the only two. The two may enjoy activities such as hiking and rowing.

Aquarius and Gemini

A Gemini and Aquarian bond well because Geminis are satisfying, encouraging, and stimulating friends. These qualities make it easy for an Aquarian to motivate a Gemini to try different activities. Since the two are always curious and energetic, they will try anything new. Geminis have a huge friend circle but are only close to some people, and an Aquarian is one. This is only because an Aquarian can fuel a Gemini's enthusiasm to try something new. Since an Aquarian expects people to arrive on time, a Gemini may need to work on this to maintain his friendship.

Aquarius and Cancer

An Aquarian may have difficulty in understanding his Cancer friend. An Aquarian enjoys challenges, so he may try his best to maintain his friendship with a Cancer. Since both Aquarians and Cancers have different wants and needs, it is hard for the two to maintain a relationship. Cancers love attention, but Aquarians want to be intellectually stimulated. Since Cancers have a sense of humor, they can sway an Aquarian's affections towards them. If Cancers can control their need to be loved, they can have a stable relationship with Aquarians; otherwise, the relationship will cease to exist soon.

Aquarian and Leo

It is difficult for people to not like Leos, but an Aquarian is the complete opposite of a Leo. Since Aquarians prefer to rest and relax, they rarely see eye to eye with a Leo, with a larger-than-life attitude. However, an Aquarian in the presence of a Leo is more enthusiastic than ever. Aquarians are great at keeping Leos in check. Since both signs enjoy activity, they may love brisk walks in the park or a workout at the gym. They may also have fun when they go to opera performances and rock shows. Leos and Aquarians, however, need to work together to keep their relationship going.

Aquarius and Virgo

Aquarians are attracted to Virgos since the latter are insightful and intelligent people who can intellectually stimulate an Aquarian. Virgos are very particular about some things in life and may be fussy occasionally, especially about things that do not matter to an Aquarian. Virgos are people who love ironing their clothes, combing their hair frequently, and washing their hands until they are spotless. An Aquarian may not even be able to find a pair of socks in their cupboard. If an Aquarian and Virgo can overlook these characteristics, they can have a long-lasting friendship.

Aquarius and Libra

Aquarians and Librans are naturally attracted to each other, and the relationship between them is amazing to behold. Since both enjoy crowds and social gatherings, they often meet each other at parties. They discuss new ideas, the news, and other trends and soon develop a friendship. Librans are impressed by an Aquarian's understanding of any subject. Since an Aquarian pays undivided attention to anybody he is talking to, a Libra finds it easy to talk to him. A Libra is conscious about their appearance, and this can strike an Aquarian's nerve. If an Aquarian can overlook these characteristics, the friendship between a Libra and Aquarian can last for a lifetime.

Aquarian and Scorpio

An Aquarius and Scorpio may not get along with each other. There is a lot of tension in this relationship, and it is why most Aquarians and Scorpios do not like being with each other. Aquarians never know what their Scorpio friends are thinking. They constantly wonder about their feelings and motives, which is often a refreshing change for them. Scorpios also enjoy spending time with Aquarians since they cannot figure them out. Each tries to decipher the other like a puzzle. Both Aquarians and Scorpios are stubborn, and this can lead to arguments and issues. However, it is easy for them to maintain their friendship if they will give each other a chance.

Aquarius and Sagittarius

Aquarians love hanging out with Sagittarians. They are the best people in the whole world, according to Aquarians. Sagittarians have an open mind, an adventurous heart, and a free spirit, and they love spending time with Aquarians because of their humanitarian beliefs and adventurous spirit. Since both Aquarians and Sagittarians are social animals, they may often meet each other at a party. They are probably the last people to leave the party. They love playing sports that require quick reflexes. Sometimes, an Aquarian may find a Sagittarian's honesty annoying while a Sagittarius may find an Aquarian's failure to notice changes annoying. The two can, however, work together and have a strong friendship if they understand each other.

Aquarius and Capricorn

Aquarians love experiments, and they may develop a relationship with a Capricorn as an experiment. While Aquarians love new things and experiment with a lot of things in life, Capricorns prefer the old ways. Aquarians love change and they hate routines, unlike Capricorns. Aquarians may think that Capricorns are ruining their lives, but then the latter may do something that would help you remember why you are fond of them. Capricorns always bring some consistency to an Aquarian's life, while an Aquarian brings some life and excitement into a Capricorn's life.

Aquarius and Aquarius

Aquarians are compatible with each other, and most Aquarians feel normal when they are around other Aquarians. They are as normal as they can be around Aquarians. Since another Aquarian cannot find the love for chocolates or sardines strange, they are often happy and calm. The friendship between two Aquarians is never boring because both are adventurous. They never tire of discussing any topic and may enroll themselves to work for charitable causes.

Aquarius and Pisces

An Aquarian and Piscean can get along easily since they both have the same humanitarian instincts. If an Aquarian and Piscean get together, they will champion the group's underdog. Aquarians and Pisceans may often meet at a rally or fundraiser. They are drawn to subjects such as numerology, tarot, and astrology. Aquarians are drawn to Pisceans, who understand these subjects. They also are musical and may enjoy sharing music or plays together.

Aquarians at a Party

Aquarians are worldly, and they love speaking to people. They enjoy intellectual conversations, and they often flex their intellect. Aquarians enjoy small groups where they can show off their skills. They enjoy debates and discuss various subjects. Aquarians love to go out by themselves also. They may go for a spirit or wine tasting, a lecture, a fancy dinner, or even a concert. They only want a place where they can voice their opinions. They can discuss their opinions even with complete strangers.

Friendship Style

Since Aquarians love being around people, they are always open to meeting new people. They want to listen to their stories. An Aquarian never feels out of place even when they find themselves in a group of new people. Since they are good listeners and always ask the right questions, they can always bring people out of their shells. People may tell Aquarians things they have told nobody before. Aquarians, however, are private. They never tell people what they are thinking about or how they feel, but it may appear that they have told people everything they need to know.

Aquarians like large groups, but they take a while to find close friends. They take time to trust anybody. They take friendships seriously, and if they are disappointed, they will take it hard. They do not take it too hard if you forget to meet them for coffee, but it will take you longer to become a part of their circle. Since Aquarians always see the best qualities in people, they are often frustrated when people cannot see those characteristics in themselves.

Aquarians often feel like cheerleaders because they like to mentor people. They, however, wish there were someone in their life who would mentor them. Aquarians love to have fun, and they are always up for an adventure.

Who is the Best Friend for an Aquarian?

Since both Aquarius and Libra are air signs, they love cultural events, spending hours debating ideas, going to rock concerts, and other fun activities. Librans are more diplomatic when compared to other people, and an Aquarian knows how to call that out. They can make Libras stick to their guns and be less diplomatic. Librans know how to break an Aquarian's barriers down easily and help them trust people more. The two signs do not have a friendship based on words, and they are happy to be together even in silence. Since both Aquarians and Librans do not hold grudges, they are easy people to be with. They understand that they each need space and have enough going on in their lives. They can pick up exactly where they left off, even if they do not speak for days or weeks. Aquarians and Librans are not known for their humor, but they can laugh for hours together.

How to Become Friends with an Aquarian

Aquarians love social gatherings and are extroverts. People often surround them, and it is easy for people to get charmed by an Aquarian's characteristics. To be friends with an Aquarian for long, you need to stick around. Be there through good and bad times. Aquarians love consistency, and when you see them at the same place repeatedly, try to break the barriers down. You can have a casual friendship with Aquarians since they are nice. If you make them laugh, they will appreciate you more. If you want a deeper friendship, you need to scratch below the surface.

How to Continue Being Friends with Aquarians

Always be the best version of yourself to be friends with an Aquarian. Aquarians do not have any time for people who are not happy with their lives. They often forgive people who forget to respond or forget their birthdays, but they never like people who are mean or lie. Hurtful words and gossip, whether directed at Aquarians or others, does not impress an Aquarian.

Tips On How to be Friends with Aquarians

In this section, we will look at ten tips to help you be friends with Aquarians.

Always Be Genuine

Since Aquarians are serious, sincere, and reflective people, they will run away from you if you are insincere. They cannot respond to disingenuous flattery, and they always know who is being honest and who isn't. If you know an Aquarius, then you should compliment them on their commendable traits. This will always have a stronger effect on Aquarians since they know that you genuinely care for them. When giving gifts, you should never shower an Aquarius with flashy or expensive items.

Get to Know Them

You should never rush things when learning more about Aquarians. They always have their guards up so it takes a while for you to learn more about an Aquarian. You need to give an Aquarian the time to understand you and feel safe around you. It is only when this happens that they will slowly open up to you. Since Aquarians are playful and love adventure, they will joke around with you.

Philanthropy

Aquarians may sometimes seem detached and cold because they do not like opening up easily. They do, however, quickly attach themselves to strangers and understand their concerns. They will also do everything in their power to help them. Aquarius may have a million problems in their head, yet they will do help someone in need. They will always give them their shoulder to cry on. To befriend an Aquarian, you need to be philanthropic.

Learn to Debate

Since Aquarians are strong-willed, they will do whatever it takes to see something through if they believe in it. They will do this even if people have a different perspective. This does not mean they are argumentative or stubborn, but it is only because they are passionate about what they believe in. If you want an Aquarian to see your side of the story, use a combination of sources and facts. He may apologize to you for not seeing things the way you saw them.

Never Lie

Aquarians always want the truth, and they can spot liars instantly. If they sense you are lying to them, they will no longer want to be around you. They are this way because of their loyalty. They have strong morals, and they expect their friends to have the same morals. You will never get a second chance with an Aquarian if you are dishonest with them. If you cannot meet your friend for coffee, tell them why and have the proof needed for the same.

Quick Wit

Aquarians are charming, smart, witty, and sarcastic. If you cannot entertain them or converse with them for hours together, or talk about worldly affairs, then you cannot hold their attention. You also need to tolerate their sarcasm and know when they're just pulling your leg. If you can do this, they will want to be around you.

Learn to Love their Views

Since most Aquarians find themselves in an existential crisis, it is important for you to support their views. They are philosophers, and they often want peace and harmony in their lives. When they listen to a tragedy or remember something that happened to them, they question everything about their lives. Most people may find this childish, but to befriend an Aquarius, you need to trust them and their ideals. If you do this, they will love you, endlessly.

Trust Them

Aquarians never like feeling trapped, and if you try to control them, they will run away from you. You need to be secure to win an Aquarius over. If you question everything they do or say, they will pull away. Since Aquarians have morals and are loyal, they will do nothing to break your trust. So, learn to trust them.

Never Give Up

It does take Aquarians a long time to let their guard down. They are afraid to let people around them know how they feel or what they are going through. When this happens, you will be glad to have them for a friend. Aquarians hate rushing into relationships, but they will stick with you forever if you try hard. However, they fear commitment, but if you love them, fight for their friendship. Let them feel secure.

Prepare for a Long-Term Friendship

When you win an Aquarius over, it means they have let their guard down. This means you never have to doubt their dedication to your friendship. Aquarians are spontaneous, and they will show you their love with sentimental gifts. They always think about what they can gift you. They lift your spirits up and encourage you to follow your passions and dreams. Since Aquarians are verbal, they will remind you about your worth. Once you develop a bond with an Aquarian, it will never break. If you do not break their trust, they will never break yours. So, stick to them, and trust them. Be there to lift their spirits because they always do it for everybody. Be their mentor and friend. You will never lose them.

Chapter Six: Aquarius in Love

Let's take a look at the love compatibility of Aquarius with other signs of the zodiac:

Aquarius and Aries

The sexual relations between Aquarius and Aries can either be exciting or stressful. These two signs get along and are supportive of each other. Both signs can follow each other with a lot of energy. However, there could be a lack of emotion with intimacy or sexual relations between the two. Aries is a sign of a lot of passion and warm emotions. Their relationship with Aquarius has the possibility of bringing out the worst in their nature. It will emphasize that the cold and unemotional Mars rules Aries.

Although this might make their relations more exciting, it will fail to bring fulfillment to either of them since they both need to feel loved. There are too much energy and masculinity in this relationship, and this could cause turbulence. It is easy to understand their roles since Aquarius has crazy ideas and widens the horizons for their partner while Aries has a lot of stamina and gives off energy. At the beginning of the relationship, things could be a lot of fun for them. However, it gets tiresome with time, and there aren't enough crazy ideas to fill the empty hole of emotions.

Aries places a lot of importance on trust, and it is easy for Aquarius to understand this. Although it doesn't mean that Aquarius will remain faithful to their partner, they might instead bring up the option of an open relationship and be honest about any indiscretions to Aries. However, this is not an option for Aries, who is ruled by Mars and wants to be the center of their partner's world. This kind of relationship will only make Aries possessive and angry as they obsess over every move made by Aquarius. Other than fidelity, trust is not an issue for this pair. They both see no need for lies since the truth can be much more interesting and easier to deal with. Both signs don't feel the need to avoid conflict, and like speaking their mind. They know that any argument or conflict can be carried out constructively so that it helps them understand their partner better and makes their relationship stronger.

The conversations between Aries and Aquarius can be so interesting that most people would want to join in. Aquarius is aware of the fact that Aries is usually serious and has boundaries that need to be respected. In turn, they like making their Aries partner laugh and let loose more. For Aries, this kind of open-minded and constantly changing partner is unimaginable at times. This is why they often end up idolizing Aquarius and love entering into any dialogue with them. For Aquarius, it is a huge boost to their ego. Since both signs are strong by nature and very energetic, they could constantly end up fighting. However, they will also overcome such fights and cherish each other at the end of the day.

Aquarius and Taurus

Taurus is a sign with a slow and tender nature, which finds the unusual and changeable nature of Aquarius annoying. These two signs are rarely attracted and find each other crazy or boring. However, if they are more open-minded about unusual sexual relations, they can help each other grow a lot. The tender nature could help the distant and independent Aquarius become more motivated and creative. This, in turn, could help Taurus become a lot more productive. If these signs are respectful enough towards each other and share their emotions, they could have a great sex life. But it rarely gets this far since these signs look for very different things in their relationships. Aquarius likes being free of any attachment while Taurus looks for an unbreakable and secure bond. It can be difficult for both parties to find a meeting point.

Aquarius often stresses out Taurus, and this tends to prevent them from being honest and true to their partner. It is difficult for Aquarius to understand the fear that Taurus has of not being good enough. Aquarius doesn't indulge in self-criticism or guilt like Taurus constantly does. Taurus finds it even more difficult to express their feelings to Aquarius because the latter's strict opinions can scare Taurus away. All of this leads to an endless circle of mistrust and lies. Aquarius seems to lack flexibility even though they make it seem like they are accepting of differences in other people. For there to be trust between these signs, Taurus has to be braver and not fear the consequences of saying the wrong thing to their partner. Aquarius has to be more compassionate towards Taurus and get rid of their self-righteous attitude.

One is an Air element, while the other belongs to the earth. This is why these two signs will find it very difficult to find something in common to talk about. Taurus is the sign of Uranus' fall, which acts as a sieve for all their Aquarian partners' bright ideas. Although this may not pose a big problem, Taurus's narrow-mindedness can make their partner feel like none of their dreams will ever come true. Taurus has to be more understanding of the need to fly that Aquarius has. If they do this, they can help Aquarius work on materializing these flighty dreams. This happens rarely since Aquarius does not find it easy to talk to or open up to Taurus. It is difficult for these two signs to reconcile, and any small issue can become big for them.

Aquarius and Gemini

Verbal stimulation can make it possible for these two signs to have good sexual relations. They don't feel the need to be free of clothes to have sex but will mostly end up without them. Both signs are more focused on finding kindred spirits, and while they continue the search, they want to have a good time. The intellectual side of this relationship will be arousing for both partners. Neither Aquarius nor Gemini like being in a relationship with a partner whom they consider stupid. Being with someone without wit would be considered only an insignificant encounter for them. Aquarius is more dominating since Gemini can be shy in certain situations, and this helps Gemini become a lot freer in expressing themselves. But if there is a lack of emotion or true intimacy between them, their relationship will fall apart as they look for it in another partner.

For this couple, trust can be a strange thing. Not that they won't trust each other, because they will. Gemini rarely feels the need to lie, and Aquarius finds dishonesty ridiculous. However, Aquarius also likes privacy, but this pair will not struggle with trust issues.

Onlookers will find a debate between this pair quite interesting. Aquarius and Gemini can have extremely stimulating conversations. The humane and rational belief systems of Aquarius will be fascinating for Gemini, while Aquarius will get a chance to relieve their ego issues.

Aquarius and Cancer

Cancer and Aquarius will have a very stressful sexual relationship. Cancer is usually the most sensitive sign, but they become quite distant and rough when they want to set boundaries. Aquarius is an innovator but tends to be set in his ways and is unchangeable. Sexual relations between the two could be stressful for Cancer, and this will make them set boundaries. Aquarius, on the other hand, will find it difficult to change just to make their Cancer partner more comfortable. Cancer cannot understand the need for Aquarius to use sex in order to feel more grounded. For them, sexual relations should only have emotions involved.

Usually, Cancer is honest and loyal. However, if they fear hurting their loved ones or fear an aggressive reaction from them, they could turn to lies. The stress in this relationship could make it difficult for Cancer to share their thoughts or feelings with Aquarius, and this can lead to trust issues between the two. Although neither partner likes lying, they have trust issues since they don't have faith in their future together.

Aquarius and Leo

Opposite signs have a lot of attraction towards each other, and this is evident between Leo and Aquarius. Aquarius seems to exist to bring down Leo, who is the king of the signs. There is a lot of passion and attraction between these strong individuals. Their sexual relations can be a struggle as well as an incredible experience. There will be liberation and warmth and passion. Aquarius will end up respecting Leo if they share true emotions for each other. These two partners will form a very strong connection with each other over time.

If you look at their partnership from a distance, everything will seem simple. However, trust always seems to be a challenge for the two signs. They are both understanding and give each other freedom. But when they are separate from each other, they realize that they know little about their partners and have very little trust in place.

Leo and Aquarius are both heroes. If they fight for the same cause together, they can bring about great change and make a real difference in the world. However, they need to stop fighting with each other if they aim to achieve such things together. If not, their energy will only be scattered in unnecessary fighting.

Aquarius and Virgo

The sexual relationship between the two signs is not easy in any way. They will not be attracted to each other unless there is some strong support in their natal charts. Both signs have natures that will not be supportive of each other. Although Virgo and Aquarius are both intellectuals, they differ greatly from each other. Their tendency to overthink will ruin the possibility of any sexual relationship between the two. The analytical nature of Virgo will be a turnoff for Aquarius, who dislikes overthinking.

Both signs have a rational nature, and this will build trust between them. Virgo usually finds it difficult to trust their partner, but they see no need for this with an Aquarius partner. However, these signs might drift apart even if they have a strong connection at the beginning. For there to be mutual trust, both signs have to be accepting of each other and try to keep their relationship fresh.

Virgo has an adaptable and changeable nature which makes it difficult to accept Aquarius's unchangeable nature. They will be good at communicating with each other and have common topics to discuss. These signs will usually share their interests and be excited about the same things.

Aquarius and Libra

Libra will find it much easier to express themselves sexually when they have an Aquarius partner. The problem with Libra is that they care too much about what other people think. In sexual relations, they will either be too subdued and come across as asexual, or they will try to do too much and make it somewhat awkward for their partner. However, Aquarius is the opposite and does not care about the opinions of others. The sexual relations between the two can be liberating for Libra but challenging for Aquarius, as they have to fight against Libra's need to fit in.

Both signs have a righteous nature, and this will make them trust each other without exception. They have the same insecurities and will help each other overcome them. However, this trust must be built and will not come all at once. These signs like being seen as attractive, and they have to tell each other this. Problems can arise between the two if Libra gets too attached and emotionally dependent on Aquarius. This is something that Aquarius will shy away from.

Both signs have an image to maintain. While Libra likes looking and acting nice towards others, Aquarius is not a crowd-pleaser and likes going the opposite way. Both are stiff in their beliefs and will be unwilling to change their minds.

Aquarius and Scorpio

The sexual relations between Aquarius and Scorpio can be very intense. Together, these signs represent the ultimate sexual freedom with no taboos or restrictions. These air and water signs are very attracted to each other. However, if they break up, they will end up with hateful feelings and despise everything they shared. These signs will find it difficult to balance rational thinking, emotions, and passion. While Scorpio is deeply emotional and has a strong need for sexual relations, Aquarius dislikes too much emotion and has trouble with someone too possessive. Their sex life will either be great or a battleground. Being fixed signs, both will struggle to adapt to a partner very different from them.

Scorpio and Aquarius are straightforward and honest people who should ideally have no problem trusting each other. However, when they get close to each other, this problem will arise: Aquarius will are expected to get tamer and commit to their Scorpio partner. If there is any sign of manipulation in the relationship, things can be out of control. Their partnership will easily break apart because of such things.

Communication is not a problem for these signs if they don't act stubbornly or are too set in their opinions. They can discuss all kinds of strange topics with enjoyment since neither likes making small talk. Small talk seems futile for them both, and they like the fact that they can discuss interesting things with each other. Their connection of depth is incredible, and both have a lot of trouble in understanding many things about society.

Aquarius and Sagittarius

The one important asset for the sexual relations between these signs is that Aquarius tends to act in the way that Sagittarius thinks. They can have a strong attraction towards each other, especially when Sagittarius is at a point where they want confirmation of their sexuality and freedom. The sexual connection between the two can be satisfying, but they are not great when it comes to intimacy. Sagittarius can bring warmth to the relationship, but their focus is easily turned. Both signs understand the need for change in their sex life and will implement it. However, their emotional bond and intimacy are not consistently strong.

Aquarius and Scorpio will understand each other's minds a little too well. Aquarius likes being free, so they can be available to others, while Sagittarius struggles with fidelity. Since both will know this about each other, it will be difficult for them to build trust. They will always question whether they should trust their partner. If they decide to commit to the relationship, they will not be able to give each other the freedom that both need.

If these signs discover a mutual interest, they will never lack subjects to discuss. Their unending discussions could even end up changing their views on a lot of things. Sagittarius is usually a little too talkative while discussing uninteresting topics as they try to connect, and

Aquarius can be distant. However, if they find a subject of interest to both, they will share stimulating conversations.

Aquarius and Capricorn

Most people assume that Capricorn is restricting and traditional, while Aquarius is the opposite. In truth, the same planet rules over both signs, which is why they have many similarities. Their different pace is the one problem in their sex life, which is usually due to their different elements. Capricorn is an earth sign that is thorough and slow. They don't jump into a relationship unless they respect their partner and are attracted to them. When they finally indulge in sexual relations, they try to give it their best. As an air sign, Aquarius is a little unreliable and flaky but being ruled by Saturn makes them a lot more reliable than other air signs. They like things to be fast and spontaneous without much overthinking involved. Aquarius will rarely have the patience to deal with Capricorn, who takes time to create a detailed plan. Their need to rush is a turn off for Capricorn. Both signs can be very passionate with the right partner, but these signs are better off as friends than lovers.

Capricorn is set in their convictions and dislikes making any mistakes, while Aquarius values truth and has no fear of confrontation. They both have a different idea of trust, and it is hard for them to accept the differences in their natures. They trust each other but don't have faith that their relationship will work out.

Aquarius and Aquarius

The sexual relationship between two Aquarians can be very interesting and full of excitement. Both will be free in expressing themselves and will also be willing to fulfill each other's fantasies. They follow no restrictions or taboos that society usually dictates. However, the lack of emotional bonding can be an issue for them. This pair will find it difficult to stay together once the initial attraction wears off. They are better suited for occasional flings.

Being from the same sign, they can understand each other without needing words. Freedom will be the foundation of their trust, and neither will want to lie. However, if either becomes too possessive, it will be the end of their relationship.

When two Aquarians have a conversation, it is very difficult for any outsider to actually understand it. They have a great connection when it comes to communication, and ideas are constantly flying around. However, their ego issues will pose a problem.

Aquarius and Pisces

Things will never get boring in the sexual relationship between Aquarius and Pisces. They may not seem like they will initially get along at all, but they can have a great sex life if Pisces avoids getting attached to Aquarius. Pisces will enthusiastically try to maintain an exciting sexual relationship, and Aquarius will follow suit.

Trust can go in two extreme directions for this couple. If they are intimate enough, they will have complete trust with each other. If not, there will be constant suspicion and lies involved. They need to take the time to understand each other if they want to build trust.

Chapter Seven: Aquarius at Work

Aquarians are very capable of many different things, but they are most suited for roles that need unconventional thinking patterns. This sign embodies a lot of professional strengths like assertiveness, social consciousness, and critical thinking. However, they also have their drawbacks, just like any other sign does.

Aquarians lack focus, and they tend to express apathy towards any task that is different from their interests. They always insist on getting their way even if it might not be the right choice while dealing with a particular task. This can have a negative impact on the professional growth of Aquarius despite their better judgment.

However, the positive traits make them great candidates for working in the fields of fine arts, politics, and service. These are some career paths that will help Aquarius flourish in the workplace. It will allow them to work in the way they like while playing on their strengths comfortably.

Aquarians love to display their unique skills, imaginative abilities, intuitive powers, and bold nature. They tend to make conscious efforts to make the world a better place.

They like to display their intellect and talents. They like to exercise these qualities and love to be in an atmosphere where they can propose new ideas and help others by being creative. Creativity and intellectual stimulation drive an Aquarius person. They are good with groups, but they will always strive to be recognized for their personal contributions too.

Aquarius people are humanitarian at heart, so they succeed immensely in occupations that allow them to bring positive changes into the world around them. They are passionate about ideas, knowledge, and new beginnings, so they are great for fields based on discovery and invention such as tech jobs, astronomy, science, etc.

Careers Options for Aquarius Individuals

Mediator

This sign brings deep thinkers who can skillfully think through any problem from an objective standpoint until they find a solution. This is a skill that is important in mediators. Mediators have to remain objective and find practical solutions while keeping a detailed record of any interaction with their clients. Their job is to help two parties communicate more effectively with each other. Mediators may work in a legal setting while helping their clients to document details in their agreement.

Teacher

Since Aquarians have a love for learning, teaching is a great fit for them. If an Aquarian works as a teacher, they can learn a lot more in that specific subject and impart the same knowledge to their students. This sign needs to live in their truth, which makes them more suitable as teachers. Aquarians will always try their best to follow the same rules that they teach their students and thereby set an example for them.

Researcher

As an avid learner and because Aquarians are inquisitive, research is another well-suited field for this sign. Research can be done in teams as well as individually. Researchers have to identify a goal and a certain objective for their research first. After this, they need to create a plan, secure research funding, and finally put their skills to work so they can carry out the project. This is the kind of job that Aquarius will find highly enjoyable and be passionate about. Their inquisitive passion will make them instantly liked by other co-workers on such research projects.

Trainer

Trainers are meant to teach certain skills, standards, or policies to individuals or a group. The assertiveness and critical thinking abilities of Aquarius will help them carry out this task well. They can use it to cleverly instill such knowledge to their students or learners while using their artistic ability to do it in an interesting way.

Actor

Actors have more opportunities than other people to express themselves in different ways. Whether or not it is at a film studio, theatre, or an elaborate set, Aquarius can occupy the spotlight as an actor. They have a very unpredictable nature, and this would make them a delight in improv acting. Their curiosity will also make them work harder at delving into a role and adapting it as their own.

Electrician

The natural curiosity of Aquarius also makes them good at working as an electrician. Their job will be to evaluate electrical failings and provide any potential solutions to their clients. But before they do this, they have to go through all the intricacies of wiring, breakers, and lighting. Playing with these delicate components will be highly enjoyable for Aquarians as they try to get to the core of the problem and then figure out a way to solve it.

Project Manager

As a project manager, Aquarians will have to define a project's objectives, create and implement a budget, and delegate all the tasks to people in the team. This will have to be done to allow the project to be completed more efficiently. Since they are self-isolators, this sign has to put in a little extra effort to be reachable for the team. However, they are great project leaders because they manage to inspire the team even when they are away. Aquarian project managers are great at motivating co-workers to work more fervently.

Scientist

A scientist is always curious, and their curiosity knows no end. This applies to Aquarius individuals as well, and it is why they are naturally suited for the job. They can work in a wide range of fields and decide which area of research they want to focus on. Aquarians will get the chance to gather new information all the time and find answers to all the questions they have.

Environmental Planner

This role's scope is quite vast, which makes the job attractive for Aquarius. Environmental planners usually have to evaluate different lands to determine how they can be used in the best way possible. Their job requires them to collaborate with people from many different professions, which allows them to learn a lot more by asking questions from different professionals and finding answers to their problems. Planners do a lot of research to figure out the advantages and disadvantages involved in using a certain piece of land for a specific purpose. Aquarians will find this job to their liking.

Aquarius in the Workplace

For an Aquarius to feel comfortable at their workplace, their abstract and deep thought process has to be welcomed. This way of thinking comes naturally to them, and if their colleagues and employers appreciate it rather than criticize it, it helps Aquarians grow professionally.

Once they feel at home in their working environment, they will always be willing to help out a colleague or take on someone else's work to lighten their load. This sign loves being helpful to those around them. Their thoughtfulness is a great asset to any workplace. However, this sign comes with some challenges that can also create problems in the workplace. For instance, despite their helpful nature, they are loners. They tend to isolate themselves while working instead of communicating with their team. This is not always acceptable to others, and most colleagues want clear communication from Aquarians.

If Aquarius suddenly goes off-grid without an explanation, it can be a hassle for others at work. To make things easier, the Aquarians should let their co-workers know in advance if they intend to take some solitary time away from work. Being more forthcoming and proactive in communication will make it easier for Aquarius to get along with coworkers. Another challenge that this sign might face is sticking to a schedule. Not all kinds of work can be done at a person's own pace.

Aquarians must overcome their aversion to a fixed routine. They cannot afford to get irritable just because there are deadlines or a schedule to follow. Work is not always aligned according to each individual's personal preferences. This is not a problem that can be fixed, and Aquarians need to learn to deal with it. Work obligations have to be met even if they are boring or difficult at times.

Aquarians usually find it difficult to do any task that is not fulfilling to them or does not bring joy. However, if they focus on the fact that getting the work done on time will give them more free time later, it can be easier for them to work through it. Aquarians will find more enjoyment in their work-life if they reciprocate what they want from work.

Workplace Compatibility with other Zodiac Signs

Aquarius is one of the best signs to have around when you need to hold a brainstorming session. They are original, innovative, and witty. They always come up with some cutting-edge ideas, and they love trying new things. Their vision is admirable and appreciated by all co-workers. However, this sign needs to be careful about who they build a working relationship with. Aquarians focus on the big picture with such intensity they often ignore how others around them feel. These are the kind of things to keep in mind when looking for a working partner. The right sign can make their work-life balance better, while others will only make things more difficult. Reading about the compatibility of Aquarius with other signs at work can be extremely helpful in navigating the professional world.

Aquarius compatibility with other zodiac signs at work:

Aquarius and Aries

The lively partnership between Aries and Aquarius will make work exciting for both signs. Aries is a sign that tends to be a pioneer, while Aquarius is always willing to embark on a new journey. While Aries finds it difficult to stick to a routine, Aquarius doesn't mind dealing with different work responsibilities. Aries has a tendency to take risks, and

Aquarius never shied away from signs of danger. They are both similar and compatible in this regard; however, neither is good at dealing with human relations.

Not that they are not sociable; in fact, Aries is quite charming, and Aquarius is a sociable type. However, they both fail to deal well with people they hurt or when confronted by some misunderstanding. These signs need to depend on a third-party water or earth sign who can advise them or take care of any human resource problems.

Aquarius and Taurus

Aquarius and Taurus appear to be complete opposites on the surface. Taurus looks for comfort in familiar things while Aquarius takes a liking to unfamiliar and strange things. Taurus is a grounded sign with their feet on the ground, while Aquarius likes building castles in the air. Taurus tries their best to save money for later while Aquarius has a free hand with spending or giving away money. These differences in their personality make it hard to imagine them working together. However, if they play to their strengths and try mitigating their partner's weaknesses, this can be done. For instance, Aquarius should be the one working on any product development at work while Taurus should be entrusted with financial matters. Aquarius should focus on advertising any services or products at work while Taurus makes their workspace a lot more comfortable to enhance productivity. These signs will work well in industries like recording, real estate development, and retail sales.

Aquarius and Gemini

Aquarius will love working with Gemini colleagues. Both these signs are innovative, witty, and sharp. If they are in the same room, there will be tons of great ideas bouncing off the walls. The one problem with this working pair is that they are not efficient at executing these great ideas. Gemini will always struggle with focusing on a single thing for too long. However, Aquarius can roll their sleeves up to get things done when it is really important. Although Gemini is not very focused, they will still do their bit while Aquarius toils away. Gemini is one of the best types to deal with any last-minute emergencies that would leave others baffled. They are an able and willing sort that Aquarius can depend on. This pair will be successful if they run a business in telecommunications, airlines, or television.

Aquarius and Cancer

Working together will require a lot of compromise from both Cancer and Aquarius. Aquarius is a very logical type, while Cancer is emotional all the time. While Aquarius likes their work environment to be very professional and stark, Cancer wants it to be cozy and familiar. Aquarius likes working with concepts, while Cancer prefers tangible products. If these two signs want to work well together, they have to bridge the gap by drawing on each other's strengths. The leadership skills of Cancer can be helpful for Aquarius. Cancer is great at championing a cause, making long-term plans, and delegating responsibilities in a way that will benefit the workplace. Aquarius is much better at finding innovative solutions for problems that are usually too difficult for others to deal with. These two signs can run a successful business together if they play to their strengths and try making a profession like teaching or catering more interesting.

Aquarius and Leo

Aquarius will find the experience of working with Leo interesting. These two signs are actually the complete opposite of each other. While Leo works just to get the glory, Aquarius likes working for their own satisfaction. While one is more into style, the latter cares about substance. Aquarius is an extremely logical kind, while Leo tends to be too emotional. All these differences make it difficult to imagine that these signs would have a common factor. However, they are both fixed signs, and this means that they look for a secure job. Both generally want constant intellectual stimulation, but they won't seek this at the risk of losing their job. Both signs are also great at working through any difficult projects and making sure they get done to everyone's satisfaction. Their reasons for working hard may be different, but they still get the job done with their incredible stamina. If these signs go into a business together, they should consider a field in film, radio, or television. Aquarius should be the one working on the technical side of things while Leo would be a great performer.

Aquarius and Virgo

Virgo has little common ground with Aquarius. However, there is mutual respect between these two colleagues. Virgo prefers to focus on the little details, while Aquarius is better at looking at the bigger picture. These two co-workers don't allow their emotions to run havoc at the workplace. They stick to their work even if other co-workers go on an ego trip or have a temper tantrum. The methods employed by Virgo can often seem too stuffy for Aquarius. Virgo, on the other hand, finds Aquarius a little inefficient when it comes to working. Despite these differences, their working partnership can be remarkably productive. Some of the most suitable businesses for these two signs to run together are a recycled product store, health food store, or yoga studio. However, if both are employed under someone else, Aquarius should take care of any promotional campaigns while Virgo deals with money matters.

Aquarius and Libra

The work compatibility between Libra and Aquarius is harmonious. When these two signs work together, they have fun even while being productive. While Libra might be a little too clingy for Aquarius at times, their team spirit is admirable. Aquarians should let their Libran partner run free with decorating the workspace. Libra will love to spruce up the space with some pictures, plants, and other things that will allow both to work more comfortably. Most Aquarians don't believe that such things matter when it comes to work and productivity. But once you let your Libra co-worker do this, you realize just how much difference it can make compared to a barren workspace. Both these signs are better at working with concepts than with products. If the business involves scientific research, patents, or intellectual property, these signs will do well. If both signs work under an employer, Libra should be the one dealing with clients while Aquarius handles the authority figures at the office. Aquarius is a lot better at dealing with pushy people and standing their ground. For Libra, this can be too much to handle, and they tend to crumble under pressure.

Aquarius and Scorpio

Both Scorpio and Aquarius are fixed signs. This means that the work dynamic between them can be quite interesting. Both these signs always feel like they are undoubtedly right, and the other person involved is wrong. They have a firm conviction that their work methods are better. Aquarius relies more on cold hard facts, while Scorpio is more emotional. Both signs are gifted in their own way. Aquarius is better at dealing with straightforward things. Scorpio is better able to notice any deception or ferret out a secret. Scorpio should be the one handling any dirty work while Aquarius should handle human-relations matters. It is important for Aquarius to listen to the advice given by their Scorpio colleague or partner since the latter has an uncanny intuition that helps them avoid any scams or fraud. This can be immensely useful for the gullible Aquarius.

Aquarius and Sagittarius

The work compatibility between Sagittarius and Aquarius is actually quite effective. Working together can bring a lot of satisfaction for both signs. Sagittarians admire the innovation, intelligence, and independence of Aquarius. The latter loves the high spirits, humanitarianism, and humor brought by Sagittarius to the workplace. There might be some trouble when Sagittarius starts acting flaky at work because of their lack of focus. However, Aquarians can be insufferably picky about small things like keeping stationery organized or setting the room's temperature. These signs can form a very lucrative partnership if they try to overlook each other's idiosyncrasies. Teaching, Law, or some import-export businesses can be successful ventures for this pair. If both are employees at the same workplace, Aquarians should work on the long-term projects while Sagittarians are better suited for short-term ones. Dividing work in this way will allow both to perform well together.

Aquarius and Capricorn

While Aquarius likes trying new things and changing the old ways, Capricorn is the opposite. However, the old-fashioned Capricorn pairing up with Aquarius is not necessarily a bad idea. Not every old method is outdated or ineffective, and not everything new is productive. If Aquarius can be open to suggestions from their Capricorn colleague, their working relationship can be quite stable. Although Aquarians like shaking things up, they have to admit that a certain security level is necessary for a successful career. Working with a Capricorn can bring this sense of stability. If Aquarians show appreciation for Capricorn's leadership skills, the latter will be a lot easier to work with. They will be much more open to accepting new ideas or innovative strategies from Aquarius at the workplace.

Aquarius and Aquarius

Aquarians are hard to startle, but another member of the same zodiac can manage this. Pairing two people from this zodiac sign together will create a wealth of creativity. The creative capacity of these two colleagues will be endless. Both are interested in cutting-edge technology, and this is why they love working with computers. Radio, telecommunications, and television are possible avenues for a successful career for Aquarius. An Aquarius employee works better alone and should just have only the minimum contact with their employer.

For instance, meeting at the start of the day for a briefing and ending the day with another short meeting is a good option. In the middle, Aquarians should work by themselves to get things done. Both Aquarian colleagues will be independent and can produce great ideas if they are left to work by themselves instead of being forced to work in pairs. Being a fixed sign, the mind of an Aquarius is extremely difficult to change. In any other aspect, this pair can work productively together.

Aquarius and Pisces

Aquarius is usually amused by the quirky techniques Pisces employs at work. Pisces admires the tremendous vision of Aquarius. Although Pisces colleagues can be a little flaky sometimes, Aquarians have their own weaknesses. For instance, Aquarians are not very effusive, and it can be difficult for anyone to understand if they like, hate, or are indifferent towards a project. However, if Aquarians put in a little effort at building a better connection with Pisces colleagues, the latter will work much harder to perform well. If both these signs work under an employer, Aquarius should stick to the analytical aspect of a project while Pisces can deal with any social niceties required at work.

Conclusion

As we come to the end of the book, I would like to thank you for reading it. I hope you found it interesting and useful. There is a lot to learn from the world of astrology and zodiac signs.

By now, you have gained in-depth knowledge about the sign of Aquarius. Each chapter in this book was aimed at providing vital information about the personality of Aquarians and other aspects of their lives.

I hope the information in this guide was helpful in revealing the strengths, weaknesses, and traits of Aquarians. You now know a lot about the best career options suited for people from this sign as well. Learning about the compatibility of Aquarius with other signs will help to navigate relationships with other people.

If used correctly, this book can promote good relationships between an Aquarius and people from other zodiac signs. It will also help Aquarians understand themselves better and improve mental, physical, spiritual, and financial wellbeing. Thank you again for making it to the end. Please recommend it to any friends or family who might benefit from the book as well.

Part 12: PISCES

The Ultimate Guide to an Amazing Zodiac Sign in Astrology

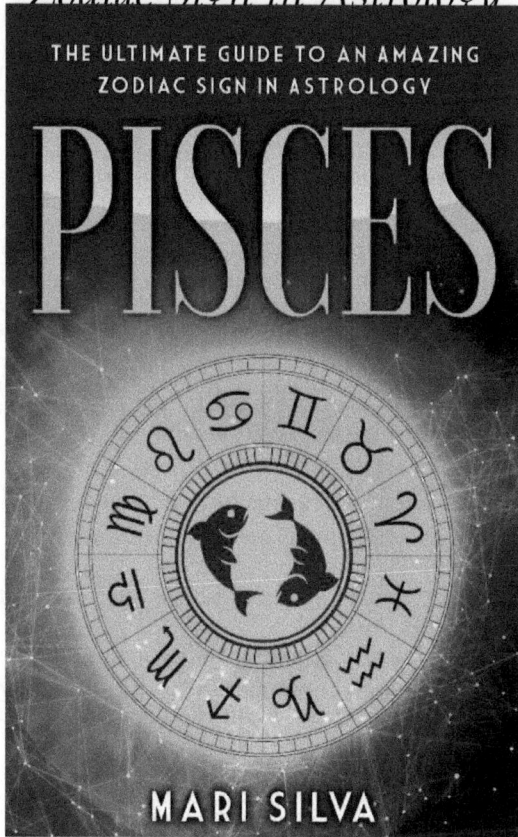

Introduction

Like all the signs of the Zodiac, the symbol for Pisces explains a great deal about those who are born under it. Two fish appear to swim in opposite directions, indicating tension in the character of Pisces people.

I prefer to look at the fish differently. I see them as swimming in an eternal loop, ever-rotating around the mysteries of the universe, penetrating and illuminating them. This idea is probably more in line with the dreamy, mystical nature of Pisces.

Ever-seeking the beautiful and the numinous, Pisces people don't spend their time daydreaming for nothing. They're people of creativity and ideas whose imaginations take them places others have no idea are even out there. Like cats, they see what we don't see.

Empathetic to a fault, Pisces wants everyone around them to feel good. They want people in their immediate circle and those on their peripheries to feel as though they belong. Of all the traits of this fascinating sign, empathy is probably one of the most prominent.

But isn't it true that most people with interest in astrology know that? Yes! This is why this book is intended to be a much more intimate exploration of Pisces, and how the people of this sign navigate the treacherous waters of human relationships.

In this book, we'll learn:

> • The astrological reasons for the behavior of Pisces people
>
> • How Pisces people grow into life by interpreting it in their own special way
>
> • How their relationships with people under other signs in the Zodiac play out
>
> • The meaning of rising signs, decanates, and cusps
>
> • Why astrology continues to be turned to by millions to understand other people better and why it's dismissed by just as many

More than a superficial survey of Pisces, this book will help you understand this amazing sign in the zodiac more fully. And if you're a Pisces yourself, you'll be gaining more knowledge about what makes you tick, your relationships, and how you live your life.

I hope you enjoy this in-depth exploration of watery Pisces. Thank you for reading and thank you for your interest in astrology!

Chapter One: Meet Pisces – February 19 – March 20

In our first chapter, we'll meet the Pisces, discovering the astrological nuts and bolts that make them tick. Then, we'll encounter Pisces in their native habitats at work, in their social lives, and at home.

We will begin by examining the semiotics of the sign, consisting of assigned symbols, the ruling planet, and other important details governing Pisces.

Getting a Handle on Pisces

The first thing I want to share with you about Pisces concerns the two fish in the sign's symbol.

These are derived from the Greek myth of Aphrodite/Venus, born from the sea. In Greek mythology, the fish are called "Ichthyocentaurs." These mythical beasts bore the upper body of a human, the forelegs of a horse, with the rest of the body consisting of a fish's tail. A Byzantine writer, Ioannes Tzetzes, is said to have been the first to use the term in the 12th Century. Elsewhere, you'll find the mythical creature described as a "sea-centaur."

These beings can also be found in Syrian mythology and are involved with the birth from the sea of the goddess Astarte.

The symbol of the fish was adopted by the Early Christians to represent Christ. Called the "Ichthys" in Greek, the ancient meaning of the fish is connected to the mythology about water, which emanated from many early belief systems and which became the basis for the Christian Rite of Baptism. The christened is submerged under the water—representing the waters from which the earth was born, in the Book of Genesis—emerging as a new creature, born into the death and the resurrection of Jesus.

In its position as the final sign of the zodiac, Pisces represents the cumulative experiences of all the other 11 signs. This is both a tremendous burden and an extravagant gift. Tied up with ancient beliefs about the world and its creation, Pisces is a sign which represents both death and new life. Its position in the zodiac can be understood to represent the cyclical and ever-changing nature of human life and its mystery.

Pisces represent the completion of the year, and the point at which another orbit around the sun commences.

Feminine? Mileage May Vary

Zodiac signs are considered either feminine or masculine, and Pisces is considered feminine. The sex associated with the signs of the zodiac tends to indicate extroversion versus introversion. We'll be talking about the sexed zodiac in Chapter Seven, especially with respect to the understanding of gendered notions attached to biological sex in the Ancient World.

So, Pisces is an introvert, compounded by the fact this mutable (changeable) sign has water as its elemental signifier, and if there's one thing you can say about water, *it's a changeable element.* While water is indispensable, bringing life to all things, it can also be extremely destructive. But don't let that scare you too much! Just know that the implied duality of the fish can manifest when other planetary

---

619

circumstances are in play. With Pisces, water is more of a friendly element than anything and not just to Pisces but to those around them.

Pisces shares its status as a feminine sign with Capricorn, Taurus, Virgo, and Scorpio, while the signs Aries, Gemini, Leo, Aquarius, and Leo are considered male. While feminine signs like Pisces are said to be inner-focused, the masculine signs are said to deploy their energies toward the world around them. While the feminine draws in, the masculine strikes out. But this is not an assessment of the intrinsic value or the rich nature of those under these signs. So, signs are sexed to describe their energetic quality. We all carry traits considered either masculine or feminine, living in harmony. But we tend to be raised according to gendered expectations of what it means to be a man or a woman, which can muddy the waters. Again, we'll be having a critical look at the sexed zodiac later on in this book.

Astrology is about humanity, not about the sexes, except in this particular instance, which comes down to us from the Ancient World. That's important to note here, as our anthropological dimorphism (dual expression of humanity via the sexes) is rooted in a gendered understanding of what the sexes mean and how they move through the world. Gender concerns self-expression, which is not governed by biology.

Preview of Chapter Seven: I hereby challenge astrology to abandon sex stereotypes about the nature of biological reality! Let's bring astrology into the 21st Century together!

Neptune and Jupiter

The two planets which rule Pisces are both named for male gods in the Ancient World. Jupiter was considered the Piscean ruling planet by the ancients, but Neptune has since taken its place.

So, how does this work when we're talking about a "feminine" sign? Shouldn't Pisces be ruled by planets named for goddesses?

The explanation perhaps lies in the establishment of male rule in religious life. Before the rise of the major monotheistic religions, women were charged with human spirituality, but all that changed, with the birth of monotheism in Judaism, then Christianity, and finally, Islam.

For Pisces, Neptune makes sense, as this is the planet named for the God of the Seas. You'll see Neptune everywhere you go in Europe but nowhere more frequently than in Rome, Italy, where myriad public art pieces, like the Fontana de Trevi and the magnificent fountains in Piazza Navona, were fashioned in his likeness.

But Neptune was officially discovered in 1846, long after Jupiter was in 1610. Neptune is associated with many aspects of the Piscean personality. Governing intellectual and spiritual life, Jupiter proposes exploration driven by curiosity and fearlessness. Reigning over matters religious and philosophical, it seems a good fit for the nature for Pisces. Their introverted, introspective nature echoes the traits of the planet which rules over their sign.

In the 12th House

As we've discussed earlier, Pisces is the last of all the signs in the zodiac. And each sign, of which there are 12, denotes a unique ambiance. Each house bears in it the sign it represents, and each house in the Pisces sign governs a certain sector of your life. To determine your houses, you must create a chart based on both the date of your birth and the time. We'll explore astrological houses and what they govern in greater detail later in this book, but here are the basics.

- First house—how people read you

This house is concerned with what people see when they look at you. This is the house of first impressions.

How you respond when threatened or venturing into places you've never been is also governed by this house, which is the House of Aries. And Aries is very concerned with the superficial and the self.

- Second house - what matters to you

This is the house of what is important to you in life, with a focus on money and valuables. It also determines who you think about and how you live with money and possessions, and what kind of importance you place on them.

This house represents Taurus, which is concerned with ownership. It also governs how you see yourself and how much you value yourself in relation to other people.

- Third house—how you communicate

This is the "thinking house," determining your communication style and the thought processes which define it. This house governs how you interact with and talk to the people around you, including family members.

Gemini is represented by this house, determining both the nature of your voice and how it's communicated and in the media.

- Fourth house—your foundation

The fourth house represents Cancer, which is all about feelings. The fourth house governs your sense of "home" and what it means, with the moon in charge. How secure you feel in the world and how grounded you are in your sense of self is determined by this sensitive house.

- Fifth house—the child within

The way we are as children is usually carried with us through life, for better or worse. Governing all the best stuff in life from play to pleasure to joy and creativity and romance, here's where your self-expression lives.

Leo is represented by this House. Leo is an active sign that demands you come to the party it's hosting and that you bring that child you once were along for the ride.

- Sixth house—daily life

Representing Virgo, the analytical sign, the sixth house determines how you conduct your daily life, your health, and how you organize yourself. Your problem-solving abilities, habits, and diligence live in this house.

Under this house, you'll also find your beloved pets, your ability to schedule, and your personal routines.

- Seventh house—relationships with others

"Relationships" here can mean everything from partnerships in business to marriages, friendships, and how you manage them.

But enemies are also governed by this house, with vanity and envy under its auspices. This is the house of Libra, so any legal issues that arise in life are influenced by the sign of the scales. "Balance" is the operative word.

- Eighth house—dynamic change and desire

Scorpio is the sign represented by this House, and that sign governs sexuality. But it's not all fun and games here. Crisis is governed by the eighth House, as well as addiction.

This house influences the nature of change and how you respond to it in life. While change means rebirth or transformation, it may also mean death or crisis.

- Ninth house—learning

The ninth house emanates from Sagittarius, which is the zodiac sign of possibilities. Ruling over your spirituality, systems of belief, and personally held philosophy.

Adventurous Sagittarius also governs commerce, culture, publishing languages, and long-distance travel. Optimism and seeing beyond what's in front of your face are traits governed by the ninth House.

- Tenth house—reputation and what you leave behind you

Practical Capricorn is represented in this house, defining what you achieve, your chosen career, and the legacy you leave in the world. The tenth House governs financial success, notoriety, and ambition.

Your relationship to authority is also ruled by this House, as well as your attitude toward the potential in your life for the achievement of various kinds.

- Eleventh house—your hopes, dreams, and purpose

What you most hope for, wish for, and what you see as your life's purpose are all governed by this house, Aquarius.

Your friends, acquaintances and personal networks are determined by the influence of this House. This is the House of connection and community.

- Twelfth house—your spirituality

This, of course, is the house of Pisces. It rules over the sectors of your personality unseen by others, including your secrets and your subconscious.

This is the house in which the self is deconstructed, resulting in spiritual growth. In the deconstructing of the self is the truth of spirit—something ardently sought after by Pisces.

Importantly, your Houses can only accurately be defined by preparing an astrological chart. For this, you must either create a chart for yourself or turn to a professional. If you plan to do this, I strongly suggest that you consult an astrological professional to obtain the most accurate reading possible. No, you can't do an accurate astrological chart without your time of birth, so get that information first! There are many places online to have a chart done, but the most reliable of these is Astro.com.

Gemstones and Colors

Aquamarine is the gemstone most popularly associated with Pisces. But it's not the only one.

Aquamarine is joined by bloodstone, amethyst, jade, jasper, and ruby. Aquamarine is Pisces' planetary stone, specifically referencing the planet Neptune. Its light blue color is reminiscent of the sea. This stone represents Pisces' powerful empathic powers and emotional richness.

Amethyst is a purple gemstone, imparting peace, love, and happiness to the wearer.

Ruby is the talismanic stone associated with Pisces, its bright red color recalling blood and passion. Ruby brings those who wear their wisdom and the ability to live in peace with others.

Internationally acknowledged as a lucky stone, Jade rewards the goodness of the wearer. It's believed that those who are kind and loving will benefit most abundantly from this stone. It represents the heart chakra and brings those who wear it vivid dreams, healing, and a more robust spirituality.

Bringing increased creativity, Bloodstone can help Pisces regain personal power following a life crisis. This stone also enhances Pisces' already highly developed intuitive skills.

Jasper soothes the restless, sensitive, Piscean soul. Assisting Pisces with emotional management, this stone is also rumored to reveal information about past lives to the wearer.

Pisces colors are blue, teal, and variations of purple, lilac, and mauve. Ethereal and watery, picture Pisces drifting into the party in a flowing magenta caftan or a diaphanous, tie-dyed extravaganza from head to toe. Men may not show up in such an extravagantly dramatic outfit, but you can bet they'll be wearing the same palette and probably a few embroidered elements. With Pisces, it's all about wearing your heart on your sleeve in your favorite color!

Now, let's find out about cusps, as these are important, and this section will explain why.

Teetering on the Brink

Being born on the cusp means that you've been born on the boundary between two zodiac signs. If you're a Pisces born on the Pisces-Arie cusp, your birth date falls between March 17 and March 23. And if you're born on the Aquarius-Pisces cusp, it falls between February 15 and February 21.

Cusp people are likely to sense internal conflict due to the fact they're essentially teetering on the brink between two very different signs. Both the examples above have specific names to describe them. The Pisces-Aries cusp can be called the "Cusp of Rebirth", while the Aquarius-Pisces cusp is described as the "Cusp of Sensitivity". Let's examine what being born during these two cusp periods means for "edgy" Pisceans.

The Pisces-Aries "Cusp of Rebirth" presents the intuitive Pisces with the aggressive nature of the first sign of the zodiac. With Pisces being the concluding sign and Aries being the beginning of the 12-sign sequence, this is an Alpha/Omega situation. This is the point at which the astrological wheel turns, and the astrological year begins.

While Pisces longs for peace and communion with all that is, Aries wants to butt heads. Aries is a fire sign, with a continual urge to move ever forward, without hesitation or impediment, and that is not the Pisces way at all!

It is important to note while these two signs are energetic opposites, the Pisces on the cusp benefits with an almost uncanny sixth sense. There's something about the Cusp of Rebirth, which makes the intuitive abilities of a Pisces even more awe-inspiring.

Sensitive Pisces further benefits from being on the cusp by having an enhanced ability to defend themselves when needed. Instead of dissolving into tears of frustration, the Cusp of Rebirth Pisces is much more likely to put up the proverbial dukes and rumble!

The Cusp of Sensitivity—Aquarius-Pisces—Brilliant and innovative, Aquarians bring Pisces born on the Cusp of Sensitivity even more unique energy, combined with exceptional creativity and intuition, which rivals even the abilities of those born on the Cusp of Rebirth.

Free spirits, ever seeking innovation, and new horizons, the Aquarian influence on Pisces on the cusp is profound. The sensitivity of Pisces is tempered by Aquarius. Pisceans born on the Cusp of Sensitivity are also much more able to erect strong boundaries that people take seriously because they're less likely to allow them to be breached.

The influence of Aquarius also focuses dreamy Pisces less on the value of psychic forecasting and more on their powerful intuition. That intuitive aptitude becomes a weapon in the hands of a Pisces born on the cusp with Aquarius.

Later we will move into the more complex aspects of astrology, including rising signs, decanates, and the importance of the planets—especially the moon in astrological charts—to the character of individual Pisceans.

Now that we've covered the astrological nuts and bolts that affect the way this sign moves through the world, let's explore a few of Pisces' most iconic traits, both positive and negative. Not even Pisces are all sunshine and lollipops.

Chapter Two: Who are these People?

"It's tougher to be vulnerable than to actually be tough."

Rihanna (Pisces)

Anyone lucky enough to have a Pisces friend has plenty of stories, and I'm no exception. Knowing a Pisces, whether male or female, is an experience like none other. While not the easiest people to get to know well, they're well worth the effort.

In this chapter, describing classical traits of Pisces, I will paint a picture of a close friend. I hope to explain how a Pisces is most likely to approach life.

After reading the first chapter, you'll understand that mileage may vary from Pisces to Pisces. The role of the other planets in any given Pisces' chart, and where they're born in the sign, is highly influential. Other environmental factors must also be actively and carefully considered.

It's quite reasonable to say that while there are differences between male and female Pisces, sex doesn't have a tendency to change the characteristics of people born under this sign. These differences are less important than the sign itself. Remember that Pisces concludes the zodiac, containing trace attributes and lessons from the preceding 11 signs. This means that Pisces soul is the eldest of all 12. Having traversed through all the other signs to arrive at the karmic terminus of the astrological wheel, the Piscean soul has reached spiritual mastery and wisdom.

It's not all sunshine and roses under the sign of the fish, though. Pisces waters can be just as dark and dysfunctional as those of any other sign.

Tough to be Vulnerable

The quote above from Piscean chanteuse, Rihanna, is so typical of Pisces. While they wear their vulnerability on their sleeves, they do so from a place of strength. This is the gift of wisdom, which all Pisces are heir to.

Vulnerability is represented by the exposure of our emotions. This is a tremendous part of what it means to be a Pisces. This is a sign with little interest in cloaking its feelings. While many read Pisces as slippery—like fish slipping through the water—Pisceans tend to splash as far away as possible, if a confrontation looms. They know all too well that bald confrontation is an emotional exposure that can leave them reeling for days, if not weeks. So, even that "slippery" quality is a manifestation of wisdom. It's both a survival strategy and a boundary.

That's because the Pisces understands the potential pain confrontation can present. Pisces also understands that, when pushed too far, they are perfectly capable of giving it to someone, yanking their chain with both barrels.

Because of this sign's abundant creativity, vulnerability translates almost like a superpower, allowing Pisces to tap into a wellspring of emotional scenarios from which they've learned to share their insights with others via their chosen form of expression.

The empathic nature of Pisces makes them something of a psychic sponge for the currents of emotion around them. In the presence of people with dark energy, Pisces is likely to flee. The discomfort of finding themselves around this type of energy can be extreme.

Their vulnerability makes it impossible for them to spend much time around the toxic, narcissists, attention seekers, liars, and manipulators. With the most porous of emotional boundaries, Pisces can be overwhelmed when in the wrong place at the wrong time, for this very reason. They may just get up and leave without warning if they find themselves face-to-face with someone who sets off their alarm bells.

But the flip side of Pisces' vulnerability is their ability to comfort and nurture those around them. There is no broader shoulder to cry on than that of a Pisces and no ear more willing to listen to your woes.

Remember: Pisces has been there—wherever "there" is.

Understanding without Knowing

Sharing honors with the two other water signs, Cancer and Scorpio, Pisces is undoubtedly the most empathic of all the signs. Pisceans have a unique ability to talk people "off the ledge," understanding what's going on, emotionally, with other people, without being apprised of the situation. They just know.

The friend I mentioned earlier is a perfect example. Her ability to comfort those in crisis is legendary in our circle of friends. She always seems to know what to say and how to approach someone having a rough time. Without being too overbearing, she empathizes with their suffering.

And how else could it be for the Piscean soul, the culmination, and satisfaction of the astrological journey? They have inhabited all the other signs. They have felt all the feelings there is to feel. Perhaps that's why they're so emotionally open—they've learned all the lessons our emotions have to teach us about life; they have already lived what the sufferer is living.

It's said that all human life originated in the ocean. But Pisces is the ocean's messenger. While the rest of us have crawled to shore, Pisces still slaps its tail in the water, admiring the reflection of empathic wholeness. All that exists is part of this sign, and so Pisces' ability to feel what others are feeling is part of the magic of the fish and one reason people misunderstand Pisces so often.

There's something a little uncanny about a being someone able to see within the hearts of others without seeing, understanding them without knowing. There is no analysis. There is only that mysterious ability to know without understanding, through the many incarnations that have come before, as the Pisces soul moves through the zodiac to its terminus.

Pisces knows this life is not forever and that, when it ends, the sea will become the home of all.

Unbound Creativity

While dreaming has a bad name in our highly industrialized and mechanized society, without dreamers, where would we be as a species? It's the dreamers among us who make the changes that bring us forward. Dreamers like Steve Jobs - a Pisces, of course!

And here's where Piscean dreaming has a tremendous impact. With an imagination that never shuts off, Pisces are always searching for the connection between that imagination and the interconnectedness of the Piscean soul.

With the sense that they're connected to all that is and ever has been, Pisces has a plumb line that drills down through human history to discover the roots of truth, beauty, and purpose. Fearlessly, the Pisces are often unaware of where the ideas that pop into their heads come from. Their imaginative intellectual doodling may be called flights of fancy by a few, but Apple stands in testament to the power of Steve Jobs' dreams.

The traditional modes of thinking are, for Pisces, a prison. In the very fabric of their lives, they're able to create new ways of living, seeing, acting, creating, and being in the world that may seem out of step.

They're out of step with social conventions, for one. Again, my friend is a perfect example. She has never been one to stay in a place for too long, preferring to move freely about the world. But she's no tourist. When she finds a place she loves, she stays. She puts down roots for as long as she believes she should rightfully and properly be there, learns the language and the culture, and then she moves on.

One of my favorite quotes from her is this: "People aren't trees." While we may put down roots—as my friend is known to, occasionally —we are not rooted to the spot forever. In her opinion, people are made to move from place to place, experiencing the world from other perspectives and learning from the experience. She finds bliss in this rootlessness, a bliss that provokes the mystery of creativity. She knows she's connected to all that is, and so she lives that truth to the fullest.

This willingness to step outside the bounds of what's considered "normal" inspires my friend, allowing her to translate her dreaming, intuition, and sense of connectedness into her work—which is, of course, creative.

These are three of the dominant, classical, positive traits of the Pisces. But as any Pisces will happily tell you, the universe is held in tension. Where there is light, there is also darkness.

So, get ready for Pisces' negative traits!

When Fish Get Cold

Piscean sensitivity is a double-edged sword. While their sensitive nature allows them to "read" people and to navigate social situations based on their ability to do so, it also makes them highly susceptible to being hurt or offended.

The Pisces connects with people they've "read" as safe to be around. This can lead to the idealization of the people they have connected with in any capacity. And when that idealization happens, Pisces will respond poorly to perceived slights.

A slight can be anything from canceling a date or social outing at the last minute to not calling when you said you would. Because you're on the Piscean pedestal as a friend, lover, family member, or colleague, they will shut down, forcing the person who's disappointed them to make the first move.

But if you've messed with Pisces deliberately, you will encounter a wall of utter silence. Once the Pisces has identified you as a liar, manipulator, cheater, or any other type of person the Pisces actively avoids, don't even expect an acknowledgment of your existence.

You have died to them. You are no more. You are an ex-person.

When the fish goes cold, it stays cold. If you're not the person Pisces thought you were, you will encounter the dark chill of the ocean's depths, and you'd better get used to it because there's no going back. Pisces does not tolerate people who live by any code of conduct other than one founded on decency and kindness.

But if whatever happened between you was not intentional on your part, Pisces will thaw out eventually. A word to the wise:—when dealing with Pisces, be exactly who you say you are. Pretending to be something or someone you're not will earn you the eternal contempt of Pisces.

And I know this to be 100% true because I've seen my Pisces friend do this with more than one person. One was a cheating ex-husband. She did not attempt to work the relationship out. She did not give him a second chance. She moved out, started over, and divorced him. Those who mention his name in her presence regret it. There was also the case of the friend who threw her overboard for the sake of a lover. My Pisces friend had taken one look at the guy and knew at once what he was—an opportunist, trying to get a free ride on her friend's back. She tried to explain this, but her friend wouldn't listen, so Pisces walked out the door and never looked back. To this day, she doesn't speak to this friend, who kicked the opportunistic boyfriend out of her luxury condo seven times in nine months, took him back, then kicked him out again. During their split, he spent time with two other women, and behaved in the same manner. My Pisces friend knew all this, and we talked about it. She said "People choose what they believe they deserve and what she believes she deserves a gigolo."

The matter was never spoken of again, and to this day, this friend is not mentioned. When Pisces slams the door and you're on the other side, don't expect to get back through it.

"Where the heck did I put my phone?"

With the Piscean propensity to avoid the cruelty of the world, they can be found dreaming and are often by dreaming comes a flighty, which can be unsettling for others who cross their path.

It's one thing to be disorganized. It's something entirely more problematic when you're leaving your cell phone in the backseat of a taxi, just because you were preoccupied, or you leave your car keys in plain sight, just to forget where you put them five minutes later.

And this is a common Pisces negative trait. In fact, this is one trait that can make people around them crazy. When important items like a cell phone are lost, all hell can break loose rather quickly.

But they don't do it on purpose. Pisces' mind is always full of thoughts, dreams, and visions, so their cell phones are the furthest things from their minds, most of the time. That's especially true when they're gazing out the window at the world going by without a care to be had.

Pisceans struggle with this tendency that can cost them jobs, friends, and lovers. It's frustrating for those around them because Pisces tends to take losing important items like cell phones in stride, usually laughing off the loss.

Enter my Piscean friend again. While, like all Pisces, she's adorable, fun, intelligent, and witty, she's also scatterbrained. She has lost at least three cell phones in the past two years. I bought her a cell phone tether for her purse for Christmas. When she saw it, she was overjoyed, saying, "Well, you know I need this, right?" We laughed heartily at that one.

But she doesn't use it, which is classic Piscean behavior.

And that's why people who know and love Pisces stick around. They're who they are, and most of us find my friend's scatterbrained behavior endearing. It also makes for a great dinner party conversation! And no, Pisces won't mind if you laugh at their antics. They'll laugh right along with you.

Mañana!

One of Pisces' greatest life challenges is a tendency to be lazy. Sorry to be so blunt, but it must be said. Ask any Pisces you know whether they're lazy, and they may protest to endless industry, but only momentarily. In the end, they'll agree that they're only too happy to lay about and dream.

To be fair, though, Piscean laziness isn't just about being distracted by their active imaginations or not wanting to work. What it's really about is boredom. This is the leading reason that Pisces needs to choose the right line of work. A job that doesn't interest them is a living hell for Pisces.

Unfortunately, our culture continues to advance the notion of hard work as the panacea for all that ails us. And while it's true that working hard to achieve something is noble, it's not necessarily the way a Pisces sees life unfolding. Not all hard work is interesting, noble, or rewarding. Hard work is just backed being broken to make other people wealthy, and Pisces doesn't play that.

The moral universe of the Pisces bends toward justice. It's the nature of the fish. It's crucial that Pisces not be tempted by economic circumstance or a hefty paycheck to sign on for work they don't emotionally connect to.

My Pisces friend has learned this about herself. She once told me that she'd taken more than one job out of sheer desperation to get the rent paid, resenting having to do so bitterly. A bitter Pisces is a Pisces who you'll find staring out the window instead of doing what he or she is being paid to do.

And laziness isn't the only thing that can have a damaging effect on Piscean productivity. Procrastination is another challenge for this sign. If they don't want to do something, they'll put off doing it until the last possible moment. Whatever that something is, it will creep down the Piscean "to do" list until it drops right off the page, as Pisces has forgotten about it. This can create a lot of unnecessary conflict in work settings.

For Pisces, the environment at work is extremely important. They need engagement and stimulation to keep them interested in what they're doing. More than that, they need to believe in what they're doing and find joy and satisfaction in whatever that is.

So, there you have it. These are the most notable and universal traits of people born under the sign of Pisces. Other facets of Pisces will pop up as we move through the book, but these are the most iconic.

Nobody's perfect. We all have our flaws and our growing edges. It should give us all comfort that even the spiritually aware and karmically experienced Pisces has a few warts among their silvery scales.

In our next chapter, we'll stalk Pisces in their natural habitats at work, play, and home. Let's see if you recognize anyone!

Chapter Three: Peeking into the Spheres of Pisces

The woman with the silk flower in her hair. The man who's always smiling and remembers no one birthday. The teen who fills notebook after notebook with intricate drawings. The child who seems to know much more about life than she should.

Any of them may be a Pisces.

In this chapter, we'll peek into the world of Pisces. These brief portraits summarize Piscean behaviors in the three dominant spheres of life—work, home, and leisure. We'll look at what to expect from Pisces in each of these contexts. Let's start our journey into the world of Pisces with work.

The Pisces Boss

Many of you will find the title of this section oxymoronic. But then, you'd be forgetting about Pisceans like the USA's first President, George Washington, Director Spike Lee, and Steve Jobs.

So, while many Pisces shrink from the spotlight and the extreme level of responsibility inherent in leadership, that's not true of all Pisces. Again, influences on their sign, like rising signs and the moon they're born under, have a tremendous impact on temperament. The moon can have a striking impact on any of the signs of the zodiac. Many say it's the most important element of the astrological birth chart, and others go so far as to say that the moon sign is more important than the sun sign.

The Pisces boss exists, and sometimes, you'll be surprised to hear that leaders you know and interact with are fish. It seems to out of character, and yet, it's an undeniable reality.

But it may only be a reality when the Pisces has found the niche that highlights all the most prized qualities of this zodiac sign. That's when Pisces' unquenchable passion comes out to play, never tiring of the work, never failing to inspire, and always a dynamic influence on those who work with them.

One of the most compelling attributes of the Pisces boss is the absence of micro-management. A Pisces boss won't be found standing behind you, trying to find errors in your work or screaming at you for coming in a few minutes late. That's not their style.

Their style is to "read" their employees to make sure that they're getting everything they need to recognize their potential. Pisces, who struggle with procrastination or laziness, are keenly aware of what coworkers need to stay fully engaged. Of all the other signs, a Pisces is most likely to recognize boredom and bullying, when it occurs on their watch.

The Pisces is oriented toward the good in matters of human relations and fervently desires to make those they supervise feel not only comfortable in the workplace but valued and appreciated. They know it hurts to be overlooked. They know it hurts to be ignored and misunderstood. It happens to them a lot.

So, the Pisces boss is like a lighthouse seen in stormy seas—reassuring, inspiring, and ready to encourage employees to be their very best. The Pisces boss sees well ahead. That ability to see what others don't, while unnerving, is also the hallmark of leaders who change the world for the better and transform workplaces from productivity mills to centers of excellence.

Pisces understands that when their unique vision of a certain project or goal is articulated to employees, that they catch fire, and so, Pisces' communication skills are deployed actively to ensure that all employees share in that unique vision and its purpose.

Because the Pisces boss is an intuitive, empathic leader, they know employees need to be liberated from arcane regulations to do their best work. Pisces knows that when this happens, their employees will become part of a leadership team that is collaborative instead of hierarchical.

Instead of micro-managing employees, the Pisces boss lets them out of the barn and into the field, knowing that free-range employees produce more satisfying results and those results are more likely to conform with the vision in play when they're not smothered.

But make no mistake; this isn't about being "nice." A consultative leader who encourages a less marked hierarchy is strategically aware. This leader understands that hanging over people doesn't get the job done; intuitive Pisces knows exactly how to extract the desired performance and results.

And all that sounds a little like Steve Jobs, doesn't it? Well, it does—and doesn't. Steve Jobs has also seen a heavy-handed leader, but he is undeniably the most successful entrepreneur of the last half-century. Many variables in astrology can impact the characteristics of the signs, so you may see a different outcome. At the same time, there are overarching truths that usually bear out.

I'm not about to lie—there are downsides to having a Pisces boss, too. I've just mentioned Steve Jobs, who was known to centralize power around his office, demanding total control from the top down. It should be told that Steve Jobs was born with an Aries moon, and Mars was also in Aries. The aggressive ram is known for butting heads, and Jobs rejected the contention that employees had any right to do that with him. He was known simultaneously as "mean and intimidating" and "inspiring and motivating." Keep him in mind as you read the rest of this section.

The Pisces is not keen on being the bearer of bad news—especially the news that an employee has been fired. Administrative nuts and bolts are the biggest bore in the world to the Pisces boss. Functions like performance reviews and payroll cause the Pisces boss's eyes to glaze over in about 10 seconds flat. A Pisces boss may even slip out the side door to avoid such important facets of working life.

Just know that if you work with a Piscean manager or other leader, you'll see the best of humanity and also a little childish flight from responsibility. What the Pisces boss needs more than anything is administrative support to *get the boring end of the job done*. When this is in place, a Pisces boss is inspirational, productive, and exceptional.

HINT: Just don't try to drive the agenda. That Pisces tail may well come out to slap you back into line!

The Pisces Employee

Much like the Pisces boss, the Pisces employee is a force of a creative nature. There is no sign more imaginative, bringing innovative and novel thinking to any table. While the corporate world or politics might seem like the last place, you'd find a Pisces, they're out there. The late Congressman John Lewis, a lifelong civil rights firebrand, was a Pisces, as was the late Senator Ted Kennedy and—believe it or not—Senate majority leader Mitch McConnell.

Pisces individualism and disinterest in conformity for the sake of "fitting in" is what makes them valuable assets in the workplace. These brilliantly unconventional thinkers might not be at home in chartered accounting, but wherever new ways of doing things are welcome, they'll excel. And who knows, a Pisces might invent chartered accounting software that makes the entire affair less boring!

The adaptability of the Pisces is where employers will find a star. Wherever Pisces go is home, so their ability under this star sign to turn on a dime is certainly a selling point. Part of that adaptability is Pisces' tendency to welcome change as a cure for the mundane. Easily bored, Pisces love it when you move the goalposts! While change is unwelcomed by many, Pisces embraces it, making them extremely easy to work with.

Any employer who can harness the limitless potential of the Piscean imagination, creativity, and adaptability will benefit tremendously. But many employers are conventional thinkers stuck in a mechanistic and rules-based past. This can create a lot of problems for Pisces at work.

For this reason, the Pisces should think about careers like consulting or freelancing that offer them the freedom they need to grow and to know satisfaction in their working lives.

Naturally, the creative arts are a Piscean playground, but here are a few other careers which fit the temperament of the fish well.

- **Filmmaker**—The Pisces imagination is tailormade for Tinsel Town.

- **Counselor** - The empathic nature of Pisces makes them ideal for this role. Their ability to "read" people and to feel with others are prerequisites.

- **Caregiver**—Compassionate to a fault, Pisces make exceptional caregivers and nurses.

- **Charity**—Pisces' passion comes out to play in this sector, driving their ability to bring in those donations, deploying their exceptional communication skills

- **Marketing**—Companies who hire a Pisces to craft their branding via marketing and advertising have hired a genius who will build a consistent, powerful brand. Pisces love to bring the unseen to life and creating a persona for a commercial brand is exactly that kind of magic.

There are so many types of work were Pisces can excel. The trick is finding that special place that represents the perfect fit for these unconventional, exceptional people.

Pisces at Play

You're at a party. The music's playing, the drinks are flowing, and everyone's having a terrific time. You look around the patio to see who's out there, and you see a man sitting quietly, sipping a cold drink, smiling, and enjoying the scene before him.

As you watch, he raises his hand and waves at a woman across the room. Seeing him a wave, she stops in mid-conversation, excuses herself, and hurries over to greet the man, as though compelled by the sheer force of his personality.

This is how the Pisces does parties. Not the most social of the signs, Pisces will not be that "life of the party" who starts conversations with random people. Pisces will socialize with those at the party willing to socialize with them—preferably making the first move. That wave across the room? That's about as far as Pisces goes until feeling more comfortable about the overall social whirl around them.

That Pisces friend I introduced to you earlier in this book is a perfect example of the foregoing. I have been to many parties where she's also been a guest. And you know what? At almost every party, she has sat in the same chair all night, rising only to replenish her drink, hit the snack table, and visit the washroom. Despite that, almost every single person in the room went over to where she was sitting and chatted with her. By the end of the party, she was surrounded by others, all of whom were discussing the current state of the world.

While my friend is quite a middling consumer of alcoholic beverages, that may not be said of all Pisces, by any means. Pisces are either a teetotaler (having learned their lesson about booze) or a madcap, dancing on the pool table with a lampshade on their head. This is the default truth about Pisces at a party.

Part of that truth is the pleasure Pisces takes in observing other people. This is Pisces' most beloved party game. Capable of picking up on the emotional landscape of others, Pisces takes mental notes about who they might like to meet and chat with, who to avoid like the plague, and who might be having a bit of a rough time and need a little support.

And Pisces will most likely wind up being the person to provide that support and a shoulder to cry on when the boozy, cathartic tears come later in the evening.

They'll often be found enjoying the music wafting through the room, the sound of laughter, and the pleasure of those surrounding them.

But when Pisces indulges in the social lubricant known as alcohol, he might propose a game of spin the bottle—especially if he's emptied the bottle.

Something Pisces should avoid is becoming dependent on substances. Trying to make social interaction less about competing emotions and more about the people surrounding them and having fun. Because of their finely tuned empathy, Pisces may believe they need liquid courage to cleave the perilous waters of social situations. It helps them dull the energies coming at them, and focus on enjoying their time, instead.

While it has a place, Pisces needs to be careful not to become enmeshed in behaviors like substance abuse. Pisces' potential for addiction to drugs and alcohol can be legendary, with the late Elizabeth Taylor standing as *Exhibit A*. When Pisces know the dangers, they're able to enjoy parties to the fullest—especially when their environment is filled with fun and laughter!

Pisces will run to the dance floor alone, when the mood is right, and the rest of the party will follow. Again, my Pisces friend is always the first to hit the dance floor and has been known to zone out completely, as she closes her eyes and moves blissfully to the music. Although she could never be described as the life of the party, she is most certainly can be described as the soul.

Pisces at Home

The main goals of Pisces are balance, tranquility, comfort, and beauty.

Spiritually attuned Pisces conceptualizes their living space as a sanctuary from the world, where they can kick back, relax, and let the groove move them. There is nothing more important for Pisces, who needs time to recharge their batteries in a nurturing, pleasant space that speaks to them.

An interesting feature of the Pisces way of being in the world is that their home is something like an extension of them. You might even think of the Pisces home as a cocoon.

A firsthand look into the Pisces mindset about their home living habits comes from my friend. Her home is an oasis of warmth and cushy comfort. Color and art fill every room, and much of the art you'll see on her walls is "outsider" art. This is art made by those who normally get little attention; she loves the originality these works. She likes supporting an unseen, unacknowledged art community. Again, the empathy of the Pisces drives even aesthetic choices.

Going even deeper, it's interesting to consider a bit of what signifies home to the Pisces. My friend, as a child, would travel with her family to various locations in her city. She often noticed small groves of trees here and there and used to fantasize about living in them on her own. To her, this was the ultimate lifestyle. Of course, people grow and change. She'd always had a dream of living by a rushing river, with trees lining it on either side and birds flitting through the trees' dense branches. She now lives by a river, in a small, comfortable home.

In the Pisces home, you'll find pets—usually more than one and often adopted out of an animal support/rescue agency. There is no such thing as a Pisces who can ignore the cries of kittens and puppies. They might not give them all a home, but Pisces will never pass by an animal in need, so a Pisces home will always be graced by the gentle presence of animals, from birds to dogs and cats to baby goats.

Pisces people love being in their homes. Taking great care to decorate to their tastes as, habitually, they spend a great deal of time there. Expect beautiful, rich color. The walls will all be painted and not necessarily with the blues and greens of the ocean. Pisces also adores the colors seen in the natural world beyond the water element, finding inspiration in the colors of flowers, plants, the sunset, sunrise, and the bright yellow of the sun itself.

Expect throw cushions. There's no avoiding them in a Pisces household, and you can bet that Pisces has a memory foam bed topper or mattress. Comfort and self-nurture are so crucial to sensitive Pisces' wellbeing. They love the sense that their home is a world that may only be fully understood by themselves, their beloved pets, and their closest friends.

You may even see your Pisces friends and neighbors decorating their walls with colorful murals and designs. While not everyone may understand this practice, Pisces understands the home as the root of the soul, where they live in perfect contentment and peace. In that nurturing, regenerating state, they ready themselves for what's expected of them in the world.

Married or cohabiting Pisceans will need quiet time to dream or practice their chosen art. While embracing and loving, Pisces can only sustain the level of intensity required by a relationship when able to enjoy ample time alone. So, the Pisces home is one of great love. But it's also one where respect for the individual needs of both partners is paramount. If Pisces' need for time alone is respected, harmony will reign in their peaceable kingdom. If not, Pisces becomes withdrawn, resenting their partner's inability to allow them the regenerative time they so desperately need. The Greta Garbo's of the zodiac, Pisces "want to be alone," as it's what keeps their spirit in balance.

And you'll almost always find Pisces at home. People born under this sign are what I like to call "semi-social." They love their social time, but without their precious time alone, they wither. When given the space, they need in their private oasis of calm and eye-appealing pleasure, they'll return to social life well-rested and ready to engage.

Only the closest of Pisces' friend group will be invited to share in the delights of the Pisces home. Extremely private and selective about their associations, Pisces operates on trust. When trust is not in place, don't expect an invitation to share a bottle of wine on their cozy terrace, crowded with plants, and awash with homey comforts.

Pisces is a sign with many levels, creating the layers of an Old Soul like none other found in the zodiac. Those who work, play, and live with these cosmically attuned creatures wouldn't want to exist in a world without them. Many of us have spirit animals. The lucky among us have Pisceans to guide us.

In our next chapter, we'll look at the Pisces child and how parents can support them growing into the unique people they are.

Chapter Four: Bringing up Baby Pisces

The Pisces child is sometimes a bit of a mystery to parents. All children are a little weird, to be sure, but Pisces out-weirds every other kid on the planet!

My Pisces friend is a perfect example. The only girl in her family, she was always a little different. For one, she rarely cried as an infant. She was not given to the epic tantrums of most toddlers, either. Quiet and watchful, she observed everything she saw and everyone she saw.

Learning to read by the age of two, she was remarkably thirsty to understand the world around her. She wanted to do everything there was to do, studying piano, ballet and painting.

From the time she could talk, it was clear that she was imaginative, as she was always the neighborhood ringleader when it was time for the kids to put on a show. She encouraged her playmates to do what they were best at, which often included singing, dancing or putting on a show.

By the time she got to high school, she was even more of a force of nature, sticking her finger in every pie of knowledge she could find, especially if that pie was concerned with creativity or spirituality. She constantly wrote, inventing characters and little worlds for her hyperactive imagination to inhabit.

She's told me that one of her favorite shows while growing up was I Dream of Jeannie. She loved it because Jeannie lived in an exotic-looking bottle lined with cushions. It never occurred to her that her "master" would send her into the bottle when she was naughty and refuse to let her out. Critical thinking didn't enter into it, though. Neither did the abusive patriarchal overtones of keeping a woman in a bottle. Rather, she focused on the privacy of the space and the coziness of it. That's Pisces for you; it was all about that exotic bottle, with its plentiful, luxurious throw cushions for my friend!

Not Your Average Bear

Pisces children are evidence of Plato's claim that all people are born bearing the knowledge of previous lives. They have a knowing quality not seen in other children. This correlates to the position of the sign at the end of the karmic astrological cycle. All knowledge gained in the other signs is carried within their little souls. How they express that reality is exactly as I described in the case of my friend. Their eyes are always looking. Their minds are always inquiring.

Piscean creativity is a huge part of who children born under this sign are. Pisces children will manifest their creativity early in life, demanding constant encouragement, freedom to explore, and the art supplies they need to let their active imaginations run wild.

While Pisces children make friends easily, they're also content to stay in their own little worlds, finger painting, banging away on a toy piano, or dancing to their favorite tunes on the radio. And if they dance, you'd better watch and then, applaud!

And, like all other Pisces, your fish baby is sensitive. Easily hurt and discouraged from shining as they know they're born to, your support, as a parent, is crucial to the healthy development of the Pisces child. They need you to tell them they can choose creativity and call on it as an emotional and spiritual wellspring all their lives.

Take care of your emotional setting around your Pisces child. Born as mega-empaths, they will often cleave to your emotions to reinforce their connection to you and further, to comfort you. They know when you're not feeling quite right, and they'll be only too happy to join you in your temporary funk. So, it's important that you temper your emotions around them.

Of course, because you're the adult in the relationship, that doesn't go both ways, so your baby Pisces will tell you how they're feeling. Open about their emotions, they want you to know when they're upset or hurt. Pisces aren't shy about letting others know when they're not happy.

In our post-emotional world, that's often an unwelcome trait. But with Pisces, feelings are important, and sharing them with those they trust even more so. While you should support the right of your child to express less than ideal emotions, it's also crucial that you talk to them about emotional management, and what behaviors are expected outside the home.

A Pisces child at school will always be the first to stand up for someone being bullied. They'll be the first to comfort another child in tears, and they won't stand for meanness, lying, or manipulation of any kind. This is one of Pisces' most noble traits—advocacy for others, which springs from the sign's endless compassion.

Sometimes, the Piscean imagination can be a little overwhelming. Many are a little taken aback by the stories Pisces children tell, so filled with detail and adventure; they almost seem like delusions. But don't worry, this is normal for Pisces children. Great outlets for their storytelling are creative writing or creating and improvising impromptu plays with their family and friends. Pisces children will entertain you at the drop of a hat.

My friend tells a story of once escaping from her mother's grasp following her bath and racing to the living room, still wet and completely naked. She then launched herself into a wild dance performance as her father yelled that she was blocking the football game on television, and her brothers rolled on the floor laughing.

One thing's for sure. When you parent a Pisces child, the only dull moments are those your child spends in the private world they love to retreat to. These, you will come to be grateful for. Pisces children are also big talkers, always ready to tell you about what they've learned, their new friend, or their latest fantasy project. They will rotate childhood love interests on the regular, breaking up, making up, flitting from favorite to favorite like the little butterflies they are.

What the Pisces child sees is learned. As visual learners, they pick up things quickly. This will typify their learning style throughout their lives, so encourage them by boning up on visual learning. Learn more about it in the Resources section at the end of this book.

Something genuinely wonderful about the Pisces child is their natural tendency to want to help. While other children hang back, the Pisces will immediately offer to lend a hand.

"Me" and "mine" aren't part of Pisces Baby's vocabulary. They love to share what they have with others. When they see that someone around them doesn't have something everyone else has, they'll do what they can to fix the problem. They are socialists by nature, who believe that everything should be shared with everyone else and that no one should go without while others have more than they need.

As I said earlier, the Piscean moral universe bends toward justice naturally, and that starts as soon as they're able to reason and to note inequality and injustice in their immediate environment.

One of the most endearing traits of the Piscean child is their love of cuddling. This tells them, clearly and unequivocally, that they're loved. Your cuddles are prized by your Pisces child. A lack of them can stunt their development, so be extravagant in showing your water baby how much you love them.

Get your little Pisces outdoors often. Pisces love the natural world, with all its colors, textures, and scents. They love to experience nature, explore bugs, and learn about everything concerned with animals, plants, and flowers. Their curiosity is endless.

If there were a childhood mantra for Pisceans, it would be "don't fence me in." Pisces love its freedom to dream, explore, create, and go to the places their imaginations take them. You may not always understand your fishy little person, but a Pisces child will richly bless with surprise after surprise, bringing the fruits of imagination and fancy into your life.

Give them all the unstructured time they need to pursue their secret worlds, curiosity, and creativity. You'll find that they're most comfortable with either a small group of other children or on their own. As I've related, Pisceans are "semi-social." They can't be forced into a mold that doesn't fit them. Trying to do that is the wrong approach.

Pisces children are also, unfortunately, subject to bullying at times by other children. My Piscean friend experienced this as a child and throughout high school. Even in adulthood, she's sometimes bullied by grown women at work. Sensitive Pisces is a favorite target of bullies. But children in this sign will stand up for themselves as much as they will for other children when the moment presents itself. Sometimes, they shock even themselves with the ferocity of their counterattack. This can lead to unfortunate incidents on the playground. That may take a little finesse on the part of parents. Your job is to instill in your child that there are better ways of dealing with a bully than hitting him over the head with a twirling baton.

True story. My Piscean friend answered a bully this way in third grade. A bully threw a chair at her when the teacher had left the classroom, and she responded by cracking him over the head with her newly gifted baton. She was sent home from school for her efforts. The bully was not. Because when the Pisces child goes off, neutron bombs pale in comparison!

While expressing anger so viscerally can be a problem, it's important to understand that Pisceans internalize negative emotions. This isn't a healthy response to negative emotions. Retaining those feelings is corrosive. Because of this, be sure to work with your Pisces child on containing their temper and also on learning to name and release negative emotions.

You can also spend time with them when they come to you complaining of controlling schoolmates, or manipulative, mendacious ones. Even in childhood, Pisces children have no time for people who engage in such behaviors. Remind them that many people are best bullying.

All this will serve your water baby well in life.

In our next chapter, we will be diving into the adventurous love life of Pisces, exploring their compatibility with other signs. Their style of loving, which is Byzantine in its complexity, boundless in its practice, and thrilling to those lucky enough to know love with this sensual sign.

Chapter Five: Pisces in Love

There is no romantic more hopeless than Pisces. Pisces lives and breathes romance, dreaming of sharing themselves and their lives with a cherished other.

The intensity of the Pisces in love is something not everyone is prepared for. It can seem almost surreal how far they're willing to go to give their all to those they love. Experiencing love with a Pisces is a once in a lifetime experience that has no equal.

Intuitive and spiritual, Pisces reads their lover like a book and then translates what they've read into that person's needs. So be sure you're serious. Because when the Pisces reads any hint of deception or falsehood, they will be shattered, and they will make sure that you share in at least a small portion of the pain you've caused.

Pisces are not people to trifle with. The scars of love can run deep in them, creating rafts of scar tissue that can be opened easily when they detect that you're being dishonest or equivocating with them.

But if you're the real thing, you'll be enveloped in an unparalleled experience of love, replete with the soaring emotions of two beating hearts that won't be stilled. The honest lover with serious intentions is the key to Piscean bliss.

For those reading who have become enchanted by a sensual Pisces, remember that you're the one who must make the approach. Shy Pisces would never presume to do so. That's a small price to pay to experience the fullness of what romantic love is all about. Because you've hooked this fish, you're in for the most delightful experience of your life. And Pisces will remain at your side, even when things go wrong. The emotional investment they make in their partners is not made lightly. It's made for the long haul. For Pisces, the heart and its ways are second nature, and love is all there is.

Let's visit the other signs of the zodiac to discover which of them is most compatible with the most romantic and emotionally available of all the signs.

Aries (March 21-April 19)

Probably the most aggressive of all the signs of the zodiac, Aries can be described as ambitious and bold.

Drawn to each other like magnets, there's chemical attraction aplenty between gentle Pisces and the audacious ram. Aries will move heaven and earth to get at Pisces. But that's Aries. These guys get what they want.

The problem for a dreamy Pisces is that the energy of the ram can be as destructive as it is energetic. Tending to insensitivity, Pisces will have difficulty maintaining emotional balance in a relationship with someone born under Aries.

Sexually, Aries loves sex as an athletic event. There's little of the tender romance that Pisceans live for. With compromise, this part of an Aries can encouraged, but does the ram sound interested in compromise?

As with everything else in astrology, the star sign can be tempered by other elements present in the birth chart, like the moon your love interest is born under.

However, Aries may make for a fun Pisces fling, but there's little to suggest that the opposing energies of these two signs can coexist in loving harmony in the context of a relationship.

Taurus (April 20—May 20)

Represented symbolically by the bull, this star sign loves serenity and sensuality. While reliable and of an inherently stable disposition, Taurus also believes in the principle of mañana—don't rush these bovine behemoths. They prefer to take their time, relax, and take in the sounds, scents, and scenery.

Pisces and Taurus can be serenely happy together, so long as Taurus doesn't attempt to change Pisces. Flexibility is not Taurus's strongest suit. But if Taurus accepts Pisces dreamy, freewheeling ways, there's a lot of potential in this match.

The stability of the bull is a wonderful complement to Pisces. Knowing what they want and when they want it helps Pisces focus on the here and now, instead of the ethers beyond the earth.

One recommendation for this pairing is the dedication both signs have to loyalty and commitment. In addition, both the fish and ram are reserved and introverted, with both tending to a sentimentality that brings mutual joy.

Pisces is deeply connected to the emotional component of sex, while Taurus focuses on its physical nature. While this may sound like a roadblock, it represents the ying-yang of coupling that can bring great happiness to both partners. Both understand sex as a serious matter, representing the expression of a love bond between two people.

In summary, Pisces in love with Taurus often finds the blissful realization of their dream, and if both partners are aware of and willing to work on their differences, this match has the potential to last a lifetime.

Gemini (May 21-June 20)

Like the two fish, the twins of Gemini represent duality. But they also represent a dynamic and active sign that can't find enough hours in the day to do everything they have in their fevered imaginations to do.

The problem here is that the vitality of Gemini brings with it a tendency to flip from one priority to another at the drop of a dime. Pisces can be thrown off balance by this, and that disorientation can be the source of pain for the sensitive fish.

The activity level of Gemini is also something of a problem for Pisces. The fish needs time to recharge their batteries, and the hyperactive nature of the twins will leave them feeling depleted.

While Gemini is sexually passionate, they often regard their sexuality as a toy. And they may include sensitive Pisces in that column, much to Pisces' detriment. Sex is much more than fun for Pisces, having strong emotional and spiritual components. While Gemini will appear fly-by-night to Pisces, Pisces will seem a bit of a millstone to Gemini.

The energies of these two signs may be mitigated by other factors in the birth chart, but ultimately, they work against one another, making for an unfavorable outcome.

Cancer (June 21-July 22)

If Pisces has something like a twin in the rest of the zodiac, it's Cancer. Represented by the crab, Cancer boasts a similar ability to read the emotional currents in the surrounding people. At home in both earthly pursuits and those of the spirit, Cancer is a truly excellent match for Pisces.

Sexually, this is a match made in heaven and mandated by the stars. Dreamy, tender, romantic, and full of welcome surprises, the fish and crab know exactly how to make each other happy.

The spiritual, emotional, creative, and intellectual bond between Pisces and Cancer is the epitome of holistic, healthy sexuality that satisfies both partners on every level of their beings.

Cancer provides an anchor in the real world for Pisces. While Pisces doesn't care to plan, Cancer is concerned with creating the right conditions for the match to thrive into the future.

This is an exceptional pairing, providing both partners with the bliss, emotional satisfaction, and intuitive—almost psychic—connection both crave.

For money, this is one of Pisces' best shots at the sort of love they desire; love that's almost supernatural.

Leo (July 23-August 22)

Many call people born under this sign the narcissists of the zodiac, and that's not far wrong. Expect Leo not only to claim the spotlight but demand it. Dramatic and expressive, you can't miss the lion. Reigning over all the other signs, Leo doesn't play second fiddle to anyone.

Because Leo likes to lead and control every aspect of their lives, they'll probably want that in your relationship, too. This, for obvious reasons, can be a problem in a Leo-Pisces match.

Sensitive Pisces won't care for Leo's steam roller approach to life, under which are squashed Piscean autonomy, along with Pisces' vibrant emotions. Pisces also is an introvert, while Leo is the extroverted life of every party they go to, in the spotlight from start to finish. This tendency can crush sensitive Pisces.

The success of a match between Pisces and Leo rests on Leo's willingness to temper their need for attention. Pisces may also have difficulty with the materialistic nature of Leo.

Sexually, these two find much to enjoy in each other. Leo's intensity and theatricality complement Pisces' love of fantasy, bringing both sexual satisfaction. Beyond that, this is a match that will require a great deal of accommodation and compromise from both parties.

Virgo (August 21-September 22)

Perfectionist Virgo is rooted in the material world. Practical, logical, and consistent, the Virgo loves to spend time making themselves masters of whatever they strive to master.

Cogito ergo sum—I think, therefore I am—is Virgo's mantra. On the other hand, Pisces *feel*. This is one of the greatest challenges of a match between these two. While Virgo relies on the intellect to guide, Pisces' intuition is their compass for navigating the world.

With feet firmly planted on the ground, Virgo's analytical nature mystifies Pisces, whose primary concerns are the meaning of things and the potential inherent in each day. This drives the practical, calculating Virgo mentally.

Pisces can be maddening for the painstaking Virgo, but Pisces may also be capable of balancing the obsessive-compulsive nature of the sign, while Virgo may be able to reign in a few of Pisces "less desirable" traits, organizing and tempering them.

Physically, sex for this pairing is excellent. Both partners will be highly satisfied by the emotional bonding their combined sexuality can create. But Virgo's analytical nature can get in the way, as they'll always be wondering if this is the best they can do.

And frankly, that's not enough for emotional Pisces, whose commitment to their partners is all-encompassing.

Libra (September 23-October 22)

Fun fact: only Libra is denoted by a manmade symbol. The scales represent the balanced nature of this sign, and people born under it reflect the nature of the scales, which is symmetry in all things.

While this pairing is desirable, both signs require a partner who is somewhat more stable and stronger. With both being intensely idealistic, this celestial coupling might be better off with a little more real. As always, this factor may be mitigated by other influences in the charts of both.

Libra's diplomacy, combined with the Pisces preference for flexibility, can be at odds. But fortunately, the communicative styles of both signs are focused on reaching an agreement. Diplomacy and flexibility are two sides of the same coin, realized via different methodologies and strategies for each.

Libra tends to be analytical, while Pisces' heart leads the way, on a path forged by that dominant Piscean trait, intuition. Libra has trouble letting go of rationality, while Pisces has learned to trust intuition above all. This can lead to head butting. That both signs can encounter difficulties arriving at decisions further complicates the interaction between the two.

Because of the analytical side of Libra, Pisces may interpret their words and actions as emotionally detached or even cold. And while Pisces is introverted, Libra tends to be extroverted, creating potential lifestyle conflicts.

There's plenty of chemistry popping between these two, but that may show strain, eventually, as Libra takes a less serious approach to sex than Pisces, who requires an emotional and spiritual sexual connection.

If both partners are committed to understanding the needs of the other, this pairing can endure. But that commitment is necessary for the relationship to stand the test of time.

Scorpio (October 23-November 22)

This powerful, dynamic sign is so full of fire, people often believe it couldn't possibly be a water sign, but like Pisces and Cancer, that's exactly what Scorpio is.

And when Pisces gets together with Scorpio, the phrase "a match made in heaven" comes to mind. Equivalent to a pairing with Cancer, there is no match more perfect for the romantic fish than Scorpio. Reading each other's minds, this is the match that Pisces prays for.

Scorpio is committed, by nature, to protecting those nearest and dearest to them. They're leaders who apply their leadership skills to relationships, but not in a dictatorial way. They seek to make sure that no harm comes to those they love most, and for Pisces, this is a stellar trait in a partner. Scorpio, like Pisces, can intuit the motivations of others, tempering Pisces' trusting nature with an ability to identify red flags in other people.

But Pisces needs to be patient with the level of sensitivity modeled by Scorpio. This can border on paranoia. Pisces can draw Scorpio out, allowing somewhat moody Scorpio to open up and share.

There is a distinct aura to this relationship. Cocooned together, these two water signs are a mystery to others, but Pisces and Scorpio find in each other the epitome of normality. Other people are weird!

For this coupling, sex is transcendent. Meeting each other's unspoken needs by telepathy, the Pisces-Scorpio romantic couple transcends what most people think of as love. This astrological combination is intensely spiritual, going far beyond the mundane.

Sagittarius (November 22-December 21)

Represented by the archer, Sagittarius aims its bow at adventure and knowledge. This sign is dedicated to adventures of all kinds, whether travel, intellectual or spiritual.

A roadblock in the success of a relationship with a Pisces-Sagittarius couple is the direct, unfiltered nature of the archer. Sensitive Pisces isn't the biggest fan of that characteristic. It's also of note that Sagittarius gets things done, whereas Pisces needs to dream about actions before undertaking them. While this may seem lazy, this aspect of Pisces is more about envisioning the road forward than not wanting to move. Sagittarius' decisive and active nature can feel a little vulgar to the fish.

For all the hippie-dippy vibes of Pisces, people born under this sign are, by nature, conservative. Pisces thinks before speaking and looks before leaping. Not so Sagittarius. They are impulsive, appearing wild and reckless to the careful Piscean.

The Sagittarian's intensely social nature is also alien to Pisces, who desires the cocoon more than the social whirl. Sagittarius is often also non-committal about romantic relationships, which the Pisces will invariably read as an insult.

While the physical attraction between Pisces and Sagittarius can be powerful, Pisces will feel the absence of an emotional or spiritual component. Sagittarius thinks of sex in very physical terms, which can be frustrating for Pisces, for whom sex is almost a sacrament.

While this relationship can have a chance under the right conditions—mutual attentiveness being indispensable—Sagittarius is not the best match for Pisces.

Capricorn (December 22-January 19)

While Capricorn is an earth sign, they're represented by the sea-goat. This mythical creature has a tail, so it finds itself at home in both the realm of emotion and that of the material, tangible world.

Solid, practical Capricorn is an excellent complement to the emotional, mystical nature of Pisces, bringing the fish back to reality with patience, understanding, and deep love. These two find common ground with ease.

Capricorn brings romantic Pisces needed stability. With the sea-goat able to move between the realms of the material and the far-off ethers, Pisces find quiet strength in a Capricorn lover. And Capricorn, not being that affected by romantic notions, finds in a Pisces a doorway to this world of emotion and spirituality, allowing them to step into a world they sometimes shy away from.

A potential conflict between these two is money. Capricorn is keenly aware of practical, real-world concerns, while Pisces is more likely to be less than concerned with this aspect of life. This can be frustrating for both parties, with Capricorn skittish about the Piscean tendency to generosity and charity and Pisces inhibited in this respect by the care taken around money by the sea-goat.

Sexually, Capricorn loves the fun aspect of sex, entering into this side of the relationship with gusto. Pisces will love this, adding romanticism and an emotional constancy that Capricorn finds reassuring. This pairing has a great chance to succeed because of the balance between the two signs.

Aquarius (January 20-February 18)

The water bearer is an air sign which replenishes the earth, creating abundant life. Great humanist thinkers, Aquarius' most pressing concern is to mend what's broken and to heal what's hurting.

Pisces and Aquarius have little to recommend them as a match. However, Pisces' willingness to compromise may serve any relationship pursued between the two. And if Pisces can get Aquarius out of the realm of intellect that is its natural home, the two may make their pairing work.

Pisces is drawn to the intellectual nature of Aquarius, finding an outlet for its own intellectual nature, which strongly trends toward the metaphysical—an interest that many Aquarians are likely to share.

Ultimately, the cool detachment of Aquarius will puzzle a Pisces, and frustrate the fish's need for intimacy. Aquarius's many distractions and preoccupation will drive Pisces nuts, as there may seem to be no time to be fully present for the active, inquisitive Aquarian. Pisces may also feel that they're being put last, as Aquarius often gets caught up in the many interests that attract people born under this sign to the detriment of all else, including their partners.

Pisces will also have difficulty maintaining a strong connection with the water bearer, sexually. Aquarians, while adventurous and inventive lovers, will seem too detached and physically oriented to Pisces. For this reason, Pisces may wind up feeling unsatisfied with their failure to connect emotionally with Aquarius.

Pisces (February 19-March 20)

As we have learned earlier in this book, Pisces are the realization of all the 11 other signs of the zodiac's lessons. Intensely spiritual and emotional, Pisces lives in a tension between the fantastic and the concrete.

It may seem so at first but, two fish joined in a romantic union is not a walk in the park. With two of these dreamy romantics locked in a loving embrace, the going can get a little weird.

The most dangerous aspect of a Pisces-Pisces relationship is the tendency of the two to become completely lost in each other, to the detriment of all else. The emotional tendencies of Pisces are magnified when there are two in a relationship. That can lead to severe negativity, as they feed off one another in a toxic loop.

However, if one or both Pisces in the relationship has a moon in an earth sign, there is greater hope of a successful match. With the moon being (arguably) as important as the sun in any sign, Pisces gains need stability, feet planted on the earth as they explore the ethers.

Sex for a Pisces dual coupling is almost supernatural, with the intuition of the two leading to erotic transcendence well beyond what most couples experience.

While this relationship can work, both parties should take the time to explore their respective charts before they become intimate. Two Pisces can live lives of harmonious bliss when the planets are well aligned.

Because we've discussed romantic relationships in this chapter, next, we should delve into the more complex aspects of astrology to understand how the planets in individual charts might affect the character of Pisces. As I've mentioned, the moon is a particularly strong influence that should be considered, as it's right up there with the sun. We'll also be looking into decanates to gain a more well-rounded understanding of what makes Pisces tick.

Chapter Six: Going Deeper into the World of Astrology to Understand Pisces

Many people are skeptical about astrology because its public representation is shallow. Many people believe that the sun sign determines the overall character of the zodiac.

This is a very superficial understanding of what makes astrology tick. While the sun is determined by the date of birth, other aspects of the signs are determined by far more subtle indicators, including the position of other planets in the birth chart.

While we've covered the aspects of astrology from this deeper method of inquiry in Chapter One, essential to understanding the meaning of any sign is a knowledge of other influences present during birth. So, it's not merely the date on which you were born that counts. Knowing where all the other planets were at the exact time of your birth is essential to gaining a more accurate picture of those born under the various signs.

First, let's discuss the decanates, also called "decans" in astrological circles.

A Matter of Degree

But isn't degree everything? A few inches this way, a few inches that way, and everything not only feels but looks different.

Astrology is simply a dynamic discipline of reading the movement of the planets during the specific timeframes that we were born under. This can be refined further by knowing the time. Because planets don't just swish around the solar system willy-nilly, their positions vary by degrees.

Before we move into a discussion of decans, let's get a handle on triplicities.

Every zodiac sign is ruled by one of the four physical elements—earth, air, water, and fire:

- Earth: Capricorn, Taurus, Virgo
- Air: Gemini, Libra, Aquarius
- Water: Cancer, Scorpio, Pisces
- Fire: Aries, Leo, Sagittarius

It's easy to see why these groupings are referred to as *triplicities*, with three signs in each of the four elements.

As the subtitle suggests, decans concern degrees—specifically, degrees in multiples of ten. In each sign, there are three decans, representing ten degrees each. Each of these decans, in turn, is governed by the movements of a specific planet. This is a powerful influence on people born under any sign in the zodiac. The planet your decan is ruled by is as influential as the sun sign itself. But the deeper you go into astrology, the more extraordinarily specific you'll find it is.

The first decan is a part of the same triplicity in the element of the sign in question. For example, the first decan of a planet appearing in Pisces applies to the first decan or ten degrees. This indicates the most undiluted expression of the traits for which Pisces is best known. It's the same story for all the signs.

Let's take a detailed look at the decans of Pisces. Once we understand the planetary influences on Pisces from this standpoint, it will give us a more developed picture.

February 19-February 29, First Decanate, Pisces-Pisces

In this decan (NB: the terms are interchangeable and refer to the same three ten-degree sections of Pisces), Neptune is the planetary influence, making people born during this decan double Pisces, as it is also the planet governing the sign, as a whole.

This the decan of imagination and intuition. Pisceans born in this decan can practically read your mind and predict what you'll do in any situation. These fish will also have lives full of change and adventure.

Double Pisces will have many lovers. Passionate and sensual, this variety of Pisces wants to experience everything there is to know the meaning of life better. At the heart of their explorations is spirituality. Who they click with is usually someone of tremendous energy, with superior communication skills. Pisces-Pisces also wants to know that their lovers believe in healthy living.

Double Pisces are loyal lovers who need a little nudge to pitch in, but once that nudge is received, they're in for the long haul.

Because this Pisces demands the pursuit of a healthy lifestyle, these fish will not look their age. Their health contributes to their need to explore and experience life to the fullest.

Pisces-Pisces is also driven by philanthropy and service to their community. Humility is a hallmark of this decanate, as is self-sacrifice for the good of others. Pisceans were born to be caretakers, not just those who raise children, but to care for anyone who comes into their lives.

March 01-10, Second Decanate, Pisces-Cancer

Ruled by the moon, people in this decanate enjoy the combined influences of Neptune and the warm, comforting moon. Those born in this position have a distinct sensitivity to the needs and emotions of others.

This is where you'll find Pisces at its most balanced, emotionally. In collaboration with Cancer and its ruling planet, fish in these ten degrees of their sign has a sense of humor that keeps people rolling on the floor. Wacky and eccentric, these Pisceans always have a far-out creative idea to share. You'll say it's nuts, and then you'll see that someone else made it happen decades later. Do not laugh at these unusual but brilliant people!

For the Pisces-Cancer, love is all. It transports and transforms them, satisfying their romantic natures. And the moonstruck Pisces-Cancer adores all things beautiful, from other humans to art to nature. They'll find common ground with others who take note of the details, while most miss them in the rush of life.

But this decanate is anything but lonely when alone. Comfortable in their skins and in their own company, they cherish their quiet times of solitude. Anyone wanting to get to know this special slice of Pisces will need to understand this aspect of the Pisces-Cancer.

Lest you think that Pisces-Cancer is a navel-gazing hippie, understand that these people are observers of all they see. Transformative thinkers, they build better mousetraps.

While not being particularly extroverted, Pisces-Cancers' natural charm endears them to others. Quick-witted, they're engaging conversationalists. They're also by nature obliged to be ingenious and creative.

Pisces-Cancer is the Piscean who proclaims, "Don't dream it, be it!" because that's what they do best. When their destiny rears up, they're swept forward by it, almost in the blink of an eye.

March 11-March 20, Third Decanate, Pisces-Scorpio

Ruled by the forceful, "get er' done" planet, Mars, Pisces in the third decanate satisfy the Piscean need to work off the steam that can build up in them. Because this is the last decanate in the zodiac's last sign, these Pisces are forces of nature. The momentum provided by the astrological cycle rebooting in adjacent Aries is powerful, making these Pisces dynamic information processors. Like soft computers, they suck up the data, spitting it out in a creative action once they've analyzed the input.

Love is the word that matters most to Pisces-Scorpio people. It motivates their actions and drives their decisions. Understanding those around them almost uncannily, they are the empaths.

While this sign is very expressive with their views and opinions, they are also passionate listeners. Pisceans have a remarkable talent to interpret the fundamental meanings behind other people's opinions and therefore accept them.

Pisces-Scorpio needs to feel they matter, and anyone who can do this for them will find a deep and abiding connection with this love-focused iteration of Pisces. Sensual and with a great appreciation of comfort, Pisces-Scorpio takes domestic bliss to a whole new level. If people were hugs, it would be these people.

Third decanate Pisces are visionaries, with a strong orientation toward the practical. They're often gifted in science and technology. But mostly, these folks just want to give of themselves wherever they discern a need.

Fate is more active in the lives of Pisces-Scorpio than planning. They know that the best-laid plans can go to pot in a heartbeat and so they answer the calls of life as they come, often journeying to places others would never imagine, intellectually, spiritually, and physically. Adventurers of the mind, spirit, and body, third decanate Pisceans don't suffer from the fear other mortals do. They've been there and done that. All of it.

Next, I'd like to guide you through a discussion of the moon's influence on Pisces (beyond the second decan) and how it can create an interesting synergy and a rather different breed of what we believe is the stereotypical Pisces.

How About That Moon?

As everyone reading knows, astrological skeptics abound. You know them. I know them. One of their principal beef is the claim that they're nothing like what their sun sign claims they're supposed to be like.

And that is an argument from ignorance. As I've been hinting throughout and stating clearly here and there, astrology isn't only concerned with the dates between which you were born. As we've just read in the discussion of the decans, the influence of elemental planets is a matter of degree, and a factor that makes a tremendous difference. So, we've already busted the myth.

The trouble with astrology is not that it deals in generalizations, but that people who don't understand it make generalizations about it. For many of us, that contingent bases its understanding on the popular conception of astrology, which is often considered nonsense that can be found in a newspaper column.

But when you take an interest in astrology, it rapidly becomes apparent that there's a lot more to it than two dates on the calendar. The day of your birth is as crucial to a deeper understanding and then the time of your birth.

It's the time of your birth that can produce a natal astrological chart, revealing the position of all the other signs at the moment you were born, as represented by planets. And, of all those planets, the moon is one of the most important.

It's often said in astrological circles that the moon is more influential on some people. Not knowing what moon you've been under can lead to apparent anomalies like a Taurus hula hoop artist or a Piscean chartered accountant. These are the people who will tell you, "Astrology isn't accurate! I'm the complete opposite of my sign!"

Because they're more influenced by the moon under which they were born.

While your sun sign influences external features of you as a person, like personality, the moon is what rules in the inner you. This is the part of you that's less overt and perhaps even, secret. The subconscious is ruled by the moon, for example.

Your less obvious but possibly more personally important traits and features are in the province of the moon. Only shining by night, the moon can tell us a lot about ourselves. It's simply more subtle, perhaps, than the sun.

Interestingly enough, is to think of the sun as active and the moon as reactive, reflecting back the light of the sun. Your moon sign, then, is concerned with your emotional response to the world around you.

Let's explore the influence of the moon on Pisces, occurring under the various signs. Remember, to discover your moon you must know your time of birth.

Moon in Aries

The ram paws the ground, snorting through its nostrils, head down. Likely to pick a fight when cornered, Aries wants what it wants, and charges forward to get it. They love thrills, chills, and winning. The Pisces with a moon in Aries is less likely to pass up opportunities and is markedly more extroverted than introverted.

Moon in Taurus

Slow and steady wins the race, with the patient, stable bull. When a Pisceans moon is in Taurus, they will benefit from an emotional equilibrium, and the strength to achieve their objectives in life. Because Taurus is another lover of beauty, Pisceans with their Moon in this sign will create beauty in whatever medium they choose.

Moon in Gemini

Pisces are emotional as a way of life. Others prefer to contain their emotions as a private matter. With Moon in Gemini, Pisces is demonstrative and forthcoming about their feelings at any moment and in any setting. This is a Gemini trait, as this sign values emotional openness.

Moon in Cancer

Since both signs are water elements, the Pisces with the moon in Cancer is what some individuals would classify as psychic. They know what you're thinking, what you're planning, and what motivates others to behave the way they do. Pisces with this lunar influence need to take special care to find time away from others to clear out all the emotional flotsam and jetsam they accumulate on their travels.

Moon in Leo

When artistic Pisces is born with a moon in Leo, expect fireworks – the good kind. This is a creative dynamo, destined to ascend the heights of creative achievement. Expressive and demonstrative, this drama queen creates artistic excellence.

Moon in Virgo

This is a difficult moon for a Piscean to be born under the influence of. Virgo's incessant ambition and focus on achievement can leave emotional Pisces feeling alone. Pisceans under this moon need to be more in touch with themselves, which may require serious internal work. That way, they can wrangle the conflicts inherent in this lunar influence and be at their best. Self-knowledge is crucial.

Moon in Libra

Because relationships matter to Pisces people as much as they do to balanced Librans, Pisces with the moon in Libra may wear themselves out trying to give everything they have to their partner. Pisceans under a Libra moon will often find they need to be open and honest with their potential partners about their expectations in a relationship. They will want to explain their acceptable behaviors, boundaries, and deal-breakers.

Moon in Sagittarius

Pisceans with their moon in Sagittarius will be hungry for knowledge and adventure. They will be passionate about seeing all the world offers and discovering anything beyond what is considered "normal." Pisces absorb the world, and with this moon, they're like super-absorbent sponges. This is Pisces unleashed, adventuring through life with gusto.

Moon in Capricorn

Industrious Capricorn gets Pisces rooted in reality and the need to do the work to get to their dreams. When influencing dreamy, esoteric Pisces, the effect is startling. Pisces are at their most creatively productive and potent with their moon in Capricorn. The only concern is the tendency to work themselves to death, instead of attending to other needs and priorities in a balanced way.

Moon in Aquarius

A Pisces whose moon is in Aquarius is actively engaged in doing good for humanity. This is the influence of Aquarius, which is most noble, and, when taken up by the empathic Pisces, it becomes a movement unto itself. With Pisces' creativity and innovative thinking, this lunar influence is extremely dynamic.

Moon in Pisces

This is the Old Soul's Old Soul. People born under both the sun and moon of this sign will often find the world a rude place to be, with their otherworldly, spiritually intense natures. But when this archetypal, almost totemic Pisces understands what he or she is sitting on and knows how to deploy it, expect magic.

I hope everyone reading is beginning to get a feel for the intricate, multi-faceted discipline that astrology is. Anything but superficial, I hope that people approach it with respect. It has much to reveal to us about our motivations, emotional and psychological landscapes if only we approach it with an open and respectful mind.

In our next chapter, we'll be talking briefly about astrology and biological sex. While clear that men and women are all made of the same cloth, the way we are raised, and the biological truth of who we are affects how we express those traits associated with our astrological charts.

But before you roll your eyes at me, let me just give you a hint – biological sex makes little difference beyond socially mandated assumptions about what sex means and the individual's acceptance of those assumptions as gospel. Let's talk about a 21st Century approach to astrology, which leaves behind the specter of gendered assumptions about biological sex.

Chapter Seven: What Does Sex Have To Do With Astrology?

Despite the public discourse on cerebral differences between human males and human females, I'm here to tell you there is only one kind of brain.

That brain is human. Its capabilities are not defined by biological sex. Nor is a preference for pink or blue trucks or Barbie dolls. That said, every cell in our bodies is permeated by the chemical cocktails associated with our respective sexes. Those cocktails do not affect the quality of this brain or its innate intellectual value.

So, no. Women are not from Venus. Men are not from Mars. We're all earthly creatures, and our biological sex is just one means by which we're identified by other people and one factor governing our interactions with and experience of the world.

Despite what folks tell you, the majority of the perceived differences between men and women, intellectually, are imposed by social structures and long-accepted stereotypes which have no meaning, other than to define what we, in our sexed bodies, are designed to do. These structures and stereotypes have represented, for millennia, a straitjacket demanding that humans find their place within certain societally prescribed parameters of behavior, appearance, and purpose.

All the signs of the zodiac are sexed, male or female. But let's consider the times in which astrology was established as a discipline.

A Little History for You

In Croatia, in 2012, the oldest known astrologer's board, used to provide personalized horoscopes, was discovered. The board depicted three sun signs, namely Cancer, Gemini, and Pisces.

Said to be over 2,000 years old, the board comes late to the astrology party, which started in the Ancient Near East, specifically, Babylonia. But even Babylon isn't far enough back.

The history of humans looking to the stars to guide their decision-making process and to make sense of their lives is estimated to be as old as 25,000 years.

It was in the Neolithic period that people began to understand the cyclical nature of the world, including the heavens above. Relying on these events to predict the outcomes in both agriculture and weather anomalies.

But astrology as a discipline did not take a form recognizable to us today until about 3,000 BCE in Mesopotamia. But it would be another 1,000 years until early astrology came to be the sophisticated discipline we know in modern times.

That's a long time ago, and if we understand the position of women in the Ancient Near East at about this time, we might have a better understanding of why the signs of the zodiac are sexed.

Women, once seen as religious leaders in society, have always been defined by their reproductive capacity and have been defined as the pillar of the home and the source of life. Because of this, women have been relegated to a divergent status and deemed as having less value than men. Men went to war. Men worked in physical labor. Men led societies. Men did things outside the home. Women did things inside the home, especially raising children.

In many societies, the earliest theories of what the sexes propose have endured even until the present day. And those ideas are no more potently expressed than in astrological signs sexed either male or female.

To see what I mean, let's look at the zodiac through the eyes of biological sex and see if we can't detect the enduring themes.

- Sexed male: Aries, Gemini, Leo, Libra, Sagittarius, and Aquarius
- Sexed female: Taurus, Cancer, Virgo, Scorpio, Capricorn, and Pisces

Applying the knowledge we've gained in our discussion about the influence of the planets ruling decans and the influence of the moons of various signs, it's not difficult to see what's going on here. The signs sexed male are extroverted, while the signs sexed female are introverted. The masculine signs are aggressive, while the feminine signs are peaceful. The male signs tend to action, while the female signs tend to passivity.

Are all these claims about the signs not rooted in stereotypes about male and female roles in society?

And, if we take astrology seriously, understanding the nuanced meanings attributed to signs in all our respective charts, then are these socially constructed assumptions of any actual value?

This is controversial, but I will answer that question with an unequivocal "no." While there may be physical distinctions between male and female brains primarily concerned with brain size, corroborating with general size differentiation between men and women, there is no distinction between brain quality or capability.

Confirmed through significant research - information not accessible to the inventors of astrology in the Ancient Near East. Specifically, Gina Rippon's book, The Gendered Brain, has dismantled the assumption that "gender," which asserts that males and females have specific roles and behaviors expected of them, has anything to do with biological sex.

Rippon's work as a neuroscientist led to an intensive study of the human brain, seeking out potential differences in male and female examples. What she discovered - size, related to the broad differentials found in male and female bodies, is the sole difference. Otherwise, our brains have the same potentialities, regardless of the sex of the body in which they're found.

Why am I telling you all this? Because I am of the firm opinion that the only differences between males and females regarding astrology are the same stereotypes and other social constructs associated with a biological sex-now debunked and considered the products of earlier, less scientifically sophisticated times.

And that is why I have not included a discussion of sex differences in this book. Any sex discrepancies between men and women, and their respective behaviors, result directly from socialization as to the meaning of biological sex and not its inherent operative value.

If modern astrology is to be taken seriously it must, like all other disciplines, be developed. The components of the practice, which indicate that it embraces the beliefs of the past, must be shed. The gendered astrological sign is surely at the extreme edge of its usefulness in the 21st Century.

Not all women are passive. Not all men are aggressive. Not all males drive action in their contexts. Many women do exactly that.

The stereotypes of the past have been debunked and now is the time for astrology to acknowledge this. You may think this is arcane, but astrology is enjoying a renaissance right now and has been since about 2017. In fact, the discipline has not been as popular since the 1970s.

Perhaps it is time for astrology to evolve and finally become a comprehensive discipline rooted in the real actions of the cosmos. Would that not enhance their influence by confirming its understanding of humans beyond that achieved by the Ancients?

To illustrate further what I'm trying to share with you, let's look at what is considered the most masculine sign in the zodiac – Leo - and how two women, one globally famous and the other an acquaintance of mine, live out their roles as not kings but queens of the jungle. Recognized as the most feminine sign, we will do the same exercise with Pisces.

Queen of the Literary Jungle, J.K. Rowling

Author of the best-selling literary series in history and the only person to become a billionaire from writing, J.K. Rowling is a Leo and a woman. Not only does she fully model all the traits of the sign, but she also does so in an uncompromising, socially engaged, and philanthropic way.

She is no longer a billionaire. That's not because she blew her billions on private planes and other extravagances or because she made poor investment choices – she gave the money away.

Facing a tremendous challenge from supporters of the gender identity lobby, she has shown grace under pressure, while still producing literary works for both children and adults.

Unlike many authors whose books become films, J.K. Rowling has maintained an iron grip on her content, having creative control and right of approval on all scripts. It doesn't get much more Leo than that. It is not commonplace for an author to be given that much distinction in the production of films based on their work.

Beyond that, J.K. Rowling clawed her way to global literary success. She was on social assistance and a single mother and was a survivor of domestic abuse and sexual assault when she wrote the first of the Harry Potter books. Not only that, but she was also rejected by at least a dozen publishing houses before finding her success story.

But like a typical Leo, she didn't even blink. She knew what she had, and she kept sending it to publishers until one of them saw the value of her work. Leo doesn't give up. Leo doesn't give in, and Leo takes on all challengers, without hesitation.

Rowling is a perfect example of gender missing the mark for defining the signs of the zodiac and the characteristics of those born under them. She's lived the life far too many women are consigned to, emerging not only prosperous but victorious and gracious in her prosperity.

Money! Rosalind

Many years ago, I had a rather extraordinary Leo friend. Rosalind was a professional dancer, among other things. But the most extraordinary thing about her was the force of her personality and its effect on other people.

She insisted on being in the spotlight. It didn't matter whether she was dancing, singing, acting, or teaching; she was a force of nature and one you could not ignore. If you were lucky enough to share the stage with Rosalind, or even be in the same room with her, you were there only to bask in her glory.

Rosalind was a brand unto herself. When you said her name, most people smiled, but a few made a face. Others, who were challenged by her fame and fortune, would find themselves on her bad side.

Rosalind was not to be challenged about money under any circumstances. She collected it, eschewing the formal banking system for rolls of large denomination bills she hid all over her house.

By sheer force of her personality, and her status as an entertainer- people served her in many ways. Rosalind had an entourage behind her, from professional chefs, assistants, even a masseuse for her every desire.

Unlike Rowling, Rosalind was disinterested in any charitable endeavor from which she did not directly benefit. Male or female, the enduring love for money is a human trait, not a sexed trait. Both sexes can be as greedy, egotistical, and self-interested as the other, and Rosalind made that clear to all who knew her.

Personality is not governed by gender; it is formed by the lives we lead. And these two Leos are great examples of modeling the sign's propensity for the spotlight – one positively and one somewhat negatively. Both women described have achieved incredible heights in their careers and incredible fiscal returns. But they have done so in different ways, in a different spirit, and with a different agenda.

They're both still women, but they are classical Leos.

Now let's meet two male Pisces to challenge the sexed zodiac of the Ancients further.

The Fish Goes to Washington

People don't tend to peg Pisceans as leaders. It's a feminine sign, right? And leadership is inherently masculine! Not just that, but aren't Pisces supposed to "introverted" and "feminine"?

Well, here's a factoid for you, four US Presidents have been Pisceans. Also, in the Oval Office were James Madison, Andrew Jackson, and Grover Cleveland. Of their number, George Washington was a first decanate Pisces, with the other three being born in the second decanate.

Tell me that's not intriguing! The Pisces-Cancer decan is the segment in which transformative thinking and leadership are probably most powerful.

Putting aside the fact these were men of their times, with all the attendant prejudices one might expect, it's especially interesting to consider that two of the Founding Fathers of our nation were Pisceans. Leading people toward that more "perfect union" mentioned in our Constitution's preamble is not as strange a Piscean occupation as it seems at first glance. Without a doubt, both Washington and Madison were idealistic leaders with a compelling belief in the blooming experiment of their fledgling nation.

And then there's Andrew Jackson. Not remembered as the most sensitive or empathic leader, he is known for his infamous policy of removing Native Americans from their traditional territories, giving rise to the shameful Trail of Tears.

Again, it's important to remember the times and imperatives these presidents lived in and with. All the same, let's just admit this policy of the Jackson administration sucked and certainly doesn't sound like something a Pisces would sign off on.

As for Grover Cleveland, he was the last Pisces to be President, and he did so in two non-consecutive terms in office, as the 22nd and 24th President. Widely admired, even by his fellow GOP at the time, Cleveland was an enemy of corruption and a champion of honesty and integrity.

The 20th and 21st Centuries have deprived the USA of Piscean leadership, but it's hoped that a little of that Pisces magic will make its way back to the White House at an opportune time.

My Cousin, Bob

Bob is not discernable as a Pisces to any but his nearest and dearest. Gruff and disinterested in philosophy, religion, the meaning of life, or basically anything except sports, he would seem to be your typical redneck.

Bob is always right, even when he's wrong. Bob will fight you over a perceived slight, faster than you can blink. Bob is always demanding apologies for those perceived slights. I have not spoken to Bob for almost five years, and it's unlikely that I will again.

As a kid, Bob was fond of attacking me with a variety of weapons, from ballpoint pens to his fingernails, which he kept long for precisely that purpose. When I saw my cousins pulling up to our front door, I knew that I'd have a few scars at the conclusion of the visit.

The most Piscean trait of Bob is his raw, almost self-pitying sensitivity. Like an open wound, the slightest glance can set him off on a rant about what a horrible person you are. Going back to his childhood again, Bob was known for soaring tantrums, which featured physical feats of strength like levitation. On all fours, Bob could get daylight as he pounded the floor with his fists and knees.

I don't know of any neurological reasons for Bob's personality. He is just Bob, and that's the way it has always been. Why is Bob like this? Bob is like this because, at his root, he is a sensitive child who demands you respect him, his authority, his grudges, and his insistence on apologies for things that may or may not have happened.

Permanently set to "disgruntled," the only aspect of Bob, which is even vaguely Piscean, is his pathological sensitivity. Incurious as the day is long, Bob is content to drink beer in front of the TV when he's not driving a rig.

So, not only is Bob the least inquisitive, dreamy Pisces I've ever met, he is also the only redneck, trucker hat and flannel-shirt-wearing Pisces I believe to exist.

So, four US Presidents and a truculent, hypersensitive redneck – all of whom were and are Pisceans. All are men. And they all represent something of a departure from what we anticipate from the supposedly "feminine" Pisces.

While a few may continue to disagree, assigning sex to a zodiac sign in recognition of gendered assumptions about men and women-only confuses the discipline of astrology further.

With our knowledge today about dimorphic, biological sex – which is that all people have personalities and experiences which guide their actions and choices in life – it's risky to believe in the notion that masculinity and femininity have anything at all to do with astrology. Whether we're accepting the sexing of the signs of the zodiac by the ancient founders of the discipline, or claiming that men and women live out the traits of their zodiac signs differently, I continue to assert that it is time to let those old beliefs go.

As we stand on the cusp of the Age of Aquarius – rumored by astrologers to begin on December 01, 2020 – perhaps this is a project whose time has come. As we transition from the Age of Pisces, during which Age monotheistic religion and philosophy rooted in the same gendered assumptions and too often guided by them arose, maybe this is an opportunity for the astrological community to lead.

As I've said throughout this exploration of Pisces, so many factors affect the way you exhibit the traits of your sun sign. From the era you're born in, to your personality, to the movement of the planets in your sign, the date and time, all these factors have a strong influence on the way we model the associated traits.

But one factor is not, to my knowledge, biological sex. As we learn more about biological sex, and begin to understand that men and women are defined by this, it becomes clearer that we cannot continue the practice of sexing the zodiac. It is misleading and harmful to the deeper understanding of astrology's true work - which is in the stars, not the flesh.

A fresh start without a sexed zodiac? I'm in!

Our next chapter will explore Pisces and friendship. Who they love to hang out with, who they avoid and who they can change the world with!

Chapter Eight: Pisces Friends, Enemies, and Collaborators

Pisces, while inherently introverted, is, as I've mentioned before, semi-social. While fond of spending plenty of time at home with their nearest and dearest (especially their beloved pets), Pisces also loves to spend time with people they feel understood and appreciated by – just like everyone else! However, semi-social Pisces will need time and solitude to recharge after every foray into the world. When that's not available to the shy fish, they're liable to get a little cranky.

In this chapter, I'd like to take a walk through the zodiac to identify a few of Pisces' most likely cronies, enemies, friends, and collaborators. Synergies happen, and each synergy between people's specific application bears significant fruit, under the right circumstances.

Let's find this cast of astrological characters and see what they're most likely to do - or not do - with Pisces when they're around. My standard disclaimer applies here – rising signs (which we'll examine in the next chapter, with a deeper look at the Houses) and the planetary influences associated with them, as well as the moons, decanates, and cusps, can strenuously influence all signs. So, it's important to remember that we're all under the auspices of the planets, as they make their way through the sky.

But before we get started, know that Pisces, while shy and retiring, is also one of the best friends you'll ever have. The empathic nature of a Piscean compels them to be the shoulder to cry on, the source of good advice, and the compassionate friend that always knows what to say.

But Pisces has needs that not everyone understands or cares about. Being sensitive and emotionally driven, this sun sign relates best with the other sun signs, which understand them on a deeper level. Let's find out who Pisces really clicks with, becoming fast friends for life.

Best Friends Forever

Pisces are sensitive, not just to the things people around them say and do. They're sensitive to social and emotional undercurrents like no other sign. Arch-empaths, they possess a unique quality to sense the emotional landscapes of other people. This is both a blessing and a curse because being in large groups of people or even in conversation with one other person encountering difficult emotions can leave them drained.

For this reason, Pisces needs to know that they can trust their friends implicitly. They need to be sure that their closest confidants will keep their confidences, as Pisces keeps theirs. No matter who you are, I'm sure you'll agree that people like that are few and far between. For this reason, we will take great care in choosing those around us who we associate with on a personal level.

And Pisces takes that selection process so seriously that others can interpret their reticence as coldness or snobbery. But Pisces will vet you harder than a political party's machinery will a candidate for public office. They need to be 100% convinced that their emotional investment in you will not blow up in a fiery inferno of disappointment and betrayal.

So, don't take it personally if you catch Pisces observing you from the other side of the room. They'll probably wave at you, smile, and then go back to observing you. They don't care if you notice. And once you've passed the audition, you'll find that Pisces is as loyal and nurturing a friend as you could ever hope to find.

And if you don't make it? I suppose it depends on what the issue is! If you're a bold, aggressive type, it's likely Pisces won't want to have much to do with you. They won't slam the door in your face, but they probably won't invite you inside, either.

Important to remember: Manipulation, lying, unfair gossip, character assassination, and other unfortunate social behaviors will slam that door in your face before you know it. Any hint of these behaviors under the surface of a personality can set Pisces off.

Pisces has a sixth sense for problem people, toxic people, narcissists, exploiters, and anyone else who doesn't have the best of intentions. They can smell it, and if they smell it on you, you're over. You're done. Pisces will see you coming and walk on the other side of the street. You have been warned.

Taurus

Stable, patient Taurus brings Pisces the solid friendship they long for. Strongly rooted in the real world, Taurus is practical and will serve as a great advisor to the fish.

Both signs are deeply tolerant of the foibles of others and incredibly compassionate. These two take having each other's backs to a new level. Intensely loyal, they create a bond that's founded on mutual trust and positive feedback.

Pisces helps Taurus unwind, while Taurus is likely to keep Pisces laughing. In each other's company, they don't even notice how comfortable they are with each other, as this is a given in their friendship and why they love each other too pieces.

While Pisces may find Taurus to be a little too focused on the material, Pisces will frustrate the bull with the notorious fishy forgetfulness. They get over these minor details to form a lifelong bond.

Cancer

Both these signs are water babies, so there's an immediate attraction by both to their respective similarities. Pisces and Cancer have an almost unconscious synergy, with Cancer bringing the ideas and Pisces bringing the imagination to transform them.

These two are a team who love sharing "in-jokes" and plans to improve the world around them. Both intensely emotional and connected to the collective unconscious, they see a problem and join forces to fix it, deploying their complimentary gifts.

Pisces has the insight to help Cancer learn to compromise, while Cancer has the tools to help Pisces understand that doing one thing at a time is probably more effective than doing, say, twenty!

These two are friends for life, sharing an intense loyalty and belief in the sanctity of friendship. Together, they're a force to be reckoned with.

Scorpio

A water sign like both Pisces and Cancer, Scorpio forms a bond with Pisces that's almost at a spiritual or soulmate level. While they may not become instant best friends, in discovering each other, they often will find a kindred spirit.

Scorpio's depth of thinking is highly attractive to the fish. They find in this an excellent outlet for their love of analytical thinking about the motivations of others. As Scorpio plots a course forward, Pisces rides shotgun, looking for the esoteric, hidden details Scorpio may have overlooked in the passion of the moment.

Both signs have a tendency to go inward. While this quality can be annoying to people born under other sun signs, these two forgive it in each other. They know why the other is doing it and understand that the hijinks they get up to together – which are often in the realm of personal or public politics – require that level of reflection before action.

Scorpio's extreme idealism is a good match for a Pisces friend, with Pisces smoothing off the often rough edges of the intense scorpion, intuiting the truth of the matter. Scorpio's dog, with a bone approach, when combined with the Piscean connectivity to a deeper level of reality, can achieve amazing things. This friendship is a keeper and a gift to humanity.

Capricorn

The stubborn goat finds a fast friend in compassionate Pisces, and while on the surface, this seems an odd pair, their friendship is often enduring and fruitful.

Because Pisces is so highly intuitive, the fish knows that the Capricorn's sharp elbows are just part of the package, laughing off the goat's gruff exterior. Pisces knows there's a big softie in there and then brings that aspect of Capricorn forth, with their familiar patience and love.

In fact, Pisces is in charge of this relationship managing its emotional aspects, while Capricorn puts their nose to the grindstone, achieving and accumulating the comfort this sign enjoys. Meanwhile, Capricorn reminds Pisces that the earth appreciates having the fish's feet on it occasionally.

And Pisces tempers Capricorn's gravitas by injecting an element of fancy into this serious, hardworking sign's life. There is tremendous balance in this friendship that serves both parties well.

Now that we've got a handle on Pisces' BFFs, it's time to look at the other side of the coin.

While Pisceans are easy to love and generally well-liked, not everybody can be close friends with this sun sign's denizens. Many people in our lives are a passing nod in the street or a beer at the corner bar. Others are thorns in Pisces's scaly sides, inflicting unpleasant emotions that need to be avoided at all costs. They rub the fish the wrong way, and when that's the case, Pisces will keep on swimming to get away. This next section addresses people Pisces should stay away from as much as possible.

Virgo

The virgin is someone the fish should avoid. Unless Pisces is willing to tailor themselves to the demands of this obsessive-compulsive, nitpicky, perfectionist sign, they will quickly be at odds and feel suffocated.

Rigid in their decision-making process, Virgo is unlikely to take the consultative, communal approach to life. It's their way or the highway which leaves the fish feeling unwelcome, unloved, and disrespected.

The precipitously high standards of the Virgo – a function of their obsessive perfectionism – seem unfair and unduly harsh. Virgo also tends to have very fixed ideas about what constitutes the truth and reality, while Pisces' fluidity rejects that kind of thinking.

Even with Pisces' innate flexibility, dealing with Virgo can be disorienting and soul-crushing for the sensitive fish.

Leo

The audacious, spotlight loving lion and shy Pisces are polar opposites. And while, on a distant planet, these two may somehow find common ground, on this planet, they're unlikely to get along.

The lion may find Pisces' shyness intriguing, wanting to understand it better, while the fish may admire the bombastic Leo's ability to command a room. But the disparities between their character traits can wear thin with time; familiarity has bred contempt.

Leo's monolithic ego grates on sensitive, humble Pisces. They're unable to process the continual proclamations of superiority and tales of victory, eventually identifying these as the smoke and mirrors they are.

Ultimately, the egotism and self-centered preening of Leo will drive the quiet, reflective Pisces away.

But keep reading because you're about to get a big surprise regarding Pisces and Leo. While true that these guys don't get along, pair them on a project at work or in the community, and watch the hostile sparks turn into the right kind of fireworks. These two, when working shoulder to shoulder, are quite a tasty match.

As I said a little earlier, the Pisces is hard not to like. Gregarious, while shy, entertaining, while humble, Pisceans make great friends for many people. But those people are not usually born under Virgo or Leo. As with everything else in this book, the mileage may vary. When the planets are aligned, everything you've just read can prove either untrue or partially true.

However, these two signs are bad bets for Pisces, and with the sensitive, emotional framework of Pisceans, they can prove to be highly corrosive influences. As acquaintances, you can enjoy each other's company, but pursuing an up close and personal relationship with these two signs is a bad bet for Pisces.

Next, let's have a look at the better collaborators for Pisces in the zodiac. These may not prove to be lifelong friends. They may be present in the life of the Pisces for only a brief time, teaching them important lessons and sharing a moment the relationship may have been expressly created to address.

For work, personal developments, and even political engagement, these signs are a few of Pisces' most influential and valuable collaborators.

Leo

Whether producing a charity gala or managing a project at work together, Pisces will find collaboration with a Leo like a trip to an amusement park. Leo wants to ride the gnarliest rollercoaster possible, and Pisces is coming along for the ride.

Thrills! Chills! Abject terror! These are all part of the experience when you're working alongside risk-taking Leo.

The advantage of this collaboration for Pisces is that Leo is perfectly willing to do all the heavy going, while Pisces plugs along in the background. Pisces couldn't care less about fame and fortune, while Leo lives for them, so putting the lion out front is a winning strategy for shy, reflective Pisces. An effective collaboration if ever there was one!

Libra

Light-hearted Libra is usually a good match for Pisces, on the job, or working at other projects. Libra loves a good laugh, so they'll make an entertaining company for Pisces.

Sometimes, though, Libra may seem less than engaged with the project at hand. A Piscean can learn from this; finding they need not put themselves last by constantly trying to please those around them.

And while Libra isn't the glory hound that Leo is, they do better on the front end of things than sensitive Pisces, especially if we're talking customer service or prickly clients. Libra's diplomacy covers those bases, while Pisces keeps the back end moving along as it should.

Aquarius

The philanthropic water bearer makes Pisces' best collaborator when working on humanitarian projects. Whether that's a non-profit dedicated to saving water resources or a school for children with learning disabilities, the two balance each other well.

Aquarius can facilitate the visionary prognostications of Pisces, creating a unique synergy that improves outcomes by injecting creativity into the work. With logical Aquarius at the controls, Pisces may dream their visions into being.

An emotional Pisces meets a brilliant collaborator in the logical Aquarius, joining rationality to intuition, often with exemplary results.

The discussion in this chapter is about specific signs and who they are to Pisces. Pisces natives will find there are many others out in the world they're able to form strong friendships with and work with. While people under signs they wouldn't normally find difficult can become resolute enemies.

Astrology is complex. As I've been trying to communicate throughout this book, this discipline is not as cu-and-dried as it may appear in a quarter-inch newspaper column. Planetary influences, such as the operation of the moon on your sun sign, and other key effects can change the game.

So, this is intended to share with you the more obvious personalities and their potential roles in your life. With astrology, nothing is written in stone. Just as the course of planetary motions brings continual change to the universe, it brings variety to every sign of the zodiac. This is a crucial point that should always be remembered.

In our next chapter, we'll discuss the work of rising signs and houses, what they mean and how they might affect Pisces. I've given it a chapter all its own because it's another interesting, deeper way of approaching astrology as a discipline for understanding other people and what makes them tick.

Chapter Nine: Rising Signs, Houses and What They Mean to Pisces

Before we dive in, I should make readers aware that the rising signs and Houses are other aspects of astrology for which you must know your time of birth. If you're interested, I highly recommend having your astrological chart done. This is a metaphorical choice that will help you understand yourself, and the significance of your sun sign with much more clarity. And if you have read this far, I will assume you are!

Your rising sign is also called your "ascendant." It refers to the planet associated with any given astrological sun sign, which is rising in the eastern sky at the exact time and place of your birth.

And ascendents don't refer solely to people. They also refer to events.

Interestingly, Donald Trump's rising sign is Leo. I mean, the hair, right? Never mind everything else. If only we'd done his chart right after that announcement in New York, back in the year BTD (Before The Donald). We might have noticed this Gemini ran a little hot.

What Does it All Mean?

The rising sign governs the way you look at the world, as well as your outward appearance. This is the key factor that is responsible for the first impression you make on people. So, what people see in you isn't necessarily what they'll eventually get if they stick around. It's just the surface of you and what you project.

So, let's visit the rising signs and how they manifest in the astrological chart and the lives of individuals they impact in the birth chart. Remember that what we're referring to in this chapter are general attributes and effects of the rising sign. Without a natal birth chart for everyone reading, I can't get any further than that. If you want to know – and it's important – then you must get a chart done, and to do that, you'll need your time of birth. Once you know your exact time of birth, you can get an accurate chart online at Astro.com.

While reading, remember that the attributes bestowed by ascendents will seem out of character for Pisces, but these are general attributes, having similar – but not precisely the same – impacts on all those they rise upon. Other influences in the chart will also be in play, as always.

PRO-TIP: Don't rely on mom and dad for the time of your birth. They may be a little fuzzy on that point. Instead, obtain a long-form birth certificate, as this document will give you the precise time you were born.

Aries

With Aries as your ascendant, you make quite a strong impression, with many believing you to be intimidating at the first meeting. People will initially find you to be opinionated.

Aries being both the first sign of the zodiac and a fire sign, your ascendent in Aries means you see your life and the world around you as one long competition. Impulsive Aries operates from instinct, blazing trails others can't imagine.

Taurus

Even a Pisces can seem willful and perhaps a little ferocious with a Taurus rising sign. While the ram has a softer side, you emit a warning that you are not to be messed with.

Taurus loves the finer things in life, from beautiful clothes to sumptuous home décor and haute cuisine. This can lead others to believe they're materialistic. For Taurus, seen as first earth element in the zodiac sign, what others believe is materialism is really sensuality. That's especially true for and Aries rising Pisces.

Gemini

Pisces, under the ascendant of the twins, is seen as a busy bee, undertaking multiple projects at once and facing them all. You're a bolt of lightning at work, home, and in your social group.

This rising sign creates energy in the languid fish, making Pisces the center of the creative universe, transforming ideas into reality. The only problem is the potential for burnout. Pisces with this ascendent should take care to focus on a couple of things at once to avoid that effect.

Cancer

With Cancer rising, Pisces is augmented, shifting from best friend to mother of whichever company you're part of. Your warm nature gets even warmer, taking on the characteristics of a luxuriously fuzzy blanket, ever at the ready to wrap itself around someone needing comfort.

Home, comfort, and stability are important to those with Cancer rising. You present to others as a nurturing port in the storm, or someone who is always willing to listen when a problem occurs.

Leo

Leo rising brings fire to even the fiercest of fire signs. For Pisces, the presence of this ascendant means that everyone knows when you've walked into the room. This is the sign of the presence and the eternal sun of summer, and you shine it happily on the world around you.

Leo rising can also be a little overwhelming at times, as the lion has needs. Like a baby, those needs will be met. Take care to remember you're an adult and that your friends, lovers, and workmates aren't your nannies.

Virgo

This ascendant sometimes brings "fuzzy on the details" fish the organizational skills needed to complement their creative, intuitive spirit. People also sense your immovable reliability when your rising sign is Virgo.

The earthiness of this rising sign augments Pisces' love of nature and animals and enhances a belief in the sanctity of this planet we all live on. Virgo rising transforms external perceptions of you to acknowledge a stable foundation.

Libra

The scales represent balance and equal justice, and that's reflected in a Libra rising sign by investing Pisces with the spirit of diplomacy. You're perceived as someone pleasant to be around.

While many find Libra indecisive, what's really at work is that they're trying to arrive at the best outcome for all concerned. So, perhaps the scales are more about socialism than diplomacy. Either way, this pragmatic sign needs to understand that no matter the outcome, someone will always feel unhappy. Work on accepting that.

Scorpio

Pisceans with Scorpio rising are perceived as mysterious, reticent, and attractive in every way possible. Already somewhat mysterious, Pisces becomes someone people are immediately curious about with Scorpio as their ascendant.

But you aren't all that easy to get to know. You take your time with people, vetting them as political parties might vet their potential candidates for office. You don't take chances with close relationships, which can be off-putting until people get to know you.

Sagittarius

Pisces gets a healthy dose of optimism with the sea-goat as their ascendant. Fun-loving and adventurous, Sagittarius is the explorer of the zodiac, taking you where no Pisces had gone before – unless they were Sagittarius rising!

You'll be heard saying what others are reluctant to say because you have strong opinions. This can blow up in your face if care isn't taken with the notorious Sagittarian "tell it like it is" method of communication.

Capricorn

Often equated with the sure-footed, solitary mountain goat, Capricorn rising is seen by others as dependable and mature. Ever prepared and ready for anything, they insist on excellence from themselves, as they do from others.

Capricorn's quest for achievement takes them places others fear. This ascendent removes any doubt from the sensitive Pisces soul, investing it with courage and the resolve to reach the greatest heights possible.

Aquarius

Aquarius' philanthropic intellect is a great complement to Pisces when it's your rising sign. Concerned with collective action and the communal good, the water bearer is about sharing the wealth.

Marching to the beat of your own drum, you can be intimidating, but only those who are threatened by your resolute idealism and self-confidence. While concerned with the greater good, you're every inch a head-turning individual, when Aquarius is the rising sign you're born under.

Pisces

At birth, Pisces are even odder when the rising sign is the same as their sun sign. This sign's psychic nature is richly fortified by this rising sign, making them a little difficult for others to understand.

Pisces rising Pisceans may seem as though they're on another planet to the rest. But what's actually going on is that they're collecting data and forming an analysis. This can be unnerving for many. The Pisces need be careful to keep their thoughts clear, specific to that person, and leave the mind-reading for another day.

Now that we've taken a walk through the rising signs and their significance, it's time to talk about another important aspect of astrology we discussed earlier – the Houses. As promised in Chapter One, we'll get to the heart of what the Houses mean here.

Everything floating around out in the heavens, transit the signs of the zodiac, and each is significant in your birth chart. Each of the Houses these celestial bodies transit has much to tell you about yourself.

The twelve houses of the zodiac represent sectors of your life. That said, none are isolated from the others completely. The twelve Houses comprise a 360-degree totality, symbolizing the cosmology of the individual concerned.

Again, you'll need your time, date, and location of birth to produce a chart before you can get a clear picture of Houses' impact on your chart. For the purposes of this book, I will keep this section simple. It must be known that the Houses are quite complicated in their operation, so please do further research to raise your consciousness about this subject.

What are They?

Twelve, as you may have noticed throughout this book, is a mystical number that is foundational to the discipline of astrology. This number also appears in a variety of religions, including Judaism, Christianity, and Islam. In Judaism, particularly, numbers are invested with a deep, spiritual significance.

So, like the sun signs, there are twelve sections in your birth chart, including the twelve astrological houses.

That is not to say that the Houses are analogous to the sun signs, which are based on the annual solar rotation. The Houses are based on the rotation of the earth, which occurs every 24 hours. For accuracy, the Houses rotate on the earth's axis, necessitating the need for the time of birth.

The astrological Houses shift every four minutes, which leaves little room for error. This explains why even those born on the same day can have wildly divergent charts.

Every House stands for a different area of your life. It also reveals notable obstacles you may face in your life and the gifts you've been born to exploit. So, whatever you do, if you're genuinely interested in an accurate reading, get that time of birth and make sure it's 100% accurate by requesting a long-form birth certificate.

Reading Your Natal Chart

To accurately read your natal chart, you must adapt to a new language, and that language is governed by the Houses. To further understand it, you will need to locate your rising sign. This is the crux of the astrological chart, appearing at the radical left of the horizon line dividing the chart in half.

You know from reading this far that the sun is your truth, the moon is your inner life, and the rising sign is your public face, revealing your personality and determining the perceptions others harbor about you, as discussed earlier in this chapter.

The rising sign or ascendant is of primary importance to your chart because it determines its unique form.

Natal charts are intended to be read counterclockwise. The horizontal line of the rising sign marks the first House. Following on from there, the Houses proceed to the right side of the horizon. This takes you through all the Houses until you get to the twelfth House, which abuts your rising sign.

Many of you reading learning how to interpret your natal charts may find numerous planets in various of your Houses. Others will see no planets in a few Houses. All you're seeing is a celestial "Polaroid" of where the planets all were at the exact moment you came into the world. Their positions in your chart illuminate your personality, your life challenges, and your areas of expertise (gifts). And each House of the zodiac will manifest in your life at certain times, as the planets continually move, affecting disparate life sectors at certain times.

Next, let's go through the twelve Houses and figure out what they mean.

First House

This is the House of your appearance and how you present yourself to others. The planet in your 1st House is a powerful influence on your life. This House corresponds to the first sign in the zodiac, Aries, and impacts goals, ideas, or attitudes that are part of who you are, defining your purpose.

Second House

This House, corresponding to Taurus, governs money, the value you attach to things, and what you own. Planets in this House at your birth determine security and financial stability. Those planets are just passing through this House express changes, particularly to your self-esteem and monetary success.

Third House

Gemini's energy is infused into this House, governing your community, transportation, and matters pertaining to communication. Planets at the time of your birth in this House are concerned with the way you express yourself and the relationships you build with those around you. Planets transiting the third House bring crucial information about the people in your most intimate circles.

Fourth House

You'll find this Cancerian House located at the bottom of your chart. It's concerned with family and the home, especially with respect to domestic life. When planets are moving through this House, we're urged to take care of our personal infrastructures, re-envisioning them as more nurturing and intimate.

Fifth House

Invested with the energy of Leo, the Fifth House is all about romance, creativity, and the children in your life. This is also the House of artistic pursuits. Transiting planets bear epiphanies that lift us up and fortify our confidence.

Sixth House

This is the House of Virgo, concerned with wellness, your daily life, and health. Your lifestyle choices impact the physicality expressed in the First House, which is concerned with the body you're born with. Natal planets here govern the structure, organization, and time management. Transiting planets support us in forming good habits and intelligent scheduling.

Seventh House

The diplomacy and pragmatic gifts of Libra create the energy influencing this House, which is the descendent, located opposite the ascendent of your First House. You'll note that so far, in our discussion of astrological Houses, each House has governed a specific sector of your life. This House is more about partnerships. Here, natal planets hone in on relationships. Those planets are transiting the Seventh House influence deal-making and binding contracts.

Eighth House

Energetically infused with Scorpio's passion, the Eighth House is the sector governing transformation. Transformation, in this instance, refers to the power of both sex and death. Natal planets cleave to the unseen world and the occult. Transiting planets reveal the unseen in any situation and remind us that life is a complicated matter.

Ninth House

The Ninth House is all about education, philosophical thinking, and, of course, travel, as this is Sagittarian turf. Exploration is the name of the game for the natal planets governing this House. Curious and inquisitive, the Ninth House is the locus of the explorer. Planets transiting it encourage us to learn new things, move somewhere unknown with a tremendous leap of faith, or to change our minds about something.

Tenth House

Positioned in the constant energy of Capricorn, this house is the pinnacle of your life's heroic tale. This House is what drives your dreams and achievements and public image. The planets in the Tenth House at the time of your birth are concerned with ambition. When planets are moving through it, you may have a profound change in your professional aspirations and path.

Eleventh House

At this point in your chart, the purpose is highlighted. With Aquarian energy at the wheel, this House governs our philanthropic work and our networks, which are further away from us. Those born in this House are the innovators, bringing fresh ideas to the world. Planets moving through the Eleventh House broaden our horizons, helping us find our rightful places in the world.

Twelfth House

This is the House of what is not seen. It's shrouded in mystery just like the sun sign, which infuses it energetically, Pisces. Governing all that is formless from our emotions to our dreams to the information we keep to ourselves, planets in this House in our charts induce extreme intuition. When planets transit this House, our karma is incarnated by people suddenly appearing in it, who are connected to that karma. Important to remember: many people in our lives are just passing through.

Now that you have a grounding in the intricacies of astrology, I'm sure you're curious about your chart. All this information you've read regarding your birth chart requires that all-important time of birth. With that information in place, you're set to discover more about who you are and what you're here to do.

In our next chapter, I'd like to spend a little time on what Pisces needs and how the Piscean energy manifests in the world when those needs are met. While we can't all have every need met all the time, we can work toward the conditions which need to exist before most of them can be, most of the time.

Let's find out how Pisces can set themselves up for the kind of lives they're capable of having when they understand themselves and what they need and get proactive to that end!

Chapter Ten: What Pisces Need to Thrive

Now that you've arrived at a more well-rounded understanding of the Pisces sun sign and how astrology influences us all as humans, it's time to talk about what Pisces needs to thrive in a world that can be unkind to the sensitive people born as fish.

It's not as though there's anything wrong with them! Quite the contrary, there's plenty to love about Pisces. The problem is the sensitivity of this sign and the shyness which plagues many if not all born Pisces.

So, this chapter will explore what Pisces need to live their best lives and how they can lay the foundation to have those needs met. Much of it has to do with personal feelings, but there's a need for Pisces to make sure that they're happy where they are, in what they're doing, and *with whom* they're doing it.

Self-Acceptance

One of Pisces' greatest life challenges is accepting who they are and being in love with all that means. The reflective nature of Pisces continually prompts them to question themselves, their decisions, even to parse the words they've said to other people to make sure they haven't said the wrong thing.

Pisces also labors under something of an inferiority complex, needing the reassurance of those around them to feel confident about who they are. But what that's really about is the Pisces tendency to neurotic self-critique and self-recrimination.

Remember my Pisces friend? She told me a story once from high school about a boy in her drama club – of course, where else would Pisces be, except maybe art class or creative writing class? This boy was always in trouble. His home life was difficult, and he was a bit off the rails because of that environment, which included absentee parents with substance abuse problems. Of course, Pisces felt for this boy. While other kids at school weren't that interested in him and avoided him, lest they be tarred with the dysfunction brush, my friend became a confidante of his.

Then, one day, my friend and this guy were in the props room at the school theater and dang it, if that boy didn't knock over and smash an old, porcelain teapot to smithereens.

The boy was terrified. He'd just come off an expulsion and knew that if he were caught for damaging a prop, the teacher would have a fit. My friend knew he was right, so when the drama teacher saw the smashed teapot, asking who had been responsible for the incident, my friend bravely raised her hand.

Her impulse to protect this boy overwhelmed her common sense. She'd been one of the top students in that class and had believed the teacher would accept her version of events. But he not only knew better – he didn't like the boy.

My noble Piscean friend was called into the drama teacher's office and dressed down. She was then kicked out of the class for the remainder of her time in senior high. This crushed her, as she loved being in plays and performing, learning lines, and taking on different characters. But the teacher would not be moved. She was kicked out.

After that, she abandoned any hope of involving herself in acting or dramatic pursuits, as the hurt never healed.

Rather than allow the errant boy to own up to his mistake, my friend took on his punishment. While she never regretted preventing her friend from getting in trouble again, she always regretted losing her connection to the drama community in her school.

This is the self-sacrificial, compassionate nature of Pisces. She took on the error of her friend, taking a fall that wasn't hers to take. And that's a serious problem. Unfortunately, one of the most pressing needs of Pisces is to believe that they are worthy of love, kindness, and compassion. Because Pisces is so deeply self-critical, many of its denizens struggle with self-acceptance. That failing can lead to acts like the one I've just described to you. Noble, yes. Smart? No.

This is why Pisceans need cheerleaders who tell them when they've done something right, that reminds them that they're good people with good intentions and worthy of all the compassion they show others. Pisces needs to understand that compassion for the self is the root of all other compassion. When it's not, Pisces can become cranky. All they need to do to fix their compassion fatigue is to apply that trait to themselves.

Friends Willing to Listen and Advise

Another pressing need for Pisces is to attract friends who will listen to Pisces as much as Pisces will listen to them.

While Pisces is happy to dispense the advice and wisdom others come to them for, it's often the case that when Pisces needs a should to cry on, it's not there. This nurturing sign is the agony aunt of the zodiac, but mothers everywhere will tell you they have the same problem as Pisces; people don't believe they need that support.

The kindness and embrace of the fish are sought out by all who know them. It's often the case, though, that no one's around when Pisces needs those gifts reciprocated. The otherworldly aura of spiritual intelligence associated with Pisces often misleads people into believing that they'll figure it out on their own - and that they're emotionally superhuman.

But fish are people, too! Pisceans need the listening ear and the sympathetic voice of caring reason as much as anyone else does. Despite their status as Old Souls who've been around the block many times, Pisces is a highly sensitive star sign. The Piscean needs to know there are people who will be there in their time of need.

This can be a huge challenge for Pisces, as many in their lives will misunderstand them. Often, Pisceans find themselves cast as flighty, out-to-lunch, and hippie-dippy. While this is true to an extent, those who do not have an open mind are missing out on the wellspring of beauty the Pisces can bring to their lives.

Their love is endless, but it's easily bruised when these delicate creatures are not treated with the tender hands they need to be well in their scaly skins. That is a problem, both for Pisces and those in their personal and professional circles.

A Piscean rejected, rebuffed, humiliated, or slighted is likely to hold a grudge. That grudge can endure until the Apocalypse if you don't clear things up with your sensitive, watery friend. You're likely to find that your phone number has been permanently lost and that you're blocked on every conceivable social media channel.

Because Pisces only gives second chances to those who ask for them. If you're walking around with your head up your backside, wondering why your Pisces friend no longer speaks to you, you're probably far too insensitive a person to be in the company of Pisces. They won't be calling any time again soon - or unblocking you!

Creative Outlets

Another key need for Pisces is an outlet for the boundless creativity of the sign. That creativity may take many shapes, from painting to sculpture to embroidery to writing to engineering to pottery to politics to dance. These guys have bright ideas about how anything you name can be improved with a dose of creative thinking.

Without a locus for their endless ideas and inspirations, Pisces can become stagnant, resentful, and even depressed. That's why it's so important that they don't just work for its own sake. While we all need to work to make a living and support ourselves, Pisces needs to find their way into work situations that give them opportunities to let their creativity shine.

And that can mean just about anything. What it doesn't mean is working at a job that's repetitive and mundane that the Pisces turns off. This is often the reason that Pisceans, especially young Pisceans, can seem lazy in the wrong environment, leading to them losing job after job.

The same is true of Pisces at home. Television isn't enough for these folks. While they'll thrill to the design genius and exceptional writing of shows like *Mad Men* and *Ratched,* they die a little inside when all their partner wants to do at night is a slouch on the couch in front of the idiot box.

Pisces would rather scribble down a great idea, refinishing a piece of furniture, or painting a mural on the living room wall, then being crushed under the mundane weight of mass media, any day. That's important for people who partnered with Pisces to remember. A bored Pisces is a listless, uninspired Pisces who is likely to bolt.

Besides work and the home, Pisces needs to seek inspiration. Curious and exploratory, Pisces loves to learn something new or interesting. Whatever their passions are, they need to have an outlet to their inner genius, and to share it with others similarly connected. Whether that's being part of a committee to beautify their town, community theater, a church choir, or a flower arranging class, Pisces must let that impulse out or lose the spark they're so well known for.

Romance

Romance isn't always about falling in love. Romance may be travel or even a wander through a local forest. It could even be a trip to the second-hand store, knocking off two birds with one stone. Beautiful vintage clothes inspire and light Pisces up and even second-hand clothes nobody else wants, Pisces sees the potential to make something beautiful out of even the lowliest polyester leisure suit. The thrill of the hunt satisfies their curiosity and the thrill of finding what they didn't even imagine they needed to add to their wardrobe or home décor repertoire, even more so.

For Pisces, when romance isn't about love, it's about the open road, or air travel to faraway, exotic places. Living their dreams is a huge motivating force for Pisces, taking them to distant, unknown places, where their only communicative tool is their brilliant smile and warm personality. Experiences and the lessons that come with them are one of the best things in life, where Pisces is concerned. These add to their natural storehouse of riches, further enhancing the mysterious wisdom of this sign.

For Pisces, there's nothing like seeing something few have seen or that they've waited to see their entire lives. My Pisces friend, for example, remembers her father taking her to the Louvre in Paris as a child. She'd always wanted to see the Mona Lisa, and standing before it on that special day is one of her most cherished childhood memories.

But when romance is about love, take care of the heart of Pisces. Intensely passionate lovers and partners, they're also deeply loyal. When these qualities are not returned by their partners, Pisces becomes morose to the point of suicide.

It's difficult for tender Pisces to understand why their partner is so incapable of returning their intensity, so think twice about not being straight with your intentions when approaching Pisces. If you're just in it for a fun night, then you'd best be very clear about that, or you may never forget what Pisces will characterize as your dishonesty. You may even discover that you're widely known as a douchebag or a trollop.

Romantic love is, for Pisces, one of the most transcendent experiences of human life. But as they get older, many Pisceans despair of the utilitarian approach to romance far too many people take. They want all the bells and whistles. They want the hearts, the flowers, the waves crashing to shores, the palm trees swaying, and the band playing a tender melody. If you're not that lover, take a pass on Pisces or regret not having done so.

To Pisces, life is one long, romantic adventure. With the Piscean ability to just roll with whatever life throws at them, they adore the surprises and sudden beauty of each day. They know the world is a rude, sharp-elbowed place. They know others don't necessarily understand their sunny smile and faraway eyes. But they don't care. They have lived through all the other signs of the zodiac. That infuses their spirits with an understanding of life's endless sweetness. While this reality makes many believe that Pisces may be a bit absurd their understanding of the romantic tale of life inspires those around them to understand where the Piscean is coming from. It's a tremendous, glorious gift and one we should all aspire to learn how to emulate.

Time to Recharge

Introspective, sensitive Pisces loves to socialize – just not all the time. If Pisces isn't left to find their center in solitude, they may become not only ill but testy. This a sign perfectly happy to sit at home, talking to their pets or creating their next great piece. Being semi-social, you'll see Pisces out and about when they're darned good and ready to do it.

Like a battery that has run down, the Pisces is never alone with their thoughts and can never rest from the world. They often have to recharge their batteries and recycle their energy. That recycling means rest, quiet, and peace; this sign needs to feel truly whole. While enjoying a happy social life and having many friends, Pisces can't be continually with other people.

Because of their intuitive nature, Pisces needs to withdraw to recharge but also to analyze what they've learned in their social interactions, about themselves and about other people.

Reflection in tranquility is how Pisces people rejuvenate themselves, re-creating their spirits. When with other people, too often the energies they intuit, both negative and positive, can deplete them, leaving them in need of rest.

While most of us take other people at face value, Pisces senses and then "reads" the undercurrents that lurk below the surface. They can spot a narcissist, for example, a mile away. This prompts them to run in the other direction, as energy vampires are Piscean kryptonite. But even people they love can wear them out. This is true of best friends, family, lovers, and even spouses and children.

For Pisces to be at their best, they need to let distance make the heart grow fonder. If this isn't understood by their nearest and dearest – and it often isn't – Pisces may rebel. While a nurturing, compassionate sign par excellence, Pisces can also turn off when they're not getting what they need. They can become cold, intolerant, and exhausted from all the human energies swirling around them.

To the rest of us, those energies may seem relatively innocuous. To a Pisces, they're an existential threat. Even a night out dancing can be difficult for Pisces to recover from. They come home over-stimulated and unable to sleep. While they might not want the night to end, they know the price they'll pay in the morning for the revelry they've indulged in.

Bad energies must also be considered. People with less than noble intentions coming into proximity with a Pisces will feel two holes burning into them from across a crowded room. These are the piercing eyes of a Pisces who has pegged them as bad news. Without a word, Pisces will know that these people are not on the menu for them or for anyone they know. That knowledge is not subject to the amendment because when Pisces has "read" ill intent, mendacity, or general nastiness, they will not be changing their vote for any reason.

They know, and while people will often scoff at Piscean intuition, it's invariably the case that their immediate read of others pans out. While those around them will poo-poo these "instant readings," the conclusion that others will inevitably draw is that Pisces' immediate read of the undesirable in question was correct. Not taking Piscean intuition seriously is a major source of frustration for this sign – yet another reason they sometimes need to jump into the depths of the ocean to sit on a rock, looking out to sea when it all gets to be too much.

Honesty and Integrity

The deep spirituality of Pisces is sensitive to those who lie, manipulate and treat others with anything less than respect. While Pisces can respectfully and even forcefully disagree, they will never disagree to the point of abuse.

But when you fail to model honesty and integrity with the sensitive fish, you will find yourself cut off. This is not done to be cruel or to punish. This is done by Pisces, to protect themselves and those around them.

No one likes to talk about this side of Pisces, but the hurt encountered by people under this zodiac sign when you do the wrong thing translates into instant ostracism. You will not speak to your Pisces again if they can help it. Pisces will avoid you until the end of the world when you bring ugliness into their peaceful, compassionate sphere.

It's not even personal with Pisces. With the fish, it's all about damage control. Intuitively equipped to read the hearts of others with precision, those who may cause trouble are distanced. But Pisces only cuts the cord once there's evidence that they were right in their intuition.

Liars are transparent to Pisces, almost at first glance. That man in the corner giving you the side-eye? He's a Pisces who has detected a misalignment between your words and your actions. You've never seen him before. So what? Pisces knows.

Got a hefty ego? Like to throw your weight around? Don't do it in front of that woman sitting at the bar, watching you in the mirror. She's going to stay as far away from you as possible, and if you get out of line, she'll make sure to tell the others. No offense. Just clean it up.

Honesty and integrity are imperative to Pisces because they know when you're lying, and they know when you're not true to yourself. A Pisces can spot a phony a mile away. And Pisces doesn't like phonies.

Honesty is a virtue that's taken seriously by Pisces. And integrity? Trusting others is right up there, and in the mind of the fish, these are the same thing. If you can't be true to yourself, you'll never be true to others, and that is fundamentally dishonest. Pisces, having moved through all the other sun signs, understands that one of the greatest goals of human life is integrity and to live as you were created to live. People who can't understand this fundamental need of Pisces – to expect the same honesty and integrity from others that they model – needn't come calling.

Respect and Understanding

One of Pisces's greatest challenges is being misunderstood. Many read Pisces as flighty or disengaged from reality. Neither claim is true.

Pisces is a dreamer. That much is true. But Pisces is also a visionary, seeing into the hearts of humans and of matters great and small. That is no mean feat. While the world around Pisces is reaching for answers, Pisces has already arrived at that goal.

But nobody listens. Pisces proposes a solution that sounds impossible or impractical. It is ignored until someone higher up the food chain clues in, and then Pisces is proven right. This may not happen for some time, but the ability of a Piscean to see beyond is usually, if not always, vindicated.

There is no explanation for this phenomenon, but that's immaterial. Once you've witnessed the prognosticating powers of Pisces, you'll never question them again. This is a predominantly third decan quality. However, all Pisces have access to this highly developed intuition, fully formed at the end of the astrological rainbow.

And that demands respect. Just because you can't find an empirical pathway to explain it does not mean to say it's not true. You have eyes and ears. Let them teach you that when Pisces says something that sounds a little crazy, you had best take notice.

Take my Pisces friend, for example. She not only "knew," in that special Pisces way, that Barack Obama would win the presidency and serve two successful terms, she knew it years before he even announced his intention. She knew that cannabis would eventually flourish as both medicine and recreation. When she confided this to a group of political operatives at a campaign training session, she was laughed at.

Who's Laughing Now?

My point is simple - place a bet on a Pisces prediction and get rich. Most people think they're crazy until they think they're geniuses. Wrong on both counts. Pisces are powerful, intuitive thinkers who process creative thinking into predictive accuracy.

So, it's much more about creativity than it is about soothsaying if you're paying attention. When you finally submit to Pisces and their processes, you'll discover a world of out-of-the-box thinking. That is the true impact of the way this sign thinks and acts. Pisces is so far out that they're right on time.

Elon Musk is not a Pisces, but that's where his Neptune lives. You do that math and tell me I'm wrong!

Respect the Pisces. Understand the Pisces and reap spillover generously splashed on you by this gentle, prescient sign. When you know a Pisces as a friend, lover, family member, or colleague, you know a portal to the weirder reaches of the universe. Through that portal are the things others don't see. We suspect the existence of these things, so we make monster movies and write ghost stories and speculative fiction about worlds we imagine might be out there, somewhere. Pisces sees those worlds with a fishy third eye.

But Pisces, if you respect and understand the beauty of a sign that lives in a type of knowledge that's not in a textbook but in the stars and the cells of their bodies, will show you amazing places.

Ultimately, what the Pisces needs more than anything is the freedom to swim in its eternal figure eight, both pulling and pushing, coming and going, being and not being. This mystically invested sign is the terminus of the zodiac, the Omega to Aries' childlike Alpha. Understanding this complex and amazing sign is key to understanding astrology itself.

Conclusion

Thank you for taking this journey with me into the heart of Pisces, the amazing zodiac sign that spiritually and in terms of karma, has seen and done it all.

I sincerely hope you've enjoyed reading more about the fish and how its natives navigate a world they can too often find unwelcoming. The shyness and reticence of this sign are unparalleled in the zodiac. That's perhaps because, on the journey around the astrological wheel, Pisces have learned lessons most of us haven't yet been exposed to.

This book was intended to be more than a look into the many traits and characteristics Pisceans exhibit. It's intended to offer you a grounding in basic astrology and the complex examination of the planets that results in a fuller understanding of individuals born under this sign. That grounding will serve you well as you move forward, hopefully creating your own chart. Maybe you'll become so adept at reading the movements of the planets; you'll become your circle's astrological expert!

Whether you read this book for pleasure or to improve your astrological knowledge, I hope I've been able to deliver both an informative and entertaining read.

Please enjoy the resources, following these few closing words. Don't forget to check out my other works on the signs of the zodiac, containing information specific to each sign, as well as broad astrological understanding.

Here's another book by Mari Silva that you might like

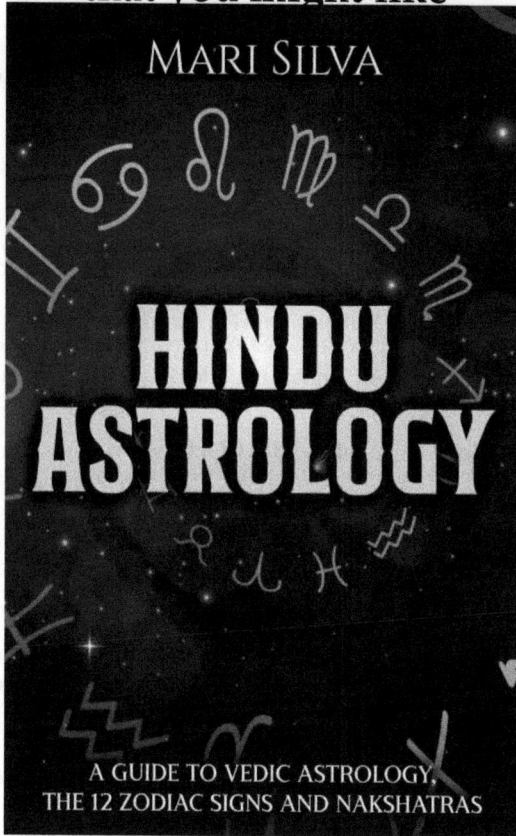

MARI SILVA

HINDU ASTROLOGY

A GUIDE TO VEDIC ASTROLOGY,
THE 12 ZODIAC SIGNS AND NAKSHATRAS

References

12 Astrology Zodiac Signs Dates, Meanings and Compatibility. (n.d.). Www.Astrology-Zodiac-Signs.Com. https://www.astrology-zodiac-signs.com/

Astrology - All Sun Moon Combinations. (n.d.). Astrology-Numerology.Com. http://astrology-numerology.com/sun-moon.html

Astrology King. (n.d.). Astrology King. http://astrologyking.com

Astrology Library. (n.d.). Astrolibrary.Org. https://astrolibrary.org/

Introduction to Astrology. (n.d.). Www.Astro.Com. https://www.astro.com/astrologie/in_intro_e.htm

Personality & Relationship Astrology: Compatibility, Attraction and Sign Personality Traits. (n.d.). South Florida Astrologer - Personality & Relationship Astrology. https://www.southfloridaastrologer.com/

Rovelli, P. (n.d.). *The Whole Astrology Workbook.* http://astronargon.us/The%20Whole%20Astrology%20Workbook.pdf

8 Things to Know About Your Aquarius Child. (n.d.). www.mom365.com website: https://www.mom365.com/mom/astrology/all-about-your-aquarius-childs-astrology

Aquarius Friendship Compatibility. (2020, October 7). Tarot.com website: https://www.tarot.com/astrology/compatibility/friends/aquarius

Aquarius relationships. (n.d.). website: https://www.compatible-astrology.com/aquarius-relationships.html

Aquarius-Pisces Cusp. (n.d.). astrologyk.com website: http://astrologyk.com/zodiac/cusp/aquarius-pisces

A, J. (2020, January 30). 5 Aquarius Celebrities Who Are Exactly Like Their Zodiac Sign (& 5 Who Aren't). TheTalko website: https://www.thetalko.com/aquarius-celebrities-fit-dont-fit-zodiac-sign/

Birthstone for Aquarius Zodiac Sign: Lucky Birthstone for 21st and about February 20th. (2019, February 1). Gemstone Blog, Diamond Article, Jewelry News, Gemology Online website: https://shubhgems.com/blog/birthstone-for-aquarius-zodiac-sign

Characteristics of Capricorn-Aquarius Cusps You Never Knew About. (2015, January 30). Astrology Bay website: https://astrologybay.com/capricorn-aquarius-cusp-characteristics

Definition of Every Zodiac Cusp Sign & Dates | Astrology.com. (n.d.). www.astrology.com website: https://www.astrology.com/on-the-cusp

Denise. (2018, April 21). The Aquarius Man: Key Traits In Love, Career, And Life. i.TheHoroscope.co website: https://i.thehoroscope.co/the-aquarius-man-key-traits-in-love-career-and-life/

Denise. (2018, April 28). The Aquarius Woman: Key Traits In Love, Career, And Life. i.TheHoroscope.co website: https://i.thehoroscope.co/the-aquarius-woman-key-traits-in-love-career-and-life/

Denise. (2018, November 12). Aquarius Qualities, Positive and Negative Traits. i.TheHoroscope.co website: https://i.thehoroscope.co/aquarius-qualities-positive-and-negative-traits/

Denise. (2018, November 11). Aquarius Weaknesses: Know Them so You Can Defeat Them. i.TheHoroscope.co website: https://i.thehoroscope.co/aquarius-weaknesses-know-them-so-you-can-defeat-them/

Denise. (2018, April 21). The Aquarius Child: What You Must Know About This Little Trendsetter. i.TheHoroscope.co website: https://i.thehoroscope.co/the-aquarius-child-what-you-must-know-about-this-little-trendsetter/

Green, I. (2018, October 29). The Aquarius Sign: A Deep Analysis of Aquarian Signs and Symbols. Trusted Psychic Mediums website: https://trustedpsychicmediums.com/aquarius-star-sign/aquarius-symbol/

Hall, M. (2019, March 20). What's the Meaning of the 11th House in Astrology? LiveAbout website: https://www.liveabout.com/the-eleventh-house-207252

Ingle, P. (2020, January 10). 10 Things That You Should Know About an Aquarius Child. parenting.firstcry.com website: https://parenting.firstcry.com/articles/10-things-that-you-should-know-about-an-aquarius-child/

Lawrence, A. (2020, July 23). Dating an Aquarius: What to Expect - PairedLife - Relationships. pairedlife.com website: https://pairedlife.com/compatibility/Dating-an-Aquarius-What-to-Expect

Leal, S. (2019, July 31). Here's Your Power Color, Based on Your Astrological Sign. Apartment Therapy website: https://www.apartmenttherapy.com/this-is-your-color-power-according-to-your-astrological-sign-36629958

Learn About Every Zodiac Cusp Sign and Dates! (2020, May 9). Medium website: https://medium.com/@meraastro.com/learn-about-every-zodiac-cusp-sign-and-dates-bad106c7d5f3

Love advice for Aquarius people. (2019, December 7). www.timesnownews.com website: https://www.timesnownews.com/astrology/aquarius-horoscope/article/love-advice-for-aquarius-people/524042

Muniz, H. (2020, January 2). The 7 Aquarius Traits You Need to Know. blog.prepscholar.com website: https://blog.prepscholar.com/aquarius-traits-personality

My Aquarius Zodiac Sign: Parent & Child. (n.d.). www.horoscope.com website: https://www.horoscope.com/zodiac-signs/aquarius/parent-child

My Aquarius Zodiac Sign: Friendship. (n.d.). www.horoscope.com website: https://www.horoscope.com/zodiac-signs/aquarius/friendship

Rubino, S. (2020, August 12). 6 Skills You Should Master This Summer. Thrillist website: https://www.thrillist.com/lifestyle/nation/6-skills-you-should-master-this-summer

Robinson, A. (2020, March 17). Aquarius Compatibility: Which Sign Is the Best Match? blog.prepscholar.com website: https://blog.prepscholar.com/aquarius-compatibility-signs

White, E. (2018, September 27). Aquarius Child: Personality Traits and Characteristics | Aquarius Baby. ZodiacSigns-Horoscope.com website: https://www.zodiacsigns-horoscope.com/aquarius/aquarius-child-personality-traits/

Capricorn Child: Capricorn Girl & Boy Traits & Personality | Zodiac Signs for Kids. (n.d.). www.buildingbeautifulsouls.com website: https://www.buildingbeautifulsouls.com/zodiac-signs/zodiac-signs-kids/capricorn-child-traits-characteristics-personality/

Capricorn Traits-Positive and Negative Characteristics | Ganeshaspeaks.com. (2016, November 29). GaneshaSpeaks website: https://www.ganeshaspeaks.com/zodiac-signs/capricorn/traits/

Faragher, A. K. (2020, July 31). Here's What the Capricorn Personality Is Really Like. Allure website: https://www.allure.com/story/capricorn-zodiac-sign-personality-traits

My Capricorn Zodiac Sign: Friendship. (n.d.). www.horoscope.com website: https://www.horoscope.com/zodiac-signs/capricorn/friendship

Thinnes, C. (2020, February 17). Capricorn Compatibility - Best and Worst Matches. Numerologysign.com website: https://numerologysign.com/astrology/zodiac/compatibility/capricorn-compatibility/

Tips on how Capricorns get to be even more awesome at life. (n.d.). www.horoscope.com website: https://www.horoscope.com/us/editorial/editorial-news.aspx?UniqueID=3310&CRC=295F9C29D08F59DE69C1D56A092D0 DCF

21 Secrets Of The Sagittarius Personality... (2017, October 19). Zodiac Fire. https://zodiacfire.com/sagittarius-personality/

Almanac, O. F. (n.d.). *Mercury Retrograde and Zodiac Signs.* Old Farmer's Almanac. Retrieved from https://www.almanac.com/content/mercury-retrograde-and-zodiac-signs

Angharad. (n.d.). *Male And Female Traits - Sagittarius.* Angharad Reese Celtic Astrology Online. Retrieved from https://www.areeseceltticastrology.com/sagittarius-girl-and-guy-personalities/

Astrology: Mercury in the Signs. (n.d.). Cafeastrology.com. Retrieved from https://cafeastrology.com/articles/mercuryinsigns_page2.html

Astrology.Care - Sagittarius Strengths and Weaknesses, Love, Family, Career, Money. (n.d.). Astrology.Care. Retrieved from http://astrology.care/sagittarius.html

Famous Sagittarius Writers. (n.d.). Www.Thefamouspeople.com. Retrieved November 7, 2020, from https://www.thefamouspeople.com/sagittarius-writers.php

Get to Know Sagittarius. (2014, November 24). Heather Beardsley Coaching. https://hbeardsley.com/get-to-know-sagittarius

Horoscopes. (2017). Bustle. https://www.bustle.com/horoscopes

Kaus Australis (Epsilon Sagittarii): Star System, Name, Constellation | Star Facts. (2019, September 18). Star-Facts.com. https://www.star-facts.com/kaus-australis/

Kaus Borealis. (n.d.). Www.Constellationsofwords.com. Retrieved from https://www.constellationsofwords.com/stars/KausBorealis.html

Keeping A Sagittarius Happy - Astroyogi.com. (n.d.). Www.Astroyogi.com. Retrieved from https://www.astroyogi.com/articles/keeping-a-sagittarius-happy.aspx

Moon in Sagittarius: Characteristics & Personality Traits. (n.d.). Stars Like You. Retrieved from https://www.starslikeyou.com.au/your-astrology-profile/moon-in-sagittarius/

My Sagittarius Zodiac Sign: Love. (n.d.). Www.Horoscope.com. https://www.horoscope.com/zodiac-signs/sagittarius/love

ophiuchus zodiac sign, Ophiuchus Traits, Celebrities, astrology, horoscopes, mythology. (n.d.). Www.Findyourfate.com. Retrieved from https://www.findyourfate.com/astrology/ophiuchus-13zodiac.html

Sagittarius Friendship Compatibility. (n.d.). Tarot.com. Retrieved from https://www.tarot.com/astrology/compatibility/friends/sagittarius

Sagittarius Horoscope: Sagittarius Zodiac Sign Dates Compatibility, Traits and Characteristics. (n.d.). Www.Astrology-Zodiac-Signs.com. https://www.astrology-zodiac-signs.com/zodiac-signs/sagittarius/

Saturn in Sagittarius. (n.d.). Tarot.com. Retrieved from https://www.tarot.com/astrology/planets/saturn-in-sagittarius

Sun in the Signs – Interpretations. (n.d.). Astrolibrary.org. Retrieved from https://astrolibrary.org/interpretations/sun/#sagittarius

The Editors of Encyclopedia Britannica. (2018). Jupiter | Roman god. In *Encyclopædia Britannica.* https://www.britannica.com/topic/Jupiter-Roman-god

The Zodiac Sign Sagittarius. (n.d.). Www.Alwaysastrology.com. Retrieved from https://www.alwaysastrology.com/sagittarius.html

This Is How Your Zodiac Sign Acts At A Party. (n.d.). My.Astrofame.com. Retrieved from https://my.astrofame.com/astrology/article/zodiac-signs-party

Top 10 Sagittarius Jobs | Money & Career | Ask Astrology Blog. (2018, November 21). Ask Astrology. https://askastrology.com/top-10-sagittarius-jobs/

12 Astrology Zodiac Signs Dates, Meanings and Compatibility. (n.d.). Www.Astrology-Zodiac-Signs.Com. https://www.astrology-zodiac-signs.com/

Astrology - All Sun Moon Combinations. (n.d.). Astrology-Numerology.Com. from http://astrology-numerology.com/sun-moon.html

Astrology King. (n.d.). Astrology King. http://astrologyking.com

Astrology Library. (n.d.). Astrolibrary.Org. https://astrolibrary.org/

Birth Chart Interpretations -Planets in Signs and Houses. (n.d.). Astrolibrary.Org. https://astrolibrary.org/interpretations/

Horoscope and Astrology - Homepage. (2019). Astro.Com. http://astro.com

Personality & Relationship Astrology: Compatibility, Attraction and Sign Personality Traits. (n.d.). South Florida Astrologer - Personality & Relationship Astrology. https://www.southfloridaastrologer.com/

The Best Online Astrology Resources. (n.d.). ♄. https://bangtanastrology.tumblr.com/post/169791137127/the-best-online-astrology-resources

Ancillette, M. 2020. "9 Best Healing Crystals for Libra's" https://angelgrotto.com/crystals-stones/libra/

Astrology. 2020. "Libra Compatibility" https://www.astrology-zodiac-signs.com/compatibility/libra/

Astrostyle. 2020. "Libra Symbol" https://astrostyle.com/libra-symbol/

Baird, C. 2013. "Science Questions with Surprising Answers" https://wtamu.edu/~cbaird/sq/2013/03/23/how-does-astrology-work/

Building Beautiful Souls. 2020. https://www.buildingbeautifulsouls.com/zodiac-signs/zodiac-signs-kids/libra-child-traits-characteristics-personality/

Café Astrology. 2020. "The Libra Woman" https://cafeastrology.com/articles/librawomanlove.html

Chatterjee, D. 2020. "5Best hobbies for the people of Libra zodiac sign" https://www.pinkvilla.com/lifestyle/people/5-best-hobbies-people-libra-zodiac-sign-556832

Fellizer, k. 2019. "This is How Long Each Zodiac Sign Takes to Fall in Love" https://www.bustle.com/p/how-long-it-takes-for-each-zodiac-sign-to-fall-in-love-19278018

Hall, M. 2020. "Teen Libra of the Zodiac" https://www.liveabout.com/libra-for-teens-zodiac-signs-206285#:~:text=If%20you're%20a%20Libra,one%20BFF%20or%20a%20crush.&text=Libra%20is%20ruled%20by%20Venus,for%20the%20art%20of%20love.

Hall, M. 2019 "The Libra Man and Love" https://www.liveabout.com/what-does-a-libra-man-want-206847#:~:text=A%20Libra%20man%20is%20attracted,honesty%20will%20win%20his%20heart.

Infinite Horoscopes. 2020. "What is my Libra Business Horoscope? https://infinitehoroscopes.com/index.php/2019/07/10/are-libra-zodiac-signs-meant-to-be-poor/

Internet Encyclopaedia of Philosophy. 2020. https://iep.utm.edu/a-taste/

Kids' Spot. 2020. https://www.kidspot.com.au/parenting/parenthood/parenting-style/raising-a-libra-baby-find-out-the-traits-and-challenges-you-may-face/news-story/b32ab960c1d92c3d5ba28b10ad943c45

Labyrinthos. 2018. "Astrology Planets and their meanings, Planet Symbols and Cheat Sheet"

https://labyrinthos.co/blogs/astrology-horoscope-zodiac-signs/astrology-planets-and-their-meanings-planet-symbols-and-cheat-sheet

Lantz. P. 2020. "Tips for Dating a Libra Man" https://horoscopes.lovetoknow.com/astrology-signs-personality/tips-dating-libra-man

Mom,365. 2020. "8 Things to Know About Your Libra Child" http://www.mom365.com/mom/astrology/all-about-your-libra-childs-astrology

Nelson, J. 2019. "Everything You Need To Know About the Libra In Your Life" https://thoughtcatalog.com/january-nelson/2016/05/everything-you-need-to-know-about-the-libra-in-your-life/

Power of Positivity. 2020. https://www.powerofpositivity.com/libras-considered-committed-partner-zodiac/#:~:text=1.,Libras%20are%20intensely%20loyal.&text=When%20you%20get%20into%20a,betray%20you%20for%20any%20reason.

Ratay, E. 2016" 5 Reasons Why a Libra is the Best Friend You Never Knew You Needed" https://www.yourtango.com/2016295845/5-reasons-libra-best-friendship-you-need-zodiac-astrology

The Rebel Coach. 2016. "Libra New Moon: Lazy Libra" https://rebelastrology.net/rebel-astrology/2016/9/30/libra-new-moon-lazy-libra

Rose, A. 2019. "How to Date a Libra" https://thoughtcatalog.com/almie-rose/2014/07/how-to-date-a-libra/

Sathya Narayanan. 2019. "Lucky Gemstones for Libra"

https://timesofindia.indiatimes.com/astrology/gemstones/lucky-gemstones-for-libra/articleshow/68205029.cms

Starlight Astrology (2020) "Libra" https://www.starlightastrology.com/libra-venus.htm

Stars Like You. 2020. https://www.starslikeyou.com.au/zodiac-strengths-your-libra-personality/

Tarot.com.2020. "Libra Friendship, Compatibility: The Great Counselor" https://www.tarot.com/astrology/compatibility/friends/libra#aries

The Famous People Guide. 2020. https://www.thefamouspeople.com/profiles/oscar-wilde-63.php

Villafane, C. 2020. "The Hobby He secretly wishes she Had Based on His Sign" https://www.thetalko.com/the-hobby-he-secretly-wishes-she-had-based-on-his-sign/

We Mystic. 2020. "The Dark Side of Libra: How to Deal with Narcissism" https://www.wemystic.com/the-dark-side-of-libra/

Your Zodiac Sign. 2020. "Libra Personality" https://www.yourzodiacsign.com/libra/personality/

12 Astrology Zodiac Signs Dates, Meanings and Compatibility. (n.d.).

Astrology - All Sun Moon Combinations. (n.d.). Astrology-Numerology.Com.

Astrology Library. (n.d.). Astrolibrary.Org.

Birth Chart Interpretations -Planets in Signs and Houses. (n.d.). Astrolibrary.Org. https://astrolibrary.org/interpretations/

Cafe Astrology .com. (n.d.). Cafeastrology.Com. http://cafeastrology.com

Horoscope and Astrology - Homepage. (2019). Astro.Com. http://astro.com

The Best Online Astrology Resources. (n.d.). https://bangtanastrology.tumblr.com/post/169791137127/the-best-online-astrology-resources

Astrologer, M. H. M. H. and Reader, T., & Hall, author of "Astrology: A. C. I. G. to the Z. " our editorial process M. (n.d.). *12 Tips for When the Sun Is in Leo.* LiveAbout. Retrieved from https://www.liveabout.com/tips-when-the-sun-in-leo-206836

Astrologer, P. L. C. H. (n.d.). *How a Leo-Virgo Cusp Sign Handles Life & Love.* Retrieved from https://horoscopes.lovetoknow.com/astrology-signs-personality/leo-cusp-traits

Astrology King. (n.d.). Astrology King. Retrieved from http://astrologyking.com/

Best Careers & Worst Jobs For Leo Zodiac Signs, Per Astrology. (2020, March 22). Your Tango. https://www.yourtango.com/2020332362/best-careers-worst-jobs-all-leo-zodiac-signs-astrology

Blog. (n.d.). The Dark Pixie Astrology. Retrieved from http://www.thedarkpixieastrology.com/blog

Damian, A. (2020, June 24). *AMAZING: Your 4 Dream Jobs if You Are a Leo.* Themagichoroscope.com. https://themagichoroscope.com/zodiac/best-jobs-leo

Find the Best Career for Your Zodiac Sign - Leo | ZipRecruiter®. (2019, May 7). ZipRecruiter. https://www.ziprecruiter.com/blog/best-career-paths-leo/

http://leohoroscope.in/. (n.d.). Retrieved from http://leohoroscope.in/

https://www.facebook.com/ZodiacFire. (2018, November 14). *21 Secrets Of The Leo Personality...* Zodiac Fire. https://zodiacfire.com/leo-personality/

Leo Friendship Compatibility: Be Patient! (n.d.). Tarot.com. Retrieved from https://www.tarot.com/astrology/compatibility/friends/leo

Leo Parent, Leo Child. (n.d.). *Baby Centre UK.* Retrieved from https://www.babycentre.co.uk/h1029981/leo-parent-leo-child

Mom365. (2020). *8 Things to Know About Your Leo Child.* Mom365.com. https://www.mom365.com/mom/astrology/all-about-your-leo-childs-astrology

My Leo Zodiac Sign: Friendship. (n.d.). Www.Horoscope.com. https://www.horoscope.com/zodiac-signs/leo/friendship

On the Cusp: What being a mix of Big Leo Energy and Virgo perfectionism means for your personality. (2019, August 20). Well+Good. https://www.wellandgood.com/leo-virgo-cusp/

Power of Positivity. (2016, August 3). *7 Things You Need To Know If You're Friends With a Leo.* Power of Positivity: Positive Thinking & Attitude. https://www.powerofpositivity.com/7-things-need-know-youre-friends-leo/

Rae, L. (n.d.). *7 Reasons Why You Should Do Business With A Leo.* Elite Daily. https://www.elitedaily.com/life/do-business-with-leos/1144979

Register, J., & Godio, M. (2020, May 7). *Your Zodiac Sign's Biggest Problem and How to Fix It.* Cosmopolitan. https://www.cosmopolitan.com/sex-love/a23490075/zodiac-sign-personality-traits-flaw/

The Leo Child: Leo Girl & Boy Traits & Personality | Zodiac Signs for Kids. (n.d.). Www.Buildingbeautifulsouls.com. Retrieved from https://www.buildingbeautifulsouls.com/zodiac-signs/zodiac-signs-kids/leo-child-traits-characteristics-personality/

The Leo Employee - Personality and Characteristics | Futurescopes. (n.d.). Futurescopes.com. Retrieved from https://futurescopes.com/astrology/leo/2767/leo-employee-personality-and-characteristics

These 10 Fascinating, Fiery Facts Will Tell You So Much About Your Leo Baby. (n.d.). Romper. Retrieved from https://www.romper.com/p/10-fascinating-facts-about-leo-babies-the-most-fiery-fire-sign-of-them-all-18366362

(2020). Theastrocodex.com. http://theastrocodex.com

Astrologer, M. H. M. H. and Reader, T., & Hall, author of "Astrology: A. C. I. G. to the Z. " our editorial process M. (n.d.). *The Meaning of the Cardinal Signs in Astrology.* LiveAbout. Retrieved from https://www.liveabout.com/cardinal-signs-aries-cancer-libra-capricorn-206724

Astrology.com - Horoscopes, Tarot, Psychic Readings. (2019). Astrology.com. https://www.astrology.com/

Cafe Astrology .com. (n.d.). Cafeastrology.com. Retrieved from https://cafeastrology.com

Cancer Horoscope: Cancer Zodiac Sign Dates Compatibility, Traits, and Characteristics. (2019). Astrology-Zodiac-Signs.com.

Cancer in Astrology. (n.d.). Www.Astrograph.com.

Definition of EMPATHY. (2009). Merriam-Webster.com.

webster.com/dictionary/empathy

Empathy Definition | What Is Empathy. (2009). Greater Good.

https://greatergood.berkeley.edu/topic/empathy/definition

Hermit Crab Successful Molting. (n.d.). Www.Hermitcrabpatch.com.

https://www.hermitcrabpatch.com/Hermit-Crab-Successful-Molting-a/138.htm#:

History.com Editors. (2018, August 21). *Summer Solstice.* HISTORY. https://www.history.com/topics/natural-disasters-and-environment/history-of-summer-solstice

https://Cancerhoroscope.in/. (n.d.). Retrieved https://Cancerhoroscope.in/

July 2017, K. A. Z. 15. (n.d.). *Cancer Constellation: Facts About the Crab.* Space.com.

Famous Birthdays. (2012). Famousbirthdays.com. https://www.famousbirthdays.com/astrology/

Majority of young adults think astrology is a science. (n.d.). UPI. https://www.upi.com/Science_News/2014/02/11/Majority-of-young-adults-think-astrology-is-a-science/5201392135954/

Mercury Retrograde Effects by Zodiac Sign. (n.d.). Horoscope.com. Retrieved from https://www.horoscope.com/mercury-retrograde/astrology/

Moon in Cancer: Characteristics and Personality Traits. (n.d.). Stars Like You. Retrieved from https://www.starslikeyou.com.au/your-astrology-profile/moon-in-Cancer/

Planetary Update by Horoscope.com. (n.d.). Www.Horoscope.com. https://www.horoscope.com

The Editors of Encyclopedia Britannica. (2018). Hera | Facts & Myths. In *Encyclopedia Britannica.*

https://www.britannica.com/topic/Hera

The Elements of Astrology: Fire, Earth, Air & Water Signs. (2016). Astrostyle: Astrology and Daily, Weekly, Monthly Horoscopes by The AstroTwins. https://astrostyle.com/learn-astrology/the-elements-fire-earth-air-and-water-signs/

Waxman, O. B. (2018, June 21). *Where Do Zodiac Signs Come From? Here's the True History Behind Your Horoscope.* Time; Time. https://time.com/5315377/are-Zodiac-signs-real-astrology-history/

What Does Your Sun, Moon, and Rising Sign Really Mean? (n.d.). Mindbody. https://explore.mindbodyonline.com/blog/wellness/what-does-your-sun-moon-and-rising-sign-really-mean

What Is Compassion? Understanding The Meaning of Compassion. (n.d.). Www.compassion.com. https://www.compassion.com/child-development/meaning-of-compassion/

Zodiac Colors And Their Meanings. (2015, March 5). Color-Meanings.com. https://www.color-meanings.com/Zodiac-colors-and-their-meanings/

Astro Dentist. (2020). Frequently asked questions. Retrieved from https://www.astro.com:

https://www.astro.com/faq/fq_fh_owhouse_e.htm

Astrology Fix. (n.d.). Expert Gemini Guide. Retrieved from https://www.astrologyfix.com:

https://www.astrologyfix.com/zodiac-signs/gemini/

Baby Centre. (2020). Gemini Child. Retrieved from https://www.babycentre.co.uk:

https://www.babycentre.co.uk/h1029254/gemini-child

buildingbeautifulsouls.com. (2020). Gemini Childe: Traits, Personality, and Characteristics. Retrieved from https://www.buildingbeautifulsouls.com/zodiac-signs/zodiac-signs-kids/gemini-child-traits-characteristics-personality/

C.Ht., P. L. (2020). Traits of a Gemini Boss. Retrieved from

https://horoscopes.lovetoknow.com/astrology-signs-personality/traits-gemini-boss

Chung, A. (2020). Compatibility Chart for Zodiac Signs. Retrieved from https://www.verywellmind.com/zodiac-compatibility-chart-4177219#history-of-astrology

Compatible Astrology, Staff. (2018). Gemini in Love. Retrieved from https://www.compatible-astrology.com/gemini-in-love.html

Green, T. (2017). 10 POWERFUL TIPS TO LEAD GEMINI TO SUCCESS. Retrieved from

https://astrologyanswers.com/article/gemini-zodiac-sign-success-tips/

Guerra, S. (2020). Top 5 Gemini Negative Traits You Need To Know. Retrieved from

https://www.preparingforpeace.org/gemini/negative-traits/#What_are_Gemini_Bad_Traits

Horoscope.com. (2018). Top 10 Careers For Gemini. Retrieved from

https://www.horoscope.com/article/top-10-careers-for-gemini/

Meade, J. (2019). Ranking The Zodiac Signs By Who Is Most Compatible With A Gemini. Retrieved from https://thoughtcatalog.com/jennifer-meade/2018/06/ranking-the-zodiac-signs-by-who-is-most-compatible-with-a-gemini/

Melorra. (2020). Zodiacal Gemstones - Gems as per Zodiac Signs. Retrieved from

https://www.melorra.com/jewellery-guide-education/gemstone/which-is-good-for/gemstones-by-zodiac-signs/

Middleton, V. (2019). A Beginner's Guide to Astrology. Retrieved from

https://www.thethirlby.com/camp-thirlby-diary/2019/5/22/a-beginners-guide-to-astrology

PeacefulMind.com. (n.d.). Air. Retrieved from https://www.peacefulmind.com/project/air/

preparingforpeace.org. (2020). Top 5 Gemini Positive Traits You Need To Know – Full Astrology Guide. Retrieved from https://www.preparingforpeace.org/gemini/positive-traits/

Prince, E. H. (2018). Six essential tips for dating a Gemini. Retrieved from

https://www.dazeddigital.com/life-culture/article/40376/1/dating-a-gemini-astrology

SCHAEFFER, A. (2020). How to Get Along With a Gemini. Retrieved from

https://classroom.synonym.com/get-along-gemini-4523008.html

Seigel, D. (2020). The 7 Fundamental Gemini Traits, Explained. Retrieved from

https://blog.prepscholar.com/gemini-traits

Tarot.com. (2020). Gemini Work Compatibility: The Thrill Seeker. Retrieved from

https://www.tarot.com/astrology/compatibility/work/gemini

The Finder, Staff. (2019). The Ultimate Guide On How To FIND LOVE According To Your Horoscope. Retrieved from https://thefinder.life/healthy-living/the-ultimate-guide-how-find-love-according-your-horoscope/

If You Are a Taurus, These Jobs Are Perfect for You ... (2017, July 12). Allwomenstalk.

https://money.allwomenstalk.com/if-you-are-a-taurus-these-jobs-are-perfect-for-you/7/

5 Ways To Overcome Your Fear Of Change During Tough Times. (2017, March 13). Molly Fletcher.

https://mollyfletcher.com/fear-of-change/

7 traits common to the strong-minded Taurus in your life. (2018, April 23). Well+Good.

https://www.wellandgood.com/taurus-personality-trait-gifs/

12 Astrology Zodiac Signs Dates, Meanings and Compatibility. (2010). Astrology-Zodiac-Signs.com.
https://www.astrology-zodiac-signs.com/

About Taurus the Bull: Astrology/Zodiac. (n.d.). Cafeastrology.com. Retrieved from

https://cafeastrology.com/zodiactaurus.html

All About Astrology: Zodiac Signs, the Planets, and Compatibility. (n.d.). Tarot.com. https://www.tarot.com/astrology

astrologer, M. H. M. H. is an, Reader, T., & Hall, author of "Astrology: A. C. I. G. to the Z. " our editorial process M. (n.d.). What are the Modalities? Cardinal, Fixed, Mutable. LiveAbout. Retrieved from https://www.liveabout.com/modalities-cardinal-fixed-or-mutable-206736

Astrologer, P. L. C. H. (n.d.). Taurus Weaknesses in Love and Relationships. LoveToKnow. Retrieved from https://horoscopes.lovetoknow.com/astrology-signs-personality/taurus-weaknesses-love-relationships

AstroTwins, T. (2017, August 6). Taurus Love Chart. ELLE. https://www.elle.com/horoscopes/love/a2231/taurus-compatibility/

Be Mine: Dealing With Possessiveness in a Relationship. (n.d.). Psychology Today. Retrieved from https://www.psychologytoday.com/us/blog/compassion-matters/201702/be-mine-dealing-possessiveness-in-relationship

Bozec, R. P., Jean-Pierre Nicola, Julien Rouger, Franck Le. (n.d.). Taurus-Scorpio: similarities and differences. Www.Astroariana.com. Retrieved from http://www.astroariana.com/Taurus-Scorpio-similarities-and.html

Compatible-Astrology.com. (n.d.). Taurus compatibility. Www.compatible-Astrology.com. Retrieved from https://www.compatible-astrology.com/taurus-compatibility.html

Constella, M. (2019, March 5). 9 Best Jobs for Taurus: Ideal Careers for Taurus Men & Women | Horoscope &

Astrology. Metropolitan Girls. https://metropolitangirls.com/best-jobs-taurus/

Cosmopolitan.com - The Women's Magazine for Fashion, Sex Advice, Dating Tips, and Celebrity News. (n.d.).

Cosmopolitan. https://www.cosmopolitan.com

Find the Best Career for Your Zodiac Sign - Taurus | ZipRecruiter®. (2019, May 7). ZipRecruiter.

https://www.ziprecruiter.com/blog/best-career-paths-taurus/

Free Taurus Kid Horoscope by The AstroTwins. (n.d.). Astrostyle: Astrology and Daily, Weekly, Monthly Horoscopes by The AstroTwins. Retrieved from https://astrostyle.com/family-horoscopes/baby-and-childrens-horoscopes/the-taurus-child/

How to Deal with a Taurus Partner's Stubbornness. (n.d.). The Femme Oasis. Retrieved from https://www.thefemmeoasis.com/astrology-zodiac/how-to-deal-with-a-taurus-partners-stubbornness/000007cc

How to Parent a Taurus. (n.d.). Www.Maisonette.com. Retrieved from https://www.maisonette.com/le_scoop/how-to-parent-a-taurus

Mom365. (2020). 8 Things to Know About Your Taurus Child. Mom365.com.

https://www.mom365.com/mom/astrology/all-about-your-taurus-childs-astrology

My Taurus Zodiac Sign: Love. (n.d.). Www.Horoscope.com. Retrieved from https://www.horoscope.com/zodiac-signs/taurus/love

PowerofPositivity. (n.d.). Power of Positivity: #1 Positive Thinking & Self Help Community. Power of Positivity: Positive Thinking & Attitude. Retrieved from https://www.powerofpositivity.com/

Rainer, M. A. (n.d.). Raising a Taurus baby? Find out the traits and challenges you may face. Www.Kidspot.com.Au. Retrieved from https://www.kidspot.com.au/parenting/parenthood/parenting-style/raising-a-taurus-baby-find-out-the-traits-and-challenges-you-may-face/news-story/0679dec1eec89d1fa8cf997dcd386b02

Taurus and their Personality and Physical Traits. (n.d.). Pointastrology.com.

Taurus Child: Personality Traits and Characteristics | Taurus Baby. (2018, September 22). ZodiacSigns-Horoscope.com. https://www.zodiacsigns-horoscope.com/taurus/taurus-child-traits-personality/

Taurus Friends & Family – Zodiac Signs. (n.d.). Retrieved from https://www.bzodiac.com/zodiac-signs/taurus-zodiac-sign/taurus-friends-family/

Taurus in Love - Sign Compatibility. (n.d.). The Love Queen. Retrieved from https://www.thelovequeen.com/taurus-love-horoscope-sign-compatibility/

Taurus Personality Traits, Characteristic, Strengths and Weaknesses. (n.d.). Your Zodiac Sign. Retrieved from https://www.yourzodiacsign.com/taurus/personality/

Taurus, Taurus Hobbies, Hobbies for taurus sign. (n.d.). Taurus.Findyourfate.com. Retrieved from

https://taurus.findyourfate.com/hobbies.html

Taurus Traits-Positive and Negative Characteristics. (2016). GaneshaSpeaks.

https://www.ganeshaspeaks.com/zodiac-signs/taurus/traits/

Taurus Weaknesses: Know Them so You Can Defeat Them. (2018, November 11). I.TheHoroscope.Co.

https://i.thehoroscope.co/taurus-weaknesses-know-them-so-you-can-defeat-them/

The Taurus Child: Taurus Girl & Boy Traits & Personality | Zodiac Signs for Kids. (n.d.).

Www.Buildingbeautifulsouls.com. Retrieved from https://www.buildingbeautifulsouls.com/zodiac-signs/zodiac-signs-kids/taurus-child-personality-traits-characteristics/

The Zodiac Sign Taurus Symbol - Personality, Strengths, Weaknesses. (2018, February 5). Labyrinthos. https://labyrinthos.co/blogs/astrology-horoscope-zodiac-signs/the-zodiac-sign-taurus-symbol-personality-strengths-weaknesses

Things You Should Know About a Taurus Child. (n.d.). Parenting.Firstcry.com. Retrieved from https://parenting.firstcry.com/articles/things-you-should-know-about-a-taurus-child/

Thinnes, C. (n.d.). Taurus Compatibility - Best and Worst Matches. Numerologysign.com. Retrieved from https://numerologysign.com/astrology/zodiac/compatibility/taurus-compatibility/

Waits, P. (2020, July 14). You Can Now Read the Four Best Professions for Taurus. Themagichoroscope.com. https://themagichoroscope.com/zodiac/best-jobs-taurus

What Sun Signs Say about Work Abilities: Taurus | News | Nexxt. (n.d.). Www.Nexxt.com. Retrieved from https://www.nexxt.com/articles/what-sun-signs-say-about-work-abilities-taurus-10871-article.html

Which Star Signs is Taurus Most Compatible With? (n.d.). AstroReveal. Retrieved from

https://www.astroreveal.com/Which-Star-Signs-Should-You-Date.aspx?a=TAU

YourTango | Smart Talk About Love. (n.d.). Www.Yourtango.com. https://www.yourtango.com

About Aries Kids & Young Ones. (n.d.). Siddhantika Astrology website: http://www.siddhantika.com/zodiac/aries-kids-teens

Aries Friendship Compatibility With Other Zodiac Signs. (2020, July 21). Revive Zone website: https://www.revivezone.com/zodiac709/aries-friendship-compatibility-with-other-zodiac-signs

Aries in love. (n.d.). https://www.compatible-astrology.com/ website: https://www.compatible-astrology.com/aries-in-love.html#:~:text=An%20Aries%20in%20love%20is%20a%20direct%20and%20forthright%20lover.&text=Overall%20the%20excitement%20of%20dating

AstroTwins, T. (2017, August 7). Aries Love Chart. ELLE website: https://www.elle.com/horoscopes/love/a56/aries-compatibility/

Davis, F. (2019, March 19). Aries Crystals: The 10 Best Zodiac Stones for Aries Sun Sign. Cosmic Cuts

Freeman, K. (2017, October 15). Most People Get This Totally Wrong When it Comes to Aries Ruling Planet. Trusted Psychic Mediums website: https://trustedpsychicmediums.com/aries-star-sign/aries-ruling-planet/

Hadikin, R. (2017, November 21). Aries Symbol astrological symbols - origin and deeper meaning - astrology-symbols.com. Astrological Symbols website: https://astrology-symbols.com/aries-symbol/

Hayes, L. (n.d.). 10 Ways to Really Love an Aries. https://www.beliefnet.com/ website: https://www.beliefnet.com/inspiration/astrology/2010/02/10-ways-to-really-love-an-aries.aspx

How to be a Successful Aries | Astrology Answers. (2017, March 21). AstrologyAnswers.com website: https://astrologyanswers.com/article/how-to-be-successful-as-an-aries/

Lapik, E. (2020, May 13). 20 Positive & Negative Aries Personality Traits and Characteristics. Astromix.net / Blog website: https://astromix.net/blog/aries-traits/#Positive_traits

Lantz C, P. (n.d.). Famous Aries Personalities and Common Traits. LoveToKnow website: https://horoscopes.lovetoknow.com/Aries_Personalities

Mesa, V. (2019, May 3). Here's What The Meaning Of The Elements In Astrology Can Reveal About Your Personality. Elite Daily website: https://www.elitedaily.com/p/the-meaning-of-the-elements-in-astrology-will-help-you-understand-your-personality-traits-17296359

Morgan. (2018, November 21). Top 10 Aries Jobs | Money & Career | Ask Astrology Blog. Ask Astrology website: https://askastrology.com/top-10-aries-jobs/

Ratay, E. (2017, May 12). 12 Reasons An Aries Is The BEST Friend You Never Knew You NEEDED. YourTango website: https://www.yourtango.com/2016294396/aries-best-friend-you-never-knew-you-needed-BFF-zodiac-astrology

Rose, E. (2019, March 22). A Beginner's Guide to Dating an Aries. StyleCaster website: https://stylecaster.com/aries-relationships/

Stone, C. (2017, March 28). Relationships Tips for Aries | Astrology Answers. AstrologyAnswers.com website: https://astrologyanswers.com/article/relationship-tips-for-aries/